OBJECTIVE HORTICULTURE

2nd Revised Edition

Objective Horticulture

(Fruit Science, Vegetable Science, Floriculture and Landscaping and Postharvest Technology)

For (ARS, NET, SET, JRF, SRF, M.Sc and Ph.D Entrance Test and Horticulture Services)

by

Anil Kumar Verma
Department of Food Science & Technology

Anju Dhiman
Directorate of Extension

Anil Gupta
Department of Food Science & Technology

Dharminder Kumar
Department of Vegetable Science

Dr. Y S Parmar, University of Horticulture & Forestry, Nauni, Solan (HP)

&

Pardeep Kumar
Department of Vegetable Science & Floriculture
Chaudhury Sarwan Kumar Himachal Pradesh Krishi Viswavidyalaya-Palampur, (HP)

A Paperback Division of

NEW INDIA PUBLISHING AGENCY

101, Vikas Surya Plaza, CU Block, LSC Market
Pitam Pura, New Delhi 110 034, India
Phone: + 91 (11)27 34 17 17 Fax: + 91(11) 27 34 16 16
Email: info@nipabooks.com
Web: www.nipabooks.com

Feedback at feedbacks@nipabooks.com

ISBN: 978-93-86546-76-0

Composed, Designed and Printed in India

Preface to the Second Edition

Horticulture, in recent years, has emerged as an important and viable diversification option in agriculture for effective landuse, nutritional security and employment opportunities and has also transformed the subsistence farming into a high value commercial enterprise.

Now it is a delightful occasion that our book, Objective Horticulture Fruit Science, Vegetable Science and Floriculture, is on the brink of second edition. The readers of this book are spread all across the Horticultural Universities.

There is an imperative growing need for knowledge in horticulture. The book entitled "Objective Horticulture" has therefore been enhancing competitive skills for M-Sc and Ph.D admission in Agricultural/Horticultural University, ICAR Institutes and other Competitive examinations. At the sametime it is hoped that this second edition may serve as an effective guide to all those aiming for further enhancement of their career in horticulture. We do hope that the book will be of appropriate use for the students in particular and teacher, scientists and farmers in general.

Authors

Preface

India has a wide variety of climate and soil on which a large number of horticultural crops such as fruits, vegetables, ornamentals, medicinal and aromatic plants, plantation crops and spices are grown. Horticultural crops cover 20.7 million hectare of area, which is nearly 11.25% of total cropped area of the country and contributes 18-20% of the gross value of India's agricultural output. Presently, our country is the second largest producer of fruits and vegetable crops in the world (surpassed only by China), accounting for about 12% of fruits and 13% of vegetables of the World's production. The country produces 41% of world mango, 27% of banana, 6% of citrus, 3.2% of apples, 2.5% of grapes, 6.94% of pineapples, 10% of papaya, 19% cashewnut, 57% of arecanut, 36% of green peas, 12% onion, 8% potato, 13% tomato, 26% egg plant, 8% cabbage, 30% cauliflower and 1.5% mushrooms. The area under flowers has also been increased tremendously. In the last three decades or so, there has been significant increase in the allocation of budgetary support for horticulture R&D resulting in sound research and development infrastructure to meet the growing needs. Horticulture is a vast subject in the field of agriculture and is divided into three major disciplines viz; *Fruit Science, Vegetable Science* and *Floriculture*. In the current Era, the competitive examinations have become pre-requisites for placements and academic goals.

The idea of preparing the book entitled "Objective Horticulture" has arisen from the fact that there is no objective type book covering all disciplines of horticulture (*Fruit Science, Vegetable Science* and *Floriculture)* as per revised syllabus prescribed by the ICAR. The book has been divided into 5 main sections viz; **Section-I**: Horticulture-Fruit Science; **Section-II**: Horticulture-Vegetable Science; **Section-III**: Horticulture-Floriculture; **Section-IV**: Important terms used in horticulture and **Section-V**: Miscellaneous.

This book will help all and serve as a comprehensive guide to those who want to prepare for competitive examinations like M.Sc. and Ph.D admission in Agricultural/Horticultural Universities, ICAR Institutes and other competitive examinations viz; ARS, SRF, JRF, Civil Services held at National and State level services. It is earnestly hoped that the students of Horticulture (fruit science, vegetable science and floriculture and post harvest technology) will find this book quite useful and prove beneficial to its readers.

Suggestions for further improvement are invited and will be immensely acknowledged.

Authors

Acknowledgement

With an overwhelming sense of legitimate pride, genuine obligation and profound personnel regard, we take this rare opportunity to express our deep sense of heartfelt gratitude to Hon'ble Vice-chancellor, Dr KR Dhiman, Dr YS Parmar, University of Horticulture and Forestry, Nauni, Solan for his immaculate suggestions, personal inspiration, constructive criticism and constant encouragement.

We also sincerely acknowledge the encouragement and guidance received from Dr SPS Guleria (retired Professor & Head, Dept PHT); Dr PC Sharma Professor and sectoral PI AICRP on PHT Deptt. of Food Sceince & Technology UHF, Nauni, Solan, Dr VK Joshi (retired Professor and Head, Department of Food Science and Technology); Dr ML Bhardwaj (Professor and Head, Department of Vegetable Science); Dr SK Chopra (retired Professor) Dr YS Parmar, University of Horticulture and Forestry, Solan; Dr RC Sharma (Prop. Hamir Supplement Foods, Hamirpur); and Dr Ashwani Kaushal (SMS, Agriculture Department, Shimla). We are thankful to Mr. Sumit Pal Jain, Prop. New India Publishing Agency (NIPA) and staff for their efforts in producing this publication.

The authors are heartly grateful to all colleagues and friends for their moral support during completion of present manuscript. The contribution of all those whose material has been used is gratefully acknowledged.

We sincerely acknowledge the help received from University Library staff especially from Sh. Mehar Chand. Our thanks are also due to Mrs Rajni Grewal and Sh Rattan Grewal for keeping everything flying when typing the manuscript painstakingly well in time.

Authors

Section – I

Fruit Science

CLASSIFICATION

Classification refers to grouping of individuals with similar identities related to genetic make up, evolution or climatic requirements. The major units are order, family, sub-family, genus, species, variety/cultivar and strain. Monocotyledonous and dicotyledonous are two major classes and most of the fruits are covered under dicotyledonous family. Different basis of classification of fruits are: *Botanical; Ecological; Stem morphology; Fruit morphology; Flowering habit; Respiration rate; Photoperiodism; Shade tolerance; Drought tolerance; Soil texture and topography; Soil reaction; Soil tolerance; Horticultural; Bearing habit; Inflorescence type; pollination types; Type of self incompatibility; Type of dichogamy; Edible parts; Center of origin; Ploidy levels; Longevity of fruit crops; Fruit size and Nutrient contents of fruits.*

1. Botanical

The fruits are classified according to their morphological and cytological similarities and dissimilarities, their place of origin, cross ability, floral biology *etc.* Fruit crops belonging to class, family, genus and species along with common English names are enlisted below:

Class/ family	Common name	Botanical name
I. Monocotyledonous		
Arecaceae	Arecanut	*Areca catechu*
	Coconut	*Cocos nucifera*
	Date Palm	*Phoenix dactylifera*
	Date Palm (Wild)	*P. sylvestris*
	Oil Palm	*Ealias guinensis*
	Palmyra Palm	*Borossus flabellifer*
Bromoliaceae	Pineapple	*Ananas comosus*
Musaceae	Banana	*Musa paradisiaca*
II. Dicotyledonous		
Anacardiaceae	Cashew nut	*Anacardium occidentale*
	Mango	*Mangifera indica*
	Pistachio nut	*Pistacia vera*
	Hog Plum	*Spondias dulcis*
	Indian Hog Plum	*Spondias pinnata*
Annonaceae	Custard apple	*Annona squamosa*
	Bullock's heart	*Annona reticulata*
	Soursop	*Annona muricata*
	Cherimoya	*Annona cherimoya*
	Atemoya	*Annona atemoya*
Apocynaceae	Karonda	*Carissa carandus*
	Natal Plum	*Carissa grandiflora*
Actinidiaceae	Chinese gooseberry	*Actinidia chinensis*
Bombacaceae	Durian	*Durio zibethinus*
Caricaceae	Papaya	*Carica papaya*
Ebenaceae	Mabola Persimmon	*Diospyros discolor D. mabola*
	Persimmon	*Diospyros kaki*
	Gaub	*D. peregrine*
	Tendu	*D. tomentosa*
	American persimmon	*D. vixgiana*
Elaeocarpaceae	Jalpai	*Elaeocarpus floribundas*
Euphorbiaceae	Aonla (Indian gooseberry)	*Phyllanthus emblica* *Emblica officinalis*
	Star gooseberry	*Phyllanthus occidus*
Flacourtiaceae	Governor's plum	*Flacourtia indicaF. ramaontchi*
	Puneala plum	*Flacourtia cataphrocta*
Guttifereae	Cow phal	*Garcinia cawa*
	Mangosteen	*Garcinia mangostana*

Contd.

Juglandaceae	Pecan nut	*Carya illinoensis*
	Walnut	*Juglans regia*
Lauraceae	Avocado	*Persia americana*
	Tamarind	*Tamarindus indica*
Malphigiaceae	Barbados cherry	*Malpighia glabra*
	West Indian cherry	*Malpighia punicifolia*
Moraceae	Bread fruit	*Artocarpus communis*
	Jack fruit	*Artocarpus heterophyllus A. integra*
	Monkey jack	*Artocarpus lakoocha*
	Fig	*Ficus carica*
	Mulberry	*Morus alba*
Myrtaceae	Guava	*Psidium guajava*
	Jamun	*Syzygium cumini*
	Rose apple	*Syzygium jambos*
Oleaceae	Olive	*Olea europaea*
	Indian olive	*Olea furruginea*
Oxalidaceae	Carambola	*Averrhoa carambola*
	Bilimbi	*A. bilimbi*
Passifloraceae	Passion fruit	*Passiflora edulis*
Proteaceae	Macadamia nut	*Macadamia ternifolia*
Punicaceae	Pomegranate	*Punica granatum*
Rhamnaceae	Indian jujube/Ber	*Ziziphus mauritiana*
	Chinese jujube	*Ziziphus jujube*
Rosaceae	Loquat	*Eriobotrya japonica*
	Quince	*Cydonia oblonga*
	Apple	*Pyrus × malus Malus × pumila*
	Almond	*Prunus communis, P. amygdalus*
	Apricot	*Prunus armeniaca*
	Sweet cherry	*Prunus avium*
	Sour cherry	*Prunus cerasus*
	Plum	*Prunus domestica*
	Peach	*Prunus persica*
	Pear	*Pyrus communis*
	Blackberry	*Rubus bruticosus*
	Strawberry	*Fragaria × versca F. × annassa*
Rubiaceae	Hog Apple/Noni	*Morinda citrifolia L.*
	Coffee	*Coffea robusta*

Contd.

Rutaceae	Bael	*Aegle marmelos*
	Kagzi lime	*Citrus aurontifolia*
	Sour orange	*Citrus aurantium*
	Pummelo	*Citrus grandis, C. maxima*
	Rough lemon	*Citrus jambhiri*
	Lemon	*Citrus limon*
	Citron	*Citrus medica*
	Grape fruit	*Citrus paradisi*
	Mandarin	*Citrus reticulata*
	Sweet orange	*Citrus sinensis*
	Wood apple	*Feronia limonia*
	Kamquat	*Fortunella japonica*
	Trifoliate orange	*Poncirus trifoliata*
Sapindaceae	Longan	*Euphoria longana*
	Akhee	*Blighia sapida*
	Litchi	*Litchi chinensis*
	Rambutan	*Nephellum lappaceum*
Sapotaceae	Sapota	*Achras zapota*
	Star apple	*Chrysophyllum cainito*
Solanaceae	Tree tomato	*Cyphomandro betacea*
	Cape gooseberry	*Physalis peruviana*
	Tomatillo	*Physalis ixocarpa*
Sterculiaceae	Cocoa	*Theobroma cocoa*
Theaceae	Tea	*Camelia sinensis*
Tilliaceae	Phalsa	*Grewia subinaequalis*
Vitaceae	Grape	*Vitis vinifera*

2. Ecological

The basic distinction on climatic tolerance helps the growers to select the fruit plants for a particular region. Fruits are categorized into four recognized groups viz; temperate, tropical, subtropical and arctic groups. India is bestowed with diverse edaphic and climatic conditions.

1	Temperate region	
a	Tree fruits	Apple, pear, peach, plum, almond, apricot, cherry
b	Nut fruits	Walnut, pecan nut, chilgoza and filbert
c	Small fruits	Blueberry, gooseberry, strawberry, blackberry, raspberry, currants and cranberry
2	Tropical region fruits	Papaya, date, coconut, banana, sapota, cashewnut, grape fruit and cape gooseberry
3	Sub-tropical region fruits	Mango, citrus, litchi, strawberry, loquat, pomegranate, persimmon, mangosteen and grape
4	Temperate fruits in sub-tropical region	Low chilling peaches, plum, pear, almond and apple
5	Arid zone	Ber, karonda and desert date
6	Semi arid zone	Custard apple, bael, fig, tamarind, phalsa and wood apple
7	Cold sandy desert	Chilgoza nut

3. Stem morphology

1	Highly developed stem	Mango, walnut and pear
2	Moderately developed stem	Apple, sapota, guava and litchi
3	Shrubs and small tree	Pomegranate, fig, peach, pummelo, sour cherry
4	Shrubs	Karonda, lemon and lime
5	Semi shrubs or bramble	Black berry and governor's plum
6	Vine	Grapes and passion fruits
7	Herbaceous perennial	Papaya, pineapple, banana and strawberry
8	Herbaceous annual	Tree tomato, cape gooseberry
9	Rambler	Cranberry and flacourtia

4. Fruit morphology

Depending on number of ovaries involved in fruit formation, fruits are usually divided into three groups: simple, aggregate and multiple fruits.

A. Simple fruits: Derived from single or syncarpous pistil of a single flower with or without accessory organ. These are further classified as dehiscent, indehiscent and fleshy type.

a) **Dehiscent:** No fruit crop only legumes, follicle, capsule and siliqua etc.

b) **Indehiscent:** Cashewnut, hazelnut, pecannut and chestnut etc.

c) **Schizocarpic:** Tamarind (lomentum type)

d) Fleshy fruits

i) **Berry:** Banana, papaya, grape, sapota, guava, gooseberry and date.

ii) **Modified berry**: Balausta (Pomegranate); Amphisarca (Bael and wood apple); Hesperidium (Citrus), Pepo (watermelon); capsule (Aonla and carambola).

iii) **Drupes/stone**: Mango, peach, plum, apricot, cherry and coconut.

iv) **Pome**: Apple, pear, loquat and quince.

B. Aggregate fruits: Derived from many ovaries of a single flower. It refers to aggregation of simple fruits borne by single flower (etaerio).

a) Etaerio of achenes (Strawberry)

b) Etaerio of berries (Annona group, custard apple, bullock heart, atemoya and cherimoya)

c) Etaerio of drupes (Raspberry, blackberry and loganberry)

C. Multiple or composite fruits: Derived from the fusion of many ripened ovaries and receptacles of many flowers.

a) Sorosis (Pineapple, jack fruit, bread fruit and mulberry)

b) Syconus (Fig)

5. Flowering habit

Kozlowaski (1971) classified the fruit plants on the basis of their season of flowering. This is presumed to the response of the fruit plants to varying photo-thermal conditions. On basis of flowering habit, the fruit plants may be of the following types.

Flowering habit	Fruits
Ever flowering	Fig and papaya
Non-seasonal flowering	Mango and coconut
Gregarious flowering	Quince
Seasonal flowering	Guava, litchi, apple and pear

6. Respiration rate

In some fruits the rate of respiration will undergo a sharp rise and fall during ripening. A sharp rise in respiration after harvesting is a phenomenon called climacteric rise and the fruits are called *climacteric fruits*. These fruits produce much larger amount of ethylene than non climacteric fruits. Whereas, a steady respiration at the time of harvesting is noticed in non-climacteric fruits. The fruits show a decline in respiration during ripening are termed as *non-climacteric fruits*.

Climacteric fruits	Non-climacteric fruits
Apple, Mango, Passion fruit, kiwi, melon, persimmon	Citrus, Grape, Pineapple, Carambola
Avocado, Sapota, Guava, Papaya	Pomegranate, Litchi, Ber, loquat
Apricot, Peach, Pear, Plum	Jamun, Cashewnut, Cherry
Banana, Ber, Annona, Fig	Strawberry, Raspberry

7. Photoperiodism

Fruit crops are classified into three groups according to their photoperiodic responses viz;

a) **Long day**: Passion fruit, apple

b) **Short day**: Strawberry, pineapple (cv. Smooth Cayenne), coffee

c) **Day neutral**: Papaya, guava, banana

8. Shade tolerance

Most of the fruit plants require much light for their growth and development, but some fruit crops are tolerant to shade and they do not require much light for their subsistence.

a) **Highly tolerant**: Carambola, bilimbi

b) **Moderately tolerant**: Banana, mangosteen

c) **Highly sensitive**: Coconut, citrus, mango and guava

9. Drought tolerance

Fruits show their varying response to moisture stress. This classification is useful to the horticulturist to select the fruit crops under specific moisture conditions.

S.No.	Drought tolerance/ Sensitive	Fruit crops
1.	Highly tolerant	Ber, bael, wood apple, karonda, custard apple, date palm, cashew nut, pomegranate, fig, persimmon
2.	Moderately tolerant	Mango, jamun, tamarind, grape fruit, grape, lemon, guava
3.	Sensitive	Apple, banana, papaya, orange, sapota, litchi, coconut, avocado, jackfruit, pummelo, carambola, pineapple

10. Soil texture and topography

Soil texture is an expression of the distribution of the various particle sizes present in soils and is important factor to select suitable plant species for a particular soil type. A soil may be coarse, medium or fine texture depending on the predominant particle size. It plays a vital role in determining the physical properties of soil. On the basis of basic soil particles, soils are grouped into *sandy, clayey and loamy*. On the basis of suitability of growing media, the fruit plants can be classified into various groups as under:

	Soil texture	Suitable fruit crops
	Sandy soil	Coconut, date palm, cashewnut, phalsa, ber, fig, wood apple, Palmyra palm.
	Loamy soil	Mango, papaya, sapota, grape, banana, apple, citrus, plum, jamun and jack fruit
	Clay soil	Palmyra palm, some species of jamun, fig and water chestnut
Soil Topography		
Undulating upland		
	- Arid temperate region	Oleaster, chilgoza
	- Semi-arid temperate area	Chestnut, pecan nut
	- Arid sub-tropical area	Ber, aonla, plum, fig, bael, wood apple
	- Semi-arid tropical area	Tamarind, custard apple
Gullied and ravinous land		Ber, custard apple, mulberry, khimi, bael, and karonda
Waterlogged and marshy land		Water chestnut, Palmyra palm
Strip land		Coconut, jamun, star-apple, rose apple, papaya, ber, karonda, governor's plum, mulberry
Degraded pasture and grazing land		Jamun, monkey jack, aonla, custard apple, banana, elephant apple, tamarind, fig
Degraded forest land		Aonla, natal palm, wild date palm, palmyra palm, lemon, lime

11. Soil reaction

This classification gives an idea about tolerance of the fruit crops to various soil reactions and an opportunity to select suitable fruit crop for particular soil reaction to raise successful orchard. According to soil reaction fruit crops may be divided into following groups.

Soil reaction	Fruit crops
Slightly tolerant to acid soil (pH 6.0-6.8)	Mango, Citrus, Banana, Guava, Papaya, Cashewnut, Carambola, Apple, Peach, Almond and Kiwi fruit
Moderately tolerant to acid soil (pH 5.5-6.8)	Pineapple, Orange, Litchi, Longan, Avocado, Passion fruit, Chestnut, Cranberry, Loquat and Jack fruit
Highly tolerant to acid soil (pH 5.5-6.8 and less)	Strawberry, Gooseberry, Raspberry, Blueberry, Fig, Bael,Elephant apple, Plum
Tolerant to alkaline soil (pH 7.2-8.0 or above)	Custard apple, Date, Coconut, Aonla, Olive, Phalsa,

12. Salt tolerance

This classification is especially important to the orchardists who plan to develop orchard in saline areas. The fruit crops may be classified on basis of their relative tolerance towards salt.

Salt tolerance	Fruit crops
High salt tolerance	Date palm, Ber, Aonla, Bael, Guava and Coconut
Medium salt tolerance	Pomegranate, Jamun, Fig, Olive, Longan, Passion fruit, Phalsa and Cashewnut
Highly sensitive to salt	Apple, Pear, Mango, Citrus, Strawberry and Avocado

13. Horticultural

Among various basis of classification horticultural basis is important because it takes into account the growing region, growing habit, tree habit and botanical relatedness of fruit crops. Broadly, on basis of their climatic requirement the fruit crops are divided as *temperate, tropical and sub-tropical.* Based on their stem characteristics fruit crops may be *tree or herbaceous.*

Temperate		Tropical and sub tropical			
Small fruits	**Tree fruits**	**Herbaceous perennial**	**Nuts**	**Citrus fruits**	**Miscellaneous fruits**
Cranberry, Grape, Raspberry, Strawberry	Apple, Pecannut, Pear, Plum, Peach Quince, apricot, Cherry, Filbert, Walnut, chestnut	Pineapple, Banana	Chestnut, Brazil nut, Macadamia nut	Oranges, Lemons, Grapes, Grape fruit, Mandarin	Loquat, Mango, Coconut, papaya, Date, Avocado

14. Bearing habit

Different bearing habits are noticed in the fruit plants. On the basis of bearing habit, fruit trees are classified into six categories to facilitate cultural operation like pruning, heading back etc.

Fruit crops	Bearing habit
Mango, cherry	Fruit buds borne terminally and giving rise to inflorescence without leaves
Apple	Fruit buds borne terminally and unfolding to produce leafy shoots which terminate in flower clusters
Guava	Fruit buds borne terminally and unfolding to produce leafy shoots with flower or flower clusters
Citrus	Fruit bud borne laterally containing flower parts only and giving rise to inflorescence without leaves
Grapes, cashewnut	Fruit buds borne laterally and unfolding to produce leafy shoots, terminally in flower clusters
Fig	Fruit buds borne laterally and unfolding to produce leafy shoots with flower clusters in leafy axils

15. Inflorescence type

Inflorescence is the reproductive shoot bearing a number of flowers. It also refers to the arrangement of flowers on the stem. It is a flower bearing shoot, which may be determinate or indeterminate or flowers may be borne in the axil of the leaf.

Inflorescence type		Fruit crops
Solitary		Almond, apricot, guava, peach, quince and trifoliate orange
Racemose	Raceme	Blackberry, blueberry, currants, gooseberry and raspberry
	Catkins	Mulberry, chestnut (Male), walnut (Male) and pecannut
	Corymb	Pear
Cymose	Solitary	Sapota, phalsa, citrus strawberry, persimmon
	Fasicle	Sweet orange, sour cherry, ber and plum
	Panicle	Grapes, litchi, loquat, mango and Pistachionut
Special type	Spadix	Coconut, date palm, banana and arecanut
	Hypanthodium	Fig

16. Pollination types

Pollination in which pollen are transferred from anther to stigma of the same flower is called *self-pollination or autogamy*. However, when pollens are transferred from anther to stigma of the other flower or cultivar or species is called *cross pollination or allogamy*.

Self pollination		Cross pollination	
Cleistogamy	Grape, Papaya, Sapota	Monoecious	Banana, jackfruit, pecan, tall coconut, hazelnut, walnut
Homogamy	Apricot, Citrus, dwarf coconut, peach	Dioecious	Chinese gooseberry, date palm, grape (muscadine), papaya, nutmeg.
		Gynodioecious	Fig

17. Type of self incompatibility

Self incompatibility is the mobility of the otherwise functional pollens to fertilize the stigma of the same flower. Pollen grains are viable in case of incompatibility but or unviable in sterility.

a) **Hetero-morphic** (No fruit crop)

b) **Homo-morphic**

i) Sporophytic: Mango, aonla and cocoa.

ii) Gametophytic: Almond, pineapple, ber, pear, apple, apricot, cherry and loquat.

18. Type of dichogamy

Dichogamy refers to the maturity of pollen and receptivity of stigma of the pistil at different periods.

Type of dichogamy	Fruit crops
Protandry	Walnut, sapota, annona, muricata, passion fruit and coconut
Protogynous	Annona species except *A. muricalo*, fig, banana, plum and pomegranate
Hetero-dichogamy	Pistachio nut
Protogynous diurnally/ synchronous dichogamy	Avocado
Duo-dichogamy	Chestnut

19. Edible parts

Fruits are used for dessert or table purpose. Pericarp is the most common edible part of fruits except nuts and dry fruits where kernel (seed) is consumed fresh or processed. Pericarp is further divided into epicarp or exocarp, mesocarp and endocarp in some fruits and hard like stone in others.

Edible part	Fruit crops
Fleshy thalamus	Apple, pear, quince, cashew apple, loquat
Aril	Litchi, rambutan, pomegranate, durian, mangosteen
Peduncle, perianth and bracts	Pineapple
Mesocarp	Papaya, mango, sapota, mulberry, passion fruit
Mesocarp and endocarp	Banana
Peduncle and cotyledons	Cashewnut
Endosperm	Coconut
Fleshy pericarp of individual berries	Custard apple
Fleshy receptacle	Fig
Thalamus and pericarp	Guava
Pericarp and placenta	Grape
Juicy placental hairs	Orange

20. Centre of origin

Centre of origin	Fruit crops
Abyssinian	Coffee
Asia Minor/ Caucasus	Apple, fig, chestnut, pistachio nut, almond, walnut, European grape
Brazil	Cashew nut, passion fruit, pineapple
China	Persimmon, quince, litchi, loquat, sweet orange, mandarin, mulberry, peach, tea, apricot, Japanese plum
Near Centre	Peach, plum, hazelnut, filbert, pomegranate, fig, cherry, *Pyrus*, *Malus*, rubber
Central America	Papaya, avocado
South/tropical America, Peru, Chile, Brazil and Paraguay	Guava, Pineapple, Cashew nut
Central Asia/ Afghanistan	Pistachio nut, apricot, almond, grape, pear
India	Jackfruit, mango (Indo-burma), bael, jamun, ber, karonda, aonla, wood apple, phalsa
South-East Asia	Banana, coconut, Pummelo, quince, lemon
Iran	Pomegranate
Japan	Plum
Man made hybrid	Atemoya, strawberry

21. Ploidy levels

Majority of the fruit crops are diploid. However, it may be diploid to octaploid. Inter-varietal ploidy differences are also found in some of the fruit species like banana, ber, apple, pineapple etc.

Allo-polyploid		Auto-polyploid	
Allo-tetraploid/ Amphidiploid	Mango	Auto-triploid	Tahati lime
Allo-hexaploid	European plum	Auto tetraploid	Aonla, bael, litchi, phalsa and rambutan
Allo-octaploid	Mango (Vellaikollamban) Strawberry	Auto-hexaploid	Persimmon and kiwi fruit
		Auto-octaploid	Ber (Gola, Illaichi)

22. Longevity of fruit crops

Longevity of the fruit crops means the complete life span of a fruit tree.

Longevity	Fruit crops
Seasonal	Cape gooseberry, tree tomato
1-2 years	Pineapple, banana
4-5 years	Strawberry, papaya, cranberry
15-30 years	Raspberry, passion fruit, annona, phalsa
20-40 years	Peach, aonla, plum, pomegranate, ber, guava, star apple, rose apple, orange
35-70 years	Apricot, fig, apple, coconut, palmyra palm.
50-100 years	Mango, avocado, pear, litchi, rambutan, persimmon, jackfruit, jamun
100-300 years	Walnut, pecan nut
1000 years	Sweet chestnut

23. Fruit size

Size of fruit is important for marketing, export and processing. It may also be termed as consumer's classification.

Size class on weight basis (g)	Fruit crops
Very light weight (50)	Cashew nut, grapes, dates, strawberry, lime, jamun, rose-apple, star-apple, cherry, peach, plum, litchi, karambola, ber etc
Light weight (50-100)	Lemon, rambutan, sapota, orange, persimmon
Medium light weight (100-250)	Banana, guava, bullock heart, apple, pear, mango (certain varieties)
Medium (250-500)	Mango, pummelo, grape fruit
Medium to heavy (500-1000)	Avocado, coconut, palmyra palm
Heavy weight (1000-5000)	Papaya, pineapple, soursap, durian
Very heavy weight (5000)	Jack fruit

24. Nutrient content of fruits

Nutrient	Fruits
Carbohydrate (%)	Apricot (72.8), Dates (67.4), Banana (36.4), Durian (34.2), Bael (30.6), Custard apple (23.9), Cashewnut (22.3)
Protein (%)	Cashewnut (21.2), Almond (20.3), Walnut 15.6)
Fat (%)	Walnut (64.5), Almond (58.9), Cashewnut (46.9), Avocado (22.8)
Vitamin A (Retinol) (I.U./ 100 g)	Mango (4800), Papaya (2020) Persimmon (1710), Jackfruit (540), Dates (600), Orange (350)
Vitamin B_1 (Thiamine) (mg/ 100 gm)	Cashewnut (630), Walnut (450), Almond (240)
Vitamin B_2, (Niacin) (mg/ 100 gm)	Litchi (122.5)
Vitamin B_3 (Riboflavin) (mg/ 100 gm)	Bael (1191), Papaya (250), Cashewnut (190), Pineapple (120)
Vitamin C (Ascorbic acid), (mg/ 100 gm)	Barbados cherry (1400), Aonla (600-700), Guava (300)
Energy (colorie/ 100 g)	Walnut (687), Almond (655), Cashewnut (596), Date (283)
Calcium (%)	Litchi (0.21), Dry karonda (0.16), Wood apple (0.13)
Iron (%)	Dry karonda (39.1), Date (10.6), Walnut (4.8), Green mango (4.5)

Note: The percent content of food constituents are presented in parenthesis.

SHORT NOTES

1. Fruit

Fruit is the matured or ripened ovary, usually develops after fertilization. Normally fruit consists of ***pericarp*** (fruit wall) formed from the wall of ovary and *seeds* formed from ovules. The pericarp may be dry or fleshy. When fleshy, it consists of outer (epicarp), middle (mesocarp) and inner (endocarp) walls. In many fruits, the division of pericarp may not be clearly visible. Sometimes, the other floral parts such as thalamus, receptacles or even calyx may develop as a part of the fruit as in apple (thalamus) and chashewnut (peduncle). These are called false fruits or pseudocarp. The fruits, which develop only from ovary, are called true fruits. A fruit that is formed without fertilization and thus without seed is called *seedless fruit* or *parthenocarpic fruit*, e.g. banana. Parthenocarpy is the development of fruit without any stimulus and by other factors. The fruit that develops out of fertilization and possess seed is termed *seeded fruits*.

2. Importance of fruits

They are a source of vitamins, minerals, organic acids, pectin and sugars.

- Because of their taste and flavour, fruits have been eaten by human beings since ancient times.
- Some of the edible fruits are either dry or can be dried, e.g. cashewnut, walnut, almond, apricot, raisins. Such dry or dried fruits can be stored for long.
- A number of fruits are used as vegetables, e.g. egg plant, okra (Lady's finger), tomato, pumpkin, gourd, cucumber, *etc*.
- Cereals are the staple food of human race. All of them are single seeded fruits.
- Fruits are important items of food for fruit eating (frugivorous) birds and some other animals.

3. Fruit-a ripened ovary

Broadly, they are divided into three groups: **simple** (formed from a flower having a single pistil), **aggregate** (formed from a flower having polycarpellary apocarpous gynaecium) and **composite** (from a whole inflorescence).

A. Simple fruits: Develops from monocarpellary or multi-carpellary syncarpous ovary of a flower, it can be dry (pericarp dry) and succulent or fleshy (pericarp fleshy).

1. **Simple dry fruits:** They have thin, hard and dry pericarp and are of three types viz; capsular, achenial and schizocarpic.

   a) **Capsular or dehiscent fruits:** These fruits are dry, many seeded and split open at maturity. These are of various types:

- **Legume or pod:** This develops from a superior mono-capillary unilocular ovary with marginal placentation it can open by both ventral and dorsal sutures. It is a characteristic of leguminosae family, e.g. gram (*Cicer arietinum*), pea (*Pisum sativum*), etc.
- **Follicle:** It resembles the legume but on ripening it opens generally along the ventral suture, e.g. madar (*Calotropis*), larkspur *etc.*
- **Siliqua:** The fruit is developed from bicarpillary, syncarpous and superior ovary that bears ovules on two parietal placenta. The ovary is unilocular but later becomes binocular due to development of a false partition wall, called replum. It dehisces from the base towards the apex by both the sutures e.g. mustard (*Brassica*). It is characteristics of family cruciferae.
- **Silicula:** It is a few seeded shortened and flattened siliqua, Candytuft (*Iberis*) Shepherd's Purse (Capsella).
- **Capsule:** It is mono or poly-capellary, dry dehiscent, many seeded fruit which develops from a superior or interior ovary. It dehisces in almost all the ways i.e. longitudinal and transverse along both the sutures. Majority of the capsules show longitudinal dehiscence which are of following types:
- **Loculicidal**: The fruit dehisces by longitudinal slit that appears along the dorsal sutures of the compound ovary so as to open into the loculli, e.g., cotton (*Gossypium herbarium*) and lady's finger.
- **Septicidal**: Longitudinal slit appears along the middle of septa and the placentae separate along the line of union, e.g., Pansy.
- **Septifregal**: Lines of dehiscence along irregular lines, but the seeds remain attached to the placenta, as in thorn apple.
- **Capsule opening by a lid**: In this type of fruit a separation layer is found in the middle of the ovary. When the latter is dry, the apical part of the pericarp separates in the form of a lid, e.g. *Anagallis* fruit.
- **Capsule opening by pores**: In this type the capsule opens by a ring of pores resulting from the incomplete separation of the stigmas at maturity, e.g. *Papaver* fruit.
- **Denticidal:** Dehiscence occurs by apical teeth e.g. pink.

b) **Achenial or indehiscent fruits:** These fruits do not burst at maturity but only the decaying of the pericarp liberates the seeds. They are single seeded fruits. These are of various types.

- **Achenes:** The thin dry pericarp remains free from seed exceptat one point. The fruit develops from a monocarpellary ovary e.g. Four O' Clock plant (*Mirablis jalapa*). Sometimes achenes occur in a group from apocarpous ovary where carpel's are many e.g. lotus (*Nelumblum*).
- **Caryopsis:** It is very small, dry and one seeded fruit that develops from a superior monocarpellary ovary. Here the pericarp is closely fused with the seed coat. It is characteristic of family Gramineae i.e. paddy (*Oryza sativa*), wheat (*Triticum aestivum*).
- **Cypsela:** It is dry, one seeded fruit that develops from an inferior, bicarpellary ovary. Here the pericarp is free from seed coat but the thalamus is fused with that forming a part of the fruit. The fruit is provided with crown of hairs at the top called pappus, e.g. sunflower (*Helianthus annus*).
- **Samara:** It is dry, one or two seeded fruit, develop from a superior mono or bicarpellary ovary. The pericarp is free from testa and produces a wing like outgrowth that helps is the dispersal of seed, e.g. Hiptage and elm etc. The wing is good device from wind disposal.
- **Nut:** It is dry, one seeded fruit which develops from a superior, bi or poly-carpellary ovary having a hard and woody pericarp, rarely leathery free from seed coat e.g. betel nut (*Areca catechu*), water chestnut (*Trapa*), *etc.*

c) **Schizocarpic fruits or splitting fruits:** They are many seeded, dry and simple fruits that break up into single seeded parts. The indehiscent single-seeded part is called mericarps while the dehiscent ones are termed as cocci (singular coccus).

- **Lomentum:** It is a dry many seeded fruit, develops from monocarpellary, superior, unilocular ovary. The fruit arises just like a legume but when ripened it forms single seeded mericarps, (*Mimosa pudica, Arachis hypogeal etc*).
- **Cremocarp:** It is a dry fruit develops from bicarpellary, syncarpous, biloccular ovary. The fruit when mature break into single seeded mericarps, which remain attached to the top of the central axis called carpophores, by means of stylopodium as in coriander (*Coriandrum sativum*) and carrot (*Daucas carota*).
- **Regma:** It is a dry fruit that develops from tri or penta-carpellary, syncarpous, superior ovary. The locules are as many as the carpel attached to carpophores and separate by splitting, as in castor (*Ricinus*) and *Euphorbia*.

- **Double samara**: Develops from multi-carpellary pistil and on maturity split and divide into winged single seeded mericarps.

2. **Succulent or fleshy fruits (simple):** The fruits are simple but the pericarp is fleshy and edible. It is differentiated into three layers-epicarp, mesocarp and endocarp. Fleshy fruits are of various types.

- **Drupe:** The fruit wall or pericarp is differentiated into three layers like epicarp, mesocarp and endocarp. The *endocarp* is stony in drupes derived from superior ovaries; the *epicarp* forms the outer skin. The *mesocarp* is thick, fleshy, juicy and edible in mango and fibrous in coconut. The endocarp is hard and stony in both the cases. The portion inner the endocarp is edible.

- **Pome:** This is false fruit as it is surrounded by a fleshy and edible thalamus. It develops from an inferior, multi-carpellary and syncarpous ovary with axile placentation. Common example is apple and pear.

- **Berry:** The fleshy pericarp is differentiated into three parts like outer most skin or *epicarp*, middle *mesocarp* and innermost *endocarp*. The endocarp is either pulpy as in grape, brinjal, red pepper, guava *etc*. The fruit is single seeded in date but many seeded in others. The seed become free from placenta and come to lie freely in the pulpy endocarp. All fruits with no hard parts excepting the seeds are called *baccate or berry* like fruit and it includes *berry, pepo, hesperidium, amphisarca* and *balausta.*

- **Pepo:** It is a special type of berry. Here the epicarp and thalamus form the outer rind of the fruit. The mesocarp, endocarp and placenta are fused together and from the pulp that is edible, seeds are many. Familiar examples are sweet gourd and cucumber.

- **Hesperidium:** This is also like a berry, but it develops from a multi-carpellary and syncarpous pistil with axile placentation. Here the outer skin is thick and leathery represents the epicarp, which contains oil glands. The fibrous portion fused with epicarp is mesocarp. The endocarp consists of many chambers with juicy glands. Common examples are lemon and sweet orange.

- **Balausta**: In pomegranate the pericarp of the fruit is tough and leathery and the chambers are made of thin wall of carpel. The edible portion is the succulent testa.

- **Amphisarca:** It develops from multi-carpellary, syncarpous, multi-chambered superior ovary. Fruit is many seeded with woody pericarp. Mesocarp, endocarp and swollen placenta are eaten as in wood apple.

B. Aggregate fruits: Develops from flowers having apocarpous pistil in which each carpel mature into fruitlets. A cluster of fruitlets on a pedicel of the flower forms the fruit. Such type of fruit is known as aggregate fruits or etaerio. These etaerio are of various types:

- **Etaerio of achenes:** It is an aggregation of achenes. The thalamus is fleshy and spongy and the achenes are embedded on its surface. Examples are rose, lotus and *Clematis* etc.
- **Etaerio of follicles:** This fruit is an aggregation of follicles developed from a flower with apocarpous pistil. Each carpel ofthe flower develops too many seeded follicle, e.g. champa, madar etc.
- **Etaerio of berries:** This fruit is an aggregation of berries, develop from a poly-carpellary, apocarpous ovary. Each carpel develops into a berry and a number of berries lie embedded in the thalamus and looks like a single fruit, as in custard apple.
- **Etaerio of drupes:** In this fruit, many small drupes, developed from different carpels and arranged collectively (in groups) on the fleshy thalamus, e.g., *Rubus idaeus*.
- **Etaerio of samara:** – e.g. Liriodendron
- **Etaerio of nuts:** – e.g. Nelumbo, Accalypha etc.

C. Composite or multiple fruits: Here the fruit is not developed from a single flower but from the total inflorescence, where the flowers are closely packed. Hence, it is called as multiple fruit. Multiple fruits are of various types.

- **Sorosis:** It is multiple and fleshy fruit that develops from a spike in pineapple, a female catkin in mulberry and a spadix in jackfruit. Pineapple fruit develops from an intercalary spike of sterile flowers with persistent bracts. The peduncle enlarges and becomes fleshy, embedding part of the sterile flowers into it. The un-embedded portion of the flowers withers away. Bracts, however, persist as small projections. Jackfruit has a spiny rind. The peduncle and perianth of individual flowers become fleshy. Achene's like fruitlets surrounded by membranous covering are embedded in the fruits. The ovaries of the individual flower develop into minute seedless fruitlets or achenes. Their perianth lobes (4 in number) become fleshy and juicy. The whole fruit is edible.
- **Syconus:** It is also a type of multiple fruit developed from the hypanthodium inflorescence. The fruit is a hollow, cup shaped, fleshy receptacle enclosing a large number of flowers. The flowers are sessile and unisexual. The male flowers are found at

the top whereas, the female flowers at the base. When the inflorescence matures, the female flower gives rise to a number of fruits or achenes. Then the syconus becomes fleshy, enclosing a number of fruits within the receptacle foe example as in peepal, banyan or fig.

4. Pome fruits

Malus (Apple), *Pyrus* (Pear) and *Cydonia* (Quince) are important genera of Pome fruits, belong to the family Rosaceae, sub family Pomoideae; and have basic chromosome number 17. *Chaenomeles* (Chiense quince), *Mespilus* (Medlar), Cratelgus, (hawthorn) and Sorbus are genera's of minor importance for their edible fruits besides their possible use as rootstocks. Plants of sub family Pomoideae are trees or shrubs. Leaves simple or pinnate, stipulate; flowers are solitary or in umbels, racemes, cymes, panicles or corymbs; 2-5 carpels, usually two ovuled, more or less united and adnate to cup shaped calyx tube forming an inferior ovary. Fruit is called fleshy pome.

5. Botanical description of apple

It is deciduous rarely evergreen tree or shrub rarely having spiny branches. Buds are ovoid with several imbricate scales. Leaves are serrate or lobed, folded or convolute in buds; flowers are white or pink in cymes. Petals are usually sub-orbicular, obovate, stamens15-50 usually with yellow anthers. Ovary inferior 3-5 cells, styles connate at base; fruit is pome usually without cells or deciduous calyx.

6. Botanical description of pear

It is a deciduous, rarely evergreen tree or shrub but sometimes thorny. Leaves are serrate, crenate or entire rarely lobed involutes in bud, petiolate stipulate, buds with imbricate buds. Flowers are with or wihout leaves in umbel like racemes white in colour or rarely pinkish. Sepals are refluxed or spreading; petals clawed sub-orbicular to broad oblong. Stamens 20-30 with red or purple anthers, styles 2-5 free closely constricted at base by the disk. Ovules two per locule; fruit is globose or pyriform pome, calyx persistent or deciduous fleshy with grit cells, walls of locules are cartilaginous.

7. Botanical description of Quince

Deciduous thornless shrub or small tree; buds small pubescent with few scales. Leaves petiole entirely stipulate. Flowers white or pink, terminal, solitary at the end of leafy shoots. Sepals 5 entire reflexed, petals 5 obovate, stamen 20, styles 5 free pubescent, ovary inferior, 5-celled each with numerous ovules. Fruit is many seeded pome pyriform. The genus consists of single species i.e. *Cydonia oblonga* Mill.

8. Stone fruits

The large genus *Prunus* includes peach, nectarine, plum & prune, cherry, apricot, almond etc. Deciduous or evergreen tree or shrub belongs to family Rosaceae and sub-family Prunoideae. Winter buds with many imbricate scales. Leaves are alternate, serrate, rarely entire and stipulate. Flowers are perfect, solitary or in fascicles or racemes. Sepals 5, petals 5 usually white sometimes pink or red, stamens are numerous or perigynous, pistil 1 with elongated style, and 2 ovules. Fruit is a drupe usually single seeded.

Prunus subgenera

a) **Amygdalus** (Peaches & Almond)

b) **Prunophora** (Plum & Apricot)

c) **Cerassus** (Cherries)

In the three subgenera, flower buds do not contain leaves but only flowers and they are always lateral buds, never terminal. Unlike the members of the subfamily Pomoideae, stone fruits do not set parthenocarpy.

a) **Amygdalus (L):** (Peach and almond)

Flowers: Sessile or short stalked, open before the leaves.

Fruit: Tomentose usually dehiscent

Stone:Pitted or smooth

Buds: 3 in each axil, the lateral one are flower buds

b) **Prunophora:** (Plum and Apricots)

Flowers: Solitary or in umbel like clusters

Fruits : Sulcate, glabrous usually bloom on epidermis

Stone : Compressed usually longer than broad and smooth

Pedicel : Usually remaining with the fruit

c) **Cerassus** (Cherries)

9. Thalamus and position of floral leaves

The thalamus is the suppressed swollen end of the floral axis on which the floral leaves are borne. In many flowers, the relative positions of calyx, corolla and androecium in respect of the ovary become distributed due to unusual growth of the thalamus. The relative position of the floral leaves is of three types:

1) **Hypogyny**: When the sepals, petals and stamens are successively and separately inserted below the ovary in the flowers, the condition is known to be hypogyny. The ovary is superior and the flowers are called *hypogynous*.

2) **Epigyny**: When the sepals, petals and stamens are successively and separately inserted above the ovary in the flower, the condition is described as epigyny. The ovary in this case is inferior and the flowers are termed as *epigynous*.

3) **Perigyny**: When the sepals, petals and stamens are inserted at the same planeas in the ovary, the condition is known as perigyny and such flowers are called *perigynous*.

10. Flower bearing habits

	Pome fruits
Apple	Terminal buds, 2 years spur
Pear	Terminal buds, 2 year spur
Quince	Terminal shoots, current year growth
	Stone fruits
Peach	Lateral buds, 1 year shoots
Almond	Lateral buds, 1 year shoots
Japanese Plum	Lateral buds, 1 year shoot
Apricot	Lateral buds, 1 year shoot + 2 year spurs
Prunes	Lateral buds, 2 year spurs + one year shoots
Cherry, sweet	Lateral buds, 2 year spurs
Cherry, sour	Lateral buds, 2 year spur
	Tree nuts
Walnut, Female	Terminals of current shoots
Walnut, male	Lateral buds, 1 year shoots
Pecan, female	Terminal of current shoots
Pecan, male	Lateral buds, 1 year shoot
Filbert, Female	Lateral buds, 1 year shoot
Filbert, male	Lateral buds, 1 year shoot
Pistachio nut	Lateral buds, 1 year shoot
	Small fruits/ berries
Strawberry	Crown buds
Blackberry	Lateral buds, 1 year canes
Raspberry	Lateral and terminal buds, 1 year canes
Cranberry	Lateral buds, 1 year canes
Blueberry	Lateral buds, 1 year canes
Currants	Lateral buds, 1 year canes
Gooseberry	Lateral buds, 1 year canes
Grape	Lateral buds, 1 year canes
Fig	Lateral buds, 1 year shoot
Persimmon	Lateral buds, 1 year shoot

11. Type of fruit and edible portion of some common fruits

S. No.	Fruit	Type of fruit	Edible part
1.	Apple, Pear	Pome	Fleshy thalamus
2.	Banana	Berry	Mesocarp and endocarp
3	Cashew nut	Nut	Peduncle and cotyledon
4.	Coconut palm	Fibrous drupe	Endosperm
5.	Cucumber	Pepo	Mesocarp, endocarp & placentae
6.	Custard apple	Etaerio of berries	Fleshy pericarp of individual barrier
7.	Date palm	One seed berry	Pericarp
8.	Fig	Syconus	Fleshy receptacle
9.	Guava	Berry	Thalamus & pericarp
10.	Grape	Berry	Pericarp and placentae
11.	Jack fruit	Sorosis	Bract, perianth and seeds
12.	Litchi	1 seeded nut	Fleshy aril
13.	Mango	Drupe	Mesocarp
14.	Melon	Pepo	Mesocarp
15.	Citrus	Hesperidium	Juicy placental hairs
16	Papaya	Berry	Mesocarp
17.	Pear	Pome	Outer portion of the receptacle bracts and perianth
18.	Pineapple	Sorosis	Fleshy thalamus
19.	Pomegranate	Balausta	Juicy outer coat of the seed
20.	Strawberry	Ataerio of achenes	Succulent thalamus
21.	Tomato	Berry	Pericarp and placentae
22.	Lady's finger (Bhindi)	Capsule	Whole fruit
23.	Orange	Hesperidium	Juicy, unicellular hairs of the endocarp

12. Important insect and pests of apple and pear

San Jose Scale: Most serious pest Less infested trees shows small greyish spots on the bark surface. Severally infested trees have the bark covered with grey layer of over-lapping scales.

Woolly Apple Aphid: The woolly apple aphid lives in colonies both on the root and aerial parts of the plants. On the aerial parts, it is seen as white woolly mass. Damage is caused by sucking of sap from stems, twigs and roots resulting in gall formation. Affected plants remain stunted with greatly reduced fruit bearing capacity.

Blossom Thirps: Very small yellow, pale brown and black slender insects feed within the flowers and floral buds.

Defoliating and fruit eating beetles: Many phytophagous species of beetles attack practically all temperate fruit plants. Beetles appear in May-June and feed on foliage and developing fruits at dusk. In case of severe damage, the plant is completely defoliated. Their immature stages (white grubs) feed on roots of many crops, vegetables and fruit trees.

Leaf roller and Fruit scraper: Green caterpillar fold apple leaves in field from April-May onwards and last generation of caterpillars attack fruits during October onwards in field/ storage and damage the fruit by scrapping the skin.

Apple Fruit Moth: Moth lays eggs at dusk in late June. The caterpillars on hatching, enter into the fruit, feed upon developing seeds upto mid August. Full grown larvae come out of the fruit after tunneling through the fruit pulp and pupate in crevices in retaining walls in the fields.

Defoliating caterpillars: Caterpillars of *Zygaena* moth, lymantrids and other hairy caterpillars, defoliate apple and other fruit trees soon after the leaves appear. The attack of these caterpillars is localized and at certain period cause severe defoliation.

Borers: Borer causes damage to roots, stems and shoots of apple and pear plants become weak or dead. Root borer makes the plant weak and shaky. Due to shot-hole borer, symptoms of the attack appear as shot-hole like perforations on the main trunk and branches accompanied with sticky appearance of the tree.

13. Important diseases of apple and pear

Seedling blight (*Sclerotium rolfsii*): Infected seedlings get killed outrightly and mustard coloured sclerotia appears at the collar region during monsoon.

Hairy root (*Agrobacterium rhizogenes*): Excessive growth of fibrous roots originates from one place and provides broom type appearance.

Crown gall (*Agrobacterium tumefaciens*): Globular, elongated or irregular tumers form at or near the graft union mainly in nursery plants.

White root rot (*Dematophora necatrix*): Affected trees show sparse foliage, slow growth, bronzing and yellowing of leaves. Such trees ultimately die. Roots turn brown and remain covered with white cottony mycelial mat of the fungus in rainy season.

Collar rot (*Phytophthora cactorum)*: Collar region near ground level turns brown, soft and spongy and on being girdled completely kills the tree. Disease infestation is maximum in poorly drained soils.

Canker and die-back: (Pink canker-*Botryobasidium salmonicolor*; European canker-*Nectria galligens*; Black rot/smoky blight-*Botryosphaeria quercum*, Nail head; *Numularia discreta*, Stem brown or stem bark canker: *Botryosphaeria dothidea*. Canker disease develops different types of symptoms on trunk and branches. Cankers usually start from the open wound and produce either deep sunken brown lesions or erupted black lesions on the bark. The bark turns papery and the portions above or below the canker get killed.

Powdery mildew (*Podosphaera leucotricha*): The disease affects the growth of buds, new shoots and leaves and produces white powdery patches. Fruits of certain varieties like Jonathan show russeting.

Leaf spots (*Mycosphaerella* sp, *Alternaria mali*, *A. alternata coniothyrium*, *Phyllostricta* sp and *Botryosphaeria quercum*): Leaf spots of different colour, size and shape are of common occurrence during late summer and rainy season. Heavily spotted leaves turn yellow and fall pre-maturily.

Apple scab (*Venturia inaequalis*): Typical scab symptoms appear on the above ground parts, particularly the foliage and fruits. Light brown or olive green spots which soon turn musty black appear on either or both sides of the young leaves in spring. Severe spotting leads to premature leaf drop. Severe and early infection results in the formation of mis-shapen fruits. Fissures of cracks often develop in scabbed area which allows the entry of other organisms causing rot of the fruit. Apparently healthy fruits which get infected in late summer (monsoon) develop small, rough black, circular lesions on their skin in the storage.

Sooty blotch and fly speck (*Gloeodes pomigene* and *Schizothyrium pomi*): Under high atmospheric humidity in rainy season, both the disease appears as sooty blemishes on the external surface of the fruits and reduces their market value.

Fruit rots: Blue mould rot (*Penicillium expansum*), Bitter rot (*Glomerella cingulata*), Brown rot (*Monilinia fructigena*), Pink mould rot (*Trichothecium roseum*), Whiskers rot (*Rhizopus stolonifer*), Bot rot (*Botryosphaeria dothidea*), Black rot (*Alternaria sp*). Apple fruits develop various types of rots either in the field or in the storage.

Virus diseases (Apple mosaic, Little leaf, Leaf pucker, Chloritic spots): Virus produces mosaic symptoms on leaves, curling, puckering, reduction in leaf size, causes reduction in vigour of the tree, excessive proliferation of buds and thereby lower fruit production.

Rubbery wood (Mycoplasma like organism): The disease causes rubberiness of shoots and such shoots drop down.

14. Predominating biochemical constituents of some stone fruits

Biochemical constituent	Peach	Plum	Apricot	Cherry
Sugars	Sucrose	Glucose & fructose	Sucrose	Glucose and fructose
Organic acid	Malic acid	Malic acid	Citric acid	Malic acid
Pigments	Anthocyanin (Cynidia-3-Monogluciside)	Anthocyanin (cydin-3-rutinoside)	Carotenoids	Di-glucoside of cynidin-keracyanin chloride
Flavouring compounds	Lactones	Benzaldehyde	Myrcene Limonene etc.	Methyl-anthranilate and Methyl salicylate
Vitamin	Vit-C	Vit-C	Vit-C	Vit-C
Phenol	Chlorogenic acid, catechin, cynidine	Neo-chlorogenic acid	Chlorogenic acid and p-Coumaric acid	Chlorogenic acid
Minerals	Potassium	Potassium	Potassium	Potassium

15. Constraints in postharvest handling of horticulture crops

- Lack of quality planting material for horticultural crops;
- High cost of establishing plantation crops and fruit orchards requires a long gestation for production.
- Low educational level coupled with poor technical training/extension facilities available to farmers.
- Poor production technologies: rainfed cultivation, improper planting, poor nutrition, old irrigation systems, plant protection and IPM management.
- Limited knowledge of maturity indices, stages of maturity, time and method of harvesting.
- Sorting and grading is done on a very limited scale, and is generally based on visual inspection.
- Limited availability of pre-cooling facilities. Pre-cooling facilities are generally available for produce such as fruits (grapes, strawberries, and mango) cut flowers (rose, gerbera, carnation, anthuriums), and vegetables (potato, onion, tomato, capsicum) which are destined for export.
- Lack of availability of transportation facilities dedicated to the horticultural sector.
- Fresh produce shipped both within the country and overseas is improperly packed and transported.

- Lack of a cold chain, inadequate storage and infrastructural facilities from the site of production to the point of consumption.
- Lack of a network of local markets and poor access to market information, results in unprecedented and unregulated arrivals in the local markets.

16. Maturity standards for important fruits

Name of fruit	Maturity standards
Mango	• Slight colour development of the shoulder or fullness of the shoulders; change in colour of pedicel from green to brown • Growth of the fibers on the stone/corrugations • Flow of latex from the stalk e.g., faster drying latex • Summation of days taken from flowering to maturity by tagging flowers • Appearance of bloom on the surface of the fruits • Computation of heat units or cumulative degree days • Change in lenticels morphology • Specific gravity of 1.0–1.02 for Alphonso and Pairi
Grapes	Heat unit concepts e.g., 3200–3600 photo-thermal units, Appearance of bloom on the berries, Colour and condition of stem cluster, Brix : acid ratio 30–35, Composition of juice thick and consistent with 18– 22% TSS, For raisins TSS should be 24–28%, Compact clusters for table purpose, e.g., Thompson Seedless
Banana	• Bunches are harvested when the top leaves starts drying • Change in colour of the axis of the fingers from dark green to light green • Brittleness of the floral ends, should fall with slight touch • Changes in the angularity of fingers from triangular to round or sharp • Number of days from emergence of inflorescence: 95–110 days • Pulp to skin ratio – 120:1.2 • Use of rings appropriate to variety.
Jack fruit	• Dull hollow sound is produced when the fruit is snapped at maturity. • The last leaf of the peduncle turns yellow • Fruit spines become well developed and wide spread • When fruit colour changes from green to yellow • An aromatic odour develops • When the rind is fairly soft, flesh is crispy and pale yellow.
Pineapple	When fruits show signs of yellowingHigh TSS and low acidity (TSS 13%; acidity 0.5–0.6%), Tips of the bracts projecting at the eyes starts drying, Acid ratio 21–27 and specific gravity 0.98–1.02. When it emits a strong flavour, attains characteristic size and a translucent appearance.Summation of days - 4½ to 5½ month and may be judged by snapping with fingers.
Papaya	Green for pickling and preparation of candy.Firm green, with moisture of 86% and TSS 10.67%, Ripe 33% for long distance market and 85.5%, colour development for local market, Harvested when fruit show signs of yellow to purple colour.
Apple	Elapsed days from bloom to harvest (100–110 days) and development of abscission layer, Textural properties are firmness, tenderness, starch and sugar content, Burst of internal ethylene production
Citrus	Change in colour (green to orange) Ease of separation, High rate of respiration, Seed-colour (green to brown) Change in organic acid, Juice content (>50%)

17. Grading of fruits and vegetables

Systematic grading coupled with appropriate packaging and storage, will extend post harvest shelf-life, wholesomeness, freshness and quality, and will substantially reduce losses and marketing cost. Horticultural produce must be sorted and graded on the basis of parameters such as maturity, size, shape, colour, weight, freedom from insects and pests, pesticide residues and ripeness.

- Mangoes are graded for export, on a weight basis as: Class A (200–350 g), Class B (351–550 g) or Class C (551–800 g).
- Pineapple fruits are graded in accordance with their weight as follows: A (1.50 kg and over), B (1.10–1.50 kg), C (0.8–1.10 kg), D (800 g) and baby (550 g).
- Papaya fruits are graded to size typically in counts of 8, 10 and 12 in to 3.50 to 4 kg net weights.
- Vegetables like onion, potato, tomato, chillies, okra and french beans are graded on the basis of size, shape, weight and maturity stage.

18. Packaging and transportation of fruits and vegetables

Large quantities of mangoes, bananas, oranges and other fruits and vegetables are transported in open trucks. Window type conical bamboo baskets designed for stacking and aeration have been developed by the CFTRI, Mysore for transportation of produce by rail.

- The use of polyethylene film bags for wrapping whole bunches of bananas for transport, has been found to be most suitable for reducing wastage.
- The use of wooden crates having internal dimensions of 42×32×29 cm has also been recommended for the long distance transportation of bananas.
- Mandarins can either be individually wrapped in cling films or are packed in consumer packages such as plastic bags, plastic mesh, trays of moulded pulp, paper board, plastic, or foamed plastic.
- Losses in first grade tomatoes can be reduced from 1.5 to 3% by using upright cone baskets together with dry grass as a packaging material between the layers of fruits. Packing of tomatoes in sealed unventilated polyethylene provides a modified atmosphere which extends storage life.
- Printed plastic bags are used to reduce light transmission to potato tubers.
- Plastic oven ventilated bags of 25 and 50 kg of capacity are used for onions and potatoes.

- Palletization and containerization will go a long way in establishing both local and international trade on a firm footing.

19. Storage of fruits

Storage life is governed by several factors. These include variety, stage of maturity, rate of cooling, storage temperature, relative humidity, rate of accumulation of CO_2, pre-packing and air-distribution systems. Optimum refrigerated storage requirements for different fruits are as follows: 1.7–3.0°C for apple, 12.8°C for banana, 0–1.7°C for grapes, 8.3–10°C for guava, 8.3–10°C for mango, 5.5–7.2°C for orange and 8.3–10°C for pineapple.

20. Public sector organizations involved in post harvest management of horticultural crops

- National Horticulture Board (NHB)
- Agricultural and Processed Food Products Export Development Authority (APEDA)
- National Dairy Development Board (NDDB)
- National Cooperative Development Corporation (NCDC)
- Ministry of Food Processing Industries (MFPI)
- National Medicinal Plants Board (NMPB)
- Indian Council for Agricultural Research (ICAR)
- National Bank for Agriculture and Rural Development
- Commodity Boards for - Spice, Coffee, Coconut, Agmark, etc.

21. Strategies needed by the Scientists, growers, industries for post harvest management of horticultural crops

Scientists

Application of conventional and biotechnological processes to the development of improved varieties having high production potential with high quality attributes and resistance to biotic and abiotic stresses.

- Mechanization of the processing of unexploited indigenous as well as exotic crop species.
- Research for farm level post harvest handling and for simple storage systems.
- Diversified and economic methods of utilizing fruits and vegetables and processing of their wastes.
- Research on traditional Indian foods with commercial value.

- Studies on biodegradable and zero oxygen permeability packaging materials.
- Development of economical methods of monitoring temperature and relative humidity in CA/MA/MAP/Low pressure storage.
- Technological improvement of the minimal processing of fresh produce.

Growers

- Adaptation of the technique of high density planting in order to increase productivity and quality for crops such as mango, pineapple, banana, tomatoes, onion, potatoes etc.
- Efficient land and input use programs – arid cultivation, fertigation, water harvesting.
- Mechanization of efficient harvesting techniques particularly for large orchards and plantations. Knowledge on post harvest biology of the produce.

Industries

- Technologies, industrial plants and machinery must be designed to suit the processing requirements of available raw materials at specific locations.
- Facilitate industrialization in production centres.
- Industry should make provision for guaranteeing stable prices to horticulturalists and reliable supplies must be provided at a reasonable price to the consumer.
- Improvement of low costing appropriate packaging material.
- Focus on the utilization of the wastage from the processing industry as by products.

22. Epithets-fruits

King of fruits → Mango
King of temperate fruits → Apple
King of Arid fruits → Ber (Poor Man's fruit)
Adam's fig → Banana
Butter fruit → Avocado
Queen of beverage fruit crops → Tea
Food of God → Cocoa

KalpaVriksha	→ Coconut
Emblem of UN	→ Olive
Five corner fruit	→ Carambola (Star fruit)
China's Miracle Fruit	→ Kiwi (Horticultural Wonder of New Zealand)

23. Edible parts of some fruits

Fruit	Edible Part
• Cucumber (Pepo)	Mesocarp, endocarp and Placentae
• Castard apple	Fleshy Pericarp
• Datepalm	Pericarp
• Fig	Fleshy receptacle
• Guava	Thalamus and Pericarp
• Grape	Pericarp and Placentae
• Jack fruit	Bracts, Perianth and seed
• Indian plum	Mescocarp including epicarp
• Tomato	Pericarp and Placentae
• Strawberry	Succulent thalamus
• Papaya	Mesocarp
• Pineapple	Fleshy thalamus
• Pomegranate	Endosperm
• Melon (Pepo)	Fleshy receptable
• Coconut Palm	Mesocarp
• Fig	Juicy out seed coat
• Litchi	Fleshy aril
• Mango	Mesocarp
• Citrus	Juicy Placental hairs
• Pear (Pome)	Outer portion of receptable bracts and perianth

24. Place of origin of some fruits

Fruits	Place of origin
• Loquat	Japan and China

- Mango South Asia
- Mango steen Malaya
- Passion fruit Brazil
- Apple South-West Asia
- Apricot Armenia
- Peach China
- Plum North America and Japan

25. Scientific names of some fruits

	Fruit Tree	Scientific Name
i)	Walnut	*Juglans regia* L.
ii)	Sour Orange	*Citrus aurantium* L.
iii)	Lemon	*Citrus limon*
iv)	Lime	*Citrus aurantifolia*
v)	Mango	*Mangifera indica*
vi)	Papaya	*Carica papaya*
vii)	Pomegranate	*Punica granatum*
viii)	Litchi	*Litchi chinensis* Sonn

26. Growth patterns of fruits

Single sigmoid growth curve	Double sigmoid growth curve	Triple sigmoid growth curve
Apple, Avocado, Pear	Apricot, Plum, Peach	Chinese goose berry
Orange, Strawberry	Sour & Sweet cherry	
Tomato	Olive	
Pineapple, Banana	Grape	
Date	Fig	

27. Type of fruit and edible portion of some common fruits.

S.No.	Name of fruit	Type of fruit	Edible portion
1.	Bael	Amphisarca	Succulent placentae
2.	Mangosteen	Amphisarca	Succulent placentae
3.	Jamun	Drupe	Epicarp and Mesocarp
4.	Longan	Berry	Mesocarp
5.	Carambola	Berry	Aril
6.	Rambutan	Berry	Aril
7.	Olive	Drupe	Epicarp and Mesocarp
8.	Wood apple	Amphisarca	Succulent placentae
9.	Karonda	Berry	Epicarp and Mesocarp
10.	Phalsa	Drupe	Epicarp & Mesocarp
11.	Aonla	Berry	Mesocarp & Endocarp
12.	Avocado	Berry	Pericarp
13.	Sapota	Berry	Mesocarp

28. Some Post-harvest diseases of fruits along with causal organism

Fruit	Disease	Causal organism
Banana	Crown rot	*Collectotrichum musae, Fusarium semitectum,*
Ber	Fruit rot	*Alternaria* sp., *Phomopsis* sp., *Colletotrichum* sp.
Citrus	Black rot	*Alternaria citri*
	Grey mould	*Botrytis cinerea*
	Green mould	*Penicillium digitatum*
	Stem end rot	*Diaporthe citri, D. medusa, D. natalensis*
Guava	Anthracnose	*Colletotrichum gloesporioides*
Kiwi fruit	Stem rot	*Botrytis cinerea*
	Ripe rot	*Botryosphaeria dithodea*
Litchi	Skin injuries	*Aspergillus* sp., *Penicillium* sp., *Rhizopus* sp.
Mango	Anthracnose	*Colletotrichum gloesporioides*
	Stem-end rot	*Botryodiplodia theobromae*
	Black mold	*Aspergillus niger*
	Dry rot	*Mycosphaerella* sp.
	Wet rot	*Phomopsis* sp.
	Alternaria spot	*Alternaria alternata*
	Fusarium rot	*Fusarium solani*
	Internal yellowing	*Enterobacter clocae*
	Anthracnose	*Colletotrichum gloesporiodes, C. dematium.*
Pear	Blossom-end rot	*Alternaria* sp., *Botrytis* sp., *Penicillium* sp.
Pineapple	Black rot	*Chalara peradoxa*
	Fruitlet core rot	*Penicillium funicalosum, Fusarium moniliform*
Pomegranate	Heart rot	*Aspergillus niger, Alternaria* sp.
	Penicillium rot	*Penicillium* sp.

29. Chemicals used to extend shelf-life of important fruits

Fruits	(Chemical concentration)	Time of application	Response
Apple	Boric acid (0.1 to 0.2%)	60 and 45 days before harvest	Improve the calcium status of fruit
	Alar (1000 ppm)	60 days before harvest	Improve the storability
	$AgNO_3$ (75 ppm) or DNP (30 ppm)	6 weeks before harvest	Improve the storability
	Diphenylamine (0.1-0.25%)	Post harvest dip for 30 seconds	Control superficial scald
Mango	Maleic hydrazide (MH) (1000- 2000 ppm)	Postharvest dip	Delayed ripening
	Calcium nitrate (1.0%) or Calcium chloride (0.6%)	Post harvest spray	Enhanced keeping quality
Banana	Tal Prolong (1 to 2%)	Post harvest dip	Extended storability
	GA_3 (50 ppm) and kinetin (20 ppm)	Post harvest dip	Retarted ripening
Ber	Calcium compounds (1.7g/L)	Post harvest spray	Delayed fruit ripening
Kinnow	Wax Emulsion (6.0%) with benomyl (0.1%)	-	Reduced weight loss during 2 months storage.
Nagpur	Waxing with benlate (0.1%)	-	Reduced rotting at ambient storage
Grape	Calcium nitrate (0.75%) Cycocel (2000-4000 ppm)	10 days before harvesting	Reduced weight loss and delay ripening. Reduced berry rot.
Guava	Calcium nitrate (1%)	Postharvest dip	Retained quality for 6 days
	Morphactin (2.5 and 5.0 ppm) & chloroflurenol methyl ester	Pre & postharvest application	Extended shelf-life

30. Mode of action of cell wall hydrolases

S.No.	Enzyme	Mode of action
1.	Pectin esterase	Acts to remove the methyl group from the C-6 position of a galacturonic acid.
2.	Polygalacturonase	Hydrolyses á (1-4) link between adjacent dimethylated galacturonic acid residues.
3.	Cellulase	Hydrolyses the â (1-4) link between adjacent glucose residues.
4.	β -galactosidase	In some cases, attacks on native galactan polymer.

31. Ethylene evolution rates of some fruits at 20-25°C

Fruits	Ethylene production rate (µl/kg/hr)
Banana	3
Litchi	1-5
Fig	1-10
Cherimoya	219
Ber	100
Pear	75-100
Citrus fruit	0.1-2.0
Pineapple	0.2-0.4

32. Methods of propagation followed in different fruit crops.

Method of propagation	Fruit crops
Layering and T-budding	Avocado, cherry, Custard apple, Grapefruit,
Patch budding	Bael
Sword sucker	Banana
Ring and T-budding	Ber, Mandarin, Olive, Peach, Pear, Plum,
Seed	Cape gooseberry, coconut, Karonda, Mongosteen, Papaya, Phalsa, Pummelo.
Soft wood grafting	Cashew nut,
Inarching	Custard apple, Guava (Stooling), Jack fruit, Loquat, Mango.
Off shoot	Date palm
Hard wood cutting	Fig, Grape, Karonda, Pomegranate,
Shield and patch budding	Jamun
Air layering	Lemon, Litchi, Loquat,
Veneer grafting	Mango
Tongue grafting	Peach, Pear, Plum,
Patch budding	Pecannut, Walnut
Suckers and slip	Pineapple
In-situ soft wood grafting	Tamarind, Wood apple

33. Inflorescence and its types

1.	**Solitary**	A flower may be borne singly in the axil of a foliage of the terminus shoot or on a specialized stalk e.g. trifoliate orange, quince, guava, peach, apricot, almond etc.
2.	**Racemes**	In this case, the peduncle continues to grow and new flower buds with their subtending brackets continue to form near the growing points, thus, producing a succession of new flowers. The lowest flowers, being the oldest are first to open and blossoming proceeds upward. There are various types of inflorescence in this class.
	Raceme	Flowers are borne on the pedicels which are about equal in length. This type is found in the wild cherry, currants, gooseberry, blackberry, blueberry, raspberry etc.
	Catkin	A spike or raceme with a slender rachis, bearing many unisexual epipetalous flower, which falls as a whole when the fruits is mature e.g. mulberry, chestnut, walnut, pecannut etc.
	Corymb	The main axis is elongated and the pedicels are of unequal length in such a way that the lower ones are the longest and the upper ones or central ones are the shortest resulting in flowers lying in a horticultural plane e.g. pear.
3.	**Cymose**	In this type at the growing point, a flower bud is produced so that the floral axis can not elongate further. The other flower buds are produced below this point on the axis towards the base. Thus this becomes determinate growth and the opening of the flower is basipetal or centrifugal. The cymose inflorescence is further of two types and these are:
	Fascicle	A cyme with flowers closely crowded on a very shorter peduncle and with pedicles of about equal length e.g. cherry (sweet and sour), plum, ber.
	Panicles	In this case main axis is indeterminate but the secondary and ultimate axis is a cymose e.g. grapes, mango, litchi, loquat, pistachio, etc.
4.	**Anomalous**	Some type of inflorescence are also observed which do not fit into the conventional types e.g. in apple. Terminal flowers open first which suggest a cyme but then the basal ones open next and then the anthesis of individual flowers proceed more or less upward to the apex which suggests a recemose type.
5.	**Special**	
	Spadix	It is a large, boat-shaped structure (spathe) enclosing an inflorescence e.g. datepalm, banana
	Hypanthodium	It is modification of capitulum in which the receptacle is hollowed into a flask. It opens to the outside by the apical pore which is borne on the inner side of the receptacle in which the male flowers lie towards the apical pore and female flowers towards the base e.g. fig.

34. Respiration

In post harvest life of fruits, respiration plays a key role. It results in biological oxidation of simple sugars. Sugars disappear with uptake of O_2 and production of CO_2 and H_2O. Energy in the form of heat is liberated. Initial phase of respiration is production of Pyruvic acid from glucose, known as glycolysis. Pyruvic acid converted to CO_2 and H_2O which is aerobic. The pathway of Pyruvic acid through various organic acids to CO_2 and H_2O is known as citric acid or Kreb's cycle.

$$RQ = \frac{CO_2 \text{ evolved}}{O_2 \text{ consumed}}$$

35. Sex-forms of flower

There are 3 sex types of flowers i.e. hermaphrodite or perfect, staminate and pistillate flowers. Hermaphrodite flowers are called perfect or complete in which both the stamens and pistils are functional. Pistillate flowers are devoid of anthers. Staminate flowers having non-functional pistils.

Flower/sex form	Fruit crops
Perfect	Apple, peach, plum, grape, mango, avocado, cashewnut, papaya, citrus, sapota, guava, etc.
Staminate	Papaya, mango, litchi, grape, date, cashewnut, pomegranate, walnut etc.
Pistillate	Papaya, walnut, grape, pecan etc.
Teratological	Papaya, mango, grape, pomegranate etc.

36. Blooming period

The blooming period of different fruit plants varies due to prevailing agro-climatic conditions in different regions of India. Broadly, blooming time of various fruit plants grown in North and South India is divided into 3 periods.

February to May	Apple, pear, peach, plum, apricot, almond, walnut, mango, citrus, grape, litchi, pomegranate and date palm flowers in North India
	Banana, Papaya, pineapple, sapota and fig flowers in South India
June to September	Guava, ber and papaya bloom in North India
	Pomegranate and citrus gives fower in South India
October to January	Guava, sapota, ber and loquat flowers in North India
	Sapota, guava, mango, ber flowers, during this time in South India

37. Flowering period in different fruits

Mango	The mango flowers late in January or in the beginning of February or even as late as March in many parts of North India
Citrus	The flowering in citrus takes place mostly in spring. In lime and lemons, flowering takes place almost throughout the year. In kinnow, flowering takes place during end February to early March in North India
Grapes	Flowers in grapes mostly develop in spring
Guava	Guava tree normally produces as many as three crops in a year. In Northern India, three distinct flowering seasons i.e. summer, rainy and autumn.
Litchi	The flowering in litchi takes place in February
Ber	The flowering period in ber lasts for about two and a half months from September to November
Loquat	The blooming period of loquat is very long lasting from mid July to January or sometimes even up to May
Datepalm	The flowering in datepalm takes place during end February to early March
Pomegranate	In evergreen pomegranate, the flower buds of the spring flush are borne on mature wood of one year old shoot, whereas the flowers which appear during July – August are borne on current year's growth. In deciduous cultivars, the flowers are borne on current years growth between July and August
Jamun	The flowering in jamun starts in the first week of March and continues upto middle of April
Phalsa	In phalsa, flowering starts from February – March and continues till May
Papaya	The papaya is found to flower throughout the year
Sapota	Sapota flowers throughout the year with main two flowering seasons i.e. July to November and against in February – March
Cashew	Normally, there are three growth flushes in cashew and in South India, the flower bud emergence commences by the middle of September and continues till the end of February, the main season being October – November
Custard apple	The flowering period of custard apple is very long commencing from March – April, continues upto July-August. The peak flowering is observed in April and May
Avocado	In moderate climate, the avocado produces flowers from November to January or three main flushes
Apple	In apple, flowering takes place in April in HP
Pear	The flowering in pear starts in last week of February and continues upto third week of March
Peach	In peach, flowering starts I the first week of February and continues till end of February
Japanese plum	Flowering in Japanese plum starts in the second fortnight of February and last upto first week of March
Almond	Almond is one of the first tree to bloom in spring. Flowering takes place in very early season occurring between January to April
Apricot	In HP, the flowering in apricot cultivars mostly occurs in the month of March
Walnut	The peak flowering period of walnut is mid April which is prolonged till the first week of May in late blooming cultivars under Shimla conditions.

38. Mode of Pollination

Pollination means the transference of the pollen from the anther to the receptive stigma whether of the same flower or of a different flower.

I.	Autogamy or self pollination	It a stigma be pollinated by the pollen of the same flower
	a) Cleistogamy	In these cases the flowers never open as opposed to most flowers which show chasmogamy (i.e. flowers open normally during anthesis). In cleistogamous flowers the pollens are shed within the closed flowers so that self pollination is obligatory e.g.grape, sapota and papaya.
	b) Homogamy	The stamens and corpels of a flower mature at the same time. So, there is a great chance of self pollination although that is not obligatory. Some homogonous flowers, however, show special mechanism for self pollination e.g. citrus, peach, apricot etc.
II.	Allogamy or cross pollination	When the pollen of a flower pollinates the stigma of another flower located on a different plant, whether at the same kind or not it is called allogamy. Special contrivances ensuring cross pollination as noted below are very compicuous.
	a) Dicliny or Unisexuality	Cross pollination is the rule among diclinous plants i.e. those bearing unisexual flowers.
	Monoecious	In monoecious plants, the only alternative is geitonogamy which, however has the same effect as self pollination e.g. banana, walnut, pecan, coconut etc.
	Dioecious	In dioecious plants nothing else can take place e.g., papaya, date, grape etc.
	b) Self-incompatibility	This is the condition when a flower cannot be fertilized by the pollen of the same flower of the same strain kof plants. Cross-pollination is obligatory in such plants e.g., almond, apple, mango, pear, pineapple, cherry, apricot.
	c) Dichogamy	When stamens and carpels of a bisexual flower mature at different times, pollination between them becomes ineffective. However, it is found that self-pollination may take place at a later stage if cross-pollination fails. Dichogamy may be of two types.
	Protandry	When the anthers ripen first. As a result when the anthers burst, it pollinates stigma of other flowers but not its own stigma which is not yet ripe, walnut, coconut. are examples
	Protogyny	The carpel matures first as in many members of Annonaceae. When the stigma is receptive, its own pollen is not ripe so that it has to ddepend on foreign pollens e.g. fig, annona, banana, plum, pomegranate and avocado.
	d) Heterostyly	In certain plants there are flowers of two (dimorphic) or three (trimorphic) different forms with anthers and stigmas of different levels. This diamorphism or trimorphism usually involves heterostyly (styles of different lengths).
	Pin type	Sapota, pomegranate
	Thrum type	Almond

39. Role of growth regulators

- For promoting rooting, the most commonly utilized hormone is IBA followed by NAA.
- GA causes inhibition of root formation on cuttings.
- Cytokinins help in quick and profuse root formation on cuttings and layers.
- By use of auxins, root formation is profuse in cuttings of guava, fig, pomegranate, Kagzi lime etc.
- Soaking seeds of fruits in 10-20 ppm solution of GA for 12 hours before sowing, significantly improves the yield and quality
- By spraying cycocel, the superfluous growth of leaves is checked.
- The use of SADH/ Paclobutrazol effective in reducing the growth of pear, peach, lemon, apple, litchi, apricot, plum and mango.
- Ethrel treatments are beneficial in mango, grape and avocado ripening.
- Ethylene is the active principle responsible for flowering in pineapple.
- Acetylene, calcium carbide, ethephon and true auxin type hormones such as NAA are used to induce flowering in pineapple.
- Commercial formulation like Planofix and Celmone are effective in induction of flowering in pineapple.
- Ethrel or ethephon at concentration of 25 ppm in combinatioin of urea (2%) and $CaCO_3$ (0.04%) is very effective for flowering in fruits.
- Paclobutrazol (PP_{333}) shows great promise for regulating, flowering and fruiting in mango and grape.
- In litchi, application of NAA replaces girdling for improved flowering by mobilization of assimilates in the trees.
- SADH promotes flowering in apple, pear, peach and lemon and reduce shoot growth.
- Grape and lemon respond to CCC treatments with increased flowering.
- Bio-regulators like IAA, IBA and phenoxy acetic acids are used to induce parthenocarpy.
- In fruits like apple, pear, peach, apricot, almond, fig, grape etc application of gibberellins produce parthenocarpic fruits.
- Parthenocarpic fruits are set with the application of cytokinins in grape.
- Application of GA, 4-CPA increases fruit set in strawberry, peach, plum and cherry.
- Spraying of NAA, TIBA and PCPA auxins on flowers increases the fruit set.
- The auxin application increases fruit size for commercial advantage in grapes, strawberry and orange.

- The combination of GA and brassino-steroids applied after fruit set had synergistic effect and increased not only the length but also diameter of the berry.
- Post-bloom applications of CPPU, a derivative of cytokinins increase the berry size more in diameter than in length
- 4-CPA treatment serve as an alternative to caprification in fig for improving fruit set
- Auxins (2, 4-D; 2, 4, 5-T and NAA) control fruit drop in citrus.
- Post-harvest berry drop of grape can be overcome by spraying 50-100 ppm of NAA a week prior to harvest.
- The fruit drop in mango can be controlled by using 10-20 ppm NAA or 10 ppm 2, 4-D after fruit set.
- Spraying with mild solution of Ethrel or morphactin reduces the fruit load by 25-30%
- Application of sodium 4, 6-dinitro-o-cresol (DNOC) at full bloom or NAA at post bloom induce satisfactory thinning in apple orchards.
- DNOC sprays are effective in apricot, plum, prune, sweet cherry and pear.
- Spraying with 2, 4, 5-T hastens ripening of apples by 1-4 weeks.
- Spray of ethephon during fruit development in apple, grapes strawberry and cranberry are promising for early fruit maturity and uniform ripening.
- Ethephon applied to citrus fruits prior to storing ensures post harvest degreening.
- In lemons, dipping in 1000 ppm ethephon result in attainment of marketable yellow colour.
- Banana, mango ripen faster with ethylene treatement.
- The propagation of green berries at harvest can be reduced considerably by the application of ethephon @ 250 ppm of colour break stage of berries.
- Cycocel (500 ppm) when applied twice (15 days interval) induces early maturity in Kagzi lime by about 20 days.
- In banana, low concentration of IAA and high level of Benzyl adenine (BA) essential for rapid growth of explants.
- In grape, BA and NAA are essential for establishment of explants, while IBA helps in rapid multiplication.
- In mango, somatic embryogenesis from nucellar explants occurs in the presence of 2, 4-D at low concentration.
- GA are used for accelerating seed germination in citrus (trifoliated orange, sweet orange, Cleopatra mandarin and acid lime), cherry, grapes, annona, apple and peach.

- Termination of bud rest by GA sprays is a commn practice in peach and apple orchards.
- GA treatment successfully reduces the period of chilling requirement.
- Gibberelins regulate fruit set, fruit development and fruit quality in grapes, particularly in Thompson Seedless grape.
- Chemical thinning of grape berries can be achieved through application of GA_3 (50-100 ppm), NAA (25-50 ppm) and Sevin (200 ppm).

40. Major disorders of fruit and plantation crops

Crop	Disorders
Almond	Gummosis
Annona	Stoning
Aonla	Fruit necrosis
Apple	Bitter pit, Water core, Jonathan spot, Russetting, Internal browning
Avocado	Dry neck, Die back
Bael	Fruit drop, cracking of fruit
Cherry	Fruit cracking
Citrus	Little leaf, Mottling leaf, Exanthema, Granulation, Yellow spot, Fruit cracking, Sun scald and Sun burn.
Cocoa	Witches broom
Coconut	Crown choking, Button shedding
Fig	Fruit splitting, Sunburn, Cracking of stem, Eruption of skin, Fruit drop
Grape	Millerandage, Hen and Chicken, Berry and Flower drop, Calyx end rot, Water berries, Pink berries uneven ripening
Jamun	Fruit and Flower drop
Litchi	Skin cracking, Sun burning, Leaf bronzing
Lime and Lemon	Splitting or Cracking
Mango	Leaf scorching, mango malformation, witches broom, spongy tissue, Seed jelly, Black tip/ Taper tip/ Tip pulp/ Girdle necrosis, Clustering/ Jhoomka, Soft nose, internal necrosis, Stem end rot, Sun burn, Sap burn
Mandarin	Fruit drop, Granulation, Decline
Mangosteen	Gamboge, Fruit splitting
Peach	Sun scald, Splitting
Pecan	Leaf scorch, Rosette
Strawberry	Albinism
Pear	Hard end, Break down
Persimmon	Calyx cavity, Fruit drop
Pineapple	Fasciation, Multiple crown, Sun scald, Excessive slip growth
Pomegranate	Fruit cracking, internal break down
Sapota	Cock's comb or Flattening of branches

41. Disorders of fruits

Aonla	**Necrosis** A physiological disorder has been observed in aonla fruits. Francis variety is highly susceptible followed by Banarasi. Incidence initiates with browning of mesocarp which extends towards the epicarp resulting into brownish black appearance of flesh.
Apple	**Scald** is one of the storage disorders in apple. Light mottling on greener surface of fruits are initial symptoms of scald. Darkening becomes more severe with elapsed time and ultimately extends to red surface also. Scald usually affects the skin only but in severe cases it may extend to fruit flesh. The immature fruits are most susceptible to scald and is aggravated by warmer temperatures in storage. **Bitterpit** is characterized by small sunken spots on the fruit surface which are more prevalent near the blossom endinitially small water soaked areas appear which shrink and turn brown with the loss of water and ultimately become brown localized areas of the dead tissue. Unlike the name, these corky tissues are never bitter in taste. The immature picked fruits and large sized fruits in 'off year' are the most affected. Golden Delicious and Yellow Newton are most susceptible varities. **Internal browning** is associated with apple variety yellow newton It is characterized by brownish streaks radiating into flesh from the core. CA storage with higher temperature can be helpful to control this disorder.
Banana	**Neer Vazhai** is malady of unknown etiology. It affects Nendran banana in Tamil Nadu. Infested plants show poor plant growth, delayed shooting, lanky bunch with few hands and immature unfilled fingers. Fruits ooze out watery fluid when cut, hence the name 'Neer' meaning 'water' and 'vazhai' - 'banana'. In infested plants, severe root damage is noted. Cause of this disorder is not known, but is of serious concern causing considerable loss. Application of growth hormone NAA improves the finger filling. It is transmitted through suckers and can be suspected to cause by virus or mycoplasma **Kotta vazhai** is also a malady of unknown etiology affecting Poovan banana. 'Kottai' means seed, referring to conspicuously enlarged ovules and immature dark green fruits. Though few studies conducted earlier with sprays of 2, 4-D @ 120 ppm enabled to obtain normal bunch, the cause of this malady is not known. It is suspected to be associated with incidence of banana streak virus.
Bael	**Fruit drop and cracking** in bael before ripening are main problems. Growth regulators 2, 4-D, GA_3 and 2, 4.5-T with various concentration check fruit drop. Cracking can be minimized by maintaining proper moisture up to full growth or maturity of fruit. **Chilling injury** develops during storage of fruits below 9°C.
Grape	Presence of green berries in a ripe bunch of coloured grapes is called **uneven ripening.** It is a varietal character and a problem in Bangalore Blue, Bangalore Purple, Beauty Seedless and Gulabi grapes. Generally inadequate leaf areas and non availability of reserves to a developing bunch is the reason. Cultural practices like cluster thinning, girdling and use of growth regulators can reduce uneven ripening. Application of Ethephon (250 ppm) at colour break stage is recommended. **Post-harvest berry drop** is due to weak pedicel attachment to the berries. Common in Anab-e-Shahi, Cheema Sahebi and Beauty Seedless. Spraying

contd.

	of NAA (50 ppm) a week prior to harvesting can minimize the post-harvest berry drop. When panicles are fully expanded, the flower buds and flower drop before the fruit set. This is common in north India but not in the south. Stem girdling prior to full bloom can reduce the problem. **Pink berry,** a common disorder in Thompson Seedless and its clone Tas-a-Ganesh in Maharashtra. Pink blush develops on a few ripe berries close to harvesting. The pink colour turns to dull red colour and the berries become soft and watery. A mixture of 0.2% ascorbic acid and 0.25% sodium diethyl dithiocarbamate at fortnightly intervals commencing berry softening.
Fig	Fig is susceptible to *sun burn, fruit splitting* and *fruit drop*. **Sun-burn** is noticed mostly in young plants and those subjected to excessive pruning. The trunk and shoots that are exposed to direct sun are prone to sun burn. The affected parts crack and the bark peels off, providing easy access for fungi and other infection. Developing a good canopy by proper pruning and coating the exposed limbs with lime protect the plants from sun burn. Fruit splitting is attributed to sudden change in atmospheric humidity during ripening. This makes the fruit unfit for consumption as the pulps is exposed to insect and microbial infection. Fruit drop may result from excessive drought and heat, cold nights or light frost. Lack of pollination also causes fruit drop in figs.
Jamun	Heavy **drop of flowers and fruits** have been observed in jamun at various stages. About 50% flowers drop within 3-4 weeks of flowering. It occurs at very young stage during 5-7 weeks of full bloom. The problem of flower and fruit drop can be minimized by spraying of GA_3 (60 ppm) twice, one at full bloom and other 15 days after fruit set.
Guava	Guava plants are attacked by wilt, which alone causes heavy losses. It is very difficult to find out on orchard of guava more than 30 years in age because most of its plants die at about 20 years of age due to wilt. Various fungi causing wilt are *Fusarium roseum oxysporum F. psidii, F. solani,* and *Gliocladium roseum*. Resistant rootstock is the only solution.
Litchi	**Sun burning** and **skin cracking** in developing fruits is a serious problem in litchi. High temperatures, low humidity and soil moisture conditions during fruit development. Inadequate moisture during early period of fruit growth results in the skin becoming hard and sun burnt. It may crack when it is subjected to increased internal pressure as a result of rapid aril growth following irrigation or rain. Fruit cracking in litchi is also favoured if temperature goes above 38ºC and relative humidity less than 60%. Growth regulators NAA (20 mg/ litre of water), GA (40 mg/litre of water), 2, 4-D (10 mg/ litre of water), 2, 4, 5-T (10 mg/ litre of water) and Ethephon (10 mg/ litre of water) reduce the incidence of fruit cracking. Spraying with $ZnSO_4$ (1.5%) weekly or $CaNO_3$ (1.5%) fortnightly from pea size to harvesting of fruit is an effective method to reduce cracking incidence.
Lime and Lemon	Cracking or **splitting** of limes and lemons is a common physiological disorder. Fruit cracking is associated with sudden changes in weather conditions, heavy irrigation or rainfall other a prolonged drought and infection of bacteria. Sometimes hot winds also cause fruit cracking. Splitting may be radial (longitudinal) or transverse, radial being more common. Lemons are more prone to fruit cracking. It can be minimized by giving timely and frequent light irrigation during summers. Irrigation after a drought should be light. Application of K also reduces fruit splitting.

contd.

Mandarin Orange	In spite of very high initial flowering and fruiting in mandarins, the ultimate yield is often low primarily owing to heavy **fruit drop**. However, all fruits that fall to mature do not drop of one time but at different times. There are more or less definite periods or stages when extensive dropping occurs in mandarins, the shedding of flowers and fruits come in more or less in three distinct waves. The first wave occurs soon after fruit setting, second during May-June known as June drop and third one known as pre-harvest drop, i.e. the drop of mature fruits before harvesting. Fluctuating temperature, low atmospheric humidity, imbalance of soil moisture, lack of proper nutrition, hormonal imbalance, incidence of insect pests and diseases are some factors causing fruit drop. Accordingly, maintenance of appropriate soil moisture level during fruit development and application of growth regulators 2, 4-D (10 ppm), NAA (5 pm), 2, 4, 5-T (5 ppm) check fruit drop. Further, application of Aureofungin @ 20 ppm helps in better retention of fruits through control of fungal diseases. **Granulation** is a physiological disorder of juice sacs of citrus including mandarins wherein they become comparatively hard, assume a greyish colour and become somewhat enlarged. The concentration of pectin substances increases, whereas there is reduction in juice content, TSS and acid content. Because of low sugar and acid content, the granulated vesicles become rather tasteless and colourless. Young, vigorous trees are more likely to develop granulated fruits than older ones. Similarly, large fruits have more granulation than small ones. In addition, granulation increases as the picking season advances. The incidence of granulation is highly specific to the type of the mandarin being cultivated. It is favoured by high relative humidity and temperature during spring. Spraying of lime reduces the extent of granulation. Reduction in irrigation also lessens its incidence. The application of 2, 4-D (12 ppm), zinc and copper reduce the incidence of granulation considerably.
Mangosteen	**Gamboge and fruit splitting** are physiological disorders in mangosteen. Gamboge is characterized by yellow exudation of gum on the fruits and branches. Fruit splitting results in swollen arils with a mushy pulp. Gamboge is more pronounced in fruits exposed to direct sunlight, and in crop that matures in summer. Heavy and continuous rains during fruit ripening favour gamboge and fruit splitting in certain locations.
Mango	**Alternate bearing** Most of the South Indian varieties are regular bearer, whereas North Indian ones alternate bearer. Paclobutrazol is a promising chemical for flower induction in mango. Soil drenching with paclobutrazol (5 g and 10 g/ tree) results in minimum outbreak of September to October. Vegetative flushes, giving an early and profuse flowering. **Mango malformation** one of the most important disorders, is causing huge losses. It is a major problem in Punjab, Delhi and Uttar Pradesh. of the two types of mango malformation, vegetative malformation is more common in nursery seedlings and young plants. Floral malformation affects trees at the bearing stage. In vegetative malformation or bunchy top, compact leaves are formed in a bunch at the apex of shoot or in the leaf axil and growth of shootlet is arrested. Floral malformation directly affects the productivity. Deblossoming alone or coupled with a spray of 200 ppm NAA lowers the number of

contd.

	malformed panicles significantly. **Black tip** is mainly noticed in Punjab, Uttar Pradesh, Bihar and West Bengal. The distal end of the affected fruits turns black and becomes hard. Fruits ripen prematurely and become unmarketable.This disorder is caused by the smoke of brick-kilns located with a distance of 600 mts. Gases like carbon monoxide and carbon dioxide, sulphur dioxide and acetylene cause these symptoms. It can be controlled by raising the height of the chimney of the brick kilns. Spraying borox (0.6%) at 10-14 days intervals (jhumka) starting from fruit set also controls it. **Clustering (Jhumka)** is characterized by a cluster at fruitlets at the tip of the panicle giving on appearance of bunch tip called *jhumka.* These fruitlets are dark green with a deeper curve in the sinus beak region compared with normally developing fruitlets. These fruitlets grow to marble size after which their growth ceases. One of the main reasons for clustering is the adverse climate during February-March, particularly the low temperature. **Spongy tissue** is specific in Alphonso mango. Fruits from outside look normal, but inside a patch of flesh become spongy, yellowish and sour. This disorder has brought down the export of this variety. Inactivation of ripening enzyme due to high temperature, convective heat and post harvest exposure to sunlight are the causes. Use of sod culture and mulching are useful in reducing its incidence. Mango hybrids Ratna and Arka Puneet which have Alphonso like characters are not suffered from this malady. Harvesting mangoes at three fourths matured stage rather than fully matured also reduces this malady.
Pear	Premature ripening begins with pink colouration near the blossom end. Consequently core breakdown (brown heart) and softening occur in affected fruit which do not ripen properly. This disorder is caused by abnormally cool growing season preceding harvest. Night temperature lower than 7.1°C and day temperature lower than 21°C for few days are sufficient to cause premature ripening. As soon as the initial symptoms appear, the fruits should be harvested and handled normally.
Peach	**Sun scald** causes severe damage to the exposed trunk and main scaffold branches. Shading of branches considerably reduces the incidence. Painting of exposed surface with lime paste and shading by wrapping straw or hay around trunk and thicker branches is quite effective . **Splitting of fruits** generally occurs at dorsal and ventral sides, mostly at the time of pit-hardening stage. Sometimes gum exudes from the fruit making it unfit for consumption. Splitting and gumming are accentuated during heavy rains after a long dry spell.
Persimmon	**Fruit drop** relates to a number of causes including excessive fruit rot, lack of pollination, water stress, excessive nitrogen application and insect damage. The first wave of drop occurs in early June just other petal fall and continues upto late July. Thereafter, no fruit drop occurs in most of the varieties. But in some varieties, late drop is also noted which is not equivalent to pre-harvest drop of apples and seems to be a unique feature of persimmon. The late drop is affected by the nutritional conditions of trees. Ringing blossom thinning, and nitrogenous fertilizer applications reduce fruit drop. All fruits drop immediately after defoliation under

contd.

	ringed conditions. This shows that fruit drop in persimmon is closely related to the nutrient status of tree. **Calyx cavity** A serious problem in persimmon. The symptoms are a sparse space or cavity that occurs directly beneath the calyx of the fruit. This cavity becomes a habitat for mealy bugs and fungal growth.Some cultivars are more susceptible than others. The incidence of calyx cavity appears to be less on trees which have heavier crop loads and where fruits have been pollinated. The avoidance of excessive N and K fertilizers, especially in later spring/ summer and close to harvest, thinning early in the season to enhance calyx growth and optimizing pollination to produce more than 3 seeds/fruit are control measures.
Pecannut	**Leaf scorch** comprises more than one type of scorch, based on appearance and cause. Necrotic (dead) areas develop on basal edges of the leaflets. As the diseases advances defoliation starts. It is most frequently associated with very wet or very dry soil. Such a soil condition causes nutrient imbalance within the plant in summer or early fall, poor filling of nuts, causing a complete crop failure takes place. It can be controlled by providing moderate shading to small trees to reduce transpiration, moderate summer cultivar, mowing or grazing of sad orchards reduce water loss through grass and weeds. Thinning of over-crowded trees is also helpful. **Rosette** is caused by the lack of Zn. There is bronzing and crinkling of leaflets. Rosette of leaves develops. In severe cases; it causes twigs and eventually branches, to die back. Growth and development of the trees are greatly retarded and the trees do not produce nuts. It can be corrected with the foliar or soil application of zinc sulphate (0.5%). Its application to the soil should be done @ 900-1,000 g/mature tree in sandy soil and in heavier soils, 2,250-4,500g /tree is enough.
Pineapple	In **fruit and crown fasciations,** fruits become totally useless. Sometimes fruits are highly flattened and twisted with innumerable crowns. Fruits and crown fasciations are associated with high vigour of the plants. Such plants take longer time to flower than the normal ones. Highly fertility of soil and worm weather, where the conditions are highly congenial for vagorous vegetative growth may favour the fasciations. The incidence of fasciations increases with advancing rations. The excessive slip growth is at the expense of the fruit, resulting in small, tampered fruits, often with knobs at the base. High nitrogen fertilization and rainfall along with relatively low temperature are congenial for this abnormality.
Pomegranate	Disintegration of arils in matured pomegranates, known as an **internal breakdown or blackening of arils** is a serious malady. This disorder can not be identified externally whereas the arils become soft, light creamy brown to dark blackish-brown and unfit for consumption. It is increasing rapidly in the pomegranate growing pockets in western Maharashtra. The incidence of internal breakdown occurs 90 days after anthesis. It immensity increases if the fruits are left on the tree for 140 days onwards. It is evident in evergreen and deciduous cultivars. The incidence is more in *ambe bahar*. It increases with increase in weight of fruits from 150-200 g (26.60%) to more than 350 g (60%). No insect or organism is associated with this malady. The TSS, acidity, reducing

contd.

	sugars, calcium, phosphorus and enzyme catalase are reduced, whereas non-reducing sugars starch, tannins, nitrogen, potassium, magnesium, boron and enzyme polyphenol oxidase and peroxidase increase in the affected arils compared with healthy ones. The exact causes are not Therefore, pomegranates should be harvested at 120 – 135 days after fruit set. **Fruit cracking**, is more intense under dry condition of the arid zone. The fully grown, mature cracked fruits though sweet, loose their keeping quality and become unfit for marketing. They are also liable to rot qualitatively. The cracked fruits show reduction in their fruit weight, grain weight and volume of juice. It is due to deficiency of calcium, boron and potash. Fully developed pomegranates crack due to moisture imbalance, as they are very sensitive to variation in soil moisture and also to day and night atmospheric moisture deficit. Prolonged drought causes hardening of peel. If this is followed by heavy irrigation or rains, the pulp grows and the peel cracks. Cracking of fruits is also due to rise in air temperature during fruit growth and development. There are some cultivars/ strains-PS 75 K 3, Appuli, Shirvan, Burachni, Krasnyl, Sur-Anar, Kurmyz-Kabukh and Francis-which are tolerant/resistant to cracking. Cracking can be managed through maintaining soil moisture and not allowing wide variation in soil moisture depletion, cultivating tolerant types, applying copious and regular irrigation during fruiting season using Pinolene (5%) as vapour guard and GA3 (15 ppm) and applying boron (0.2%) reduces cracking of fruits and improve fruit colour.
Sapota	*Wilt or die-back* is common where sapota cultivation is being extended to traditionally rice-growing regions. Due to anaerobic conditions in monsoon and post-monsoon season in such areas wilt is of common appearance aggravated by Fusarium spp. This can be controlled by effective drainage facility before planting. *Abnormal* shape of fruit is related with number of seeds in it which depend on conditions for pollination of anthesis. High temperature and rainfall during flowering cause obligation of fruits. Therefore, cultivation of sapota in areas with extreme summer temperature should be avoided. Sometimes fruits do not develop into their normal shape but develop a depression of furrow towards the calyx-end. This symptom usually appears immediately after heavy rainfall and is aggravated by high intensity of irrigation. Therefore, over irrigation should be avoided. The fruits exposed to intense sunlight do not open uniformly, developing corkiness during winter. This is probably due to killing of hydrolyzing enzymes by alternating moisture accumulation and heating of fruit surface in winter.
Cocoa	Cocoa produces a large number of flowers. But only a small percentage of flowers is successfully pollinated and too many fruits are set for the tree to carry through to maturity. The young cocoa fruit till it attains a length of 10 cm is called a 'cherelle' an over 80% of the cherelles formed on a mature tree usually wilt. This phenomenon is called **cherelle wilt.** The cherelle initially stop growing and a week later, turn yellow and then blacken and shrivel. The wilt occurs only up to about 100 days after fertilization with peak wilting of 50 and 70 days.
Strawberry	**Albinism** is due to lack of fruit colour during ripening. Fruits remain irregularly pink or even totally white and sometimes swollen. They have acid taste and become less firm. Albino fruits are often damaged during

contd.

	harvesting and are susceptible to Botrytis infection and decay during storage. It is probably caused by certain climatic conditions and extremes in nutrition.
Coffee	*Die-back* is a physiological disorder that refers to the death of young branches during dry period. Pre-mature yellowing of leaves and drying of young tertiary branches from third and fourth node progressing either ways towards tip as well as downwards are its symptoms. It occurs due to adverse environmental factors such as high temperature exposure to high light intensity, low soil moisture, low relative humidity and depletion of reserve carbohydrates. The after-effects are interveinal chlorosis and narrow, crinkled, small leaf formation with abnormal branching after the onset of first summer showers. Remove dead and whippy wood. Provide optimum shade (30%), Spray pre-blossoms and pre-monsoon bordeaux mixture (0.5%). conserve soil moisture status by thick mulch. Liming of soils to correct pH is also necessary. *Pre-mature fruit* drop usually occurs in coffee during the berry development stage, 90-120 days after blossom. The extent of fruit drop varies depending upon the field conditions (waterlogging wet feet) as well as physiological status of the bush (hormonal imbalance, carbohydrate content and nutrient deficiency), 'Wet feet' condition in the plantations is due to continuous heavy rainfall with cool ambient temperature, high relative humidity, cloudy weather and improper drainage leading to water logging. The fruit drop can be checked by adopting proper soil cultivation methods like providing good drainage, cradle pits etc. In addition, post-blossom (15 days after blossom) and pre-monsoon application of one of these growth regulators (Planofix or Agronoa or Miraculan or Atonik @50 ml/ 200 litres of water or Potozyme or Cytozyme crop plus @60 ml/ 200 litres of water) is also useful in controlling premature fruit drop. A total quantity of 1,500 litres of spray solution is adequate for a hectare crop. Bean disorders like black bean, black jolloo and normal jolloo are generally observed in Arabica coffee due to physiological factors during bean development stage. Two rounds of Bordeaux mixture as pre-monsoon and post monsoon applications (during May and September) are quite good to keep it under control. The post-monsoon application of Bordeaux mixture could be given along with urea (0.5%) and murate of potash (0.375%) (1 kg urea and 750 g of MOP/ barrel).
Rubber	**Tapping panel dryness** (TPD) is the only major physiological disorder affecting the rubber tree. This syndrome is characterized by partial or complete drying up of the panel (i.e. no production of latex) after a period of prolonged and late dripping of latex for a few days/ weeks. Some trees become dry even without late dripping. In some dry trees, tumors and necrotic bark tissues develop along the bark. The affected soft bark becomes light brown in colour and hence TPD is also known as brown bast. The outer bark gets dried and cracks open. Tumors can be seen on the panel area. Otherwise, the tree continues to grow normally. The exact cause of this syndrome is unknown, although excessive harvesting of latex seems to be a possible trigger and high yielding clones are more vulnerable. Giving tapping rest is the only recommendation at the moment, but this is not a solution. Low frequency taping is also recommended which will reduce the incidence of TPD.

43. Biochemical constituents of fruit crops

1. Mango - α-carotene
2. Barbedos cherry - Ascorbic acid
3. Bael - Riboflavin
4. Walnut - Fat
5. Date palm - Iron
6. Pineapple - Bromelin
7. Fig - Ficin
8. Papaya - Papain
9. Cocoa - Theobromine

43. Common technical terms

2, 4-D	2, 4-Dichloro-phenoxy acetic acid
2, 4-DB	2, 4-dichloro-phenoxy butyric acid
2,4,5-T	2,4,5-trichlorophenoxy butyric acid
AAR	Accumulated assured rainfall
AAS	1-aminocyclopropane-1-carboxilic acid (precursor of ethylene)
ADP	Adenosine di-phosphate
Alidochlor (CDAA)	N-N-dailly-2 chloro-acetamide
AMO1618	1-(N-piperidine carboxy)-2-isopropyl-5-methyphenyl-4 trimethyl ammonium chloride
AOA	Amino-oxy-acetic acid
APP	Ammonium polyphosphate

EXPLANATORY NOTES

APPLE

(*Malus × domestica* Barkh)

Family:	Rosaceae
Sub-family:	Pomoideae
Origin:	Asia Minor to Western Himalaya, South-West Siberia
Type of fruit:	Pome, usually without cells
Edible portion:	Fleshy thalamus
Basic chromosome number:	X=17
Somatic number:	2n = 34, 51

Predominating biochemical constituents :

Sugar:	Glucose & fructose
Organic acid:	Malic acid
Pigments:	Cynidin-3-galactoside
Flavouring compounds:	Ethyl 2-Methyl butyrate
Vitamin:	Vitamin C and A
Phenol:	Quinic acid, Cynidin-3-galactopyranoside
Mineral:	Potassium

- Apple is most widely grown as temperate fruit in the world.
- India-rank: 11th in Apple production in the world.
- Apple is a typical temperate fruit..
- Himachal Pradesh is known as "APPLE bowl of India".
- San Jose Scale got its entry into India from France in 1906.
- J&K is leading apple producing state.
- Average summer temperature should be around 21-24ºC during active growth period.
- Most critical period for water requirement: April-August.
- Flowers are white to pink in colour borne on terminal buds or 2 years spur.
- Inflorescence is Cyme and determinate type with 5 flowers.
- In India, 11 to 33% pollinizing trees are recommended for regular cropping.
- *Early fruit drop* is due to lack of pollination and competition.

- *June drop* is due to moisture stress.
- Pre-harvest fruit drop is due to development of abscissic layer (formation of ethylene).
- Scarlet Gala, Red Fuji: High yielding varieties.
- Optimum temperature for pollen germination and fruit setting is 21.1 - 26.7ºC
- J&K is leading apple producing State
- Highest yield of good quality in regions having long day hours and high light intensities and relatively very warm days with cool night and low humidity during the growing season.
- Apple is staple fresh fruit in the temperate regions of world.
- Acid content of fresh fruits helps to develop natural flavour in apple juice.
- *Malus pumila* Var. paradisiaca is paradise apple and is parent of all. Formerly, it was *M. communis* or *Pyrus malus.*
- *Malus sylvestris* is wild crab apple.
- *Malus baccata* is Siberian crop.
- Apple is a False fruit.
- Fuzi is the offspring of Ralls Janet×Delicious developed in 1939
- Granny Smith is a chance seedling and is open pollinated seedling of French crab
- Most apple varieties have chilling requirement of 1000-1600 hrs at a temperature below 7ºC to break the rest period
- Ambri is only indigenous variety grown in India.
- Baldwin is discovered as a chance seedling
- Golden delicious is commercially used as a pollinizer for delicious apples
- McIntosh is a chance seedling
- Fuzi is cross between Red Delicious × Rall's Janet (Japan) introduced in 1858 and named as Fuzi in 1962.
- Summer temperature should be 22-25ºC
- Thomas Andrews Knight produced the 1st apple cultivar of known parentage.
- Cox's McIntosh is a low hills variety.

- High temperature is more susceptible to superficial scald if grown in temperate climate.
- 300 mm rainfall is considered best from April to September.
- During growing season water-stress reduces/delays, number size of fruits and increase June Drop.
- Best root growth temperature is 18°C, best pH of soil is 6.5-6.7
- Well drained, slightly acidic and loam soils are required for better quality apples.
- *Malus sikkimenis, M. torngoides and M. hupehensis* are apomictic rootstocks of apple.
- 1870 - A.A. Lee introduced Apple at Kullu, (HP)
- 1918 - Satya Nand Stokes introduced Apple at Kotgarh, HP
- 1889 - Alexander Coatt introduced Apple at Mashobra (Shimla), HP
- Commercial method of propagation of rootstocks is stooling.
- EMCA series of rootstock resistant to viruses
- Northern spy is resistant to wooly aphid (*Eriosoma lonigerum*)
- M_{26} and MM106 rootstocks are sensitive whereas, M_{13} and M_{16} are tolerant to water logging.
- Fire blight caused due to *Erwinia amylovora*
- Conventionally propagated by seeds.
- Clonal rootstocks are commonly propagated by Stooling (Mound layering). IBA is used for rooting.
- Budding: Shield or T budding is common
- Cordons, dwarf pyramid and espalier are planting systems for HDP.
- Cordons: In this system side shoots are kept short by summer pruning.
- Dwarf pyramid: Planting distance = 1 to 1.5 meter plant to plant; 2-3 meter between rows
- Espalier: Annual pruning is done.
- Cordons: Planting distance = 2×3 meters and 60-90 cm apart in rows, planting at an angle of 45°. Supporting wire is used. This system is not suitable for vigorous seedling rootstocks.
- Calcium deficiency causes bitter pit in apple.
- Zn deficiency causes Rosette, where as Magnesium deficiency causes Interveinal Chloroses in apple
- Iron deficiency is common in semi-arid region where irrigation water is high in bicarbonates and soil pH is high.

- Boron deficiency causes internal core.
- Drip or Trickle irrigation systems are used.
- Jonathan, Golden Delicious, Rome beauty are examples of partially self-fruitful.
- Low temperature during flowering kills petal (-4°C to -2°C).
- Pollination is carried through honey bees, 2-3 hives/ hectare are sufficient.
- Spray of Amino-ethoxy vinyl glycerin (AVG increases fruit set in apple.
- 2, 4-D and 2 4 5-T are used to control fruit drop.
- NAA, carbaryl are used for thinning.
- Cold storage temperature is -1°C to 0°C at 85-90% RH.
- In CA storage O_2 (2-3%) and CO_2 (2-3%) is recommended.
- Golden Delicious, Jonathan, Granny Smith and Cox's Orange Pippin are susceptible cultivars of apple to powdery mildew.
- Apple scab caused by *Venturia inaequalis* and Fire blight caused by *Erwinia amylobora*
- Powdery mildew is caused by *Podospharea leucotricha* and Crown gall by *Agrobacterium tumefaciens* that occurs near or at graft union on nursery plant.
- *Aphilenus mali* is a predator of wooly apple aphid
- *Malus floribunda* is a small fruited species and is good pollinizer of apple
- English varieties are self-pollinated and act as suitable pollinizer for delicious group.
- Red Delicious is most popular variety of India.
- Red Gold acts as pollinizer for Red Delicious and Starking Delicious.
- Golden Delicious is a commercial variety of USA and Europe.
- McIntosh is a leading variety of Canada.
- Northern Spy: Resistant to wooly apple aphids
- Seeds stratification at 4-7°C for 60-90 days.

Scab resistant varieties :

- Prima (*M. floribunda* × Rome Beauty) released in 1970
- Priscilla: released in 1972

- Liberty: released in 1978
- Red Free (Coop-13): released in 1981
- Coop-12 (Emra): released in 1980
- Freedom: released in 1983. It is fairly resistant to powdery mildew
- Macfree: released in 1974

Apple hybrids :

Amb Royal - Starking Delicious × Ambri (Hybrid No. 54)
Amb Red - Red Delicious × Ambri (Hybrid No. 157)
Amb Rich - Rich-a-Red × Ambri (Hybrid No. 15)
Lal Ambri - Red Delicious × Ambri
Sunhari - Ambri × Golden Delicious
Amb Starking - Starking Delicious × Ambri
Chaubattia Princess - Red Delicious × Early Shanburry

Rootstocks :

- Rootstocks: Standard (MM 108), Vigorous (MM 111), Semi-vigorous (MM 106, M7) and Dwarf (M_9, M_{26}).
- In 1912, EMR Station in England developed a series of rootstock named Malling series (M series) and Malling Merton (MM series) rootstocks.
- M_9, M_{27}, M_{20} are dwarf rootstock, M_{2-}, M_7 and M_{26} are semi-dwarf rootstock whereas vigorous rootstocks are M_{12}, M_6 and M_{25}.
- Malling Merton rootstock are MM 104, MM 106 MM 109, MM 111.
- Seedling rootstock: *M. baccata* most commonly used rootstock in India.

Clonal rootstocks :

- M_9 (dwarf rootstock): suitable for high density plantation (Resistant to collar rot).
- M_4, M_7, MM106 are: semi-dwarf suitable for high density plantation and resistant to Woolly Apple Aphid.
- MM 111 (Semi-vigorous): Resistant to drought and wooly apple aphid
- M_{27} (Ultra-dwarf): $M_{13} \times M_9$
- $M_{26} = M_9 \times M_{16}$, susceptible to fire blight and collar rot
- Recommended rootstocks are M_2, M_{13}, (Vigorous); M4 (Semi-vigorous);
- Malling (M) and Malling Merton (MM) rootstocks are clonal rootstocks.

1st efforts initiated at East Malling Research Station (EMRS), Kent, England in 1912 that leads to development of Malling series of clonal rootstocks.

- Malling Merton or MM series of rootstocks were developed by East Malling Research Station Kent & John Inns Horticultural Institute Merton, England in 1928. 15 clones were numbered from 101-115 with the prefix MM from the Malling and Merton Research Station
- EMLA Series of Rootstocks: EM from East Malling and LA from Long Ashton have been developed. EMLA 9 or M9 EMLA or EMLA106 or MM106 EMLA is known as free from virus diseases.
- Polish apple rootstocks (P-series): P_{22}, P_2, P_{16} are important. All are winter hardy and resistant to collar rot.
- American apple rootstocks (MAC series)
- Canadian apple rootstock (Ottawa): OH-Ottawa Hybrid, Ottawa clonal (O) series.

The major apple producing belts/areas are :

- North West Hill Region

  Jammu & Kashmir: Srinagar, Pulwama, Anantnag, Baramullah, Kupwara.

  Himachal Pradesh: Shimla, Kullu, Sirmour, Mandi, Chamba, Kinnaur

  Uttrakhand: Almora Nainital, Pithauragarh, Tehri, Pauri, Chamoli, Uttarkashi, Dehradun

- North Eest Hill Region

  Arunachal Pradesh: Tawang, West Kanneng, Lower Subansiri

PEAR

(*Pyrus communis*)

Family :	Rosaceae
Sub-family:	Pomoideae
Origin:	Central & Eastern China & Korea
Type of fruit:	Pome
Edible portion:	Fleshy thalamus
Basic chromosome number:	X=17
Somatic number:	2n = 34, rarely 51 and 68

Predominating biochemical constituents :

Sugar:	Fructose

Organic acid:	Malic acid
Pigments:	Carotenoid
Flavourings:	Ethyl, propyl, butyl acetates
Vitamin:	Vitamin C
Phenol:	Chlorogenic acid & arbutin (seeds)
Mineral:	Phosphorus and Calcium

- *Pyrus communis* is European/common/soft pear.
- *P. pyrifolia* is Oriental/Japanese/ hard pear.
- Pear varieties are in three groups namely: European, Asian, Hybrids.
- Low chilling cultivars: Keiffer, Chinese sand pear.
- *P. communis*: Trees are pyramedial having white flowers mostly in corymbs.
- *P. pyrifolia* (Syn *P. serotina* var. Culto): White flowers appears before emergence of leaves
- *P. pashia* Linn (Mehal/ Kainth) and *Shaira* (*P. serotina*) are important rootstock of pear.
- Quince is dwarf rootstock. Chilling requirement of *P. communis* is more than *P. pyrifolia*.
- Amino acid: *Asparagine* in pear juice of variety Bartlett.
- Pear is highly delicious fruit maintaining desirable acid: base balance in the body.
- Bartlett variety found better for canning.
- Climate: Pear can tolerate as low as (-26°C), temperate in dormancy and as high as 45°C during growing period.
- Flowers are white in colour, rarely pink.
- Inflorescence is Umbel like racemes, indeterminate with 6-8 flowers.
- Fruits are globose or pyriform, pome calyx persistent, fleshy usually having grit cells.
- Flower buds appear on two year and older spurs.
- Propagation: Pear is commercially propagated by budding (Shield or T-budding) done in May-June or September.
- Little leaf in pear: Due to zinc (Zn) deficiency.
- Blossom Blast: Due to zinc (Zn) deficiency called *Pseudomonas blight.*
- Storage scab: Caused by *Venturia pirina*
- Pear decline: Caused by Mycoplasma and transmitted by pear psylla.

- Rootsocks: *P. pashia* (Kainth); *P. serotina* (Shiara)
- Planting distance = 5 × 5 mts
- High density planting = 3 × 3 mts
- Beconte, Beaure Hardy, Clappe Favorite are the improved cultivars.
- Bacterial fire blight is caused by Bacterium *Erwinia amylovora*.
- Quince (Rootstock) is used to get dwarf Pear.
- *P. pyrifolia* is susceptible to black end disorder.

Rootstocks :

- Quince A (semi-dwarf); Quince B (intermediate) and Quince C (dwarf) rootstock.
- *Pyrus pashia* (Kainth) is resistant to wooly apple aphid and fire blight.
- Old Hume or Beaurre hardy is used in interstock for pear to overcome graft incompatibility between *Bartlett* and *quince*.
- Pear exhibits vegetative parthenocarpy and produces seedless fruits.
- Pear is trained to central leader system.
- *Pyrus communis* (Soft pear) is resistant to oak root fungus *Armillaria mellea*.
- *Pyrus* is differentiated from *Malus* due to presence of gritty cells. Lenticels are very prominent in pear fruit. Flemish Beauty and Magness are free from grit cells.
- Type of incompatibility in pear is *Gametophytic*.

QUINCE

(*Cydonia oblonga* Mill)

Family:	Rosaceae
Sub-family:	Pomoideae
Origin:	Southern Europe and Asia Minor
Type of fruit:	Pome
Edible portion:	Fleshy thalamus
Basic chromosome number:	X = 17
Somatic number:	2n = 34

- Inflorescence is terminal, solitary at the end of a leafy shoot.
- Quince fruit is many seeded pome fruit, pyriform.
- Flower buds at the terminal shoot or one year shoot
- Meech, Pineapple, Champion, Orange, Van-deman, Rea are main cultivars of quince.

- Quince A is vigorous and Quince C is dwarfing rootstock of pear.
- Quince (*Cydonia oblonga*) is commonly used rootstock in Pear.
- Susceptible to oak root fungus, fire bight, excess lime and cold.
- Deciduous thornless shrubs or small tree; buds small pubescent with foud scales.
- Flowers white or pink, terminal, solitary at the end of leafy shoots sepals 5 entire reflexed, petals 5 obovate.
- Stamen 20, styles 5 flora pubescent below, ovary inferior.
- The genus consist of single species i.e. *Cydonia oblonga* Mill.

PEACH

(*Prunus persica* Batsch)

Family:	Rosaceae
Origin:	Warm areas of China or Western China
Type of fruit:	Drupe
Edible portion:	Mesocarp and epicarp
Basic chromosomes:	X = 8
Somatic number:	2n = 16

- Flower buds borne laterally on one year shoot.
- Pistil single, ovary perigynous require chilling hours 400-1000.
- Flowers are solitary.
- Most peach cultivars are self fertile.
- Peach is native to China, peach was brought to North America from Europe.
- Climate: Very hot and arid climate.
- Among temperate fruits, peach has lowest chilling requirement.
- Regular pruning is required for getting maximum fruits.
- *Prunus behmi*: A matural hybrid of Almond × Peach
- Fruits have about 8-13°Brix TSS.
- Prunacin is the principle glycoside present in peach.
- Tatura trellies system of high density plantation is followed in peach.
- Mild winter (December-January) is the best time for pruning in peach.
- Fruiting takes place laterally on previous season growth.

- Blooming period can be delayed by the application of GA_2 (200 PPM) before leaf fall or by application of ethophon to avoid risk of spring frost.
- Peach is very susceptible to Iron deficiency.
- Nectarine is merely a peach with recessive gene that results in Fuzzless fruits.
- Self-sterile varieties are J H Hale, Candoka, Halberta, Alamar and Mikado.
- Among temprate fruits, peach needs lowest chilling hours and is earliest flowering.
- Peach is prone to water logging and sunscald.
- Pruning intensity is most severe in peach. It is trained to open centre system.

Rootstocks :

- Peach-Almond hybrids
- Hard woody cutting, IBA @ 500 ppm, in the month of December for growth of rootstocks.
- Planting season is winter. Spacing is 6 × 8 meters.
- Wild Peach, Myrobalan plum are rootstocks.
- *Nematode resistant rootstocks*: Nemaguard, Shalil Okinawe, Yunnan, Neared and Shalen.
- Myran is tolerant to drought, poor soil, root knot nematode and verticillium wilt.
- Nemaguard: *P. Persia* × *P. devidiana* (Nematode resistant rootstock)

ALMOND

(*Prunus amygdalous* Batsch)

Family:	Rosaceae
Origin:	Persia-Afghanistan, Western Asia
Type of fruit:	Drupe
Edible portion:	Kernel/ Cotyledon
Basic chromosomes:	X=8
Somatic number:	2n = 16

- Flowers buds borne laterally on one year shoot
- Almost all cultivars are self-sterile and thus require a pollinizer.

- Almond blooms very early during cool and moist weather. It is important to have a number of bees in orchard for good cropping.
- Rootstocks: Bitter almond, wild peach, peach-almond hybrids are good.
- Almond is a cross pollinated (by honey bees).
- USA is the largest producer of almond in world.
- In compatibility (self and cross) is the major hinderance in production/ yield and crop improvement of almond.
- Chilling requirement: 800 hours.

PLUM

1. European Plum (*Prunus domestica* L)
2. Japanese Plum (*Prunus salicina* L)

Family:	Rosaceae
Origin:	Europe West Asia and China
Type of fruit:	Drupe
Edible portion:	Mesocarp and epicarp
Basic chromosome number:	X = 8
Somatic chromosome number:	2n = 16

- Flowering on lateral unmixed flower buds having two year or older spurs.
- Each bud produce 1-3 flowers but no leaves. All terminal buds are vegetative.
- Plum is generally propagated by shield budding on seedling rootstocks of wild apricot or peach.
- Plums that can be dried successfully with or without stone are referred as *Prunes*.
- Plum is trained to central leader system in case of spreading type and modified central system for upright growing cultivars (Santa Rose, Stanley).
- In plum, self incompatibility is mediated by multiple alleles.
- Rootstock: Myrobalan-B, St. Julein-C, Myrobalan-29 and Dwarf-1, Pixy.
- Fruits TSS at time of maturity: 12.5°Brix.
- Seedling rootstock – wild apricot (zardalu).
- Peak water requirement period in plum is: May to June.
- Open centre is oldest training system followed in plum.
- In plum heavy bearing is a problem

APRICOT

(*Prunus armeniaca* L.)

Family:	Rosaceae
Origin:	China and Siberia
Type of fruit:	Drupe
Edible portion:	Mesocarp and epicarp
Basic chromosome number:	X = 8
Somatic chromosome number:	2n = 16

- Flowers are solitary and are borne only on lateral buds.
- Fruit buds on one year and older wood.
- Apricot bears fruits on spurs and shoots.
- Apricot is propagated by shield budding on wild apricot or peach rootstocks.
- Moorpark: One of the best apricots for outdoor cultivation in small garden.
- Highly perishable fruit.
- Chilling requirement: 300-900 hrs below 7ºC for fruiting.
- Summer temperature: 16.6-32.2ºC

CHERRIES

Sweet cherry	**Sour cherry**
Prunus avium L.	*Prunus cerasus* L.
Family: Rosaceae	Rosaceae
Origin: Black Sea	Eastern Europe or West Asia
Type of fruit : Drupe	Drupe
Edible portion: Epicarp and mesocarp	Epicarp and mesocarp
Basic chromosome number: X=8	X=16
Somatic number: 2n = 16, 24, 32	2n = 32

- Cherries are divided into two groups: *Prunus avium* L. (Sweet cherry) and *Prunus cerasus* L. (Sour cherry).
- Sweet cherries are used for table purposes whereas sour cherries for processing.
- Chilling requirements: 2000-2700 hrs, highest among the temperate fruits.
- Heavy rainfall during flowering causes: 'Blossom wilt'.

- Heavy rainfall during ripening causes - 'Fruit cracking'.
- In Europe, a wine - 'Kirschwascer' is distilled from pulp of cherries.
- Most of commercial varieties of cherry are self-sterile.
- Clonal rootstock: Colt, Mazzard F-12/1 (semi vigorous, difficult to root).
- *Prunus avium* is diploid (2n = 16); *Prunus fruticosapall* (2n = 32)
- Sour cherry (*P. cerasus*) = *P. avium* × *P. fruticosa*
- Sweet cherries probably originate from the Black Sea and Caspian Sea.
- Keracyanin chloride is colouring principle of fruit skin.
- Inflorescence is a few flowered fascicles.
- Flower buds of both are borne on two year wood or at the base of one year shoot.
- Flowers are Perigynous.
- Harvesting of fruits is done with pedicel intact
- All sour cherry cultivars are self fertile and do not require pollinizers.
- Heavy rainfall during flowering causes Blossom wilt whereas; rainfall during ripening causes fruit cracking.
- Paza, Mahaleb and Mazzard are seedling rootstock
- Cherry is grown under rainfed condition in India.
- Stella is self-fertile cherry cultivar.
- In sour cherry, flowers open late that is why flowers are not attacked by frost.
- Flowers are perigynous.

Rootstocks :

- *Prunus avium*: F12/1 (commercially used), Charger (Intermediate).
- Semi-dwarf: Colt A = *P. avium* × *P. sendo cerasus*
- Dwarf rootstock: Colt and Charger.
- Mahaleb (*P. mehaleb*): Produce vigorous tree.
- Mizzard (*P. avium*): Produce dwarf tree.
- Paza (*P. cerasoides*): Show delayed incompatibility.
- Cherry is prone to sunscald.
- *Prunus avium* is diploid with somatic chromosome number 2n=16 but occasionally triploid and tatraploid are also seen.

MULBERRY

(*Morus alba* L.)

Family:	Moraceae
Origin:	China
Type of fruit:	Sorosis/ Syncarpus/ Aggregate of drulets
Edible portion:	Mesocarp
Basic chromosome number:	X = 14
Somatic number:	2n = 28, 42, 56, 84, 112, 308

- Inflorescence is many flowered catkin borne at the axils of leaves on new spring season growth.
- Female flowers contain two pistil.

FIG

(*Ficus carica* L.)

Family:	Moraceae
Origin:	West Asia
Type of fruit:	Syconus
Edible portion:	Fleshy receptacle
Basic chromosome number:	X = 13
Somatic chromosome number:	2n = 26

- *Ficin-* is an active compound present in Fig.
- *F. glomerata* (Gular) – Resistant to Nematode.
- Notching is practiced in Poona Fig for activating dormant buds.
- About 90% of the fig produced in the world is dried.
- Pruning is done in month of December.
- Inflorescence is borne at the nodes of one year shoots besides a vegetative bud that may or may not develops into new shoot.
- Fig has highest fibre content among fruits.
- Excel and Conardia are suitable for high density plantation (2.5 × 2.5 m^2)
- Sanpedro fig is intermediate between common fig and Smyrna fig.
- Common fig is grown parthenogenetically which doesn't required caprification.

- Capri fig is pistillate.
- Conardia (drying purpose); Excel (canning purpose); Deanna (table purpose).
- Excessive irrigation or heavy rains during ripening results in fruit cracking and production of insipid fruit.

WALNUT

(*Juglans regia* L.)

Family:	Juglandaceae
Origin:	South East Europe
Type of fruit:	Nut
Edible portion:	Lobed cotyledons
Basic chromosome number:	X = 16
Somatic number:	2n = 32

- The walnut is monocot.
- Male catkins are borne laterally on one year shoot.
- The female inflorescence occurs after a period of vegetative growth as a terminal raceme.
  - English or Persian walnut: *Juglans regia*
  - Northern California/ black walnut: *J. hindsii*
  - Japanese walnut: *J. ailantifolia*
- Nuts are harvested at PTB stage (when packing tissues turn brown).
- Temperature of 29-32ºC near harvesting results in well filled kernels.
- Hot summer with low humidity result in blank nuts.
- Sensitive to low temperature during spring and high temperature in summer.

HICKORY

(*Carya sp*)

Family:	Juglandaceae
Origin:	South East Europe
Type of fruit:	Nut
Edible portion:	Cotyledons
Basic chromosome number:	X =16
Somatic number:	2n = 32, 64

PECAN NUT

(*Carya illinoensis* Koch)

Family:	Juglandaceae
Origin:	Southern USA
Type of fruit:	Nut
Edible portion:	Seed or cotyledon
Basic chromosome number:	X = 16
Somatic chromosome number:	2n = 32

- Pecan is monoecious.
- Require warm temperate climate.
- Queen of nuts.
- Most important nut fruit of world, ranking 5th in production.
- The male catkins are borne laterally near the end of last season growth.
- The female inflorescence is a few flowered terminal spikes.
- All species of Genus *Carya* are together known as *Hicories* means species between pecan and other hicories are called *Hicans.*
- In Pecan, patch budding is done in May.
- Best planting time of Pecan is December-January.
- Best planting distance should be kept 8 × 10 meter.

FILBERT (HAZEL NUT)

(*Corylus sp.*)

Family:	Betulaceae
Type of fruit:	Nut
Edible portion:	Seed or cotyledon
Basic chromosome number:	X = 14
Somatic chromosome number:	2n = 28

- Filbert is monoecious.
- Male and female flower buds borne in the lateral positions on one year old shoot.

PISTACHIO NUT

(*Pistacia vera* L.)

Family: Anacardiaceae
Origin: West Asia
Type of fruit: Nut
Edible portion: Cotyledons
Basic chromosome number: X=15
Somatic chromosome number: 2n = 30

- Pistachio nut is usually dioecious.
- Both male and female flower buds occur laterally on one year old shoots.
- Inflorescence is a panicle.

CASHEWNUT

(*Anacardium occidentale* L.)

Family: Anacardiaceae
Origin: Tropical America (Brazil)
Type of fruit: Nut
Edible portion: Cotyledon & fleshy peduncle
Basic chromosomes number: X = 21
Somatic chromosome number:. 2n = 42

- USA is the largest importer of cashew kernels.
- Cashewnut is a tropical plant require moist and mild tropical climate.
- Cashew is a sun loving plant and does not tolerate excessive shade.
- Cashewnut in India was introduced by the Portuguese in Malabai coast in 16th century.
- The inflorescence of cashewnut is an indeterminate panicle of Polygamo-monoecious type.
- Cashew is restricted to altitude below 700 m where the temperature does not fall below 20°C for prolong period.
- Most popular method of roasting: Steam method
- Best quality kernels are obtained from Drum roasting – Highest whole kernel is obtained.
- Maximum recovery of oil: oil bath roasting
- Cashew is very sensitive to water logging conditions.
- 3rd important agriculture commodity exported from India.

- Commonly used drier for drying of kernel: Broma dryer.
- Cashew starts flowering in the month of November and extends upto February.
- Temperature exceeding 39-42°C during fruit development stage causes fruit drop.
- Seed is most important method of propagation for raising seedling for use as rootstock.

CHESTNUT

(Castanea spp.)

Family:	Fagaceae
Type of fruit:	Nut
Edible portion:	Kernel
Basic chromosome number:	X = 12
Somatic chromosome number:	2n = 24

- Chestnut is monoecious.
- Both male and female catkins are borne in axils of leaves of new spring shoots.

STRAWBERRY

(*Fragaria × ananassa* Duch)

Family:	Rosaceae
Sub-family:	Rosoideae
Origin:	Man-made hybrid
Type of fruit:	Etaerio of achenes
Basic chromosome number:	X = 7
Somatic chromosome number:	2n = 56

- The flower buds are borne at axils of leaves on the crown.
- The inflorescence is cymose with the early central flowers opening first and being much larger than later ones.
- The flowers are polygamy dioecious.
- Ovaries are superior.
- Strawberries are perennial, stoloniferous herbs.
- The leaves are trifoliate and arise from the "crown". The runners produce "daughter" plants at every other node.
- Fruit mature rapidly; ripening occurs in 20 to 50 days after pollination.
- Fruit of strawberry is a complete fruit with 98% edible portion.

- All cultivated varieties are octaploid.
- Mulching is an important cultural operation in strawberry cultivation.

BLACKBERRY AND RASPBERRY (BRAMBLES)

(*Rubus* Sp.)

Family:	Rosaceae
Origin:	India
Type of fruit:	Etaerio of druplets
Basic chromosome number:	X = 7
Somatic number:	2n = 21, 28, 35 — — — — 84

- Mixed flower buds of raspberry and blackberry are borne on one year old canes.
- The indeterminate racemose inflorescence is terminal on a short shoot arising from the flower bud.
- Ovaries are superior.
- The many pistilled flowers are perfect.
- White to pink flowers (1" diameter) is borne terminally on several-flowered racemes, cymes, or corymbose inflorescences on current season's growth.
- Fruit development occurs rapidly, taking only 30-50 days for most raspberries, and 40-70 days for blackberries.

CRANBERRY

(*Vaccinium macrocarpon*)

Family:	Ericaceae
Origin:	Native to cool temperate area
Type of fruit:	False Berry
Edible portion:	Fleshy thalamus
Basic chromosome number:	X = 12
Somatic chromosome number:	2n = 24

- Cranberries are self-fruitful.
- Cranberries are a group of evergreen dwarf shrubs or trailing vines.
- Cranberries have small evergreen leaves.
- The flowers are dark pink, style and stamens fully exposed and pointing forward.
- Flowers are solitary.
- Fruit is initially white, but turns a deep red when fully ripe.

- Flowers are borne singly in leaf axils on the basal portion of terminal mixed bud.
- Flowers are inverted, have four petals, inferior ovaries and are whitish pink in colour.
- The fruit is an epigynous or "false" berry, bright red with waxy bloom at maturity, giving dark red to black appearance.
- Fruit mature in 60-120 days after fertilization, depending on cultivar and weather.

BLUEBERRY

(*Vaccinium corymbosum L.*)

Family:	Ericaceae
Origin:	native to cool temperate area
Type of fruit:	Berry
Edible portion:	Pericarp and mesocarp
Basic chromosome number	X=12
Somatic chromosome number:	2n=48, 72

- Flower buds are either lateral or terminal on one year shoots
- White or cream flowers are borne on short racemes (1-2 inches).
- Flowers are urn-shaped and inverted, on very short pedicels (nearly sessile), with inferior ovaries.
- Inflorescence is dense raceme.
- The fruit is an epigynous or "false" berry.
- Fruit mature in about 90 days from bloom.
- Fruits are blue to black in colour and having good fruit quality.
- Three commercially important blueberry species are:

  Northern Highbush blueberry (*V. corymbosum L.*)

  Southern highbush (*V. corymbosum* hybrids with *V. darrowi, V. ashei*)

  Half-high highbush (*V. corymbosum x V. angustifolium*)

CURRANT BERRY

(*Ribes* spp.)

Family:	Saxifragaceae
Origin:	Asia and North America
Type of fruit:	Epigynous berry
Edible portion:	Thalamus
Basic chromosome number:	X=8
Somatic chromosome number:	2n = 16

- The mixed flower buds are lateral on one year shoot or spurs.
- Inflorescence is raceme.
- The perfect flowers have inferior ovaries.
- Red and white currants: *R. sativum* Syme, *R. rubrum* L.
- Black currant: *R. nigrum* L. Cultivars:
- Leaves of currants are 3-5 lobed, somewhat acute tips and petioled.

GOOSE BERRY

(*Ribes grossilaria* L.)

Family :	Saxifragaceae/ Grossulariaceae
Origin:	North America
Type of fruit:	Epigynous berry
Basic chromosome number:	X=8
Somatic chromosome number:	2n = 16

- Inflorescence is solitary.
- The perfect flowers have inferior ovaries.
- Gooseberries attain heights of 2-5 ft and black currants the most vigorous.
- Inflorescences contain 1-3 flowers in gooseberry. Inflorescences are racemes, commonly referred to as "strigs".
- Ovaries are inferior.
- Black currants are mostly self-incompatible, but will produce some fruit if self-pollinated.
- The fruit is usually glabrous and crowned with calyx remnants.

CANADIAN BUFFALO CHERRY

(*Shepherdia canadensis*)

Family:	Elaeagnaceae
Origin:	North America
Type of fruit:	Berry
Edible portion:	Pericarp and mesocarp
Basic chromosome number:	X = 20
Somatic chromosome number:	2n = 40

- *Shepherdia canadensis* is a woody perennial.
- *Shepherdia canadensis* can survive the coldest of winter climates with annual temperatures as low as -50° Fahrenheit.

- The berries are orange colored. It has a taste of grapes and red currant.
- Shepherdia canadensis is typically used in jelly.
- Shepherdia canadensis is dioecious, thus both a male and a female of the species are required in order to bear fruit.

GRAPE

(*Vitis vinifera* Michx)

Family:	*Vitaceae*
Origin:	Black Sea to Caspian Sea
Type of fruit:	Berry
Edible portion:	Pericarp and placentae
Basic chromosome number:	X=19, 20
Somatic chromosome number:	2n = 38, 40

Predominating biochemical constituents :

Sugars:	Glucose & fructose
Organic acid:	Tartaric acid
Pigments:	Monoglucosides of Malvidin, cyanidin and di-glucoside
Flavouring compound:	Linalool and geraniol
Vitamin:	Vitamin A
Phenol:	Tannins
Mineral:	Potassium

- "True grapes" (*Euvitis)*: the European grape *V. labrusca.*
- "Muscadine grapes" (*Muscadinia*): thick-skinned fruit, berries *V. rotundifolia.*
- 'Thompson seedless' is a major cultivar of table grape.
- Flower buds are at the nodes of one year old canes with the *racemose* inflorescence appearing opposite the leaves as the new shoot develops.
- Hypogynous flowers are usually perfect and sometime dioecious.
- Two celled ovary is superior.
- Muscadine grapes have small (2-3"), round, unlobed leaves with dentate margins.
- Flowers are small, 5 each of sepals, petals, and stamens.
- Ovaries are superior and contain 2 locules each with 2 ovules.
- Most grapes are self-fruitful.
- Grapes are true berries; round to oblong.

- Berries are often glaucous, having a fine layer of wax on the surface.
- Ideal time for planting is October.
- Rains during ripening causes berry cracking and rotting.
- Single pruning is done in North India during winter season (Dec - Jan).
- Pruning is done twice in South India:

1. April - Back or foundation pruning
2. October - Fruit or forward pruning

- Bower system of training is mostly adopted in India (High economic ratio).
- Growth regulators
- CCC: For suppressing vigour of vine & increase fruit fullness of bud.
- GA_3: For increasing berry size.
- NAA (50 PPM): To reduce post harvest fruit drop
- MH: For induction of male sterility
- Pink berry formation is common problem in Thompson Seedless and its clone.
- Average productivity of Grape in India (16.95 t/hac) and is highest in the world.
- Pruning intensity is lowest (3-4 bud) in Bangalore Blue, Bokhri cultivars.
- Pruning intensity is highest (10-14 buds) in Thompson Seedless.
- Calyptra- a cap like structure formed as a result of union of sepals and petals.
- Berry weight is obtained under bower system of training.
- Berry drop in grape is due to defective and improper pollination or fertilization.
- For Thompson Seedless, the spacing of 1.8 x 2.5 m^2 is ideal for bower system of planting.
- For Thompson Seedless, the spacing of 1.8 x 3.0 m^2 is ideal for 'y' trellies system of planting.
- Raisins are only processed product in India.
- Grape is a multi-seeded berry.
- Kishmish Beli - outstanding raisin grape cultivar.

- Back pruning/ growth pruning is the *summer pruning* in Grapes.
- Winter pruning in Grapes is also known as *forward pruning*.
- The skin of grape berry covered with wax like layer is called as cutin.
- Tartaric acid is commercially extracted from grape.
- Major Producing States: Maharashtra, Karnataka, Punjab, Andhra Pradesh and Tamil Nadu.
- Currently, in India the approximate area under different cultivars of grapes given as:
- Thompson Seedless = 55%,
- Bangalore Blue = 15%,
- Anab-e-Shahi and Dilkhush = 15%,
- Sharad Seedless = 5%,
- Perlette = 5%
- Gulabi and Bhokri = 5% of the total area under grapes in India.
- Raisin (dried seedless grape): Pusa Seedless, Thompson Seedless, Sultana are preferred for raisin making.
- Shot berries (Perlette): caused due to boron deficiency + poor pollination.
- Stem girdling: Removal of 5 mm wide ring at full bloom stage

Major grapes producing countries in world (2007-08)

Country	Area (000, ha)	Production (000, MT)	Productivity, MT/ ha
Italy	770	8519	11
France	830	6500	8
China	504	6250	12
United States of America	380	6105	16
Spain	1200	6013	5
Turkey	540	3923	7
Iran	315	3000	10
Argentina	220	2900	13
Chile	182	2350	13
India	64	1677	26
Others	2498	19043	8
Total	7503	66281	

Source FAO, except India data (Source Indian Horticulture Database, 2008)

KIWIFRUIT

(Actinidia chinensis L)

Family:	Actinidiaceae
Origin:	New Zealand
Type of fruit:	Berry
Edible portion:	Mesocarp
Basic chromosome number:	X=9
Somatic chromosome number:	2n = 18

- National symbol of New Zealand.
- Kiwi is a deciduous vine.
- Species include *A. chinensis, A. arguta and A. kolomikta.*
- The name "kiwi" or "kiwifruit" replaced "Chinese gooseberry" in the 1960's.
- Kiwifruit is dioecious, having separate male and female plants.
- 'Hayward' dominates the world industry, due to large fruit size, excellent flavour and storage qualities.
- Leaves are large (8" diameter), round, petioled, with entire margins, and light pubescence on the underside.
- Female flowers have 30 styles fused at the base into a superior ovary; each carpel contains 10-20 ovules. These flowers are usually larger than males.
- Bees are the primary pollinator for kiwifruit.
- The fruit is a many-seeded berry with a brown, hispid exocarp (peel).
- The flesh is green due to chlorophyll.
- T-bar or Pergola is adopted for planting.

PERSIMMON

(Diospyros kaki L.)

Family:	Ebenaceae
Origin:	China
Type of fruit:	Berries
Edible portion:	Epicarp and mesocarp
Basic chromosome number:	X=15
Somatic chromosome number:	2n = 90

- National fruit of Japan.
- Persimmon is dioecious.

- Female flowers are usually solitary.
- Male ones are in cymes; both are borne at leaf axils of new growth.
- The female flower is hypogynous.
- Persimmon fruit have two species: *Diospyros kaki* (Japanese persimmon) and *Diospyros virginiana* (American or common persimmon).
- Persimmon trees are dioecious.
- The colour changes from cream to pale yellow or pale green in persimmon fruits.
- Japanese persimmon varieties naturally bear astringent fruits.
- Fruits develop with or without seeds.
- Brix level at time of maturity: 14 to 17%
- Pollination is not an important factor for fruit development in persimmon.
- Predominating sugar is fructose.
- Astrigency is due to water soluble tannins.
- The best persimmon fruits judged by High sugar contents.
- Most cultivars required chilling has below 7°C.
- It is a climatric fruit.
- Calyx cavity, skin russetins and calyx end cracking are disorders.
- Flowers are bee pollinated.

NORTHERN PAWPAW

(*Asimina triloba* L.)

Family:	Annonaceae
Origin:	Eastern North America
Type of fruit:	Berry
Basic chromosome number:	X = 9
Somatic number:	2n = 18

- Pawpaws are shrubs or small trees, reaching heights of 2–12 m tall.
- The northern, cold-tolerant common pawpaw (*Asimina triloba*) is deciduous.
- The leaves are alternate, obovate, 20–35 cm long and 10–15 cm broad.
- Flowers of pawpaws are produced singly or in clusters of up to eight together.
- Six sepals and petals (three large outer petals, three smaller inner petals) of white to purple colour.

- The fruit of the common pawpaw is a large edible berry, having numerous seeds.
- Fruits are green when unripe, yellow or brown at maturity.

ATEMOYA

(*Annona atemoya*)

Family:	Annonaceae
Origin:	Man made hybrid
Type of fruit:	Etarior of berries
Edible portion:	Pericarp of individual berry

INDIAN WILD STRAWBERRY

(*Fragaria vesca* L.)

Family:	Rosaceae
Origin:	India
Type of fruit:	Etaerio of drupes
Edible portion:	Fleshy thalamus

TAMARIND

(*Tamarindus indica* L.)

Family:	Leguminosae
Origin:	Tropical Africa and India
Type of fruit:	Pod/ lomentum
Edible portion:	Pulp or mesocarp
Basic chromosome number:	X = 12
Somatic chromosome number:	2n = 24

MANGO

(*Mangifera indica* L.)

Family :	Anacardiaceae
Origin :	Indo-Burma region (South East Asia)
Type of fruit:	Drupe
Edible portion:	Mesocarp
Basic chromosome number:	X = 10
Somatic chromosome number:	2n = 40

Predominating biochemical constituents :

Sugar:	Sucrose
Organic acid:	Citric acid

Pigment:	Carotenoids
Flavouring compounds:	Z-Ocimene; E-Ocimene and B-Mycene
Vitamins:	Vitamin A & C.
Phenols:	Tannic acid
Mineral:	Iron

- Mango is the king of fruits.
- Mango essentially is a tropical fruit.
- Highest productivity is in: Venezuela
- Mango is a highly cross pollinated crop.
- Akbar established lalbagh in Dharbhanga (Bihar) having 1 lakh mango plants.
- Ain-e-Akbari was written by Abdul Fazil in 1590 AD during reign of Akbar.
- North Indian varieties are alternate bearer, mono-embryonic, self-incompatible.
- South Indian varieties are regular bearer and poly-embryonic.
- Dashehari and Alphonso cultivars are suitable for canning.
- Chausa is highly susceptible to mango malformation.
- Maturity indices (Specific gravity): Alphonso (1.01 to 1.02), Deshahari (1.0).
- Mangoes are highly susceptible to low temperature.
- VHT is recommended for disinfecting mango against fruit flies and stone weevil.
- Two crops of mango are taken in Kanyakumari district of Tamil Nadu.
- Mango hybridization work was first started by Burns and Prayag in 1911 at Pune.
- Caging technique of breeding is used in mango by Dr R N Singh.
- Good mango varieties have a TSS of 20^0Brix.
- Rumani is used for dwarfing effect in Deshehari.
- Olour is used for dwarfing effect in Langara & Himsagar.
- Villicolumban is used for dwarfing effect in Alphonso.

- Salt resistant rootstocks of mango are Kurukkan, Moovandan, Nekkare
- Number of prefect (bisexual) flower. Highest – 68.9% in Langra and Lowest – 0.74% Rumani.
- Xavier-variety has highest TSS of 24.8°Brix.
- Fruit is climacteric and shows sigmoid growth curve.
- Poly-embryonic mangoes are inferior: Bappakai, Goa, Olour, Mazagaon, Bellary, Chandrakaran, Furukan, Prior, Kirukkan, Mulgoa.
- Limiting factor for cultivation are low temperature and freezing.
- The favorable temperature range between 24-27°C but can tolerate as high as 48°C provided irrigation is regular.
- High humidity favours diseases incidence and high humidity followed by low temperature causes powdery mildew.
- Ellachi is a malformation resistant variety of Mango.
- In Mango, predominate sugar is sucrose and acid is citric acid.
- Veneer grafting is best method of propagation ideal for establishing in-situ orchards.
- Lower temperature during panicle development results into increased proportion of male flowers.
- Pollination in mango is carried by common house fly.
- Biennial bearing is synonymous to alternate bearing occurs due to genetic nature.
- Parthenocarpic varieties of Mango are Sindhu and Ratna.
- Cultivar free from floral malformation is Bhadauran.
- Sindhu = Ratna × Alphonso
- Ratna = Neelam × Alphonso
- Square system of planting is most popular in Mango.
- Disorders of Mango are enlisted as Soft nose, leaf scorch, mottle leaf, spongy tissue, malformation and black tip.
- Storage temperature: 3.9-8.9°C temperature for 4-7 weeks.
- Hypobaric storage: 76 to 152 mm Hg at 13°C, 98-100% RH in Irwin, Tommy Atkins, Kent etc.

Export specifications for mango :

Variety	Countries				
	Middle East	**Netherlands / Germany**	**UK**	**Japan**	**USA**
Alphonso	200-250 g	250-300 g	250-300 g	250-300 g	250-300 g
Kesar	200-250 g	225-250 g	225-250 g	250-300 g	250-300 g
Packing	1 Dozen/2.5 kg	1 Dozen/2.5 kg	1 Dozen / 2.5 kg	1 Dozen/ 3.5 kg	1 Dozen/ 3.5 kg
Storage Temperature	13°C	13°C	13°C	13°C	13°C
Export	By Sea	By Air	By Air	By Air	By Air

Source: Maharashtra State Agriculture Marketing Board: Website (Jan, 2009)

Important insect-pests of mango:

1. **Mango hopper** (*Amritodous atkinni*): It is serious during flowering. Both adults and nymphs suck the sap from tender shoots, leaves, inflorescence or panicle. Panicle withers a fruit setting if affected adversely. Honey dew on which 'Sooty Mould' grows on the leaves and panicle. Incidence is high in old neglected and densely planted orchards. Shade and high humidity is very favourable for development of mango hopper. Spray carbaryl (sevin) (0.03%) 2 gm/ litre at the time of panicle emergence and again at the pea stage of fruit. Application of insecticides should be avoided at full bloom stage so that the activity of pollinators does not affect.

2. **Fruit flies** (*Daucus dorsalis*): The maggot feeds on pulp and converts into off smelling rotten semi-liquid. The adult flies emerge in April from cocoons in the soil and after mating they lay eggs in clusters 150-1200 under the skin in the fruit before ripening. After 2-3 days, the maggot hatch out and start feeding on pulp. The life cycle is completed in about 10-27 days during summer. Hang traps containing 100 ml emulsion of methyl eugenol (10.1%). Malathion (0.1%) from April-June, 10 traps are sufficient for one hectare of orchard.

3. **Mango psylla:** This is a sporadic pest and when associated with mango hoppers, may cause great damage to the tree from February-April. Their presence can be noticed in the panicles as tiny oval, pale-yellow nymphs having only the wing pads. Their symptoms of attack resemble to that of mango hopper. If infestation is serious, spray twice carbaryl (sevin) (0.03%) 2 gm/ litre.

4. **Mango Mealy bug** (*Drosicha mangifera*): Causes damage to growing shoots and panicles by sucking sap from January to April. The attacked shoots wither and flowers do not set fruits or fruits drop-off

prematurely. Spray as recommended for a hopper is also effective against mealy bugs, especially the young nymphs. Prevent crawling up of nymphs by applying 5 cm wide sticky bands of 15-20 cm slippery around tree trunk about 1/2 metre above the ground level in the middle of December. Apply Ostice or Esso fruit tree grease.

5. **Stem borer** (*Batocera rufamaculata*): Damages tree by tunneling into stems. Wooden grass comes out of the surface and of holes. Remove the grass and apply cotton wick soaked in petrol or methyl parathion (0.02%) (4 ml Metacid 50 EC in 1 L water) or insert 0.5 g para-dichlorobenzene (PDCB) per hole and then plug holes with mud.
6. **Bark eating caterpillar** (*Inderbela guadrinotata*): Causes damage to bark as well as stem by feeding under the cover of its webbing. Remove webbing and treat the main limbs and trunk with 0.1% methyl parathion (2 ml Metacid 50 EC/L water) or 0.2% BHC (4 g BHC 50 WP/L water) in February-March and repeat in September-October.
7. **Shoot borer** (*Chlumetia transversa*): The young terminal shoots dry up. Remove and destroy the wilting shoots along with the borers inside. Spray the new growth with endosulfan 0.05% (280 ml Thiodan/ Endocel 35 EC).
8. **Regulation of bearing in Mango:** Regular bearing varieties such as Dashehari and Amarpali may be grown. Proper cultural practices to regulate growth and bearing like addition of fertilizers and control of diseases and insects-pests may be adopted. De-blossoming of the panicles with NAA @ 200 ppm during 'On' year may help to regulate the bearing.
9. **Fruit drop in Mango:** A spray application of 20 ppm 2, 4-D (2 g in 100 L water) in the last week of April or in the last week of May will control the summer fruit drop to some extent in Langra and Dashehari.
10. **Harvesting of Mango fruit and yield:** Fruit is usually harvested in a physiologically mature but unripe stage, 15-16 weeks after fruit setting. After harvest, the process of ripening hastens. The fruit is kept in a room for a day after harvesting and thereafter, it is wrapped between layers of straw, grass, hay, etc.

Important disease of mango :

1. **Anthracnose** (*Colletotrichum gloeosporioides*): Dark brown sunken lesions appear on leaves, twigs and fruits. Shoots wither and die back. Blossoms blight and fruits may shed.
2. **Powdery mildew** (*Oidium mangiferae*): White powdery growth covers young foliage during March/April. Leaves become distorted brown

and dry. The inflorescence may also be affected.

3. **Mango die-back** (*Botryoliplodia theobromae*): Disease affects old and young plants alike. Initially affected twigs loose the normal on luster leaves, drop and ultimately the whole branch starts drying from tip downwards or the plant above the graft union wilt and dry completely.

4. **Mottle leaf** (Zinc deficiency): On severely affected trees the leaves are small, pointed and narrow and the fruit remains small, hard and dry. Bud development is delayed.

5. **Spongy tissue:** Spongy tissue, a physiological disorder occurs in the ripe fruits and is manifested as a non-edible sour yellowish and sponge-like patch with or without air pockets, developing in the fruit during ripening and remaining small or involving the whole fruit pulp. Symptoms are not visible on external surface but affected fruits have a bad odour. Alphonso variety is more prone to this malady. The exact cause is still mystery. Arka Anmol, Ratna, Arka Puneet are resistance varieties of mango to spongy tissues. Follow sod culture, Pre-harvest dip of fruit with $CaCl_2$ (2%) solution reduces the occurrence of spongy tissue in ripe alphonso fruits. Harvest fruits at 3/4 maturity stage. Post harvest dip in 500 ppm ethephone reduces incidence and alphonso is susceptible to spongy tissues while Sindhu is free from spongy tissue.

Disorders of mango :

1. Leaf Scorch: Tips and margins of leaves particularly old mangoes shows scorching. Affected leaves fall down. The main reason is due to an excess of chloride ions which render potash unavailable. Leaf scorch is common in saline soils, or where Muriate of Potash (KCl) is used for potassium or where brackish water is used for irrigation. Spray K_2SO_4 (5%), avoid planting on saline soils and avoid brackish water for irrigation.

2. Mango malformation: It is serious in Punjab, Delhi, UP but negligible in Bihar, West Bengal and Orissa. Mango malformation affects most cultivars like Bombay Green followed by Chausa, Dhashari and least in Langra. Mango malformation is of two types i.e., vegetative and floral.

The vegetative malformation generally affects seedling in which there is a swelling of buds and formation of small shoots with short internodes at the apical end and give an appearance of Witches broom like structures.

In floral malformation, panicles become deformed, axes become deformed, axes become short due to a cluster inflorescence. Malformed panicle has bigger flowers than normal flowers and mostly male. The probable cause of malformation is fungus. Mango hopper, archaeological, physiological and biochemical causes (nutrient, soil moisture, hormonal inhibitors etc). Spray NAA @ 200 ppm in 1st week of October to check fruit drop and deblossoming of panicle once at bud brays stage, can shift the flowering to a late date.

CITRUS FRUITS

(*Citrus spp*)

Family : Rutaceae
Origin : China, India
Type of fruit: Hesperidium
Edible portion: Juicy placental hairs
Basic chromosome number: X = 9
Somatic chromosome number: 2n = 18

Predominating biochemical constituents :

Sugars: Glucose & fructose
Organic acid: Citric acid
Pigments: Carotene and Xanthophylls
Flavouring compounds: Citral (lemon); Valencene (orange)
Vitamin: Vitamin-C
Phenol: Flavonoid & titerpenes
Mineral: Potassium

- Classification of citrus was given by Tanka & Swingle (1945)
- Spain is largest exporter of citrus.
- Ultra dwarf rootstock of citrus: Flying dragon
- Sikkim is the only place where mandarins are packed in wooden boxes.
- Grapefruit is also known as forbiddin fruit or breakfast fruit.
- Citron: glucoside present Hespiredine
- Main fruits of this group: Lime/ Lemon/Mosambi/ Orange (Mandarin)
- Advanced technology: Tissue culture and micro-propagation
- Pre-cooling: Forced air
- Transport for quality: Waxing
- Sensibility: Refrigeration, ethylene and odours
- Growing areas: The major citrus producing belts are:
- Jammu & Kashmir (Jammu, Kathua, Udhampur, Rajauri), Himachal Pradesh (Kangra & Sirmour) and Uttrarchanl.

  Punjab, Haryana and Rajasthan (Shri Ganga nagar)

West Bengal (Darjeeling, Jalpaiguri), Sikkim, Arunachal Pradesh and Assam

Rajasthan (Bharatpur, Dholpur & Sawai Madhopur).

Madhya Pradesh (Mandsaur, Shajapur Chhindwara, Khandwa, Hosangabad)

Maharashtra (Amravati, Nagpur, Akola, Aurangabad)

West Bengal (Midnapur, 24 Pargana (N) and Orissa.

Andhra Pradesh, Tamil Nadu (Dindgual Anna, Trichy, Tirunalveli, Kattabomman).

Groups of citrus fruit

a. Mandarin group
   i. Kinnow: (C. *nobilis* x C. *deliciosa*)
   ii. Mandarin: *Citrus reticlata*
   iii. It is a highly polyembryonic species.

b. Orange group (sweet orange, sour orange)
   i. Sweet orange (C. *sinensis*): Tight skin orange.
   ii. Sour orange (C. *aurantium*)
   iii. Lime (C. *aurantifolia*)
   iv. Lemon (C. *limon*)
   v. Sweet orange varieties: Mosambi, Malta and Blood Red.

c. Pummelo group
   - Strain of Citron — C. *medica*
   - Pummelo — (C. *grandis*)
   - Sour Pummelo — C. *megalaxycarpa*
   - Rough lemon — C. *jambhiri*

d. Acid group
   - Lemon: — C. *limon*
   - Rough lemon — C. *jambhiri* (most important rootstock of the world).
   - Sour lemon — C. *aurantifolia*
   - *Poncirus* is trifoliate plant highly thorny.
   - Fruit are inedible, used as rootstock for citrus.
   - *Fortunella*: Small shrubbery tree, used as ornamental and for candying.

- Predominant sugar in sweet group is *glucose* and in acid group is *citric acid*.
- Rind is rich in Pectinic acid and essential oil and also contains certain glucoside.
- Hesperidium is present in orange and lemons.
- Naringin is present in grape fruit.
- Fruits contain ascorbic acid. In orange and mandarin TSS and acid ratio = 8:1 whereas, in grapefruit TSS and acid ratio = 6:1.
- USA, Spain, Israel are major citrus producing countries.
- Inter-generic hybridization: Poincirus (Trifoliate orange x *fortunella* (Kumquat)).
- Citranges: Trifoliate orange x sweet orange
- Limquats (Kumquat) = West Indian lime
- The sweet orange commonly known as Mosambi, Malta, Sathgudi.
- Sweet orange is highly poly-embryonic.
- Origin: Musambi is said to be Mozambique.
- Blood Red Malta: Introduced from Mediterranean Region.
- Sathgudi is known as Chinese orange.
- Washington Navel is originated in Brazil and introduced in 1870 into Washington (USA).
- Jaffa and Shamouth varieties of sweet orange originated from Palestine.
- Valencia Late - Origin is probably in China.
- Sweet orange is commercially propagated by budding.

Lemon group

Hill lemon (galgal): Eureka and Baramasi.

Lime: Kagzi and Baramasi

Sweet lime: Local (C. *limetoides*)

Sour lime: C. *aurantifolia*

Sour lime (Kagzi lime, Acid lime, Mexican lime)

Family: Rutaceae

Origin: Indian

Type of fruit: Hesperidium

Edible portion: Juicy placental hair

Basic chromosome number: X=9

Somatic chromosome number: n = 18

- Acid lime is tropical plant.
- Sour lime in Hindi is known as Neembu.
- India rank 5th among major lime and lemon producing countries.
- Sweet lime (*Citrus limetoides*): Native-India, self-incompatible
- Tahiti lime (*Citrus latifolia*): seedless triploid
- Rangpur lime (*Citrus lamonica*): native India.
- Pummelo (*C. grandis*): largest fruit among citrus group and is self-incompatible
- Kagzi lime is the indicator plant for tristiza and is highly susceptible to this disease.
- Citrus cankar is most serious disease of acid lime.
- Lemons are divided into 4 groups i) Eureka (ii) Lisbon (iii) Anamalous (iv) Sweet lemon.
- Sweet lime contains non-acid juice.
- Sweet lime is resistant to greening.

Grapefruit

(*Citrus paradise*)

Family:	Rutaceae
Origin:	West Indies
Type of fruit:	Hesperidium
Edible portion:	Juicy placental hairs
Basic chromosome number:	X = 9
Somatic chromosome number:	2n = 18

- Well known ancestor of grape fruit is shaddock or Pummelo (*C. grandis*).
- Grapefruit is separated from Pummelo in 1830 by James Macfadyen.
- The name has been assigned because its fruits are borne in clusters like grape.
- The mild bitterness in the juice is due to presence of Naringin.
- Grapefruit is poly-embryonic.
- Marsh seedless: introduced in India from USA. It belongs to Pallid pulp group.
- Duncan: Originated as a chance seedling in Florida. It belongs to pallid pulp group.
- Foster: Originated as bud sprout on a Walters grapefruit tree and discovered in 1906-1907 by R B Foster and developed at Sharanpur Botanic Garden.

- Ruby: It is bud sport found in Texas in 1929.
- Propagated by budding on commercial compatible rootstock in South India in Jatti Khati (*C. jambhiri*) for North India.
- Karna Khatta is an outstanding citrus rootstock.

Pummelo

(*Citrus grandis* osbeck)

Family: Rutaceae
Origin: Malaya and Polynesia
Type of fruit: Hesperidium
Edible portion: Juicy placental hairs
Basic chromosome number: X=9
Somatic chromosome number: 2n = 18

Indian Sweet Lime (Meetha Nimbu)

(*Citrus limettiodes Tanaka*)

Family: Rutaceae
Origin: East Asia
Type of fruit: Hesperidium
Edible portion: Juicy placental hairs
Basic chromosome number: X = 9
Somatic chromosome number: 2n = 18

Lemon (Bara Nimbu)

(*Citrus limon* Burn)

Family: Rutaceae
Origin: East Asia
Type of fruit: Hesperidium
Edible portion: Juicy placental hairs
Basic chromosome number: X=9
Somatic chromosome number: 2n = 18

Mandarin

(*Citrus reticulata* Balnco)

Family: Rutaceae
Origin: China
Type of fruit: Hespridium
Edible portion: Juicy placental hairs
Basic chromosome number: X=9
Somatic chromosome number: 2n = 18

- Mandarin is commercially grown in India.
- Nagpur Santra is originated in India.
- Khasi orange - Commercially grown in orange.
- Coorge orange - commercial variety of South India.
- Exotic Mandarin: Kinnow, Satsuma and Emperor Danug.
- The Mandarin group includes all types of loose jacket oranges commonly called as Santra i.e. Nagpur Santra, Coorge Santra.
- Nagpur Santra is mainly propagated by budding.
- Mandarin is largely propagated by seed.
- Jambheri is universally used for propagating *Nagpur Santra* in Maharashtra.
- Nagpur Santra successfully grown on lemon rootstock (*Citrus limon*).
- Mandarin is highly polyembryonic.
- Mandarin fruits mature after about 8-9 months of their blossoming.
- February flowering: Ambe Bahar
- June flowering: Mrig Bahar
- October flowering: Haste Bahar
- Mandarins are highly susceptible to waterlogging.
- Mandarin, Sweet orange, Acid lime and Grapefruit are highly polyembryonic.
- Pummelo, Tahiti lime, Citron are Monoembryonic.
- Rangpur lime: most promising roostock for mandarins and sweet orange.
- Trifoliate orange resistant to phytopthora and nematodes.
- Preharvest fruit drop is common in citrus. It is due to physiological and pathological factors.
- Degreening of citrus fruits is done by CaC_2 (calcium carbide)
- Sweet orange are susceptible to water logging and photopthora rot, so water stagnation in orchard should be avoided.
- Double ring method is best for irrigation.
- Deficiency of Zinc along with N_2 is major nutritional problem of sweet orange.
- Kinnow mandarin is King x *Willow* leaf *(Citrus deliciosa*).
- Kinnow was developed by HB frost in USA in 1935.
- Kinnow was introduced in India in 1959.
- Nagpur mandarin was introduced in India in 1894 by Shuji Raja Bhosle.

- Kinnow can be grown in HDP by using "Troyer Citrange" as a rootstock by spacing the plants at 1.8 x 1.8 m^2 (3000 plants/ hactare).
- Cultivation is limited due to acidity and puffiness of fruit.

Rootstocks for citrus fruits :

- Rough lemon: *C. jambhiri*
- Grape fruit: Karna Khatta
- Sweet orange: Jambhiri
- Grandis (*C. maxima*) – Pummelo or Shaddock (Mono-embryonic)

Commercial methods for propagation of citrus fruits :

- Lemon: Air layering
- Mandarin: T or shield budding
- Sweet orange: T budding
- Pummelo: Seed, T-budding
- Acid lime: Seed

Export specifications for mandarin :

Variety	Middle East	
Nagpur Mandarin	Fruit Colour:	Light orange
	Fruit weight:	150-175 g
	Grades:	65-70 mm & 40-45 mm
Packing	65 mm grade –	7 kg
	40 mm grade –	2.5 kg
Storage	5-7°C	
Transport	By Sea	

Source: Maharashtra State Agriculture Marketing Board: Website (Jan, 2009)

Diseases of citrus :

1. **Citrus canker**: Canker is a bacterial disease. The bacterium gets entry through stomata and wounds. Leaves attacked by citrus leaf minor (*Phyllocnistis citrella*), give easy entry to canker. Canker is seen in form of tiny, circular pimple like eruptions on leaves, stems and fruit. Incidence of canker is more in high rainfall area than in the dry areas. Mild temperature and wet weather are favourable conditions for canker spread. Kagzi lime is most affected. Mandarin and Lemon are least affected. Sweet orange is fully partial resistant.

2. **Citrus die-back or wither tip** (*Colletotrichum gloeosporioides*): It is caused by fungus. The branches start drying from tip downwards. Lesions may be found on the leaves. Apply Bordeaux paste (Copper sulphate 700 g + lime 1 kg + water 10 litre) on cut ends.

3. **Greening**: First discovered by Fraser and Smith in India. Plants of all ages are affected. It is caused due to mycoplasma. The leaves of spring growth flush after reaching maturity develops striking chlorotic patterns, resembling those of Zn deficiency. Green dots appear on leaves. Twigs show multiple bud formation and off shoot blooming and later the back symptom appear. Affected fruits develop orange colour first at the bottom and seed abortion takes place with gum pockets formation. Greening is transmitted by grafting and citrus psylla (*Diaphorina citri*). Sweet oranges, mandarin, lime and grapefruit are susceptible but sweet lime and pummelos are tolerant. Spray rogor (0.03%) to control citrus psylla or control psylla vector by Dimethoate or Phosphamidon. Antibiotic therapy by tepacycline or penicillin @ 1000 ppm as trunk injection is also good.

4. **Tristeza (Honey combing)**: Affected tree lacks a new growth during normal flush period. The tree looks chlorotic and sick. Leaves drop off and twigs die back. The main insect vectors are citrus aphid (*Citricidus kirki*), taxoptele and citricidus. Trisṭeza virus is both vector and bud transmissible but not through seeds. Use resistant rootstock Rangpur lime for mandarin and sweet oranges. In Punjab, Jatti Khatti, Cleopatra mandarin and sweet orange may be used as resistant rootstock to control aphid vector. Use virus free planting material. For Maharashtra, Andhra Pradesh and Karnataka, Rangpur lime is recommended. Avoid sour orange and sweet lime rootstocks.

Insect and pests of citrus :

- **Citrus psylla** (*Diaphorina citri)*: It is a kind of plant lice that suck sap from growing points. Serious damage may occur at flowering time and results in low fruit setting.
- **Citrus leaf minor** (*Phylloenistis citrella stainton*): The attack of pest is most seviour from April to September particularly in the nursery. Larvae mine through leaves.
- **Citrus fruit flies** (*Daucus* spp.): Fruit flies lay eggs on the maturing fruits by embedding them inside the pulp. The maggots feed on the fruit pulp gregariously. The fruit starts rotting and is unfit for human consumption. The fruits generally drop and the fully grown maggots leave them to pupate in soil.
- **Citrus white flies** (*Dialeurodes citri*): Suck sap and also exudes honeydew, leading to the development of a sooty mould on the infested

fruits and leaves. As a result, sweetness of the fruit is reduced. Fruit ripening and growth is retarded.

- **Citrus butterfly**: Larvae usually feed on tender leaves eating them from the edges to the mid rib. When numerous in number, they causes damage to young plants in nursery and may completely defoliate them.
- **Citrus nematodes**: Causes decline and die-back disease. The symptoms include general reduction in plant growth and vigour, yellowing and shedding of leaves and under sized fruits, the decline symptoms are often more pronounced in the upper most pronounced in the upper most portion of the tree. On the roots, the soil particles cling tightly to the gelatinous egg masses. The infestation is mainly spread either through infected nursery or irrigation water

Disorders in citrus

- **Gummosis** *(Phytophthora* spp.): The disease invades the bark which is killed through the wood. The bark ruptures lengthwise and large quantity of gum is exuded.
- **Fruit rot** (*Penicillium italicum*): Also known as blue mould rot. Soft, watery discoloured spots appear on the fruit rind. Spots enlarge and decay and get covered with blue or green spore mass.
- **Green mould rot** (*Penicillium digitatum*)
- **Sour rot** (*Geotrichum candidum*): Buff coloured water raised spots appear on the rind, fungus invades flesh of the fruit which is decomposed. It gives a sour smell and attracts fruit flies.
- **Granulation:** The juice sacs become hard enlarged and turn opaque grayish in colour. Granulation was 1st reported from California and in India from Abohar. Due to this disorder, the density of pulp get increased, juice sacs contain excess of Ca, Mg, Na, K and decreased soluble carbohydrates and organic acid. Granulation is a result of lignifications of juice cells that leads to the formation of sclerenchyma. To control granulation avoid excess moisture in field, spray 2, 4-D @ 12 ppm.

BANANA

(Musa × paradisica and *Musa × balbisiana)*

Family:	*Musaceae*
Origin:	South-East Asia
Basic chromosome number:	X=11
Somatic chromosome number:	2n = 22, 33, 44
Type of fruit:	Berry
Edible portion:	Mesocarp and Endocarp

Predominating biochemical constituents :

Sugars:	Sucrose
Organic acid:	Malic acid
Pigments:	Carotenoid (a-carotene and lutein)
Flavouring pigments:	Amyl & iso-amyl esters of acetic, propionic & butyric acids
Phenols:	Dopamine
Vitamin:	Vitamin-C
Mineral:	Phosphorus

- Banana is referred as a kalpataru (a plant of virtues).
- Temperature 20-30°C
- India's share in world production of Banana: 31.6%
- Removal of male bud after completion of the female phase is referred as denavelling.
- Banana is a moisture loving plant.
- Banana is herbaceous, monocotyledon and monocarpic fruit crop.
- Banana is a rich source of energy.
- Desuckering, propping and mettocking are important cultural practices in banana.
- Finger tip disease is serious in high density plantation.
- Tetrazolium test is used for bunchy top virus detection.
- Most of cultivated banana is triploid in nature.
- Two spray of KH_2PO_4 at fruit development stage increases the bunch weight.
- Genetic classification of banana was given by Simmond & Shephard.
- Ripe banana fruit contains over 26% of sugar.
- Temperature above 36-38°C causes scorching effect with increased transpiration.
- Furrow method of planting followed in Gujrat and Maharashtra.
- Trench method of planting is followed in Tamil Nadu.
- Trench method is especially followed in wetland system of cultivation.
- Descuckering once in 45 days is common practice in banana plantation.

- For long distance transportation, harvesting is done at 75-80% maturity.
- Banana ripening can be delayed by skin coating with waxol (12% wax emulsion).
- CBRS: Central Banana Research Station situated at Tamil Nadu.
- Seedness of banana is controlled by spraying 2, 4-D @25 PPM.
- Poovan & Ney poovan are preferred in multistorey system.
- Salt water treatment reduces duration of banana fruits
- Banana is rich source of dietary potassium (K) and good source of energy
- Rajapuri – Resistant to cold.
- Nendran – remain starchy even on ripening.
- Kanchelkela is important commercial culinary cultivars of India.
- Advance Technology: Planting of tissue cultured plants
- Pre-cooling: Forced air
- Storage temperature conditions:

(i) Holding room: 13-14°C

(ii) Ripening room: 14-20°C

(iii) Relative Humidity: 90-95%

- Mature green banana can be stored up to 3 weeks in ethylene free air or up to 6 weeks in a controlled atmosphere at 14°C.
- Ethylene application is best method to hasten ripening without loss in fruit quality or flavour.
- A pre-storage dip in E-9267 emulsifiable mineral oil at 0.4% is effective in reducing fruit decay and also prolonged storage life.
- Dipping of fruits in 1.5% or 2.5% talprolong solution delays yellow colour development by 4-8 days.

The major banana producing areas are:

- Arunachal Pradesh, Assam, Sikkim, Bihar, West Bengal.
- Maharashtra (Jalgaon, Ahmednagar, Dhule, Nanded, Parbhani), Gujarat, Madhya Pradesh, Orissa, Andhra Pradesh (Godavari), Cuddapah
- Karnataka, Tamil Nadu and Kerala.

Export specifications for banana

Variety	Middle East	
Grand Naine, Cavendish	Colour:	Green
	Weight of Bunch:	2.5kg
	Fruit type:	Preferably straight
Packing	13 kg	
Storage	13-14ºC	
Transport	By Sea	

Genus divided into 5 groups

a) Eumusa (x=11, 2n = 22, 33, 44), diploid, triploid and tetraploid (Edible banana).

b) Rhodochlamys (X=11, 2n=22) *M. ornata, M. velutina* (Ornamental banana)

c) Callimusa (X=10, 2n=20) *M. coccinea* (Ornamental)

d) Australimosa (X=10, 2n=20) *M. textiles.*

e) Incertaesedis (X=7, 2n=14) *M. ingens, M. beccarii* (X=9, 2n=18)

- Banana is staple food of South Africa.
- Ripe fruit of banana contains 27% sugars
- *Musa acuminata* – source of today's edible banana
- Male flower of banana are resistant to panama wilt but susceptible to bunch top.
- Panama wilt: Gross Michel is susceptible, Basari is immune and Poovan is resistant.
- Banana propagated through offsets: Sucker (*Sword suckers preferred).
- Due to blackening at low temperature bananas are not stored in refrigerator.

LITCHI

(Litchi chinensis Sonn)

Family:	Sapindaceae
Origin:	China
Type of fruit:	Nut
Edible portion/ part:	Fleshy aril
Basic chromosome number:	X=14, 15, 16, 17
Somatic chromosome number:	2n = 30, 32

Predominating biochemical constituents :

Sugars:	Glucose and fructose
Organic acid:	Malic acid
Pigments:	Cynidin-3-rutinoside and Malvidin – 3 acetyl glucoside
Vitamin:	Vitamin C
Phenol:	Ferulic and phydroxy-benzoic acid
Mineral:	Phosphorus

- Litchi is a delicious fruit.
- Litchi is a single seeded nut.
- Fruit consists of aril (70-85%), peel (8-15%) and seed (4-18%).
- Air layering is called "Marcottage" in China and "Gootee" in India.
- Rootstock – *Litchi philippinensis*. It is grown extensibly in Phillipines.
- IBA (500 ppm) is most effective in root promotion in air layering of litchi
- Flowers are petal less.
- Essentially an evergreen Sub-tropical fruit tree which prefers moist climate.
- Dry hot wind in summer causes Fruit cracking in litchi.
- Red pigment is due to anthocynin.
- The edible portion of the Litchi fruit is aril.
- Litchi was introduced in India through Burma at the end of 17th century.
- Frost in winter and dry heat in summer are limiting factors.
- Litchi is essentially a fruit of moist subtropical climate.
- Litchi does well in deep, well drained loam soil rich in organic matter.
- Seeds of Litchi have short viability for 4 to 5 days after extraction.
- Air layering is common method of propagation.
- Dried Litchi is called as Litchi nut.
- The litchi flowers are staminate, hermophrodite and pseudo-hermophrodite
- Pollination is essential for seedless type done by honey bees, flies and wasps.
- GA @ 50 ppm is best to reduce fruit drop when applied to flower panicles in Muzaffarpur variety.
- NAA (50-150 ppm) induces fruit drop.

POMEGRANATE

(*Punica granatum* L.)

Family:	Punicaceae
Origin:	Iran
Type of fruit:	Balausta
Edible portion:	Juicy seed coat or aril
Basic chromosome number:	X=8, 9
Somatic chromosome:	2n = 16, 18

- Leprosy patients get benefitted from pomegranate fruit juice.
- Under temperate climate, pomegranate behaves as deciduous but in sub-tropical and tropical climate it behaves as an evergreen or partially deciduous.
- Pomegranate is tolerant to slightly alkaline and limy soil conditions.
- Pomegranate may be trained as multi-stemed tree or single stemed tree.
- Flowering can be induced in June-July (Mrig Bahar), February-March (Ambe Bahar) and September-October (Hasth Bahar) such practices are known as bahar treatment.
- Mrig-bahar is taken in areas where water is enough during hot weather.
- Pomegranate fruits become ready for harvesting in 5-7 months after the appearance of blossoms.
- The most popular cultivar of pomegranate is 'Wonderful' as it is large-fruited and fruits are well-colored.
- Pomegranate is used in many ways, including juice, dyes, inks, tannins for leather (bark) and a variety of remedies for various ailments.
- Pollination is by insects or hummingbirds; cross pollination generally improves fruit set.
- Fruits are irregularly rounded pome with bright red, leathery rind and a prominent calyx.
- The attractive scarlet, white or variegated flowers may be solitary or grouped in two's and three's at the ends of the branches.
- Bahar treatment is followed in pomegranate.
- More incidence of fruit cracking (Internal break down) takes place in bahar season.
- Amlidana (Ganesh × Nanha) – New pomegranate hybrid suitable for high density plantation, have TSS-12.6°Brix, released by IIHR.

- Multi-stem training system is followed.
- It is considered to be highly drought tolerant.

AONLA

(*Emblica officinalis*)

Family:	Euphorbiaceae
Origin:	Tropical Asia (Indo-China)
Type of fruit:	Berry
Edible portion:	Exocarp and Mesocarp
Basic chromosome number:	X=7
Somatic chromosome number:	2n = 28 (tetraploid)

- Aonla is deciduous tree with deep rooted and sparse foliage.
- Time of fruit bud differentiation in aonla is March-April.
- Trifla and Chavanprash are well known indigenous medicine in Ayurvedic system using aonla.
- Irrigation should be avoided during flowering (mid March – mid April)
- Pruning is done during March-April.

AVOCADO

(*Persia americana* Mill)

Family:	Lauraceae
Origin:	West Indies/Mexico or central America
Basic chromosome number:	X=12
Somatic chromosome number:	2n= 24
Type of fruit:	Berry
Edible portion/ part:	Pericarp

Predominating biochemical constituents :

Sugars:	Glucose and fructose
Organic acid:	Malic acid
Pigments:	Carotenoids
Flavouring compounds:	C_6 alcohol and aldehyde
Vitamin:	Vitamin C
Phenol:	Catechin and Flavones
Mineral:	Potassium

- Avocado is also known as butter fruit and fruit of New world.
- It is a sub tropical fruit.

- It is most nutritive fruit among fruits.
- Avocado fruit is a single seeded berry
- Type of dichogamy is protogynous.
- Dry neck is a physiological disorder of avocado.
- It's energy value is twice as much as Banana fruits
- Most leading avocado cultivar in the world is Furete (Mexican × guatimalan)
- Avocado is classified into 3 horticultural races:

(i) Mexican – Gotfried, Duke.

(ii) West Indian – Pollock, Simmonds, Black Prince, Fushsia, Peterson, Waldin

(iii) Guatemalan – Taylor, Linda, Queen, Benit.

- Furete – (Mexican × Guatimalan) is an alternate bearer.
- Duke seedlings are resistant to root rot and cold hardiness.
- Girdling of alternate bearing varieties increase the yield.
- Indian varieties are: i) Green (Gutemalan type) – Oval shape fruit Purple (West Indian type) – Pear shape fruit.
- Above 25°C temperature, the flowers formation is inhibited.
- Cleft, whip and tongue grafting are best methods of propagation.
- Inflorescence is termed as protogynous diurnally synchronous and dichogamy.
- Dichogamy means female and male flowers mature at different times.
- Honey bees are chief pollinating agents.
- Most serious disease is *phytophthora cinnamome* (root rot).
- Treatment with ethylene hastens ripening of mature avocado.

SAPOTA

(*Achras zapota* L.)

Family:	Sapotaceae
Origin:	Mexico (Tropical America)
Type of fruit:	Drupe
Edible portion:	Mesocarp
Basic chromosome number:	X=13
Somatic chromosome number:	2n = 26

- Sapota is a climacteric fruit.

- Sapota follows double sigmoid growth curve.
- Temperature above 43°C during summer causes flower and fruitlet drop.
- Rootstock: Khirni (*Manikara hexandra*); Adam's Apple (*M. kauki*); Mahua (*Madhuca latifolia*).
- Fruit is good source of digestible sugar (12-18%).
- Propagation of sapota by inarching using Rayan as rootstock is most accepted and commercial method.
- Ethephon (1000 PPM) can be utilized at 20-25°C for uniform and rapid ripening

CUSTARD APPLE

(*Annona squamosa*)

Family:	Annonaceae
Origin:	Tropical America/West Indies
Type of fruit:	Etaerio of berries
Edible portion:	Pericarp
Basic chromosome number:	X=7
Somatic chromosome number:	2n = 14

- Ramphal (Bullock heart): *Annona reticulata* – common rootstock
- Lakshman Phal (Atemoya) – *Annona atemoya* (*A. squamosa* × *A. cherimoya*)
- Hanuman Phal: Cherimoya (*Annona cherimoya*) popular in Assam and South India.
- Pond Apple (*Annona glabra*)
- Among annonaceous fruit, custard apple is most favourite in India.
- Cherimoya: Prefers subtropical climate.
- Cherimoya is consider to be best fruit of Annonaceae family
- Custard Apple contains 20% Sugar.
- Bullock's Heart is more commonly found in South India than North India
- Cherimoya is mostly restricted to Assam.
- Mostly consumed as table fruit.
- Grafting and budding are commercial methods of vegetative propagation.
- Flowers are born on current season's growth.

- Poor fruit set due to very high and very low humidity prevailing at time of flowering.

JACK FRUIT

(*Artocarpous heterophyllus* L.)

Family:	Moraceae
Origin:	India
Type of fruit:	Sorosis
Edible portion:	Bracts/perianth/seed
Basic chromosome number:	X=14
Somatic chromosome number:	2n = 56

1. Jack fruit is a monoceious fruit tree.
2. They are considered as "Good source of Pectin".
3. Seeds are sown immediately after extraction.
4. Caulifluorus bearing habit.

CARAMBOLA

(*Averrhoea carambola* L.)

Family:	*Oxalidaceae*
Origin:	India-China
Type of fruit:	Berry
Edible portion/ part:	Mesocarp
Basic chromosome number:	X=12
Somatic chromosome number:	2n = 24

- It is also known as five corner fruit.
- Native place is Malaysia.
- Fruit cum ornamental tree, root extract used as antidote for poisioning.
- Produce flower and fruits on trunk (cauliflorus in nature).
- Sour type: 1% acid: varieties are Gold Star, Icambola.
- Sweet type: 0.4% acid: Golden Star
- It contains oxalic acid.

DATE PALM

(Phoenix dactylifera L.)

Family:	Arecaceae
Origin:	Iraq
Type of fruit:	Drupe
Edible portion:	Pericarp
Basic chromosome number:	X= 18
Somatic chromosome number:	2n = 36

- Single seeded berry and is dioecious in nature.
- Datepalm inflorescence is spadix.
- Date palm have tendency of alternate bearing.
- Datepalm is propagated by separating offshoots.
- Metaxenia is common in Date palm.
- In India – date is harvested at Doka stage.
- In other countries date is harvested at Dang stage.
- Fruits for fresh eating are preferred at Dang stage.
- Drink of Date palm is known as "Dibbis".
- Liquor prepared from date palm is 'Arrak' popular in Iraq.
- One kg fully ripe fresh dates provide approximately 3150 calories.
- "Its feet in running water and its head in the fire of the sky" is a term given to date palm.
- Ethephon is an effective fruit thinning agent.
- Date harvested at doka stage have 70-80% moisture.
- Doka stage harvested fruits are successfully processed to prepare chhuhara.
- Exploitation of metaxenia to induce earliness improvement in quality.

BER

(*Ziziphus mauritiana* L.)

Indian ber: *Ziziphus mauritiana*

Chinese ber : (*Z. jujube*)

Family:	*Rhamnaceae*
Origin:	India, China
Type of Fruit:	Drupe
Edible portion:	Pericarp (Exocarp + Mesocarp)
Basic chromosome number:	X=12
Somatic chromosome number:	2n = 24, 48, 96

Predominating biochemical constituents :

Sugars:	Glucose & fructose
Organic acid:	Malic acid
Pigments:	Carotenoids
Vitamins:	Vitamin C and A
Phenol:	Tannin
Mineral:	Phosphorus and Iron

- Ber is extremely drought hardy.
- Spraying of 3% thio-urea or KNO_3 once in 2 days before pruning induces bud sprouting from maximum number of nodes.
- Irrigation during October causes flower shedding.
- Irrigation during March-April causes fruit spoilage and delays ripening.
- Best time for pruning: May end to middle June.
- Ber also show strong self-incompatibility (Gametophytic).
- *Z. nummularia* – dwarfing rootstock for high density plantation.
- Umran: Originated from Rajasthan, processed and used as 'chhuhara'.
- Gohma Kirti (Ganesh Kirti): Selection from umran and is an early variety.
- Maturity: 150-175 days after flowering.
- Storage temperature: 3ºC + 85-90% RH.
- It is an ideal tree for arid and semi arid region.

- Budding is the commercial best method of propagation (Shield budding is best)
- Flowering: Inflorescence is axillary cyme

BAEL

(*Aegle marmelos*)

Family:	Rutaceae
Origin:	India
Type of fruit:	Amphisarica (Berry)
Edible portion:	Succulent placenta
Basic chromosome number:	X= 9
Somatic chromosome number:	2n = 36

- Richest source of Vit.B_2 (Riboflavin).
- Marmelosis – active ingradient present in bael and is extracted from bark.
- Leaves are used for offering to 'Lord Shiva'.
- Mature green fruits are ideal for harvesting.
- Ripe fruits are used for beverage making; hence they should be harvested at ripe stage.
- Storage temperature: 9°C + 85-90% RH
- Mature green or raw fruits are most suitable for making preserve.

JAMUN

(*Syzygium cumini*)

Family:	Myrtaceae
Origin:	East India-Malaya
Type of fruit:	Drupe
Edible portion:	Epicarp and mesocarp
Basic chromosome number:	X=20
Somatic chromosome number:	2n = 40

- *Syzygium jambose* – Rose Apple or Gulab Jamun.
- Generally grown as avenue or as wind break.
- Good source of Iron, used as an effective medicine against diabeties, heart troubles.
- *S. densiflora* rootstock of Jamun is resistant against attack of termites.

KARONDA

(*Carissa carandus L.*)

Family:	Apocyanaceae
Origin:	India and Java
Type of fruit:	Berry
Edible portion:	Epicarp and mesocarp
Basic chromosome number:	X= 11
Somatic chromosome number:	2n = 22

- *Carrisa grandiflora* – Natal plum
- Richest source of Iron.
- Karonda behaves as a Xerophyte plant.
- Karonda may be a) Green fruited (b) White fruited c) Dark purple fruited
- Fruit have antiscorbatic property.
- *C. ovate*-Jam preparation
- *C. edulis*: scented flowers

LOQUAT

(*Eribotrya japonica*)

Family:	*Rosaceae*
Origin:	China
Type of fruit:	Pome
Edible portion:	Fleshy thalamus
Basic chromosome number:	X=17

- Subtropical, evergreen pome fruit.
- It was introduced in India under the name of 'Japanese Medlar'.
- California Advance, Golden Yellow and Thames Pride should be harvested at 11% TSS.

COCONUT

(*Cocos nucifera)*

Family:	Palmaceae/ Areacėae
Origin:	Malaysia, Indonesia
Type of fruit:	drupe
Edible portion:	Endosperm
Basic chromosome number:	X=16
Somatic chromosome number:	2n= 32

- Coconut is known as "Kalpavariksha" or "Tree of Heaven".
- Fruit is a single seeded drupe.
- Kerala share highest in coconut production: 42%
- Productivity of coconut (7779 nuts/hac) in India is best in the world.
- Dwarf palms are self-pollinated while tall palm are cross pollinated.
- Optimum temperature for growth: 27°C
- Maximum productivity of coconut: Maharashtra (20, 621 nuts/ hac)
- Two forms of copra:
- Edible copra: Ball copra and Cup copra

  Milling copra
- Endocarp used for making toys, buttons *etc.*
- Coconut is a heliotropic plant (love sunshine)
- Kurumba: an immature coconut containing a refreshing clear liquid.
- In drip irrigation, 30-40 Litre water/day is optimum for West coast condition.
- Coconut ripens in 12-13 months from the opening of the inflorescence.
- Laccadive ordinary is suitable for making ball copra and toody extraction.
- Laccadive Micro is also suitable for making ball copra.
- It is the only one perennial source of edible oil in India.
- Nata is a zero calorie drink prepared from coconut water.

TEA

(*Camellia sinensis*)

Family:	Theaceae
Origin:	China
Type of fruit:	Capsule
Edible portion:	Leaves
Basic chromosome number:	X=16
Somatic chromosome number:	2n= 32

- Tea is a calcifuge crop (best grown in acidic soil).
- Tea is known as queen of beverage crop.
- India is largest producers, consumer and exporter of tea in the world.
- Tea is processed by CTC method (cut, tear and curl) or orthodox method.

- Orthodox method: Light strength tea.
- CTC method: Strong strength tea.
- Tea flowers are bisexual.
- In tea; stimulant is *Thein*, aroma is due to *Theol* and bitter taste is due to *Tannin*.
- Assam is leading producers of tea in India (55%)
- Skiffing is practiced in tea is a lighest form of pruning.
- Sundaram is a very high yielding clone.
- Best harvesting time: two leaves and a bud stage.
- The 1st plucking of recovering bushes is called 'tipping'.
- 1st step in processing of tea is 'withering'.
- Most of tea garden is located at altitudes ranging from 1,000 to 1,200 mts.
- The mean maximum temperatue below 30°C is good for cultivation.
- The end product of fermentation is the affavins and arubigins are responsible for brightness and colour.

COFFEE

(*Coffea arabica*)

Family:	Rubiaceae
Origin:	Abyssinian/Ethiopia
Type of fruit:	Berry
Edible portion:	Coffee cherry/seeds
Basic chromosome number:	X=22
Somatic chromosome number:	2n= 44

- *Coffee arabica*: self polliated (2n = 22)
- *Coffee roubsta*: cross pollinated (2n = 44)
- India's rank in coffee production: VIth
- *Arabica coffee* for higher elevation while *robusta* coffee for lower elevation.
- Coffee fruit with single seed called "Pea berry".
- Tree coffee (*Coffea liberica*) is resistance to leaf rust.
- Coffee contains Niacin which is useful to cure skin diseases.

- Processing: a) By wet method – to produce permanent coffee

  b) By dry method – to produce cherry coffee
- In India, *arabica* is processed as parchment coffee, while *robusta* is processed as cherry coffee.
- The cured coffee is called green coffee which is traded in the market.
- Scuffling (soil-sterring) is practiced in coffee.

ARECANUT

(*Areca catechu*)

Family: Arecaceae
Origin: Malay Archepelago
Type of fruit: Nut
Edible portion: Endosperm

- India is largest producer and consumer of Arecanut.
- It is a monoecious crop.
- Inflorescence is spadix, flowers are sessile.
- Single seeded berry.
- Arecoline – (0.1%) stimulating agent, present.
- Polyphenols and tannins are responsible for astringent taste o nuts.
- Polyphenol stanins are responsible for astringent taste of nuts.
- Plants are susceptible to sun scorch especially in south or south west direction.
- Trade type A) Kalipak – Processed green nuts
- Kottapak or chali – Dried ripe nuts (most popular trade)
- Scented supari
- Nuli is made from tender nuts.
- Young seedlings are best protected by raising banana crop during the earlier years.
- Fully-ripe nut with minimum weight of 35 gram is used for propagation.
- Mahali and Yellow leaf diseases (YLD) are major threats in southern states.

COCOA

(*Theobroma cacao*)

Family: Sterculiaceae
Origin: South America
Type of fruit: Drupe (pod)
Edible portion: Endosperm
Basic chromosome number: X=10
Somatic chromosome number: 2n= 20

- Brazil is the largest producer.
- In India, Kerala is the leading producer of cocoa, followed by Karnataka and Tamil Nadu.
- The horizontal branches are called as Fan or Jorquette.
- Vertical continuous stem is called – chupan.
- Cocoa tree grown naturally in tiers.
- It is a beverage crop, rich source of fat (3.7% and protein (7%).
- Cocoa is propagated through seeds.
- Forestero is the recommended variety by CPCRI, Kerala.
- Criolla type is less suitable than Forestero.
- Bearing habit is cauliflorous.
- Spacing of cocoa in:

i) Arecanut Garden: 5.4 x 2.7 m^2 (686 plants/ hac)

ii) Coconut Garden: 3.0 x 75 m^2 (444 plants/ hac)

- Young cocoa fruits are called as "cherelle" and its wilting prior to maturity is called "cherelle wilting" (disorder)

RUBBER

(*Hevea brasiliensis*)

Family: Arecaceae
Origin: Brazil

- Rubber Research Institute of India (RRI) is situated in Kottayam, Kerala.
- Tapping is done in rubber for extraction of latex. The technique is devised by Ridley.
- India rank 3rd in rubber production and 5th in area and 1st in productivity.
- Kerala is the highest producer of rubber in India.

- It is commercially propagated by forkert budding.
- Latex contains average 32% dry matter.
- Processed product: sheet rubber (latex + acetic or formic acid)
- In smoke house, 40-60°C temperature is maintained
- RRH-105 occupies 80% area under rubber cultivation. It is the highest yielding in world.
- Major physiological disorder: Brown blast or TPD (tapping panel dryness)
- Tapping cut (tapping pennel) should be at a slope of 30° in budded plants and 25° in seedling.
- Metrola – (latex meter) to measure percent of rubber.
- Best yield is obtained by tapping a depth of less than 1 mm close to cambium.

OIL PALM

(*Elaeis guinnensis*)

Family:	Arecaceae
Origin:	West Africa
Type of fruit:	Nut
Edible portion:	Endosperm

- It is also known as "Small holder irrigated crop".
- Oilpalm is a monoecious and cross pollinated crop.
- Oil palm is the highest edible oil yielding crop among perennial crops.
- Palmolin is prepared from crude oil.
- Types
  - i) Dura: shell is present
  - ii) Pisifera: shell is absent
  - iii) Tehera: Dura × Pisifera

1. Tonera types are only used for planting because of their high mesocarp content widely cultivated in the world.

- Oilpalm are of two types *Dura* and *Pisifera* on basis of presence or absence of shell covering and kernel inside fruit.
- The shell is presen in *Dura* and absent in *Pisifera*.

2. Palm oil is rich in palmitic acid.
3. Oil is called as crude palm oil, rich in vitamin A & E.
4. Separated kernels are dried to final moisture of 6-8%.

- Stripping is done in oil palm.
- It is commercially propagated by seed.
- Harvesting starts after 3 to 4 years after plantation.
- Harvesting done at ripe stage for oil extraction.
- Mesocarp yield (70-90% oil), kernel (10-30% oil) and mesocarp contans (45-55% oil).
- Palm oil is rich in palmitic acid.

PINEAPPLE

(*Ananas comosus* L.)

Family:	Bromiliaceae
Origin:	Brazil
Basic chromosome number:	X=25
Somatic chromosome number:	2n = 50, 75,100
Type of fruit:	Sorosis
Edible portion:	Bracts & Perianth (accessory tissue)

Predominating bio-chemical constituents :

Sugars:	Sucrose
Organic acid:	Citric acid
Pigment:	Carotenoids
Flavouring:	Ethyl acetate, butane-3-diol-di-acetate
Vitamin:	Niacin
Phenol:	P-coumaric acid, Ferulic acid
Mineral:	Potassium

- Pineapple is a monocotyledonous, monocarpic, herbaceous fruit plant
- Pineapple is non-climateric fruit
- Pineapple fruit contain an enzyme called Bromelin. It is an active constituent.
- Etheral (Ethophon) is used for inducing flowering in pineapple.
- Average sugar content in pineapple is: 10-12%
- Any acid content in pineapple is: 0.6 - 0.8%
- Earthing up is an essential operation in pineapple cultivation

- Fruits which mature in winter are acidic.
- Multiple crown disorder found in cayenne group (Kew).
- Self incompatibility is the major breeding hindrance in pineapple.

GUAVA

(*Psidium guajava* L.)

Family:	Myrtaceae
Origin:	West Indies to Peru
Basic chromosome number:	X=11
Somatic chromosome number:	2n = 22, 33
Type of fruit:	Berry
Edible portion:	Thalamus and pericarp

Predominating biochemical constituents :

Sugars:	Glucose and fructose
Organic acid:	Citric acid
Pigments:	Chlorophyll, carotene, lycopene
Flavouring compounds:	Methyl benzoate, haxenol, cinnamyl acetate
Vitamin:	Vitamin-C
Phenol:	(+) gallucatechin
Mineral:	Phosphorus

- Lucknow-49 is an important guava cultivar having excellent taste and keeping quality.
- Guava flowers twice in North however, thrice in South India.
- Double sigmoid growth curve is noticed in guava.
- Guava harvested throughout year except May and June.
- Chinese guava (*Psidium fridrichsthalianum*) – dwarfing rootstock and resistant to guava wilt and nematodes.
- Fruit quality of winter crop is best, it escapes the attack of fruit flies
- Practice of taking winter crop instead of rainy season crop is known as crop regulation.
- UP produce best quality Guava fruits.
- Vit-C contents are highest in fruit peel at mature stage.
- Bending in guava is practiced in MH.

PAPAYA

(*Carica papaya* L.)

Family:	Caricaceae
Origin:	Tropical America
Basic chromosome number:	X=9
Somatic chromosome number:	2n = 18, 36
Type of fruit:	Berry
Edible portion:	Mesocarp and endocarp

Predominating biochemical constituents :

Sugars:	Glucose & Fructose
Organic acid:	Citric acid
Pigments:	Caricaxanthin (yellow skin); b-Carotene (yellow) & Lycopene (Red flesh)
Flavouring compounds:	Methyl butanoate and linalool
Vitamin:	Vitamin C and A
Mineral:	Calcium & phosphorus

- Papaya is commercially propagated by seed.
- Yellow pigment in papaya is Caricaxanthin
- Enzyme present in dried latex of papaya (papin) is pepsin.
- Recommended spacing for Pusa Nanha is 1.25 x 1.25 m^2 (6000 plants/ hac).
- Frost is the most limiting factor in papaya cultivation in North India.
- Papaya is a polygamous plant.
- Carpine obtained from papaya is utilized as a diuretic and heart stimulant.
- Damping off is most serious disease of papaya seedlings.
- 10% male plant is planted where delicious varieties are cultivated.
- Papaya plants are very susceptible to water logging.
- Papaya is thermo-sensitive crop.

- *Carica candamarcensis* – Mountain papaya
- Highest productivity after banana.

PHALSA

(*Grewia asiatica*)

Family:	Tiliaceae
Origin:	India
Type of fruit:	Drupe
Edible portion:	Epicarp and Mesocarp
Basic chromosome number:	X= 9
Somatic chromosome number:	2n = 36 (tetraploid)

- Phalsa is most perishable fruit crop and is tolerant to drought.
- Pruning: December - January
- Self-pollinated crop.
- Suitable for multistoried cropping.
- Red colour is due to anthocynin.
- Propagation by seeds
- Highly perishable fruit
- Drought resistant crop

MANGOSTEEN

(*Garcinia mangostana*)

Family:	Guttiferae
Origin:	India
Type of fruit:	Amphisarca (Berry)
Edible portion:	Succulent placenta

- Finest fruit of the world
- Typical example of parthenogenetic development
- It is the only fruit in which glucose is available in readily form
- It contain tannins up to 13%
- Very high humid or dry condition leads to 'Gamboge' a disorder in which excessive exudation of latex take place
- Variety: Jolo

PASSION FRUIT

(*Passiflora edulis*)

Family:	Passifloraceae
Origin:	Brazil (Tropical America)
Type of fruit:	Berry
Edible portion:	Mesocarp
Basic chromosome number:	X=9
Somatic chromosome number:	2n =18

- Rich source of vitamin -A
- Vine bears hen's egg sized fruits in adundance
- Two arm kniffin system – ideal for training
- Type: (A) Purple – more productive (B) Yellow
- Hybrid Kaveri-Purple × Yellow
- Var: Noel's special

TAMARIND

(*Tamarindus indica* L.)

Family:	Leguminosae
Origin:	Tropical Africa
Type of fruit:	Pod/lomentum
Edible portion:	Mesocarp/pulp
Basic chromosome number:	X=12
Somatic chromosome number:	2n =24

- Tamarind pulp has antiscorbatic properties.
- Varieties: Urigam

RAMBUTAN

(*Nephelium lappaceum* L.)

Family:	*Sapindaceae*
Origin:	Malaya
Type of fruit:	Berry
Edible portion:	Aril
Basic chromosome number:	X=11
Somatic chromosome number:	2n = 22

OLIVE

(*Olea europea* L.)

Family: Oleaceae
Origin: Mediterranean region
Type of fruit: Drupe
Edible portion: Epicarp and mesocarp
Basic chromosome number: X=23
Somatic chromosome number: 2n = 46

WOODAPPLE

(*Feronia limonia* L.)

Family: Rutaceae
Origin: India
Type of fruit: Amphisarca (Berry)
Edible portion: Succulent placenta
Basic chromosome number: X=9
Somatic chromosome number: 2n =18

Water Chestnut

(*Trapa bispinosa*)

Family: Trapaceae
Edible part: Kernel

MAKHANA

(*Euryale ferox*)

Family: Nymphaceae

MULBERRY

(*Morus alba*)

Family: Moraceae
Origin: China
Type of fruit: Aggregate of druplets/ sorosis
Edible portion: Mesocarp
Somatic chromosome number: 2n = 308

- Plant of temperate region
- Maximum production area is in Karnataka
- Hocky sticks are prepared from *Morus spp*.

DURIAN

(*Durio zibethinus*)

Family: Bombaceae
Origin: Malaysia
Type of fruit: Drupe
Edible portion: Aril

- Odour is like rotten onion
- Devoid of root hair (absent)
- Rich in vitamin-E
- Fruit – Aphrodisiac activity

MACADAMIA NUT

(*Macadamia ternifolia*)

Family: Proteaceae
Origin: Malaysia
Type of fruit: Nut

- Australlian nut/Queensland nut
- Protein present is 10%
- Propagation: Wedge grafting
- Quality of Macadamia nut is related to oil content.
- Oil present is 78.2%.
- It is only commercial food crop indigenous to Australia.
- *Macadomia intergrifolia* is only the commercial species
- It has xerophytic characteristics.

MAHUA

(*Basia latifolia*)

Family: Sapotaceae
Origin: India

- Corolla is rich source of sugar
- Mahua oil – linoleic fatty acid-useful to reduce blood cholesterol level
- Polyembryony is found
- Highest gestation period (15-20 years)

MULTIPLE CHOICE QUESTIONS

1. Which of the following is a 'Typical Temperate Fruit'?

a) Apple b) Quince
c) Pear d) Cherry

2. The term 'Pome' relates to

a) Family of fruit b) Origin of fruit
c) Edible portion of fruit d) Type of fruit

3. Which of the following is a predominating organic acid in apple?

a) Tartaric b) Malic
c) Citric d) None of these

4. Apple is a ______type fruit

a) Berry b) Pepo
c) Pome d) Lomentum

5. Origin of apple is

a) Asia minor & Caucasus c) South-West Asia
c) Eastern Europe d) All of these

6. June Drop in Apple is due to

a) Moisture stress b) High temperature
c) High boron d) High relative humidity

7. Sanjose Scale in apple got entry into India from

a) England b) USA
c) France d) Srilanka

8. Apple scab is caused by

a) Bacteria b) Fungus
c) Virus d) Yeast

9. Which State is called as "Apple bowl of India"?

a) Sikkim b) Himachal Pradesh
c) Uttrakhand d) Arunachal Pradesh

10. Wooly apple aphid resistant rootstock of apple.

a) Northern spy b) M27

c) M16 d) M2

11. Ambred, a variety of apple is developed by crossing

a) Red Gold × Ambri b) Golden Delicious × Ambri

c) Red Delicious × Ambri d) None of these

12. Bitter pit of apple is due to the deficiency of

a) Zn b) Calcium

c) Boron d) Iron

13. The type of inflorescence in apple is

a) Cyme b) Raceme

c) Catkin d) Corymb

14. Which of the following apple cultivar is a cooking type?

a) Ambri b) Imperial

c) Golden Delicious d) Red Delicious

15. Basic chromosome number of apple is

a) 15 b) 16

c) 17 d) 18

16. Pre-harvest fruit drop in apple is controlled by

a) NAA b) Ethylene

c) Ethephon d) GA

17. In apple to control pre-harvest fruit drop, NAA is used in concentration of

a) 100 ppm b) 10 ppm

c) 0.1 ppm d) 0.01 ppm

18. The blooming period of apple is

a) June-September b) June-August

c) February-May d) October -January

19. The term '*Entomophily*' refers to

a) Pollination by birds
b) Pollination by insects
c) Pollination by animals
d) Pollination by wind

20. The condition when a flower can not be fertilized by the pollen of same is called

a) Dichogamy
b) Homogamy
c) Unisexual
d) Self-incompatibility

21. Rosette of apple is due to deficiency of

a) Zinc
b) Calcium
c) Boron
d) Iron

22. Water core disorder in apple is due to

a) Excessive water
b) Low temperature
c) Excessive exposure to sun rays
d) Water deficiency

23. Small sunken spots on apple fruit surface are symptoms of physiological disorder called

a) Internal browning
b) Scald
c) Bitter pit
d) Water core

24. Apple scab is caused by

a) Venturia inaequalis
b) Podosphaera leucotricha
c) Phytophthora cactorum
d) Sclerotium rolfsie

25. Scab symptoms appears typically on

a) Foliage
b) Fruits
c) Both foliage & fruits
d) None of these

26. Which of the following is a commercial method of propagation of apple clonal rootstocks?

a) Budding
b) Mound layering
c) Cutting
d) Cleft grafting

27. Low chilling varieties of apple are

a) Bartlett, Max
b) Michel, Schlomit
c) Prima, Liberty
d) All of these

28. MM106, a semi-vigrous rootstock of apple is susceptible to

a) Powdery mildew b) Die back
c) Collor rot d) Black spot

29. Processing cultivar of apple is

a) Tropical Beauty b) Michel
c) Schlomit d) None

30. In apple, low temperature treatment (2-5°C) treatment of seeds done to promote germination is called

a) Seed priming b) Seed Stratification
c) Seed Scarification d) Vernalization

31. Normally________ chilling hours are required in apple.

a) 400-600 b) 400-500
c) 500-1500 d) 800-1600

32. Limiting factors during flowering in apple is/are

a) High temperature & low RH
b) Hail storm and low temperature
c) Low temperature & low RH
d) All of these

33. Fruit thinning in apple is done to maintain tree vigour and regular production of quality fruits. It can be achieved by

a) NAA @ 10 ppm b) Carbaryl @ 0.075%
c) NAA @ 100 ppmd) Both a and b

34. Fire blight of apple is caused by

a) Fungus b) Bacteria
c) Virus d) MLOs

35. Bitter pit in apple can be controlled by

a) $CaCl_2$ b) NaCl
c) KCl d) Urea

36. Crown gall of apple is due to

a) Podosphaera leucotricha b) Agrobacterium tumefaciens
c) Phytophthora cactorum d) Dermatophora necatrix

37. Dwarfing rootstock of Pear is

a) Quince C
b) Kainth
c) Quince A
d) Shiara

38. Parent variety of all Delicious group of apple is

a) Red Spur Delicious
b) Golden Delicious
c) Red Delicious
d) Red Gold

39. __________variety of apple is indigenous to India.

a) Golden Delicious
b) Ambri
c) Rich-a-Red
d) Baldwin

40. Pyrus communis is a cross between

a) *P. caucasica Fed* × *P. pyrifolia* (Burm)
b) *P. ussurensis* × *P. pyrifolia* (Burm)
c) *P. pyrifolia* × *P. ussurensis*
d) None of these

41. Basic chromosome number of pomoideae is

a) 7
b) 17
c) 9
d) 8

42. Basic chromosome number of prunoideae is

a) 8
b) 17
c) 9
d) 10

43. Basic chromosome number of spiroideae is

a) 8
b) 7
c) 9
d) 6

44. Which of the following is the chief pollinator in most of the temperate fruits?

a) Honey bees
b) House flies
c) Fruit flies
d) Bumble bees

45. Woodapple is native to

a) Japan
b) India
c) Srilanka
d) Mexico

46. Liberty, Prima, COOP 12 and Freedom are scab resistant varieties of

a) Apple b) Pear
c) Quince d) Peach

47. Sunehari and Shanburry are improved cultivars of

a) Cherry b) Apple
c) Almond d) Pear

48. Akbar is a hybrid of

a) Grape b) Mango
c) Apple d) Papaya

49. The term Pomology is derived from a______ word

a) English b) Latin
c) French d) Greek

50. Cherry belongs to the family

a) Rosaceae b) Proteaceae
c) Oxalidaceae d) Sterculiaceae

51. Black Tartarian, Bing and Nepolean are cultivars of

a) Sour cherry b) Sweet cherry
c) Duke cherry d) None of these

52. Basic chromosome number of sour cherry is

a) 13 b) 15
c) 14 d) 16

53. Which of the following cultivar of sweet cherry is/are most suitable for fresh market?

a) Bing b) Napolean
c) Black republican d) All of these

54. Shiara and Kainth are used as rootstock in

a) Quince b) Pear
c) Apple d) Peach

55. Pyrus pyrifolia is susceptible to which of the following disorder?

a) Black end
b) Breakdown
c) Hard end
d) Gummosis

56. Black end in pear is due to

a) Excessive chloride
b) Water defieicncy
c) Low temperature
d) Excessive water

57. Botanically, Pear is a

a) Berry
b) Drupe
c) Pome
d) Nut

58. In Pecan, Shuck opening can be hastened by

a) Dipping the fruit in 2000 ppm ethephon
b) Spraying the fruit with 2000 ppm ehtephon
c) Dipping the fruit in 100 ppm ethephon
d) Dipping the frost in 500 ppm ehtephon

59. In Pecan, the lower branch is kept at a height of ______ meter from the ground.

a) 2
b) 1
c) 2.5
d) 5

60. Pecan belongs to the family

a) Rutaceae
b) Rosaceae
c) Juglandaceae
d) Musaceae

61. The Genus Carya belongs to

a) Walnut
b) Filbert
c) Pecannut
d) Pistachio nut

62. The term 'Hicans' refers to.

a) Natural hybrids between Pecan and other Hicorries
b) All the species of the genus Carya
c) All the varieties of pecan
d) All the species of genus Juglans

63. Pecan is native to

a) China b) Malaysia
c) North America d) India

64. Commercial method of vegetative propagation in Pecan is

a) T-budding b) Patch budding
c) Shilled budding d) Veeneer grafting

65. In Pecan, the best planting time is

a) December-March b) December-April
c) Decembe-January d) June-July

66. Walnut belongs to the family

a) Caricaceae b) Juglandaceae
c) Anacardiaceae d) Myrtaceae

67. Average yield (kg/tree) of walnut is

a) 300 b) 40
c) 400 d) >500

68. Which of the following is the richest source of Vitamin B 6?

a) Walnut b) Pecanut
c) Filbert d) Chestnut

69. Walnut is believed to be originated from

a) Iran b) India
c) China d) Srilanka

70. _________ cm annual rainfall is considered sufficient for walnut.

a) 1000 b) 80
c) 500 d) 10

71. In walnut, the best time of planting is

a) December-March b) March-July
c) August-September d) October-November

72. Which of the following rootstock of walnut is resistant to crown rot?

a) *Juglans nigra* b) *J. microcarpa*
c) *J. sieboldiana* d) *J. hindsii*

73. Which method of vegetative propagation is commercially followed in walnut?

a) T-budding
b) Patch budding
c) Ring budding
d) Shield budding

74. Best time of veener grafting in walnut is

a) July-August
b) January-February
c) March-April
d) None of these

75. Best species of walnut for raising seedling rootstock.

a) J. regia
b) J. hindsie
c) J. nigra
d) J. microcarpa

76. Bartlett is an improved variety of

a) Apple
b) Apricot
c) Pear
d) Peach

77. The largest almond producing country in the world is

a) USA
b) South Africa
c) China
d) Srilanka

78. Which of the following is a rich source of carbohydrates (%)?

a) Banana
b) Apricot
c) Bael
d) Cashewnut

79. __________ fruit contains highest fat percent.

a) Avacodo
b) Walnut
c) Almond
d) Cashewnut

80. Type of apomixis in apple is

a) Facultative
b) Obligatory
c) Non-recurrent
d) None of these

81. Which of the following is not a pome fruit?

a) Peach
b) Apple
c) Loquat
d) Pear

82. Nemaguard, a rootstock of peach is resistant to

a) Nematodes
b) Wet soils
c) Peach leaf curl
d) Alkaline soils

83. Pyrus pashia (Kainth) rootstocks is resistant to

a) Nematode
b) Wooly aphid
c) Wet soils
d) Collar rot

84. Colt, Charger and Pazza are used as rootstocks for

a) Plum
b) Peach
c) Cherry
d) Apricot

85. Wild peach is used as rootstock in

a) Almond
b) Walnut
c) Apple
d) Quince

86. The highest iron contents containing fruit is

a) Dry karonda
b) Walnut
c) Green mango
d) Date

87. The highest ascorbic acid contents are present in

a) Barbados cherry
b) Aonla
c) Citrus
d) Gauva

88. ___________ fruit is highest in vitamin A (IU/100 g)

a) Papaya
b) Persimon
c) Mango
d) Dates

89. The richest source of riboflavin is

a) Bael
b) Papaya
c) Pine apple
d) Cashewnut

90. The highest calcium content is present in

a) Dry karonda
b) Litchi
c) Wood apple
d) Green mango

91. Which of the following fruit is essentially a tropical fruit?

a) Mango
b) Grape
c) Citrus
d) Banana

92. Cock's comb is a physiological disorder associated with

a) Litchi
b) Mango
c) Pear
d) Sapota

93. Amarapali, a hybrid of mango is a cross between

a) Dashehari × Neelum
b) Neelum × Dashehari
c) Neelum × Alphonso
d) Alphonso × Neelum

94. Mallika is a cross between

a) Dashehari × Neelum
b) Neelum × Dashehari
c) Alphonso × Bangapalli
d) Neelum × Alphonso

95. Which country has the highest productivity of mango?

a) Venezuela
b) India
c) China
d) Pakistan

96. Which form of sugar is predominantly present in mango?

a) Fructose
b) Starch
c) Sucrose
d) Hemi-cellulose

97. Litchi is commercially propagated by

a) Air layering
b) Seeds
c) Tip layering
d) All of these

98. Litchi is native to

a) North America
b) North China
d) South China
d) Mexico

99. In Litchi, leaf scorching is associated with deficiency of

a) Phosphorous
b) Potassium
c) Calcium
d) Molybdenum

100. Which of the following variety of litchi is susceptible to sun burn and fruit cracking?

a) Dehradun b) Calcuttia
c) Muzaffarpur d) China

101. The edible portion of the Litchi is

a) Drupes b) Aril
c) Pome d) Berry

102. Litchi is a crop of ____________ areas

a) Temperate b) Tropical
c) Sub tropical d) Moist sub-tropics

103. Litchi is a good source of

a) Phosphorus b) Calcium
c) Vit.-A d) All of them

104. State which of the following statements is incorrect about successful cultivation of litchi

a) Freedom from frost
b) High humidity
c) Rich deep soil and abundant moisture
d) Low humidity

105. Best soil for Litchi cultivation should have pH between

a) 3.5-5.5 b) 6.0 – 6.5
c) 7.5 – 10.5 d) 3.5 – 4.5

106. Major physiological disorder in Litchi is

a) Fruit cracking b) Black tip
c) Soft nose d) Mottle leaf

107. Litchi seed under ambient condition lose viability within

a) 1-2 weeks b) 3-4 weeks
c) 4-5 days d) 10-18 days

108. Fruit cracking in Litchi Cv Rose Scented can be reduced by spraying

a) 0.4% Boron b) 200 ppm 2, 4, D
c) NAA 200 ppm d) None of these

109. Dried Litchi is called

a) Aril
b) Pome
c) Raisin
d) Litchi nut

110. Hong-Kong, Rose Scented and Seedless Late are the varieties of

a) Loquat
b) Litchi
c) Sapota
d) Ber

111. The biggest litchi producing country in the world is

a) India
b) China
c) Sri Lanka
d) New Zealand

112. Which of the following State is leading in pomegranate production?

a) Maharashtra
b) Gujarat
c) Himachal Pradesh
d) Rajasthan

113. Pomegranate belongs to the family

a) Ebenaceae
b) Punicaceae
c) Caricaceae
d) Sapotaceae

114. Origin of pomegranate is

a) Iran
b) India
c) Brazil
d) Australia

115. Anardana is

a) Soft Seeded Variety
b) Dried Seed with pulp
c) Smooth seed variety
d) Wild variety

116. Queen is the variety of

a) Grape
b) Guava
c) Pineapple
d) Mango

117. In orchards the wind breaks are planted in

a) South-West
b) West-North
c) North-East
d) None of these

118. Jaffa is a variety of

a) Mango
b) Banana
c) Malta
d) Jackfruit

119. Seedlessness in grapes is due to

a) Parthenocarpy
b) Excess nitrogen
c) Embryo abortion
d) All of these

120. Yellow colour in onion is due to the pigment

a) Anthocyanin
b) Carotene
c) Quercetin
d) Both (a) and (b)

121. Which one of following is a monocot in nature?

a) Mango
b) Papaya
c) Citrus
d) Pineapple

122. Green revolution programme was introduced in the year

a) 1966-67
b) 1969-70
c) 1967-68
d) 1968-69

123. Injury caused by relatively low temperature above freezing point is.

a) Freezing injury
b) Chilling injury
c) Mechanical injury
d) None of these

124. Multi-storey cropping system is practiced in

a) Jammu & Kashmir
b) Bihar & Madhya Pradesh
c) Karnataka & Kerala
d) Rajasthan & Haryana

125. Which is the most important factor considered while establishing an orchard?

a) Topography
b) Approach road
c) Location
d) Availability of water

126. Very important constituent in fruits for preparing Jelly is

a) Sugar
b) Pectin
c) Cellulose
d) Vitamin

127. Marmalade is prepared successfully from

a) Citrus fruits
b) Guava
c) Apple
d) Mango

128. Spacing between fruit plant is determined on the basis of

a) Choice of farmer
b) Spreading behavior of plants
c) Availability of land
d) All of these

129. Maximum number of fruit plants can be planted in the orchard by

a) Digonal system
b) Square system
c) Hexagonal system
d) Rectangular system

130. Most popular method of planting fruit trees in orchards is

a) Square system
b) Diagonal system
c) Hexagonal system
d) Rectangular system

131. In hilly area, which system of fruit planting should be followed?

a) Strip cropping
b) Wind strip cropping
c) Contour system
d) None of these

132. Which hormone is found in ripened fruits?

a) Ethylene
b) Auxin
c) GA_3
d) IAA

133. Name the fruit crops which is used as hedge.

a) Duranta plumeri
b) Karonda
c) Kikkar
d) Tecoma stans

134. The farming which takes place without season is known as

a) Enforced farming
b) Rabi farming
c) Kharif farming
d) None of these

135. Which of the following is the variety of sweet orange?

a) Nagpur
b) Foster
c) Blood Red
d) Marsh seedless

136. Which is the popular and cheapest method of asexual propagation?

a) Budding
b) Cutting
c) Layering
d) Grafting

137. Ideal pH for orchard crops is

a) 6-8 b) 5-7
c) 4-6 d) 9-13

138. In grafting, upper part of stem is called

a) Stock b) Scion
c) Bud d) Appical bud

139. In cutting ______ inches long part of one year age should be used.

a) 6-9 b) 12-16
c) 1-2 d) 15-20

140. Which of the following growth promoter can develop the roots in mango?

a) GA_3 b) IAA
b) 2,4,5-T d) IBA

141. ______ ppm 2, 4-D spray can increase the yield of tomato three times.

a) 25-35 b) 100-150
c) 50-100 d) 1-5

142. Size of grapes can be increased by spraying

a) 20 ppm GA_3 b) 1000 ppm GA_3
c) 1 ppm GA_3 d) 2 % GA_3

143. Which of the following is not an auxin?

a) GA_3 b) NAA
c) 2, 4-D d) IAA

144. Which of the following is not a growth promoter?

a) Auxin b) Gibberellin
c) Abscissic acid d) Cytokinin

145. Which of the following is a growth inhibitor?

a) NAA b) BA
c) IAA d) GA_3

146. For arid climatic conditions which fruit should not be selected?

a) Date palm
b) Ber
c) Pomegranate
d) Banana

147. __________is not preferred for wind break in orchard.

a) *Casuarina equisetifolia*
b) *Prosopise juliflora*
c) Dalbergia sisso
d) Syzygium cumini

148. Planting distance of individual fruit species provides

a) Uniform growth
b) Easy orchard operation
c) Proper utilization of orchard space
d) Proper supervision

149. Water requirement is a ratio between

a) Water used and plant material produced
b) Water transpired and plant material produced
c) Water evaporated and plant material produced
d) Water percolated and plant material produced

150. Most popular method of propagation of mango is.

a) Veneer grafting
b) Inarching
c) Forkert budding
d) Epicotyl grafting

151. Date palm should be propagated by

a) Suckers
b) Seeds
c) Offshoots
d) Rhizomes

152. Most economic method of irrigation of orchard under water scarcity conditions is

a) Flood system
b) Sprinkler system
c) Both a and b
d) Drip system

153. According to flowering habit, date palm is

a) Monoecious
b) Dioceious
c) Hermophrodite
d) Andramonocious

154. Latest hybrid mango variety released from Maharashtra is

a) Amrapali b) Mallika
c) Ratna d) Nileshwari

155. For Malta blood red the best root stock is

a) Citrus jambhiri b) Karna khatta
c) Rangpur lime d) Cleoptera mandarin

156. The best time for pruning of ber in Rajasthan is

a) Mid of April to mid of May
b) Mid of March to mid of April
c) Mid of May to mid of June
d) None of the above

157. Seedlessness in grapes is due to

a) Lack of pollination b) Parthenocarpy
c) Aneuploidy d) Embryo abortion

158. Out of following which fruit plants need 'Bahar' treatment.

a) Lichi and loquat b) Guava and pomegranate
c) Ber and date palm d) Grape and Aonla

159. Gros Michel is a variety of banana which is

a) Triploid b) Diploid
c) Tetraploid d) None of the above

160. Kohir safed and safed jam are the varieties of

a) Pomegranate b) Guava
c) Date palm d) Mango

161. Asepsis means

a) Exclusion of air
b) Exclusion of moisture/ water
c) Exclusion of dust and spray
d) Exclusion of micro-organism

162. Canning in a method of

a) Heat processing
b) Non heat processing
c) Sterilization
d) Any other

163. Which of the following fruit crop is not belongs to temperate region?

a) Apple
b) Pea
c) Strawberry
d) Lemon

164. Which of the following is a temperate fruit crop?

a) Walnut
b) Lime
c) Sweet orange
d) Pummelo

165. Which of the following is not a sub-tropical fruit crop?

a) Phalsa
b) Grape
c) Papaya
d) Fig

166. Which of the following is a tropical fruit crop?

a) Sapota
b) Walnut
c) Strawberry
d) Mandarin

167. Which of the following is not a tropical fruit crop?

a) Banana
b) Cashewnut
c) Fig
d) Mango

168. The ideal temperature for coffee crop is.

a) 15°C - 30°C
b) 5°C - 20°C
c) 25°C – 40°C
d) 30°C - 50°C

169. Which of the following is a variety of coffee?

a) S-306
b) S-288
c) S-308
d) S-541

170. Which of the following is a variety of Rubuster Coffee?

a) S-274
b) S-795
c) S-288
d) S-307

171. Coffee plants are matured at the age of ______ years.

a) 15
b) 10
c) 20
d) 4

172. Coffee plants begin yielding a small crop from

a) 4th year
b) 8th year
c) 2nd year
d) 10th year

173. In apples small, narrow and mottled leaves are primarily because of the deficiency of

a) Zinc
b) Iron
c) Potassium
d) Iodine

174. Amimgola is a variety of

a) Guava
b) Banana
c) Mango
d) Grape

175. Sonar Bahisth is a variety of.

a) Ber
b) Mango
c) Fine apple
d) Papaya

176. Fruit drop in mango can be controlled by spraying

a) 2, 4-D
b) B.H.C
c) NaCl
d) KCl

177. A perfect jelly has an acidity of

a) 1.5%
b) 1.0%
c) 1.25%
d) 2.0%

178. Vegetables are subjected to drying after

a) Blanching
b) Washing
c) Sulphiting
d) None of these

179. Tomato sauce is preserved by using

a) Acetic acid
b) Sodium Benzoate
c) Salt
d) All of these

180. Fruit candy is

a) Agra-ka-Petha
b) Aonla ka murabba
c) Toffees
d) Sugar candy

181. Cordial is generally taken by mixing with

a) Water and ice
b) Tea
c) Coffee
d) Gin

182. For pickle making one can use maximum of

a) 40% salt
b) 30% salt
c) 75% salt
d) 35% salt

183. Tomato sauce must not have less than

a) 16% TSS
b) 10% TSS
c) 5% TSS
d) 12% TSS

184. Marmlades must have

a) 2% pectin
b) 1.25% pectin
c) 0.75% pectin
d) 1.0% pectin

185. Jam is prepared with

a) Fruit pectin and pulp
b) Fruit pulp alone
c) Fruit pectin alone
d) Pectin, pulp, seed and skin mix

186. Qualitatively good fruit juice is one which is

a) Extracted from healthy fruit
b) Extracted from healthy fruit and mixed with sugar, acid, colour and essence
c) Extracted from healthy fruit and added with sugar alone
d) Extracted from healthy fruit and added with essence alone

187. Soft wood cutting is a propagation material used in.

a) Coleus
b) Rose
c) Licthi
d) Mango

188. Semi-hard wood cutting is a propagating material used in

a) Bagonia
b) Grape
c) Pomegranate
d) None of these

189. Hard wood cutting is a propagating material used in

a) Date
b) Fig
c) Grape
d) Litchi

190. Which of the following is not a kind of detached graft?

a) Wedge b) Saddle
c) Tongue d) None of these

191. Which of the following is the kind of detached grafting?

a) Venner b) Saddle
c) Tongue d) All of these

192. Which of the following is the kind of budding?

a) Shield b) Patch
c) Ring d) All of these

193. In grafting, lower part of plant is known as

a) Stock b) Scion
c) Both of them d) None of these

194. Root cutting for propagation is used in

a) Dog wood b) Blackberry
c) Fig d) Apple

195. The nitrogen requirement of one year old plant is

a) 150 grams b) 50 grams
c) 2 grams d) None of these

196. Which of the following is not a self-pollinated fruit crop?

a) Guava b) Grape
c) Peach d) None of these

197. Which of the following is not a cross pollinated fruit?

a) Mango b) Litchi
c) Peach d) None of these

198. Which of the following is not a self accompability fruit crop?

a) Pear b) Almond
c) Apple d) Guava

199. Amimgola is a variety of

a) Apple b) Guava
c) Ber d) Mango

200. Date palm is propagated by

a) Off shoots
b) Suckers
c) Both a) and b)
d) Seeds

201. Which of the following is not a suitable fruit crop for arid climatic conditions?

a) Date palm
b) Pomegranate
c) Banana
d) Ber

202. Kinnow is a cross between

a) Mandarin x Sweet orange
b) Willow leaf x Wilking
c) King x Willow leaf
d) King x Sweet orange

203. Kohir Safed and Safed jam are varieties of

a) Guava
b) Pomegranate
c) Mango
d) Fig

204. Root cuttings are used as propagation materials in

a) Fig
b) Litchi
c) Apple
d) Mango

205. Farming which takes place without season is known as

a) Enforced farming
b) Kharif farming
c) Profitable farming
d) All of these

206. Which one of the following is not a variety of apple?

a) Rome beauty
b) Red Delicious
c) Winter banana
d) Roma

207. Tangela is a cross between

a) Tangerin x Grape fruit
b) Tangerin x Sweet orange
c) Tangerin x Pummelo
d) Tangerin x Mandarin

208. In India, maximum area under cashew nut is in

a) West Bengal
b) Andhra Pradesh
c) Orissa
d) Kerala

209. Wind breaks are planted in orchards towards

a) South-west b) North-west
c) East-South d) North-east

210. Chief pollinator of Mango is

a) House flies b) Honey bees
c) White fly d) None of them

211. Variety of Mango immune to malformation.

a) Dashehari b) Langra
c) Bahaudran d) Alphonso

212. Mango is a native of

a) Mexico b) Indo-Burma Region
c) Sri Lanka d) Pakistan

213. Mango is rich in

a) Vitamin-C b) Vitamin-B
c) Vitamin-E d) Vitamin-A

214. Soft-nose in mango is associated with deficiency of

a) N b) Ca
c) P d) K

215. Mango a drupe fruit belongs to family

a) Rosaceae b) Rutaceae
c) Anacardiaceae d) Tiliaceae

216. Spongy tissue is considered to be one of the most important physiological disorder of Mango, most common in

a) Alphonso b) Arka anmol
c) Langra d) Ratna

217. Mango variety highly susceptible to malformation

a) Alphonso b) Bombay Green
c) Langra d) Fazli

218. The most popular variety of mango grown in West Bengal.

a) Dashehari b) Zardalu
c) Himsagar d) Langra

219. Neelum is widely cultivated in

a) Western Region b) Northern Region
c) Eastern Region d) Southern Region

220. Ratna is a cross between

a) Neelum × Alphonso b) Neelum × Dashehari
c) Neelum × Bombay d) Bombay × Kalapadi

221. Mango flowers are borne on terminal inflorescence that is called

a) Cyme b) Racema
c) Panicle d) Corymbose

222. Neelum a late variety of mango is widely cultivated in

a) Northern India b) South India
c) Western India d) Eastern India

223. Arka Aruna is a hybrid of

a) Mango b) Litchi
c) Sapota d) Passion fruit

224. Tapka is associated with maturity of.

a) Papaya b) Grapes
c) Guava d) Mango

225. A disease which can transform 'on year' of fruiting to 'off year' in Mango.

a) Powdery mildew b) Leaf blight
c) Anthracnose d) Stem canker

226. A serious physiological disorder of mango orchards near brick kilns is

a) Black tip b) Spongy tissue
c) Black rot d) Malformation

227. 'Parthenocarpy' in few varieties of mango may be due to

a) Prevailing low temperature during flowering
b) Reduced activity of pollinators
c) Absence of pollinating tree
d) All of these

228. Mango varieties most suitable for pickle making.

a) Ramkela b) Kesar
c) Kitki d) All of these

229. Specific gravity is the most common method to determine maturity stage of mango. The specific gravity should be

a) 1.01 - 1.02 b) 1.08 - 2.1
c) 1.5 - 2.0 d) 2.0 - 2.5

230. pH range of soil for growing mango is around

a) 2.3 - 4.5 b) 7.2 - 7.8
c) 7.0 - 7.5 d) 5.5 - 7.0

231. Powdery mildew, a serious disease of mango is caused by

a) *Indarbola quadrinotata* b) *Bactocera rufamaculata*
c) *Oidium mangiferae* d) *Apsylla cistellata*

232. Deblossoning is practiced in

a) Mango b) Citrus
c) Apple d) Guava

233. Commercial method of grafting in mango.

a) Whip grafting b) Veneer grafting
c) Tongue grafting d) Side grafting

234. Sap burn is a post harvest disorder of

a) Papaya b) Banana
c) Mango d) Apple

235. Biennial bearing is synonymous to

a) Alternate bearing b) Deblosssoming
c) Regular bearing d) Parthenocarpy

236. Which pair is wrong?

a) Mango : King of fruit and essentially a tropical fruit
b) Langra : Mass selection
c) Powdery mildew : High humidity favoured by low temperature
d) Mallika : Dhashehari x Neelam

237. Which of the following is true?

a) Mallika and Amrapalli developed at IARI
b) Pollination in Mango is carried by honey bees
c) Mango is a self-pollinated crop
d) Mango fruit is non-climacteric

238. Which pair is incorrect?

a) Anthrachose : *Colletotrichum gloesporiodes*
b) Alternaria rot : *Alternaria alternata*
c) Dry rot : *Mycosphaerella sp.*
d) Black mould : *Asperigillus niger*

239. Botanically mandarins are

a) *Citrus reticulata*
b) *Citrus limettoides*
c) *Citrus aurantium*
d) *Citrus sinensis*

240. Mandarins are commercially propagated by

a) Seed
b) Shield budding
c) Grafting
d) Air layering

241. Kinnow is a hybrid between.

a) Sweet lime × Lemon
b) Kagzi lime × Sour orange
c) Sweet orange × Lemon
d) King × Willow leaf

242. What is the name of ancestor of grapefruit?

a) Shaddock
b) Mosambi
c) Lemon
d) Sour lemon

243. What is the best method for propagation of grapefruit?

a) Seeds
b) Budding
c) Cutting
d) Layering

244. Duncan, Foster and Ruby are important cultivars of

a) Pummalo b) Mandarins
c) Grapefruit d) Lime

245. Grapefruit was separated from Pummelo in the year.

a) 1830 b) 1730
c) 1825 d) 1810

246. Marsh seedless is a variety of which of the following citrus fruit.

a) Mandarins b) Pummelo
c) Sweet orange d) Grapefruit

247. Name of glucoside present in grapefruit is

a) Naringin b) Hesperidin
c) Catechin d) Gallocatechin

248. Marsh seedless, a variety of grape fruit was introduced in India from

a) England b) USA
c) Italy d) Japan

249. Citrus canker is caused by

a) Mycoplasma b) Fungus
c) Bacteria d) Virus

250. In citrus, greening is a diseased caused by

a) Mycoplasma b) Bacteria
c) Fungus d) Virus

251. Sweet orange is commonly known as

a) Mosambi b) Malta
c) Sathgudi d) All of these

252. Jaffa, a variety of sweet orange was introduced in India from.

a) Brazil b) Palestine
c) Florida d) China

253. The origin of sweet orange is

a) China b) Sri Lanka
c) California d) Brazil

254. Which among the following is the richest source of acid?

a) *Citrus megalaxycarpa* b) *Citrus reticulata*
c) *Citrus sinensis* d) None of these

255. The monoembryonic citrus is/are.

a) *Citrus latifolia* b) *Citrus medica*
c) *Citrus maxima* d) All of these

256. *Citrus grandis* is synonymous to

a) *Citrus maxima* b) *Citrus sinensis*
c) *Citrus reticulata* d) *C. medica*

257. Granulation, a physiological disorder of citrus fruit was first noticed at

a) California b) China
c) Florida d) India

258. A nocturnal serious pest of citrus fruit is

a) Mites b) Fruit sucking moth
c) White flies d) Aphids

259. Which of the following is correctly matched?

a) Grape fruit : Marsh seedless, Duncan. Foster
b) Mandarin : Mosambi, Pine apple, Blood Red
c) Sweet orange : Kinnow, Srinagar, Nurpur Local
d) Sweet lime : Eureka, Baramasi, Lucknow Seedless

260. Which of the following is important mandarin of North-west India?

a) Coorg Santra b) Desi Santra
c) Khasi Orange d) Kinnow

261. Seedling utilized to detect the infection of viral diseases are called as

a) Indication plants b) Resistant plants
c) Susceptible plants d) Hardy plants

262. Indicator citrus plant to detect virus disease 'Tristeza' is

a) Sour orange b) Kagzi lime
c) Sweet orange d) Blood Red

263. Granulation is a _______ disease/ disorder.

a) Physiological
b) Bacterial
c) Fungal
d) MLO

264. Citrus fruits are successfully stored at temperature of

a) 0°C
b) 8-10 °C
c) 13 °C
d) >5 °C

265. Family of coconut is

a) Arecaceae
b) Musaceae
c) Rutaceae
d) Bromiliaceae

266. Coconut is often termed as

a) Kaja Vriksha
b) Kalpa-Vriksha
c) Dharam-Vriksha
d) Karma-Vriksha

267. The word 'Copra' is related to

a) Arecanut
b) Pecannut
c) Coconut
d) Walnut

268. Which part is used to extract coconut oil and contains 65 to 75 percent oil.

a) Immature nut
b) Dry copra
c) Wet meal
d) Liquid endosperm

269. Coconut thrives best in

a) Hot and humid climate
b) Mild and moist climate
c) Sub tropical climate
d) Arid and semi arid climate

270. Godhavari Ganga, a hybrid of coconut, is recommended for which State of India?

a) Karnataka
b) Tamil Nadu
c) Kerala
d) Andhra Pradesh

271. Laksha Ganga, Ananda Ganga and KeraSree are important varieties of

a) Cashewnut
b) Arecanut
c) Coconut
d) Pecannut

272. A waste product obtained during extraction of fibre from coconut husk is known as

a) Nata-de-coco
b) Coconut jam
c) Coconut vinegar
d) Coirpith

273. White kernel of fresh mature coconuts, shedded and dried to about 2.5% water content is called

a) Desiccated coconut
b) Coconut cream
c) Coconut milk
d) Virgin coconut oil

274. Convenience product from raw coconut kernel is/ are

a) Dessicated coconut (DC)
b) Coconut cream
c) Coconut milk
d) All of these

275. What are milling copra and edible copra?

a) Varieties of coconut
b) Forms of copra
c) Harvesting stages of coconut
d) Quality parameters of coconut

276. In coconut, multi-storey cropping system is followed to

a) increase productivity
b) protect from warm condition
c) improve soil status
d) conserve soil moisture

277. In multi-story cropping system, the coconut palm serves as

a) Ground floor
b) Mid story
c) Top floor
d) None of these

278. In fully dried copra, the maximum moisture content is

a) 1%
b) 6%
c) 8%
d) 3%

279. Coconut oil obtained from coconut milk is called as

a) Virgin oil
b) Cosmetic oil
c) Dietary oil
d) Industrial oil

280. Botanically, arecanut is known as

a) *Anacardium occidentale* L.
b) *Theobroma cacao* L
c) *Areca catechu* L.
d) All of these

281. Arecanut belongs to family

a) Rosaceae
b) Rutaceae
c) Palmae
d) Anacardiaceae

282. Arecanut is said to be native to

a) South America
b) Phillipines and East Indian Islands
c) Brazil
d) China

283. Arecanut is an essential ingredient of

a) Gutka
b) Panmasula
c) Both a & b
d) None of these

284. The cultivation of arecanut is mostly confined to

a) 28° North and South of equator
b) 15° East and West of equator
c) 20° North and West of equator
d) 15° North and South of equator

285. Mangala, an important variety of arecanut was introduced from China in the year

a) 1980
b) 1975
c) 1973
d) 1990

286. Which of the following variety of arecanut is an indigenous collection?

a) Mangala
b) Sumangala
c) Sreemangla
d) Mohit Nagar

287. Arecanut is only propagated by

a) Cutting
b) Seeds
c) Budding
d) Layering

288. Optimum spacing for arecanut (meter)

a) 2.7 × 2.7 b) 5 × 5
c) 1.5 × 1.5 d) 4 × 4

289. Chali or Kottapak in arecanut are the terms related to

a) Fresh nuts b) Tender nuts
c) Mature nuts d) Dried ripe nuts

290. The economic produce of arecanut is its fruit, which is called as

a) Betel nut b) Areca husk
c) Moti d) Jini

291. The husk of arecanut constitutes ________ to ________% of total weight of fresh nut.

a) 40 - 45 b) 30 - 40
c) 50 - 60 d) 60 - 80

292. Botanically cocoa is called as

a) *Theobroma cocoa* L.
b) *Cocos nucifera* Linn.
c) *Hevea brasiliensis*
d) None of these

293. Arecanut thrives well in a soil type which is

a) Laterite b) Alluvial
c) Loam d) All of these

294. The largest arecanut country in the world is

a) India b) Bangladesh
c) Indonesia d) Thailand

295. A product prepared from immature green arecanut is called

a) Kalipak b) Chali
c) Kattapak d) None of these

296. White supari and Red supari are the varieties of

a) Walnut b) Hazelnut
c) Arecanut d) Theobroma

297. Cashewnut tree needs

a) Warm moist and tropical climate
b) Dry and temperate climate
c) Humid climate
d) Humid tropical climate

298. Cashew starts flowering in the month of _______ and extends upto February.

a) December b) January
c) November d) October

299. The cashew apple juice is a rich source of

a) Vitamin C b) Vitamin A
c) Iron d) Fats

300. Botanically, ceshewnut is known as

a) *Cocos nucifera* Linn b) *Theobroma cocoa* L.
c) *Areca catechu* L. d) *Anacardium occidentale* Linn

301. The cashew is said to be native of

a) Brazil b) Phillipines
c) India d) Srilanka

302. In the 16th century, the cashewnut was introduced in India by _____ in Malabar Coast and planted to check the soil erosion

a) The Mughals b) The Portuguese
c) Japanese d) Romans

303. The high quality oil obtained from cashewnut is known as

a) Cashew nut shell liquid (CNSL)
b) Fenny
c) Challi
d) Natta-do-Coco

304. Oil-protein-water emulsion obtained by squeezing grated fresh coconut kernel is known as

a) Cream b) Coconut sap.
c) Coconut wine d) Coconut syrup

305. Which of the following pair is a wrong statement?

a) Coconut water - Vinegar, Natta-do-Coco
b) Coconut shell - Charcol powder
c) Coconut milk - Desserts, sweet
d) Fermented sap - Burfi, cookies

306. ________is a traditional high sugar coconut food.

a) Jam
b) Vineger
c) Nata-de-Coco
d) Wine

307. The largest coconut producing state in India.

a) Karnataka
b) Kerala
c) Tamil Nadu
d) Andhra Pradesh

308. Natural fibre extracted from mesocarp tissue is known as

a) Coir
b) Activated carbon
c) Dessicated coconut
d) Coconut sugar

309. The largest cocoa producing country in the world.

a) Indonesia
b) Malaysia
c) Brazil
d) West Africa

310. Roasting, grinding, refining, conching and tempering are terms used in cocoa are related with

a) Chocolate making
b) Drying
c) Maturity
d) Quality evaluation

311. The art of tansforming liquid chocolate into a solid is

a) Roasting
b) Shellory
c) Tempering
d) Conching

312. Fermentation of cocoa beans is carried by

a) Heap method
b) Tray method
c) Bore method
d) All of these

313. In Cocoa, development of pod takes _____ month from fertilization to full ripening.

a) 5 - 6
b) 1 - 2
c) 2 - 3
d) 3 - 4

314. On ripening, the green Cocoa pods become ____ in colour.

a) Light green b) Yellow
c) Orange d) Draft green

315. Each pod of cocoa will have ______ beans embedded in white pulp (mucilage).

a) Less than 5 b) 25 - 45
c) 10 - 20 d) More than 60

316. Chicklet is obtained from latex of

a) Fig b) Mango
c) Sapota d) Papaya

317. Pineapple is mainly propogated by

a) Crowns b) Crown slips
c) Stumps d) Suckers

318. Artificial ripening is very difficult in

a) Lemon b) Papaya
c) persimmon d) Plums

319. Cardamon hills are located in

a) Nilgiries b) Kerala
c) Himalayas d) Satpura

320. Which sugar is obtained from grapes?

a) Sucrose b) Lactose
c) Maltose d) Glucose

321. Which of the following is called the 'King of fruits'?

a) Mango b) Grapes
c) Banana d) Pomegranate

322. Which of the following is a diocious fruit free?

a) Walnut b) Date
c) Litchi d) Jackfruit

323. Which of the following is heterostyly?

a) Walnut
b) Fig
c) Date
d) Litchi

324. In hexagonal method of tree planting, about percent more trees can be planted than triangular method.

a) 25
b) 40
c) 10
d) 15

325. The interfiller tree in mango garden is

a) Papaya
b) Litchi
c) Guava
d) Loquat

326. Square method of planting is most common in

a) Mango
b) Litchi
c) Citrus fruit
d) All of these

327. Rectangular system of planting is most common in

a) Peach
b) Falsa
c) Grape
d) All of these

328. Evergreen fruits like Mango, Guava and Jackfruit should be planted in the month of

a) February - March
b) June - July
c) September - October
d) December

329. Temperate fruits like apple, peach, pear and plum should be planted in the month of

a) March - April
b) December - April
c) July - August
d) September - October

330. Upper stem of banana is called

a) Sucker
b) Rhizome
c) Pseudostem
d) None of these

331. Maximum production of banana is in

a) Maharashtra
b) Tamil Nadu
c) Kerala
d) U.P.

332. The recommended distance for banana planting is

a) 5 × 5 meters
b) 10 × 10 meters
c) 8 × 8 meters
d) 3 × 3 meters

333. Fruiting in banana occurs after

a) 2 years
b) 10-16 months
c) 4 months
d) None of them

334. Fruits of banana mature after……months of fruit setting.

a) 1-2
b) 2-3
c) 9-10
d) 3-4

335. The origin place of papaya is

a) South America
b) Pakistan
c) Russia
d) Canada

336. The seed of papaya for seeding should be shown in

a) August-September
b) April-May
c) February-March
d) June-July

337. Salad crops are those crops used for

a) Canning
b) Latex extraction
c) Raw consumption
d) Ornamental purpose

338. Removal of undesired branches by picking auxiliary buds is known as

a) Clipping
b) Nipping
c) Building
c) Topping

339. How much of the total area under fruit is occupied by mango?

a) 25%
b) 40%
c) 60%
d) 75%

340. Rose mix is having the NPK in the ratio of '

a) 2:5:5
b) 3:8:5
c) 5:8:18
d) 10:15:20

341. Quincunx in horticulture refers to

a) Pruning method of grapes
b) De-suckering method of banana
c) Planting method of trees
d) Harvesting fruits from trees

342. Banana suckers arise from

a) Underground rhizomes b) Underground corms
c) Stolons d) Pseudostems

343. Muscat Red is a variety of

a) Grapes b) Pomegranate
c) Plums d) Apple

344. One hectare of banana plantation yields fruits weighing.

a) 2,000 – 25,000 kg b) 26,000 – 55,000 kg
c) 10,000 – 20,000 kg d) 70,000 – 90,000 kg

345. A coconut tree will start fruiting after _____ of planting.

a) 2 years b) 1 year
c) 6 years d) 4 years

346. A cashewnut tree will start fruiting after ______ of planting.

a) 4 years b) 9 years
c) 1.5 years d) 10 years

347. Grape tree will start fruiting after ______ of planting.

a) 4 years b) 5 years
c) 1.5 years d) 2.5 years

348. Guava tree will give the fruits after ______ of planting.

a) 4 years b) 2 years
c) 7 years d) 10 years

349. Which of the following fruit is cured in smoke for ripening?

a) Orange b) Banana
c) Jack fruit d) Mango

350. A fruit plant which bears fruits only once in its life is

a) Banana b) Plum
c) Arecarnut d) Custard apple

351. Veneer grafting is the best method of propagation in

a) Banana b) Lime
c) Guava d) Mango

352. Grapes contain which of the following acids?

a) Malic acid b) Tartaric acid
c) Hydro-cyartic acid d) Glutonic acid

353. The edible part of pomegranate fruit is

a) Testa of fruit b) Endosperms of seed
c) Fleshy ovary d) Juicy embryo

354. One hectare of pineapple crop may yield upto

a) 175 tonnes b) 125 tonnes
c) 50 tonnes d) None of these

355. Which of the following fruits are drupe?

a) Ber b) Mango
c) Both a and b d) Raspberry

356. The food crop which is not thoroughly propagated by vegetative means is

a) Orange b) Banana
c) Grapes d) Pineapples

357. The fruit which does not exhibit flowers is

a) Guava b) Grapes
c) Jack fruit d) Orange

358. Air layering is practised usually with

a) Grapes b) Persian lime
c) Mango d) None of these

359. Die back of citrus can be controlled with the application of.

a) Bordeaux mixture b) Endosulfan
c) Zinc sulphate d) B.H.C.

360. Himrod and Perlette are the improved cultivars of

a) Guava b) Mango
c) Papaya d) Grape

361. Gold Delight is a variety of

a) Guava b) Papaya
c) Grape d) Mango

362. The arbour system of training the grape vine is recommended for

a) Perlette b) Thompson seedless
c) Anab-e-Shahi d) None of these

363. The pruning in grape should be done in

a) January b) April
c) July d) October

364. Banana, Papaya and Jack fruits are used as

a) Fruits b) Vegetables
c) Both a and b d) Salad

365. Scientific name of Sapota or Chiku is.

a) *Achras zapota* b) *Phyllanthus emblica*
c) *Oryza sativa* d) None of these

366. Major source of water used by the plants is

a) Gravitional water b) Capillary water
c) Hygroscopic water d) Interspace water

367. The citrus disease namely 'Reclamation' and 'Dieback' are caused by the deficiency of

a) Zinc b) Iron
c) Copper d) Molybdenum

368. The chemical name of "Vitamin A" is

a) Retinol
b) Thiamine
c) Riboflavin
d) Cynocobalamin

369. "Calciferol" name is given to

a) Vitamin-C
b) Vitamin-D
c) Vitamin-A
d) Vitamin-E

370. Common name of "Thiamine" is

a) Vitamin-A
b) Vitamin-B1
c) Vitamin-C
d) Vitamin-K

371. "Retinol" is also known as

a) Vitamin-A
b) Vitamin-C
c) Vitamin-B4
d) Vitamin-B2

372. Common name of "Ascorbic acid" is

a) Vitamin-D
b) Vitamin-K
c) Vitamin-B12
d) Vitamin-C

373. "Tocopherol" is a chemical name of which vitamin?

a) Vitamin-E
b) Vitamin-B7
c) Vitamin-B9
d) Vitamin-B5

374. Common name of "Riboflavin" is

a) Vitamin-B9
b) Vitamin-B8
c) Vitamin-A
d) Vitamin-B2

375. Which mineral is needed for making "Haemoglobin"?

a) Iron
b) Iodine
c) Calcium
d) Phosphorus

376. Which mineral is required for making the "Thyroid hormone"?

a) Iodine
b) Calcium
c) Sodium
d) Potassium

377. Which mineral salts are required to maintain the osmotic pressure of body fluid?

a) Salt of sodium
b) Salt of potassium
c) Both (a) and (b)
d) Salt of calcium

378. Which carbohydrate is present in maize?

a) Starch
b) Glucose
c) Fructose
d) Cellulose

379. Which of the following item can not be digested by human body?

a) Glucose
b) Fructose
c) Starch
d) Cellulose

380. A balance diet means

a) A diet free of proteins
b) Which sypply all the nutrients necessary for growth & development
c) A fat containing diet
d) Carbohydrate rich diet

381. Proteins, fats and carbohydrates are called

a) Macronutrients
b) Micronutrients
c) Minor nutrients
d) Major nutrients

382. Food energy is measured in

a) Calories
b) Grams
c) Ampere
d) Watts

383. Starch and sugar are source of

a) Fats
b) Carbohydrates
c) Hormones
d) Vitamins

384. The richest source of proteins are

a) Pulses
b) Fruits
c) Vegetables
d) Cereals

385. Cereals are rich in

a) Vitamins
b) Minerals
c) Carbohydrates
d) All of these

386. Nuts and oil seeds are a good source of

a) Vitamins b) Fats
c) Proteins d) All of these

387. How many calories of energy is obtained from one gram of protein?

a) 9 b) 4
c) 7 d) 30

388. The highest calories energy value is in

a) Fats b) Proteins
c) Carbohydrates d) Minerals

389. Which of the following minerals is a part of haemoglobin of blood?

a) Calcium b) Iron
c) Magnesium d) Manganese

390. Which element is essential for chlorophyll formation?

a) Iron b) Manganese
c) Calcium d) Magnesium

391. Softening of fruits during ripening is due to the breakdown of

a) Starch b) Sugars
c) Organic acids d) Pectic substances

392. The diameter of the plunger for measuring apple firmness is

a) 8 mm b) 11 mm
c) 14 mm d) 17 mm

393. A typical example of non-climacteric fruits is

a) Cherry b) Plum
c) Peach d) Apricot

394. The starch-iodine test for judging apple maturity results in the formation of

a) Dark red colour b) Dark bluish red colour
c) Dark bluish black colour d) Dark reddish blue colour

395. Ripening of fruits is caused as a result of

a) Synthesis of new enzymes
b) Breakdown of starch
c) Breakdown of pectic substances
d) Increase in respiration rate

396. The aroma of a ripe apple is due to

a) Ethylene b) Eugenol
c) Valencene d) Ethyl-2-methyl butyrate

397. The oldest method of preservation of foods is

a) Canning b) Drying
c) Fermentation d) Processing

398. Which of the following varieties of apricot is most suitable for drying

a) Shakarpara b) New castle
c) Early Shipley d) None of these

399. During dehydration of apple, the yield varies from

a) 5-10% b) 10-15%
c) 15-20% d) 20-25%

400. Most vegetables are dehydrated at a temperature of

a) 55°C b) 65°C
c) 75°C d) 85°C

401. Fruit coatings prolong shelf life of commodities by reducing

a) Respiration b) Transpiration
c) Microbial spoilage d) All of these

402. The process of rapid removal of field heat is called

a) Pre-cooling b) Pre-freezing
c) Pre-heating d) None of thesse

403. The recommended temperature for the storage of banana is

a) 0°C b) 4°C
c) 8°C d) 13°C

404. The storage life of fruits is reduced by higher

a) Respiration
b) Transpiration
c) Ethylene
d) All of these

405. Which of the following substance is useful in increasing firmness of fruits

a) $CaCl_2$
b) KCl
c) NaCl
d) All of these

406. Firmness of fruits can be measured by a

a) Penetrometer
b) Refractomete
c) Altimeter
d) Techometer

407. Which of the following is the most effective in initiating ripening of fruits?

a) Ethylene
b) Calcium Carbide
c) Propylene
d) Acetylene

408. Fruit cordial is a type of

a) Fermented beverage
b) Orange squash
c) Fruit concentrate
d) Lime juice product

409. Mohr titeration method is used for estimation of

a) Salt
b) Pectin
c) Calcium
d) Sugar

410. Which of the following is categorized as class-I preservatives?

a) Citric acid
b) Sulphur dioxide
c) Benzoic acid
d) Sugar

411. Which is the latest technique in food preservation?

a) Canning
b) Freezing
c) Hurdle technology
d) Drying

412. Canning is invented by

a) Louis Pasteur
b) Nicholas Appert
c) NW Desrossier
d) Peter Durand

413. In apple starch Iodine test gives

a) Dark bluish black colour
b) Dark red colour
c) Dark Redish blue colour
d) Dark bluish red colour

414. Carotenoid pigments are synthesized during

a) Flower bud stage b) Pea stage
c) Development stage d) Senescence stage

415. The term climacteric rise was first stated by

a) Kidd & West b) Haard & Salunke
c) Hulme d) Ryall & Pentzer

416. Recommendations are made for increasing shelf life of apple is

a) $CaCl_2$ b) $CaNO_3$
c) Ethephon d) GA

417. Which of following contributes maximum in fruit fresh weight?

a) Carbohydrate b) Acid
c) Lipid d) Water

418. A seed receptacle developed from an ovary is called

a) Fruit b) Flower
c) Modified stem d) Leave

419. Which of the following fruits have single large seed surrounded by fleshy mesocarp?

a) Apple b) Apricot
c) Cherry d) None of these

420. Type of fruit in citrus is called

a) Berry b) Pome
c) Drupe d) Hesperidium

421. Which are two major respiratory substrates found in fruit?

a) Sugar & acid b) Minerals & fat
c) Protein & CHO d) None of these

422. Which of the following contains both ascorbic and citric acid serving the same purpose?

a) Pineapple juice
b) Apple juice
c) Orange juice
d) Lemon juice

423. When sugars are heated above their melting points, they darken to a brown colouration is Known?

a) Colourization
b) Caramelization
c) Exidative degradation
d) None of these

424. Freezing preceded by partial dehydration is known as

a) Sharp freezing
b) Quick freezing
c) Dehydro freezing
d) Freeze drying

425. Sun drying is slow as evaporation takes place

a) Uniformly
b) Non-uniformly
c) Continuous
d) Intercepted

426. Which one of the following is not a traditional type packaging?

a) Metal cons
b) Glass bottles
c) Microwaveable containers
d) Cartons & boxes

427. Which of the following is not an antioxidant?

a) TBHQ
b) CMC
c) PG
d) BHT

428. Which of the following is not a stabilizer/ thickner?

a) Starch
b) Carboxy methyl cellulose
c) Gelatin
d) MSG

429. Pigment present in Papaya is

a) Xanthophyll
b) Carotine
c) Caricaxanthin
d) None of these

430. Spongy tissue is associated with which variety of mango

a) Alphonso
b) Amarpali
c) Rumani
d) Neelam

431. Which one is non-climacteric?

a) Pineapple
b) Mango
c) Avocado
d) Banana

432. Best method of preservation is

a) Deaeration
b) Dehydration
c) Pasteurization
d) None of these

433. Photophosphorylation is

a) Hill reaction
b) Formation of ATP in presence of light
c) Formation of NADP in presence of light
d) None of the above

434. Fruits and vegetables with yellow coloured skin are rich in

a) Vitamin-E
b) Vitamin-B
c) Vitamin-C
d) Vitamin-A

435. Freezing point depression of a solution is measured with

a) Viscometer
b) Calorimeter
c) Osmometer
d) Spectrophotometer

436. Fruits stored in cold stores exhibit longer storage life due to

a) An increase in humidity
b) Decrease in respiration rate
c) Increase in CO2 only
d) Increase in O2 only

437. Lemon squash is preserved for long duration without discolouration by using

a) Citric acid
b) Potassium meta-bi-sulphite
c) Benzoic acid and citric acid
d) Malic acid and benzoic acid

438. Jelly and marmalade must have

a) 2.5% pectin
b) 1.25% pectin
c) Pectin 0.75 to 1.5%
d) 1.0% pectin

439. Wax coating enhances shelf life of fruits as it blocks

a) Respiration
b) Transpiration
c) Ripening process
d) Maturation

440. Chemical formula of potassium metabisulphite preservative is

a) $K_2S_2O_3$ b) KMS
c) KSO_2 d) K_2SO_2

441. Pungency in mustard oil is due to

a) Acid b) Amino
c) Glucosilates d) None of these

442. Sunflower oil is rated as good quality oil because it contains

a) Low saturated fatty acids
b) High unsaturated fatty acids
c) Low unsaturated fatty acids
d) High saturated fatty acids

443. The most commonly used disinfectant in water treatment

a) Calcium b) Sulphur
c) Magnesium d) Chlorine

444. Gritty cells are associated with

a) Pear b) Apple
c) Apricot d) Cheery

445. Removal of outer cover of fruits is known as

a) Lying b) Peeling
c) Cutting d) Lye peeling

446. Vitamin which shortens blood clotting time

a) Vitamin-A b) Vitamin-B
c) Vitamin-D d) Vitamin-K

447. Juice and bark of pomegranate fruit is useful for treatment of

a) Cancer b) Leprosy
c) Diarrhoa d) Dysentry

448. Grape belongs to the family

a) Vitaceae b) Caricaceae
c) Bromileaceae d) Palmaceae

449. Place of origin of grape is

a) Sri Lanka
b) Armenia
c) India
d) Japan

450. Grape is believed to be introduced in India by the invaders from Iran and Afghanistan about

a) 1200 AD
b) 1576
c) 1300 AD
d) 17th Century

451. Grape is commercially cultivated in

a) Gujarat
b) Andhra Pradesh
c) Himachal Pradesh
d) Orissa

452. The discovery of ________________ by R. Shankar Pilay at Hyderabad in 1930 has resulted in a new awareness of grape growing in India.

a) Anab-e-Shahi
b) Perlett
c) Beauty Seedless
d) Delight

453. Which of the following fruit is used for raisin making?

a) Apple
b) Pear
c) Grape
d) Grapefruit

454. The name of Sardar Bahadur Lal Singh and R. Shankar Pilay are associated with

a) Mango
b) Citrus
c) Banana
d) Grape

455. Arka Kanchan is a cross between

a) Anab-e-Shahi × Queen of the Vineyard
b) Banglore Blue × Black Champa
c) Black Champa × Thompson seedless
d) Bangalore Blue × Anab-e-Shahi

456. Which of the following statement is incorrect?

a) Arkavati (Black Champa × Thompson Seedless
b) Arka Kanchan (Anab-e-Shahi x Queen of the Vineyard)

c) Arka Shyam (Anab-e-Shahi x Black Champa)
d) Arka Hans (Bangalore Blue x Anab-e-Shahi)

457. How many seeds are present in grape berry?

a) 4 b) 8
c) 10 d) 12

458. Who has developed the Kniffin system of grape vine training?

a) Shakespeare Kniffin b) William Kniffin
c) Hellery Kniffin d) Johnson Kniffin

459. In grapes, pruning involves the removal of

a) Canes b) Shoots
c) Leaves d) All of these

460. In grapes, the ripened shoots of the past season is called

a) Short b) Canes
c) Lateral d) Spur

461. The main stem of plant in grapes is called

a) Trunk b) Shoot
c) Lateral d) Cane

462. In grapes, the new leafy growth of the current season is

a) Cane b) Spur
c) Short d) Lateral

463. Which of the following statement about grapes is incorrect?

a) Lateral - The side branch of a shoot or cane.
b) Spur - The basal portion of the cane left after pruning.
c) Fruit spur - The spur intended to bear fruit.
d) Trunk - The ripened shoot of the past season

464. In grapes, varieties are required to be pruned to varying number of buds based on their

a) Fruiting habits b) Climatic condition
c) Maturity d) None of these

465. Telephone system was first introduced in the vineyards of natural cure centre at Urulikanchan Poona in 1960 by

a) Prof. KP Singh
b) Prof. N Gopal Krishanan
c) Prof. RP Singh
d) Prof. Gopal Rao

466. India ranks in fruit production next only to ________ in the world.

a) Bangladesh b) The USA
c) China d) Egypt

467. Nearly ______ percent of the total population in India depend on agriculture

a) 37-40 b) 65-70
c) 50-60 d) 20-30

468. India is the largest __________producing country in the world.

a) Mango b) Banana
c) Sapota d) All of the above

469. The largest Apple producing country in the world is

a) China b) USA
c) Italy d) Brazil

470. The largest Guava producing country in the world is

a) China b) Brazil
c) Thialand d) India

471. The largest Pineapple producing country in the world is

a) China b) Brazil
c) Thailand d) None of these

472. The largest Papaya producing country in the world is

a) China b) Brazil
c) Thailand d) India

473. Cluster bearing improved cultivar of acid lime in

a) Vikram
b) Rangpur lime
c) Seedless lime
d) Persian lime

474. According to ripening behavior which of the following is/are climacteric fruit (s).

a) Banana
b) Mango
c) Persimon
d) All of these

475. Active compound in bael fruit is

a) Marmelosin
b) Annonine
c) Ficin
d) Bromelin

476. Apple variety indigenous to India is

a) Ambri
b) Ambrich
c) Liberty
d) Red Gold

477. Among citrus fruits __________ is the richest source of acid content.

a) Rangpur lime
b) Amilbed
c) Pummelo
d) Sweet lime

478. Among temperate fruits which is pruned severely?

a) Apple
b) Pear
c) Peach
d) Quince

479. Aridosols are one of the characteristics of soils mostly found in

a) Arid tract of Gujarat
b) Costal Karnataka
c) Andhra Pradesh
d) Indo-Gigantic Plain

480. Vertisols soils refers to

a) Rich in fertility and low to medium in organic content
b) Poor organic content and maganese may add black colour to the soils
c) Rich in salts
d) None of these

481. The largest mandarin-producing country in the world is

a) USA
b) China
c) Mexico
d) South Africa

482. The largest grape producing country in the world is

a) USA
b) Italy
c) Mexico
d) South Africa

483. The major agro-processed product exported from our country is

a) Mango pulp
b) Banana pulp
c) Apple pulp
d) None of these

484. Which of the following fruit is major source of fat (g/100g edible portion)?

a) Avocado
b) Aonla
c) Bael
d) Jack fruit

485. *Carissa carandus* is originated in India while *C. grandiflora* is native to

a) Australia
b) Mexico
c) South Africa
d) Japan

486. Washington Navel is a variety of

a) Pummelo
b) Sweet orange
c) Grape fruit
d) Kinnow

487. Which of following is used for blocking evaporation in harvested fruit to improve shelf-life?

a) Ethylene
b) GA_3
c) Wax
d) MH

488. Viviparous seeds are reported in

a) Jamun
b) Loquat
c) Jack fruit
d) Phalsa

489. The term 'Adam's fig' is association with

a) Mango
b) Apple
c) Banana
d) Avocado

490. The term 'Butter fruit' is associated with

a) Avocado b) Banana
c) Cocoa d) Apple

491. The term five corner fruit is associated with.

a) Cocoa b) Carambola
c) Kiwi d) Ber

492. Which of the following fruit is the horticultural wonder of New Zealand?

a) Kiwi b) Banana
c) Carambola d) Durian

493. The Emblem of the United Nations is like

a) Apple b) Olive
c) Banana d) Ber

494. Which of the following statement is incorrect?

a) Akbar is an apple hybrid
b) Pusa Urvashi is anthracnose resistant variety of grape
c) Akshay is a regular bearing mango strain
d) Pusa Navrang is a high yielding variety of Banana

495. Which state in India is the largest producer of sapota?

a) Karnataka b) Assam
c) Tamil Nadu d) Bihar

496. Which state in India is the largest producer of Pineapple?

a) Andhra Pradesh b) West Bengal
c) Bihar d) Tamil Nadu

497. Lal Bagh is associated with one lakh plants/varieties of which fruit.

a) Apple b) Persimmon
c) Mango d) Citrus

498. Yield of banana is highest in __________ in the world.

a) USA b) India
c) Mexico d) Brazil

499. The 1st book on Litchi was written in

a) 1056 AD
b) 1059 AD
c) 1156 AD
d) 1066 AD

500. Sun scald, a physiological disorder is associated with which fruit

a) Tomato
b) Brinjal
c) Watermelon
d) Must melon

501. Conservation of water through creative landscaping is called

a) Xeriscaping
b) Aesthetic landscaping
c) Wrenching
d) Xyloporosis

502. Oxisols type of soils that are

a) Highly weathered mineral soils
b) Found in arid tracts of Gujarat, Rajasthan
c) Laterite soils
d) Red soils

503. Yellow spot of citrus is due to ____________ deficiency.

a) Copper
b) Boron
c) Zinc
d) Molybdenum

504. Wood apple is native to

a) South Africa
b) India
c) Australia
d) Mexico

505. Yellow colour of papaya is due to

a) Phyton
b) Carotenoid
c) Caricaxanthin
d) Chlorophyll

506. ______ bahar guava crop is preferred in guava.

a) Mrig
b) Ambe
c) Hasth
d) None of these

507. Wilt resistant species of guava is

a) P. guajava
b) P. friedrichsthalianum
c) Both (a) & (b)
d) None of the above

508. Date palm contains 10.6% iron, whereas Karonda contains

a) 50% b) 39.1%
c) 30% d) 28.5%

509. The National Research Centre for grapes at Pune was established in.

a) 1995 b) 1993
c) 1997 d) 1991

510. National Research Centre for grapes is at

a) Gujarat b) Pondicherry
c) Maharashtra d) Goa

511. Coconut Research Station at Kasargod was established in

a) 1916 b) 1933
c) 1945 d) 1954

512. Which of the following statement is incorrect?

a) Coconut Research Station is at Kasargod
b) Central Coconut Research Station is at Kayangulan
c) Rubber Research Institute of India is at Kottayam
d) National Research Centre for banana is at Bikaner

513. Central Coconut Research Station (CCRS) is in

a) Kerala b) Karnataka
c) Bihar d) Rajasthan

514. Pepo is a modified berry type in

a) Papaya b) Wood Apple
c) Carambola d) Watermelon

515. Etaerio of achenes is a type of fruit in

a) Strawberry b) Blackberry
c) Custard apple d) Atemoya

516. National Research Centre for citrus at Nagpur in Maharashtra was established in

a) 1988 b) 1986
c) 1990 d) 1985

517. A separate full fledged Horticulture and Forestry University established in the year 1985 is in

a) Himachal Pradesh
b) Haryana
c) Bihar
d) Rajasthan

518. Central Institute of Horticulture for North Indian Plains established in the year 1984 is at

a) Godhra
b) Lucknow
c) Bangalore
d) Nagpur

519. Central Plantation Crop Research Institute (CPCRI) is at ________

a) Kasargod (Kerala)
b) Kodaikanal (TN)
c) Lucknow (UP)
d) Jodhpur (Rajasthan)

520. Thin walled aluminium layer formed at the base of the organ is

a) Marcottage
b) Adventitious layer
c) After ripening
d) Abscission layer

521. Specific gravity is an index of maturity in

a) Mango
b) Papaya
c) Sapota
d) Banana

522. Flattening of eyes is an index of maturity in

a) Banana
b) Pineapple
c) Litchi
d) None of these

523. Juice content is an index of maturity in

a) Citrus
b) Banana
c) Jack fruit
d) Mango

524. Rooting of an attached stem by excluding light under moist condition from a portion of the stem is

a) Air layering
b) Marcottage
c) Chinese layering
d) All of these

525. A plant growing attached to an aerial portion of another plant is

a) Xerophyte
b) Serophyte
c) Aerophyte
d) Mesophyte

526. Most affected fruit by cracking is

a) Apple b) Mango
c) Cherry d) Citrus

527. Substances used to prevent oxidation or discolouration of foods are

a) Anthocyanins b) Antioxidants
c) Desiccant d) Absorbents

528. The tip of a stem, shoots *etc* is called

a) Apical b) Anthesis
c) Allele d) Axillary

529. The pollen producing organ of the flower is called

a) Ovary b) Anther
c) Cyme d) Cuticle

530. A class of water soluble pigments including most of those imparting red or blue colour to fruit or flower is known as

a) Chlorophyll b) Anti-transpirants
c) Anthocyanins d) Antioxidant

531. Chemicals which form a thin film over the produce and check water losses through transpiration are

a) Anthocyanins b) Anti-transpirants
c) Chelates d) Adsorbends

532. Exanthema in peach and citrus is due to the deficiency of

a) Zinc b) Boron
c) Copper d) Molybdenum

533. Directly damaging insect of citrus is

a) Fruit sucking moth
b) Citrus leaf miner
c) White flies
d) Aphids

534. Plants adapted to drought conditions are

a) Mesophytes
b) Xerophytes
c) Serophytes
d) Aerophytes

535. A basic nitrogenous compound related to uric acid, one of the purines is.

a) Xanthin
b) Xanthophyll
c) Zinc oxide
d) Zinc chloride

536. Ber is an ideally suited to _____ zone cultivation.

a) Temperate
b) Tropical
c) Sub-tropical
d) Arid

537. Ficin an important compound is present in

a) Aonla
b) Litchi
c) Fig
d) None of these

538. Which fruit crop is resistant to salt and drought

a) Fig
b) Litchi
c) Date palm
d) None of these

539. Chirmi, Rutab, Tamer are the developmental stages of

a) Avacado
b) Date palm
c) Ber
d) Bael

540. Drink of date palm is known as

a) Perry
b) Dibbis
c) Syrup
d) None of these

541. "Arrak" is a liquor prepared from

a) Date palm
b) Avocado
c) Both (a) & (b)
d) Pear

542. Doka is harvesting stage in

a) Avacado
b) Ber
c) Date palm
d) Mango

543. Date palm variety suitable for juice

a) Hayane b) Halawy

c) Barhae d) Sevi

544. Storage temperature of Ber is

a) 3°C b) 5°C

c) 10-11°C d) 13-14°C

545. Marmelosin present in which fruit crop

a) Ber b) Bael

c) Karonda d) Jamun

546. Richest source of Riboflavin

a) Loquat b) Jamun

c) Bael d) Karonda

547. Cane pruned variety of grape is

a) Pusa Seedless b) Beauty Seedless

c) Early Muscat d) Delight

548. Basrai Dwarf is a variety of

a) Mango b) Banana

c) Ber d) Grape

549. Barren nuts are formed due to deficiency of

a) N and B b) Mo & Zn

c) P and Cu d) Ca & P

550. Barlette is an improved variety of

a) Peach b) Apricot

c) Pear d) Cherry

551. Barbados cherry, the richest source of Vitamin-C belongs to the family.

a) Rosaceae b) Malphigiaceae

c) Rutaceae d) Musaceae

552. The latex exudated from the unripe papaya fruit having proteolytic activity is called

a) Papain b) Pectin
c) Latex d) Glucoside

553. Regulation of flowering and fruiting in fruit crops by cultural and mechanical means is called

a) Auxin treatment b) Chemical treatment
c) Mechanical treatment d) Bahar treatment

554. Method of inducing early flowering in plants with very low temperature is

a) Scarification b) Vernalization
c) Stratification d) Photo-periodism

555. The stage of full growth, development or ripeness is termed as

a) Maturity b) Ripeness
c) Senescence d) Aging

556. Ability of seeds to germinate is called as

a) Vernalization b) Viability
c) Variation d) Vivipary

557. A condition in which the internodes get shortened and the leaves have a clustered appearance is termed as

a) Rosetting b) Rouging
c) Ringing d) Resting

558. The planting of fruit trees at closer spacing to accommodate more number of plants per unit area refers to

a) Planning of orchard b) High density orcharding
c) Plant density d) Clean culture

559. A substance produced in a very small quantity in one part of plant and translocated to another plant where it induces a physiological response is called

a) Hormone b) Anthocyanin
c) Chlorophyll d) Xanthin

560. The practice of removing banana pseudostem after harvesting fruit is termed as

a) Layering b) Mulching
c) Mattocking d) Leaching

561. Which of the following fruit follows single sigmoid growth curve?

a) Grape b) Perch
c) Apple d) Guava

562. Fruit which follows a double sigmoid growth curve is

a) Apple b) Mango
c) Pear d) Fig

563. Which of the following fruits follow triple sigmoid growth curve?

a) Aonla b) Orange
c) Chinese gooseberry d) None of these

564. Bitterness in citrus juice is due to

a) Limonin b) Citric acid
c) Acid : Sugar ratio d) Glucosides

565. Bitterness in peach juice is due to

a) Malaic acid b) Hydrocyanin
c) Prunasin acid d) None of these

566. Nectarines are

a) Died plums b) Smooth skinned apricots
c) Smooth skinned peaches d) Smooth skinned plums

567. Technique to detect virus infection of a plant by grafting or budding it on an indicator plant known to be highly susceptible to that virus infection is known as

a) Indexing b) Counting
c) Plating d) Culturing

568. Sorting of produce according to size or quality refers to

a) Quality evaluation b) Labeling
c) Grading d) Sorting

569. Any fruit served after meals is

a) Solid fruit
b) Staple fruit
c) Ripened fruit
d) Dessert fruit

570. Under developed seedless berry of grape that fails to enlarge due to boron deficiency or poor pollination termed as

a) Sweet berry
b) Sour berry
c) Sap berry
d) Shot berry

571. The largest litchi producing state of India is

a) Haryana
b) Bihar
c) Karnataka
d) West Bengal

572. Coconut water is a source of which hormone?

a) Cytokinin
b) Ethylene
c) IBA
d) NAA

573. Edible portion of litchi is

a) Aril
b) Bracts
c) Perianth
d) Thalamus

574. Fruits with very low ethylene production

a) Grape
b) Passion fruit
c) Apple
d) Sapota

575. Edible part of almond is

a) Cotyledon
b) Mesocarp
c) Pericarp
d) Endosperm

576. Cashew nut shell liquid (CNSL) is

a) Pericarp fluid of cashew nut
b) Epicarp fluid of cashewnut
c) Mesocarp fluid of cashewnut
d) None of these

577. Natural ripening hormone is

a) Ethylene
b) Amino oxyacetic acid
c) Methoxyvenyl glycyne
d) Aminoethoxy glycine

578. Ethylene stimulates

a) Ripening of fruit
b) Pigment synthesis
c) Senescence
d) All of these

579. Molecular weight of ethylene

a) 28.05
b) 30.05
c) 29.05
d) 32.05

580. Boiling point of ethylene

a) 75°C
b) 98.4°C
c) 100°C
d) 103.7°C

581. Which of following is/are multiple fruits?

a) Pineapple
b) Fig
c) Jack fruit
d) All of these

582. Which of following is an aggregate fruit?

a) Mango
b) Papaya
c) Custard apple
d) Litchi

583. Which of following is simple fruit?

a) Banana
b) Bread fruit
c) Fig
d) Custard apple

584. Crops with sharp rise in respiration after harvesting

a) Mango
b) Apple
c) Banana
d) All of these

585. Highly salt tolerant crop

a) Mango
b) Apple
c) Citrus
d) None of these

586. Highly salt sensitive crop is

a) Coconut
b) Date palm
c) Ber
d) None of these

587. Medium salt tolerant crop is

a) Phalsa
b) Strawberry
c) Citrus
d) Pear

588. Hafus mango is also known as

a) Langra
b) Chausa
c) Alphonso
d) None of these

589. A disorder of citrus trees associated with an alkaline soil reaction resulting in a peculiar type of growth is

a) Crinkle
b) Corky core
c) Crazy top
d) Sun scald

590. Plants suited to grow on acid soils are called

a) Calcifuge
b) Serophytes
c) Unfruitful
d) Xerophytes

591. Group of varieties of mango whose flowering and cropping spread around the year is called

a) Biennial
b) Annual
c) Baramasi
d) Perennial

592. An organism with chromosome number not the exact number of basic number is

a) Aneuploid
b) Octaploid
c) Diploid
d) Polyploid

593. Excessive fruit drop is a problem in which of the following fruits.

a) Mango
b) Citrus
c) Grape
d) All of above

594. More number of chromosome creating big problem in genetical analysis in

a) Ber
b) Mulberry
c) Both (a) & (b)
d) Mango

595. Taking a genotype or a group of genotypes into a new environment where they were not being grown before is called

a) Introduction
b) Hybridization
c) Germplasm conservation
d) Micro-propagation

596. Banana cv Lady Finger was introduced from Australia whereas Grand Naine is from

a) USA b) France

c) Peru d) Egypt

597. Florda Sun, Sun Red and Florda Reel cultivars of Peach are introduced in India from

a) Italy b) USA

c) Australia d) Kenya

598. In Mango, cultivars Haden, Sensation, Julie were introduced from USA whereas Caribao from

a) Italy b) Philippines

c) USSR d) Brazil

599. Solo Sunrise, Sunset, Wilder, Soniyimma Malinchly are cultivars of

a) Mango b) Guava

c) Papaya d) Pear

600. Lambert, Francis, Emperor are introduction from USA and belong to which fruit

a) Walnut b) Sweet cherry

c) Pomegranate d) Grape

601. Hachiya, Flat Seedless and Hykumo cultivars of persimmon were introduced from

a) USA b) Japan

c) Kenya d) Australia

602. Sabohar Madhu and Sabohar Priya are the varieties of

a) Guava b) Mango

c) Litchi d) Sapota

603. Pusa Delicious, Pusa Majesty, Pusa Giant and Pusa Dwarf are the varieties of

a) Papaya b) Litchi

c) Sapota d) Bael

604. Prickly pear refers to the fruit of

a) Pear
b) Opuntia
c) Longan
d) Carambola

605. Seedless in banana is due to

a) Vegetative parthenocarpy
b) Stimulative parthenocarpy
c) Stenospermocarpy
d) All of these

606. Most susceptible citrus to cold is

a) Sweet orange
b) Sour orange
c) Lime
d) Lemon

607. The chromosome number of Umran ber is.

a) 96
b) 80
c) 75
d) 50

608. The original home of Dashehari is

a) Malihabad
b) Lucknow
c) Banaras
d) Kanpur

609. The best breeding method to incorporate disease resistance is

a) Introduction
b) Back cross
c) Selection
d) Polyploidy breeding

610. Inarching is also known as

a) Simple approach grafting
b) Simple inarching
c) Embracing
d) All of the above

611. Removal of the back and phloem tissues from a stem is called

a) Grafting
b) Etiolation
c) Girdling
d) Inarching

612. Process of injuring the hard seed coat by any means to accelerate the water absorption and to improve the gaseous exchange for hastening the germination is termed as

a) Scarification
b) Stratification
c) Quiescence
d) Cryo-preservation

613. The operation of removal or trimming of some parts of a plant with a view to give it a particular shape is called

a) Training b) Grafting

c) Layering d) Separation

614. The growth appearing on rootstock portion is called

a) Water shoot b) Water sucker

c) Scaffold branches d) Leader

615. Modified leader training system is found most suitable for

a) Cherry b) Plum

c) Peach d) Apple

616. Open centre training system is found suitable for

a) Peach b) Apple

c) Pecan d) Walnut

617. The main stem growing from ground level upto the tip dominating all other branches is called

a) Water shoots b) Leader

c) Head d) Trunk

618. The point on the trunk from which first branches arise is called

a) Head b) Leader

c) Water sucker d) Trunk

619. The terms heading back, thinning out and dehorning are related with

a) Training b) Emasculation

c) Pruning d) Weeding

620. The term thinning refers to

a) Removal of extra fruit from the tree before its maturity to avoid over-crowding

b) Removal of shoots from the base of a branch

c) Removal of all the wood after leaving 7-10 cm thick stub all over the tree

d) None of the above

621. Which of the following chemicals are used for thinning in different fruits?

a) Ethephon
b) Naphthalene acetic acid (NAA)
c) Sevin
d) All of these

622. Based on quantity of nutrients in plants, the basic nutrient is/are

a) C
b) H
c) O
d) All of these

623. The formula for auxin is

a) $C_{18}H_{32}O_5$
b) C_7H_8O
c) $C_{12}H_{22}O_{11}$
d) C_2H_5OH

624. *Vitis* species most tolerant to salt in soil is

a) *V. labrusca*
b) *Vitis champini*
c) *Vitis vinifera*
d) None of these

625. Best propagation material in pineapple is

a) Offset
b) Slips
c) Rhizomes
d) Crowns

626. Which of the following pair is incorrect?

a) Basic nutrients ------ C, H, O
b) Macro-nutrients ---- N, P, K, Ca, Mg, S
c) Micro-nutrients ---- Fe, Zn, Cu, P, Mo, Cl
d) Secondary nutrients ---- N, P, K

627. Which of the following statement is incorrect about the mobility of nutrients within plant?

a) Highly mobile -- Mo
b) Moderately mobile -- Zn
c) Less mobile --- S, Fe, Mn, Cl
d) Immobile ----- Ca, B

628. Mineral sources of chlorine is

a) Apatite b) Olivine
c) Biotite d) Micas

629. The Coconut Development Board is located at

a) Calicut b) Gurgaon
c) Lucknow d) Cochin

630. The ability of a somatic cell to reproduce the entire plant somatically is called

a) Transformation b) Totiopotency
c) Tapping d) Syngamy

631. Which of the following has the highest somatic chromosome number?

a) Custard apple b) Mango
c) Jamun d) Mulberry

632. Pineapple is suited to ______ climate.

a) Humid tropics b) Temperate
c) Sub-tropical d) Arid

633. Pin and thrum types of flowers are found in the inflorescence of

a) Apple b) Mango
c) Carambola d) Loquat

634. Salt tolerance limit of citrus is

a) 1000 ppm b) 2000 ppm
c) 1500 ppm d) 1800 ppm

635. Strawberry is usually propagated by

a) Runners b) Offsets
c) Rhizome d) Corm

636. Sugar Loaf is a variety of

a) Mango b) Peach
c) Pineapple d) Strawberry

637. The acid content _________ with ripening in banana fruit.

a) Decreases
b) Increases
c) Remain unchanged
d) 1st increases and later on decreases

638. Original home of Thompson Seedless grape is

a) Mexico b) Brazil
c) USA d) Asia Minor

639. How many species are there in mango?

a) 50 b) 30
c) 45 d) 69

640. Apple seeds are stratified at _______ for 2-3 months.

a) 1-2°C b) 2-3 °C
c) 0°C d) -1°C

641. Ber is commonly propagated by

a) T-budding b) Shield budding
c) Patch budding d) None of these

642. Fruit belonging to amphisarica group is

a) Wood apple b) Sweet orange
c) Pomegranate d) Custard apple

643. Regular bearing improved variety of mango is

a) Alphonso b) Chausa
c) Langra d) Amrapali

644. Grape famous for local wine production in Kinnaur (HP) is

a) Perlett b) Angoori
c) Anab-e-Shahi d) Early Muscat

645. Apomictic seedlings are also known as

a) Nucellar seedlings b) Vigorous seedling
c) Dwarf seedling d) Ultra seedling

646. Aonla fruit contains __________ mg of Vitamin C/100 g of fruit content.

a) 1000 b) 600

c) 800 d) 50

647. Atleast __________% pollinizers are recommended in apple orchards.

a) 20 b) 15

c) 33 d) 40

648. How much percentage of edible portion exist in strawberry

a) 88% b) 95%

c) 98% d) 78%

649. Fruits those can only ripen on tree after harvesting

a) False fruits b) Non-climacteric

c) Climacteric d) True fruits

650. On the basis of vitamin-C content present in fruits which statement is true

a) Aonla > Barbados Cherry > Chilli > Guava

b) Barbados cherry > Aonla > Guava > Chilli

c) Barbados cherry > Guava > Aonla > Chilli

d) None of these

IMPORTANT CULTIVARS

Fruit crop	Cultivars/Varieties
Acid lime/ kagzi lime	Pramalini (Canker tolerant), Chakradhar (Seedless), Sai Sarbati (Tolerant to tristeza and canker), Jai Devi (Pleasant aroma).
Almond	Sloh (Peach × Almond)- **self-fertile** Drake, Katha, Dhebar- **Self fruitful** Makhdoom, IXL, Ne Plus Ultra, Merced, Non-Pareil (Most popular variety), Eureka, Kaparil, Thompson, Texas, Shalimar, Mission, Prabhat, Waris. **Self-fertile:** Ne Plus Ultra and Drake **Cross sterile:** IXL and Non-Pareil **Pollinizers:** Ne Plus Ultra, Drake (self-fertile)
Aonla	Banarasi (early maturity, best cultivar for muramba)Francis (HathiJhool), Chakiya (alternate bearer), Kanchan (NA-4) (Seedling selection from Chakiya), NA-6, NA-7 (Amrit), NA-9 (Neelum), NA-5 (Krishna): selection from Banarasi, Balwant, Anad-1, Anand-2, GA-1.
Apple	**Early:** Tydeman's Early, Irish Peach, Benoni, Early Shanburry **Mid:** Red Delicious, Rich-a-Red, Top Red, Lord Lambourne (P), Red Chief, Red Gold, American Mother, Jonathan, Rome Beauty, McIntosh, Cortland, Golden Delicious **Late:** Yellow Newton, Winter Banana, Granny Smith, Lal Ambri, Buckingham **Green English varieties:** Baldwin, Cox's Orange Pippin, Black Ben Davis, Pippins. **Spur type varieties:** Star Crimson, Well Spur, Red Chief **Standard colour mutants:** Top Red, Skyline Supreme, Hardyman. **Scab Resistant Varieties:** Prima, Priscilla, Sir Prize, Jonafree, Florina, Macfree, Nova easy grown, Red Free, Liberty, Freedom, Florina (France). **Low-chilling varieties:** Michael, Schlomit, Anna, Vared, Neomi, Tropical Beauty, Parlin's Beauty (suitable for processing). **Good seed viability:** Golden Delicious, Yellow Newton, Northern Spy. **Hybrids:** Amb Royal, Amb Red, Amb Rich, Lal Ambri, Sunhari, Amb Starking, Chaubattia Princess.
Apricot	Kaisha, Royal, Moorpark, New Castle, Nugget, St. Ambroise, Early Shipley, Royal, Chaubattria Alankar, Shakarpara, Alfred, Chaubattria Madhu, Kaisha, Halman, Chaubattria Kesari, Charmagz, Khante.
Arecanut	Mangla, Sumangla, Sreemangla and Mohit Nagar are high yielding varieties.Sreevardhani (*A. catechu* × *A. triandra*), Mangla (Indonesian introduction); Sumangla (Srilankan introduction); SreeMangla and Mohit Nagar (Singapore introduction); Samrudhi.
Bael	Kagzi Gonda, Kagzi Etawah, Kagzi Banarasi, Gorakhphur, Sewan Large, Deoria Large

contd.

Banana	-Planted at 2.1 x 2.1 (m^2) spacing: Poovan, Rasthali, Nendran and Robusta -Planted at 1.8 x 1.8 (m^2) spacing: Basari, Khulhan, Jawari.-Dwarf Cavendish (AAA): Safed Velchi (diploid variety) -Lady Finger (AB-diploid variety)-Robusta (AAA): Bombay green, Harichal (Highly susceptible to sigatoka leaf spot but resistant to panama wilt).-Grand Naine (AAA): Tall mutant of dwarf Cavendish requires propping.-Poovan (AAB): Rasthali, Amripani, Mortman (choicest table banana).-Poovan Mysore (AAB): susceptible to banana streak virus, leading cultivar of South India.-Nendran (AAB): French plantain, Rajeli (Good for making banana chips). Most prized cooking variety used in Kerala.-Hill banana (AAB): Virupakshi, Sirumalai, Ladan. **Hybrids:** FHIA-1 (Gold Finger), CO-1 (Keller Laden × *M. balbasiana* × *Kadali*)-Poovan: resistant to panama wilt and bunchy top virus.-Kanchankela: Kitchen garden best cultivar, bunch weight 10-15 kg.-Dwarf Cavendish: The cultivar is suitable for high density plantation. Average bunch weight is 20 kg.Harichal (sweeter), Nandran (*Plantain*), Hill Banana, Amrit Sagar, Gros Michel (1st position among table bananas)
Ber	**Extremely dry area** (early maturing varieties): Gola, Seb **Dry area** (Late maturing varieties): Umran, Ilaichi **Humid area**: Mehrun **Mid maturing varieties:** Rashmi, Mundia, Banarasi **Sanur2:** resistant to powdery mildewChhurara, Kareka, Seo, Thornless, Jogra Gola are other varieties.
Cashewnut	Ullal-1, Chintamani-1 (Karnataka); Dhana, Madakhathara, Priyanka (export variety) (Kerala); Vengurla-1 to 7 (Maharashtra); VRT-1 to 3 (Tamil Nadu). **Hybrids:** Ven-3 (Ven 1 × Ventore 56); Ven-4 (Midnapur Red × Vetore 56); Ven-6 (Venore 56 × Ven 1).
Cherries	Black Heart, Nepolean White, Stella, Lambert, Pink Early, Black Republican, White Heart, Compact Stella, Governors Wood, Sunburst, Summit, Sam. **Sweet cherry varieties**: Black Tartarian, Napolean, Windsar, Bing, Compact Stella, Bing, Compact Lambert, Sun Burst, Sue, Sun, Victor, Van Jubilee and Lapins.
Cocoa	Forestero, Criollo (produce best quality cocoa), Trinitarion (Criollo × Forestro)
Coconut	**Tall**: West Coast Tall, Laccadive Ordinary, Andaman Ordinary, Pratap **Dwarf**: Chowghat Green Dwarf, Chowghat Orange Dwarf, Ganga Bandam, Gudanjali, Mangipod and Nulaka.
Coffee	S-795 (Robusta): Most popular variety, occupy 70% of total coffee area.Cauvery, San Ramon (mutant), Kent (mutant variety), Cauvery, Blue Mountain.
Currants	**Red currants**: Jonkheer van Tets (Holland), Earliest of Fourlands, Laxton's No. 1 (England), Perfection, Wilder, Red Cross. **White currants**: Werdavia, Zitavia, Meridian, Victoria, White Imperial, White Grape.

contd.

	Black currants: Baldwin, Blackdown, Ferdoti 1, Noir de Bourgogne (for brandy in France), Topsy, Kerry, Magness, Consort
Custard apple	Balanagar, Barbados Seedling, British Guinea, Kakarlapahad, Mahaboob Nagar, Washinghton. **Hybrids:** Arka Sahan (*A. atemoya* × *A. squamosa*): less seeds, high brix-31°B. African Pride (Cherimoya × Custard Apple).
Date palm	Khadrawy, Medjool, Sharan (Chuhharah making)Halawy, Barhee, Khalas, Sevi, Khunezi (Fresh eating)Pind Khajoor (soft-dates), Sharan (Uneven ripening) Cane sugar date (semi dry date): Dayari, Deglet Noor, ZahidiInvert sugar date (soft date): Halawy, Khadrawy, Barhee, Medjool
Fig	**Edible Fig** (Long styled pistilate flower): Kadota, Mission, Conardia, Poona Fig, Brown turkey. **Smyrma Fig** (Long styled pistilate flower): Calimyrna, Zidi, Taranimt **San Pedro Fig**: San Pedro, King Gentile, Lampreiria, Dauphine. **Wild Fig** (Short styled pistilate flower): Brawley, Samson, Stanford **Important Cvs**: Marseille, Black Ischia, Kabul, Bangalore, Lucknow
Grapefruit	Duncan, Marsh Seedless, Foster, Red Blush, Triumph, Sharanpur Special
Grapes	Thompson seedless, Sonaka, Anab-e-Shahi, Perlette, Bangalore Blue, Pusa Seedless, Beauty Seedless, Arkavati, Arka Hans, Arka Kanchan, Arka Neelmani, Sharad Seedless, Dilkush, Kishmish, Black Hamburg, Black Prince, Delight, Perllete. **Coloured seeded**: Bangalore Blue, Gulabi (Muscat) **Coloured seedless**: Beauty Seedless, Kishmish Charm, Sharad Seedless **White seeded**: Anab-e-Shahi, Dilkhush (clone of Anab-e-Shahi) **White seedless**: Perlette, Pusa Seedless, Thompson Seedless, Sonaka and Manik Chaman. **Cane pruned varieties**: Gulabi, Pusa Seedless, Kishmish Charini and Thompson Seedless **Spur pruned varieties**: Bangalore Blue, Black Champa, Beauty Seedless. Bhokri, Delight and Perlette. **Commercial use of grape varietiesTable grapes:** Anab-e-shashi, Perlete, Pusa Seedless, Beauty Seedless **Raisin grapes**: Gold, Kishmish Beri, Thompson Seedless **Wine grapes**: Banglore Blue, Beauty Seedless, Early Muscat, Thompson Seedless. **Juice grapes**: Champion, Beauty Seedless. **Canning grapes**: Pusa Seedless, Kishmish Charm, Kishmish Beli, Seedless White, Thompson Seedless.
Guava	Lucknow-49 (Sardar)- Chance seedling from Allahabad Safeda in 1927 by Dr Cheema. Hafsi (Red fleshed guava), Chittidar, Harijha, Allahabad Surkha, Allahabad Round (Parthenocarpic), Behat Coconut (Seedless Guava), Arka Mridula (soft seeded), Saharanpur Seedless and Nagpur Seedless, Lalit, Banarasi Red.

contd.

	Hybrids: Kohir Safed: Kohir × Allahabad Safeda Safed Jam: Allahabad Safeda × Kohir
Jackfruit	Gulabi, Champa, Hazari, Rudrakshi Jack, Singapore or Ceylon Jack, Muttam Varikka, Monkey Jack.
Jamun	Raj Jamun, Paras (large size), Nerandra Jamun-6 (Seedless)
Kiwifruit	Abbott, Bruno, and Monty are female cultivars.Hayward, Matua, Tomouri, Allison are Male (pollinizers).
Lemon	Eureka, Lisbon, Villa France, Lucknow Seedless, Kagzikalan, Nepali Oblong, Nepali Round.
Litchi	Muzaffapur (early variety); Dehradun (famous variety grown in UP, Punjab); Calcuttia is a hardy variety. Rose Scented, Elaichi, Saharanpur are important cultivars.Early Seedless (Early Bedana), Rose Scented, Dehradun, Gulabi, Purbi, Shahi, Bombai, Late Seedless (Late Bedana), Swaran Roopa (non-cracking).
Loquat	**Mid varieties**: Fire Ball, Large Agra, Mammoth, Matchless, Safeda **Early varieties**: Golden Yellow, Pale Yellow, Thames Pride **Late varieties**: California Advance, Tanaka
Mandarin	Coorag: Most important commercial variety in South India.Khasi: Locally known as Sikkim or Kamla mandarin.Nagpur (Ponkan): Finest mandarin in the world.Satsuma (seedless): Commercial mandarin of Japan.Emperor and Fuetrellis (Australia), Sutwal: Introduction from Nepal.
Mango	Bombai (Biennial bearing, susceptible to malformation), Himsagar (biennial, heavy bearing variety), Langra (excellent sugar:acid ratio), Fazli (fruit quality is not good), Dashehari (Most popular northern Indian cultivar), Alphonso (high demand for processing), Banganpalli (Popular south Indian variety).
Papaya	Pusa Delicious, Pusa Majesty (highest papain yielder), CO-3, Coorge Honey Dew, Sunrise Solo (Pink flesh), Taiwan (Blood red colour).Pusa Giant: Suitable for tooty fruity and candies.Pusa Nanha: extremely dwarf, suitable for HDP (Pot garden).CO-1, CO-2; (dwarf); CO-6: Selection from Pusa Majesty.Sunrise Solo type of papaya produces no male plants.
Peach	**Early:** Alton, World's Earliest, Red Haven, Starkred Gold, Early Candor, Quetta and Saharanpur Prabhat **Mid:** July Elberta, Alexander **Late:** J.H. Hale, Parrot Deluxe, Peregrine **Self-sterile cultivars**: J H Hale, Halberta, Mikado, Candoka, Alamar.July Alberta, Alaxander, Sharbati, Kamto-5, Shan-e-Punjab, Nectarine Florida Red, Early White Giant. **Low chilling cultivars**: Sharbati, Saharanpur, Prabhat, Florida Prince, Floridason and Shan-e-Punjab. **Improved cultivars**: Shan-e-Punjab, July Elberta, Red Heaven, Kanto-5, Shimizo Hakuto, Florida Red. **Subtropical region**: Flordasun, Down Rambler, Down Rose, and Sharbati
Pear	**Early:** Early China, Fertility, Sackle and Laxton's Superb

contd.

	Mid: Bartlett, Max-Red, Starking Delicious, Dr Julis Buyot and Conference. **Late**: Easter, Beurre Hardy, Winter Nellis, Clapp's Favourite, Flemish Beauty. **Low hills and valley areas**: Pather Nakh, Kieffer China pear. **Pollinizers:** Fertility and Flemish Beauty **High chilling hours**: Anjou, Bartlett, Conference, Flemish Beauty **Low chilling hours**: Keiffer, Gola, Patharnakh **European and Asian pear:** Bartlett, Flemish Beauty, Starkrimson Delicious, Anjon, Max Red Bartlett, Winter Nellis, Laxton's Superb. **Hybrids**: Kiffer (French Pear × Oriental Pear), Leconte, **Pear varieties free from grit cell:** Flemish Beauty and Magness
Pecannut	Mahan, Nellis, Barkett, Stuart, Desirable, Cheyenne, Wichita
Persimmon	**Non astringent varieties**: Fuyu, Jiro, 20th Century and Mastumoto **Astringent varieties**: Hachiya, Nightingale, Triumph, Hiratanenashi
Pineapple	Kew-leading commercial variety valued particularly for canning.Giant Kew, Queen, Mauritious (mainly in Kerala), Jaldhup & Lakhat (queen group), Cayenne (triploid variety), Sugar Loaf (sweetest).Jaldhup has characteristic alcoholic flavour.
Plum	**Japanese plum**: Sweety Early, Methley, Kelsey, Burbank, Titron, Beauty Aloocha, Satsuma and Mariposa.
Pomegranate	Paper shelled (South India), Muskati Red, Spanish Ruby, Alandi (Maharashtra), Madhugiri, Dholka (Gujrat), Jalore Seedless, Chawla, Ganesh (Selection from Alandi), G-137 (Clonal selection from Ganesh). **Hybrids**: Mridula (Ganesh × Gul-a-Shahi Red), Jyoti (Basein Seedless × Dholka); Ruby (Ganesh × Kabul × Yercaud) **Soft-seeded varieties**: Jyothi, Ganesh, Basein Seedless, Paper Shell **Hard-seeded varieties:** Khandhari and Alandi
Sapota	Kirti Bharti: Popular in AP, thick skin, good transport value.Cricket Ball, Kalipatti, CO-2, PKM-1, Calcutta Special Round, Murrabba and Baramasi. **Hybrids**: CO-1: Cricket Ball × Oval PKM-2: Guthi × Kirti Bharti PKM-3: Kalipatti × Cricket Ball DSH-1 and 2: Kalpatti × Cricket Ball
Strawberry	Chandler, Tioga, Torrey, Belrubi, Pajaro, Premier, Red Cot, Dil Pasand
Sweet lime	Mitha Chikna, Mithotra
Sweet orange	Hamlin, Jaffa, Pineapple, Valencia, Mosambi, Salgudi (Most popular in Andhra Pradesh), Blood Red, Shamouti (Seedless variety), Washington Navel. Pineapple and Valencia – indicator of greening
Tea	Sundaram, Singra, Athrey, Jayaram, Golconda.
Walnut	Lake English, Gobind, Eureka, Placentia, Wilson, Chakrata, Roopea, Karan

Commercial mango varieties in different states

States	Varieties
Andhra Pradesh	Banganapalli, Swaran Rekha, Neelum and Totapuri
Bihar	Bombay Green, Chausa, Dashehari, Fasli, Gulab Khas, Himsagar, Zardalu and Langra
Gujarat	Kesar, Alphonso, Rajapuri, Jamadar, Totapuri, Neelum, Dashehari and Langra
Haryana	Chausa, Dashehari and Langra
HP	Chausa, Dashehari and Langra
Karnataka	Alphonso, Totapuri, Banganpalli, Pairi and Neelum
Madhya Pradesh	Alphonso, Bombay Green, Dashehari, Fazzi, Langra and Neelum
Maharashtra	Alphonso, Kesar and Pairi
Punjab	Chausa, Dashehari and Malda
Rajasthan	Bombay Green, Chausa, Dashehari and Langra
Tamil Nadu	Alphonso, Totapuri, Banganpalli and Neelum
Uttar Pradesh	Bombay Green, Chausa, Dashehari and Langra
West Bengal	Fazli, Gulabkhas, HimSagar, Kishan Bhog, Langra and Bombay Green

Mango hybrids and their characters

Hybrid	Important characters
Mallika (Neelum × Dashehari)	Regular-bearer, high TSS, good colour, uniform fruits, moderate keeping quality.
Amrapali (Dashehari × Neelam)	Dwarf, regular-bearers, duster bearing, small sized fruits, good keeping quality
Ratna (Neelam × Alphonso)	Regular bearer, free from spongy tissue and fibre
Arka Puneet	Regular bearer, attractive skin colour, medium sized, free from spongy tissue, good keeping quality, good sugar acid blend.
Sindhu (Ratna x Alphonso)	

Recommended varieties of apple in different states

Season	Himachal Pradesh	Jammu & Kashmir	Uttrakhand
Early season	Tydeman's Early (P)	Irish Peach	Early Shanburry (P)
	Michael Molies	Benoni	Fenny Benoni
	Delicious Schlomit	Starkrimson	Chaubattia Princess
Mid season	Starking Delicious	American Mother	Red Delicious
	Red Delicious	Jonathan (P)	Starking Delicious
	Vance Delicious	Cox's Orange	McIntosh (P)
	Top Red, Rich-a-red	Pippin & Red Gold (P)	Cortland
	Red Chief	Queen's Apple	Golden Delicious (P)
	Oregon Spur	Rome Beauty	
	Red Spur, Red Gold (P)	Scarlet Siberian	
Late season	Golden Delicious (P)	King Pippin	Rymer
	. Yellow Newton (P)	American Apirouge	Buckingham (P)
	Winter Banana	Kerry Pippin	
	Granny Smith (P)	Golden Delicious (P)	
		Red Delicious	
		Ambri Baldwin	
		Yellow Newton (P)	

(P) = Pollinizer

Banana cultivars grown in different States

State	Cultivars
Andhra Pradesh	Dwarf Cavendish, Robusta, Rasthali, Amritpani, Thellachakrakeli, Karpoora Pooven, Chakrakeli, Monthan and Yenagu Bontha
Assam	Jahaji (Dwarf Cavendish), Borjahaji (Robusta), Honda, Manjahaji, Chinia (Manohar), Kanchkot, Bhamkot, Attikot, Jatikot, Digjowa, Kulpait and Bharat Moni
Bihar	Dwarf Cavendish, Alpon, Chinia, Chini Champa, Malbhog, Muthia, Kothia and Gauria
Gujarat	Dwarf Cavendish, Harichal (Lokhandi) and Gandevi Selection, Karnataka Dwarf Cavendish, Robusta, Poovan, Rasabata (Rasthab), Monthan & Elakkibale
Kerala	Nendran, Palayankodan (Poovan), Rasthaa, Monthan & Red Banana
Maharashtra	Dwarf Cavendish, Basrai, Robusta, Lal Veichi, Safed Veichi, Nendran
Tamil Nadu	Virupakshi, Robusta, Red Banana, Poovan, Rasthali, Nendran, Monthan, Karpuravali, Sakkai and Matti
West Bengal & Orissa	Champa, Mortman Rasthaa, Amrit Sagar, Giant Governor, Lacatan, Monthan

Grapes clone and hybrid varieties

	Clone	Parents	Hybrid	Parents	Character
1.	Pusa Seedless	Thompson Seedless	Arkavati	Black Champa × Thompson Seedless	Good for raisins making
2.	Tash-A-Ganesh	Thompson Seedless	Arka Neelmani	Black Champa × Thompson Seedless	Good for Red wine
3.	Manik chaman	Thompson Seedless	Arka Krishna	Black Champa × Queen of Vineyard	Juice
4.	Sonnaka	Thompson Seedless	Arka Hans	Bangalore Blue × Anab-a-Shashi	White wine
5.	Dilkhush	Anab-A-Shahi	Arka Trishna	Bangalore Blue × Convent Large Black	Wine
6.	Rao Sahebi	Cheema Sahebi	Arka Shweta	Anab-a-Shahi × Thompson Seedless	Table
7.	Cheema	Pandari	Arka Majestic	Anab-a-Shahi × Black Champa	Table
8	Sharad	Kishmis	Pova Urvashi	Har × Beauty Seedless	Tolerant to anthracnose
	Seedless	Charni	Pusa Navrang	Madeline Angavine × Ruby Red	Tenturier

HINTS FOR SELF-CONFIDENCE

- Mango malformation was 1st observed in 1891 in Bihar.
- Spongy tissue was 1st observed by Cheema and Dhani in 1934.
- Bunchy top of banana was 1st observed in 1891 in Fiji.
- Coconut root wilt – 1st observed in 1882 in Kerala.
- Black tip – 1st observed in 1909 by Woodhouse.
- Sigatoka leaf spot disease of banana – 1st observed in 1913.
- 1st hybrid between tall and dwarf coconut was released in 1932.
- Banana improvement work was started in 1949 in Tamil Nadu.
- Guava improvement work was started in 1907 in Pune.
- Oil palm improvement work was started in 1976 in Andhra Pradesh.
- Cocoa improvement work was started in 1980 in Karnataka.
- The word Horticulture derived from *Hortus + culture* is a Latin word meaning garden and cultivation.
- Scientific names are written in Latin.
- International Institute of Horticulture is at Brazil.
- China is the largest producer of fruits in the world.
- World conference on Horticulture Research in 1998 held at Rome.
- Venezuela is the country having highest productivity of Mango.
- Mango is referred as Bathroom fruit.
- Agricultural Research Services started in 1975.
- Agricultural Scientists Recruitment Board (ASRB) was established in 1973.
- Decandolle is the father of systematic pomology.
- Ultra-violet light has direct influence on colour development of apple fruit.
- Ruby is an improved cultivar of pomegranate.
- National Horticulture Board (NHB) was established in 1984.
- Indian Institue of Horticultural Research was established in 1968.
- Agricultural & Processed Products Development Authority (APEDA) was established in 1985.
- Coconut Development Board belongs to Ministry of Commerce.
- ICAR is an autonomous registered society.

- Ganesh Kirti is a variety of Ber.
- Kiwi fruit is known as Miracle fruit of China.
- International Society for Horticultural Science (ISHS) has head quarter in Belgium.
- Custard apple is *essentially a sub-tropical fruit*.
- Guava and avocado are native to West Indies.
- Ber, phalsa and mango fruits are drupe.
- Papaya, sapota, custard apple are native to tropical America.
- Loquat is *strictly sub-tropical crop*.
- Ellaichi is Malformation resistant variety of Mango.
- Central Plantation Research Institute established in 1965.
- Central Tuber Crops Research Institute established in 1963.
- CPRI shifted to Shimla in 1948.
- NBPGR established in 1976.
- Calyptra is associated with grapes.
- Furete is an improved variety of Avocado.
- Black Corianth is parthenocarpic grape variety.
- Hen and chicken disorder is observed in grape.
- Mangla is an improved variety of Arecanut.
- Laksha Ganga is improved variety of coconut.
- Hesperidium is botanical form of fruit in citrus.
- Tamarind fruit is botanically a pod (Lomentum).
- Adventious polyembrony occurs in Mango.
- Strawberry is propagated through stolon.
- Suckers are used in date palm for vegetative propagation.
- CO-6 of papaya provides maximum papain contents.
- Homogygosity in early generation is fast due to selfing.
- Soft nose is a disorder of mango.
- Sapburn is a post harvest disorder in mango.
- Chestnut grown in temperate region.
- Mango malformation is reduced by NAA @ 200 ppm.
- Granulation is a disorder of citrus.

- Calyx end rot-due to calcium deficiency occurs in Persimmon.
- Pineapple is highly suited for tropical humid.
- Papaya fruit botanically is called berry.
- Hogplum belongs to family Anacardiaceae.
- Perlette is an early variety of grape suited for North India.
- Vikram is an improved cultivar of Acid lime.
- Anab-e-Shahi is popular grape variety of Andhra Pradesh.
- Neelphonso is a cross between Neelum × Alphonso.
- Lalit is improved variety of Guava.
- Thompson seedless is grown in Maharashtra.
- Skiffing is practiced in Tea.
- Dormex/ Hydrogen cyanide is used in grape for early bud break.
- D-leaf is best indicator of nutrient status of pineapple.
- Ber is heavily pruned fruit crop.
- Strawberry starts bearing in one year of planting.
- Meristem culture is used for getting disease free plant through mass propagation.
- Wood apple is not botanically a fruit.
- Protandry is a problem in walnut.
- Yellowing of new leaves is due to deficiency of Iron.
- NAA is a fruit thinning growth regulator.
- Rangpur lime is best rootstock for citrus in South India.
- Chloride toxicity caused leaf scorching in mango.
- Palm oil is obtained from Mesocarp.
- Bitterness in citrus is due to glucoside.
- Barbados cherry is richest source of Vitamin-C, belongs to family *Malphagaceae*.
- Bartlett is an improved variety of Pear.
- Aphid is a vector of papaya mosaic.
- White flies are vector for leaf curl of papaya.
- Calcium carbide induces artificial ripening in mango.
- Mauritius is mid-season variety of pineapple.

- Bombay Green is highly susceptible to mango malformation.
- Papaya is most susceptible to waterlogging.
- Bower training system in grape vines is effective for maximum cost benefit ratio.
- Burrowing nematode is a serious problem in banana.
- California Advance is a variety of Loquat introduced from Australia.
- Cane drying is a serious problem in Gold variety of grapes.
- Cashew apple is a modified peduncle.
- Cashew was introduced in India by Portuguese.
- Capacity of individual cell to regenerate into full plant is called totipotency.
- Citron is botanically named as *Citrus medica.*
- Coconut water is source of cytokinins.
- CO-1 banana is a cross between *Laden* × *M. balbisiana* and Kadali.
- Citrus species having aroma similar to eucalyptus is *C. assumensis.*
- Citrus granulation is associated with Zn, Cu, Mn deficiency.
- Citrus canker is most serious problem of acid lime.
- Carotenoids and Vitamin C = reduce cancer risks, enhance tumour surveillance.
- All rootstocks of MM series are resistant to Woolly Apple Aphid (WAA).
- Papaya is 2nd richest source of vitamin-A after Mango.
- Aonla variety NA-4 (Kanchan): Chance seedling of chakiya. Suitable for processing.
- Aonla variety NA-9 (Neelam): Suitable for candy and preserve making.
- Woolly Apple Aphid (WAA) predator: *Aphilenus mali.*
- Richest sources of Riboflavin = Bael
- Triploid varieties of Apple are: Baldwin, Mutsu, Bramlay's seedlings.
- Nandran (Banana) is most suitable for making *Banana chips.*
- Mango varieties resistant to malformation are: Bhadauran, Illaichi, Alis.
- Caprification: Pollination of common fig with Capri fig.
- Capri fig has male flower used for pollination.
- Hardiest species among papaya is: *Carica quercifolia*

- Thoory is a dry type of date (Bread type).
- Avocado is a Single seeded berry.
- In India, Date is harvested at Doka stage. Pind Stage never attained by date in India.
- India is the largest producer, consumer and exporter of Tea in world.
- Decanting: Pouring off clear supernatant liquid.
- True solution: a homogenous mixture of two or more substances.
- Solvent: Liquid medium in which the solid, liquid or gas dissolved.
- Solute: is the dissolved material.
- Endothermic: When solute dissolves in a solvent, heat absorbed.
- Exothermic: When solute dissolves in a solvent, heat given off.
- Suspension: Contains large particles, visible to the eyes.
- High density plantation in pomegranate 5×2 m accommodates 1000 trees/ hectare.
- High density plantation in banana 1.5×1.5 m accommodates 3000 – 4500 plants/ hectare.
- High density plantation in Amarpali mango 2.5×2.5 m accommodates 1600 plants/ hectare.
- High density plantation in Dashehari mango 3.0×2.5 m accommodates 1333 plants/ hectare.
- Tristeza virus indicator plant is Kagzi lime.
- Marmelosin is the active ingredient present in all parts of bael tree.
- *Prunes* are the plums dried successfully with or without stones.
- Nectarines are the smooth skinned peaches.
- Sindhu is a seedless mango variety (Stenospermocarpic parthenocarpy).
- Mango hopper is the most serious and damaging insect.
- *M. decandra* & *M. incarpoides* rootstocks are suitable for water logged conditions.
- Mango is highly cross pollinated having chromosome number 2n = 40.
- Rosica is the only mutant cultivar of mango.
- Rumani variety of Mango has apple shape fruit.
- Malbhog variety of mango is most susceptible to water logging.

- ✍ Dasheheri has high fruit retention; even langra has highest number of perfect flower.
- ✍ Citrus type of fruits belongs to a very big group belongs to family Rutaceae.
- ✍ Ripe orange and mandarin juice contains = 8-12% sugars.
- ✍ 1 ton of lemon fruit yields 4-9 kg essential oil.
- ✍ Tanaka (1969) specifies 159 species, Swingle (1943) discussed 16 species and Hodgson (1961) specifies 16-31 species.
- ✍ *Citrus aurantium* rootstock is highly susceptible to tristeza virus.
- ✍ Kinnow is a cross between King × Willow Leaf.
- ✍ Eureka cultivar of lemon is famous in world.
- ✍ Citrange = Sweet orange × trifoliate orange.
- ✍ Citrumelo = Grape fruit × trifoliate orange.
- ✍ Kagzi lime is the indicator plant for Tristeza virus.
- ✍ Sour and sweet orange are indicator plants for Psorosis.
- ✍ Rangpur lime is an indicator plant for Exocortis.
- ✍ Tristeza virus in citrus fruits cause sudden decline of plants.
- ✍ Pineapple is a true xyrophytic crop.
- ✍ Papaya is a good filler crop in orchards.
- ✍ Selection No.7 is a good papain yielding cultivar.
- ✍ Papain is a proteolytic enzyme used as meat tenderizer.
- ✍ Cashew nut kernel contains highest protein contents of 20 percent.
- ✍ Protein is the main building block of human cells.
- ✍ Protein forms antibodies (important for disease resistance).
- ✍ A protein containing/ composed of more amino acids is considered as best quality protein for nutrition.
- ✍ Protein, fats and carbohydrates are the major dietary components and release energy in the human body.
- ✍ Cooked starches are easily digested because they breakdown into sucrose and glucose easily during digestion.
- ✍ Dietary fibres like cellulose and hemi-cellulose in human diet prevents constipation.
- ✍ Requirement of food in body is generally estimated in terms of energy (calories to be produced in body).

- Iron is a major and essential component of RBC and stored in liver and spleen.
- Anaemia, a common physiological imbalance among women is due to iron deficiency.
- Iodine deficiency cause goiter and sometimes may cause mental retardation during fatal stage.
- Vitamin-A is necessary for clear vision in dim light and its deficiency causes night blindness.
- Vitamin-E is also known as tocopherols and it acts as an anti-oxidant.
- Vitamin-K prevents blood coagulation and prevents blood hemorrhage.
- 'Ascorbic acid' is not synthesized in the human body, but is important for formation of collagens.
- Collagen: a protein widely distributed in body, acts as a cementing material holds the body cells together.
- Cooking cause more loss of vitamins particularly vitamin-B but dry cooking like frying or roasting does not cause loss of nutrients.
- Limonene is an anticancer compound present in custard apple.
- Father of plant taxonomy = Linnaeus
- Climacteric and non-climacteric are the classification of fruit crops on rate of respiration basis.
- Classification on basis of performance under different light intensity are i) Sun loving = Heliophytes and Shade loving = Sciophytes.
- The response of plants to day light period is known as photoperiodism.
- Hexagonal system of plantation accommodates 15% more trees per area as compare to square system.
- Diagonal system of plantation is also known as quincunx system and it accommodates 1.5 to 2 times more plants.
- Contour system of plantation is followed in the hills, slopes or soil erosion prone areas.
- Production of horticultural crops in plant growing structure is known as 'Plant Forcing".
- Development of seeds without complete sexual process is known as apomixes.
- Tetrazolium test is capable of determining seed viability within 6 to 10 hours.
- Scalding is a hot water treatment useful in breaking seed dormancy by placing seeds in 77ºC - 100ºC hot water.

- Scarification is a process of injuring the hard seed coat mechanically by hammer or rubbing with sand paper and by acid scarification.
- Stratification is also known as moist chilling in which seeds are exposed to low temperature.
- Orthodox seeds are those seeds which can be dried to a low moisture level and shows loss of viability with rise in moisture contents, these seeds are usually long lived e.g. apple, ber, grapes, lemon etc.
- Recalcitrant seeds require relatively high moisture contents for longevity and loose viability if dried below critical moisture level e.g. avocado, barbados cherry, litchi, mango, jackfruit etc.
- Cryopreservation is defined as preservation of seeds by immerging them in liquid nitrogen at very low temperature (-196 ºC) and relatively low moisture contents.
- Etiolation is the development of plants or plant parts in absence of light.
- Inter-stock is a plant part placed between stock and scion to overcome incompatibility.
- Insertion of inter-stock between stock and scion is known as double working.
- Colt, Charger, Mahalab, Paja and F 12/1 are important rootstocks for cherry.
- Karna khatta is a rootstock for citrus fruits.
- Chemically thinning is done with: Ethephon, NAA and Sevin.
- T-budding is also known as shield budding.
- Pollination by wind = Anemophilly is prominent in papaya, date palm, pomegranate, and coconut.
- Pollen viability is checked through Acetocarmine test (1-2% acetocarmine straining).
- Date palm is a single seeded berry.
- Olive is the only drupe with exception where there are the flowers having 2 carpals and 4 ovules although only one carpel develops.
- Ethylene is the active principle responsible for flowering in pineapple.
- Paclobutrazol is effective for regulating flowering and fruiting in mango and grape.
- Hen and chicken is a disorder of grapes caused due to boron deficiency.
- Black heart of apple is caused due to low temperature.

- Jhoomka in mango is a disorder due to improper pollination and fertilization.
- C_3 plants have lower water use efficiency.
- C_4 plants use low concentration of CO_2.
- Intercropping means growing of 2 or more crops simultaneously on same piece of land with a defined row pattern.
- Mixed cropping is the growing or 2 or more crops simultaneously intermingled without any row pattern.
- Relay cropping is a pattern in which crops are grown in quick succession. Second crop is sown between rows of first crop which is ready to harvest.
- Sequence cropping means growing 2 or more crops in sequence on the same piece of land in a farming year.
- Mixed farming is a system of farming which includes crop production, raising livestock, poultry, fisheries etc.
- In Papaya, papain contain 72.2% protein
- Pusa giant variety of papaya have good wind resistance
- Defoliation cause maleness
- Defoliation cause – Femaleness
- Female flower contain more amino acid (AA) than male flower
- Vivipary : Grape fruit, Cocoa, Jackfruit
- Heterostyly: 1. Litchi 2. Cashew 3. Walnut 4. Pomegranate 5. Sopota
- Ethylene application to climacteric fruit: 0.1 – 1.0 µl/ litre
- Most popular method of Breeding in India – Pedigree method.
- Addition of methanol to persimmon fruits aid ripening
- Punjab safed, Pusa reshmi are Asiatic or tropical type radish varieties
- Bridge grafting is generally useful for repair purposes
- Carrot is an excellent source of Vitamin-A and Iron
- Chekiananis is commonly known as multi-vitamin leafy vegetable or 'multi—mineral packed'
- Cracking in tomato skin associated with deficiency of baron
- Damping off is most commonly occurring disease in nursery
- Starch is degraded to sugars during fruit ripening, and add sweetness to fruits

- Brinjal is known as an appetizing vegetable
- Ethylene strongly promotes ripening activities by stimulating the climacteric rice
- Generally 11% pollinizers are considered sufficient for deciduous fruit trees
- Ethylene stimulates respiration even in non-climacteric fruits like citrus and oranges
- Only 5-10% of the blossoms develop into fruits on a full blossoming apple or pear tree
- Kinnow is the first generation hybrid of King Sweet Orange
- Litchi is a heterostyled fruit tree
- Maleic hydrozide (MH) lowers the fruit drops, possibly due to its ability of checking respiration rate
- Mango malformatioin is a disorder took place due to imbalance between growth promoters and inhibitors
- Pollination is not an important factor for fruit development in persimmon
- Proper ripening of date palm fruits needs a temperature of over 30ºC for not less than 30 days
- Pseudostem is the upper stem of banana
- Punjab Chhuhara is a determinate variety of tomato
- Commercial production of cabbage is done by seed to seed method
- Potato tuber production totally stops at 36 ºC
- CaC_3 is suitable for hastening ripening of fruits
- Leafy vegetables are richest source of vitamin-A
- Bird eye is a disease of apple
- Sylria is a variety of pea having edible pods
- Veni is a special type flower arrangement used in south India to decorate hair
- Plantation crops are also known as high value industrial crops
- Productivity of coconut in India in terms of nuts/ hac is highest among major coconut growing countries
- Malaysia is the largest palm oil producer in the world
- Arecanut is an essential ingredient of 'gutka' and 'Pan masala'
- 'Kalipak' is a cut and processed product of arecanut

- National Research Centre for grapes (Pune, Maharashtra) was established in the year 1997.
- National Research Centre for oil palm (Elurn, Pedeegi AP) was established in the year 1995.
- National Research Centre for Banana (Tiruchirapadi, Kerala) was established in year 1993.
- Central Institute for Temperate Horticulture (CITH) Srinagar, J&K was established in the year 1991.
- Walnut richest in fat (64.5%) followed by Almond (58.9%)
- Cashewnut richest in protein (21.2%) and thiamin 630 mg/100 gm.
- Dry Apricot is richest in calcium, phosphorous and niacin.
- Dry Karonda is richest in iron (39.1%) followed by date palm (10.6%).
- Mango is richest in vitamin-A followed by papaya.
- Bael is richest in riboflavin.
- Barbados cherry richest in vitamin-C (Ascorbic acid) followed by aonla.
- Litchi is richest in calcium content.
- Banana gives highest calories/unit area.
- Walnut produces highest calories per unit of edible portion.
- Cashewnut is third most important agro-commodity exported from the country.
- Higher humidity and higher temperature are needed in banana and pineapple.
- Water is major constituent of protoplasm.
- Apomixes employed in citrus, mango and grape.
- Seed coat is known as testa.
- Sexual propagation is done in phalsa and papaya.
- In citrus, moisture content of 4 to 6% is favourable.
- After ripening takes places in grapes, after harvesting dry period is required that is called after ripening.
- Avocado is sensitive to salt concentration.
- Ber, aonla and date palm are tolerant to salt.
- Apple, pear, mango, citrus avocado are highly sensitive to salt tolerance.
- Stratification is done in apple, pear and cherry at temperature 32 to 45°C for 1-4 months

- Scalding is done in guava for 2 weeks.
- Vegetative propagation is done in pineapple, guava and banana.
- Mound layering is done in mango, guava and rootstocks of apples.
- Flute budding is done in cashew nuts and ber.
- Karonda and chillari used in fencing.
- Pineapple and papaya are used as filler tree in citrus plants.
- Phosphorus is constituent of nucleic acid, phospholipids.
- Magnesium is constituent of chlorophyll.
- Sulphates are taken by roots, SO_2 by leaves.
- Head system is used for weak growing varieties of grapes.
- Kniffin system of training is suitable for Thompson Seedless and Kandhari.
- Strawberry, cherry, citrus, grapes are non-climateric fruits.
- Avocado, sapota, kiwi fruit, cherimoya, are typically climactric fruits.
- Nitrate and Ammonium are two major source of nitrogen taken up by roots.
- Chilgoza (Pinus gerardiana) is an evergreen temperate fruit.
- Alphonso is an export variety of mango.
- Sindhu is a seedless variety of mango.
- Max Red Bartlett is bud sprout of Bartlett or Bud Mutant.
- In Peach, July Alberta is most commonly grown variety.
- CNSL stands for Cashew nut shell liquid.
- Coconut milk is used as RTS.
- Papain yield is 1.5 to 5 gm/fruit from papaya.
- Astringency in persimmon is due to leuko-anthocyanin.
- Pineapple is a C4 food plant.
- Banana yields highest calories per unit area
- Yield of banana is highest in India in world
- Yellow color of papaya is due to Caricaxanthin
- Wood apple (Feronia limonea) is native to India
- Wilt resistant species of Guava is P. fried richs thaliancim
- Karonda have 39.1% Iron, date palm contain 10.6 percent
- Washington Navel is a variety of sweet orange

- Blastophage psens (Wasp) is associated with caprificative of fig
- Jamun, Mango and Citrus are polyembryonic species.
- Aphid and white flies are vactors of Papaya mosaic and Leaf curl respectively.
- Pear has highest lenticels in fruit.
- Calcium carbide induces artificial ripening in Mango
- Mauritius is the mid season variety of pineapple.
- Loquat is an evergreen pome fruit.
- Bombay Green is highly susceptible to 'Malformation'.
- Dilkhush is the clonal selection of Anab-e-shahi.
- Mango pulp is the highest exported fruit processed product
- Papaya is the most susceptible crop to water logging condition.
- Banglore mango has stable flavour hence used for processing.
- Peach leaf curl a fungal disease is caused by *Taphrina deformens.*
- Exanthema is a disorder causes yellowing in fruit trees due to copper deficiency.
- Pre-harvest leaf fall in apple is caused by fungus *Morosinina coronaria.*
- Rosetting in apple is due to Zn deficiency.
- Little leaf in walnut is due to Zn deficiency.
- Bitter pit-a storage disorder in apple, is associated with calcium deficiency.
- Granulation is a physiological disorder of citrus due to Zinc + copper deficiency.
- Northern spy is a resistant root stock of apple to wooly apple aphid (WAA).
- Apple scab is caused by fungus *Venturia inaequalis.*
- Rootstock *Malus zumi* is resistant to apple scab.
- Fruit cracking in litchi is caused by hot winds and low moisture content.
- VAM stands for Vascular Arvascular Mycorrhiza.
- In peach scorch injury caused by low temperature.
- Corky spot in pear caused due to boron & calcium.
- Albinism is a physiological disorder of strawberry in which fruits turn white.

❑❑❑

Section – II

Vegetable Science

CLASSIFICATION

Vegetables are rich source of vitamins, minerals than other than nutrients. In India, vegetables occupy only 2.8% of the total cropped area. Vegetables are (except mushroom) grown for their succulent and edible parts such as the roots, stems, leaves, young tops, fruits or seeds which are used in culinary preparations either fresh or preserved in the fresh state.

These crops are further classified into different groupings according to similarities in edible parts, growth habits, methods of culture and botanical family. Different basis of classification are :

1. Botanical

Class/ family	Common name of vegetables
MONOCOTYLEDONEAE	
Amaryllidaceae	Onion, leek, shallot, garlic, welsh onion, chive
Araceae	Arvi, taro, elephant's foot
Dioscoreaceae	Dioscorea yam, potato yam
Liliaceae	Asparagus
DICOTYLEDONEAE	
Aizoaceae	New Zealand spinach
Chenopodiaceae	Beetroot, palak, Swiss chard, spinach
Compositae (Asteraceae)	Chicory, endive, artichoke, lettuce, head lettuce
Crucifereae (Brassicaceae)	Kale, Brussels sprout, cauliflower, sprouting broccoli, knol-khol, rutabaga, turnip, Chinese cabbage, mustard.
Cucurbitaceae	Watermelon, wax gourd, round melon, snap-melon, long

Contd.

	melon, cucumber, pumpkin, bottle gourd, ridge gourd, bitter gourd, chow-chow, pointed gourd.
Convolvulaceae	Sweet potato
Euphobiaceae	Tapioca or cassava
Leguminoseae (Fabaceae)	Cluster bean, Indian bean, soybean, lima bean, French bean, kidney beans, fenugreek, broad bean, cowpea.
Malvaceae	Okra
Solanaceae	Sweet pepper, hot pepper, tomato, brinjal/egg plant, potato
Umbelliferae/ Apiaceae	Celery, carrot, parsnip, parsley

2. Hardiness

1. **Hardy**: Asparagus, broccoli, Brussels sprouts, knol-khol, cabbage, chives, garlic, kale, leek, onion, parsley, peas, radish, turnip etc.
2. **Semi-hardy**: Beetroot, carrot, cauliflower, celery, globe artichoke, lettuce, palak, parsnip and potato.
3. **Tender**: Amaranthus, chilies, tomato, cluster been, colocasia, cowpea, cucurbits, sweet potato, tapioca and yams.

3. Edible part

1. **Leafy vegetables:** The vegetable crops which are grown mainly for their leaves. They are rich in vitamins and minerals and also look decorative. Examples are spinach, amaranth, lettuce, horse radish, cabbage, green onion etc.
2. **Shoot vegetables:** The vegetable crops which are grown primarily for their edible shoot, mainly the young, succulent stem. Examples are asparagus, bamboo, celery etc.
3. **Pod and seed vegetables:** Generally *Leguminosae* or *Fabaceae* family plants are grown for their young pods and seeds. Example are, snap-bean, winged bean, okra etc.
4. **Root and bulb vegetables**- Vegetables grown for their swollen underground roots and stems. Examples are carrot, potato, onion, raddish, beet root, elephant foot etc.
5. **Flower vegetables**: Vegetable plants having flowers as edible part. Examples are horse raddish, squash, rose, sunflower etc.
6. **Fruit vegetables**: The vegetables grown for their fleshy, succulent fruits. Examples are eggplant, tomato, peppers, melons etc.

4. Growth season

- **Cool season vegetable:** Beet root, cabbage, carrot, cauliflower, celery, kale, knol-khol, lettuce, methi, onion, palak, pea, radish, spinach, winged bean and turnip.
- **Hot/warm season vegetable:** Bean, cluster bean, lima bean, brinjal, cassava, colocasia, cucumber, melons, pumpkin, okra, pepper, sweet potato and tomato.

5. Family

- **Cole crops or crucifers:** These vegetable crops belong to the Cruciferae or Brassicaceae (mustard) family having edible leaves or heads. Examples are cabbage, cauliflower, mustard, Chinese cabbage, radish etc.
- **Cucurbits:** Cucurbits belong to the cucurbitaceae family. They are grown mainly for their fruits but some have edible young shoots and flowers also called vine crops. Examples are bottle gourd, charantia, cucumber, melons, squash etc.
- **Legume vegetables:** The members of the leguminosae or fabaceae family. The seeds are rich in protein. Examples are French bean, kidney & lima bean, peas etc.
- **Solanaceous crops:** Vegetables belong to the Solanaceae family and with the exception of white potato, are also called *Fruit Vegetables*. Examples are eggplant, tomato etc.

6. Photo-periodism

Long day vegetables: Beet, Chinese cabbage, Lettuce, Raddish, Spinach

Short day vegetables: Potato, Sweet potato

Day neutral vegetables: Asparagus, Beans, Peas, Cucumber, Chilies, Tomato

7. Respiration rate

- **Very high:** Asparagus, broccoli, peas, spinach
- **High:** Beans and lettuce
- **Moderate:** Beet, carrot, celery and cucumber.
- **Low:** Cabbage, sweet potato, turnip, muskmelon, pepper and tomato.

8. Photosynthesis

- C_3: Bean, spinach, lettuce, carrot, potato, sweet potato, tomato and sugar beet.

- C_4: Amaranthus

9. Isolation distance

- **Self-pollinated:** Tomato, lettuce, glove artichoke, broad bean, green peas, cowpea and fenugreek.
- **Often cross pollinated**: Okra, brinjal, chilli and lima bean.
- **Cross pollinated**: Onion, leek, garlic, arvi, taro, asparagus, spinach, palak, Brussels sprout, cauliflower, sprouting broccoli, knol-khol, turnip, mustard, cucumber, pumpkin, bottle and bitter gourd, carrot, parsley and other vegetable crops.

10. Transplanting

- **Easy to transplant:** Brinjal, tomato, lettuce, Cole crops.
- **Transplanted with care:** Onion, chilli, celery.
- **Not transplanted:** Okra, beans, peas, cucurbits, turnip, amaranthus and fenugreek.

SHORT NOTES

1. Classification of functional foods

Functional food is any modified food or food ingredient that may provide a health benefit beyond traditional nutrients it contains. They are similar in appearance as conventional foods.

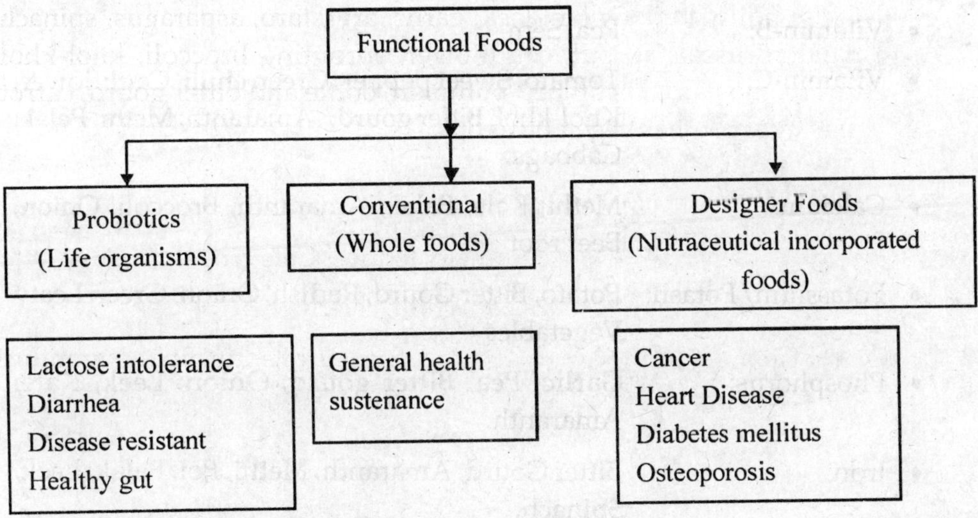

2. Type of glucosinolate in Cole crops

- Isothiocyanate: Cauliflower, cabbage, knolkhol
- Sulphoraphane: Broccoli-most important in preventing cancer
- Glucobrassicin: Cabbage and broccoli
- GluconastrinL: Cabbage
- Indole-3-carbinol: Cabbage
- Sinigrin: Brussels sprout and broccoli.

3. Bio-active compounds in vegetables

- Vitamin C: Cabbage, broccoli
- Vitamin A: Broccoli
- Beta carotene: Orange colour cauliflower

- Anthocyanin: Red cabbage, purple broccoli.
- Protein: Pea, French bean, Cowpea, Cluster bean, Amaranth, Broad bean
- Carbohydrates: Potato, Sweet Potato, Dry Beans, Yam, Tapioca
- Vitamin-A: Carrot, Palak, Amaranth, Pumpkin, Methi, Green Pea, Paprika
- Vitamin-B: Pea, Sem
- Vitamin-C: Tomato, Sweet pepper, Green chilli, Cauliflower, Knol-khol, Bitter gourd, Amaranth, Methi, Palak, Cabbage.
- Calcium: Methi, Kale, Palak, Amaranth, Broccoli, Onion, Beet root
- Potassium/Potash: Potato, Bitter Gourd, Radish, Onion, Green Leafy Vegetables
- Phosphorus: Garlic, Pea, Bitter gourd, Onion, Leek, Kale, Amaranth.
- Iron: Bitter Gourd, Amaranth, Methi, Poi, Palak, Leek, Spinach.

4. Phyto-chemicals in vegetables

Vegetables	Phyto-chemicals	Benefits
Beans	Flavonoids (saponins)	Protect against cancer, lower cholesterol
Broccoli	Indoles, isothiocyanates	Protect against cancer, heart disease and stroke
Carrot	β-carotene	Protect against certain cancers and heart disease, boost the immune system
Sweet potato	β -carotene	Antioxidant
Tomato	Lycopene, Flavonoids	Protect against cancer, fight infection
Bitter gourd	Momordicin and Charantin	Diabetes, Blood purifier, Hypertension, Dysentery, Anathematic
Radish	Isothiocyanates	Jaundice, Liver infection, Piles
Chilli	Capsaicin, Oleoresin	Anti-diarrhoeal, Anti-rheumatic

5. Source of anti-oxidants

- Lycopene: Watermelons, tomatoes, guava & pink pomegranate
- Anthocyanins: Black carrots, blueberries, bilberries, red grapes, strawberries
- β-carotene:
- Carotenoids: Pumpkin, carrots, kale, yellow corn & seaweed
- Lutein & Zeaxanthin: kale, spinach,beet,mustard greens & sweet green pepper
- Capsaicin: Chilli, peppers
- Isothiocyanates: Cruciferous vegetables

6. Natural colour rich vegetables

Vegetable	Variety	Uses
Carrot	Pusa Ashita	Natural Dye and mixing in food products
Paprika	KTPL-19	Natural Dye and mixing in food products
Amaranth	Pusa Lal Chaulai	Natural Dye and mixing in food products
Beet root	Deyroit Dark Red	Natural Dye and mixing in food products
Red Cabbage	Red Cabbage	Natural Dye and mixing in food products
Purple Broccoli	Palam Vichitra	Natural Dye and mixing in food products
Purple Sem	Sem	Natural Dye and mixing in food products

7. Natural pigments present in vegetables

Colour	Principle Compound	Vegetables
Red	Lycopene	Tomato, watermelon
Yellow/Orange	â-carotene	Carrot, melon, green leafy vegetables like red pepper, yellow & orange-fleshed sweet potato
Green	Chlorophyll	Broccoli, palak, other green leafy vegetables
Blue/Purple	Anthocyanins	Red cabbage, brinjal, poi, purple tomato, purple sweet potato, black carrot
White/Tan Brown		Garlic, onions, green onions, shallots, chives

8. Registered Pesticides used in vegetables

Name of pesticide	Name of vegetables
2,4-D amine salt	Potato
Aureofungin	Potato
Captan	Cabbage, tomato
Carbaryl	Brinjal, cabbage
Carbendazim	Brinjal, cucurbits
Carbofuran	Brinjal, cabbage, tomato, potato
Chlorpyriphos	Brinjal, cabbage, onion
Cypermethrin	Brinjal, okra
Cypermethrin + Quinalphos	Brinjal, cabbage
Dicofol	Okra
Dimethoate	Brinjal, tomato, potato, onion
Dinocap	Okra, Chilli
Endosulfan	Brinjal, onion
Fenitrothion	Brinjal, tomato, potato, onion
Fenthion	Cucurbits, onion
Gibberelic Acid	Onion, Brinjal, cabbage
Lindane	Brinjal, cabbage, tomato, okra, potato, cucurbits, onion
Malathion	Brinjal, tomato
Monocrotophos	Pea, Brinjal, tomato
Phorate	Brinjal, tomato, potato
Ziram	Tomato

9. Acts and rules for regulation of the pesticide manufacture and use in India

- The Insecticides Act 1968 and Rules 1971 (replaced by Pesticides Management Bill 2008).
- Prevention of Food Adulteration Act 1954, is now been transferred to Food Safety and Standards Authority, (FSSA- Act, 2006).
- The Environment (Protection) Act 1986
- The Factories Act 1948
- Bureau of Indian Standards Act
- Air (Prevention & Control of Pollution) Act 1981
- Water (Prevention & Control of Pollution) Act 1974
- Hazardous Waste (Management & Handling) Rules 1989

10. Sex Forms

- Cleistogamy: Lettuce
- Chasmogamy: Tomato, capsicum
- Protogyny : Cole crops
- GMS : Tomato, Muskmelon, Watermelon, Cole crops, Beet root, onion
- CMS: Carrot, Sweet Pepper, Cucumber
- CGMS : Onion, Carrot, Radish, Beet, Tomato
- Protandry: Onion, Carrot
- Herkogamy: Lima Bean
- Peas and Beans are self pollinated crop due to presence of Keel
- Hermaphrodite: Ridge Gourd, Cucumber – Original form.
- Andromonoecious: Muskmelon.
- Gynoecious: Cucumber
- Monoecious: Cucumber.
- Trimonoecious: Cucumber, Muskmelon, Ridge Gourd

11. Anthesis

1. Bottle gourd – 5-8 PM
2. Snake gourd – 6-9 PM
3. Ridge gourd – 5-8 PM
4. Muskmelon –5.30 – 6.30 AM
5. Cucumber: Morning
6. Sponge gourd – Morning

12. Inflorescence type

1. Recemose: Peas Beans, Tomato, Cole crops
2. Panicle: Cassava, Drumstick
3. Umbel: Celery, Onion, Garlic
4. Spike: Beet, Amaranthus, Palak
5. Capitulatum: Globe artichoke
6. Spadix: Taro, Elephant foot yam
7. Catkin: Cabbage

13. Carotenoids and Cancer Chemoprevention:

- Inhibits human breast cancer.
- Lycopene inhibits prostate cancer.
- Carotenoids reduce lung cancer in females.
- β-carotene inhibits cell proliferation in carcinogenesis. Inhibits cervical, lung, prostate, colorectal and stomach cancers.
- Lycopene-rich foods reduce prostate cancer risk in human. Enhance cell-to-cell communication by up-regulating gap junctions.
- Lutein and zeaxanthin intake linked to reduced risk of prostate cancer.

14. Anthocyanins and associated flavonoids

- Responsible for red to blue colours in the plants.
- Found dissolved uniformly in the vascular solution of epidermal cells.
- Distribution of six most common anthocyanins in the edible plant parts.
- Cyanidin (50%), Pelargonidin (12%), Peonidin (12%), Delphinidin (12%), Petunidin (7%), Malvidin (7%).
- Most widespread anthocyanin in fruits is cyanidin-3-glucoside.
- Main sources of anthocyanin: brinjal, onion, purple cabbage, black carrot etc.

15. Genetic marker

- Genetic markers represent genetic differences between individual organisms or species.
- Generally, they do not represent target genes themselves but act as 'signs' or 'flags'.
- Genetic markers that are located in close proximity to genes (i.e. tightly linked) may be referred to as gene 'tags'.
- Such markers themselves do not affect the phenotype of the trait of interest because they are located only near or 'linked' to genes controlling the trait.
- All genetic markers occupy specific genomic positions within chromosomes (like genes) called 'loci.
- **Morphological markers**: Visually characterized phenotypic characters such as flower colour, seed shape, growth habits or pigmentation.
- **Biochemical markers**: include allelic variants of enzymes called isozymes.

- **Isozyme markers:** are differences in enzymes that are detected by electrophoresis and specific staining.
- **DNA (or molecular) markers:** which reveal sites of variation in DNA.

16. List of chemicals used to extend the shelf-life of vegetables

Vegetables	Chemical (concentration)	Time of application	Response
Onion	Maleic hydrazide (2000 to 3000 ppm)	Two weeks prior to harvest	Reduced sprouting in storage
	Maleic hydrazide (2000 ppm)	Pre-harvest spray	Reduced storage losses
Okra	GA_3 and ascorbic acid (each at 100 or 250 mg/L) and packed in polyethylene bags	Post harvest dip for 10 months	Extended shelf-life for 9-12 days at ambient temperature.
Tomato	CME 74050 (10 ppm)	Post harvest dip for 5-10 min	Extended shelf-life

17. Maturity Standards for Vegetables

Name of vegetable	Maturity standards
Tomato	• Mature green, pink or breaker and red ripe • Pulp surrounding the seeds is jelly-like, seeds slip away from the knife • For long distance shipment tomato is harvested at mature green stage • The ripe stage indicates that most of the surface is pink or red, and fruits are firm.
Okra	• Pods are still young, tender, exhibiting maximum growth • Pods should be readily shaped when they are picked • When mature pods are fibrous, and tough.
Asparagus	• Spears grow above the ground • They should be harvested when spear are not too long. • Before the tops begin to spread.
Cauliflower	• Head attains proper size and before they become discoloured, loose or blemished. • Over mature flowers become too long, flower stocks elongate, resulting fuzzy, ricyness.
Carrots	• Size is the primary consideration and at least ¾ diameter • Proper colour development without zoning.
Green Peas	• Sugar content >5–6% at maturity, sugar decline with increase in starch/ protein • Tenderness and appearance of pods should be well filled with young tender peas. • Changing in colour from dark to light green with firmness of 5 kg/cm^2

18. Export specifications for vegetables

Commodity	Parameters for Export
Okra	3-5 inch length, green tender, packing 5 kg
Bottle Gourd	12 inch length, greenish tender, straight, packing 5 kg
Peas	5-6 inch length, green tender, straight, packing 5 kg
Gowar	4-5 inch length, not over matured packing 5 kg
Suran	Cleaned, weighing around 5-10 kg
Green Chilli	3-4 inch length, straight, thick, packing 5 kg
Drum sticks	24 inch length, straight, thick, packing 5 kg
Lime	20-25 mm, green, packing 5 kg, gunny bags20 kg wooden boxes
Mode of Transport	By Air or By Sea

Source: Maharashtra State Agriculture Marketing Board: Website (Jan, 2009)

19. Major vegetable producing countries in the world (2007-08)

Country	Area (000, ha)	Production (000, MT)	Productivity, (MT/ ha)
China	23936	448983	19
India	7803	125887	16
United States of America	1333	38075	29
Turkey	996	24454	25
Russian Federation	970	16516	17
Egypt	598	16041	27
Iran	641	15993	25
Italy	526	13587	26
Spain	379	12676	33
Japan	379	12676	33
Others	16957	222625	13
Total	54573	946774	

Source: FAO, except India data (Source: Indian Horticulture Database 2008)

20. Centers of origin

Center	Horticultural crops
South Mexican and Central American Center	Common bean, lima bean, winter pumpkin, chayote, sweet potato, arrowroot, pepper, papaya, guava, cashewnut, wild black cherry, cherry tomato, cacao.
South American Center	Lima bean, common bean, potato, tomato, pumpkin, pepper, cocoa, passion flower, guava, Common potato, strawberry, pineapple, Brazil nut
Mediterranean Center	Green pea, lupine, olive, garden beet, cabbage, turnip, lettuce, asparagus, celery, chicory, parsnip, rhubarb.
Middle East	Alfalfa, fenugreek, fig, pomegranate, apple, pear, quince, cherry.
Central Asiatic Center	Chickpea, onion, garlic, spinach, carrot, pear, almond, grape, apple.
Indian Center	Eggplant, cucumber, radish, taro, yam, mango, orange, tangerine, citron, tamarind, black pepper, sandalwood, pummelo, banana, breadfruit, mangosteen, coconut palm, sugarcane, clove, nutmeg black pepper.
Chinese Center	Chinese yam, radish, Chinese cabbage, onion, cucumber, pear, Chinese apple, peach, apricot, cherry, walnut, litchi

EXPLANATARY NOTES

POTATO

(Solanum tuberosum)

Family:	Solanaceae
Origin:	South America
Type of vegetable:	Tuber crop
Edible portion:	Stem tuber
Basic chromosome number:	X=24
Somatic chromosome number:	2n =48

- Potato is a self-pollinated crop, propagated vegetatively.
- Potato was introduced in India from Europe in early 17th century.
- Harvesting of potato is done before the temperature rise from 30°C.
- 4th major food of the world after rice, wheat and maize
- China ranks 1st in area and production.
- It is grown in all states of India except Kerala.
- Maximum day temperature below 35°C while maximum night temperature below 20°C.
- Late blight is most devastating disease in potato occurs every year in the hills but occasionally in plains.
- Most of varieties don't tuberize when night temperature is more than 23°C.
- Potato tuber dormancy 8-10 weeks.
- Hills accounts for only 5% of area under potato.
- About 50% of the potato produced in the world is utilized as human food.
- Ridge and furrow system are most popular methods of potato planting.
- Seed plot technique in potato was developed by Dr Puskarnath.
- Dehaulming in potato is done 10-12 days before harvesting.
- Tubers are treated with 1% thiourea + 1 PPM GA3 for 1 hour to break dormancy.
- For best yield, potato needs long day condition during growth and short day condition during tuberization.
- Upto date is most popular variety of potato in India.
- Potato is unfit for consumption if solanin is greater than 20 mg/ 100 g.

- Earthing up of potato is done 40 days after sowing.
- Central Potato Research Institute (CPRI) was established in the year 1949.
- Kufri Chipsona 1 and 2 are suitable for processing and producing light colour chips and French fries.
- International Potato Centre (1971) is an autonomous scientific institute at Lima in Peru.

TOMATO

(*Solanum lycopersicum*)

Family:	Solanaceae
Origin:	South America
Type of vegetable:	Berry
Edible portion:	Whole fruit
Basic chromosome number:	X=12
Somatic chromosome number:	2n =24

- Botanically tomato is Lycopersicon esculentum now changed to Solanum lycopersicum.
- Tomato is universally treated a "Protective food".
- Number 1 processing vegetable extensively grown as annual crop all over world.
- Tomato puree and tomato paste have great export demand.
- Tomato is a climacteric fruit.
- Tomato have 5 forms like i) Cherry tomato, (ii) Pear tomato, (iii) Common tomato, (iv) Potato leaf type, (v) Upright tomato.
- Lycopene is responsible for red colour in tomato and its production is highest at 21-24°C.
- Production of lycopene pigment drops rapidly above 27°C.
- Seed treatment with 2, 4 D @ 2-5 PPM increase early fruit set and parthenocarpy.
- Training and pruning are followed in indeterminate type of tomato (Single stem system).
- Staking is followed in indeterminate type of tomato.
- Excessive rains adversely affect its fruit set, causing flower drop.
- It has tap root system. Moderately tolerant to acid soils.
- Breaker stage: (10% lycopene) suitable for long distance transport.

- B and Zn are important micronutrient required for tomato cultivation.
- Foliage spray of PCPA (20 PPM) is very effective in increasing fruit set.
- Cluster of flowers known as "Truss".
- Determinate type plants are dwarf and growth restricted with appearance of terminal flower.
- Indeterminate type plants continue growth and less initiation of flower and fruit on the stem takes place.
- Ethrel (1000 ppm) enhances the ripening of tomato fruits.
- Sel-120 is the first root-knot nematode resistant variety of tomato.

BRINJAL

(*Solanum melongena*)

Family:	Solanaceae
Origin:	Indo-Burma
Type of vegetable:	Berry
Edible portion:	Whole fruit
Basic chromosome number:	X=12
Somatic chromosome number:	2n =24

- India ranks 2nd after China in brinjal production.
- It is a often cross-pollinated crop.
- Brinjal fruit is a berry. Dry brinjal fruits contain goitrogenic principle.
- Anthocyanin pigment present in brinjal.
- Hetero-style is common in brinjal.
- Brinjal is a day neutral plant.
- 2, 4-D chemical is used to control weed in brinjal.
- Dark purple skin binjal have more vitamin-C than those of white skin.
- Maximum fruit setting takes place in `long styled flowers' (70-80%).
- 14% area under brinjal is covered by hybrid varieties.
- Brinjal fruits are good source of Vitamin-B.
- White brinjals are preferred by diabetic patients.
- There is no fruit setting in pseudo-short and short-styled flowers.
- Aphid resistant variety of brinjal : Annamalai
- Extra early maturing variety of brinjal: Pusa Purple Long

- Pusa Ankur: New variety
- Little leaf of brinjal resistant varieties: Arka Sheel, Manjari Gota.
- Orobanchae spp a root parasite is a serious weed of brinjal crop.

CAPSICUM And CHILLI

(*Capsicum annum*)

Family:	Solanaceae
Origin:	Mexico
Type of vegetable:	Berry
Edible portion:	Whole fruit
Basic chromosome number:	X=12
Somatic chromosome number:	2n –24

- Capsaicin is responsible for pungency in chilli.
- *C. annum* and *C. frutescence* have "white flower" while *C. pubescence* have purple flowers.
- China is the major capsicum (bell pepper) producing country.
- India is a major producer, consumer and exporter of chilli in the world.
- June-October is the major chilli growing period in South India.
- Dry chilli generally contains about 6% stalks + 40% pericarp + 54% seeds.
- Paprika (*Capsicum frutescence*), variety Arka Abir is suitable for colour extraction.
- NAA and triconitinol control fruit drop.
- Punjab Lal, Punjab Surakh are Multiple disease resistance varieties.
- Bacterial wilt resistant variety Utkal Rashmi, Arka Gaurav.
- Jwalamukhi: Suitable for High density plantation.
- Pusa Sadabahar variety of *C. frutescence* is perennial in nature.
- Punjab Lal: suitable for colour extraction.
- Varieties with thin pericarp, less seeds, strong spike is suitable for drying.
- Pusa Meghdoot: First F1 hybrid by public sector.
- Fruit rot resistant variety : K-2
- Leaf curl resistant variety. Pusa Jwala, Pusa Sadabahar, Pant C-1

OKRA

(*Abelmoschus esculentus*)

Family: Malvaceae
Origin: Africa
Type of vegetable: Berry
Edible portion: Whole fruit
Somatic chromosome number: 2n =130

- Okra is a tropical crop.
- India is the largest producer of okra in world.
- The roots and stems are used for clearing cane juice during preparation of Gur.
- High iodine content of fruit help in control goiter.
- Bhindi flowers are self fertile.
- Arka Abhay is a sister line of Arka Anamika.
- Perkins Long Green: Suitable for hilly region of North India.
- Punjab Padmani: Possesses field resistance to yellow vein mosaic virus (YVMV) and tolerance to jassids and cotton boll worm.
- Export standard: 6-8 cm long fruits.
- Dr. Harbhajan Singh started systematic research work on bhindi.
- At temperature above 42°C, flower bud drops.
- The major breeding objective in Okra is resistance to YVMV.
- Jassid is the most serious pest.
- Ethephon reduces vegetative growth at 100-150 ppm.
- Pusa Sawani has tolerance to salinity.
- Okra Abhay and Pusa A-4 give quick branching after pruning.
- Pusa A-4: Resistant to YVMV and tolerant to jassids, fruits and shoot borer
- Varsha Upkar: Suitable in disease prone areas (YVMV).

PEA

(*Pisium sativum*)

Family:	Leguminoceae
Origin:	Central Asia
Type of vegetable:	Pods/leguminous
Edible portion:	Fleshy and tender seeds
Basic chromosome number:	X = 7
Somatic chromosome number:	2n =14

- Field pea (P. arvense) are having coloured flowers and garden pea (P. sativum) have white coloured flowers.
- Pea is an herbaceous winter annual.
- Arka Ajeet is resistant to powdery mildew and rust.
- Arkel is most popular exotic pea introduced from England.
- Training or stacking is an important cultural operation in tall varieties.
- Tenderometer is the instrument used to test the maturity of peas in processing industries.
- Delayed harvesting results in conversion of sugars into starch and pods become coarse.
- Peas are rich source of proteins (25%).
- Bonneville is the large seeded peas, most suitable for drying.

FRENCH BEANS

(*Phaseolus vulgaris*)

Family:	Leguminoceae
Origin:	Mexico
Type of vegetable:	Pods/leguminous
Edible portion:	Pods and seeds
Basic chromosome number:	X = 11
Somatic chromosome number:	2n =22

- 94% of the pods are edible.
- It is also known as kidney bean, snap bean and is most important leguminous crop.
- Pusa Parvati is resistant to powdery mildew and is developed through mutation breeding.
- Most of the varieties are day neutral, semi-pole varieties are short-day types.

- It is a shallow rooted crop.
- Staking is an important operation for pole beans.
- GA3 sprayed at 50-200 ppm is effective in improving crop growth.
- Blossom drop and ovule abortion are common problems at high temperature (35°C).

CABBAGE

(*Brassica oleracea var capitata*)

Family:	Crucifereae
Origin:	Mediterranean region
Type of vegetable:	Leafy vegetable
Edible portion:	Head
Basic chromosome number:	X = 9
Somatic chromosome number:	2n =18

- *Brassica oleraceae* var sylvastris: wild cabbage
- *Brassica oleraceae* var sabuda: savoy cabbage
- Cabbage covers 4% of total area under vegetables.
- India rank 3rd in cabbage production.
- Hybrids occupy 30% of the area under cabbage production.
- It has anticancer property due to presence of Indole-3-carbinol.
- Cabbage bear seed in special kind of bicarpillary pod called as `Siliqua'.
- Round head variety mature earliest followed by conical varieties.
- Spraying 50 ppm boric acid at flowering enhances the seed yield.
- Sauerkraut: Value added product prepared from white cabbage, used to cure scurvy.
- Ctyoplasmic and genetic male sterility found in cabbage is also helpful for the production of F1 hybrid.
- Cabbage grown in saline soil is more prone to black leg disease.
- A spray of CCC or SADH increases the low temperature resistance in cabbage.
- Cabbage produce seed in the temperate areas only.
- Pusa Ageti: 1st tropical variety developed for cultivation under high temperature conditions.
- Growth of most of cabbage varieties is arrested when temperature rise above 25°C.
- Cabbage is hardier than cauliflower and can withstand frost.

CAULIFLOWER

(*Brassica oleracea var botrytis*)

Family:	Crucifereae
Origin:	Mediterranean region
Type of vegetable:	Leafy vegetable
Edible portion:	Curd
Basic chromosome number:	X = 9
Somatic chromosome number:	2n =18

- Cauliflower is only crop in group of Cole crops in which the intermediate stage of curding lies between vegetative and reproduction stage.
- Blanching is a method to protect curd from attaining yellow colour after their direct exposure to sun.
- Most of late type (Snowball) has self blanched habit.
- Cauliflower was introduced in India in 1822 by Dr Jemson from London.
- It requires 5-8 irrigation during growth.
- Pusa Himjyoti is only variety which can be grown from April to July in the hills.
- Scooping: Removal of central portion of curd for easier initiation of flower stalk in cauliflower.
- Cauliflower is thermo-sensitive crop.

KNOL KHOL

(*Brassica caulorapa*)

Family:	Crucifereae/brassicaceae
Origin:	Mediterranean region
Type of vegetable:	Leafy vegetable
Edible portion:	Swollen stem called knob
Basic chromosome number:	X = 9
Somatic chromosome number:	2n =18

- In India, knol-khol is more popular in Kashmir.
- Khol-khol (a) for seed production - Annual
  (b) for flowering and fruiting ? Biennial
- Brussels Sprout and knol-khol are typically biennial crop.
- Best time for planting is: October.

- Inflorescence in Knol-khol is racemose.
- Early varieties of knol-khol are more prone to pre-mature bolting.

BRUSSEL'S SPROUT

(*Brassica oleracea var gemmifera*)

Family:	Crucifereae/brassicaceae
Origin:	Mediterranean region
Type of vegetable:	Leafy vegetable
Edible portion:	Swollen axillary bud/sprouts
Basic chromosome number:	X = 9
Somatic chromosome number:	2n =18

- It has sporophytic self-incompatibility.
- Brussels sprout is a cool season, moisture loving vegetable.
- Late varieties can withstand temperature as low as -10°C.
- The inflorescence type is racemose.
- It is a frost resistant crop.
- Excess application of potash imparts bitter taste to sprouts.
- Excess nitrogen results in loose sprouts due to quick vegetative growth.

SPROUTING BROCCOLI

(*Brassica oleracea var italica*)

Family:	Crucifereae/brassicaceae
Origin:	Mediterranean region
Type of vegetable:	Leafy vegetable
Edible portion:	Flower bud
Basic chromosome number:	X = 9
Somatic chromosome number:	2n =18

- USA is the largest producer.
- Rich source of sulphoraphane- compound which reduces the risk of cancer.
- Palam Samridhi: released from CSKHPKV, Palampur.
- Broccoli, an Italian word derived from Latin 'Brachium' means an arm or branch.
- Early type is 'annual' while late type is 'biennial' in nature.
- It has 130 times more vitamin A than cauliflower and 22 times more than cabbage.

- Excessive use of cole crops results in swelling of thyroid glands and goiter disease.
- In dry condition the crop becomes fibrous.
- Inflorescence type is cymose.
- Mass selection is most common method used in cross pollinated crop for the improvement of qualitative characters governed by single or few genes.
- Back cross method is used to transfer resistance governed by one or few dominant or recessive genes.

KALE

(*Brassica oleracea var acephala*)

Family: Crucifcreae/brasslcaceae
Origin: Mediterranean region
Type of vegetable: Leafy vegetable
Edible portion: Leaves and shoots
Basic chromosome number: X = 9
Somatic chromosome number: 2n =18

- It is the hardiest crop and can withstand temperature as low as -10 to -15°C.
- Karam Sag is mostly grown in J & K.
- Kale is propagated by seed.
- Karam Sag is medium tall variety, mostly grown in J&K.

RADISH

(*Raphanus saivus*)

Family: Crucifereae
Origin: Europe
Type of vegetable: Root cum leafy
Edible portion: Root and leaves
Basic chromosome number: X=9
Somatic chromosome number: 2n =18

- Radish is suitable for tropical and temperate climate.
- Edible portion develops from both primary root and hypocotyls.
- It is a cross pollinated vegetable.
- Arka Nishant is pithiness resistant radish.
- Tropical variety can produce seed both in tropical and temperate region of India.

- Akashin is a physiological disorder of radish caused due to boron deficiency.
- Hollow root is a physiological disorder due to high temperature.

CARROT

(*Daucus carota*)

Family:	Umbelifereae
Origin:	Afganisthan
Type of vegetable:	Root
Edible portion:	Root
Basic chromosome number:	X=9
Somatic chromosome number:	2n =18

- Carrot is an annual herb for roots, biennial for flowering and seed production.
- Carrot flowers are protendrous and inflorescence type is umbel.
- Splitting of carrot root occurs when sudden change in soil moisture status.
- Asiatic types are high yielding, produce seeds under tropical conditions.
- Asiatic types are poor in carotene contents.
- Chantaney is an excellent cultivar for canning and storage.
- Cavity spot is a disorder of carrot due to calcium deficiency.

ONION

(*Allium cepa*)

Family:	Amaryllidaceae
Origin:	Central Asia
Type of vegetable:	Bulb crop
Edible portion:	Bulbs and leaves
Basic chromosome number:	X=8
Somatic chromosome number:	2n =16

- India ranks second in area and production in world.
- Netherlands is the leading exporter of onion, 21% of world export.
- Inflorescence is an umbel. Onion flowers are white.
- The shallot is a perennial onion.
- Onion is highly cross-pollinated crop, chiefly pollinated by honey bees.

- Almost all cultivars grown in plains in India are short-day cultivars.
- The best harvesting time for Rabi onion is one week after 50-70% neck fall.
- Lasalgaon in Maharashtra is the biggest onion market in India.
- Indian export is about 12% of world's onion demand.
- Anthesis starts in Allium cepa at 7AM.
- Cytoplasmic genetic male sterility was first found in onion.

GARLIC

(*Allium sativum*)

Family:	Amaryllidaceae
Origin:	Central Asia
Type of vegetable:	Bulb crop
Edible portion:	Cloves
Basic chromosome number:	X=8
Somatic chromosome number:	2n =16

- It has higher nutritive value as compare to other bulb crops.
- Diallyl disulphide possesses true garlic odour.
- G 282 is suitable for export purposes.
- It is a frost-hardy plant, produced vegetatively by cloves.
- Curing is an additional treatment given to bulb crops to remove excess moisture.
- Irradiation with 6 krad of cobalt 60 gamma rays recommended for successful storage of garlic.
- Garlic is used as a spice throughout India.

LEEK

(*Allium porrum*)

Family:	Amaryllidaceae
Origin:	Central Asia
Type of vegetable:	Leafy vegetable
Edible portion:	stem and leaves
Basic chromosome number:	X =16
Somatic chromosome number:	2n =32

- Leek is a non-bulb forming member of family Amaryllidaceae.
- It is grown especially for its blanched stem and leaves.

- It is a biennial crop.
- Seeds are produced in higher altitudes in the hills.

BITTER GOURD

(*Momordica charantia*)

Family:	Cucurbitaceae
Origin:	Indo-Burma
Type of vegetable:	Cucurbitaceous fruit
Edible portion:	Fruit
Basic chromosome number:	X = 9
Somatic chromosome number:	2n =18

- The fruits are rich in iron and are also known as bitter cucumber.
- Anthesis occurs very early in the morning.
- White coloured varieties are less bitter in taste and are preferred in South India.
- .terness is due to momodicidin.
- Female flower production increases at low temperature of 20°C under short day and above 36°C poor flower production takes place.
- MH 50-150 ppm and CCC 50-100 ppm increases female: male ratio.

CUCUMBER

(*Cucumus sativus*)

Family:	Cucurbitaceae
Origin:	India
Type of vegetable:	Cucurbitaceous pepo
Edible portion:	Fruit
Basic chromosome number:	X = 7
Somatic chromosome number:	2n =14

- It is the second most widely cultivated cucurbit after watermelon.
- Immature fruits are used as salad and also for pickling.
- Cucumber is extensibly grown in glasshouse.
- Open pollinated cultivars are monoecious in sex form.
- Himangi is resistant to bronzing.

- It prefers slightly low temperature as compare to watermelon.
- Ethrel, 150-200 ppm increases the number of female flower.
- The yield can be doubled by using tropical gynoecious F1 hybrid.
- Chilling injury, a physiological storage disorder noticed below -10°C for prolonged period.
- Gynoecious line can be maintained by induction of male flower through gibberellic acid (1500-2000 ppm), silver nitrate (250-400 ppm) or silver thiosulphate (400 ppm).
- Sex expression largely depends on environmental conditions and short days, lower temperatures, high humidity and low nitrogen status tend to increase female flower.
- Honeybees are the major pollinating agents of cucumber
- Ideal conditions for honeybee pollination include clear skies and low wind speed, low humidity for more bee activity. The optimum time for pollination is between 7:00 a.m. to 9:00 am.
- Carotenoid pigment and ascorbic acid are the major bioactive compound in cucumber and musk melon.

WATERMELON.

(*Citrullus lanatus*)

Family:	Cucurbitaceae
Origin:	Tropical Africa
Type of vegetable:	Cucurbitaceous pepo
Edible portion:	Fruit
Basic chromosome number:	X = 11
Somatic chromosome number:	2n =22

- Cool nights and warm days are ideal for accumulation of sugars in watermelon.
- Arka Manik is highly resistant to powdery and downy mildew.
- It is grown in relay system just before digging potatoes.
- Application of TIBA (25-250 ppm), boron (3-4 ppm) and calcium (20-25 ppm) is recommended to increase fruiting.
- Average TSS is recorded around 9-10% in watermelon.

MUSKMELON

(*Cucumis melo*)

Family:	Cucurbitaceae
Origin:	Tropical Africa
Type of vegetable:	Cucurbitaceous pepo
Edible portion:	Fruit
Basic chromosome number:	X = 12
Somatic chromosome number:	2n =24

- It is a climacteric fruit.
- Mature fruits are round in shape.
- Anthesis takes place at 22-29°C at 5 to 6.30 am.
- Keeping quality of Arka Rajhans is excellent.
- It requires tropical climate and fairly high temperature of 35-40°C.
- Cool nights and warm days are ideal for accumulation of sugars in muskmelon.
- It is more tolerant to soil acidity.
- Exogenous application of silver thiosulphate 300-400 ppm induces the male flowers in gynoecious muskmelon.

PALAK (LOCAL)

(*Beta vulgaris var bangalensis*)

Family:	Chenopodiaceae
Origin:	Indo-China
Type of vegetable:	Leafy vegetable
Edible portion:	Leaves
Basic chromosome number:	X = 9
Somatic chromosome number:	2n =18

- Palak is a leafy vegetable and it requires more N2 for crown growth.
- Palak leaves contain low oxalic acid.
- It is a rich source of Vitamin A and C, also contains protein and iron.

VILYATI PALAK/ SPINACH

(*Spinacea oleracea*)

Family:	Chenopodiaceae
Origin:	Iran
Type of vegetable:	Leafy vegetable
Edible portion:	Leaves
Basic chromosome number:	X = 6
Somatic chromosome number:	2n =12

- It is a long day plant
- It has very high respiration rate which is due to the presence of large leaf surface
- Prickly seeded variety best suited for hilly regions.
- Smooth seeded variety best suited for plains.
- Virginia Savoy is a prickly seeded cultivar of spinach.
- It tolerates frost better than most other vegetables.

AMARANTHUS

(*Amaranthus sp*)

Family:	Amaranthaceae
Origin:	India
Type of vegetable:	Leafy vegetable
Edible portion:	Leaves and stem
Basic chromosome number:	X = 16
Somatic chromosome number:	2n =32

- Warm season crop (most common vegetable grown in summer and rainy season)
- Susceptible to water logging conditions.
- It is a C4 plant.
- It can be grown in soil pH as high as 10.

LETTUCE

(*Lectuca sativa*)

Family: Chenopodiaceae
Origin: Mediterranean region
Type of vegetable: Leafy vegetable
Edible portion: Leafy heads and leaves
Basic chromosome number: X = 9
Somatic chromosome number: 2n =18

- It is a cool season crop.
- Thermo-dormancy is found in lettuce.
- It is a major salad crop of North America.
- Mulching is recommended for lettuce.
- Lettuce is of four types

a) Crisp head b) Butter head
c) Leaf type d) Romine type

- Seed don't germinate properly when soil temperature is more than 22°C.
- High temperature causes a bitter taste of leaves and induces tip burn injury.
- White Boston is butter head type cultivar of lettuce.
- Pre and post harvest spray of BA @ 15-10 ppm help in delaying senescence in storage and improve the shelf life.
- It is better not to harvest lettuce immediately after rain, because leaves being crisp and brittle break easily while handling.

CHINESE CABBAGE

(*Brassica campestris var. pekinensis*)

Family: Brassicaceae
Origin: China
Type of vegetable: Leafy vegetable
Edible portion: Leafy heads and leaves
Basic chromosome number: X = 10
Somatic chromosome number: 2n =20

- Low O_2 (2%) in combination with CO_2 (2%) improves shelf life of Chinese cabbage

PARSLEY

(*Petroselinum crispum*)

Family:	Umbelliferae
Origin:	Ethiopia
Type of vegetable:	Leafy vegetable
Edible portion:	Leafy stalks and petioles
Basic chromosome number:	X = 11
Somatic chromosome number:	2n =22

- Rich source of Fe and Vitamin-C
- Seed rate: 250-300 g/ hac
- 3 types: Plain leafed, double curled and moss curled

CELERY

(*Apium graveolens*)

Family:	Umbelliferae
Origin:	Ethiopia
Type of vegetable:	Leafy vegetable
Edible portion:	Fleshy leaf stalks
Basic chromosome number:	X = 11
Somatic chromosome number:	2n =22

- Propagation by seeds
- Yellow or self blanched: Florida golden, Golden
- Green leaved: Preferred in India. Wrights grove giant, ford hook emperor
- Exposure to high temperature: leads to bitterness in leaves
- Below 15°C bolting takes place

SWEET POTATO

(*Ipomea batata*)

Family:	Convolvulaceae
Origin:	Mexico-Guatemala
Type of vegetable:	Tuber vegetable
Edible portion:	Fleshy leaf stalks
Basic chromosome number:	X = 11
Somatic chromosome number:	2n =22

- India is largest producer in South-East Asia and VIth largest in the world

- It is a perennial vine
- Moderately draught tolerant crop
- Ridge and furrow - best for raising crop
- Excessive rainfall and long photoperiod encourage vide growth, reducing tuber yield
- China - rank 1st in area and production of sweet potato
- Cercospora leaf spot of sweet potato was first reported in Africa
- Propagation by vine cutting (40000 vine cutting/hac)

CASSAVA Or TAPIOCA

(*Manihot esculenta*)

Family:	Euphorbiaceae
Origin:	Brazil-Paraguay
Type of vegetable:	Tuber vegetable
Edible portion:	Tubers
Basic chromosome number:	X = 36
Somatic chromosome number:	2n =72

- Major starchy root crop of tropics (tropical crop)
- The plant is perennial shrub
- Yellow colour of flesh is due to presence of carotene
- It is drought tolerant crop
- Vascular blue lining or `Vascular streaking' is present in cassava
- Cassava is photo insensitive crop
- Sago important food product derived from cassava starch

YAMS

(*Dioscorea spp*)

Family:	Dioscoreaceae
Origin:	Indo-Burma, Malaya
Type of vegetable:	Tuber vegetable
Edible portion:	Tubers
Basic chromosome number:	X = 20
Somatic chromosome number:	2n =40

- Greater Yam: also known as Ratalu (water yam)
- Fuyu is a product made from yam

- Yam flour is also used for human consumption as Kokoote
- Africa alone produce 90% tuber and cover 95% area
- Chinese Yam, Asiatic Yam are common name of lesser yam
- Lesser Yam matures early as compare to other spp.
- Lesser Yam is sweeter than other yam

ELEPHANT'S FOOT

(*Amorphophallus campanulatus*)

Family:	Araceae
Origin:	Indo-Burma
Type of vegetable:	Tuber vegetable
Edible portion:	Tubers
Basic chromosome number:	X = 13, 14
Somatic chromosome number:	2n =26, 28

- Blood purifier
- Propagation - By tubers
- Harvest : 7-8 months after planting
- Paste of this yam is used to reduce pain

COLEUS (CHINESE POTATO)

(*Solenostemon rotundifolius*)

Family:	Labiatae
Origin:	Africa
Type of vegetable:	Tuber vegetable
Edible portion:	Tubers

Propagation - By vine cuttings, Sucker, tuber

QUEENSLAND ARROWROOT

(*Canna indica L.*)

West Indian Arrowroot

(*Maranta arundinacea L.*)

Origin:	South America
Type of vegetable:	Tuber vegetable
Edible portion:	Tubers

- It is used for production of carbonless paper for computer print
- Biscuit of it is popular in India

JERUSALEM ARTICHOKE

(*Helianthus tuberosus*)

Origin:	United States
Type of vegetable:	Tuber vegetable
Edible portion:	Tubers

- It is commercial source of levulose, used as sweetening agent by diabetic patients
- Glucofratons - Principle carbohydrates in tubers

COLOCASIA Or TARO

(*Colocasia esculenta*)

Family:	Araceae
Origin:	Indo-Burma
Type of vegetable:	Tuber vegetable
Edible portion:	Tubers

- Propagation - By cormels
- Africa Rank 1st in area and production of taro
- Eddoe type is most prevalent as vegetable

YAM BEAN

(*Pachyrrhizus erosus*)

Family:	Leguminoseae
Origin:	Indo-Burma
Type of vegetable:	Tuber vegetable
Edible portion:	Fleshy Tubers
Basic chromosome number:	X = 11
Somatic chromosome number:	2n =22

- Propagation - By seeds
- Eddoe : Colocasia esuenta var. antiquorum.
- Desheen/ Bonda : Colocasia esculenta var esculenta.

BREAD FRUIT

(*Artocarpus altilis*)

Family:	Leguminoseae
Origin:	Malaysia
Basic chromosome number:	X = 28
Somatic chromosome number:	2n =56

- Variety: Yellow Heart
- Stimulative parthenocarpy is found in bread fruit
- Propagation - By root cuttings

DRUMSTICK

(*Moringa Oleifera*)

Family: Moringaceae
Origin: Indo-Burma, Malaya
Basic chromosome number: X = 14
Somatic chromosome number: 2n =28

- In India, it is commercially grown in Tamil Nadu.
- Deciduous crop, flowers are white in colour.
- Drought tolerant crop. It is a tropical crop.
- Fruit weight - 230 g containing 10-20 seeds each.
- It contains an oil called behen oil.

ASPARAGUS

(*Asparagus officinalis L.*)

Family: Liliaceae
Origin: Mediterranean region
Type of vegetable: Leafy vegetable
Edible portion: Spears, stems

- Tender shoots called `spears' are used as vegetable
- Spear contain `asparagine' which is used in medicine as diuretic in cardiac dropsy and chronic gout
- Blanching is done to produce white asparagus.

GLOBE ARTICHOKE

(*Cynara scolymus*)

Family: Asteraceae/compositae
Origin: United States
Type of vegetable: Leafy vegetable
Edible portion: Flower head/buds

RHUBARB

(*Rheum rhaponticum*)

Family: Polygonaceae
Origin: Mediterranean region
Type of vegetable: Leafy
Edible portion: leaf stalk or petiole

- It is a cold resistant plant
- Propagation - By corns

CHOW - CHOW

(*Sechium edule*)

Family:	Cucurbitaceae
Origin:	Mexico
Type of vegetable:	Green vegetable
Edible portion:	Pear shaped fruits
Basic chromosome number:	X = 14
Somatic chromosome number:	2n =28

- Single seeded fruit
- Richest source of nutrition among gourds
- Fruits are vivipary in nature
- Propagation - by sprouted fruits

CHEKURMANIS (MADURA KEERA)

(*Sauropus androgynus*)

Family:	Leguminoseae
Origin:	India
Type of vegetable:	Leafy vegetable
Edible portion:	Leaves and tender shoots
Basic chromosome number:	X = 11
Somatic chromosome number:	2n =22

- It is also known as vegetable of 21st centry
- Due to high nutritive value, it is commonly called as "Multivitamin greens"
- Propagation : By stem cuttings

MULTIPLE CHOICE QUESTIONS

1. Vegetables on the basis of nutrition are called

   a) Staple foods b) Protective foods
   c) Health foods d) Organic foods

2. Which of the following is a root vegetable?

   a) Onion b) Garlic
   c) Carrot d) Leek

3. The mushrooms are

   a) Algae b) Fungi
   c) Seed sprouts d) None of these

4. Potato, sweet potato and tapioca crops falls in group of

   a) Tubers b) Roots
   c) Bulbs d) Pods

5. The green pigments of leaves and stem usually held close to the cell wall in small bodies called

   a) Carotenes b) Anthocyanin
   c) Xanthophylls d) Chloroplasts

6. First commercial transgenic crop is

   a) Tomato b) Cotton
   c) Soybean d) Brinjal

7. Water insoluble pigment(s) is/are

   a) Chlorophyll-a b) Chlorophyll-b
   c) Carotenoids d) All of these

8. Which of the following carotene is valuable in the synthesis of vitamin-A?

   a) α-carotene b) β-carotene
   c) γ-carotene d) None of these

9. Flavonoids are classified into

   a) Anthocyanins b) Anthoxanthins
   c) Both a & b d) None of these

10. The anthoxanthins are ____________ in colour.

a) Blue
b) White
c) Red purple
d) Black

11. Anthocyanins are present in the ______________ of the plant cells.

a) Vacuole
b) Chloroplast
c) Chromoplast
d) Golgi bodies

12. Beta-cyanins and Beta-xanthins are together known as

a) Anthoxanthins
b) Betalains
c) Enzymes
d) Carotenoids

13. On which type of soil sweet pepper grows best

a) Black
b) Sandy loam
c) Clay
d) Red latrite

14. Capsicum seedlings are transplanted at a spacing of

a) 60 x 30 cm
b) 40 x 40 cm
c) 1 x 1 m
d) 80 x 45 cm

15. A common practice before shipping to check moisture loss and bruising during transit is

a) Tenting
b) Thinning
c) Waxing
d) Pruning

16. Bitter taste in brinjal fruit is due to

a) CN glycocides
b) Solasodine
c) Anti-vitamin-E factor
d) Trypsin inhibitors

17. Edible portion of artichoke

a) Root
b) Fruit
c) Leaves
d) Flower buds

18. Edible portion of cucumber

a) Fleshy receptacle
b) Placentae
c) Mesocarp, endocarp, placentae
d) Pericarp, endocarp

19. The limiting amino acid in green vegetables

a) Methionine
b) Tryptophan
c) Lysine
d) Argnine

20. Edible podded cultivar of Pea

a) Arkel
b) Bonneville
c) Perfection new line
d) Sylvia

21. Compound responsible for medicine value in green chilli

a) Rutin
b) Resin
c) Capsaicin
d) Solanum

22. Potato tuber production is maximum at

a) 15ºC
b) 20ºC
c) 25ºC
d) 30ºC

23. The young potato plant grows best at

a) 16ºC
b) 20ºC
c) 24ºC
d) 25ºC

24. In general, potato needs ________ mm irrigation water for the optimum production.

a) 500
b) 600
c) 700
d) 800

25. Elephant yam corms weigh 6.8-9.0 kg at the end of

a) Fourth year
b) Third year
c) Second year
d) Fifth year

26. One gram of onion generally contains – – – seeds.

a) 180
b) 240
c) 300
d) 360

27. Garlic freezes at the average temperature of

a) -2ºC
b) -5ºC
c) -3ºC
d) -4ºC

28. The best storage temperature for garlic is 0 to 2.2°C with relative humidity of

a) 60 %
b) 50 %
c) 40 %
d) 30 %

29. Garden pea was an important crop in eleventh century in – – –

a) England
b) Poland
c) Holland
d) New Zealand

30. Garden pea was probably distinguished from field pea in 1536, but their common use began after the year

a) 1586
b) 1600
c) 1775
d) 1700

31. One gram of celery seed holds about ....seeds.

a) 1570
b) 2470
c) 2000
d) 2070

32. Celery seed takes nearly ____________ to germinate.

a) 10 days
b) 20 days
c) 30 days
d) 40 days

33. Chromosome number of Globe artichoke is

a) 2n=34
b) 2n=32
c) 2n=24
d) 2n=28

34. Browning of cauliflower is caused by the deficiency of

a) Zinc
b) Manganese
c) Copper
d) Boron

35. Fastening of vines to an upright support of a tree called Pangare (*Erithrina indica*) is known as– – – –

a) Kniffin system
b) Head system
c) Single-stake system
d) Cordon system

36. The cold storage temperature for melons is 0^0C and having relative humidity of

a) 50-60% b) 60-70%
c) 40-50% d) 80-90%

37. The seed rate of long melon is _______ kg/ ha)

a) 1 - 2 b) 2 - 3
c) 2 - 4 d) 4 - 5

38. Cucumber (*Cucumis sativus* Var kheera) was demonstrated by the ancient Greeks and Romans in about _____BC

a) 100 b) 500
c) 200 d) 400

39. Flowering in pumpkin (*Cucurbita moschata*) starts ________ days after sowing.

a) 60 – 80 b) 50 – 60
c) 30 – 40 d) 85 – 95

40. Bottle gourd was being cultivated in India even before

a) 500 BC b) 2000 BC
c) 1500 BC d) 1000 BC

41. _________ is the cultivar of bottle gourd.

a) Pusa Meghdoot b) CO-1
c) Australian Green d) Straight Eight

42. The number of seeds per 100 g bitter gourd is about ______.

a) 350 b) 450
c) 550 d) 650

43. Turnip (*Brassica campestris*) was introduced in England probably in ______ while in 1606 in USA.

a) 1590 b) 1490
c) 1390 d) 1290

44. One gram of turnip seed holds _______ seeds.

a) 460 – 500 b) 360 – 460
c) 560 – 660 d) 260 – 360

45. One gram radish contains about _____ seeds.

a) 650 b) 550

c) 750 d) 850

46. Carrot seed will not germinate below _____.

a) 7.9°C b) 5.9°C

c) 6.9°C d) 3.9°C

47. On weight basis _____ kg of cutting of sweet potato are required per hectare.

a) 300 b) 400

c) 500 d) 600

48. The seed rate (g/ha) of tomato is

a) 400-500 b) 600-900

c) 1000-1100 d) 100-150

49. The yield of tomato (tones/ ha) is

a) 40-45 b) 20-25

c) 10-15 d) 50-55

50. Which of the following is not a variety of tomato?

a) Pusa Ruby b) Best of all

c) Roma d) Pusa Kranti

51. Which of the following are the varieties of tomato?

a) Kalyanpur Angurlata b) T-1

c) Pusa Early Dwarf d) All of these

52. The yield of brinjal (tones/ha) is

a) 15-20 b) 25-30

c) 30-40 d) 40-50

53. Which of the following is not a variety of brinjal?

a) Pusa Purple Long b) Pusa Kranti

c) Black Beauty d) Pusa Jawala

54. Which of the following are the varieties of sweet chilly?

a) Pant C-1 b) California Wonder
c) Arka Mohini d) All of these

55. The seed rate of onion is

a) 10-12 kg/ ha b) 15-20 kg/ ha
c) 1-2 kg/ha d) None of these

56. Which of the following are the varieties of onion?

a) Pusa Red b) Arka Pragati
c) Arka Niketan d) All of these

57. The seed rate of radish is

a) 12 kg/ ha b) 5 kg/ ha
c) 25 kg/ ha d) None of these

58. The yield of radish is

a) 2-5 tonnes/ ha b) 20-30 tonnes/ha
c) 15-40 tonnes/ ha d) None of these

59. Which of the following are the varieties of radish?

a) Pusa Himani b) Rapid Red White
c) Fresh Breakfast d) All of these

60. Edible part of potato is scientifically termed as

a) Tuber b) Rhizome
c) Corn d) Chisome

61. Edible part of onion is called

a) Corm b) Tuber
c) Bulb d) Rhizome

62. Among vegetables ____ has more of vitamin-A and vitamin-C

a) Potato b) Tomato
c) Brinjal d) Table chilies

63. What constitute bulb of onion?

a) Fleshy scales
b) Fleshy sepals
c) Fleshy corolla
d) Fleshy petals

64. Sweet potato is propagated by

a) Seeds
b) Buddings
c) Root cuttings
d) Vine cuttings

65. Garlic is propagated by

a) Cloves
b) Seeds
c) Scales
d) Bulbs

66. Branch of science that deals with study of principles of propagation and production of fruits is called

a) Olericulture
b) Floriculture
c) Pomology
d) Entomology

67. The plants bearing male and female flowers on the same plant are called

a) Monophrodite
b) Monoecious
c) Bisexual
d) Hermophrodite

68. Raw carrots are good source of

a) Vitamin A
b) Vitamin B
c) Vitamin K
d) Vitamin E

69. Edible part of Chinese cabbage is

a) Young shoots
b) blanched stem and leaves
c) Heads consisting of flower buds
d) loose leafy heads

70. Beri-Beri and Anaemia are caused by the deficiency of

a) Vitamin-A
b) Vitamin-B
c) Vitamin-C
d) Vitamin-D

71. For preparing tomato ketchup, the tomato should have

a) Green colour
b) Yellow colour
c) High TSS
d) None of these

72. The most important quality of an onion for dehydration for export should have

a) Red colour
b) White colour
c) Brownish yellow
d) None of these

73. The most serious disease of okra is

a) Powdery mildew
b) Root rot
c) Yellow vein mosaic
d) None of these of the above

74. DCT-1, DCT-2 and Cherry wonder are the important varieties of

a) Lettuce
b) Chinese cabbage
c) Cherry tomato
d) Sprouting Broccoli

75. Per hectare yield of asparagus is

a) 4-5 tonnes
b) 8-10 tonnes
c) 1-4 tonnes
d) 10-15tonnes

76. Blue colour tags are used for ________ seed production

a) Nuclear
b) Certified
c) Foundation
d) Registered

77. Blue colour tags are used for

a) Nuclear seed
b) Certified seed
c) Foundation seed
d) Registered seed

78. Cat face is a physiological disorder of

a) Potato
b) Cabbage
c) Tomato
d) Chillies

79. Ideal trap crop for tomato fruit borer is

a) Marigold
b) Tobacco
c) Mustard
d) Potato

80. White colour tags are used for ________ seed production

a) Nuclear
b) Certified
c) Foundation
d) Registered

81. The physiological disorder caused by Boron deficiency in tomato is

a) Puffiness
b) Cracking
c) Blossom end rot
d) Silvering

82. In our diet, staple vegetable is

a) Brinjal
b) Chillies
c) Tomato
d) Potato

83. Pusa Sawani, 'Pusa Makhmali' and Perkin's Long Green are varieties of

a) Bhindi
b) Squash melon
c) Cluster Bean
d) Lobia bean

84. Vitamin that is said to be essential for clotting of blood is

a) A
b) E
c) K
d) A and E

85. Lady finger can be grown throughout the year in

a) Central India
b) Southern India
c) Both a and b
d) Northern Indian Plains

86. Scientific name of painted bug in Cole crop is

a) *Plutella xylostella*
b) *Bagrada cruciferum*
c) *Brevicoryne brassicae*
d) *Agritis segetum*

87. *Trialeurodes vaporariorum* is known as

a) Cut worm
b) Fruit fly
c) Fruit borer
d) Green house whitefly

88. Potato tuber production is the maximum at

a) 15 ºC
b) 20 ºC
c) 25 ºC
d) 30 ºC

89. Scientific name of Pea leaf minor is

a) *Helicoverpa armigera* b) *Eteilla zinckenella*
c) *Caliothrips indicus* d) *Chromatomyia horticola*

90. One gram of onion contains _____ seeds.

a) 180 b) 300
c) 240 d) 360

91. Edible part of sweet potato is.

a) Underground stem b) Underground root
c) Both these d) None of these

92. 'Elephant Yam' corms (buds) weighing 100-200 g are used for planting of the ____ years crop.

a) First b) Second
c) Three d) Fourth

93. Where we have to contact to produce fresh seeds of Potato?

a) New Delhi b) Shimla
c) Lucknow d) Darjeeling

94. Vegetables are rich source of

a) Carbohydrates b) Proteins
c) Vitamin d) None of these

95. Vegetables are packed in cans and processed by heat in

a) Retort b) Water bath
c) Sun d) None of these

96. In cucurbits, the crop which is dioecious in nature is

a) Bottle gourd b) Pointed gourd
c) Muskmelon d) Watermelon

97. Scientific name of Chinese chive is

a) *Allium porrum* b) *Allium cepa* var. *viviporum*
c) *Allium tuberosum* d) *Allium fistulosum*

98. In onion, bolting takes place due to

a) High temperature
b) Low temperature
c) High nitrogen
d) Deficiency of nitrogen

99. In potato 'Hollow heart' is due to

a) Excessive water and fertilization
b) Excessive watering & high temperature
c) Excessive watering and cutting
d) Excessive watering & low temperature

100. Samutsen is also known as

a) Indra's heaven
b) Wooden house
c) Curved stream
d) None of these

101. The minimum isolation distance of okra for certified seed should be

a) 100 m
b) 400 m
c) 500 m
d) 200 m

102. How many types of seed legislation in India is/are available?

a) 3
b) 2
c) 1
d) 4

103. *Momordica balsamina* is also known as

a) African cucumber
b) Balsam Apple
c) Balsam pear
d) All of these

104. The type of seed legislation

a) Control legislation
b) Sanctioning legislation
c) Both a & b
d) None of these

105. The Central Seed Testing Laboratory (CSTL) is located at

a) Patna
b) New Delhi
c) W.B.
c) None of these

106. The minimum purity percentage for labeling purpose of Chinese cabbage should be

a) 89% b) 98%
c) 95% d) 70%

107. The minimum purity percentage for seed standards of lettuce should be

a) 70% b) 85%
c) 98% d) 96%

108. Under the Seed Act 1966, which section is related to the "forfeiting of property"

a) Section 18 b) Section 21
c) Section 20 d) Section 15

109. In which year the "criminal procedure code" was passed

a) 1988 b) 1898
c) 1899 d) 1989

110. *Solanum lycopersicon* is a __________ crop

a) Cross pollinated b) Self pollinated
c) Self incompatible d) a & b

111. Asian Vegetable Research Development Centre (AVRDC) is situated at

a) India b) Geneva
c) Taiwan d) New York

112. For hybrid seed production of tomato favourable day temperature should be

a) 15-20°C b) 21-25°C
c) 10-15°C d) 28°C

113. The moisture required for safe storage of tomato seeds

a) 5% b) 6-8%
c) 14% d) 5-6%

114. Generally the sex ratio in cucurbits varied from 1:20 to

a) 1:30 b) 1:45
c) 1:34 d) 1:40

115. The seed requirement for one hectare planting of Palak is

a) 5-9 kg b) 15-20 kg
c) 25-30 kg d) 2-3 kg

116. Which variety of tomato is suitable for long distance transportation

a) Hisar Lalima b) Pant Bahar
c) Punjab Chhuhara d) SL 120

117. Brinjal is a __________ crop

a) Self pollinated
b) Cross pollinated
c) Often cross pollinated
d) Self fertile

118. The minimum isolation distance for foundation & certified seed production of brinjal is

a) 200m & 400m b) 100m & 200 m
c) 200m & 100m d) None of these

119. Yield of brinjal per hectare for hybrid seed is

a) 150-200 kg b) 150-200 g
c) 4 kg d) 400 kg

120. The variety with less seeded fruit is

a) Pusa Kranti b) Arka Navneet
c) Arka Kusumakar d) a & b

121. Which of the following is the biennial vegetable

a) Muskmelon b) Tomato
c) Onion d) Chilli

122. The amount of natural cross pollination for brinjal is

a) 10% b) 12.5%
c) 16.5% d) 18%

123. The gene responsible for the colour of brinjal is

a) Capsaicin
b) Anthocyanin
c) Beta carotene
d) None of these

124. For induction of mutations, seeds to be treated should have moisture of

a) 10%
b) 13%
c) 18%
d) 2%

125. The planting ratio of male : female for sweet pepper is

a) 1:4
b) 1:5
c) 2:1
d) 2:5

126. The planting ratio of male : female for chilli pepper is

a) 1:5
b) 1:20
c) 1:10
d) None of these

127. After seed extraction the drying in the seed drier should be done at

a) 15°C
b) 20°C
c) 25°C
d) 30°C

128. The optimum temperature for pollen germination is

a) 15-18°C
b) 20-25°C
c) 25-30°C
d) 10-15°C

129. 1000 seed weight of pungent type peppers is

a) 5 g
b) 3.5 g
c) 7 g
d) 10 g

130. Maturity time of Muskmelon in North India is

a) June-July
b) Sept-Oct.
c) Nov-Dec
d) Feb-March

131. The amount of natural cross pollination in okra is up to

a) 10%
b) 19%
c) 16%
d) 39%

132. The minimum isolation distance for certified seed production of okra is

a) 400 m b) 200 m
c) 1000 m d) 1600 m

133. In cabbage for seed production, a minimum of ______ inspections should be made.

a) 3 b) 5
c) 2 d) 6

134. Garden pea is a ____________ crop.

a) Cross pollinated b) Self pollinated
c) Self incompatible d) Both a & b

135. The minimum isolation distance for foundation seed production of pea is

a) 100 m b) 20 m
c) 10 m d) 200 m

136. In French bean rouging is done for____ time(s).

a) 4 b) 2
c) 3 d) 1

137. Seed weight of 1000 French beans is

a) 150 g b) 250-600 g
c) 400-800 g d) 100- 200 g

138. Seed yield per hectare in French bean is

a) 200-400 kg b) 1000 kg
c) 1500-2000 kg d) 500 kg

139. Which of the following varieties have the highest yield in French bean

a) Contender b) Arka Komal
c) Pant Anupama d) VL Boni 1

140. An isolation distance of_____ is sufficient to avoid cross pollination in cowpea.

a) 50 m b) 3 m
c) 20 m d) 4 m

141. A siliqua of a cauliflower contains________ seeds.

a) 4 b) 10-30
c) 40 d) 9

142. One quintal of sugar beet contains ________ of sugar.

a) 8 kg b) 10 kg
c) 12 kg d) 17 kg

143. The minimum isolation distance for certified seed production of cauliflower is

a) 200 m b) 1600 m
c) 1000 m d) 500 m

144. Which of the following cauliflower variety belongs to late group?

a) Early Kunwari b) Snowball-16
c) Pusa Deepati d) Pusa Subhra

145. The yield obtained from one hectare of cauliflower production is

a) 80 quintals b) 400 kg
c) 700 kg d) 100 quintals

146. The best temperature for curding in cabbage is

a) 20°C b) 12-16°C
c) 10°C d) 4°C

147. In cabbage for raising nursery for one hectare area, seed rate is

a) 500-600g b) 1 kg
c) 100g d) 1.5kg

148. The seed yield of cabbage per hectare area is approximately

a) 700 kg b) 1000 kg
c) 300 kg d) 400 kg

149. "Pride of India" is a variety of

a) Tomato b) Chilli
c) Cabbage d) Cauliflower

150. Chenopodiaceae is the family of

a) Potato b) Sweet Potato
c) Okra d) Spinach

151. Which seed production method is used for radish?

a) Seed - Seed b) Root – Seed
c) Both a & b d) None of these

152. Purple colour variety of sprouting broccoli is

a) Italian Green b) Palampur Samridhi
c) Green Head d) DBPG-1

153. The minimum isolation distance for certified seed production of radish is

a) 1600 m b) 1000 m
c) 400 m d) 500 m

154. Seed production of onion is done by_______ method.

a) Stump to seed b) Bulb to Seed
c) Core intact method d) Both a & b

155. Seed maturity for onion takes _________ days after anthesis.

a) 20-30 b) 15-20
c) 35-50 d) 50-60

156. Seed yield per hectare for open pollinated cultivars of onion is

a) 100-500 kg b) 500-1000 kg
c) 2000 kg d) 1500 kg

157. The minimum isolation distance for cucumber certified & foundation seed production is

a) 400 & 800 m b) 200 & 400 m
c) 500 & 800 m d) 600 & 700 m

158. Muskmelon produces inviable seed when crossed with

a) Water melon b) Cucumber
c) Squash melon d) both a & b

159. Which of the following is the variety of watermelon

a) Pusa Jyoti b) Arka jyoti
c) Arka Nishant d) None of these

160. Average yield (qt/ha) of Okra in Kharif season is

a) 60-70 b) 100-150
c) 250-300 d) 500

161. Arka Niketan (Red Onion) developed at

a) IARI, New Delhi b) IIHR,Banglore
c) PAU, Ludhiana d) UHF-Nauni

162. The sum total of all the attributes that gives effective plant stand in the field is called

a) Seed lot b) Seed Germination
c) Seed vigour d) None of these

163. Dapog is a term associated with

a) Seed-bed preparation b) Inter Cultivation
c) Digging of soil d) Nursery raising

164. Which of the following seed programmes consist of establishing a national agency

a) Official seed programme b) Semi- official
c) Private d) Both b & c

165. Isolation distance maintenance falls under which principles

a) Agronomic b) Genetic
c) Both a & b d) None of these

166. The minimum isolation distance for certified seed production of spinach is

a) 200 m b) 1000 m
c) 400 m d) 800 m

167. The seed yield (kg/ ha) of spinach is

a) 500-700 kg b) 1500-2000 kg
c) 1000-1500 kg d) 400-500 kg

168. A growth hormone sprayed for fruit setting in tomato under adverse condition is

a) Cycocel (CCC) b) 2, 4-D

c) PCPA d) Etheral

169. The amount of cross pollination in lettuce varies between

a) 25-30% b) 1-6%

c) 10-12% d) 30-35%

170. The minimum isolation distance for foundation seed production of lettuce is

a) 50 m b) 25 m

c) 10 m d) 100 m

171. Lettuce is harvested when _______ per cent of the seeds in the heads show white pappus.

a) 20-25 b) 30- 50

c) 10-15 d) 40-80

172. The seed yield (kg/ ha) of the variety "Great Lakes" of lettuce is

a) 500-600 kg b) 100-125 kg

c) 200-400 kg d) 1000 kg

173. The minimum isolation distance for certified seed production of Amaranthus is

a) 400 m b) 200 m

c) 500 m d) 1000 m

174. The seed rate (kg/ ha) in Amaranthus is

a) 15-25 kg b) 1.5-2.5 kg

c) 10 -12 kg d) 50 kg

175. The seed yield (per ha) of Amaranthus is

a) 200 kg b) 2-3 quintals

c) 500 kg d) 1000 kg

176. The minimum isolation distance for methi foundation seed production is

a) 100 m
b) 10 m
c) 5 m
d) 50 m

177. Seed plot technique is used for the seed production of

a) Tomato
b) Potato
c) Brinjal
d) Pepper

178. There are about_______ organized seed companies in India in 2011.

a) 150-200
b) 500
c) 400
d) 250

179. TPS technique is done in which vegetable

a) Tomato
b) Potato
c) Bitter gourd
d) All of these

180. For the production of TPS, the extracted seeds are treated with

a) HCl
b) NaOH
c) HNO_3
d) H_2SO_4

181. The minimum isolation distance for growing TPS is about

a) 50 m
b) 100m
c) 1000 m
d) 1600 m

182. Cassava is a___________ crop.

a) Self pollinated
b) Cross pollinated
c) Self fertile
d) All of these

183. The minimum isolation distance for foundation seed production of bitter gourd is

a) 400 m
b) 800 m
c) 200 m
d) 1000 m

184. Seed rate per hectare for tomato is

a) 100 – 200 gm b) 900 – 1000 gm
c) 400 – 500 gm d) 800 – 900 gm

185. Dehauling in potato is done to obtain

a) Quality seed tuber b) Higher yield
c) High protein & carbohydrate d) High starch contents

186. The air distribution systems used for seed drying is

a) Main & lateral duct system
b) Single central perforated duct
c) Perforated false floor
d) All of these

187. A seed drier requires ....of heat output to evaporate 1 pound of water.

a) 2000 BTU b) 1000 BTU
c) 500 BTU d) 1500 BTU

188. Seed rate (Kg/hectare) for long melon is

a) 6-8 b) 8-10
c) 3-7 d) 1.5-2.0

189. The final seed sample which is used for further test purposes is called

a) Primary sample b) Composite sample
c) Working sample d) Submitted sample

190. The total working sample for brinjal seed test is

a) 400 g b) 150 g
c) 200 g d) 100 g

191. ________ bean is the only winter season leguminous crop.

a) Broad b) Sem
c) Lobia d) Guar

192. The equipment used for germination of seeds is

a) Cabinet type germinator b) B. O.D.
c) Walk-in-room germinator d) Both a & c

193. Solan Nirog and Bonneville are important varieties of

a) French bean
b) Capsicum
c) Tomato
d) Green Pea

194. Embryo Excision Test is done to determine the viability of

a) Vegetable seed
b) Tree seed
c) Flower seed
d) All of above

195. The direct vigour test can be done by

a) Brick gravel test
b) Paper piercing test
c) Accelerated ageing test
d) All of these

196. In accelerated ageing of vigour test, the seeds are aged at a temperature of

a) 100°C
b) 40-45°C
c) 50°C
d) 20°C

197. Seed moisture is determined by

a) Phosphorus pentoxide
b) Karl Fischer
c) B. O.D.
d) Both a & b

198. Phosphorus pentoxide method of soil moisture determination was given by

a) Karl Fischer
b) Leendertz
c) Richharia
d) N.K. Nair

199. International Crop Improvement Association was organized for the first time in

a) 1950
b) 1919
c) 1920
d) 1947

200. The Seed Act came into existence in India in

a) 1966
b) 1969
c) 1963
d) 1956

201. In a balanced diet _______ of vegetables are needed.

a) 120g b) 300g
c) 92g d) 150g

202. The deficiency of Vitamin A causes

a) Pneumonia b) Diarrhoea
c) Night blindness d) All of above

203. The deficiency of Vitamin B_1 causes

a) Beriberi b) Diarrhoea
c) Night blindness d) Pneumonia

204. The deficiency of Vitamin C causes

a) Rickets b) Pellagra
c) Scurvy d) Beriberi

205. Leafy vegetables like cabbage, lettuce and vegetable oils are main source of

a) Vitamin C b) Vitamin B_1
c) Vitamin D d) Vitamin E

206. Pusa Naveen is a variety of

a) Bottle guard b) Bitter gourd
c) Peas d) Cauliflower

207. Which state in India is the largest producer of vegetables?

a) Karnataka b) Gujarat
c) Punjab d) Uttar Pradesh

208. In polyhouse, gynoecious cucumber usually come in bearing within _____ days of transplanting.

a) 60-80 days b) 60-70 days
c) 20-25 days d) 30-40 days

209. Vegetables neutralize the ______ formed during digestion of meat and other fatty foods.

a) Gases b) Toxins
c) Acids d) None of these

210. _______ is/are the main source of Vitamin D.

a) Sun
b) Leafy vegetables
c) Potato
d) All of above

211. How many dicot vegetable families are important to human beings?

a) 5
b) 6
c) 4
d) 7

212. How many monocot vegetable families are important to human beings?

a) 7
b) 9
c) 10
d) 13 or morc

213. Typical characters of gymnospermae plants are

a) Ovules naked only
b) Ovules naked, not enclosed in an ovary
c) Ovules enclosed in ovary
d) None of these

214. Typical characters of angiospermae plants are

a) Ovules enclosed in a carpel
b) Ovules not enclosed in an ovary
c) Ovules naked
d) None of these

215. According to respiration rate, cucumber is a_______ vegetable.

a) Climacteric
b) Non climacteric
c) Both a & b
d) None of these

216. __________ is a climacteric plant

a) Tomato
b) Cucumber
c) Potato
d) Cabbage

217. The Indian Patent Act was passed during the year

a) 1993
b) 1994
c) 1992
d) 1970

218. The Protection of Plant Varieties and Farmers Right (PPVFR) Act was passed in the year

a) 1856 b) 2001
c) 1999 d) 1956

219. Which of the following is/are long day plant

a) Cabbage b) Lettuce
c) Carrot d) All of these

220. Solanaceous crops are

a) Day Neutral b) Short Day
c) Long Day d) None of these

221. Highly tolerant plant (pH = 6.0 - 8.5) to soil acidity

a) Potato b) Watermelon
c) Okra d) Fennel

222. Whiptail in cauliflower is caused by

a) Excess of boron b) Deficiency of boron
c) Deficiency of Molybdenum d) Deficiency of Calcium

223. Yellow coloured fruits and vegetables are rich source of

a) Vitamin-E b) Vitamin-B
c) Vitamin-A d) Vitamin-C

224. Which of following has very high lime requirement?

a) Chilli b) Onion
c) Both a and b d) Cucumber

225. The largest brinjal producing country in the world is

a) India b) Nigeria
c) Africa d) China

226. The largest chilli producing country in the world is

a) India b) Nigeria
c) China d) USA

227. Hydro-priming is mainly used for

a) Tomato b) Radish
c) Cauliflower d) All of these

228. The induction of flowering due to low temperature is called

a) Chilling b) Vernalisation
c) Germination d) Etiolation

229. For fruit setting in tomato, optimum temperature is

a) 15 - 20°C b) 21 - 23°C
c) 25 -30°C d) 25°C

230. For subsequent growth and tuberization, a temperature of______ is needed.

a) 15° C b) 25° C
c) 18 – 20° C d) 20 – 25° C

231. In onion, formation of bulb is favoured by

a) Low temperature b) High temperature
c) Moderate d) None of these

232. In potato Black Night Shade is a weed host responsible for

a) White rust b) Black leg
c) Stem rust d) Wilting

233. Optimum temperature for curd formation in cauliflower

a) 17° C b) 20° C
c) 30° C d) 25° C

234. In sweet potato, sweetness is enhanced by high RH of

a) 75% b) 70%
c) 80% d) 85%

235. Tomato leaf curl virus is transmitted by

a) Aphid b) Whitefly
c) Butter fly d) Grasshopper

236. Which of the following is a stem vegetable ?

a) Sweet potato
b) Knol khol
c) Carrot
d) Radish

237. The striking effect of photo-periodic flowering was discovered by Garner and Allard

a) 1915
b) 1920
c) 1910
d) 1925

238. How many nutrient elements are essential for plant growth ?

a) 16
b) 17
c) 14
d) 13

239. Which of the following option is not a macro-nutrient?

a) Nitrogen
b) Calcium
c) Boron
d) Magnesium

240. Which of the following is a micro nutrient ?

a) Sulphur
b) Zinc
c) Phosphorus
d) Potassium

241. Onion bulb is constituted from

a) Flesh petals
b) Fleshy sepals
c) Fleshy scales
d) All of these

242. ________________ promotes rapid early growth and accelerates development

a) Nitrogen
b) Zinc
c) Phosphorus
d) Boron

243. __________ helps in the formation of starch and translocation of sugar

a) Hydrogen
b) Carbon
c) Potassium
d) Magnesium

244. Formation of oil is due to

a) Magnesium
b) Molybdenum
c) Chlorine
d) Calcium

245. Blossom end rot in tomato is due to the deficiency of

a) Mo
b) Ca
c) Mg
d) Zn

246. Manganese helps in formation of

a) Oil
b) Sugar
c) Chlorophyll
d) Starch

247. Iron deficiency causes

a) Shortened internodes
b) Browning
c) Defoliation
d) Intervienal chlorosis

248. Nitrogen fixing ability in plants is due to

a) Magnesium
b) Manganese
c) Iron
d) Molybdenum

249. Molybdenum effect was first demonstrated in 1939 by

a) Warington
b) Garner and Allard
c) Arnon and Stout
d) None of these

250. Physiological role of auxins is

a) Apical dominance
b) Removal of dormancy
c) Induction of parthenocarpy
d) Stimulation of cell enlargement

251. Function of Gibberellins is

a) Shedding of leaves
b) Cell elongation
c) Breaking seed dormancy
d) Cell division

252. Ethylene is a gaseous hormone, it

a) Induces dormancy
b) Inhibits seed germination
c) Promotes senescence
d) Induces ripening

253. Which of the following has more of vitamin A and vitamin C ?

a) Brinjal
b) Cauliflower
c) Table chilies
d) Tomato

254. Surface irrigation includes flooding and

a) Drip irrigation b) Sprinkler irrigation
c) Furrow irrigation d) Trickle irrigation

255. In which method of irrigation, non-corrosive perforated tubes are placed on the soil surface or in furrows ?

a) Sprinkler irrigation b) Basin irrigation
c) Furrow irrigation d) Drip irrigation

256. Water requirement in leafy vegetables is

a) High b) Low
c) Moderate d) Very low

257. Irrigation method by which water is saved is

a) Sprinkler irrigation b) Drip irrigation
c) Basin irrigation d) Surface irrigation

258. When two or more crops are grown at the same time on a piece of land, it is called

a) Sequential cropping b) Relay cropping
c) Inter cropping d) Mixed cropping

259. 1st herbicide produced in world is

a) 2, 4-D b) Banavel-D
c) Semazin d) Atrazine

260. Which one of the following is an odd cropping system

a) Turmeric + Maize b) Potato + Radish
c) Cabbage + Radish d) Cauliflower + Cabbage

261. The active principle causing 'Sorghum poisoning' is

a) Aspirin b) Caffein
c) Dhurrin d) Capsaicin

262. A crop having high water requirement is followed by a crop having

a) Low water requirement b) Non-water requirement
c) High water requirement d) None of these

263. The system involving raising of crops on interspace between rows of the main crop on the same land is known as

a) Intercropping
b) Companion cropping
c) Both a and b
d) Multiple cropping

264. The growing of a second or third crop in one year on the same piece of land after the previous crops that have been harvested is

a) Crop rotation
b) Relay cropping
c) Crop succession
d) Vertical cropping

265. Cultural practices __________ pests and pathogens.

a) Reduce
b) Increase
c) Spread
d) All of these

266. Which one of following vegetable is monocot in nature?

a) Garlic
b) Spinach
c) Radish
d) Pointed gourd

267. Borers are found mostly in

a) Cole crops
b) Fruit vegetables
c) Bulbous vegetables
d) Root crops

268. Bacterial spot of sweet pepper is caused due to

a) *Pythium aphanidermatum*
b) *Phomopsis vexans*
c) *Xanthomonas campestris* pv.*vesicatoria*
d) None of these

269. Which of the following is a critical example of andromonoecious sex form ?

a) Water melon
b) Pumpkin
c) Musk melon
d) Bittergourd

270. Aphids do not attack __________.

a) Onion
b) Cabbage
c) Garlic
d) Potato

271. The disease found in French beans is

a) Anthracnose
b) Powdery mildew
c) Downy mildew
d) Damping off

272. Which irrigation system causes O_2 deficiency in root system, increase nematode attack?

a) Sprinkler
b) Drip
c) Both a and b
d) Furrow

273. A disease that does not occur in brinjal

a) Anthracnose
b) Powdery mildew
c) Downy mildew
d) Damping off

274. *Septoria rolfsii* in tomato is responsible for

a) Bacterial blight
b) Collar rot
c) Powdery mildew
d) Damping off

275. The important insect vector for chilli leaf curl is

a) *Myzus persicae*
b) *Bemisi atabaci*
c) *Aphis gossypii*
d) All of these

276. The important insect vector for Yellow Vein Mosaic Virus of okra is

a) *Aphis gossypii*
b) *Myzus persicae*
c) *Hishimonu sphycitis*
d) None of these

277. Nematodes that affect tomato are

a) Stem and root nematode
b) Cyst nematode
c) Root knot nematode
d) Both b and c

278. Needle nematode is common in

a) Cabbage
b) Water melon
c) Tomato
d) Carrot

279. Cyst nematode affects mostly

a) Potato
b) Pea
c) Brinjal
d) All of these

280. The insect vector for little leaf of brinjal is

a) *Hishimonu sphycitis*
b) *Bemisi atabaci*
c) *Myzus persicae*
d) *Aphis gossypii*

281. Late blight of potato is caused by

a) *Rhizoctonia solani*
b) Aphids
c) *Phytophthora infestans*
d) *Erwinia crotovera*

282. Powdery mildew in cucurbits is caused by

a) Fungus
b) Bacteria
c) Mycoplasma
d) Virus

283. Web light in beans is caused by

a) *Coletotrichum spp*
b) *Erysiphae spp*
c) *Uromyces pisi*
d) *Rhizoctonia solani*

284. Fusarium disease is caused by

a) Mycoplasma
b) Fungus
c) Virus
d) Bacteria

285. *Ditylenchus* nematode is very common in

a) Onion
b) Garlic
c) Potato
d) Both "a" and "b"

286. Zinc increases weight of fruit in

a) Carrot
b) Brinjal
c) Turnip
d) Cabbage

287. Phosphorus increases number of ________in tomato.

a) Flowers
b) Fruits
c) Leaves
d) Seeds

288. Tomato variety suitable for processing and fresh market

a) Pusa Ruby
b) Angur Lata
c) Arka Saurabh
d) Kalinpur

289. In Asiatic type of carrot, core is

a) Indistinct
b) Distinct
c) Stump
d) Blunt

290. Cercospora leaf spot in sweet potato was 1st reported in

a) Africa b) China
c) India d) USA

291. Longest storage life among cucurbits is of

a) Water melon b) Bottle gourd
c) Ash gourd d) Cucumber

292. __________ is compulsory in beet root and turnip.

a) Chilling b) Vernalization
c) Thinning d) None of these

293. Early maturing variety of potato is

a) Kufri Ashoka b) Kufri Sutlej
c) Kufri Jyoti d) Kufri Red

294. Late maturing variety of potato is

a) Kufri Sutlej b) Kufri Deva
c) Kufri Jeevan d) Kufri Moti

295. Kufri Sheetman is a hybrid cross of

a) S-4485 × Kufri Kuber
b) Phulwa × Chaigs Defence
c) Kufri Sindhuri × Kufri Red
d) Kufri Red × Kufri Kundan

296. Variety resistant to late blight, early blight in potato is

a) Kufri Kuber b) Kufri Deva
c) Kufri Sheetman d) Kufri Badshah

297. Vegetable known as "Protected Food".

a) Potato b) Brinjal
c) Tomato d) Chilli

298. Sugar baby is a variety of

a) Bitter guard b) Muskmelon
c) Watermelon d) Sugarcane

299. Brinjal is a good source of

a) Vitamin C
b) Vitamin B
c) Protein
d) Vitamin E

300. Growth regulator used to control fruit drop is

a) NAA
b) Ethylene
c) Auxin
d) None of these

301. First tropical variety of cabbage developed for cultivation under high temperature is

a) Pusa Himjyoti
b) Pusa Ageti
c) Pusa Snowball K-1
d) Pusa Shubhra

302. Growth of most cabbage varieties is arrested when temperature

a) below 25°C
b) above 40°C
c) above 25°C
d) below 15°C

303. The only Cole crop in which the intermediate stage of curding lies between vegetative and reproductive stage is

a) Cabbage
b) Cauliflower
c) Broccoli
d) Knol Khol

304. __________ induces male flowers on gynoecious cucumber

a) GA_4
b) Ethylene
c) Abscissic acid
d) GA_3

305. Buttoning in cauliflower is caused due to

a) Excessive N_2
b) N_2 deficiency
c) Mg deficiency
d) Mo deficiency

306. Fruit drop controller and fruit set enhancer is

a) 2-4 D
b) Ethylene
c) CCC
d) IBA

307. CCC (Cycocel) is used for

a) Senescence delayer
b) Colour enhancer
c) Fruit ripening
d) Root inducer

308. NAA, growth regulator is used as

a) Fruit set enhances
b) Root inducer
c) Post harvest fruit drop preventer
d) All of these

309. Essential elements which acts as regulators and carriers.

a) K, Ca, Mg
b) Mn, Zn, Cu
c) N, S, P
d) Ca, B

310. N, S, P are useful elements as

a) Energy storage
b) Regulators
c) Catalysers
d) Activators

311. Best time of fertilizers application is

a) March – April
b) February – March
c) May – June
d) January – February

312. Select the ectotrophic mycorrhizae bio-fertilizer

a) Basidiomycetes
b) Glomus
c) Gigaspore
d) *Penicillium*

313. Phosphorus solibilizers bio-fertilizers include

a) *Pseudomonas*
b) *Aspergillus bacillus*
c) *Penicillium*
d) All of these

314. Onion, okra, asparagus, summer squash etc chiefly supply

a) Iodine
b) Calcium
c) Protein
d) None of these

315. Growth regulator used to reduce period of chilling requirement

a) NAA
b) Cytokinin
c) IBA
d) GA_3

316. *Vigna unguiculata* is the botanical name of

a) Cluster bean
b) Cowpea
c) French bean
d) Garden pea

317. Which of the following vegetable requires more amount of N_2 as compared to others?

a) Potato
b) Brinjal
c) Tomato
d) Palak

318. Sweet potato is a

a) Short Day Plant
b) Long Day Plant
c) Day Neutral Plant
d) None of these

319. Green leafy vegetables are rich source of

a) Citric acid
b) Folic acid
c) Malic acid
d) All of the above

320. ICMR recommendation consumption of vegetable/capita/day is around

a) 200 g
b) 250 g
c) 300 g
d) 400 g

321. Which of the following vegetable is non-climacteric ?

a) Musk melon
b) Tomato
c) Water melon
d) Cucumber

322. Bioflavonoids (Quercetin) are present in which vegetable crop ?

a) Onion
b) Garlic
c) Both
d) None of these

323. In India, vegetable crop occupies ______ percent area of total cultivated area?

a) 1.8%
b) 3.8%
c) 2.8%
d) 4.8%

324. India's contribution in world production of vegetables is

a) 43.38%
b) 23.38%
c) 13.38%
d) 33.38%

325. Which of the following vegetable crop is a C_4 plant?

a) Carrot b) Bean
c) Potato d) Amaranthus

326. Which vegetable crop contribute maximum to earn foreign exchange as fresh vegetables?

a) Potato b) Onion
c) Tomato d) Garlic

327. Storage temperature of brinjal is

a) 5 - 6°C b) 10 - 11°C
c) 7 - 8°C d) 13 - 14° C

328. Wart disease of potato is caused by

a) Fungus b) Virus
c) Bacteria d) Mycoplasma

329. Tomato leaf curl is transmitted by

a) Thrips b) White Fly
c) Aphids d) All of these

330. Little leaf of brinjal is caused due to

a) Fungus b) Virus
c) Bacteria d) Mycoplasma

331. *Aulacophora foveicollis* is the scientific name of which pest

a) Tuber moth b) Stem fly
c) Mustard saw fly d) Red pumpkin beetle

332. Leucinodis or banalis is the major pest of

a) Tomato b) Potato
c) Brinjal d) Chilli

333. Hollow heart in potato is due to

a) Moisture deficiency b) Poor ventilation
c) Excessive N_2 d) Low temperature

334. Pusa Mukta is the variety of

a) Cabbage b) Kholkhol
c) Cauliflower d) Tomato

335. Punjab Chhuhara is a variety of

a) Date b) Banana
c) Brinjal d) Tomato

336. Wolf Apple is the common name of

a) Apple b) Chilli
c) Tomato d) Brinjal

337. In which state, potato is generally not grown?

a) Andhra Pradesh b) Kerela
c) Uttar Pradesh d) Tamil Nadu

338. Sweet potato is commercially propagated by

a) Seed b) Root cuttings
c) Tubers d) Vine cuttings

339. Average yield (t/ ha) of turnip

a) 10 – 20 b) 30 – 40
c) 20 – 30 d) 40 – 50

340. Krishna is the hybrid variety of

a) Tomato b) Chilli
c) Brinjal d) Potato

341. Root-knot nematode resistant variety of tomato is

a) Selection-120 b) Pusa Sheetal
c) Pusa Uphar d) Pusa Ruby

342. Aphid resistant cultivar of brinjal is

a) Annamalai b) Vaishali
c) Pusa Purple Long d) Arka Shrish

343. Resistant variety for black rot of cabbage is

a) Pusa Sambandh b) Pusa Ageti
c) Pusa Mukta d) None of these

344. "Palam Samridhi" is a known variety of

a) Knol-khol b) Brussels sprout
c) Sprouting broccoli d) Cabbage

345. Excellent variety of Carrot for canning is

a) Pusa Kesar b) Pusa Maghali
c) Pusa Lal d) Chantaney

346. Brinjal hybrid "Pragati" is a cross between

a) Arka Kusumakar × Manjiri Gola
b) PPC × Manjiri Gola
c) Vaishali × Manjiri Gola
d) Manjiri Gola × Arka Kusumakar

347. __________is a single seeded cucurbitaceous vegetable.

a) Chayote b) Karkoli
c) Karkrol d) Ivy gourd

348. Delayed harvesting in radish may cause

a) Forking b) Deformed root
c) Pithiness d) All of the above

349. Golden nematode is a serious pest of

a) Tomato b) Brinjal
c) Potato d) Cabbage

350. Potato Seed Rate per hectare is

a) 1 g b) 10 g
c) 5 g d) 15 g

351. Sweet Potato contains ________ % of starch.

a) 10 b) 14
c) 12 d) 16

352. The largest area under chilies is in

a) Maharashtra b) Andhra Pradesh
c) Tamil Nadu d) Uttar Pradesh

353. The turnip belongs to the family

a) Umbelliferae b) Cruciferae
c) Chenopodiaceae d) Convolvulaceae

354. Whip tail disorder is controlled by

a) Application of Boron in soil b) Gypsum addition
c) Liming soil d) Late sowing

355. Which state occupies 1st position in India under sweet potato production?

a) Bihar b) Meghalaya
c) Orissa d) Assam

356. The largest vegetable growing state in India

a) West Bengal b) UP
c) Orissa d) Maharashtra

357. Bacterial spot of tomato and capsicum is caused due to

a) *Alternaria solani* b) *Ralstonia solanacearum*
c) *Oidiopsis taurica* d) *Rhizotonia* sp.

358. The vegetable crop tops in share of total vegetable production is

a) Brinjal b) Potato
c) Tomato d) Cauliflower

359. Phytic acid, a toxic substance is present in

a) Leafy vegetables b) Root vegetables
c) Peas and Beans d) Cucurbits

360. Coleus is commonly known as

a) Indian Potato b) Chinese Potato
c) White Potato d) Irish Potato

361. The sweet potato is a native of

a) Asia b) Peru
c) Mexico d) Tropics of America

362. Sprouting during onion storage can be prevented by using

a) NAA b) MH
c) GA_3 d) Thiourea

363. Exposure of potato tuber to sunlight causes

a) Black heart b) Browning
c) Hollow heart d) Greening

364. The Economic Threshold Level of aphid population in case of potato is

a) 20/100 leaves b) 10/100 leaves
c) 30/100 leaves d) 40/100 leaves

365. The growth regulators in cucurbits are mostly applied at

a) 2 - 4 leaf stage b) Flowering stage
c) 4 - 6 leaf stage d) Fruiting stage

366. TIBA, a chemical is exogenously applied in case of

a) Cucumber b) Muskmelon
c) Water melon d) Bitter gourd

367. The recommended seed rate (kg/ ha) of bottle gourd is

a) 2.0-3.0 b) 8
c) 3-6 d) 10-12

368. Which of the following chemical is used to induce maleness in gynocious cucumber?

a) $AgNO_3$ b) IAA
c) NAA d) IBA

369. The vegetable which is the richest source of Vitamin A is

a) Turnip leaves b) Pumpkin yellow
c) Carrot d) Drumstick leaves

370. The vegetable which is the important source of iodine to human diet is

a) Tapioca b) Okra
c) Tomato d) Brinjal

371. Botanically fruit type of Okra is

a) Pod b) Capsule
c) Berry d) Siliqua

372. The type of inflorescence in onion is

a) Umbell b) Panicle
c) Spadix d) Raceme

373. The optimum temperature for seed germination in pea is

a) 5° C b) 30° C
c) 10° C d) 22° C

374. White brinjal is a good remedy for

a) Diabetes b) Heart disease
c) Cancer d) Skin problems

375. Edible podded cultivar of Pea is/are

a) Sylvia b) Bonneville
c) Arkel d) All of these

376. Blotchy ripening in tomato is associated with deficiency of

a) Nitrogen b) Phosphorus
c) Potassium d) Calcium

377. The per capita consumption of potato in India/year is

a) 15 kg b) 30 kg
c) 20 kg d) 50 kg

378. The vegetable producing maximum amount of nutrient/unit area/ unit time is

a) Potato b) Tomato
c) Carrot d) Onion

379. The optimum temperature requirement for snowball group for curd initiation and development in cauliflower is

a) 20-27° C b) 20-25° C
c) 12-16° C d) 10-16° C

380. Maximum area and production of cauliflower is in

a) West Bengal b) UP

c) Bihar d) Tamil Nadu

381. Bitterness in carrot is associated with

a) Isopentanol b) Iso-coumarin

c) Carotene d) Sulphoraphane

382. Cucumber Green Mottle Virus is transmitted through

a) Insect b) Water

c) Soil d) Air

383. The leading Okra producing country in the world is

a) Africa b) India

c) China d) Netherlands

384. Which of the following variety of okra is recommended for cultivation in disease prone area?

a) PusaSawami b) Punjab Padmini

c) Pusa Mukhmali d) Varsha Upkar

385. *Colletotrichum capsici* causes which disease in chilli?

a) Anthracnose b) Die back

c) Fruit rot d) All of these

386. The largest sprouting broccoli producing country in the world is

a) China b) USA

c) India d) Japan

387. The biggest onion market in India is in which state?

a) UP b) Maharashtra

c) MP d) Karnataka

388. Seed plot technique in potato is developed by

a) G.Kallo b) Puskarnath

c) Harbajan Singh d) None of these

389. Main chemical content of black pepper oil is

a) Ceneol b) Eugenol
c) Peperine d) Linalool

390. Cinnamon belongs to family

a) Lauraceae b) Iridaceae
c) Fabaceae d) Araceae

391. Terbein is the important chemical content in

a) Sweet Flag b) Nutmeg
c) Cinnamon d) Curry leaf

392. Per capita consumption of spice in USA is

a) 2 times of Indian consumption
b) ½ times of Indian consumption
c) 3 times of Indian Consumption
d) 4 times of Indian consumption

393. The leading fenugreek producing state in India is

a) Rajasthan b) Madhya Pradesh
c) Gujarat d) Uttar Pradesh

394. Which of the following is leading Ginger producing country in the world?

a) China b) Italy
c) Sri Lanka d) India

395. Which of the following is the highest production of spices in which state?

a) Himachal Pradesh b) Madhya Pradesh
c) Andhra Pradesh d) Uttar Pradesh

396. Family of clove is

a) Myrtaceae b) Alliaceae
c) Apiaceae d) Fabaceae

397. Botanical name of currant tomato

a) *Lycopersicon pimpinellifolium* b) *L . esculentum*
c) *L. peruvianum* d) *L. cheesmani*

398. Self incompatible but self fertile sps. of tomato

a) *Lycopersicon hirsutum* *b)* *L. cheesmani*

c) L . peruvianum d) L. penneli

399. Most serious disease of okra is

a) Powdery mildew

b) Yellow vein mosaic

c) Root rot

d) None of these

400. Pusa Sawani and Pusa Makhmali are cultivars of

a) Lady's finger b) Bean

c) Peas d) Labia bean

401. Tomato variety suitable for seacoast cultivation is

a) Sabour Suphala b) Arka Meghali

c) Hissar Arun d) Pusa Rohini

402. Leaf curl resistant source of tomato

a) *L. hirsutum fsp. Glabratum* b) *L. cheesmani*

c) *L. pimpinellifolium* d) *L. peruvianum*

403. Most common breeding method of tomato

a) Introduction b) Selection

c) Pedigree d) Single seed decent method

404. Top cross refers to

a) Inter varietals cross b) Intra hybrid cross

c) Inter specific cross d) Inter generic cross

405. Fertility is less in distant hybridization technique that is due to

a) Due to polygenic character b) Less recombination ability

c) Both a and b d) None of these of the above

406. Isolation distance for hybrid seed production of tomato

a) 50 mt b) 100 mt.

c) 200 mt. d) 400 mt.

407. Male sterility of tomato is due to

a) Staminal sterility
b) Positional sterility
c) Exerted stigma
d) All of the above

408. Bitterness in colocasia corms is due to presence of

a) Calcium oxalate
b) Calcium chloride
c) Potassium oxalate
d) Calcium carbonate

409. Brinjal is a

a) Self pollinated
b) Cross pollinated
c) Often cross pollinated
d) None of these

410. Purple colour of brinjal is ________ over green colour.

a) Dominant
b) Recessive
c) Complementary
d) Supplementary

411. Maximum fruit set in brinjal occurs on ________ style.

a) Long
b) Medium
c) Short
d) Pseudo short

412. Bacterial wilt donor sps. of brinjal

a) *Solanum xanthocarpum*
b) *S. incanum*
c) *S. toxicarpum*
d) All of these

413. Phomopsis blight resistant variety of brinjal

a) Florida Market
b) Pusa Bhairab
c) Both a and b
d) None of these

414. Bt. Brinjal contains which gene

a) Cry 1 ab
b) Cry 1 ac
c) Cry 1bc
d) Cry 1 ad

415. Most important breeding goal of any breeding programme is/are

a) High yield
b) Earliness
c) Resistant to pest
d) All of these

416. Capsicum was introduced by the

a) Portuguese
b) English
c) French
d) Chinese

417. *Capsicum annum* is originated from

a) Mexico b) Amazonia
c) Peru and Bolivia d) Europe

418. In which cross viable seeds are produced –

a) *Capcicum annum* × *C. chienense*
b) *Capsicum annum* × *C. frutesence*
c) *C. annum* × *C. pendulum*
d) *C. annum* × *C. pubescens*

419. Which Spp. of Capsicum produce purple colour flower

a) *Capsicum annumm* b) *Capsicum baccatum*
c) *Capsicum frutesence* d) *Capsicum pubescens*

420. Cross pollination percentage in pepper

a) 7.6-36.8% b) 7.62-34.8%
c) 15-20% d) 15-25%

421. Diploid apogamic is reported in which vegetable

a) Onion b) Brinjal
c) Cassava d) Cucumber

422. Metamorphic plant is extensively observed in which family

a) Brassicaceae b) Solanaceae
c) Rutaceae d) Cucurbitaceae

423. Which sex form is dominant in Asparagus?

a) Maleness b) Femaleness
c) Both d) None of these

424. Which vegetable is tetramorphic in sex form?

a) Spinach b) Lettuce
c) Cucumber d) Potato

425. Trimonoecious sex form is found in which vegetable.

a) Cucumber b) Muskmelon
c) Ridge gourd d) All of above

426. In which breeding method selection is absent up to F_6 generation

a) Pure line
b) Pedigree
c) Mass selection
d) Single seed descent Method

427. Multi-line are

a) Homogeneous and homozygous
b) Homogeneous and heterozygous
c) Heterogeneous and Heterozygous
d) Heterogeneous and Homozygous

428. Synthetic and composite varieties are

a) Homogenous and homozygous
b) Homogenous and Heterozygous
c) Heterogeneous and Homozygous
d) Heterogeneous and Heterozygous

429. Which variety of cauliflower is more Self incompatible?

a) Early variety
b) Mid variety
c) Mid late variety
d) Late variety

430. On the basis of flowering potato is a/ an

a) Short day
b) Long day
c) Day neutral
d) Intermediate

431. Which type of male sterility found in cabbage?

a) GMS
b) CMS
c) CGMS
d) None of these

432. GCA test is done for developing

a) Synthetic var.
b) Composite var.
c) Both
d) None of these

433. Which variety of tomato having highest lycopene?

a) Pusa Rohini
b) Pusa Early Dwarf
c) Pusa Meghdoot
d) Hissar Unnat

434. Protandry is a common phenomenon of which vegetable.

a) Onion b) Carrot

c) Beet d) All

435. Centre of Origin of Carrot is

a) India b) Pakistan

c) Afghanistan d) Africa

436. Selfing and massing techniques of onion is first given by

a) Jones and Mann b) Rick

c) Jones and Clark d) Joneson

437. Pusa Chetki a var of Raddish is developed through

a) Introduction from Denmark

b) Selection from IARI

c) Hybridization from IARI

d) Pedigree Method from IARI

438. Parents for Hybridization Technique selected on the basis of

a) Phenotypic performance b) Genotypic performance

c) GCA test d) All of above

439. 'Hollow Heart' in potato caused due to

a) Excessive watering and fertilization

b) Excessive watering and high temperature

c) Excess watering

d) None of these

440. Clonal population is

a) Homozygous and Homogenous

b) Homozygous and Heterogeneous

c) Heterogeneous and Homozygous

d) Heterogeneous and Heterozygous

441. Mass selection is rarely used in

a) Cucumber b) Tomato

c) Cassava d) Chilli

442. Heterosis can be fixed by

a) Asexual reproduction
b) Apomixis
c) Polyploidy
d) All of above

443. Anthesis time in Chilies is

a) 5 AM
b) 6 AM
c) 7 PM
d) 7 AM

444. First F_1 Hybrid was developed by any Private sector in India

a) Bharat
b) Meghana
c) Vidyut
d) Rupali

445. YVMV resistant variety of Okra

a) Pusa Sawani
b) Arka Abhay
c) Arka Alok
d) Punjab Padmini

446. YVMV resistant gene controlled by

a) Single dominant gene
b) Single recessive gene
c) Duplicate dominant gene
d) Duplicate recessive gene

447. Arka Mohini is a variety of capsicum developed through

a) Mutation breeding
b) Introduction
c) Selection
d) Pedigree method

448. YVMV resistant gene is transfer from which sps of okra

a) *Abelmoschas esculentus*
b) *A. tetraphylus*
c) *A. fisculens*
d) *A. moschatus*

449. In *Brassica* resistant to cabbage aphid is related to

a) High saponin in leaves
b) High tannin in leaves
c) Low sinigrin in leaves
d) All of these

450. Multiline Cvs are deliberate mixture of

a) Isogenic line
b) Closely related line
c) Unrelated line
d) All of these

451. All species of chilli having basic chromosome number12 except

a) *C. pendulum*
b) *C. baccatum*
c) *C. ciliatum*
d) *C. pubesens*

452. Botanical name of field pea

a) *Pisum sativum* b) *P. elatius*
c) *P. hortens* d) *P. arvense*

453. Spinach belongs to family

a) Umbellifereae b) Crucifereae
c) Chenopodiaceae d) Oleraceae

454. Arka ajit is a variety of pea resistant to __________ developed through __________.

a) Fusarium wilt, back cross
b) Fusarium wilt, pedigree
c) Powdery mildew, back cross
d) Powdery mildew, hybridization

455. Mutant variety of pea is

a) Acacia b) Bonneville
c) Ooty 1 d) Jahawar Matar 3

456. Botanical name of snap bean is

a) *Phaseolus vulgaris* b) *P. lunetus*
c) *P. coccineus* d) *Dolichos lablab*

457. Chromosome number of Kidney bean is

a) 22 b) 24
c) 14 d) 18

458. Moringa is also known as

a) Drum stick b) Horse radish tree
c) Radish tree d) All of these

459. *Pusa Parvari* is a variety of ________ and is developed through_____

a) Lablab bean, pedigree
b) French bean, mass selection
c) French bean, mass selection
d) French bean, mutation breeding

460. Most of the French bean cultivars are classified as

a) Short day b) Long Day
c) Day Neutral d) Intermediate

461. Botanical name of Asparagus bean is

a) *Vigna cylindrical* b) *Vigna unguiculata*
c) *V. radiate* d) *V.sesquipedilis*

462. Photo-thermo insensitive variety of cowpea

a) Pusa rituraj b) Arka Garima
c) Pusa Dofasli d) Arka Suman

463. Origin of cluster bean is

a) India b) Mexico
c) China d) Guatemala

464. Ancestor of cluster bean is

a) *Cyamopsis tetragonoloba* b) C. *indica*
c) C. *senegalensis* d) C. *mesensii*

465. Pusa Sadabahar is a variety of

a) Cluster bean b) Fenugreek
c) Chilli d) All of the above

466. Arka Jaya and Arka Vijaya are varieties of

a) Clusterbean b) Lablab bean
c) French bean d) Runner bean

467. Botanical name of butter bean is

a) *Phaseolus lunitus* b) *P. vugaris*
c) *Dolichos lablab* d) *Vigna radiata*

468. Hopi and Wilbur are varieties of Lima bean are

a) Pole type b) Semi pole type
c) Bush type d) None of these

469. Favism is related to which crop

a) Lablab bean b) Broad bean
c) Cucumber d) Ginger

470. Isolation distance of okra is

a) 400 mtr b) 200 mtr
c) 100 mtr d) 50 mtr

471. Winged bean is

a) Short day b) Long day
c) Day neutral d) Intermediate

472. Export variety of Okra is

a) Varsa Uphar b) Parbhani Kranti
c) Pusa A4 d) All of these

473. Fruit and shoot borer resistant sp of okra is

a) *A. tetraphylus* b) *A. ficulneus*
c) *A. manihot* d) *A. esculentus*

474. Cauliflower was introduced in India by a botanist from

a) Kew garden, 1822 b) Kew garden, 1832
c) Italy, 1822. d) Italy, 1832

475. Resistant to black rot in Cole crops was found to be governed by

a) Dominant single gene b) Dominant polygene
c) Recessive single gene d) Recessive poly gene

476. Reason behind lack of development of cauliflower hybrid

a) Selfing and sibmating probability
b) Less effective self incompatibility in cauliflower than other
c) Non synchronous flowering of male and female parent
d) All of these

477. To develop any hybrid, We use tester having

a) Broad genetic base b) Narrow genetic base
c) Medium genetic base d) None of these

478. Ogura type of male sterility is found in

a) Cauliflower b) Brinjal
c) Chilli d) Okra

479. Pusa Kartik Shankar is a/an ________ season variety of cauliflower.

a) Early
b) Mid
c) Mid late
d) Late

480. Black rot resistant variety of cauliflower is

a) Pusa Shubra
b) Pant Shubra
c) Pusa Early Synthetic
d) Narendra Gobi 1

481. Botanical name of kitchen kale is

a) *Brassica oleracea var. fimbriata*
b) *B. O. var. acephala*
c) *B. O. var fruticosa*
d) *B. O. var. medulosa*

482. Cymose type of inflorescence is found in

a) Broccoli
b) Cabbage
c) Cauliflower
d) Knolkhol

483. Strongest self incompatibility found in which vegetable.

a) Kale
b) Cauliflower
c) Broccoli
d) Radish

484. Pusa sambandh is a ______ variety of cabbage

a) Hybrid
b) Selected
c) Synthetic
d) Mutant

485. Pumpkin is a

a) Triploid
b) Diploid
c) Amphi-diploids
d) None of these

486. H-64 is a variety of cabbage developed by using

a) CMS line
b) Selection Method
c) CGMS Line
d) Inbreeding Method

487. Which of the cabbage variety grown in tropical condition

a) Pusa Agethi
b) September
c) BSS-115 (Sudha)
d) Pusa Mukta

488. Hacuran is manmade hybrid developed by crossing between

a) Cabbage × Chinese cabbage
b) Chinese Cabbage × Cabbage
c) Cabbage × Brussels Sprout
d) Cabbage × Kitchen Kale

489. Ogura type of male sterility in *Brassica oleracea* transferred from

a) Kitchen Kale b) Japanese Radish
c) Temperate carrot d) Indian Radish

490. Cole crop are highly

a) Heterogeneous and Homozygous
b) Heterogeneous and Heterozygous
c) Homogenous × Heterozygous
d) Homogenous × Homozygous

491. Which of the following variety of broccoli have yellowish green head?

a) Palam Kanchan b) Palam Bitchitra
c) Palam Samridhi d) Pusa Broccoli kt sel-1

492. King of North is a variety of

a) Cabbage b) Knol-khol
c) Cauliflower d) Brussels sprout

493. Origin of the *Cucumis melo*

a) Sahara desert b) Kalahari desert
c) Central Asia d) Desert area of Afghanistan

494. Chromosome number of *Cucumis ficifolius*

a) 24 b) 48
c) 12 d) 72

495. Anthesis time of muskmelon is

a) 5.30-6.30 AM b) 4.30-5.30 PM
c) 7.30-8.30 AM d) 8.30 -9.30 AM

496. Which is not cross compatible?

a) Water melon × Musk melon b) Muskmelon × Long melon
c) Musk melon × Gherkin d) Musk melon × Phoonte

497. How many sex form are found in cucurbits?

a) 5 b) 6
c) 7 d) 8

498. *Cucumis* melo is

a) Monoecious b) Dioecious
c) Andromonoecious d) Gynomonoecious

499. Fusarium wilt resistant var. of muskmelon

a) Harela b) Durgapur Madhu
c) Punjab Sunehri d) All of the above

500. Fruit fly resistant sp of *Cucumis is*

a) *C. melo var callosus* b) *C. melo var momordica*
c) *C. figarei* d) *C. meeusii*

501. Lesser yam is botanically known as

a) *D. esculenta* b) *D.rotundata*
c) *D.floribunda* d) *D.alata*

502. Which is male sterile hybrid of muskmelon?

a) Hara Madhu b) Punjab Sunehri
c) Punjab Hybrid . d) Pusa Rasraj

503. Cucumber is native to

a) India b) Africa
c) Central America d) None of these of the above

504. The open pollinated cultivars of cucumber are

a) Monoecious b) Gynomonoecious
c) Dioecious d) Gynoecious

505. Maleness in gynoecious lines of cucumber is induced by

a) $AgNO_3$ b) NAA
c) IBA d) ABA

506. Ancestor of watermelon

a) *Citrulus colosynthes* b) *C. vulgaris*
c) *C. edulis* d) *C. naudiniam*

507. Multiple disease resistant variety of watermelon is

a) Pusa Bedana b) Arka Manik
c) Durgapur Metha d) Arka Jyoti

508. A cucurbitaceous crop considered to be perennial is

a) Parval b) Chow - chow
c) Snake gourd d) None of these

509. Gynoecious line of cucumber is maintained by applying

a) GA_3 (1500 ppm) b) Silver nitrate (200-300 ppm)
c) Both a & b d) None of these

510. Calabreeze is a variety of

a) Green Sprouting b) Broccoli
c) Cauliflower d) None of these

511. Export potential variety of bottle gourd

a) Pusa Summer Prolific Long b) Pusa Hybrid 3
c) Samrat d) All of these

512. Femaleness of cucurbits is promoted by

a) Short days b) Moderate temp.
c) High humidity d) All of these

513. Flower colour of Ridge gourd is

a) Deep yellow b) Fade yellow
c) White d) Creamy

514. Pusa Manjari is a variety of

a) Bottle gourd b) Bitter gourd
c) Pumpkin d) Cucumber

515. Chromosome number of kakrol is

a) 28 b) 24
c) 22 d) 4

516. Which fruit colour is dominant in bitter gourd?

a) Green b) Yellow
c) White d) Creamy

517. White colour variety of bitter gourd is/are

a) Priya b) Preethi
c) Coimbatore Long Green d) All of above

518. Botanical name of Chappan kaddu

a) *Cucurbita pepo* b) C. *maxima*
c) C. *moschata* d) C. *martinezii*

519. Multiple diseases resistant sp of *Cucurbita* is

a) *C. ecuadorensis* b) *C. maxima*
c) *C. moschata* d) *C. martinezii*

520. Pusa Alankar is a hybrid of

a) Summer squash b) Winter squash
c) Pumpkin d) Snake gourd

521. Interspecific hybrids are not popular in *Cucurbita sp* because

a) The produced hybrids are sterile
b) These are cross incompatible
c) These shows inbreeding depression
d) All of these

522. Chromosome number of mitha karela is

a) 32 b) 24
c) 22 d) 38

523. Genomic constituent of *Cucurbita moschata*

a) ABBB b) AAAB
c) AAAA d) AABB

524. Botanical name of Buffalo gourd

a) *C. ficifolia* b) *C. moschata*
c) *C. maxima* d) *C. pepo*

525. Tendrils are absent in which cucurbit

a) Summer squash
b) Winter squash
c) Ivy gourd
d) Snake gourd

526. Bridge sps. of the genus Cucurbita

a) *C. lundeliana*
b) *C. ficifolia*
c) *C. mixta*
d) *C. angrosperma*

527. Dioecious species of cucurbits is/are

a) Spine gourd
b) Ivy gourd
c) Pointed gourd
d) All of above

528. Multiple diseases resistant variety of radish is

a) Arka Nishant
b) Pusa Chetki
c) Punjab Safed
d) Scarlet Globe

529. Centre of origin of Carrot is

a) Afghanistan
b) China
c) India
d) Africa

530. Inflorescence of Carrot is

a) Compound umbel
b) Simple umbel
c) Corymbs
d) Spike

531. Brown anther and petaloid anther are found in

a) Carrot
b) Radish
c) Onion
d) Cucumber

532. Pusa Madhabi is a variety of onion developed through

a) Selfing and Massing
b) Hybridization
c) Selection
d) Polyploidy breeding

533. Which Carrot variety has high carotene contents?

a) Pusa Meghali
b) Pusa Kesar
c) Pusa Asita
d) Pusa Yamdagnii

534. Major breeding method of beet root is

a) Mass selection
b) Inbreed line selection
c) Hybridization
d) Recurrent selection

535. Which variety of carrot is suitable for kanji preparation?

a) Pusa Asita
b) Pusa Rudhira
c) Pusa Bristi
d) Pusa Nayanjyoti

536. Breeding objective of turnip is/are

a) Uniform size and shape
b) Tolerant to pest and disease
c) High yield and earliness
d) All of above

537. Extra early variety of Turnip is

a) Early Milan Red Top
b) Golden ball
c) Pusa Chandrima
d) Pusa Swarnima

538. Onion variety resistant to purple blotch

a) Arka Kalyan
b) Arka Niketan
c) Pusa Red
d) Arka Bindu

539. Long day onion variety is

a) Early Grano
b) Brown Spanish
c) Both a & b
d) None of these

540. Spinach beet produces only ________ flowers.

a) Hermaphrodite
b) Staminate
c) Pistillate
d) None of these

541. Spinach can be classified as

a) Short day plant
b) Long day plant
c) Day neutral plant
d) Intermediate plant

542. Which species of amaranths is predominant in India?

a) *A. tricolor*
b) *A. dubious*
c) *A. tristis*
d) *A. hypocondriachus*

543. Amaranths is a ________ plant.

a) Short day
b) Long day
c) Day neutral
d) Intermediate

544. King of salad crop is having chromosome number of

a) 18
b) 20
c) 24
d) 32

545. Lettuce is essentially

a) Short day b) Long day
c) Day neutral d) Intermediate

546. The CPRI was established in

a) 1949 b) 1946
c) 1956 d) 1959

547. Potato late blight resistant sp is

a) *S. demissum* b) *S. stoloniferum*
c) *S. bulbocartanum* d) All of these

548. New Leaf, a transgenic variety of potato is resistant to

a) Colorado beetle b) Spindle tuber moth
c) Potato virus d) Late blight

549. Frost resistant variety of tomato is

a) Kufri Sheetman b) Kufri Bahar
c) Kufri Alankar d) Kufri Jyoti

550. Potato variety resistant to early blight is/are

a) Kufri Chamatkar b) Kufri Pukhraj
c) Both a & b d) None of these

551. Most of the open pollinated varieties of black pepper developed through

a) Selection b) Introduction
c) Hybridization d) Mutation

552. Root knot nematode resistant variety of black pepper is

a) Poornima b) Sreekara
c) Panchami d) Panniyur -2

553. Which variety of cardamom is tolerant to Azukal diseases?

a) MCC 61 b) Mudigree 1
c) ICRI 1 d) All of these

554. In ginger, flowers are borne on

a) Spike b) Racemes
c) Cymose d) Umbel

555. Origin of ginger is

a) India b) China
c) Pakistan d) Peru

556. Mutant variety of ginger is

a) Surari b) Suprabha
c) Varda d) Mahima

557. Turmeric is a

a) Sterile triploid b) Sterile diploid
c) Tetraploid d) Sterile tetraploid

558. Somatic chromosome number of fenugreek is

a) 16 b) 22
c) 24 d) 48

559. Delayed harvesting in radish may cause

a) Forking b) Pithiness
c) Deformed roots d) All of above

560. Mutant variety of turmeric is

a) Co-1 b) BSR-1
c) Suroma d) Krishna

561. Coriander is

a) Andromonoecious b) Monoecious
c) Gynoecious d) Andro-dioecious

562. Coriander variety resistant to stem gall

a) Rajendra Swati b) Rajendra Kranti
c) Swati d) CO 3

563. Somatic chromosome number of cumin is

a) 14 b) 22
c) 24 d) 48

564. Non lodging variety of coriander

a) Pant Haritma b) Hissar Anand
c) Gujrat Coriander 2 d) Co1

565. Rajendra Kranti variety of fenugreek is developed through

a) Mass selection b) Pure line selection
c) Recurrent selection d) Mutation

566. Which crop is protendrous?

a) Cumin b) Coriander
c) Turmeric d) Clove

567. Which is not similar according to flowering?

a) Turmeric b) Curry leaf
c) Garcinia d) Ivy gourd

568. Flower colour of vanilla is

a) Green b) White
c) Yellow d) Pink

569. Distant hybrid of vegetables are produced through

a) Embryo Culture b) Anther culture
c) Somaclonal variation d) Mutation

570. Diverse cytoplasm can be fixed together by

a) Protoplast fusion b) Embryo abortion
c) Micro-propagation d) Anther culture

571. Male sterile *Brassica napus* developed as cybrids, contain

a) Mitochondria of *R. sativus* b) Chloroplast of *B. campestris*
c) Nucleus of *B. napus* d) All of these

572. Europe is primary centre of

a) Lettuce b) Cabbage
c) Radish d) Okra

573. Pusa Nasdar is a variety of

a) Ridge gourd b) Bottle gourd
c) Amaranths d) Brinjal

574. Primary centre of origin of Sweet potato is

a) South America
b) Near East
c) Central Asia
d) Africa

575. Edible part of cucumber (pepo) is

a) Pericarp
b) Fleshy receptacle
c) Monocarp, endocarp, placenta
d) Placenta

576. Which of the following having polygenic inheritance

a) Resistance to Cabbage yellow
b) Resistance to phomopsis blight
c) Resistance to black rot
d) All of above

577. Resistant to Fusarium wilt in pea is governed by

a) Single gene inheritance
b) Poly-gene inheritance
c) Oligo-gene inheritance
d) None of these

578. Chayote is generally raised by planting

a) Seed
b) Tuber
c) Vine cutting
d) Entire fruit

579. Pleiotropy of okra was found in

a) Calyx colour and petal vein colour
b) Resistance to powdery mildew
c) Pod per plant
d) Resistance to YVMV

580. Which breeding method is not used in self pollinated crops?

a) Recurrent selection
b) Mass selection
c) Family breeding
d) Mutation

581. Pant Subhra variety of cauliflower is developed through

a) Recurrent selection
b) Introduction
c) Pure line selection
d) Inbreeding method

582. Transgenic are produced in tomato for

a) Modifying ripening
b) Resistant to virus
c) Resistant to herbicide
d) All of these

583. Tomato variety Money Maker was introduced in India from

a) USA b) Denmark
c) Philippines d) Israel

584. Purple colour of Broccoli is controlled by

a) Single dominant gene b) Single recessive gene
c) Complementary gene d) Duplicate recessive gene

585. Flower of brinjal may be

a) long- styled b) Medium- styled
c) Pseudo- short styled d) All of above

586. Flowers of beet leaf are

a) Staminate b) Pistillate
c) Hermaphrodite d) All of above

587. First commercial transgenic crop is

a) Tomato b) Cotton
c) Soybean d) Brinjal

588. Breeding objective of Leek is

a) Winter hardiness b) High yield and earliness
c) Resistant to early bolting d) All of above

589. Complementary gene ratio of di-hybrid cross is

a) 9:7 b) 9:3:4
c) 9:6:1 d) 9:3:3:1

590. Chromosome number of black pepper is

a) 128 b) 44
c) 63 d) 22

591. The chromosome number of okra is

a) 50 b) 150
c) 130 d) 80

592. The chromosome number of globe artichoke

a) 36 b) 34
c) 9 d) 18

593. The term appertizing is used for

a) Canning
b) Dehydration
c) Syruping
d) Sterilization

594. Who is called 'Father of canning'?

a) M.S. Swaminathan
b) Nicholas Appert
c) De Candole
d) Mendel

595. Which of the following plastic is the biodegradable

a) Poly-hydroxy butyrate
b) LDPE
c) Polypropylene
d) Polythene

596. Carrots are rich in

a) Vitamin A
b) Vitamin B
c) Vitamin C
d) Vitamin D

597. Red colour of tomato is due to

a) Anthocyanin
b) Carotene
c) Xanthophyll
d) Lycopene

598. During sealing of the can, temperature should not fall below

a) 50°C
b) 40°C
c) 64°C
d) 74°C

599. Type of food having a pH range of 4.5-5.0 is classified as

a) Acidic
b) Alkaline
c) Medium acidic
d) Non-acidic

600. Vodka is prepared from

a) Tomato
b) Cashew
c) Potato
d) Coconut

601. FPO was promulgated in

a) 1945
b) 1955
c) 1965
d) 1970

602. Which of the following vitamin is a thermo-sensitive vitamin

a) Vitamin A
b) Vitamin B
c) Vitamin C
d) Vitamin D

603. Fruit and tomato products should be sterilized at

a) 90°C for 30 minutes b) 80°C for 25 to 30 minutes
c) 100°C for 30 minutes d) 85°C for 5 to 10 minutes

604. KMS is most effective against ---------- than yeast.

a) Yeast b) Mould
c) Bacteria d) None of these

605. Modified atmospheric packaging (MAP) of fruit and vegetables prevent the building up of the following

a) Protein b) Sugar
c) CO_2 and acetylene b) None of these

606. TSS of tomato sauces should be

a) 50% b) 58%
c) 30% d) 70%

607. Solution of salt in water is called as

a) Brine b) Vinegar
c) Juice d) Cider

608. Commonly used sprout suppressant in potato in India is

a) MH b) Cycocal
c) Alar d) All of these

609. Acidifying agent used in vase solution is

a) Sucrose b) Citric acid
c) Quinoline d) All of above

610. Which of the following is the permanent method of preservation of fruits and vegetables

a) Exclusion of moisture b) Canning and bottling
c) Pasteurization d) Blanching

611. Treatment of fruits and vegetables with low temperature for short time is known as

a) Pasteurization b) Blanching
c) Sterilization d) None of these

612. Vacuum cooling is mostly used for which type of vegetables.

a) Tuber crops
b) Cole crops
c) Leafy vegetables
d) Bulb

613. Under CA storage, generally acidity of the stored products will

a) Decrease
b) Increase
c) Remain constant
d) None of these

614. Darkening of potatoes is due to deficiency of

a) Phosphorous
b) Potassium
c) Calcium
d) Iron

615. Among the following Riboflavin is more in

a) Gourds
b) Potato
c) Melons
d) None of these

616. Lactic bacteria is used in

a) Chutney
b) Murabba
c) Pickle
d) Jelly

617. In pre-cooling mostly water is removed by

a) Distillation
b) Evaporation
c) Conduction
d) None of these

618. In freezing which principle is followed

a) Condensation
d) Drying
c) Crystallization
d) All of these

619. During storage of potatoes internal blackening is due to

a) <8°C or > 20°C
b) <2°C or >10°C
c) <4°C or > 15°C
d) None of these

620. Tenderometer is a device which can measure

a) Maturity of beans
b) Maturity of peas
c) Specific gravity of gourds
d) Wind velocity

621. Formation of abscission layer is maturity index of

a) Melons
b) Tubers
c) Peas
d) None of these

622. Solidity is the maturity index for which type of vegetables.

a) Melons b) Tuber Crops
c) Leafy vegetables d) All of these

623. CFTRI is situated at

a) Mysore (Karnataka) b) IARI (New Delhi)
c) Chandigarh (Punjab) d) Mumbai (Maharashtra)

624. Which of the following is a precursor of Vitamin A?

a) Vitamin B b) Alpha Carotene
c) Beta-carotene d) Methionine

625. Which among the following is temporary method of preservation?

a) Preservation by sugar b) Pasteurization
c) Preservation by salt d) Drying

626. Cobalt is present in which of the following vitamins

a) Vitamin B_1 b) Vitamin B_{12}
c) Vitamin B_5 d) Vitamin D

627. In onion, which of the following is the major post harvest problem?

a) Sprouting b) Bolting
c) Flowering d) None of these

628. Vegetables are rich in

a) Proteins b) Fats
c) Vitamins d) Minerals

629. Most of the vegetables are __________ in nature.

a) Acidic b) Alkaline
c) Neutral d) None of these

630. In cold storage, potato is stored at

a) 2.2°C and 60%RH b) 2.0°C and 75%RH
c) 2.2°C and 75% RH d) 2.9°C and 60% RH

631. Chilies are rich sources of

a) Vitamin A b) Vitamin A and B
c) Vitamin A and C d) Vitamin A and B

632. Onion is a good source of

a) Vitamin B
b) Vitamin D
c) Vitamin A
d) Vitamin C

633. Curcumin is extracted from

a) Capsicum
b) Onion
c) Cucumber
d) Turmeric

634. For canning purpose, tomato is harvested at

a) Immature stage
b) Fully ripe stage
c) Mature stage
d) Half ripe stage

635. Vitamin A is abundantly found in which type of vegetables.

a) Tuber crops
b) Cole crops
c) Leafy vegetables
d) Half ripe stage

636. For canning, tomato fruits are picked at

a) Immature green stage
b) Mature green stage
c) Half ripe or pink stage
d) Red ripe stage

637. Ripe watermelon when thumped gives

a) Metalic sound
b) Dull sound
c) Both a and b
d) No sound

638. Ripe tomato is a good source of

a) Vitamin A
b) Vitamin B
c) Vitamin C
d) Vitamin D

639. Curing of sweet potato is done at one of the following temperature and RH

a) 60°C and 30%RH
b) 80°C and 30%RH
c) 60°C and 40% RH
d) 80°C and 70% RH

640. Outer skin colour of onion bulb is due to

a) Quercetin
b) Carotene
c) Anthocyanin
d) Xanthoyl

641. Vegetables are dehydrated at the temperature (°C) of

a) 60-66 b) 40-45
c) 50-55 d) 70-75

642. Quick freezing is done at 0-4°C for

a) 10 minute b) 15 minute
c) 20 minute d) 30 minute

643. The cheapest preservation method of fruits and vegetables

a) Canning b) Freezing
c) Drying d) Fermentation

644. Best quality 'Oleoresin' is extracted from

a) Onion b) Chilli
c) Castor d) Garlic

645. Sauerrubem is the fermented product of

a) Turnip b) Cabbage
c) Beetroot d) Orange.

646. First picking in bitter gourd can be done after

a) 50-60 days b) 70-80 days
c) 80-90 days d) None of these

647. Lye peeling is done at a temperature of

a) 75°C b) 84°C
c) 93°C d) 105°C

648. Which of the following is the precursor of Ethylene?

a) ABA b) Methionine
c) Tryptophan d) AA

649. Fresh unshelled peas can be stored well for 2 weeks at

a) 5°C & 85 % RH b) 0°C & 90-95% RH
c) 15°C & 60-70 %RH d) 4°C & 100% RH

650. Which of the following is associated with 'browning' disorder?

a) Apple b) Cabbage
c) Cauliflower d) Citrus

651. In carrot, commercially peeling is done by

a) Lye peeling
b) Hand Peeling
c) Mechanical Peeling
d) Steam Peeling

652. National Horticulture Board (NHB) was established in the year

a) 1981
b) 1982
c) 1983
d) 1984

653. Which one of the following is the anti-sterility vitamin

a) Vitamin A
b) Vitamin E
c) Vitamin C
d) Vitamin D

654. In cucumber, chilling injury symptoms are occurred at

a) <7°C
b) 7°C
c) <10°C
d) 10°C

655. Amaranthus leaves are rich in

a) Vitamin A
b) Vitamin B
c) Vitamin C
d) Vitamin D

656. How many tubers or sets will be needed to raise the yams on one hectare area

a) 14,300
b) 15,300
c) 13,300
d) 16,000

657. Which variety of lima bean needs support?

a) Pole type
b) Semi- pole type
c) Bush type
d) All of these

658. The drying rate is affected by

a) Surface area
b) RH
c) Air Velocity
d) All of these

659. Black heart of potato occurs when storage temperature is

a) 5°C
b) 0°C
c) -5°C
d) 10°C

660. Carrot is a rich source of

a) Protein b) Fat
c) Carotene d) Carbohydrate

661. Cauliflower curds can be stored for a month at

a) 0° with 85-90%RH b) 15°C with 60-80% RH
c) 15°C with 60-65 %RH d) 20°C with 50-70 % RH

662. Which can be used for canning pea

a) SR can b) AR can
c) Plain can d) None of these

663. Sublimation is associated with

a) Vacuum drying b) Spray drying
c) Freeze drying d) Foam mat drying

664. Which of the following is a rapid one-cooling method?

a) Evaporative cooling b) Hydro cooling
c) Forced air cooling d) Vacuum cooling

665. 'Elephant's Foot Yam' is a rich source of vitamin

a) A and B b) B and C
c) C and D d) Only B

666. Family of Basella is

a) Solanaceae b) Basellaecae
c) Chenopodiaceae d) None of these

667. In pickle, white cottony surface is due to

a) Rhizopus b) Lactobacilus
c) Mycoderma d) Mucor

668. A pea variety which gives 50% produce during 1st picking

a) Arkel b) Meteor
c) Mattar Ageta-6 d) None of these of above

669. Melons for distant marketing are picked at

a) Half-slip stage b) Full-slip stage
c) Green mature stage d) None of these

670. The optimum temperature for growth of thermophillic bacteria is

a) 20°C b) 55°C or above
c) 40°c d) 75°C or above

671. For distant marketing, tomato fruits are harvested at

a) Immature green stage b) Red ripe stage
c) Turning stage d) Mature green stage

672. For drying of pea, tendrometer reading should be about

a) 85-90 b) 95-106
c) 105-110 d) 115

673. Browning in cabbage stored in cellar storage is due to

a) Polyphenotoxidase b) Catalase
c) Oxidase d) None of these

674. What is the temperature of cellar storage

a) 0-5°C b) >15°C
c) -18to-40°C d) None of these

675. For long-term storage, potato should be stored at

a) 0-5°C b) 5-10°C
c) 10-15°C d) 15-20°C

676. Tomato fruits for processing are picked at

a) Over ripe stage b) Pink stage
c) Half ripe stage d) Mature stage

677. For longer storage of cucumber fruits, the temperature should be kept at

a) 5°C b) 20°C
c) 25°C d) 10°C

678. The Limiting Amino Acid in green vegetables is

a) Methionine b) Lysine
c) Tryptophan d) Arginine

679. Which of the following is the staple vegetable in Indian diet

a) Cauliflower b) Potato
c) Tomato d) Chilli

680. Spinach is a rich source of

a) Vitamin A b) Vitamin E
c) Vitamin C d) Vitamin B

681. Which bean is used for extraction of gum

a) Hyacinth bean b) Cluster bean
c) French bean d) Broad bean

682. Cryo-preservation is associated with

a) Liquid oxygen b) Liquid potassium
c) Liquid CO_2 d) Liquid nitrogen

683. Chromosome number of Basella is

a) 2n=70 b) 2n=26
c) 2n=24 d) 2n=18

684. Red colour of carrot is due to

a) Lycopene b) Quercetin
c) Anthocyanin d) Carotene

685. The term 'Cold sterilization ' is also known as

a) Ultra filtration b) Irradiation
c) Refrigeration d) Ultra-filtration

686. In storage, soft rot is caused by

a) Erwina b) Agrobacterium
c) Xanthomonas d) Penicllium

687. Broccoli is the modification of

a) Swollen inflorescence b) Main bud
c) Auxiliary bud d) Stem sprout

688. Which of following is a stem vegetable?

a) Carrot b) Knol -khol
c) Sweet potato d) Radish

689. How much vegetables (%) is utilized by processing industries

a) >1% b) 1%
c) <1% d) 5%

690. Katrain station transferred to IARI, Delhi

a) 1945 b) 1955
c) 1947 d) 1973

691. Per hectare seed rate of basella is

a) 8-10 kg b) 12-15 kg
c) 10-12 kg d) 20-25 kg

692. In case of tomato, drained weight is

a) 40% b) 50%
c) 55% d) 60%

693. Raw material used for 'Gherkin' is

a) Tomato b) Cabbage
c) Soybean d) Cucumber

694. Which cans are used for canning of cauliflower and sweet potato?

a) AR Cans b) Plain
c) SR Cans d) All of these

695. Pungency in onion is due to the presence of

a) Allyl propyl disulphide b) Capsaicin
c) Diallyl disulphide d) Solanin

696. Controlled Atmosphere Storage was invented by

a) James Harrison b) Gane
c) Kidd and Wert d) Wade

697. Who introduced the term 'pH'?

a) Plummer (1987) b) Chang (1979)
c) Sorenson (1909) d) Van Holde (1885)

698. Amaranthus belongs to the family

a) Chenopodiaceae b) Amaranthaceae
c) Portulaceae d) None of these

699. Pusa Kiran, Pusa Kirti and Badi Chaulai are important varieties of

a) Basella b) Amaranthus
c) Lettuce d) tomato

700. Storage temperature for asparagus is

a) 0-5°C b) 5-7°C
c) 7-10°C d) 10-15°C

701. For direct sowing of Amaranthus, per hectare seed rate is

a) 2 kg b) 4 kg
c) 1 kg d) 3 kg

702. Vegetable which is not blanched before drying is

a) Palak b) Cauliflower
c) Tomato d) Onion

703. Moisture content in dried vegetable is

a) 2% b) 3%
c) 5% d) 16%

704. Vitamin which is not found in fruits and vegetables is

a) Vitamin A b) Vitamin B_1
c) Vitamin B_6 d) Vitamin B_{12}

705. After processing cans are cooled rapidly at a temperature of

a) 10°C b) 25°C
c) 39°C d) 49°C

706. Potato can be placed in the group of

a) Highly- perishable b) Semi- perishable
c) Perishable d) Non-perishable

707. Which of the following is a medium acidic food

a) Asparagus b) Limabean
c) Pear d) Com

708. National pickle of India is

a) Cucumber pickle b) Carrot pickle
c) Mango pickle d) Lime pickle

709. Who coined the term vitamin?

a) Kohn b) Funk
c) Darwin d) Muller

710. Brinjal protects against the

a) Cancer b) Allergy
c) Diabetes d) Fever

711. Packaging film which is used for better modified atmospheric packing (MAP) is

a) LDPE b) HDPE
c) Polypropylene (PP) d) LLDP

712. Amaranthus is a

a) Self pollinated crop b) Often cross pollinated crop
c) both (a) and (b) d) Cross pollinated crop

713. Brine concentration for canning of vegetables is

a) 1-1.5% b) 2-2.5%
c) 3-3.5% d) 4-4.5%

714. The horticulture Society of India was established in the year

a) 1942 b) 1945
c) 1955 d) 1962

715. Ideal storage temperature of Cucumber is

a) 0°C b) 3-4°C
c) 10-13°C d) 13-15°C

716. In which of the following process enzyme is inactivated

a) Sulphitation b) Canning
c) Asepsis d) Blanching

717. Which of the organization is engaged in exporting of processed product

a) NAFED b) APEDA
c) NABARD d) FCI

718. Highest quantity of carotene is available from

a) Fenugreek leaf b) Spinach leaf
c) Colocasia leaf d) Carrot

719. Which colour onions are used for dehydration?

a) Yellow b) Red
c) White d) Pink

720. What is the ideal storage temperature for peas?

a) 0°C b) 10°C
c) 12°C d) 13°C

721. Among root crops, the application of potassic fertilizers is essential in

a) Radish b) Carrot
c) Turnip d) None of these

722. An early maturing variety of potato which does not degenerate rapidly is

a) Up-to date
b) Kufri Sindhuri
c) Kufri Chandramukhi
d) None of these

723. Onion can be stored best at a temperature of

a) 0°C b) 4-5° C
c) 7°C d) 10-13° C

724. Arka Abhay is a variety of

a) Brinjal b) Chilli
c) Tomato d) Bhindi

725. Bean variety Pusa Parvati is evolved through

a) X-rays b) Gamma -rays
c) EMS d) MMS

726. During balancing, vitamin C loss is

a) 5-10% b) 10-15%
c) 10-50% d) 30-60%

727. Best temperature for storing tomato fruits is

a) 12 -15°C b) 4-5°C
c) 5-10°C d) 15-20°C

728. The major mineral which is present in fruit and vegetables is

a) Na b) K
c) Ca d) Mg

729. *Cucumis melo* var.*acidulus* is

a) Weed melon b) Sour melon
c) Summer tough melon d) Rock melon

730. Vegetable, which is rich in niacin is

a) Sweet potato b) Peas
c) Avocado d) Ginger

731. Among the following which is rich source of vitamin C.

a) Tomato b) Amaranthus
c) Bitter gourd d) Cabbage

732. Iron content is highest in which vegetables

a) Mustard leaves b) Amaranthus
c) Beet d) Spinach

733. The daily requirement of vitamin for normal man is

a) 20mg b) 30mg
c) 50mg d) 100mg

734. Ethylene Forming Enzyme (EFE) is presently known as

a) ACC Synthase b) ACC Oxidase
c) ACC Transferase d) None of these

735. Bitter taste in brinjal fruit is due to

a) Anti Vitamin E b) CN glycosides
c) Solasodine d) Trypsin inhibitor

736. The rate of chemical reaction approximately doubles for each rise in temperature of

a) 5°C b) 10°C
c) 15°C d) 22°C

737. Carotene content is highest in

a) Amaranthus b) Fenugreek leaves
c) Coriander leaves d) Lettuce

738. Which of the following is rich source of calcium?

a) Amaranthus b) Tomato
c) Spinach d) Curry leaves

739. In fruits and vegetables waxing is done to reduce

a) Respiration b) Photosynthesis
c) Transpiration d) Evaporation

740. Betalins is an active pigment which found in

a) Beet root b) Rose
c) Avocado d) Citrus

741. Black rot in cauliflower is caused by

a) Fungal diseases b) Bacterial diseases
c) Viral diseases d) None of these

742. Black rot in cabbage is transmitted by

a) Mechanical means b) Seeds
c) Vectors d) None of these

743. Which of the following vegetables contains highest amount of sodium?

a) Tomato b) Spinach
c) Lettuce d) Chow-chow

744. Vegetables are referred as protective food because they are rich in

a) Vitamins and minerals b) Proteins
c) Carbohydrates d) Acid

745. Browning occur in

a) Tomato b) Onion
c) Brinjal d) Chilli

746. Which of the following plant hormone enhance senescence

a) Ethylene b) NAA
c) Cytokinin d) ABA

747. Yellow colour of onion is due to the presence of

a) Allicin b) Quercetin
c) Malvelin d) None of these

748. Which of the following vitamin is sensitive to heat?

a) Vitamin A b) Vitamin C
c) Vitamin D d) Vitamin E

749. Bitter principle in bitter gourd is

a) Terpenoids b) Tannin
c) Cucumis d) None of these

750. What should be the ideal temperature for storage of brinjal

a) 15-17°C b) 10-12°C
c) 5-7°C d) 14-15°C

751. What is the acidity of cucumber pickles

a) 0-5-1.4 b) 0.6-0.8
c) 0.7-1.5 d) 1.0-1.5

752. 'Sauerkraut' is prepared from

a) Cauliflower b) Cucumber
c) Cabbage d) Tomato

753. TSS range for a mature a watermelon's is

a) 8-10°B b) 10-12°B
c) 14-16°B d) 18-20°B

754. 'Khalpi' is prepared by fermentation of

a) Radish b) Cucumber
c) Cabbage d) Carrot

755. An F1hybrid of cucumber recommended by IARI is

a) Pusa Sanyog b) Poinsette
c) Straight Eight d) None of these

756. Main aim of pre-cooling is

a) Reduce microbial load b) Improve quality
c) Remove field heat d) None of these

757. In pre-cooling, water is mostly removed by

a) Convection b) Conduction
c) Radiation d) None of these

758. Formation of abscission layer is maturity index of

a) Leafy vegetables b) Onion
c) Tomato d) Melons

759. 'Solidity' is the maturity index for

a) Seed vegetables b) Leafy vegetables
c) Root vegetables d) Cucurbits

760. For best storage of cucumber temperature should be

a) 1-2°C b) 4-5°C
c) 85°C d) 10-13°C

761. For processing, vegetables requires a temperature of

a) 100°C b) 105-110°C
c) 110-115°C d) 115-121°C

762. Protein content in potato is about

a) 1.4% b) 1.8%
c) 2.2% d) 2.5%

763. After cooking the vegetables, nutrients generally

a) Increase b) No Change
c) Decrease d) None of these

764. Which is a non-climacteric vegetables

a) Watermelon b) Cucumber
c) Muskmelon d) Tomato

765. *Cucumis melo* var.*chito* is also known as

a) Lemon cucumber b) Mango melon
c) Melon apple d) all of these

766. Chemical preservative which is used in tomato ketchup is

a) Sodium benzoate b) Salt
c) KMS d) Acid

767. Heat treatment of vegetables in boiling water for few minutes is known as

a) Pasteurization b) Blanching
c) Sterilization d) Cooking

768. Which of the following is a ripening hormone

a) Auxin b) IBA
c) NAA d) C_2H_4

769. Which one of the following vegetables is acidic in nature?

a) Cucumber b) Rhubarb
c) Onion d) Potato

770. Arka Jyoti is an improved variety of

a) Muskmelon b) Watermelon
c) Bottle gourd d) Snapmelon

771. Arka Jeet is a popular cultivar of

a) Muskmelon b) Bitter Gourd
c) Bottle gourd d) Watermelon

772. Mosture content in dried vegetables is

a) 2% b) 3%
c) 5% d) 7%

773. Bulking rate is very high in potato variety

a) Kufri Chandramukhi b) Kufri Alankar
c) Kufri Naveen d) None of these

774. Vegetable having high calorific value is

a) Fenugreek b) Potato
c) Amaranths d) Tomato

775. Cabbage is a heavy feeder of

a) N, K b) N,P,K
c) N, P d) P, K

776. California Wonder is an important variety of

a) Hot pepper b) Sweet pepper
c) Bird Pepper d) None of these

777. Beet root fruit botanically is capsule which contains

a) 2-6 seeds b) 12-14 seeds
b) 8-10 seeds d) 12-14 seeds

778. Cowpea is probably a native of

a) India b) China
c) Central Africa d) None of these

779. At what temp green beans can be stored for several days?

a) 3.4^{0}c b) 4.4^{0}c
c) 5.2^{0}c d) 5.5^{0}c

780. Blanching time for French beans is

a) 2 minute b) 3 minute
c) 5 minute d) 7 minute

781. Most of the post harvestel losses of vegetables occur during

a) Canning b) Grading
c) Transportation d) Cooling

782. Vegetables are graded according to

a) Shape b) Size
c) Colour d) All of these

783. Which method is effective in delay senescence and maintain quality of mushrooms after harvesting

a) Modified atmospheric packing (MAP)
b) Controlled atmospheric storage
c) Modified humidity packing
d) Refrigeration

784. Toxin thiocyanate is more in

a) Potato b) Tomato
c) Kale & Cauliflower d) Onion

785. Leaf changes is important maturity indices for

a) Cole crops b) Tuber crops
c) Root crops d) None of these

786. Plastic low tunnel is suitable for off season cultivation of

a) Solanaceous crops b) Cucurbits
c) Leguminous crops d) Cole crops

787. Plastic low tunnel technology is a boon for off season vegetable cultivation in

a) Hilly areas b) Hot deserts
c) Cold deserts d) Plains

788. Cucumber Mosaic virus is spread by

a) Seeds b) Aphids
c) Mites d) Whiteflies

789. Earthing of potato is done

a) 40days after sowing b) 20 days after sowing
c) 50 days after sow d) None of these

790. Exceptionally large potato tubers may have more chances of

a) Black-heart b) Brown-heart
c) Hollow-heart d) All of above

791. Challenger is a variety of

a) Indian bean b) Hyacinth bean
c) Cluster bean d) Lima bean

792. Chemical used for controlling root knot nematode in brinjal is

a) Aldrin b) Chloropyriphos
c) Nonagon d) None of these

793. CH-1 was evolved at

a) CSAUA &T (kanpur) b) PAU Ludhiana
c) CCSHAU (Hissor) d) IARI New Delhi

794. Cluster bean belongs to genus

a) Phaseolus b) Dolichos
c) Cyanopsis d) None of these

795. The nets used in net houses are available in which three colours.

a) Black, green, white b) Violet, green, yellow
c) Pink, red, yellow d) Blue, red, yellow

796. In shading nets, shade intensities range from _______ to ______ percent

a) 20-40 b) 40-60
c) 25-75 d) 35-55

797. Which type of vegetable crops are preferably grown under shade nets

a) Cucurbits b) Leafy vegetables
c) Solanaceous d) Cole crops

798. Insect proof nylon nets are available in different intensities of perforations (in mesh)

a) 25-60 b) 35-70
c) 20-40 d) 60-80

799. Cluster bean produces an amide

a) Aspargine b) Allantoin
c) Glycoprotein d) Allantonic

800. The shade nets are manufactured from

a) LDPE b) PVC
c) Teflon d) HDPE

801. Term Biotechnology was coined by

a) Karl Ereky (1919) b) Karl Ereky(1909)
c) Hanninng(1907) d) Zieber and Brink(1905)

802. Perfection and selection-8 are the introduced varieties of

a) Cabbage b) Carrot
c) Asparagus d) Radish

803. The most commonly used method for transformation of plant is

a) Agrobacterium medited transformation
b) Protoplast method
c) Electrotransformation
d) Micro-injection

804. In order to obtain protection against Tomato Yellow Leaf Curl Virus which of the following approaches are used

a) Coat protein mediated resistance by inoculation with a mild TYLC clone.
b) Use of antisense or catalyst (ribozyme) RNA
c) Plant transformation with partial or defective viral sequence
d) All of the above.

805. A synthetic gene coding for an insecticidal crystal protein (ICP) of *Baccilus thuriengiensis* have been transferred to Brinjal is

a) Cry 1 A gene
b) Cry 1 Ab gene
c) Cry 1 Aa gene
d) Cry 1AB gene

806. Bt stands for

a) *Baccilus sp*
b) *Agrobacterium tumfacience*
c) *Baccilus thuringiensis*
d) None of these of the above.

807. A major short coming of isozyme in analysis of chilli

a) Small number of isozyme loci available
b) large number of isozyme loci available
c) Both of the above
d) None of these of the aabove

808. In capsicum research RFLP refers to

a) Study genetic diversity
b) Study linkage
c) Provide moleculer marker for mapping
d) Distinguish homozygous from heterozygous individual

809. RFLP stands for

a) Restriction Fragmented Length Polymorphism
b) Restriction Fragment Length Polymorphism
c) Restricted Fragment Length Polymorphism
d) Restricted Fragmented Length Polymorphism.

810. RADP in chili used for

a) To study genetic diversity
b) To study linkage
c) To provide molecular marker for mapping
d) All of these

811. Contender is a variety of

a) French bean b) Broad bean
c) Lima bean d) None of these

812. Transgenic cauliflower is effective against infection of

a) *Xyllostella pluttela* b) *Myzus persicae*
c) Painted bug d) None of these

813. Bt Brinjal is effective against

a) Phomopsis blight
b) Shoot and fruit borer
c) Root and Fruit borer
d) Root and Shoot borer

814. ICP stands for

a) Insecticidal Crystal Protein
b) Insecticide Crystal Protein
c) Insect Crystal Protein
d) Insecticidal crystallization protein

815. Biochemical methods would be of great value for cultivar identification

a) Isozyme analysis b) RFLP
c) Both d) None of these

816. RAPD stands for

a) Randomly Amplified Polymorphic DNA
b) Random Amplified Polymorphic DNA
c) Randomly Amplification Polymorphic DNA
d) Randomly Amplified Polymorphic DNA

817. The techniques to clone 1st gene were developed in

a) 1972 b) 1978
c) 1987 d) 1974

818. Soil bacteria often posses Ri Plasmid is

a) *A. rhizogenes* b) *A. tumifaciens*
c) *R. solunuceurum* d) None of these

819. Synthetic seeds are

a) Protoplast b) Somaclones
c) Cybrids d) Somatic embryos

820. Manipulation of the genetic material towards a desired end is a directed and Re-determined way is called

a) Genetic engineering b) Gene cloning
c) Reconibinent DNA technology d) All of these

821. Introduction of Tobbaco Mosaic Virus transgene into plants in 1986 was used to demonstrate

a) Cross expression b) Co-inoculation
c) Co -transformation d) Co protein

822. The first transgenic plant was

a) Produced in 1956 in tomato b) Produced in 1953 in tomato
c) Produced in 1956 in tobacco d) Produced in 1953 in tobacco

823. Flavour savr was the first genetically engineered– – – – – – –

a) Tomato b) Potato
c) Brinjal d) Capsicum

824. RAPD molecular markers are

a) Dominant b) Co dominant
c) Recessive d) Neutral

825. AFLB molecular marker are

a) Co-dominant b) Recessive

c) Dominant d) Neutral

826. Which of the following protein has toxic effect on Coleoptera including Collardo Potato Beetle

a) Cry 3A protein b) Cry 3 Ab protein

c) Cry 3B protein d) Cry 3AB protein

827. Maize transposable elements have been successfully introduced into

a) Tobacco cell culture b) Potato cell culture

c) Carrot cell culture d) Tomato cell culture

828. In brinjal ____________ species, is a source of resistance to Verticillium wilt and bacterial wilt

a) *Solanum scabrum* b) *Solanum xanthocarpum*

c) *Solanum torvum* d) *Solanum sisymbrofolium*

829. Hild's Ideal is a variety of

a) Brussels Sprouts b) Carrot

c) Wheat d) Rye

830. Totipotency of plant cells was demonstrated for first time by using

a) Tomato b) Potato

c) Turnip d) Carrot

831. *Agrobacterium*-mediated transformation of hypocotyl explant of cauliflower

Variety is

a) Pusa Snowball K1 b) Pusa Snowball

c) Both d) None of these

832. Haploid production cannot be done through

a) Pollen culture b) Callus culture

c) Anther culture d) Hybridization

833. First interagenic cross between radish & cabbage was made by

a) Jennings
b) Hull
c) Karpenchenko
d) Richy

834. Tolerance of low temperature, resistance to cucumber mosaic virus and *Botrytis cineria* was transferred from *S. lycopersicoides* in tomato by using

a) Protoplast fusion
b) Protoplast culture
c) Embryo culture
d) Ovule culture

835. *L. peruvianum and L. esculentum* are self incompatible and these can be overcome by using

a) Embryo culture
b) Somaclonal variation
c) Distant Hybridization
d) Embryo rescue technique

836. Purpose of embryo culture of *Abelmoschus esculentus*× *Abelmoschus moschatus* hybr

a) Study of embryo development
b) Induce embyo growthin the the absence of symbiotic fungus
c) Study of self and cross adaptability relationship
d) Overcome non viability

837. Non viability in *Abelmoschus esculentus* × *A. moschatus* , *A. tulerculatus* × *A. moschatus* hybrid can be overcome by

a) Embryo culture
b) Somaclonal variation
c) Protoplast fusion
d) Anther culture

838. Purpose of embryo culture in *Allium cepa and A. fistolosum is*

a) Study of embryo development
b) Study of soma-clonal variation
c) Anther culture
d) Protoplasm fusion

839. Self serility of seeds in *Colocassia esculentum*× *C. centequarum* can be overcome by

a) Potoplasm fusion
b) Somaclonal variation
c) Embro culture
d) Distant hybridization

840. Study of self and cross incompatibility in cucumis spp (*C. metriferus*×*C. melo*) can be overcome by

a) Protoplasm fusion b) Embryo culture
c) Distant hybridization d) Somaclonal variation

841. In *P. vulgaris and P. acutifolium* embryo culture was done to

a) Overcome non viability b) Over self-incompatibility
c) Over self sterility d) All of above

842. Distant hybridization is mainly followed to

a) Overcome presynganic and postsyngamic barriers
b) Exchange of genome between cultivated and wild sp
c) Transfer of resistant gene(s) from wild sp. To cultivated sp.
d) All of the above.

843. For long storage, potato tubers should be kept at

a) 5-10°C b) 10-15°C
c) 15-20°C d) 20-25°C

844. Hyrid between *Brassica napus and B. compestris* can be obtained by

a) Distant hybridization b) Protoplast fusion
c) Somaclonal variation d) Embryo culture

845. Hybrid between *Solanum melongena and Solanum sisimbrifolium can be* obtained by

a) Protoplast fusion b) Somaclonal variation
c) Distant d) None of these

846. Cross between *S. tuberosum* and *S. breudents* can be made by

a) Somaclonal variation b) Embryo rescue technique
c) Protoplast fusion d) All of the above

847. Hybrid between *Solanum tuberosum* and *L. esculentum* can be get by

a) Protoplast fusion b) Somaclonal variation
c) Embryo culture d) All of above

848. The non conventional genetic procedure involving fusion between isolated somatic protoplast (wall less naked cell) under in vitro condition and subsequent development of their product (hetero karyon) to a hybrid plant is known as

a) Cybridization b) Mitotic hybridization
c) Protoplast fusion d) Somatic hybridization

849. Breeding posses a nuclear genome from only one parent but cytoplasm gene from both parents known as

a) Somatic hybridization b) Protoplast fusion
c) Embryo cultured d) Cybridization

850. In Somatic hybridization the most preferred plant part is/are

a) Root cells b) Stem cells
c) Mesophyll cells d) All of these

851. Hybrid between *D. carota and petroselinum* can be obtain by

a) Somatic hybridization b) Protoplast fusion
c) Distant hybridization d) All of these

852. Phomopsis blight, fruit rot, Verticillium wilt and bacterial wilt are the important diseases of

a) Tomato b) Potato
c) Brinjal d) Chilli

853. *S.tuberosum and S.phureja* can be crossed by using

a) Embryo rescue b) Embryo culture
c) Protoplast fusion d) Somaclonal variation

854. *S. tuberosum and S. melongna* can be crossed by using

a) Protoplasm fusion b) Embryo culture
c) Somaclonal variation d) Embryo rescue

855. Di haploid *S. acaule* and tetraploid *S. tuberosum* can be crossed by using

a) Somatic hybridization b) Embryo rescue
c) Embryo culture d) Somaclonal variation

856. *Lectuca debilis and L. indica* can be hybridized by

a) Protoplasm fusion
b) Somatc *hybridization*
c) Embryo culture
d) None of these

857. *Brassica napus* and *B. compestris* can be crossed by using

a) Protoplast fusion
b) Somatic hybridization
c) Embryo culture
d) None of these

858. *B. oleracea and B. compestris* can be crossed by using

a) Somatic hybridization
b) Embryo culture
c) Protoplasm fusion
d) None of these

859. Poor fruit set and seed production in *Cucumis moschata and C. maxima is* due to

a) Self incompatibility
b) Cross incompatibility
c) Poor pollen tube growth
d) None of these

860. Poor fruit set in C.*maxima and C.moschata* due to

a) Self incompatibility
b) Cross incompatibility
c) Poor pollen tube growth
d) None of these

861. Poor fruit set in C. *maxima and* C. *pepo* is due to

a) Self incompatility
b) Cross incompatibility
c) Poor pollen tube growth
d) None of these

862. Lettuce is a ______crop.

a) Self pollinated
b) Often cross pollinated
c) Highly cross pollinated
d) None of these

863. Intergeneric crosses between *B. compestris* and *Raphanus sativus* crossability is generally poor due to

a) Slow growth of pollen tube
b) Structural barrier
c) Strong incompatibility reaction at stigma
d) None of these

864. Hybridization barriers can be overcome by using

a) Embryo culture
b) Bridge cross
c) Use of growth substances
d) All of above

865. *C. sativus* × *Cucumis melo* have

a) Post syngemic incompatibility
b) Pre syngemic incompatibility
c) Both
d) None of these

866. Most common sex expression in cucurbits is

a) Monoecism b) Dioecism
c) Andromonoecism d) None of these of above

867. *S. bulbocadtanum and S.tuberosum* incompatibility can be overcome by using

a) Embryo rescue b) Growth hormones
c) Bridge cross d) Protoplast fusion

868. Bridging sp in *S. bulbocatum and S. tuberosum* is

a) *S. pennatesectum* b) *S.phureja*
c) *S.acaule* d) All of above

869. Virus restant varities in potato were developed by utilizing *S.tuberosum ssp andigema and S.stoloniferum as donor* parent. The technique used was

a) Distant hybridization b) Embryo culture
c) Somatic hybridization d) Endosperm culture

870. A variety resistant to *Pseudomonas solanacearum* was developed by using *S.phureja and S.vernei* has been ideal source *of Globodera pallida* resistance developed by using

a) Embryo culture b) Somatihybridization
c) Endosperm culture d) Distant hybridization

871. Muskmelon crosses with __________

a) Cucumber b) Watermelon
c) Long melon d) None of these

872. In lettuce downy mildew resistant varieties were developed through

a) Endosperm culture b) Embryo culture
c) Embryo rescue technique d) Distant hybridization

873. Distant hybridization between *L.serryola* and *L. viosa* result in

a) Vanguard b) Sioux
c) Improved meeruthi d) None of these

874. In lettuce mosaic resistant varieties can be developed by using

a) Protoplasm fusion b) Distant hybridization
c) Embryo rescue d) All of above

875. In lettuce virus resistant varieties can be developed by using

a) Distant hybridization b) Protoplasm fusion
c) Embryo rescue d) All of above

876. Pollen of which type of bean are allergic to some people

a) Broad bean b) Cluster bean
c) Sword bean d) None of these

877. Male sterility was recovered from the cross of *Brassica nigra* and *B. oleracea* by

a) Distant hybridization b) Protoplasm fusion
c) Embryo rescue d) All of these

878. In *Phaseolus vulgaris* resistance *to Pseudomonas phaseoli* was transferred *Phaseolus coccineus* through

a) Protoplasm fusion b) Embryo culture
c) Distant hybridization d) Ovule culture

879. The toleance to root rot in varieties Georgia, Roza,Viva and Refws NW-59,

NW-63 was derived from *P. coccineus* through

a) Distant hybridizataion b) Embrryo culture
c) Ovule culture d) All of above

880. In Okra , *A. manihot* has been successfully used to develop YVM Virus resistant varieties by

a) Distant hybridization b) Embryo culture
c) Ovule culture d) None of these

881. Cucumber Mosaic Virus (CMV) is transmissible by

a) Sap
b) Aphis spp
c) *Myzus persicae*
d) All of above

882. Cross between *L. esculentum* and *L. chilense* follows

a) Embryo culture
b) Protopasm fusion
c) Distant hybridization
d) Endosperm culture

883. Cross between *L.esculentum* and *L.lycoperciodes* follows

a) Embryo culture
b) Protoplasm fusion
c) Distant hybridization
d) Endosperm culture

884. Cross between *L. esculentum and L. peruvianum* follows

a) Embryo culture
b) Protoplast fusion
c) Distant hybridization
d) Endosperm culture

885. Cross between *A. esculentus and A. ficuleneus* follows

a) Embryo culture
b) Protoplasm fusion
c) Distant hybridization
d) Endosperm culture

886. Cross between *A. esculentus and A. moschatus* follows

a) Embryo culture
b) Protoplast fusion
c) Distant hybridization
d) Endosperm culture

887. Cross between *A. moschatus and A. manihot* follows

a) Embryo culture
b) Protoplast fusion
c) Distant hybridization
d) Endosperm culture

888. Cross between *Glycine max and G. tomentella* follows

a) Embryo culture
b) Protoplast fusion
c) Distant hybridization
d) None of these

889. *Phaseolus vulgaris* and *Phaseolus accutifolius* follows

a) Embryo culture
b) Protoplasm fusion
c) Distant hybridization
d) All of these

890. *Brassica oleracea* and *B. compestris* follows

a) Embryo culture
b) Protoplasm fusion
c) Distant hybridization
d) All of these

891. *Brassica compestris* and *Brassica oleracea* follows

a) Embryo culture b) Protoplasm fusion
c) Ovule culture d) None of these

892. *B. chinensis* and *B. perkinensis* follows

a) Embryo culture b) Protoplast fusion
c) Ovule culture d) None of these

893. *C. melo* and *C. moschata* follows

a) Embryo culture b) Protoplasm fusion
c) Ovule culture d) None of these

894. *Phaseolus accutifolius* and *P.vulgaris* follows

a) Embryo culture b) Protoplast fusion
c) Ovule culture d) None of these

895. *P.coccineus* and *P. vulgaris* follows

a) Embryo culture b) Protoplasm fusion
c) Ovule culture d) None of these

896. *P. vulgaris* and *P.retensis* follows

a) Embryo culture b) Protoplasm fusion
c) Ovule culture d) None of these

897. *P.vulgaris* and *P.lanatus* follows

a) Embryo culture b) Protoplasm fusion
c) Ovule culture d) None of these

898. General dose of radiation for mutation in *S. tuberosum* is

a) 5-6 krd b) 3-15 krd
c) 15-25 krd d) 10-20 krd

899. General dose of radiation for mutation in *Ipomea batata* is

a) 5-6 krd b) 3-15 krd
c) 15-25 krd d) 10-20 krd

900. Tomato variety Pusa Lal Meeruti was evolved by

a) X-rays b) gamma- rays
c) EMS d) MMS

901. Of the following general dose of radiation (Krd) is used for mutation in *S. melongena*

a) 5-6 b) 3-15
c) 15-25 d) 10-20

902. General dose of radiation (Krd) used for mutation in *C. annum*

a) 5-6 b) 8-10
c) 10-20 d) 15-20

903. General dose of radiation (Krd) used for mutation in *Pisum sativum*

a) 15-25 b) 10-20
c) 10-15 d) 15-20

904. General dose of radiation (Krd) used for mutation in *Vicia faba*

a) 5-10 b) 10-15
c) 10-20 d) 5-15

905. General dose of radiation (Krd) used for mutation in *C. sativus*

a) 25-40 b) 30-35
c) 15-20 d) 10-25

906. General dose of radiation (Krd) used for mutation in *Daucus carota*

a) 30-50 b) 50-70
c) 10-30 d) 15-20

907. General dose of radiation (Krd) used for mutation *in Brassica* sp

a) 60-80 b) 80-100
c) 90-100 d) 110-120

908. *L. esculentum* using gamma rays as mutagen result in

a) Early and high yielding b) 6-10 days earlier ripening
c) Early flowering mutant d) All

909. C. *annum* using gamma rays as mutagen result in

a) A productive mutant b) A inferior mutant
c) No effects of gamma rays d) None of these

910. *Pisum sativum* using gamma rays as mutagen result in

a) Early and low yield
b) Ten days earlier yield
c) Early but unsatisfactory seed production
d) None of these

911. *Pisum sativum* using X- rays and neutron as mutagen result in

a) Early and low yield
b) Ten days earlier yield
c) Early but unsatisfactory seed production
d) None of these

912. *Pisum sativum* using DES as mutagen result in

a) Early and low yield
b) Ten days earlier yield
c) Early but unsatisfactory seed production
d) None of these

913. *Pisum sativum* using X ray and EMS as mutagen result in

a) Early and low yield
b) Ten days earlier yield
c) Early but unsatisfactory seed production
d) None of these

914. X ray used mutagen *in P. vulgaris* result in

a) Early and high yield
b) Late but high yield
c) Early but less yield
d) Late and less yield

915. Which mutagen is used to increase yield in S.*tuberosum*

a) Irradiation
b) Chemical mutagen
c) x rays and gamma rays
d) All

916. Parentage of Pusa Ruby (Tomato) are

a) Sioux X S-12
b) Sioux X Red cloud
c) Sioux X Pusa Early Dwarf
d) Sioux X Improved Meeruti

917. *Pisonia grandis* is

a) Indian lettuce
b) Indian spinach
c) Water cabbage
d) Letture tree

918. Which of the following mutagen help in increasing yield in *C. annum*

a) Gamma rays
b) DES
c) Chemical mutagen
d) All of these

919. Which of the following mutagen play role in increasing yield *in P. vulgaris*

a) Gamma rays
b) X rays
c) Irradation
d) All of these

920. Mutagen used for increasing yield in *Vicia faba*

a) Irradation
b) Chemical
c) Both a and b
d) None of these

921. Mutagen used for resistant traits in *S. tuberosum* against *Phytophthora infestens*

a) Gamma rays
b) X-rays
c) WEU
d) All

922. Mutagen used for resistant traits in *S. tuberosum* against *Alternaria solani*

a) Gamma rays
b) X-rays
c) WEU
d) Spontaneus

923. Mutagen used for resistant traits in *S. tuberosum* against *Synchytrium endobioticum*

a) X-rays
b) Gamma rays
c) EMS
d) None of these

924. Mutagen used for resistant traits in *S. tuberosum* against *Pseudomonas solanacearum*

a) Gamma rays
b) EMS
c) Both a and b
d) None of these

925. Mutagen used for resistant traits in *Ipomea batatas* for cold tolerance

a) Gamma rays
b) X-rays
c) Both
d) None of these

926. Mutagen used for resistant traits in *Lycopersicon spp* against *Phytophthora infestans*

a) Gamma rays b) X-rays

c) Chemical mutagen d) All

927. Mutagen used for resistant traits in *Lycopersicon* spp against *Phytopathora infestans* against Race T_0

a) Gamma rays b) X-rays

c) Chemical mutagen d) All

928. Mutagen used for resistant traits in *Lycopersicon spp* against *Phytopathora infestans* against Race T_1

a) Gamma rays b) X-rays

c) Chemical mutagen d) All

929. *Cucumis melo* var. *momordica* is

a) Snap melon b) Cucumber

c) Bittergourd d) All

930. *Limnocharis flava* is

a) Water cabbage b) Lungru

c) Watercress d) All

931. *Parkia roxburghii* is

a) Tree bean b) Winged Bean

c) Ivy Gourd d) drumsticks

932. *Solanum indicum* is

a) Bush Tomato/ Indian nightshade

b) Agathi

c) Horse radish

d) All

933. Pant Sabji Matar-4 is resistant to

a) Powdery mildew b) Fusarium wilt

c) Root rot d) All

934. Early Badger variety of pea is resistant to

a) Fusarium wilt b) Rust
c) Powdery mildew d) None of these

935. Mutagen used in *Phaseolus vulgaris* against bacterial disease

a) X-rays b) Gamma rays
c) Beta rays d) All

936. Mutagen used in *Phaseolus vulgaris* against Golden Mosaic virus

a) X-rays b) EMS
c) Gamma rays d) All

937. Mutagen used in *Phaseolus vulgaris* against Yellow Mosaic virus

a) X-rays b) EMS
c) Gamma rays d) Both b and c

938. Mutagen used in *Phaseolus vulgaris* against *Uromyces phaseoli*

a) X-rays b) Gamma rays
c) EMS d) Both b and c

939. Mutagen used *in Phaseolus vulgaris* against *Xanthomonas phaseoli*

a) X-rays b) Gamma rays
c) EMS d) Both b and c

940. For getting High dry matter and sugar *S. lycopersicon* treated with

a) X-rays b) Gamma rays
c) EMS d) All

941. *C. annum* treated with Gamma rays result in

a) High capsaicin content b) High colour
c) Vitamin C d) All

942. For increasing High capsaicin and amino acid composition in seed of *Capsicum annum* is treated with

a) X-rays b) Gamma rays
c) Neutron d) All

943. Treated with Sodium azide, EMS in *Capsicum annum* result in

a) High capsaicin content b) Good colour
c) High protein d) All

944. Treatment with Sodium irradiation in *Capsicum annum* result in,

a) High capsaicin content b) Good colour
c) High protein d) All

945. In *Phaseolus vulgaris* treatment with X-ray result in

a) Yellow to green pod b) High yield
c) Good quality d) All

946. In variety Moskovsky of bean released by USSR E1, DMS result in

a) Increase protein content b) Yellow to green pod
c) High yield d) All

947. *Vicia faba* when treated with Irradiation result in

a) Increase protein content b) Yellow to green pod
c) High yield d) All

948. *Vicia faba* when treated with chemical mutagen result in

a) Increase protein content b) Yellow to green pod
c) High yield d) All

949. *Trigonella foenumgraceum* when treated with EMS result in

a) High crude oil content b) Increase in protein
c) Both d) None of these

950. *Brassica pekinensis* when treated with E_1 result in

a) Increase in ascorbic acid
b) Decrease in ascorbic acid content
c) No effects on ascorbic acid content
d) None of these

951. *Brassica pekinensis* when treated with DMS result in

a) Increase in ascorbic acid
b) Decrease in ascorbic acid content
c) No effects on ascorbic acid content
d) None of these

952. *S. tuberosum* when treated with gamma rays result in

a) Change in tuber colour
b) Increase in protein content
c) Increase in carbohydrate content
d) Form deep eyes

953. *S. tuberosum* when treated with radio isotopes result in

a) Change in tuber colour
b) Increase in protein content
c) Increase in carbohydrate content
d) Form deep eyes

954. Blossom End Rot in tomato is due to the deficiency of

a) Ca b) P
c) Fe d) I

955. *Ipomea batatas* when treated with Gamma rays result in

a) Change in tuber colour b) Increase in protein content
c) Increase in tuber size d) None of these

956. *Cyclenthera pedata* is

a) Sweet Bittergourd b) bitter melon
c) Spine gourd d) None of these

957. Sioux variety of tomato when treated with X-rays result in variety

a) S-12 b) Improved meeruthi
c) Pusa Lal Meeruthi d) None of these

958. S-12 is superior over Sioux in

a) Large number of fruits b) High yield
c) Both a and b d) None of these

959. Meeruthi dry seeds when treated with 30 Krd gamma rays result in

a) Improved meeruthi b) Pusa Lal Meeruthi
c) S_{12} d) None of these

960. Pusa Lal Meeruthi is superior over Meeruthi in

a) Uniform fruit ripening
b) Increase yield
c) Uniform colour
d) All

961. Kloster variety when treated with .... results in Stralart variety in tomato

a) X-rays
b) Gamma rays
c) Chemical mutagen
d) Neutron

962. The dose of X-rays used when Kloster variety treated with X-rays to form Stralat variety in tomato (Krd)

a) 10
b) 20
c) 15
d) 25

963. Arka Suphal, Arka Meghana, Arka Sweta and Arka Harita are the hybrids of

a) Chilli
b) Tomato
c) Capsicum
d) Okra

964. In Navy bean, Michelite when treated with............ result in Sanilic.

a) X-rays
b) Gamma rays
c) Chemical mutagen
d) None of these

965. Sree Ohara is an improved variety of

a) *coleus*
b) sweet potato
c) colocasia
d) cassava

966. Priya is a selection of which cucurbit

a) bottle gourd
b) bitter gourd
c) sponge gourd
d) ridge gourd

967. In Navy bean Michelite when treated with X-rays result in

a) Sea farer
b) Sea Way
c) Sanilac
d) All of these

968. Sea Farer is superior over Michellite in

a) Very early type
b) Increase Yield
c) High protein
d) All

969. Wax poded bean when treated with X-rays result in

a) Pusa Parvati b) Sea Farer

c) Sea Way d) All

970. French bean is a native of

a) Asia b) South & Central America

c) Mediterranean region d) None of these

971. Fruits of okra are rendered unmarketable due to the attack of

a) Aphids b) Mites

c) Painted bug d) All of above

972. Sugar Baby is a variety of

a) Cucumber b) Water melon

c) Summer squash d) None of these

973. Garlic having largest bulb size

a) Gede b) Madrasi

c) Tabiti d) Jamunanagar local

974. Great Lakes is a variety of

a) Crisp head lettuce b) Butter head lettuce

c) Leaf type lettuce d) None of these

975. Harvesting of chaulai is done

a) 2-3 weeks after sowing b) After 3-4 weeks

c) After 5-6 weeks d) None of these

976. In tomato, for fruit setting in adverse climatic conditions, spray

a) 2, 4-D b) PCPA

c) Ethrel d) Cycocel

977. In yams, poisonous alkaloids, volatile acids & calcium oxalate are present in the

a) Leaves b) Roots

c) Tubers d) Flowers

978. Indian cauliflowers are primarily

a) Self- incompatible b) Self- compatible
c) Self- sterile d) Cross- incompatible

979. Japanese White is a variety of

a) Carrot
b) Radish
c) Turnip
d) None of these of above

980. Leaf curl virus in nature is spread by

a) Aphids b) Whitefly
c) Leaf hopper d) Jassids

981. Leek is mainly propagated by

a) Seed b) Bulb
c) Root cutting d) Leaf cutting

982. Lima bean can be planted ________ in a year.

a) Once b) twice
c) Thrice d) All of these

983. Lycopene development in tomato is adversely affected when temperature is above

a) 30°C b) 25°C
c) 20°C d) 10°C

984. Number of irrigations generally applied to chilli is

a) 3-4 b) 6-8
c) 5-10 d) 15-16

985. Which species of potato is a source of high starch

a) *S. vernei* b) *S.stoloniferum*
c) *S. chacoense* d) *S. Acaule*

986. Which species of potato is a source of Bacterial resistance

a) *S.chacoense* b) *S. spasipilum*
c) *S. prureja* d) *S. stenotomum*

987. Which species of potato is a source of resistance for Potato Virus Y

a) *S.chacoense* b) *S. stoloniferum*

c) *S. phureja* d) All of these

988. Which species of potato as a source of resistance for Potato Leaf Roll Virus

a) *S. acaule* b) *S.brevidens*

c) *S.tuberosum* d) All of these

989. In Potato, gene designation for colourless peel is

a) y b) Y

c) c d) d

990. In Potato, gene designation for *Verticilium* resistance is

a) Ve b) V

c) VE d) v

991. Australian Green is a variety of

a) Summer squash b) Pea

c) Bean d) all of above

992. In chilli gene symbol................indicate pointed fruit

a) P b) p

c) D d) d

993. In chilli gene symbol................indicates male sterility

a) ms b) MS

c) Ms d) ms

994. In chilli gene symbol................indicates resistance to *M. incognita*

a) N b) R

c) M d) n

995. In chilli gene symbol................indicates phenotype capsaicin

a) C b) c

c) Cc d) CC

996. Which of the following gene symbols indicates hairless in chillies

a) H_1 b) H
c) H_2 d) h

997. In chilli gene symbol................indicates yellow or orange mature fruit Colour

a) W b) X
c) Y d) Z

998. Which of the following gene symbols indicates high beta carotene in chillies

a) T b) t
c) Tt d) tt

999. Biodiversity is study of:

a) Diverse species in nature
b) Number of living organisms
c) Variety of all living organisms on earth
d) All of the above

1000. The Great Columbian exchange relates with :

a) Tomato , maize , potato , wheat
b) Cole crops and tomato
c) Maize wheat and potato
d) Tomato and potato

1001. In which year FAO, technical council has proposed the creation of global gene bank to store representative collection of main varieties of food plants

a) 1972 b) 1967
c) 1961 d) 1983

1002. CBD (The Convention on Biological Diversity) was adopted in June 1992 at Rio de Jeneiro at earth summit and is effective from:

a) 1992 b) 1995
c) 2000 d) 1993

1003. Objectives of CBD are

1) To conserve the biodiversity
2) Sustain and adequate sharing of benefits arising out by utilization of genetics :
3) Transfer of technology and appropriate funding

a) Only 1 and 2 b) 1 and 3 only
c) None of these d) All above

1004. Country that signed the CBD require to integrate consideration of

a) Sustainable use of biodiversity b) Fund to different plan itself
c) Cannot share technology d) All above

1005. International Treaty on Plant Genetic Resources (ITPGR) for food and agriculture is effective from

a) 1 march 2004 b) 29 June 2004
c) 2 July 2004 d) 5 June 2004

1006. ITPGR become effective after ratification of 40 countries and treaty has over

a) 45 countries b) 72 countries
c) 84 countries d) 115 countries

1007. Objectives of ITPGR are

a) Conservation and sustainable use of bio resources for food and agriculture
b) Fair and adequate sharing of benefits
c) Biodiversity conservation
d) All of the above

1008. Institution mechanism of BDA (The Biological Diversity Act) of India involves participation of

a) National biodiversity authority
b) State biodiversity board
c) Biodiversity management committee d)
d) None of these

1009. Which of following is not true about NBA (National Biodiversity Authority)

a) It deals with matter related for access by foreign individual, institutes, and companies
b) Imposition of conditions to secure and faire use of bio resources
c) Approval for IPRs
d) All of the above

1010. LMO in contest of biodiversity stands for :

a) Level of molecular organization
b) Lab modified organisms
c) Land mass organization
d) Living modified organisms

1011. Punjab hybrid-1, MH-10 are the hybrids of

a) Muskmelon b) Water melon
c) Summer squash d) Cucumber

1012. Resources to be exempted from NBA

a) Rare bio-resources
b) Resources traded as commodity
c) Extinct bio-resources
d) All above

1013. The monesty benefits and fee royalty receive as a result of approval by NBA deposited in

a) National biodiversity fund
b) State biodiversity fund
c) Govt. of India
d) International biodiversity fund

1014. For each contracting party of ITPGR there are some undertakings

1) Survey and inventory of PGRFA
2) Promote and support local communities
3) Minimize or eliminate the threat to PGRFA
4) In situ and ex-situ conservation of wild type

a) All above are false b) Only 1and 4 are true
c) Except 2 all d) All above true

1015. The BDA of India passed by Indian parliament in

a) July, 2002 b) December, 2002
c) Nov., 2002 d) July, 2005

1016. Objectives of BDA of India are

1). To conserve and protect local communities
2). Respect and protect local communities
3). Rehabilitation of species
4). Implementation through constitutional committees

a) All of the above b) All except 1
c) 1, 2 and 3 d) All except 3

1017. National Heritage Sites Important from the stand point of Biodiversity will proposed in NBA by

a) International Biodiversity Agencies
b) Central Government
c) Local Self Governments
d) State Governments

1018. Biodiversity Act 2002 divided into

a) 12 sections b) 7 sections
c) 15 sections d) 8 sections

1019. Benefits of sharing for PGR and Traditional Knowledge has been well taken care of at National level by following acts

a) Protection of plant varieties and Farmer's rights
b) Patent act 2006
c) Both a and b
d) National Biodiversity Act

1020. Protection of Plant varieties and Farmer's rights act come into light

a) 1985 b) 2001
c) 2005 d) 1995

1021. Key issues which needed to be consider for TRIPS agreement for harmonization with the provision of CBD are

a) Disclosure of sources and country of origin of biodiversity
b) Evidence prior to approval to authorities
c) Fair and equal sharing under relevant national regime
d) All of the above

1022. National Valvian Research Institute of Plant Industry was established in

a) 1960s b) 1894
c) 1943 d) 1974

1023. N I Valvian research institute is situated in

a) Italy b) U.S.A
c) Russia d) U.K

1024. NATIONAL SEED STORAGE LAB Fort Collin U.S.A set up in

a) 1947 b) 1899
c) 1965 d) 1935

1025. The Institute of Plant Genetics and Crop Plants Genetic Resources, Gatersleben Germany was established in

a) 1897 b) 1947
c) 1974 d) 1943

1026. First gene bank was introduced in

a) 1920s b) 1950s
c) 1960s d) 1910

1027. IBPGR, now IPGRI was established in

a) 1974 b) 1928
c) 1947 d) 1966

1028. A gene bank

a) Provide potential solution of gene erosion and genetic wipeout
b) Provide degree of in-situ and ex-situ conservation of gene pool
c) All of the above
d) None of these

1029. Seed gene bank is the conservation of

a) All type of crops
b) Root crops only
c) Species with seeds tolerant to low temperature
d) None of these

1030. Recalcitrant seed is

a) True seed
b) Nucleus seed
c) Vegetative propagule
d) Certified seed

1031. Stigma receptivity of capsicum is

a) 3-days after anthesis
b) 2-days after anthesis
c) 4-days after anthesis
d) None of these

1032. Advantages of cryopreservation are:

a) Preservation of short life seed for long time
b) Require minimum space
c) Prevent contamination
d) All of the above

1033. Botanical gardens are

a) Site of conservation of living species
b) Centre of important research
c) Centre of taxonomy and identification
d) All of the above

1034. Total no of botanical gardens all over the world are:

a) 1500
b) 2000
c) 2500
d) 2400

1035. Pusa Alankar is a hybrid of

a) Ridge gourd
b) Bottle gourd
c) Bitter gourd
d) Summer squash

1036. DNA preserve for long duration at temperature

a) 2°C
b) 7°C
c) 4°C
d) -196°C

1037. Germplasm documentation is effective in

a) Utilization of gene bank
b) Exchange of genetic information among between different countries
c) To manage and conserve bio-resources
d) All of the above

1038. Oblong fruited hybrid variety of bottle gourd is

a) Pusa Meghdhut b) Pusa Summer Prolific Long
c) Pusa Manjari d) None of these of the above

1039. The concept of ideotype was developed by

a) Resell (1978) b) Andrew knight (1800)
c) Golden d) Donald

1040. Over dominance hypotheses of heterosis was proposed by

a) Shull and East (1908) b) Andrew Knight (1800)
c) H. J. Muller (1927) d) Thomas Fairchild (1717)

1041. The term genotype and phenotype was coined by:

a) Johansen b) Corren
c) Robison d) Rusell

1042. The term heterosis was coined by

a) East b) Shull
c) Jones d) Daoport

1043. Who first used the term horizontal and vertical resistance

a) Jenning b) Thoday
c) Vander Plank d) Robinson

1044. The term recurrent selection was coined by

a) Hull b) Mathur
c) Rimphu d) None of these

1045. Blotchy ripening of tomato due to deficiency of

a) Nitrogen b) Magnesium and potassium
c) Copper d) Calcium

1046. Development of seed without sexual process is known as

a) Polyembryony b) Apomixes
c) Both a and b d) None of these

1047. Autpolyploidy is known as

a) Hybrid polyploidy b) Simple polyploidy
c) Segmental polyploidy d) All of above

1048. Introduction of mutation in crops by X-ray is done by;

a) Broke (1971) b) Stadler (1928)
c) H.J. Muller (1927) d) Aureback (1929)

1049. First intergenic hybrid between radish and cabbage made by

a) Rimphu (1880) b) Hull (1945)
c) Adam (1982) d) Karpenchinko (1927)

1050. Tomato fruit borer

a) *Phytophthora infestans* b) *Trialeurodes vaporariorum*
c) *Bactrocera tau* d) *Helicoverpa armigera*

1051. Capsicum variety of red colour is

a) California Wonder b) Bharat
c) Orobelle d) Indira

1052. Cross pollinated crops associated with

a) Diachogamy b) Cleistogamy
c) Chasmogamy d) None of these

1053. Asexual reproduction involves

a) Autogamy b) Allogamy
c) Amphimixes d) Apomixes

1054. The genetic constitution of *Gossypium hebaceum* is

a) AA b) BB
c) DD d) Both a and b

1055. The process of gametophyte development from somatic cell is called

a) Apospory b) Diplospory
c) Apogamy d) Angiogamy

1056. Single gene affecting more than one character

a) Phenotropy b) Polymorphism
c) Pleistogamy d) None of these

1057. Sugar found in DNA is

a) Ribose b) Fructose
c) Maltose d) De-Oxyribose

1058. Complementary gene produce phenotype was given by

a) Lamark b) Weisman
c) Darwin d) Bateson

1059. Theory of acquired character was given by

a) Lamark b) Weisman
c) Darwin d) Bateson

1060. Mendel was born in year

a) 1820 b) 1821
c) 1828 d) 1822

1061. Law of parallel variation was given by

a) Johenson1903 b) Davenport, 1908
c) Shull and East, 1908 d) Vavilov, 1926

1062. Gene pool consists of

a) Land races b) Obsolite cultivars
c) Modern cultivar d) All of these

1063. Genetic assortative mating useful in developing

a) Inbred b) Extreme phenotype
c) Sources population d) None of these

1064. Cytoplasm sterility is governed by

a) Cytoplasm and genetic gene b) Plasma gene
c) Nuclear gene d) None of these

1065. Who discover cell

a) Palade b) Claddy
c) Robert Hook d) Robert brown

1066. Restore gene is

a) Double top crop b) Single cross hybrid
c) Synthetic varieties d) None of these

1067. Which of following is wheat and maize research institute

a) IARI b) CAZRI
c) CSWRI d) CIMMYT

1068. Phototropism is

a) A plant's response to gravity b) A plant's response to light
c) A plant's response to water d) None of these

1069. Emasculation means

a) Removal of anther b) Removal of gynoecium's
c) Both a and b d) None of these

1070. ICRISAT deals with

a) Maize b) Shorghum
c) Cotton d) Mustard

1071. CIMMYT is situated at

a) Mexico b) India
c) Spain d) Nigeria

1072. CAZRI deals with

a) Arid crops b) Tropical crop
c) Sub tropical crops d) None of these

1073. Short-day Plants are

a) onions & garlic b) pea&potao
c) lettuce&garlic d) ginger&cabbage

1074. Microsporogensis occur in

a) Root b) Leaf
c) Stem d) Anther

1075. Pigment responsible for skin colour

a) Glutin b) Melanin
c) Fatty acid d) Amino acid

1076. Which of following material make protein chain

a) Amino acid
b) Fatty acid
c) Carbohydrates
d) None of these

1077. The transfer of pollen grain from anther to a flower stigma of same flower is known as

a) Cross pollination
b) Self pollination
c) Often pollination
d) Fertilization

1078. Root pressure is maximum when

a) Transpiration and absorption are low
b) Transpiration and absorption is high
c) Transpiration is high absorption is low
d) Transpiration slow absorption is high

1079. In the mechanism of opening and closing of stomata, the important factor is

a) Shape of gourd cell
b) Protein content of cell
c) Starch content in cell
d) All of the above

1080. Formation of lycopene in tomato is inhibited if temperature is

a) Below 13°C
b) Beyond 38°C.
c) At 20°C
d) Exceeds 32°C

1081. In green vegetables, the amino acid is

a) Methionine
b) Lysine
c) Arginine
d) Tryptophan

1082. Photophosphorylation is a process in which

a) CO_2 is reduced into carbohydrates
b) NADP is formed
c) Chemical energy is converted into light energy
d) Light energy is converted into chemical energy

1083. Photosynthesis does not take during night because

a) Optimum temperature is not available
b) Light is not present
c) More CO_2 evolved during night
d) Conc. of O_2 is less

1084. Term used to indicate the wind pollination is

a) Entomophily b) Zoophily
c) Anemophily d) Hydrophilic

1085. Monoecious condition is

a) An adaptation for cross pollination
b) An adaptation for self pollination
c) An adaption for vegetative propagation
d) None of these

1086. Optimum soil pH for tomato is

a) 6.0 to 7.0 b) 5.5 to 6.0
c) 7.0 to 8.0 d) None of these

1087. Mature Green stage of tomato is preferred for

a) Local market b) distant market
c) Processing d) None of these

1088. Recurrent selection is mostly used in

a) Self pollination b) Cross pollination
c) Vegetative propagation d) None of these

1089. Anthesis time of chilli is

a) 10:15AM to 11:00AM b) 5:15AM to 07:15AM
c) 7:15AM to 11:15AM d) None of these

1090. Isolation for chilli for Foundation Seed and Certified Seed genotype

a) 400m & 200m b) 1600m & 800m
c) 800m & 400m d) 1000m & 500m

1091. Spacing for Indeterminate varieties of tomato is

a) 60 × 45 cm b) 90 × 30 cm
c) 90 × 90 cm d) None of these

1092. Seed rate for Open Pollinated Varieties of tomato is

a) 100-200g/ha b) 150-250g/ha
c) 200-300g/ha d) 400-500g/ha

1093. Pure line is

a) The progeny of self heterozygous plant
b) The progeny of self homozygous plant
c) The progeny of vegetative propagation
d) The progeny of nucleus seed

1094. Sum total of genes in a species is called as

a) Gene bank
b) Gene pool
c) Gene sanctuaries
d) All of these

1095. Which of the following organizations are associated with germplasm

a) CGIAR
b) IPGRI
c) NBPGR
d) Both b and c

1096. NBPGR was established by

a) ICAR
b) FAO
c) CGIAR
d) NHB

1097. Which of the following organizations are associated with the working of Quarantine

a) NBPGR
b) BSI
c) FRI
d) All of these

1098. Indian Institute of Vegetable Research (IIVR) is located at

a) Port Blair, Andaman & Nicobar
b) Pusa, New Delhi
c) Varanasi, U.P.
d) Bangalore, Karnataka

1099. Conservation of Germplasm in form of seeds in cold storage is called

a) Field Gene Bank
b) Seed Gene Bank
c) Gene Sanctuaries
d) Gene Pool

1100. The goal of CBD

a) Conservation of biodiversity
b) Sustainable use of its components
c) Fair and equitable benefit sharing
d) All of these

1101. The subsidiary centers of diversity are

a) Indo-Malaysia b) Chile
c) Brazil and Paraguay d) All of these

1102. Introduction that can be used for commercial cultivation without any change in original phenotype

a) Primary Introduction b) Secondary Introduction
c) Direct Introduction d) Indirect Introduction

1103. In 1909, who coined the term Genotype and Phenotype

a) Vavilov, N.I. b) Mendel, G.J.
c) Johannsen, Wilhelm d) Nilsson, H.

1104. Cran (1915) first of all reported male sterility in

a) Capsicum b) Brinjal
c) Tomato d) Radish

1105. Mutation that occur naturally is called

a) Somatic Mutation b) Forward Mutation
c) Spontaneous Mutation d) Induced mutation

1106. Regeneration of whole plant from naked single cell in culture medium is called

a) Meristem culture b) Protoplast culture
c) Cell culture d) Organ culture

1107. Central Tobacco Research Institute (CTRI) is located at

a) Karnal b) Jhansi
c) Rajahmundry d) Nagpur

1108. Cultivation of crop regrowth after harvest on same field in the same year is called

a) Sequential Cropping b) Inter Cropping
c) Multiple Cropping d) Ratoon Cropping

1109. A technique of determining order of bases of DNA molecule which constitute a gene is called

a) Gene Cloning b) Gene Sequencing
c) Gene Splicing d) Genetic Engineering

1110. Asian Vegetable Research and Development Centre (AVRDC) is located at

a) Columbia b) India
c) Taiwan d) Mexico

1111. Which of the following are the main centers of crop diversity as proposed by Vavilov

a) South America b) China
c) India d) All of these

1112. Development of seed by cross pollination is called

a) Autogamy b) Apogamy
c) Allogamy d) Apospory

1113. Genetic improvement of crop plants through use of various physical and chemical mutagens for various economic use is called

a) Molecular Breeding b) Transgenic Breeding
c) Polyploidy Breeding d) Mutation Breeding

1114. In cryopreservation, tissues are stored in liquid nitrogen at

a) 4°C b) 0°C
c) 20°C d) -196°C

1115. In Heterosis Breeding, one should capitalize on

a) Homozygosity b) High seed cost
c) Over dominance d) Inbreeding depression

1116. *Eulycopersicon* is characterized by

a) green-fruited species b) yellow-fruited species
c) red-fruited species d) None of these

1117. Khatta palak is

a) *Rumex vesicarius* b) all of these
c) *R. acetosella* d) *R. scutatus*

1118. Polyploidy can be induced by

a) Colchicine b) Nitrous acid
c) Methyl methane sulphonate d) Ethylmethane sulphonate

1119. Two basic steps of breeding programme are

a) Mutation and Selection
b) Hybridization and Selection
c) Pollination and Fertilization
d) Variation and Selection

1120. The somatic chromosome numbers in Pea are

a) 7
b) 14
c) 28
d) 48

1121. The cornerstone of all breeding programmes is

a) Introduction
b) Selection
c) Selfing
d) Hybridization

1122. The hereditary material in chromosome is

a) DNA
b) RNA
c) ADP
d) ATP

1123. Inbreeding is deleterious in

a) Maize
b) Cucumber
c) Onion
d) Tomato

1124. National Research Centre for Spices (NRCS) OF 1986 is reorganized as IISR in

a) 1995
b) 1990
c) 1992
d) 1988

1125. Vegetables are called 'protective food' as they are rich in

a) Fats
b) Proteins
c) Vitamins and minerals
d) Sugar

1126. 'Green house cultivation' is mostly applied for growing of

a) Cut flowers
b) Vegetables
c) Vine crops
d) Shade loving trees

1127. 'Heterosis' is commercially exploited in

a) Self pollinated crops
b) Cross pollinated crops
c) Sexually propagated crops
d) Vegetatively propagated crops

1128. Pusa Manjari is a hybrid of

a) Bottle gourd b) Bitter gourd
c) Pumpkin d) Musk melon

1129. The term 'Epistasis' is given by

a) Bateson b) Mendel
c) Halman d) Hull

1130. Cucumber variety 'Olympian' is a

a) Asian varietiy b) Slicing variety
c) Pickling varietiy d) None of these

1131. Central Research Institute for Dryland Agriculture (CRIDA) is located at

a) Nagpur b) Bikaner
c) Jodhpur d) Hyderabad

1132. The leading producer of spices in the world is

a) Brazil b) Mexico
c) India d) Indonesia

1133. All India Spices Development was established in

a) 1971 b) 1990
c) 1963 d) 1966

1134. The cheapest method of preservation is

a) Preserving b) Canning
c) Freezing d) Drying

1135. Cucumber variety 'Socrates' is a

a) Asian variety b) Pickling cucumber
c) Special cucumber d) Seedless cucumber

1136. Mass selection is essentially a

a) Clonal selection b) Population movement
c) Hybridization technique d) Mutation breeding

1137. RRII headquarter is located at

a) Calicut b) Kottayan
c) Kasargod d) Bangalore

1138. Maximum fruit setting in tomato occurs at night temperature

a) 25-28°C b) 15-20°C
c) 10-20°C d) 22-29°C

1139. 'Breeder style' is the source of

a) Certified seeds b) Foundation seeds
b) Registered seeds d) Nucleus seeds

1140. In tomato flowers fails to set fruit if temperature is below and above

a) 10 °C & 25°C b) 13°C & 38°C
c) 8°C & 15°C d) 11°C & 28°C

1141. The full form of B. V.O. is

a) Brown Virus of Orange
b) Browning of Vegetables Crops
c) Bacteria like Viral Organisms
d) Brominated Vegetable Oil

1142. National Horticulture Board (NHB) was established during

a) 1984 b) 1986
c) 1976 d) 1980

1143. In India, first book on horticulture was written by

a) B. P.Paul b) W.B.Hayes
c) M.S.Randhawa d) J.E.Knott

1144. Sandy soil is suitable for

a) Late crop b) Early crop
c) Mid crop d) None of these

1145. Indian Botanical Garden, Kolkata is an example of

a) Italian style b) Mughal style
c) Japanese style d) English style

1146. The most effective method for transfer of oligogenic character is

a) Pedigree breeding b) Back cross breeding
b) Bulk breeding d) None of these

1147. In tomato,Lycopene is highest at

a) 11-14 °C b) 21-44 °C
c) 21-24 °C d) None of these

1148. Pedigree selection is a principle of

a) Rootstock b) Method of breeding
c) Plant breeding d) Scion

1149. Chromosome Number of tomato is

a) 22 b) 20
c) 26 d) 24

1150. Person related with 'Green Revolution' in India is

a) Dr. M.S. Swaminathan b) Dr. N.S. Randhawa)
c) Dr B. P. Pal. d) Dr. R.S. Paroda)

1151. First 'State Agricultural University' of India is situated at

a) Kanpur b) Pant Nagar
c) Solan d) Banglore

1152. Vegetables are dehydrated at a temperature of

a) 60-66°C b) 80-85°C
c) 40-50°C d) 90-95°C

1153. To check the variability in the root stocks one should opt for

a) Seedling b) Clonal rootstock
c) Seasonal rootstock d) All of above

1154. Cauliflower variety 'Early Kunwari' comes under which maturity group

a) October maturity group b) September maturity group
c) November maturity group d) None of these

1155. Pusa Snowball - 1(Cauliflower) is a

a) Selection from triple cross
b) Selection from the cross 12012 X 12013
c) Selection from local collection
d) None of these

1156. The crop showing greatest inbreeding depression

a) Onion b) Lettuce

c) Tomato c) Lima bean

1157. Storing of seed at freezing temperature

a) Orthodox b) Recalcitrant

c) Ex-situ conservation d) In-situ conservation

1158. Pusa Snowball K-1(Cauliflower) is

a) Resistant to black rot b) tolerant to powdery mildew

c) Tolerant to black rot d) None of these

1159. Pusa Kartik (Cauliflower) is resistant to

a) Downy mildew b) Powdery mildew

c) Black rot d) none of these

1160. In cauliflower, prominent introduction is

a) Pant Gobhi - 3 b) Early Kunwari

c) Dania d) None of these

1161. To reduce soil erosion, what is preferably done

a) Planting of crops with fibrous roots

b) Planting tall trees with long spacing

c) Keeping gentle slope to land

d) Dividing form in smaller areas

1162. Which is/are rare seed spices

a) Fennel b) Fenugreek

c) Cumin d) All of them

1163. The state leads in vegetable production is

a) U.P. b) Punjab

c) Bihar d) West Bengal

1164. An individual lacking one pair of chromosome from a diploid set (2n-2) is called

a) Monosomic b) Nullisomic

c) Trisomic d) Terasomic

1165. Spice crop largely exported from India is

a) Canine b) Black Pepper
c) Turmeric d) Cardamom

1166. Pure line selection is mainly applicable in

a) Self pollinated crops b) Cross pollinated crops
c) Often cross pollinated crops d) All of them

1167. Plantation and spices are main crops of

a) Eastern plateau and hill zone
b) Western plateau and hill zone
c) Central plateau and hill zone
d) Southern plateau and hill zone

1168. Vegetables require a sterilization temperature of

a) 105°C b) 116°C
c) 100°C d) 121°C

1169. IARI was shifted from Pusa (Bihar) to Pusa (New Delhi) in

a) 1905 b) 1936
c) 1952 d) 1942

1170. In cauliflower, curd and inflorescence blight is caused by

a) *Peronospora parasitica* b) *Alternaria brassicicola*
c) *Xanthomonas campestris* d) None of these

1171. In cauliflower, Black rot is caused by

a) *Alternaria brassicicola* b) *Peronospora parasitica*
c) *Xanthomonas campestris* d) None of these

1172. CBD was adopted in

a) 1994 b) 1986
c) 1991 d) 1992

1173. The 13th meeting of Subsidiary Body on Scientific, Technical and Technological advice (SBSTTA) held at

a) Italy b) Greece
c) Germany d) France

1174. Pusa Shubhra (Cauliflower) is a selection from

a) Double cross b) Local collection

d) Exotic Snowball group d) Triple cross

1175. Plant analysis is used if done at

a) Harvest b) Grain Formation

c) Early stage d) both 'a' and 'b'

1176. Seed coat peroxidase test is used for

a) Wheat b) Soy bean

c) Sorghum d) Ground Nut

1177. "Hydroponics Food Production." was written by Dr. Howard during the year

a) 1975 b) 1978

c) 1976 d) 1980

1178. Seed plot technique of potato is used to produce

a) Virus free seeds b) Fungus free seeds

c) Big size tuber d) Insect free seeds

1179. Rockwool is produced by burning a mixture of

a) Cock, basalt and perlite b) cock, basalt and limestone

c) Cock, basalt and cocopeat d) None of these

1180. Sodium is utilized essentially by

a) Cabbage b) Cauliflower

c) Okra d) Knol-kohl

1181. 90% of total photosynthesis in the world is carried out by

a) Trees b) Herbs

c) Shrubs d) Algae

1182. Fluchloralin is used as

a) Post plant b) pre emergence

c) Pre plant d) After 60 days

1183. Root mist and Fog feed technique comes under

a) Aeroponics b) Solid media culture
c) Liquid hydroponics d) None of these

1184. First herbicide produced in the world is

a) 2, 4, 5-T b) 2, 4,-D
c) Atrazin d) Semazin

1185. Difference between seed and grain is

a) Seed Processing b) Seed quality
c) Cost d) Genetic Purity

1186. The growth in plant is measured by

a) Microscope b) Auxanometer
c) Potometer d) Barometer

1187. Individual lacking one chromosome from diploid set (2n-1) is called

a) Nullisomic b) Monosomic
c) Trisomic d) Tetrasomic

1188. Number of chromosomes in wheat endosperm is

a) 21 b) 42
c) 63 d) 14

1189. National Agricultural Science Museum was inaugurated on 3rd Nov, 2004 by

a) A. B. Vajpayee b) Sonia Gandhi
c) Dr. Man Mohan Singh d) Dr. A. P.J. Abdul Kalam

1190. NIAM (National Institute of Agriculture Marketing) is located at

a) Hisar b) Jaipur
c) New Delhi d) Meerut

1191. Storage protein in beans is

a) Insulin b) Tripsin
c) Phaseoline d) Globulins

1192. Vegetables are canned in

a) Brine b) Syrup
c) Distilled Water d) None of these

1193. The term self incompatibility was originally coined by:

a) Koelreuter b) Frankel and Galun
c) Stout d) None of these

1194. The inability of a plant with functional pollen to set seeds when self pollinated called

a) Self incompatibility b) Male sterility
c) Self pollination d) None of these

1195. Koelreuter first reported self incompatibility in

a) *Lythrum soliearia* b) *Verbasum phoenieum*
c) *Nicotiana sanderae* d) None of these

1196. Equipment for Hydroponics are

a) Water Pumps, Timer and Oxygen Detection Sensor
b) PVC Pipes, pH and Ec Meters, Blowers
c) Pollinators, Nurtimeter
d) All of the above

1197. Based on flower morphology self incompatibility system is-

a) Heteromorphic system b) Homomorphic system
c) Both (a) and (b) d) None of these

1198. Heteromorphic system is of-

a) Distyly type b) Tristyly type
c) Both (a) and (b) d) None of these

1199. Distyly system operates in the family-

a) Primulaceae b) Lythraceae
c) Both (a) and (b) d) None of these

1200. In primula, types of flower-

a) Thrum b) Pin
c) Both (a) and (b) d) None of these

1201. In homomorphic system self incompatibility results due to-

a) Flower morphology
b) Physiological causes
c) Environmental causes
d) None of these

1202. Homomorphic system is of:

a) Gametophytic system
b) Sporophytic system
c) Both (a) and (b)
d) None of these

1203. Gametophytic system was first discovered by:

a) Hughes and Babcock
b) Koelreuter
c) East and Mangelsdorf
d) None of these

1204. Gametophytic system permits production of

a) Homozygotes
b) Heterozygotes
c) Both (a) and (b)
d) None of these of these of these

1205. Complementary hypothesis was proposed by

a) Bateman
b) William *et al*
c) Richards
d) Brewbaker

1206. Site of gene expression for self incompatibility may express in

a) 1 location
b) 2 location
c) 3 location
d) 4 location

1207. The stigmatic inhibition is found in:

a) Radish
b) Bougainvillea
c) Lillium
d) None of these

1208. Self incompatibility promotes

a) Autogamy
b) Allogamy
c) Homogamy
d) None of these

1209. Self incompatibility can be overcome by:

a) Bud pollination
b) Delayed pollination
c) Late season
d) All of the above

1210. Sporophytic self incompatibility was first discovered by

a) East and Mangelsdorf
b) Hughes and Babcock
c) Grestel
d) Both (b) and (c)

1211. In gametophytic self incompatibility a cross between S1 x S2 would be

a) Partial fertility
b) Full fertility
c) No progeny
d) None of these

1212. Self incompatibility reaction may occur

a) On the stigma
b) In the style
c) Ovary
d) All of the above

1213. Nurtimeter is used to measure

a) fertility status of soil
b) nutrient contents of the solution
c) Atmospheric pressure
d) None of these

1214. Self incompatibility promotes

a) Inbreeding
b) Out breeding
c) Both (a) and (b)
d) None of these

1215. Recovery of male parent only in

a) Sprophytic self incompatibility
b) Gametophytic self incompatibility
c) Both (a) and (b)
d) None of these

1216. Self incompatibility in which the inhibition of pollen germination or pollen tube growth occurs on the stigma known as

a) Monollelic self incompatibility
b) Polyllelic self incompatibility
c) Diallelic self incompatibility
d) Stigmatic self incompatibility

1217. In sporophytic self incompaibility the crosses between S1S2 X S1S2 would be

a) No progeny b) Partial fertility

c) Full fertility d) None of these

1218. Complementary hypothesis was proposed by-

a) Bateman (1952) b) Allard (1960)

c) Nettancourt (1972) d) None of these

1219. Koelreuter first reported male sterility in flowering plant in

a) 1789 b) 1806

c) 1888 d) None of these

1220. Most recent work on male sterility has been received by:

a) Frankel and Galun b) Kaul

c) Both (a) and (b) d) None of these

1221. A condition in which pollen is either absent or non functional in flowering plants

a) Self incompatibility b) Male sterility

c) Cytoplasmic male sterility d) None of these

1222. Blackleg of Cole crops is caused by

a) *Peronospora parasitica* b) *Phoma lingam*

c) *Xanthomonas campestris* d) none of these

1223. Male sterility results from the action of action of:

a) Allogamy b) Autogamy

c) Homozygosity d) All of these

1224. In species presense of male sterility leads to

a) Heterozygosity b) Homozygosity

c) Inbreeding d) None of these

1225. Tip burn in cabbage is caused by inadequate supply of

a) Boron b) calcium

c) Zn d) None of these

1226. In male sterility pollen is

a) Abortive b) Shrivelled
c) Non functional d) All of these

1227. Bolting is

a) Development of vegetative parts
b) Development of root system
c) Both a and b
d) Development of flower stalks

1228. Leek (*Allium porrum*) is a

a) Warm climate vegetable b) both a and c
c) Cool climate vegetable d) none of these

1229. Leek plant is similar to

a) Garlic b) Radish
c) Carrot d) Onion

1230. Commercially important variety of leek is

a) Large Long Summer b) DDR
c) Kt-5 d) None of these

1231. In leek, White tip is caused due to

a) *Phytophora porii* b) Higher temperature
c) *Alternaria porri* d) All of these

1232. The male sterility which is controlled by the only nuclear genes is

a) Cytoplasmic male sterility
b) Genetic male sterility
c) Cytoplasmic genetic male sterility
d) None of these

1233. Pant Uphar is a variety of peas whereas Varsha Uphar is a variety of

a) Tomato b) Okra
c) Brinjal d) Capsicum

1234. The restorer line is represented as

a) A- line b) B- line
c) R- line d) None of these

1235. The male sterile line is represented as

a) A- line b) B- line
c) R- line d) None of these

1236. Leeks are mature after– – – – days after transplanting

a) 30-45 days b) 45-50 days
c) 50-65 days d) 90-110 days

1237. Male sterility is transferred with the help of

a) Back cross b) Random mating
c) Inbreeding d) None of these

1238. Coexistence of female and hermaphrodite individuals in a population is known as

a) Male gametocides b) Gynodieocy
c) Isogenic line d) None of these

1239. Moss Curled is a variety of

a) Leek b) Parsley
c) Sugarbeet d) None of these

1240. Chemicals which are used for induction of male sterility is known as

a) Gynodioecy b) Isogenic line
c) Male gametocides d) None of these

1241. Artificial induction is difficult in case of

a) Male sterility b) Self incompatibility
c) Both a and b d) None of these

1242. Parsley is mainly propagated by

a) Crown b) Tuber
c) Both b and d d) Seed

1243. Heritable features of a host plant which suppresses or retard development of a pathogen or insect is

a) Genetic resistance b) Phenotypic resistance

c) Both a & b d) None of these

1244. Specific resistance of a host to the particular race of a pathogen is known as

a) Vertical resistance b) Genetic resistance

c) Horizontal resistance d) All of the above

1245. During harvesting of parsley it must be cut at least

a) 0.25 to 1.0 inches above the crown

b) 1.5 to 2.25 inches above the crown

c) 1 to 1.25 inches above the crown

d) All of the above

1246. For excellent Broccoli, soil Ph should be

a) 6.5 – 8.0 b) 5.0 - 6.0

c) 5.0 – 7.0 d) 5.5 – 6.5

1247. The concept of gene for gene hypothesis was first given by

a) Allard, 1960 b) Day, 1974

c) Fehr,1987 d) Flor,1956

1248. Sweet potato belongs to family

a) Euphorbiaceae b) Convolvulaceae

c) Cruciferae d) Solanaceae

1249. In broccoli, molybdenum deficiency causes which type of symptom

a) Black rot symptom b) Soft rot symptom

c) Downey mildew symptom d) Whiptail symptom

1250. Seeds of fenugreek mainly contain

a) *Trigonelin* b) *Diosgenin*

c) *Eugenol* d) *Cheratin*

1251. *Brevicoryne brassicae* is

a) Cabbage looper b) Aphid

c) Cabbage web worm d) All of above

1252. The mode of inheritance in genetic of resistance is:

a) Oligogenic b) Polygenic
c) Cytoplasmic d) All of these

1253. Pollination in radish is done by

a) Bees b) House fly
c) Wind d) None of these

1254. Which is the vegetable cum spice crop

a) Fenugreek b) Cumin
c) Coriander d) Curry leaf

1255. Inbreeding is deleterious in

a) Potato b) Maize
c) Cucumber d) Tomato

1256. Bitterness in cucumber due to effect of external pollens and is called

a) Glycosides b) Acids
c) Alkaloids d) Metaxenia

1257. The term vertical and horizontal resistance was coined by

a) Vander plank b) Flor
c) Painter d) None of these

1258. What is gene architecture

a) The underlying genetic basis of a phenotypic trait
b) Genotype phenotype map
c) Both a & b
d) None of these

1259. The choice of breeding methods mainly depends on the mode of

a) Pollination b) Reproduction
c) Gene action d) All of above

1260. In which crop anthesis takes place in evening?

a) Bottle gourd b) Bitter gourd
c) Snake gourd d) Ivy gourd

1261. Ivy gourd is propagated by

a) Seed
b) Root cutting
c) Tuberous root
d) Stem cutting

1262. Which vegetable crop requires mulching?

a) Lettuce
b) Chilli
c) Potato
d) Tomato

1263. A population of genetically similar plants such as pure line F1 between 2 pure lines and progeny of a clone is known as

a) Homozygous population
b) Heterozygous population
c) Homogenous population
d) None of these

1264. The method is used for transferring somc desirable genes from wild species to cultivated ones is:

a) Transgenic breeding
b) Clonal selection
c) Polyploidy breeding
d) None of these

1265. 'Jade Cross' is a hybrid of which vegetable

a) Cabbage
b) Broccoli
c) Cauliflower
d) Brussel sprouts

1266. Single seed descent method was given by

a) CA Brim
b) Newman
c) J.B Harrington
d) None of these

1267. Seed rate of Brussel sprouts per acre is

a) 100-250 gm
b) 450-500 gm
c) 500 gm
d) None of these

1268. The term pure line selection was first given by

a) Johannsen
b) Simmonds
c) Fehr
d) Allard

1269. Single seed descent is modified form of

a) Bulk method
b) Pure line method
c) Pedigree method
d) None of these

1270. Recurrent selection was restricted to

a) Self pollinated crop b) Cross pollinated
c) both a and b d) None of these

1271. Mass pedigree method was proposed by

a) Johannsen b) Harrington
c) Fehr d) None of these

1272. The term recurrent selection was coined by

a) Hayer and Garber,1919 b) East and Jones,1920
c) Jenkins,1940 d) Hull, 1945

1273. Simple recurrent selection is also known as

a) Phenotypic recurrent selection
b) Reciprocal recurrent selection
c) Reccurent reciprocal half sib selection
d) None of these

1274. Garlic contains amino acid namely

a) Alliin b) Allicin
c) Di-allyl disulphide d) Allinage

1275. The F2 population to be evaluated is smaller in

a) Pedigree method b) Bulk method
c) Back cross method d) None of these

1276. The crossing is done repeatedly with recurrent parent in

a) Pedigree method b) Bulk method
c) Back cross method d) None of these

1277. The term biotechnology was coined by

a) Chain Weizmann b) Karl Ereky
c) Alexander Fleming d) None of these

1278. First attempt in plant tissue culture was done during the year

a) 1904 b) 1925
c) 1902 d) 1900

1279. Publication of first handbook on plant tissue culture during the year

a) 1960 b) 1952

c) 1941 d) 1959

1280. During which year, in tomato Gamberg *et al* designed shoot regenaration protocap where nodal and shoot explants were used, giving rise true to type plants bearing normal flower

a) 1995 b) 1997

c) 1998 d) 1994

1281. Okra is considered as

a) Allopolyploid b) Autopolyploid

c) Tetraploid d) Triploid

1282. *Plasmodiophora brassicae* is

a) Clubroot disease

b) Fusarium yellow disease

c) black rot disease

d) None of these

1283. The first country to commercialize transgenic in the early 90s with the introduction of virus resistance tobacco, later followed by tomato was

a) Japan b) China

c) India d) None of these

1284. The insect control protein genes is isolated from

a) *Bacillus thuringeinsis*

b) *Pseudomonas syringae* pv *tabaci*

c) *Bacillus amyloliquefaciens*

d) None of these

1285. In Brussel sprouts, sprouts are harvested when

a) Upper leaves begin to turn yellow

b) lower leaves begin to turn yellow

c) Both a & b

d) None of these

1286. The production of transgenic plants with male sterility and fertility restoration genes has become available in

a) *Brassica napus* b) *Brassica nigra*
c) *Brassica sativus* d) *Brassica juncea*

1287. Starch content of sweet potato is

a) 16% b) 6%
c) 26% d) 50%

1288. Pencil strip is a physiological disorder of celery due to deficiency of

a) P b) N
c) K d) Ca

1289. *Brassica napus* is an amphidiploids of

a) *B. nigra* × *B.compestris* b) *B.compestris* × *B.rapa*
c) *B.rapa* × *B.oleracia* d) *B.oleracea* × *B.nigra*

1290. ________can be developed for enhanced nutritional value of vegetable hybrids

a) Transgenic parental line b) Higher yield
c) Both a & b d) None of these

1291. The technique which is utilized for development and maintenance of self incompatible and inbred lines is

a) Protoplast culture b) Anther culture
c) Plant tissue culture d) None of these

1292. Chinese Cabbage can be use as

a) A potherb and a salad crop b) Salad crop
c) A potherb crop d) None of these

1293. The chemical which induced male sterility

a) Male gametocide b) Ethidium bromide
c) Both a & b d) None of these

1294. In tomato,*Lycopersicon pimpinellifolium* is resistant to

a) Early blight b) Buck eye rot
c) Soft rot d) Septoria leaf spot

1295. In tomato,*L.hirsutum* is resistance to

a) Foot rot b) Early blight
c) Leaf mould d) None of these

1296. Male sterility results from the action of

a) Nuclear gene b) Chloroplast genes
c) Mitochondrial genes d) All of above

1297. Genetic male sterility is controlled by

a) Nuclear genes b) Plasma genes
c) Mitochondrial genes d) None of these

1298. In male sterility the pollen is

a) Functional b) Non-functional
c) Both a & b d) None of these

1299. What are Isogenic lines

a) Line having single gene different
b) Line having double gene diff
c) Both a & b
d) None of these

1300. A good amount of male sterility in flowering plants was reported by

a) Koelreuter b) Frenkel and Galun
c) Allard and Duvick d) None of these

1301. The scientific name of Chinese cabbage is

a) *Brassica oleracea* var *italica* b) *Brassica oleracea* var *capitata*
c) *Brassica oleracea* var *acephala* d) *Brassica chinensis*

1302. Host resistance for bacterial canker of tomato is

a) PI 126408 b) PI 126955
c) Oksitu Sozai –I d) None of these

1303. Elimination of viruses to produce indexed plant material through __________coupled with heat therapy

a) Tissue culture b) Meristem culture
c) Both a & b d) None of these

1304. Pant C-I cultivars of hot pepper is resistance to

a) Fusarium wilt
b) Internal cork
c) Flea beetle
d) *Phytopthora capsici*

1305. RFLP is a

a) Molecular marker
b) Gene
c) Both a & b
d) None of these

1306. High quality Chi-nese cabbage is obtained at temperature of

a) 5°C to 10°C
b) 10°C to 15°C
c) 15°C to 20°C
d) None of these

1307. Biotechnological tools have been employed for

a) New varieties
b) Produce transgenes
c) Resistance to diseases
d) Both b & c

1308. The molecular markers used in crop improvement of lettuce are

a) RAPD
b) RLFP
c) Both a & b
d) None of these

1309. Biotechnological methods in cassava has been used for elimination of

a) Aphids
b) Cassava mosaic virus
c) Cucumber mosaic virus
d) None of these

1310. Which biotechnological method is used for resistance towards pathogen *Septoria apii* in celery

a) Embryogenic suspension culture
b) Embyo rescue
c) Meristem tissue culture
d) Protoplast fusion

1311. Which biotechnological method is used for resistance against *Phytophthora infestans* in potato

a) Micropropagation
b) Protoplast
c) Embryogenic cell suspension
d) Somatic embryogenesis

1312. Biotechnological method used in resistance against Tobacco mosaic virus in tomato is

a) Protoplast
b) Callus
c) Explants
d) None of these

1313. Mass selection procedure is used in

a) Self- fertilizing crops b) Cross fertilizing crops

c) Both a & b d) None of these

1314. Which transgenic product is used to reduce the insect pest attack in tomato crops

a) Bt protein b) Chitinase

c) Acetolactate synthase d) 2, 4-D monooxygenase

1315. Which type of gene is used to reduce cucumber mosaic virus in cucumber

a) Chitinase b) Viral coat protein

c) Bromoxynil nitrilase d) Bt protein

1316. Which transgenic product is used to improve storage capacity of tomato

a) Viral coat protein b) Bt protein

c) Antisense polygalacturonase d) Bromoxynil nitrilase

1317. Which organization first initiated the International Centre for Genetic Engineering & Biotechnology (ICGEB)

a) WHO b) UNESCO

c) NBPGR d) UNIDO

1318. By which breeding method in potato, the inferior progenies & plants can be eliminated in early generations

a) Bulk method b) Asexually propagation

c) Line breeding d) Back cross

1319. Name a variety of potato which bred properly through asexually propagation

a) Kufri Sindhuri b) Kufri Sheetman

c) Kufri Alankar d) All of these

1320. Mass selection or polycross nurseries of sweet potato are grown on

a) Nursery beds b) Trollies

c) Pots d) Coconut pots

1321. In cross pollinated crops, mass selection is used to maintain

a) Purity
b) Superiority
c) Both a & b
d) Germination percentage

1322. In cauliflower selection of plants on the basis of progeny testing & mass pollination is followed to

a) Maintain purity
b) Develop new varieties
c) Both a & b
d) Resistance to salt

1323. Varietiy released for onion improvement by mass selection is

a) Arka Kalyan
b) Arka Niketan
c) Arka Pragati
d) All of these

1324. Name a variety of sweet potato released by mass selection derived from a complex cross.

a) B 6172
b) CIP 440127
c) B-90
d) None of these

1325. Give a classical example of vegetable of the utilization of gene cytoplasmic male sterility for hybrid seed production.

a) Cucumber
b) Garlic
c) Onion
d) Both b & c

1326. Source of disease resistance in buck eye rot of tomato is

a) *Lycopersicon pennelii*
b) *L. esculentum*
c) *L. pimpinellifolium*
d) *L. hirsute*

1327. Source of resistance in late blight of tomato is

a) Utah 737
b) Utah 20
c) Rossol
d) Bulgarian 21

1328. Source of resistance against Phytophthora leaf blight of bell pepper is

a) CI
b) B-79
c) PI 123469
d) Paprika & Lorai

1329. Source of resistance against powdery mildew of bell pepper is

a) Padasali
b) AC- 2258
c) Lorai
d) PM-702

1330. Source of resistance against Black rot of crucifers is

a) Avans b) EC-177283
c) KN-81 d) Fuji

1331. Source of resistance against stalk rot of crucifers is

a) PI-208474 b) Lawyana
c) Budger d) Super Snowball

1332. Source of resistance against Ascochyta blight of pea is

a) Virco b) Kinnauri
c) Tall white sugar d) Boretes 2040

1333. F1 hybrids are mainly manifested for

a) Higher yield b) Early yield
c) Disease resistance d) Better quality

1334. High degree of heterosis in water melon was observed for

a) Yield b) High TSS
c) Proper fruit size & weight d) All of these

1335. Hybrid cultivar dveloped using male sterile lines is

a) Abundance b) Bonanza
c) Aristocrat d) All of these

1336. Summer squash has mainly

a) 5 groups b) 3 groups
c) 4 groups d) 6 groups

1337. Donors for damping off disease in okra is

a) Nigeria b) Round selection
c) Pusa Makhmali d) Red Ghana

1338. Donors for Fusarium wilt in okra is

a) Pusa Sawani b) Long Green Smooth
c) Crimpson Smooth Long d) Red 1

1339. Interspecific hybridization in Phaseolus is aimed at

a) Disease resistance b) Podding character
c) Alteration of seed size d) All of these

1340. Salt tolerant lines have been isolated in *Lycopersicon* by

a) Tissue culture b) Molecular markers
c) Both a & b d) None of these

1341. Which tomato species are salt tolerant

a) *L. pennellii* b) *L.esculentum*
c) *L. pimpinellifolium* d) All of these

1342. Which method is used to eliminate the common viruses in potato?

a) Protoplast fusion b) Meristem
c) Explant d) All of these

1343. Germplasm is maintained by

a) Seed b) Vegetative cuttings
c) Both a & b d) Grafting

1344. Host resistance against phomopsis blight & fruit rot of brinjal is

a) V-1200 b) V-1196
c) Manjari Gota d) Florida Hill Bush

1345. Host resistance against Sclerotinia wilt is

a) V-1740 b) Junagadh Sel.1
c) Black Round d) Aruna

1346. Host resistance against Alternaria blight of carrot is

a) IHR 244 b) Parsnip
c) IHR 231 d) IHR 232

1347. Method used for germplasm conservation is

a) Cryopreservation b) Rapid freezing
c) Slow freezing d) All of these

1348. Slow growing method used for germplasm storage is done by

a) Lowering the temperature b) Increasing the temperature
c) Freezing d) None of these

1349. *Cucurbita pepo* is

a) Summer squash b) Watermelon
c) Cucumber d) None of these

1350. In order to produce homozygous diploid plants, _______technique is used to produce haploids in tomato and capsicum is

a) Anther culture
b) Embryo rescue
c) Micropropagation
d) All of these

1351. Taxonomy & origin of cole crops have been investigated based on

a) Structures
b) Genes
c) Molecular markers
d) None of these

1352. Genetic engineering gives complete control over the characters of the

a) Explant
b) Genes
c) Transgenic plants
d) Both a & c

1353. Potato meristems can be preserved in liquid nitrogen for

a) Half a month
b) 2 years
c) 3 days
d) 10 years

1354. Donors for resistance for angular leaf spot of French bean is

a) FC 1
b) JP 83
c) PM 2
d) SVM 1

1355. Fruits of *Zucchini* and *Cocozelle* are

a) Elongated
b) Flattened
c) Cylindrical
d) Both a & c

1356. The mechanisms for resistance constitutes

a) Antibiosis
b) Tolerance
c) Antixenosis
d) All of these

1357. Non preference is an alternate name of

a) Antixenosis
b) Tolerance
c) Antibiosis
d) Both a & c

1358. Harvesting of individual F2 plants & selfing the bulk progeny of each plant to a high level of homozygosity is called

a) Pure line
b) Pure line family
c) Bulk
d) Single Seed Descent

1359. ________ is a clonal selection from the variety Darjeeling in potato

a) Kufri Alankar b) Kufri Chandramukhi
c) Kufri Red d) Kufri Safed

1360. Institute maintaining germplasm of ginger

a) NBPGR b) UHF Nauni
c) BCKV d) All of these

1361. Multiple disease resistant varieties in pea breeding is

a) JP 179 b) JP 9
c) JP 15 d) All of these

1362. JP 9 variety of pea is resistant to

a) Powdery mildew b) Leaf miner
c) Rust d) All of these

1363. *Pseudoperonospora cubensis* is

a) CMV b) Powdery mildew
c) Both a and b d) Downy mildew

1364. In *Beta vulgaris*, there are ___ loci involved

a) 4 b) 5
c) 2 d) 1

1365. In genus Lycopersicon, _____ is a self incompatible species.

a) *L. esculentum* b) *L.hirsutum*
c) *L. pimpinellifolium* d) Both b & c

1366. In self incompatible species of Lycopersicon, the cessation of pollen tube growth takes place in

a) Pistil b) Stamen
c) Upper part of style d) Upper part of stigma

1367. Self-incompatible phenotype of________ is temperature dependent

a) *L.peruvianum* b) *L.esculentum*
c) *L.chilense* d) *L.pimpinellifolium*

1368. Fluorescence Microscopy Technique is used for distinguishing ________population in Indian cauliflower.

a) Disease resistant b) Compatible & incompatible
c) Abiotic stress resistant d) All

1369. International Board for Plant Genetic Resources (IBPGR) is situated at

a) Chile b) Taiwan
c) Germany d) Rome

1370. NBPGR is situated at

a) Rajasthan b) M.P.
c) New Delhi d) Patancheru

1371. A variety______ resistant to powdery mildew of pea has been devloped at UHF, Nauni.

a) Solan Nirog b) Solan Garima
c) Solan Kanchan d) None of these

1372. Factors responsible for disease resistance in plants

a) Environmental factor b) Hereditary factors
c) Both a & b d) Genetic facors

1373. Host resistance against cercospora leaf spot is

a) Laetitia
b) Nagano
c) 3 hydroxytyramine content of leaves
d) None of these

1374. Pure line selection was first employed to improve seed weight in

a) Pea b) French bean
c) Okra d) Tomato

1375. Host resistance against purple blotch of onion is

a) IIHR 56-1 b) HG 1
c) Autumn keeper d) All of these

1376. In Single seed descent method main limitation is

a) Slow method
b) Labour extensive
c) Expensive
d) All of these

1377. Biotechnological method used against little leaf disease in egg plant is

a) Callus from infected tissue
b) Embryo rescue
c) Suspension cells
d) None of these

1378. Cytoplasmic male sterility in________ is manifested as petaloidy, where stamens are transformed into petal or leaf like structures which lack pollen forming tissue

a) Carrot
b) Tomato
c) Potato
d) Bean

1379. Double backcross method was adopted in tomato for combining

a) Large fruit size
b) Earliness
c) High yield
d) Both a & b

1380. Biotechnological method used against *Pseudomonas solanacearum* in tomato is

a) Secondary embroids
b) Callus
c) Suspension cells
d) Explants

1381. Technique used for genetic transformation in celery is

a) *Agrobacterium tumefaciens*
b) Electroporation
c) Both a & b
d) None of these

1382. The DNA transformation method by transforming roots in cucumber is done by using

a) *A. tumefaciens*
b) *A. rhizogens*
c) Bt
d) All of these

1383. In which crop(s) micro-propagation method is mostly used for developing disease resistance

a) Carrot
b) Ginger
c) Garlic
d) Both a & b

1384. Hybrids produced between tomato & potato, method used was

a) Embryo rescue
b) Micro-propagation
c) Somatic hybridization
d) None of these

1385. Vectors used in delivering genes in somatic hybridization is

a) Ti plasmids
b) Cosmids
c) Viruses
d) All of these

1386. Uptake of genes is detected by using

a) RLFP
b) Luciferase enzyme
c) RAPD
d) All of these

1387. Gene responsible for delaying ripening in tomato is

a) NOR
b) RIN
c) Virus coat protein
d) All of these

1388. Method used for transferring alien genes

a) Microinjection
b) Uptake of DNA
c) Both a & b
d) None of these

1389. Gene used for blocking the action of fruit ripening for increasing shelf-life is

a) NOR
b) RIN
c) Antisense
d) Bt gene

1390. Which of the following tomato variety has been developed by antisense RNA technique

a) Flavr Savr
b) Endless Summer
c) Pusa Ruby
d) Punjab Chhuhara

1391. Ideotype of capsicum plant constitute

a) High capsaicin
b) Vitamin A
c) Ascorbic acid
d) All of these

1392. Artificial selection generally makes crop species

a) More useful to humans
b) More likely to survive in nature
c) Less likely to survive in nature
d) Both a and c

1393. Kinner Red is a variety of

a) Cauliflower b) Carrot
c) Chinese cabbage d) Red cabbage

1394. Italian Green and Green Head Cultivars/hybrids belongs to which crop

a) Onion b) Lettuce
c) Spinach d) Broccoli

1395. The concepts of centers of origin of crop plants was proposed by

a) N. I .Vavilov b) C linnaeus
c) J.R. Harlan d) J.B. Hutchinson

1396. Turnip cultivar Pusa Swarnima is a cross between

a) Golden Ball x Japanese White
b) Snow Ball x Japanese White
c) Purple Top White Globe x 4-White),
d) None of these

1397. Leaf Lettuce

a) Great Lakes b) Iceberg
c) Both a and b d) Chinese Yellow

1398. Vavilov proposed

a) Mega-centers of origin b) Primary centers of origin
c) Centers of diversity d) Micro-centers

1399. Pusa Harit is a variety of

a) Palak b) Swiss chard
c) Kale d) Beetroot

1400. In temperate carrot first hybrid 'Pusa Nayanjyoti' developed at Katrain has been released during____________by utilizing the CMS system

a) 2009 b) 2008
c) 2011 d) 2010

1401. The number of centers of origin initially proposed by Vavilov.

a) 6 b) 8
c) 12 d) 9

1402. The institute of plant industry, where Vavilov worked, is located at

a) Moscow
b) Verkhoyansk
c) Leningrad
d) Canberra

1403. Muslim invaders introduced cherries and grapes in India from

a) Afghanistan
b) Iran
c) Iraq
d) Turkey

1404. Heterosis breeding in vegetables was initiated as early as 1908 in tomato followed by————————————— in 1916

a) Capsicum
b) Brinjal
c) Radish
d) Cucumber

1405. The Botanical Survey of India was established in the year

a) 1880
b) 1930
c) 1890
d) 1840

1406. Jones and Clarke,1943 works with onion on

a) Genic-cytoplasmic male sterility
b) Cytoplasmic male sterility in
c) Male sterility
d) None of these

1407. The Calcutta botanic gardens was established in the year

a) 1871
b) 1781
c) 1791
d) 1841

1408. First F_1hybrid of eggplant was released during 1924 in __________ (Nishi, 1967)

a) Japan
b) China
c) India
d) France

1409. The quarantine of germplasm pertaining to agricultural and horticultural crop species is done by the

a) Entomologist
b) Plant pathologists
c) Nematologists
d) All of these

1410. In India, exotic collections of germplasm carry the prefix

a) EC
b) IC
c) IW
d) EG

1411. Self-incompatibility system in cabbage was studied by

a) Jones and Clarke. 1943
b) Liedle and Anderson, 1993
c) Pearson, 1932
d) Nishi, 1967

1412. Vavilov was the Director at Institute of Plant Industry during the period

a) 1920-1915
b) 1916-1926
c) 1926-1936
d) 1916-1936

1413. East India Company introduced cabbage, cauliflower etc. from

a) China
b) South America
c) Mediterranean region
d) U.K

1414. NBPGR is responsible for the introduction and maintenance of germplasm of

a) Agricultural crops only
b) Agricultural and horticultural crops
c) Horticultural crops only
d) Agricultural, horticultural and forest species

1415. The extent of acclimatization observed in an introduced material is dependent on the

a) Genetic variability present
b) Mode of pollination
c) Duration of its life cycle
d) All of these

1416. Newness of a variety is known as

a) Uniformity
b) Novelty
c) Stability
d) Distinctiveness

1417. The process of quarantine at NBPGR takes at least

a) Two weeks
b) Three weeks
c) Five weeks
d) Four weeks

1418. The seed Act 2004 is linked to

a) Agriculture b) Horticulture
c) Forestry d) All of the above

1419. The first report of hybrid vigour in chilli came in 1933 from

a) PAU, Ludhiyana b) IARI, New Delhi
c) GB, Panatnagar University d) None of these

1420. F_1, hybrid Pusa Meghdoot of bottle gourd was developed at IARI, Regional Research Station, Katrain and released in ________

a) 1973 b) 1970
c) 1972 d) 1971

1421. ________ has started marketing of seeds of first tomato hybrid, Karnataka

a) Indo-American Hybrid Seed Company
b) Syngenta
c) Century seed
d) Tokita

1422. In 1883, late blight of potato was inadvertently introduced in India from

a) USA b) Mexico
c) Europe d) South America

1423. Plant introduction scheme was expanded as the plant introduction and exploration Organization during

a) 1948 b) 1956
c) 1965 d) 1971

1424. Asian Vegetable Research and Development Centre maintains the germplasm collection of

a) Mungbean b) Soyabean
c) Mungbean, pepper and tomato d) All of these

1425. In IARI the division of plant introduction was established in the year

a) 1957 b) 1961
c) 1951 d) 1967

1426. Exploration would be the most successful if it is targeted at

a) Farmers field
b) Primary centre of origin
c) Micro-center
d) Secondary centre of origin

1427. The quickest method for developing an improved variety is

a) Primary introduction
b) Mass selection
c) Secondary introduction
d) Domestication

1428. The division of plant introduction, IARI New Delhi was reorganized as National Bureau of Plant Genetic Resources in the year

a) 1961
b) 1968
c) 1971
d) 1976

1429. Kanyakumari represents

a) Arid zone
b) Subtropical zone
c) Tropical zone
d) Temperate zone

1430. Indo-American Hybrid Seed Company, Bangalore started marketing of seeds of first tomato hybrid, Karnataka and first bell pepper hybrid Bharat in

a) 1962
b) 1970
c) 1985
d) 1973

1431. Plant introduction consists of

a) Procurement and quarantine
b) Cataloguing and evaluation
c) Multiplication and distribution
d) All of these

1432. In India, indigenous collection of germplasm of wild relatives of crop plants carries the prefix

a) EC
b) WC
c) IW
d) WG

1433. Potato germplasm collection is maintained at

a) Shimla
b) Nainital
c) Srinagar
d) Patna

1434. F_1 hybrids of summer squash is

a) Pusa Alankar
b) Pusa Meghdoot
c) Pusa Sanyog
d) None of these

1435. Plant Breeder's Rights are operating in

a) Germany
b) Denmark
c) Netherlands
d) All of the above

1436. The world collection of coffee germplasm is maintained at

a) Senegal (Africa)
b) Ethiopia (Africa)
c) Kerala (India)
d) New Delhi (India)

1437. International centers for tropical agriculture maintains the germplasm collcction of

a) Cassava
b) *Phaseolus spp*
c) Tropical pasture species
d) All of these

1438. Flag smut of wheat came into India from

a) Australia
b) USA
c) Mexico
d) UK

1439. Physical purity of spinach seed for foundation & certified seed should be

a) 95%
b) 96%
c) 97%
d) 98%

1440. ———————-crop provides one of the rare examples of very early recognition of male sterility (Jones and Emsweller, 1936)

a) Onion
b) Cabbage
c) Radish
d) Carrot

1441. Kaul (1988) classified male sterility in—————-major groups

a) 3
b) 4
c) 2
d) 5

1442. Germplasm is also called

a) Gene pool
b) Genetic resources
c) Gene bank
d) World collection

1443. Mechanism,Hand emasculation + hand pollination is used in

a) Cucumber

b) Bitter gourd,

c) Tomato, eggplant, sweet pepper

d) Summer squash

1444. Mechanism, Male sterility + natural pollination is used in

a) Onion, cabbage, cauliflower

b) Tomato, hot pepper, sweet pepper

c) Cucumber, muskmelon

d) Cole crops

1445. A germplasm collection can be maintained in the form of

a) Seed bank b) Seed or field bank

c) Shoot tip bank d) Any of these

1446. Genetic drift is also called

a) Genetic erosion b) Random drift

c) Genetic slippage d) Either of these

1447. Beltsville (USA) maintains germplasm of

a) Small grains b) L egumes

c) Sugar crops d) Oilseeds

1448. The institute of plant industry, Leningrad has

a) 1,00,000 accessions b) 2,40,000 accessions

c) 1, 60,000 accessions d) 1, 90,000 accessions

1449. The Royal Botanic Gardens is located at

a) Kew (England) b) Ontario (Canada)

c) Senegal (Africa) d) Florida (USA)

1450. Atanassova, 1999 in tomato studied

(a) Positional sterility b) Functional male sterility

(c) Microsporogenesis d) None of these

1451. Functional male sterility in eggplant was studied by Phatak and Jaworski in

a) 1971 b) 1953

c) 1989 d) 1972

1452. Gene bank is best maintained as

a) DNA bank b) Seed bank

c) Field bank d) Shoot-tip bank

1453. Soyabean, brinjal, radish and buckwheat has

a) Central American centre of origin

b) Asia minor centre of origin

c) Central Asia centre of origin

d) China centre of origin

1454. Germplasm collection of a crop consists of

a) Land races and obsolete varieties

b) Land races, wild forms, exotic collections

c) High yielding varieties, transgenic lines and land races

d) All of these

1455. Environmental sensitive male sterile mutants in Cabbage

a) TGMS(Thermosensitive genic male sterility), TCMS (Thermosensitive cytoplasmic male sterility)

b) TGMS,PGMS(Photoperiod sensitive genic male sterility)

c) TGMS

d) None of these

1456. In 1876, coffee rust came into India from

a) USA b) Ceylone

c) Africa d) South America

1457. IR 36 variety of rice was introduced from

a) Taiwan b) Philippines

c) Africa d) Japan

1458. Seed collections disturbed only for regeneration are called

a) Base collection b) Active collection
c) Working collection d) Field collection

1459. Recalcitrant seeds are produced by

a) Mango and rubber b) Cocoa and coconut
c) Coffee and oil palm d) All of these

1460. The identification of fertilizing cytoplasm for specific nuclear male sterile gene reported by

a) Rundfeldt, 1961 b) Nieuwhof, 1968
c) Rick, 1948; Sawhney, 1983 d) Horner and Palmer, 1995

1461. In 1900, potato moth came into India from

a) Ireland b) Italy
c) England d) USA

1462. A top cross hybrid "H 44" of cabbage by using SI has been developed

a) UHF-Nauni
b) CSK HPKV,Palmpur
c) IARI, Regional Research Station, Katrain
d) PAU, Ludhiyana

1463. The PPV & FR Act 2001 was approved in

a) 1999 b) 2001
c) 2004 d) 2005

1464. The PPV & FR Act 2001 provides protection of

a) Plant varieties b) Farmer's rights
c) Plant breeder's rights d) All of above

1465. Criteria for registration of plant varieties include

a) Novelty b) Distinctiveness
c) Uniformity and stability d) All of above

1466. The PPV & FR Authority is located at

a) New Delhi b) Chennai
c) Hyderabad d) Kolkata

1467. The PPV & FR Act 2001 came into force in

a) 2004 b) 2001
c) 2005 d) 2002

1468. In its legislative structure, PPV & FRA Act involves representatives of

a) Farmers b) Women industry
c) Seed industry d) All of above

1469. Headquarter of Asian Vegetable Research Development Centre (AVRDC) is located in

a) Taiwan b) Indonesia
c) India d) Malaysia

1470. Any plant part used for commercial multiplication of a crop is called

a) Seed
b) Seedling
c) Variety
d) Vegetatively propagated part

1471. Improved seed reveals the

a) Breeder seed b) Foundation seed
c) Certified seed d) All of above

1472. Initial seed of an improved variety is called

a) Nucleus seed b) Breeder seed
c) Foundation seed d) Certified seed

1473. The Royal Commission on agriculture was set up in

a) 1930 b) 1945
c) 1925 d) 1927

1474. The Grow More Food Enquiry Committee was started during the

a) First Five year plan b) Second Five year plan
c) Third Five year plan d) Sixth Five year plan

1475. The multiplication of nucleus seed into foundation seed at Block level was introduced to the farmers in

a) Fifth year plan b) Second year plan
c) Sixth year plan d) First year plan

1476. High Yielding Variety Programme (HYVP) was launched in India in

a) 1963 b) 1976
c) 1966 d) 1965

1477. ISST means

a) International Society of Seed Testing
b) Indian Society of Seed Technology
c) Indian Society of Seed Testing
d) International Society of Seed Technology

1478. Grow out tests are done to maintain

a) Physical purity b) Genetic purity
c) Seed multiplication d) Seed certification

1479. Rouging is done to remove virus affected plants at

a) Flowering stage b) Vegetative stage
c) Maturity stage d) Harvesting stage

1480. The disinfection of bags used for storage of raw seeds is done by

a) Thiram b) Malathion
c) DDT solution d) Streptocycline

1481. Registered seed is the progeny of

a) Nucleus seed b) Foundation seed
c) Certified seed d) Breeder seed

1482. Maintenance of Breeder's seed of established varieties is done by

a) Independent selection b) Individual selection
c) Bulk selection d) Pedigree selection

1483. The Virus Y & A of potato can be detected by

a) Phloroglucinol test b) Visually
c) A6 test d) Serological test

1484. The Potato Leaf Roll Virus is detected by

a) A6 test b) Phloroglucinol test
c) Serological test d) Visually

1485. Separation of tomato seed by fermentation controls

a) Bacterial rot
b) Bacterial canker
c) TMV
d) Wilt

1486. To control bacterial canker in the extracted tomato seed, it is treated with

a) 0.8% pure acetic acid
b) 100 ml HCl
c) Boiling water
d) Washing soda

1487. The isolation distance for foundation seed production in cucurbits is

a) 500 m
b) 1200 m
c) 1000 m
d) 200 m

1488. The present Seed Replacement Rate for various crops is

a) 15-20%
b) 30-35%
c) 25-35%
d) 40-45%

1489. The isolation distance for self pollinated crops is

a) 3-10m
b) 100-200m
c) 80-90m
d) More than 200m

1490. The Seed Bill 2004 with latest amendments was introduced in Indian parliament in

a) 17th July 2010
b) 17th May 2009
c) 14th April 2009
d) 23rd April, 2010

1491. The device used to measure dry & wet bulb temperature for seed drying is

a) Thermometer
b) Sling psychrometer
c) Inferometer
d) Tachymeter

1492. Freedom from inert matter & defective seeds is known as

a) Genetic purity
b) Physical purity
c) Inviable seed
d) Fresh seed

1493. Certification is not required for

a) Breeder seed
b) Foundation seed
c) Certified seed
d) All of the above

1494. Progeny of nucleus seed is referred as

a) Certified seed
b) Foundation seed
c) Registered seed
d) Breeder seed

1495. Physical purity of 95% is permissible for the foundation & certified seed of

a) Soybean
b) Groundnut
c) Spinach
d) Carrot

1496. Seed meant for general distribution to farmers for commercial crop production refers to

a) Foundation seed
b) Breeder seed
c) Certified seed
d) Nucleus seed

1497. Breeder seed is the progeny of

a) Foundation seed
b) Registered seed
c) Certified seed
d) Nucleus seed

1498. Seed certification requires

a) An improved variety
b) Genetic purity
c) Physical purity
d) All of the above

1499. 'SVRC' is

a) Seed Variety Release Committee
b) State Variety Release Committee
c) Seed Variety Research Committee
d) State Variety Research Committee

1500. Headquarter of Union for the Protection of New Plant Varieties (UPOV) is situated at

a) Washington
b) Geneva
c) Bangkok
d) Moscow

1501. Seeds which do not absorb water are

a) Fresh ungerminated seed
b) Inviable seed
c) Hard seed
d) Dead seed

1502. National Seed Project was Ist introduced in which state of India

a) U.P b) New Delhi
c) M.P. d) West Bengal

1503. The objectionable weed seed of Methi is

a) *Convolvulus arvensis* b) Sengi (*Melilotus spp.*)
c) *Cuscuta spp* d) *Argemone maxicana*

1504. The germination percentage of pigeon pea for foundation seed should be

a) 90% b) 85%
c) 75% d) 65%

1505. Absence of seeds of other variety of the same & other crops in a seed lot refers to

a) Physical purity b) Genetic purity
c) Defective seed d) Improved seed

1506. A legal system which ensures production of high quality seed in terms of purity & germination is called

a) Seed law b) Seed certification
c) Seed testing d) All of above

1507. Separation of the field of a variety to the prescribed distance from that of another variety to avoid contamination is called

a) Rouging b) Grow out test
c) Isolation d) Spacing

1508. A Plant Breeder's Right holder of a variety can

a) Distribute seeds b) Import seeds
c) Export seeds d) All of above

1509. For PBR (Plant Breeder's Rights), the PPV & FR Act recognizes the contribution of farmers in

a) Conserving b) Improving
c) Exchange d) All of above

1510. According to PPV and FR Act, for the purpose of farm produce, the farmers have right to

a) Save b) Use
c) Sow d) All of above

1511. Basic requirements for protection of a variety include

a) Novelty b) Distinctiveness
c) Uniformity d) All of above

1512. The Plant Breeder's Rights Act provides

a) Breeder's exemptions
b) Farmer's exemptions
c) Both a & b
d) None of these

1513. PBR's provides exclusive rights to the breeder for

a) Commercial production b) Marketing
c) Export & import d) All of above

1514. In field crops, a variety can be protected maximum for

a) 5 yrs b) 10 yrs
c) 15 yrs d) 20 yrs

1515. New varieties of trees & vines can be protected maximum for

a) 10 yrs b) 15 yrs
c) 18 yrs d) 20 yrs

1516. The Farmer's Rights are also known as

a) Farmer's privilege b) Farmer's exemptions
c) Both a & b d) None of these

1517. Plant Breeder's Rights are also known as

a) Breeder's privilege b) Research exemptions
c) Both a & b d) None of these

1518. PBR can be granted to

a) Breeder of a variety b) Legal owner of a variety
c) Both a & b d) None of these

1519. PBRs may lead to

a) Unhealthy practices
b) Increase in price
c) Monopoly
d) All of the above

1520. PBR may also lead to

a) Faster seed industry development
b) Improvement of quality due to competition
c) Reduction in genetic variability
d) All of above

1521. A single dominant gene regulates-------- in cucumber (Hazra and Som, 1999)

a) Dioeciousm
b) Monoecism
c) Both a and b
d) Gynoecism

1522. The concept of Farmer's rights was endorsed by FAO conference in

a) 1979
b) 1989
c) 1996
d) 1999

1523. A variety that is used for comparison of a particular character is called a

a) Candidate variety
b) Example variety
c) Reference variety
d) Extant variety

1524. Any seed which is not genuine or true-to-type is called as

a) Impure seed
b) Inviable seed
c) Hard seed
d) Spurious seed

1525. The major share of cost involved in seed production is

a) Input cost
b) Land rent
c) Harvesting
d) Crop & Field management practices

1526. International Seed Federation (ISF) is an organization merged from

a) FIS
b) ASSINSEL
c) Both a & b
d) None of these

1527. The first International Seed Congress was held at

a) Budapest (1930) b) London (1924)
c) Paris (1929) d) Bologna(1928)

1528. New Policy on Seed Development (NPSD) was established on

a) 1998 b) 1988
c) 1989 d) 1980

1529. WTO was first officially commenced in

a) 1948 b) 1950
c) 1995 d) 1985

1530. The predecessor of WTO was

a) WHO b) GATT
c) ITO d) NPSD

1531. The World Vegetable Centre (WVC) is the

a) AICRP b) AVRDC
c) NPSD d) WTO

1532. First private seed company was

a) Monsanto b) Namdhari
c) Sutton & Sons d) Takii

1533. Seed coat is derived from

a) Testa b) Embryo
c) Endosperm d) Nucellus

1534. There are _______ seed testing laboratories in India

a) 301 b) 103
c) 205 d) 302

1535. Standards of germination for seed certification in chillies is

a) 70% b) 90%
c) 80% d) 60%

1536. In flowering plants, second seed coat is known as

a) Integument b) Aleurone layer
c) Tegamen d) Inner ventral scale

1537. The hybrids developed by Govt. agencies, Govt. institutions & Agri Institutions are the

a) Private hybrids
b) Institutional hybrids
c) Public hybrids
d) Govt. hybrids

1538. Maximum seed moisture range in vegetable crops stored in sealed containers varies between

a) 15-20%
b) 30-40%
c) 1-2%
d) 9-12%

1539. The first private seed company came into existence at

a) Mumbai
b) Kolkata
c) Lucknow
d) New Delhi

1540. Cotyledons in monocots are called

a) Endosperm
b) Mega gametophyte
c) Embryo
d) Integuments

1541. Presently ICAR has________ breeder seed production units

a) 45
b) 54
c) 92
d) 107

1542. The quality of seed is considered superior if purity is above

a) 95%
b) 97.5%
c) 98%
d) 96%

1543. The solution required to determine the genuineness of pea varieties for colour of seeds is

a) Peroxidase
b) Ferrous sulphate
c) K2Cr2O7
d) $CuSO_4$

1544. SDS-PAGE (Poly-acrymide gel electrophoresis for denatured proteins) refers to

a) Separation of carbohydrates
b) Separation of ions
c) Separation of sodium
d) Separation of proteins

1545. The amount of working sample collected according to ISTA rules is

a) 1000 seeds
b) 800 seeds
c) 400 seeds
d) 100 seeds

1546. The optimum pH of the filter paper for the purpose of germination of seed is

a) 5-6
b) 6-9
c) 6-7.5
d) 4-6

1547. The optimum temperature range for germination of onion seeds is

a) 10-15°C
b) 20-30°C
c) 15-20°C
d) 30-40°C

1548. The intensity of light requirement of all light requiring plants should be

a) 250 lux
b) 500 lux
c) 400-700 lux
d) 750-1250 lux

1549. The chemical used to overcome physiological dormancy of seeds is

a) $FeSO_4$
b) KNO_3
c) $CuSO_4$
d) HCl

1550. Seed viability can be determined by

a) Tetrazolium test
b) Enzyme test
c) Cool germination test
d) A6 test

1551. Seed borne plant viruses can be detected by

a) Direct seed test
b) Double diffusion test
c) Radial diffusion test
d) All of the above

1552. ELISA is a test for

a) Detecting bacteria
b) Seed viability
c) Seed vigour
d) Detecting viruses

1553. ELISA stands for

a) Enzyme-linked immunosorbent antiserum
b) Enzyme linked immunity antigen
c) Enzyme linked immunosorbent assay
d) Enzyme linked immunity antibodies

1554. The most common moisture meter used in India is

a) Universal OSAW moisture meter
b) Indian OSAW moisture meter
c) Dessicator
d) b & c

1555. The International Crop Improvement Association (ICIA) was changed to

a) AOSCA b) AOSA
c) ISTA d) IBC

1556. For self pollinated crops, the number of inspections at the field for certification is

a) 1 b) 3
c) 2 d) 5

1557. For Cole crops, the number of inspections required is

a) 2 b) 4
c) 6 d) 3

1558. The minimum isolation distance of cucurbits for foundation seed should be

a) 500 m b) 200 m
c) 1000 m d) None of these

1559. One gram of onion seed generally contains _______ seeds.

a) 180 b) 240
c) 300 d) 360

1560. Onion variety suitable for kharif crop is

a) Pusa Red b) Agrifound Dark red
c) Agrifound light red d) Pusa Ratnar

1561. Orange coloured varieties of carrot are rich source of

a) Carotene b) Lycopene
c) Anthocyanin d) None of these

1562. Pear shaped variety of tomato is

a) Punjab Kesri b) PNR-7
c) Punjab Chhuhara d) Punjab Tropic

1563. Perfection is a cultivar of

a) Fenugreek b) Asparagus
c) Celery d) Basella

1564. Plant part of celery consumed as salad is

a) Stem b) Leaf blade
c) Pelide d) None of these

1565. Potato is ______ plant for its tuber.

a) Short- day b) Long- day
c) Day- neutral d) None of these

1566. Purple Vienna is __________ variety of knol-khol.

a) Early b) Mid
c) Late d) All season

1567. Pumpkin varieties mature in ________

a) 60-70 days b) 70-80 days
c) 80-90 days d) 110-120 days

1568. Root system of sweet potato is

a) Shallow b) Medium
c) Deep d) None of these

1569. Salt tolerant variety of onion

a) Punjab Selection b) No. 404
c) Nasik Red d) N-53

1570. Seeds of radish remain viable up to

a) 1-2 days b) 2-3 days
c) 3-4 days d) 4-5 days

1571. Attack of pea stem fly is maximum in

a) September b) November
c) January d) February

1572. The bean used for extraction of gum is

a) Cluster bean b) Hyacinth bean
c) Yard-long bean d) None of these

1573. The best pH of soil for tomato cultivation is

a) Below 5.0 b) 8.0 & above
c) 6.0 -7.0 d) 7.0 -8.0

1574. The best temperature for colour development in carrot is

a) 10-15°C b) 15-20°C
c) 20-25°C d) None of these

1575. The best temperature for growth of cucumber is

a) 10-15°C b) 18-24°C
c) 25-35°C d) 35-40°C

1576. The colour of Pusa Sunehri variety of sweet potato is

a) White b) Yellow
c) Light orange d) Golden

1577. Turnip crosses easily with

a) Radish b) Mustard
c) Cabbage d) All of these

1578. The flowers in brinjal are

a) Hermaphrodite b) Staminate
c) Pistillate d) Solitary &Hermaphrodite

1579. The flowers of spine gourd are

a) White b) Yellow
c) Purple d) Green

1580. The most popular salad crop is

a) Lettuce b) Celery
c) Parsley d) Asparagus

1581. The most suitable time for transplanting sweet pepper

a) Mar- Apr b) Mid - Feb
c) Apr - May d) June - July

1582. Most common pest of spine gourd is

a) Hadda beetle b) Fruit borer
c) Blister Beetle d) Leaf miner

1583. Triploid variety of watermelon is

a) New Hampshire Midget b) Pusa Bedana
c) Charleston Grey d) None of these of above

1584. Vegetables are packed in cans & processed by heat in

a) Retourt b) Water bath
c) Sun d) Any other means

1585. Virus free potato seeds are produced at

a) New Delhi b) Shimla
c) Lucknow d) Uttar Pradesh

1586. Root to seed method is preferred for the production of

a) Nucleus seed b) Foundation seed
c) Certified seed d) All of above

1587. Vegetables are rich source of

a) Vitamins b) Minerals
c) Both a and b d) Fats

1588. Which of the following is a non-climacteric

a) Watermelon b) Muskmelon
c) Cucumber d) Tomato

1589. When knol-khol is grown for seeds it becomes

a) Annual b) Biennial
c) Perennial d) All of these

1590. Watermelon seeds do not germinate satisfactorily below

a) 15°C b) 21°C
c) 35°C d) None of these

1591. Which is the correct sequence of floral parts of pumpkin

a) Ovary, corolla & stigmatic lobes
b) Corolla, stigmatic lobes & ovary
c) Stigmatic lobes, ovary & corolla,
d) Corolla, ovary & stigmatic lobes

1592. Which crop is self-pollinated

a) Bottle guard b) Cauliflower
c) Radish d) Tomato

1593. Which of the following is fruit & vegetable crop

a) Sweet Potato b) Okra
c) Potato d) Spinach

1594. Which growth regulator is used to check sprouting of onion under storage

a) NAA b) MH
c) GA d) PCPA

1595. Seed rate of TPS is recommended for planting one hectare area is

a) 150 g b) 250 g
c) 350 g d) 450 g

1596. Which of the following is not correctly matched?

a) Ginger-Rhizome b) Garlic-Bulb
c) Potato-Tuber d) Sweet Potato-Stolen

1597. Major disease of onion in India is

a) Leaf Blight b) Smut
c) Purple blotch d) White rot

1598. Generally best soil for vegetable cultivation is

a) Sandy b) Sandy Loam
c) Clay Loam d) Clay

1599. Which of the following vegetable produces maximum seeds per fruit

a) Tomato b) Pea
c) Beans d) Capsicum

1600. Which of the following vegetable is richest source of protein

a) Pea b) Fenugreek
c) Pointed Gourd d) Cucumber

1601. Who studied the heterosis in brinjal

a) B.S. Tomar b) N.Basavaraja
c) H. Singh & T.S. Kaler d) All of these

1602. Wind pollination plays an important role in seed production of

a) Radish b) Turnip
c) Garden Beet d) None of these

1603. Yellow coloured vegetables are rich source of

a) Vitamin E b) Vitamin C
c) Vitamin A d) Vitamin B

1604. How many types of flower have been described in brinjal

a) 4 b) 3
c) 2 d) 5

1605. Place of origin of dolichos bean

a) India b) Asia
c) Africa d) China

1606. Deficiency of boron in turnip causes

a) Black Leg b) Brown Heart
c) Black Heart d) None of these

1607. Sex expression of Asparagus plants are

a) Monoecious b) Dioecious
c) Hermaphrodite d) None of these

1608. Arka Chandan is a variety of

a) Pumpkin b) Cucumber
c) Spine gourd d) Watermelon

1609. Tuber production in potato stops totally at temperature

a) 15°C b) 30°C
c) 16°C d) 32°C

1610. During summers, round gourd should be irrigated at an interval of

a) 7-8 days b) 8-9 days
c) 9-10 days d) 8-10 days

1611. Harvesting stage of round gourd is

a) Tender b) Ripe
c) Fully Ripe d) None of these

1612. Most commonly occurring diseases in nursery is

a) Powdery mildew b) Downy mildew
c) Damping off d) None of these

1613. Ivy gourd is propagated by

a) Stem Cutting b) Tubers
c) Suckers d) All of these

1614. Lettuce mosaic is transmitted through

a) Aphids b) Thrips
c) Seeds d) Insects

1615. Nursery of lettuce is sown in

a) Jan-Feb b) Oct-Nov
c) Sep-Oct d) Sep-Nov

1616. Optimum pH for growth of okra is

a) 7.0-7.5 b) 5.0-6.0
c) 6.0-6.8 d) 4.0-4.5

1617. Rhubarb is grown for its

a) Stem b) Leaves
c) Stalk d) Roots

1618. Commercial production of cabbage seeds is done by

a) Seed-Seed b) Head-Seed
c) Both (a) & (b) d) None of these

1619. Leaves or seed stalk of onion fall down from the point of attachment is

a) Stemphylum blight b) Purple Blotch
c) Both (a)&(b) d) None of these

1620. Sweet potato is tolerant to _______ soil.

a) Acidic b) Alkaline
c) Sandy loan d) Clayey Soil

1621. Usual size of seed piece in potato

a) 100-150 g b) 40-50 g
c) 70-80 g d) 80-90g

1622. Yield of radish is

a) 100-150 q/ha b) 100-200q/ha
c) 250-300 q/ha d) 50-60 q/ha

1623. How many groups are there in lettuce

a) 3 b) 4
c) 5 d) 6

1624. Wine is also prepared from which bean

a) Dolichos bean b) Hyacinth bean
c) Faba bean d) French bean

1625. Fenugreek, Spinach and Mountain spinach are rich in

a) Vit A b) Vit B1
c) Vit C d) None of these

1626. Tuber production of potato is maximum in

a) Hilly areas b) Low land areas
c) Plains d) None of these

1627. Protandry is very much common in

a) Onion b) Garlic
c) Radish d) Carrot

1628. Protogyny is common in

a) Elephant foot yam b) Cole crops
c) Globe artichoke d) None of these

1629. Chromosome number of cassava is

a) 36 b) 38
c) 40 d) 42

1630. Pollarding is mainly done in

a) Moringa b) Cassava
c) Curry leaf d) Chekurmanis

1631. Chromosome number of Jerusalem artichoke is

a) 100 b) 102
c) 109 d) 60

1632. Chinese Water Chestnut is propagated by

a) Corms b) Tubers
c) Roots d) None of these

1633. Largest area is among salad crops.

a) Lettuce b) Parsley
c) Both d) None of these

1634. Spinach is_________ plant.

a) A long day b) A short day
c) A day neutral d) None of these

1635. Seed colour of ridge gourd is

a) White b) Brown
c) Black d) None of these

1636. Scooping is a practice that facilitates bolting in

a) Cabbage b) Brussels sprout
c) Cauliflower d) Broccoli

1637. Type of parthenocarpy in colocasia is

a) Vegetative b) Stimulative
c) Both a and b d) None of these

1638. Which palak variety is developed through spontaneous mutation

a) Pusa Palak b) Jobner green
c) Pusa Harit d) Pusa Jyoti

1639. Little leaf of brinjal is transmitted by

a) Mites b) Aphids
c) Thrips d) Leaf hopper

1640. Potato witches broom is caused by

a) MLO's b) Bacteria
c) Fungus d) Virus

1641. London Flag is an improved variety of

a) Leek b) Garlic
c) Onion d) Welsh onion

1642. Which of the following cucurbit is less affected by powdery mildew

a) Luffa b) Cucumis
c) Bottle gourd d) Bitter gourd

1643. Highest production of vegetables in India is from

a) West Bengal b) Assam
c) Punjab d) Sikkim

1644. How many tubers or sets will be needed to raise the yams on one hectare area

a) 14,300 b) 15,300
c) 13,300 d) 16,000

1645. Which variety of lima bean needs support

a) Pole type b) Semi- pole type
c) Bush type d) All

1646. A pea variety which gives 50% produce during 1st picking

a) Arkel b) Meteor
c) Mattar Ageta-6 d) None of these of above

1647. Which of following is a stem vegetable

a) Carrot b) Knol -khol
c) Sweet potato d) Radish

1648. According to All India Medical Science report, the per capita vegetable requirement in India is

a) 500g b) 400g
c) 200g d) 300g

1649. All Cole crops belongs to the family

a) Cruciferae b) Brassicaceae
c) Umbelliferae d) None of these

1650. Amaranthus belongs to the family

a) Chenopodiaceae b) Amaranthaceae
c) Portulaceae d) None of these

1651. Among root crops, the application of potassic fertilizers is essential in

a) Radish b) Turnip
c) Carrot d) None of these

1652. An early maturing variety of potato which does not degenerate rapidly is

a) up-to date b) Kufri Sindhuri
c) Kufri Chandramukhi d) None of these

1653. An edible podded variety of garden pea is

a) Mattar Ageta-6 b) Mithi Phali
c) Bonneville d) None of these

1654. Arka Abhay is a variety of

a) Brinjal b) Chilli
c) Tomato d) Bhindi

1655. Asparagus is

a) Monoecious b) Dioecious
c) Staminate d) Hermaphrodite

1656. Badi chaulai belongs to species

a) *Blitun* b) *Tricolor*
c) *Caudatus* d) None of these

1657. Bean variety PusaParvati is evolved through

a) X-rays b) Gamma -rays
c) EMS d) MMS

1658. Best temperature for storing tomato fruits is

a) 12 -15° b) 4-5°C
c) 5-10°C d) 15-20°C

1659. Bitter taste in brinjal fruit is due to

a) Anti Vitamin E
b) CN glycosides
c) Solasodine
d) Trypsin inhibitor

1660. Black heart is a physiological disorder of

a) Tomato
b) Chilli
c) Cabbage
d) Potato

1661. Black rot in cauliflower is caused by

a) Fungal diseases
b) Bacterial diseases
c) Viral diseases
d) None of these

1662. Black rot in cabbage is transmitted by

a) Mechanical means
b) Seeds
c) Vectors
d) None of these

1663. An F_1hybrid of cucumber recommended by IARI is

a) Pusa Sanyog
b) Poinsette
c) Straight Eight
d) None of these

1664. Arka Jyoti is an improved variety of

a) Muskmelon
b) Watermelon
c) Bottle gourd
d) Snapmelon

1665. Arka Jeet is a popular cultivar of

a) Muskmelon
b) Bitter Gourd
c) Bottle gourd
d) Watermelon

1666. Bulking rate is very high in potato variety

a) Kufri Chandramukhi
b) Kufri Alankar
c) Kufri Naveen
d) None of these

1667. Cabbage is a heavy feeder of

a) N, K
b) N, P
c) N, P, K
d) P, K

1668. California Wonder is an important variety of

a) Hot pepper
b) Sweet pepper
c) Bird Pepper
d) None of these

1669. Carrot is pollinated by

a) Insects b) Wind
c) Water d) All of above

1670. Cowpea is probably a native of

a) India b) China
c) Central Africa d) None of these

1671. Cucumber Mosaic virus is spread by

a) Seeds b) Aphids
c) Mites d) Whiteflies

1672. Directorate of Vegetable Research is at

a) Bhopal b) New Delhi
c) Varanasi d) Ludhiana

1673. Earthing up of potato is done

a) 20days after sowing b) 40 days after sowing
c) 50 days after sow d) None of these

1674. Exceptionally large potato tubers may have more chances of

a) Black-heart b) Brown-heart
c) Hollow-heart d) All of above

1675. Fauvism is related to

a) Indian bean b) Cluster bean
c) Broad bean d) Cowpea

1676. Carrot yellow disease is caused by

a) Fungus b) Bacterium
c) Virus d) None of these

1677. In potato, gene designation for colourless peel

a) y b) Y
c) c d) d

1678. In Potato gene designation for *Verticillium* resistance.

a) Ve b) V
c) VE d) v

1679. In chilli gene symbol...............indicates dwarf plants

a) Dw_1 b) Dw_2
c) Both d) n

1680. In chilli gene symbol...............indicates phenotype capsaicin.

a) C b) c
c) Cc d) CC

1681. Cross pollination percentage in pepper

a) 7.6-36.8% b) 7.62-34.8%
c) 15-20% d) 15-25%

1682. Diploid apogamic is reported in which vegetable

a) Onion b) Brinjal
c) Cassava d) Cucumber

1683. Metamorphic plants is extensively observed in which family

a) Cucurbitaceae b) Solanacae
c) Rutaceae d) Brassicaceae

1684. Which sex form is dominant in Asparagus

a) Femaleness b) Maleness
c) Both d) None of these

1685. Which vegetable is tetramorphic in sex form

a) Spinach b) Lettuce
c) Cucumber d) Potato

1686. Tri-monoecious sex forms is found in which of following vegetable

a) Cucumber b) Muskmelon
c) Ridge gourd d) All of these

1687. Homozygous gynoecious line can be developed by inducing formation of male flowers on gynoecious plants with the help of

a) GA b) Silver thiosulphate
c) NAA d) None of these

1688. 'Heterosis' is commercially exploited in

a) Self pollinated crops
b) Cross pollinated crops
c) Sexually propagated crops
d) vegetatively propagated crops

1689. Which is the most suitable for quick colour development in a garden

a) Annuals
b) Trees
c) Shrubs
d) Climbers

1690. Crossing over during meiosis results in

a) Breaking linkage
b) Help in mutation
c) Promoting linkage
d) None of these

1691. The leading producer of spices in the world is

a) Brazil
b) Mexico
c) India
d) Indonesia

1692. All India Spices Development was established in

a) 1971
b) 1990
c) 1963
d) 1966

1693. An individual lacking one pair of chromosome from a diploid set (2n-2) is called

a) Monosomic
b) Nullisomic
c) Trisomic
d) Terasomic

1694. Spice crop largely exported from India

a) Canine
b) Black Pepper
c) Turmeric
d) Cardamom

1695. Pure line selection is mainly applicable in

a) Self pollinated crops
b) Cross pollinated crops
c) Often cross pollinated crops
d) All of these

1696. Plantation and spices are main crops of

a) Eastern plateau and hill zone

b) Western plateau and hill zone

c) Central plateau and hill zone

d) Southern plateau and hill zone

1697. Pusa Manjari is a variety of

a) Bottle gourd b) Bitter gourd

c) Pumpkin d) Cucumber

1698. Chromosome number of kakrol is

a) 28 b) 24

c) 22 d) 4

1699. White colour variety of Bitter gourd is/are

a) Priya b) Preethi

c) Coimbatur Long Green d) All of the above

1700. Multiple diseases resistant species of *Cucurbita* is

a) C. ecuadorensis b) C. maxima

c) C. moschata d) C .martinezii

IMPORTANT CULTIVARS

Vegetable	Cultivars
Amaranthus	Pusa Kirit, Pusa Kiran, Pusa Lal Chaulai, Chhoti Chaulai, Badi Chaulai, Arka Saguna.
Bitter gourd	Pusa Vishesh, Coimbatore Green, Coimbatore Long Round, Priya, Priyanka, Arka Harit, Phule Green.
Brinjal	**Selection:** Pusa Purple Long (PPL), Pusa Purple Cluster (PPC), Pant Samrat, Pusa Purple Round (PPR), Arka Shirish and Arka Kusumbar (Green type), Punjab Chamkila, Punjab Neelum, Punjab Bahar (Round type), Azad Kranti, Arka Nidhi. **Hybrid** Pusa Kranti: PPL × Hyderptore × Wynad Local → long type Pant Rituraj: T-3 × Pusa Purple Cluster → Round type Pusa Arupam: Pusa Kranti × Pusa Purple Cluster → long type Punjab Barsati: Pusa Purple Cluster × H-4 **Public sector hybrid:** Pusa Anmol, Arka Navneet, Vijay, Azad. **Private sector hybrid:** Vardan, Nisha, Suphal, Shiva and Vaishali (Bicolour variety) **Bacterial wilt resistant varieties:** Pusa Anupam, Pusa Purple Cluster, Arka Nidhi, Arka Keshav, Neelkantha, Pant Rituraj **Phomopsis blight resistant varieties:** Pusa Bhairav, Pusa Anupam, Florida Market. **White coloured cultivar:** KKM-1
Brussel's sprout	Hilds ideal, Rubine-F_1 hybrid, Jade Cross, Danish Prize, Long Island, Early Mom, Pearl Crystal, Oliver, Rogor, Royal Marvel, Rasmunda, Rider, Dwarf Improved.
Cabbage	**Introduction:** Golden Acre, Copenhagen Market (Early variety), Glory of Enkhuizen, Red Acre **Selection:** Pride of India (Early and round), Pusa Ageti **Hybrids:** Pusa Drum Head: F_1 hybrid from Japan → Black leg or dry rot resistant variety. Pusa Mukta: Black rot resistant variety Pusa Sambandh: Suitable for high density planting, early maturing and synthetic variety. Pusa Synthetic **Private sector hybrids:** Sree Ganesh Gol, Uttam, Bajrang, Green Boy and Green express, Sudha , Stone Head, Green Challenger and Green Cornet.
Capsicum	**Introduction:** California Wonder, Yolo Wonder, World Beater, Chinese Giant, Golden Wonder, Sweet Banana. **Selection:** Arka Mohini, Arka Gaurav, Arka Basant **Public sector hybrid:** Pusa Deepti, Green Gold **Private sector hybrid:** Early Boonty , Bharat, Hira, Lario
Carrot	Pusa Kesar: Local Red × Nantes Half Long Pusa Meghali: Pusa Kesar × Nantes Chantaney, Danvers, Zero, Ooty-1, Pusa Yamdagini
Cassava/tapioca	Sree Harsha (tropical clone from Sree Sahya), Sree Prakash, Sree JayaSree Vijaya, Nidhi.

contd.

	Hybrid: Sree Vishakam, Sree Sahya.
Cauliflower	**Introduced:** Improved Japanese **Selection:** Pusa Himjyoti, Pusa Snowball K-1, Pune Ketki, Pusa Deepali, Pant Shubhra, Pusa Aghani. **Hybrid:** Pusa Shubhra, Pusa Aghani **Synthetic:** Pusa Early Synthetic, Pusa Synthetic, Pusa Gobi-3 **Private sector hybrid:** Candid Charm, White Flash, Early Himlata, Himani, Nath Vijaya, Nath Shweta. **Black rot, curd and inflorescence blight resistant varieties:** Pusa Shubhra, Pusa Snowball K-1 **Early variety:** Early Kunwari, Pusa Early Synthetic, Pusa Deepali, Pusa Ketki. **Mid variety:** Improved Japanese, Pusa Sharad, Pusa Aghani **Late variety:** Pusa Snowball, Pusa Snowball K-1 (black rot tolerant).
Chilli	**Selection:** Kalyanpur Yellow, Sabour Angar, Arka Lohit, Bhagya Laxmi, Sindhur, Pusa Sadabahar. **Hybrid:** G-S, Bhaskar, NP-46A , Pusa Jwala, Punjab Lal , Pant C-1 **Private sector hybrid:** Tejashwini, Champian, Gayatri, Agni, Delhi Hot, Skyline.
Colocasia/taro	Setamukhi, Saharsmukhi, Sree Rashmi, Sree Pallavi.
Cucumber	Japanese Long Green, Pusa Sanyog, Poinsette, Himangi, Solan Hybrid, Sheetal, Arka Jyoti.
Elephant's foot	Gajendra, Santragachi, Kovvur, Sree Padma
French Bean	Pusa Parvati, Kentuchy Wonder, Tweed Wonder, Pusa Himlata, Contender, Arka Komal, IIHR 220, Arka Suvidha, Giant Stringless.
Garlic	Yamuna Safed, G 282, Agrifound Parvati, Godavari, Sweta.
Kale	Dwarf Green, Dwarf Moss Curled, Hamburger Market, Karamsag, Scotish, Siberian.
Knol-khol	White Vienna, Large Green, Purple Vienna, King of North, Golith White (Sadashiv), Sutton's Earliest Purple, Purple Speck.
Leek	London Flag, American Flag
Lettuce	Great Lakes and Imperial-559 (Crisp head type, resistant to tip born.Slowbolt, Chinese Yellow, White Boston, Dark Green, Punjab Lettuce No. 1 (Crisp head type).
Muskmelon	Pusa Sharbati, Pusa Madhuras, Pusa Rsaraj, Hara Madhu, Punjab Sunheri, Punjab Rasila, Arka Rajhans, Arka Ajeet, Pusa Sharbati.
Okra	**Selection:** Pusa Makhmali, Gujrat Bhindi No. 1 **Introduction:** Clemon's Spineless, Perkin's Long Green **Hybrid:**Pusa Sawani: Pusa Mukhmali × IC-1542Punjab Padmani: *A. esculantus* × *A. manihot* sp. manihotArka Anamica: *A. esculantus* × *A. manihot* sp. tetraphyllusArka Abhay: *A. esculantus* × *A. manihot* **Private sector hybrid:** Panchali, Adhunik, Supriya, Varsha **YVMV resistant varieties:** Arka Anamika, Arka Abhay, Parbhani Kranti, Punjab Padmani, Pusa Sawani, Varsha Upkar, Hissar Barsati.
Onion	Pusa Red, Pusa Ratnar, Pusa Madhavi, Agrifound Dark Red, N53, Arka Bindu, Brown Spanish, Pusa White Round, Punjab 48, Patna Red, Arka Niketan, Punjab Red Round, Pusa White Flat, Arka Pragati.

contd.

Palak	Selection: Pusa Jyoti, Pusa Bharti (Polyploid variety), Punjab Green, All green. **Hybrids: Pusa Palak** (Swish chord x Local Palak) **Pusa Harit** (Sugar beet x Local Palak), **Benerjee's Giant** (Local Palak x Beer root). **Mutant variety**: Jobeer Green
Peas	Arka Ajit, Bonneville, Arkel, Jawahar Matar 3, Arka Ajeet, Jawahar Matar 1, Harbhajan, Lincoln, Pant Uphar, Sylvia, Little Marvel, Early Superb, Perfection New Line.
Potato	**Early maturing**: Kufri Chandramukhi, Kufri Lavkar, Kufri Ashoka, Kufri Jawahar. **Late maturing**: Kufri Deva, Kufri Megha **Mid maturing**: Kufri Sindhuri , Kufri Jyoti, Kufri Lalima, Kufri Swarna, Kufri Chipsona, Kufri Badshah, Kufri Sutlej, Kufri Giriraj. **Clonal Selection**: Kufri Red, Kufri Safed **Hybrids:** Kufri Chandramukhi: (S-4485 × Kufri Kuber) Kufri Sheetman: (Phulwa × Craig's Defance) Kufri Sindhuri: (Kufri Red × Kufri Kundan) Kufri Badshah: (Kufri Jyoti × Kufri Alankar) Kufri Sutlej: (Kufri Bahar × Kufri Alankar) Kufri Alankar, Kufri Chamatkar, Kufri Jyoti, Kufri Naveen, Kufri Jeevan, Kufri Khasigaro, Kufri Moti and Kufri Kundan **Late blight resistant varieties**: Kufri Jyoti, Kufri Moti, Kufri Megha, Kufri Kundan, Kufri Jeevan, Kufri Naveen. *Kufri Thenamalai* (Cyst nematode and late blight resistant), *Kufri Kuber* (Resistant to black scurf), *Kufri Chipsona II* : (Tolerant to frost and late blight), *Kufri Suvarna, Kufri Badshah* (Resistant to late blight), *Kufri Chipsona 1 and II*: Suitable for processing purpose.
Pumpkin	Arka Chandan, Ambli, Pusa Vishwas, Pusa Vikas, Pusa Hybrid-1
Radish	**Asiatic**: Pusa Chetki, Pusa Desi, Pusa Rashmi, Arka Nishant, Punjab Safed, Japanese White. **European**: Chinese Pink, Rapid Red, Scarlet Long, Scarlet Globe, White Icicle. **Hybrid**: Pusa Himani: Radish Black × Japanese White Pusa Safed: White-5 × Japanese White
Rhubarb	Strawberry, Macdonald, Valentine, Victoria, Cherry Red
Savoy cabbage	Perfectain, Chieftain, Wake Field, Charlatan, Jercy.
Spinach	Virginia Savoy, Early Smooth Leaf, Banarasi, Khara Palak.
Sprouting broccoli	Palam Samridhi, Mars, Green Lofi, Packman, Decicco, Greenbud, Spartan Early, Green Mountain, Italian Green, Green Head, Costal Atlantic, Pusa KTS-1
Sweet potato	Kalmegh, Samrat, Kiran, Gouri, Sankar, Varsha, Bhuban, Sree Vardhani, Sree Bhadra, Sree Nandni, Pusa Suffaid, Pusa Lal, Pusa Sunderi and Sree Arun & Sree Varun are new released varieties. Shree Bhadra: Excellent trap crop for root knot nematode.
Sweet potato	Kalmegh, Varsha, Sree Vardhini, Samrat, Kiran, Gouri, Sankar, Sree Nandini, Rajendra Sakarkand.
Tomato	**Introduction:** Roma, Sioux, Best of all, Marvel, Money Maker, Ageti, **Selection:** Arka Vikas , Sonali, Pant Bahar, Arka Saurabh

contd.

	HybridsPusa Ruby: Sioux × Improved Meeruti Pusa Gaurav : Glamour × Watch Marglobe: Marvel × Globe Pusa Red Plum: *L. esculantum* × *L. pimphifolium* Sweet-72: Pusa Red Plum × Sioux Pusa Sheetal, Hissar Lalima, Hissar Lalit, Punjab Chhuhara Pusa Uphar: Suitable for processing **Public Sector Hybrid:** Arka Vishan, Arka Vardan, Arka Abhijit, Rajshree, Pusa Divya (F_1 Hybrid). **Private sector hybrid:** Naveen, Avinash, Meenakshi, Manisha **Bacterial wilt resistant varieties:** Shakti, Arka Alok, Arka Vikas, Pant Bahar, Best of All, Sloux, Pusa Divya **Low temperature region:** Pusa Sheetal, Pusa H-1, Pusa Sadabahar. **Extreme early variety:** Hissar Arun Hissar Anmol and Pusa Red Plum are **Inter-specific hybrid.** Arka Meghali: Suitable for **rainfed condition** Arka Vikas: Suitable for **drought condition.**
Turnip	Pusa Swarnima, Pusa Chandrima, Pusa Top White Globe, Golden Ball, Pusa Kanchan, Local Red Round.
Vilayati palak/ Spinach	Prickly seeded cultivar → Virginia Savoy Smooth seeded cultivar → Early Smooth Leaf Banerjees Giant, Khara Lucknow, Khara Palak.
Watermelon	Sugar Baby, Arka Jyoti, Arka Bedana, Arka Manik, Durgapur Kesar, Pusa Bedana.
Yams	**Greater yam varieties:** Sree Kirthi, Sree Roopa, Sree Shilpa- 1st hybrid variety of Greater Yam. **Lesser Yam varieties:** Sree Latha, Sree Kala, Konkan Kanchan. **White Yam varieties:** Sree Subhra, Sree Priya, Sree Dhanya.

HINTS FOR SELF-CONFIDENCE

- Vegetables are called protective foods due to presence of vitamins, minerals and phyto-chemicals.
- A protein found in bitter gourd, momordin, has clinically demonstrated anti-cancerous activity.
- In tomato, *Lycopene* is the red pigment and major carotenoid.
- In Brussels sprout, edible part is *swollen axillary buds* called Sprouts.
- In Knol-Khol, the edible part is *swollen stem called* tuber or knob whereas in Kale edible part is *fleshy leaves*.
- All the Cole crops originate from wild ancestors *Brassica oleracea* var. sylvestris L. commonly known as wild cabbage, cliff cabbage, or Colewort.
- India is the 2nd largest producer of cauliflower and cabbage in the world.
- Cole crops are rich sources of Flavonoids and Hydroxy cinnamoyl derivatives as well.
- The most important objective of breeding is crop uniformity.
- Recently *Brassica* hybrid breeding has been using the sporophytic self-incompatibility mechanism since there is no cytoplasmic male sterility in *B. oleracea*.
- Appearance including colour and shape is an important extrinsic trait and the only major breeding objective that is addressed to the consumers.
- Nutraceutical = Nutrition + Pharmaceutical.
- Water-soluble anthocyanins found in red, blue, purple flowers, fruits, vegetables etc are the most preferred natural colourants.
- Spirulina and Hematococcus, the micro-algae are also rich source of food colourants.
- In vegetables specially Cole crops, Glucosinolates convert to isothionates (contain sulfur) and indoles (contain no sulfur) when vegetables containing them are cut.
- Antioxidant enzymes namely superoxide dismutase (SOD), glutathione peroxidase and catalase are made by the body and Superoxide radical inactivates viruses and bacteria.
- Nitric dioxide (NO) is a vasodilator and kills parasites.
- Hydrogen peroxide causes oxidative damage in cells.

- Food derived antioxidants help in detoxification of harmful free radicals.
- Raw broccoli rich source of glucosinolates, flavonoids, lutein, zeaxanthin, carotenes and fibre and also excellent source of Vitamin C, B2, B3, B5, B6, Vitamin E, K, Mg, Zn etc.
- Acylated anthocyanins give to the black or purple carrots their dark violet colour.
- Bioactive compounds in pepper: Ascorbic acid, carotenoids, flavonoids, capsaicinoids.
- The heat values measured by Scoville Heat units (SHU).
- Assam region has declared as world hottest chilli 1,001,304 (SHU).
- The capsaicin content in red dry chili varies between 0.03% to 1.819 %.
- The capsainthin content in red chilies varies between 0.08 % to 0.419 %.
- Chilli oleoresin is the single largest oleoresin used for natural color in the world.
- Betalains are water-soluble, nitrogen containing plant pigments.
- Found in cytoplasm of plant tissue (red beets, portulaca, bougainvillea, etc.)
- Betalains provide insect-repelling signals in cactus thorns.
- Betacyanins imparts the red-violet colour. Provide protection from UV light in ice plants.
- Betacyanin-rich beets are most efficient to scavenge free-radical.
- Beetroot extract have the chemo-preventive properties against lung and skin cancers.
- Betalains have slightly higher protection against skin and lung tumours than anthocyanins and carotenoids.
- Carotenoids are important in human health i.e., â-carotene, á-carotene, lycopene, lutein and zeaxanthin.
- Carotenoids are nutritionally important for eye health, normal cell regeneration and other health aspects linked to free radicals.
- Lutein is generally referred as 'the eye-protective nutrient'. It protects cells from lipid peroxidation. Protects from AMD and cataracts.
- Lycopene, lutein, and zeaxanthin are excellent antioxidants.
- Chlorophyll-a (bluish black) and chlorophyll-b (dark green).
- Pigment curcumin is found in turmeric, curry, mustard, etc. and acts

as an anti-inflammatory agent.

- Turmeric has anti-mutagenic and anti-carcinogenic properties as well as lowers blood cholesterol levels and improve LDL/HDL ratio
- In Capsicum, attractive red color is due to carotenoids, capsanthin and â-carotene and also contains phenolics & quercetin - powerful antioxidants known to protect against cardiovascular & cancer.
- Nasunin – a potent flavonoid present in brinjal.
- Broccoli: Highest cross pollination (95%)
- Spinach: 5 sex forms present.
- Anemophily : Spinach, Beet Root, Palak, Amaranthus
- Entomophily: Onion, Carrot, Radish, Cole crops
- Savoy Cabbage: *Brassica oleraceue* var. sabauda, (conical in shape).
- Pusa snowball K-25: Field resistance to Sclerotia rot.
- Onion bulbs having Red colour– Anthocyanin.
- Onion with yellow skin – Quercetin.
- Iodine rich vegetables are Onion and Okra.
- Tapioca contains highest carbohydrates.
- Incidence of *colletotrichum* and Purple Blotch is more severe in kharif and late kharif onion.
- Nematode: Ditylenchus is very common in onion and garlic.
- 1st commercial hybrid in cucumber in Japan (1940).
- 1st commercial hybrid by IARI in vegetable – Pusa Meghdoot, Pusa Manjari (1971).
- 1st commercial hybrid of tomato – Karnataka hybrid.
- 1st commercial hybrid sweet pepper – Bharat.
- Sweet potato is cheapest source of calorie.
- Cool season crop are hardy while warm season crops are tender.
- Recalcitrant seeds: Pointed gourd, chow-chow
- Pedigree method: Most popular breeding method in India.
- Highest mineral: Amaranthus > Bathua leaves > Coriander.
- Highest Mg: Chilli > Amaranthus > Spinach.
- Highest Cu: Pointed gourd.
- Highest Mn and Mo: Cowpea.

- Highest S: Cauliflower > Brussels sprout > Fenugreek > Cowpea
- Oxalic acid: Amaranthus > Spinach.
- Highest calorific value : Tapioca > Garlic > Lima bean
- Highest Carbohydrates: Tapioca > Garlic > Sweet potato > Potato.
- Highest Proteins: Lima bean > Pea > Garlic.
- Highest B complex: Chilli > Fenugreek leaves > Beet leaves.
- High vitamin C: Bathua leaves > Colocasia leaves > Amaranthus > Turnip green > carrot.
- High P: Garlic > lime bean > colocasia > Drumstick.
- High Fe: Amaranthus > Knol-khol< Spinach.
- High K : Spinach > Potato > Colocasia > Garlic > Lima bean.
- Major mineral nutrients obtained from leafy vegetables are: Ca, Fe and P.
- Bitter gourd: Useful for patients with week nervous system.
- Radish: Used in urinary trouble.
- Cheratin: Bitter gourd – effective against diabetes.
- Celery is effective against hypertension.
- Thinning is compulsory in best root and turnip
- Dr. Kihara developed Pusa Bedana (seedless variety of watermelon) in 1972
- Cercospera leaf spot of sweet potato – 1st report in Africa
- Spineless variety of Okra – Pusa Sawani
- All vegetables comes under category – Spermatophyta
- All vegetables lack fat content (0.1%)
- Mature seeds of Pea and Bean contain Phytic acid
- Inter-specific hybrid of tomato:
- Hissar Anmol: *Hissar Arun* × *L. hirsutum*.
- Pusa Red Plum: *L. esculantum* × *L. pimpillifolium*
- Ash gourds have longest storage life among cucurbits.
- Yellow coloured onion varieties are mostly grown in the world.
- Tomato'! Pusa Ruby, Angur Lata are suitable varieties for Juice extraction.
- Phosphorous increase number of flowers in Tomato

- Cu increase number of flower in Brinjal
- Zn increase weight of fruit in Brinjal
- Little leaf of Brinjal is due to mycoplasma and Zn deficiency
- 6 Stames are present in Cruciferae and Alliaceae family of vegetables
- 5 Stamen are present in Solanaceae family of vegetables
- Cabbage trap crop –mustard (25:1) prevent attack of Red Pumpkin beetle
- The seed rate of tomato is 400-500 gm/ ha.
- The yield of tomato is 20-25 tonnes/ ha.
- Origin place of groundnut is South America.
- Sugar beet is a long day plant.
- 2, 4-D degrades rapidly in the presence of MCPA.
- The dormancy of weed seed is a characteristic that enables weeds to persist for decades and even for centuries.
- The seeds of tobacco are positively photoblastic.
- The seeds of palm require as high as 10-20ºC temperature to break the dormancy.
- The botanical name of Pea is *Pisium sativum.*
- Punjab Chhuhara is a determinate type variety of tomato.
- Whiptail is a disease of cauliflower.
- Pusa Ruby is a variety of watermelon.
- Longevity of brinjal seed is four years.
- The botanical name of watermelon is *Citrullus vulgaris.*
- Cabbage is a cross pollinated crop.
- Dahlia is propagated by bulbs and bulbils.
- Most commonly occurring disease in nursery is damping off.
- Most ideal variety of radish grown in summer and rainy season is Pusa Chetaki.
- Pusa Sawani is a variety of okra.
- Addition of methanol to persimmon fruits aid ripening.
- Aponixes is the development of seeds without complete sexual process is a form of vegetative/ non-sexual propagation.
- Punjab Safed, Pusa Reshmi are Asiatic or tropical type radish varieties.

- Bridge grafting is generally useful for repair purposes.
- Carrot is an excellent source of Vitamin-A and Iron,
- Chekurmanis is commonly known as multi-vitamin leafy vegetable.
- Cracking in tomato skin associated with deficiency of boron.
- Damping off is most commonly occurring disease in nursery.
- Starch is degraded to sugars during fruit ripening, and adds sweetness to fruits.
- Brinjal is known as an appetizing vegetable.
- Ethylene strongly promotes ripening activities by stimulating the climacteric rise.
- Generally 11% pollinizers are considered sufficient for deciduous fruit trees.
- Ethylene stimulates respiration even in non-climacteric fruits like citrus and oranges.
- Only 5-10% of the blossoms develop into fruits on a full blossoming apple or pear tree
- Pollination is not an important factor for fruit development in persimmon.
- Pulsing is a pre-shipment treatment emrloyed by growers.
- Maleic hydrazide (MH) lowers the fruit drops, possibly due to its ability of checking respiration rate.
- Mango malformation is a disorder took place due to imbalance between growth promoters and inhibitors.
- Potato tuber production totally stops at 36°C temperature.
- Proper ripening of date palm fruits needs a temperature of over 30°C for not less than 30 days
- Leafy vegetables are richest source of vitamin-A
- Malaysia is the largest palm oil producer in world.
- Punjab Chuhara is a determinate type variety of tomato.
- Commercial production of cabbage is done by seed to seed method.
- Vegetables are rich source of vitamins and minerals than other nutrients.
- Vegetable consumption/capita/day
- Recommended '! 300 gram
- Available '! 145 gram in India

- 300 gram recommended vegetables consumption includes (125 g green leafy vegetables + 100 g roots + 75 g other vegetables).
- India is the 2nd largest producer of vegetable after China.
- Vegetable crops in India occupy only 2.8% of the total cropped (cultivated) area.
- India accounts for 13.38% of total world production of vegetables.
- Productivity of vegetables in India is 14.9 tonnes/hectare.
- State having largest area under vegetables in India '! West Bengal
- State having maximum production of vegetables in India '! West Bengal
- State having maximum productivity of vegetables in India '! Tamil Nadu.
- Home or kitchen gardening is most ancient type of gardening.
- Market gardening is very intensive method of vegetable cultivation.
- Truck gardening is very extensive method of vegetable cultivation.
- Green leafy vegetables are rich source of Folic acid.
- Major mineral present in fruits and vegetables is'! potassium.
- Countries which are highest consumer of vegetables per capita
  1. Greece '! 377 kg/ year
  2. Turkey '! 327 kg/ year
- Late blight of potato is caused by *Phytophthora infestans.*
- Black heart of potato is caused due to unfavourable oxygen conditions during storage.
- Colocasia leaves contain highest amount of carotene and cabbage has the least among all the green leafy vegetables.
- In green vegetables, drying and withering reduces B-vitamin.
- Chlorophyll-a, is present in the florets of blue green broccoli and chlorophyll-b is present in stalks of broccoli.
- Chlorophyll is mostly insoluble in water and dominant in unripe fruits.
- Carotenoids are group of yellow, orange, red and fat soluble pigments.
- In plants carotenoids are present in á-carotene, ß-carotene, ã-carotene, xanthophylls and crypto-xanthin.
- Anthocyanin and anthoxanthins are important cyanidin based compounds.
- Anthocyanins are pelargonidin (Red), cyanidin (Reddish blue) and delphinidin (blue).

- Alaksha and Resistant Surprise are fusarium wilt varieties of pea.
- Soybean is native to South-east Asia.
- Spinach is native to South-west Asia.
- Oxalic acid is present in spinach.
- Origin of Hyacinth bean is India.
- Celery seed rate – 250 gm/ha
- Sweet potato – spacing 45 x 30 cm
- Bottle guard seed rate - 3-4 kg/ ha
- Methi seed rate – 25 kg/ ha
- Colocasia – Asterpency is due to calcium oxide.
- Radish is photo-neutral plant.
- Colocasia is photo-phobic plant.
- Tomato is photo-philic plant.
- Horsh Radish – Pungency due to Allyl isothiocynate.
- Nets of 40 and higher mesh are effective means to control the entry of flying insects and save the crops from viral diseases.
- In plastic low tunnel, polyethylene film of 30-40 microns thickness is used.
- In plastic mulch, silver and yellow coloured films are successively used for repelling the aphids and whitefly respectively.
- LDPE and LLDPE plastic films are commonly used for mulching.
- Black plastic mulch films are more popular due to opacity.
- Trench cultivation technology has been found sustainable for the production of vegetables around the year in cold climate.
- Floating plastic covers are used to cover large open fields to protect vegetables from frost, snow and low temperature.
- Greenhouse technology is also known as protective cultivation.
- In low cost Greenhouses, for covering UV, stabilized plastic film of 200 microns thickness is used.
- Semi-climate controlled GH are suitable for vegetable cultivation during mild summer and winter season.
- Wooden structure of poly-house is vulnerable to the attack of termites.
- For green house growing, low volume and high value type of vegetables are mostly preferred.

- For GH fabrication, galvanized steel or zinc coated pipes are preferred to avoid corrosion.
- Plastic film began to be manufactured after World War II.
- Double layer acrylic transmits about 83% of light and reduces heat loss by 20-40% over single layer.
- Fibre and polycarbonate has high rate of expansion and contraction.
- Polythene film treated with UV inhibitors will last for 12-24 months longer than untreated ones.
- Polyester films can last upto 15 years.
- Designing of green house should be such that the angle of incidence of solar radiations is never greater than 40 degrees.
- Designing of GH is that the structure should be able to transmit maximum possible sunlight during winters.
- Greenhouses are normally designed for a service life of 25 years.
- Locate service structure to the North of GH.
- Separate and guttor or connected structures are two basic methods for GH arrangement.
- Drip or sprinkler system of irrigation is used in modern green houses.
- The transparent covering should be at 90°angle to the sun rays for maximum transmission of solar radiations into a GH.
- North-South orientation has a good radiation distribution.
- Transitivity decreases as the number of span increases.
- The East-West arrangement is preferable during winters above 40-45° latitude.
- Evaporative cooling type of cooling is the most efficient and economical way to reduce GH temperature.
- GH crops grow best in light with wavelength ranging from 400-700nm.
- PAR stands for photosynthetic active radiation.
- Shading and high pressure Na lamps are the ways of controlling light intensity and photoperiod in green house.
- When RH is high, it inhibits the uptake of nutrients especially calcium.
- The maximum yield can be achieved by injecting 1000-1500 ppm carbon dioxide in GH.
- The term Hydroponics was used by Gerick, 1940.
- In India, Hydroponics was first introduced at Kalimpong, Darjeeling, West Bengal.

- The vegetable crops which are adapted to Nutrient Film Technique are tomato and cucumber.
- Sphagnum moss is derived from *Sphagnum pappilosum* and *S. palustre*.
- Particle size of fine sand ranges from 0.05-0.25mm.
- Vegetable crops which are difficult to transplant are cucurbits and weet corn.
- Combination of ingredient used for raising nursery is coco peat, vermiculite and perlite (3:1:1).
- The pH of the water used for plug transplants should be 5.5-6.5.
- Bicarbonate is a measure of water hardness.
- The plants show very definite purple colouration along the stem and underside of leaves due to the deficiency of phosphorous.
- Indeterminate type of tomato cultivar is grown under greenhouse.
- The minimum temperature required for tomato seed germination is 8-10°C.
- The ideal range of temperature for colour development in tomato is 18-25°C.
- Beefsteak cultivar of tomato produces slicing type of fruits.
- The most popular cvr of tomato currently grown are trust and match.
- Cherry tomato varieties have TSS of 6.8 to 7.7.
- Single main stem type of training system is used in tomato.
- Tomato plants under green house are supported by nylon threads.
- The plants are 30-35 feet longer in their 10-11 months life cycles of cultivation.
- Removal of excess fruits leads to increase in the fruit size of the plant.
- Tomato is a self-pollinated crop.
- In tomato, bumble bees are the perfect pollinator even under environmental stress conditions.
- Tomato is sensitive to water stress condition during flower formation and fruit enlagement.
- Calcium deficiency in tomato cause blossom end rot.
- For correction of Ca deficiency calcium nitrate mixture is given.
- Most of the tomato varieties are ready for first picking after 75-85 days.
- The optimum night temperature for quality production in Capsicum is 18-21°C.

- In capsicum, thick fleshed ones are best for roasting and cooking while, thin ones are suitable for salads.
- A very low night temperature (10°C) in capsicum ensures high percentage of fruit set with a few seeds.
- Pepper is a non-climacteric fruit.
- Cucumber fruit is berry and pepo.
- In cucumber, air and soil temperature influences germination, vegetative growth, flower initiation, fruit growth and fruit quality.
- Cucumber varieties grown in green house are usually European type.
- Gynoecious, predominating gynoecious and monoecious are three types of cucumber varieties.
- Drip irrigation system is used in cucumber production under green houses.
- Most of the varieties of muskmelon grown under green houses are andro-monoecious.
- Muskmelon is usually planted in green house in November-December months.
- Transparent plastic of 30-50 microns (infra-red) is commonly used for making low tunnels.
- Cherry tomato crop can be planted at a spacing of 30×60 cm.
- Lower intensity of light in pepper cause flower bud abscission.
- Lower light intensity in tomato reduces the content of ascorbic acid.
- High temperature in pepper cause abscission of flower and reduce fruit yield.
- In cucumber, maximum rate of biomass production is achieved at a constant air temperature of 30-35°C.
- In tomato, enrichment of the green house with carbon dioxide results in increase in vitamin A.
- The development work on drip irrigation was initiated in Israel during 1940.
- The concept of Drip Irrigation was given by Symcha Blass.
- Drip irrigation was used in India since 1970.
- To get rid of DBM, tomato and carrot crops can be inter-planted with cabbage.
- *Helicoverpa armigera* is the name of tomato fruit borer.

- *Crysoperla carnea* the predator used for the control of aphid, jassids and eggs of some lepidopterous insects.
- *Bacillus thuringiensis* is the bio-control agent extensively used in vegetables.
- Diamond black moth (*Plutella xylostella*) damages the leaves of cabbage, cauliflower, mustard.
- Damping off is caused by *Pythium* spp., *Rhizoctonia* spp. *Fusarium* spp.
- Downy mildew is caused by *Pseudopernospora cubensis.*
- Early blight is caused by *Alternaria solani.*
- Bacterial wilt in tomato is caused by *Pseudomonas solanacearum.*
- Leaf curl virus in tomato is transmitted by white fly.
- *Agaricus bisporus* is a cultivated mushroom.
- *Pleurotus ostreatus* is *an Oyster* mushroom.
- *Volvariella volvacea is a* Paddy straw mushroom.
- Shitake mushroom is *Lentinus edodes.*
- Dhingri mushroom is *Pleurotus eryngii*
- Paddy straw mushroom is popularly known as tropical mushroom.
- Mushrooms contain 20-35 % proteins (dry wt.)
- Mushrooms are rich in Lysine and tryptophan.
- Mushrooms are almost free from fall except from linoleic acid.
- Chlorosis refers to yellowing of the leaves.
- Brown coloured dye is obtained from *Polyporus bispidus.*
- *Amanita muscaria* species of mushroom is recommended for the remedy of epilepsy.
- *Aricularia auricula* is used against the inflammation of Eye and throat.
- Yellow coloured vegetables are rich in vitamin A.

❑❑❑

Section – III

Floriculture

CLASSIFICATION

Floriculture is the aesthetic branch of horticulture which deals not only with the cultivation of ornamentals, annuals, biennials and perennial plants but also with their marketing. Flowers symbolize beauty, purity, peace and love. In India, it is a dynamic and expanding industry showing an impressive annual growth rate.

Classification of Flower Crops

The flowering plants can be classified broadly on the basis of their species, genus, family, plant part used or type of flower plants. They are further classified as cutflowers, cut foliage, turfgrasses, groundcovers, hedges, accents, specimen plants, avenue trees, screens, topiaries, fillers and others.

1. Classification on basis of life span

(i) **Seasonal flowers:** These complete their life cycle within one calander year and need to replant every year. These flowers have short life span ranging from 4-6 months. For example; marigold, chrysanthemum, gladiolus, aster etc.

(ii) **Perennial flowers:** The flowers have life span extending beyond one calendar year and do not need replacement year after year. The life span ranges from 2 years in case of tuberose; 5 years in case of crossandra, to over 8 years in case of rose or over 10 years in some jasmine varieties.

2. Classification on basis of end use

(i) **Traditional flowers:** These are offered in religious and social ceremonies, used as an adornment by womens, offered for worship at home or temples. Flowers are used singly or in form of garlands or strung together loosely. Examples are jasmine, rose, chrysanthemum, marigold, crossandra and tuberose.

(ii) **Non-traditional flowers:** Non-traditional flowers are used strictly for decorative purposes. These flowers are referred as cut flowers and are generally harvested with a long stem. The flowers in non-traditional use are arranged in vases, pots, bouquets and are mostly consumed during social functions. These flowers are also known as modern flowers. Examples are gladiolus, rose, carnation, gerbera, orchids.

(iii) **Industrial use flowers**: Some flowers are used as raw material in the industries for extraction of essential oil, perfumes and cosmetic products and also for preparation of some edible products like gulkand, rose oil, rose water, jasmine oil, concretes, gulkand and attar are some of the commercial products manufactured in processing units/ perfumeries.

3. Classification on basis of their use

(i) **Lawn or Turf grasses:** The grasses grown for aesthetic purpose in the landscape or for any outdoor recreational use. They are usually maintained at a low height. Examples: Bermuda grass, carabao grass, zoysia grass, creeping bent grass, perennial rye grass.

(ii) **Cut flowers**: The plants grown for their attractive flowers with long shelf life. Examples: anthurium, chrysanthemum, gladiolus, orchids, rose.

(iii) **Cut foliage**: The plants grown for their attractive foliage which are cut for floral decoration. Examples: ferns, fishtail palm, Song of India, Song of Jamaica.

(iv) **Edge Crops**: The short statured plants grown to serve as barrier between the lawn and garden, to highlight gardens, or to create stand-alone gardens; also called *border plants*.

(v) **Groundcovers**: The aesthetically appealing plants grown in the landscape primarily to suppress weed growth and to control, retard or prevent soil erosion by covering and binding loose, bare soil. It is oftenly used to produce a carpeting effect. Examples: *Alternanthera versicolor*, *Cuphea*, travelling jew, creeping peanut, Vietnam rose.

(vi) **Hedges-** The plants grown at the edges of pathways or boundaries and continuously pruned to knee-high height or upper but below eye level. Examples: *Duranta,* hedge bamboo, Chinese holly, dwarf santan.

(vii) **Specimens**: The plants having showy features, or with unique characteristics which make them pieces of conversation or botanical curiosity, or otherwise desired as collector's item. They are ideally planted in isolation rather than massed with other plants, and easily become focal point in the landscape. Examples of potential specimens: queen of flowering trees (*Amherstia nobilis*), palms.

(viii) **Shade crops:** These are generally trees, shrubs, trellised vines and lianas which are grown mainly to provide shade singly or with supporting trellis.

(ix) **Avenue Trees**: The trees and shrubs grown, more or less equidistant, beside roads and streets. Palms are also used. Examples: acacia (raintree), katuray, narra, date palm.

4. Classification on the basis of plant type

a) **Woody plants**
   i) Trees
   ii) Shrubs
   iii) Vines and ground covers

b) **Herbaceous plants**
   i) Flowers
   ii) Vines and ground covers
   iii) Grass/turf

c) **Potted plants, houseplants, gift plants**

SHORT NOTES

1. Scooping

It involves 'Removing' of basal plate and destroying the 'Central Shoot' of the bulb, thus encouraging the formation of bulblets round the cut edges of the scale leaves. Scooping is achieved by using a special knife or a spoon with a 'Sharpened edge' to leave a 'Concave depression' at the base of bulb. The depth of the cut is important, because the bulblets are formed on 'cell tissues' at the lowest point of the 'scale leaves'. If the cut is too deep, the 'basal cells' responsible for meristem development will be removed, resulting in poor bulblet formation. If the basal plate is not adequately removed, it will inhibit 'bulblet formation'. The time required to reach flowering is 3 to 4 years, bulb size is 8-12 cm in diameter.

2. Scoring

Scoring is almost identical to scooping, except for the preparation of the "Base" of the bulb. Scoring is generally used on large-diameter bulbs (16-20 cm) where scooping is difficult. The Base of the bulb is prepared by making 2 or 3 incisions through the "base plate", sufficiently deep to destroy the Central growing shoot and to "induce" the dormant axillary buds to sprout. Proliferation of the bulblets from the base of the scale is far "less" generous than with scooping but their growth rate is greater, reducing the time needed to reach flowering to "2 to 3 years".

3. Tunicate bulbs (Laminated bulb)

- Laminate or tunicate bulbs (Daffodil, Tulip).
- True bulbs have fresh modified leaves called scales.
- A disk of hardened stem tissue is called basal plate.
- Laminate bulbs have outer bulb scales which are dried and membranous provide protection from drying and mechanical injury to the bulb.
- The fleshy scales are in the continuous concentric layers, so that structure becomes more or less solid.

4. Non-tunicated or scaly bulbs

- Typically represented by lillium species.
- These bulbs do not possess the enveloping dry covering.
- The scales are separate and are attached to the basal plate.
- In general, the non-tunicated bulbs are easily damaged and must be handled more carefully than the tunicated bulbs.

- They must be kept continuously moist/wet because they are injured by drying
- Scales are thicker and loosely wrapped i.e., in Lillies

5. Senescence

Senescence is the final phase in the ontogeny of the organ, in which a series of normally irreversible events are, initiated that leads to the cellular breakdown and death of organ. In higher plants it is of three types i.e., Population senescence; individual plant senescence; and determinate organ senescence. Senescence is also defined as the deteriorative processes that are natural cause of death.

6. Aging

Aging refers to the Processes Acquiring Maturity with the passage of time. Normally an increment of time, which may or may not be accompanied by physiological changes including senescence. Aging thus includes a much 'wider span' of physiological processes, which may either "weaken the organism or to be neutral" (with respect to the capability of biological organism to survive. Senescence in contrast refers to changes providing for the 'endogenous regulation' of death.

7. Growth pattern of corm

Gladiolus and crocus growth pattern are typical examples of corm, with gladiolus semi-hard to tender. In areas with severe winter, the corm must be stored over winter and planted in spring. At time of planting the corm is a 'vegetative structure', new roots develop from its base, one or more buds to develop leaves. Flower initiation takes place within `few weeks' after the shoots begins to grow, and at the same time the base of `shoot apex' thickened. Succeeding year, new corm begins to form above the old corm. Stolons like structure bearing miniature corm or cormels on the tips develop from base of new corm. The new corm continues to make food material. At the end of summer when the foliage dries, there are one or more new corms and a great number of cormels. The corms are dug out and stored over winter until they are planted in the next spring.

8. Growth pattern of rhizome

Rhizomes grown by elongation of the growing points, at terminal ends and on lateral branches. Length also increases by growth in the intercallary mesostem, in the lower part of internodes. As the plant continues to grow and the older parts die, several branches arising from a plant may eventually become separated to become 'individual plant' of 'a single clone'. Rhizomes exhibit consecutive vegetative and reproductive stages, but growth cycle differs in two ways:

i) In patchymorph rhizomes of 'Irish', a growth cycle begins with the initiation of growth of 'lateral branches' on a flowering section. This flowering stock dies but these new lateral branches produce leaves and grow vegetatively during the remainder of that season. Continuous growth of underground stem, storage of food and production of floral bud at conclusion of vegetative period depends on photosynthesis. Consequently, foliage should not be removed during these periods. A flowering stock is produced in a 'following spring' and no further terminal growth can take place. In general, plant with this structure, flowers in spring and grows vegetatively during summer and fall.

ii) Plants with heptomorph habit as a general rule with exception grow vegetatively during beginning of growth period and flowers later in the same period. The length of time during which individual rhizome remain vegetative varies with kind of plants. Some bamboo species remain vegetative for many years but then they change abruptly and the entire plant produces plant. In some rhizomes plants like blueberry, rhizome development is increased by higher temperature and long photoperiod and is correlated with vigorous above ground growth.

9. Important annual flowers

S.N.	Popular name	Scientific name	Family	Native
1.	Acroclinum (Paper flower)	*Acroclinum roseum*	Asteraceae	Australia
2.	Ageratum (Floss flower)	*Ageratum houstonianum*	Asteraceae	Central America
3.	Anchusa	*Anchusa capensis*	Boraginaceae	South Africa
4.	Chrysanthemum	*Chrysanthemum sp*	Asteraceae	North Africa, Europe
5.	Snap dragon, dog flower	*Antirrhinum majus*	Scrophulariaceae	South America
6.	African daisy	*Arctotis stoechadifolia*	Asteraceae	South Africa
7.	Aster	*Callistephus chinensis*	Asteraceae	China, Japan
8.	Bells of Ireland	*Molucella laevis*	Labiateae	Mediterranean region
9.	Brachycome	*Brachycome iberidifolia*	Asteraceae	Australia
10.	Calendula	*Calendula officinalis*	Asteraceae	South Europe
11.	California poppy (Pot marigold)	*Eschscholzia californica*	Papaveraceae	California (USA)
12.	Candytuft	*Iberis sp*	Crucifereae	Europe
13.	Carnation	*Dianthus caryophyllus*	Caryophyllaceae	Europe
14.	Cineraria	*Senecio cruentus*	Asteraceae	Canary Islands
15.	Clarkia	*Clarkia elegans*	Onagraceae	California, USA
16.	Parrot Bill	*Clianthus dampieri*	Leguminoseae	California, USA
17.	Teak seed	*Coreopsis tinctorea*	Asteraceae	California, USA
18.	Corn flower	*Centaurea cyanus*	Asteraceae	Europe, Britain
19.	Cosmos	*Cosmos bipinnatus*	Asteraceae	Mexico

contd.

20.	Dahlia	*Dahlia variabilis*	Asteraceae	Mexico
21.	Daisy	*Bellis perennis*	Asteraceae	Europe
22.	Dimorphotheca (African daisy)	*Dimorphotheca aurantiaca*	Asteraceae	South Africa
23.	Gamolepsis	*Gamolepsis tagetes*	Asteraceae	South Africa
24.	Gazania	*Gazania splendens*	Asteraceae	South Africa
25.	Baby breath	*Gypsophila elegans*	Caryophyllaceae	Caucasus region
26.	Everlasting or Straw flower	*Helichrysum bracteatum*	Asteraceae	Australia
27.	Hollyhock	*Althea rosea*	Malvaceae	China
28.	Ice Plant	*M. criniflorum*	Aizoaceae	South Africa
29.	Lady's lace	*Pimpnella monoica*	Umbelliferae	India
30.	Larkspur	*Delphinium hybridum*	Ranunculaceae	Europe
31.	Linaria	*Linaria bipartita*	Scrophulareaceae	Spain, Morocco
32.	Linum (flax)	*Linum grandiflorum* Var. *rubrum*	Linaceae	North Africa & Europe
33	Lupin	*Lupinus hartwegis*	Luguminoseae	North America
34.	Mignonette	*Reseda odorata*	Residoceae	North Africa
35.	Mimulus (Monkey flower)	*Mimulus tigrinus*	Scrophulariaceae	Western part of North & South America
36.	Nasturtium	*Tropaeolum majus*	Tropaeolaceae	Mexico & South America
37.	Nemasia	*Nemasea strumosa*	Scrophuliaraceae	South Africa
38.	Nigella	*Nigella damascene*	Ranunculaceae	North Africa
39.	Pansy	*Viola tricolor* Var. *hortensis*	Violaceae	Europe
40.	Petunia	*Petunia hybrids*	Solanaceae	South America
41.	Phlox (Strawflower)	*Phlox drummondii*	Polemoniaceae	USA
42.	Rudbeckia (Cone flower)	*Rudbeckia bicolour*	Asteraceae	North America
43.	Salvia (Sage flower)	*Saliva splendens*	Labiateae	South America
44.	Saponaria (Soapwart)	*Saponaria vaccaria*	Caryophyllaceae	Europe
45.	Butter fly flower, Poor Man's orchid	*Schizanthu-s wisetonensis*	Solanaceae	Chile& Peru
46.	Shirley Poppy (corn poppy)	*Papaver rhoeas*	Papaveraceae	Europe
47.	Statice (Sea lavender)	*Limonium sinuatum*	Plumbaginaceae	Mediterranean Region
48.	Stock	*Matthiola incana*	Crucifereae	Mediterranean Region
49.	Sweet Alyssum	*Alyssum mauritimum*	Crucifereae	Western Asia and Europe

contd.

50.	Sweet pea	*Lathyrus odoratus*	Leguminosae	Europe
51.	Sweet Sultan	*Centaurea moschata*	Asteraceae	Caucasus region
52.	Sweet William	*Dianthus barbatus*	Caryophyllaceae	Northern France
53.	Venidium	*Venidium fastvosum*	Asteraceae	South Africa
54.	Verbena	*Verbena hybrida*	Verbenaceae	South America
55.	Wall flower	*Cheiranthes cheiri*	Crucifereae	Europe

10. Status of floriculture

World

Total area = 3, 60,000 hectare

Area under greenhouse = 46,000 hectare

Existing auction centres (world)

- Alsmeer (The Netherlands)
- Miami (USA)
- Bagota (Columbia)
- Tel Aviv (Israel)

New emerged markets (world)

- Japan
- Thailand
- Mauritius

Top ten in the Floriculture Trade (world) (Year 2007)

Exporters		Importers		Producers	
Country	Share (%)	Country	Share (%)	Country	Share (%)
Netherlands	58.0	United Kingdom	19	Netherlands	13
Colombia	14.0	Germany	18	Japan	11
Ecuador	7.0	US	16	Italy	6
Kenya	5.0	The Netherlands	9	Colombia	3
Italy	3.0	France	9	China	3
USA	2.0	Japan	4	France	2
Belgium	1.7	Italy	4	Germany	2
Denmark	1.6	Switzerland	3	South Korea	2
Costa Rica	1.6	Belgium	2	USA	2
Israel	1.5	Russian Federation	2	Ecuador	2

Top ten Cut Flower	Top ten Pot plants	Top ten countries in per capita consumption of flowers
Rose	Ivy	Switzerland
Tulip	Kalanchoe	Norway
Chrysanthemum	Ficus	Holland
Gerbera	African violet	Germany
Lilly	Potted chrysanthemum	Belgium
Alstroemeria	Spathiophyllum	Italy
Freesia	Hyacinth	Japan
Carnation	Dracaena	Swedan
Iris	Potted Rose	France
Gypsophilla	Primrose	Denmark

(Source: Floriculture International)

India

- Total area = 1, 60,720 hectare
- Loose flower production = 8.70 MT
- Cut flower production = 4.3 million tones
- Annual growth rate = 7-10 percent
- India has a great tradition of growing flowers.
- The total area under flower production is 1, 60,720 hectare.
- Flower production is concentrated mostly in Tamil Nadu, Andhra Pradesh, Maharastra, West Bengal, UP, Delhi, Haryana and Rajasthan.
- In India, nearly 98.5% flowers are grown under open conditions and only 1.5% is grown under green house.
- India's share in floriculture trade is 0.49% and total value of exports is $66 million.
- The domestic market is of Rs. 500 crores and is growing at 25% annually in the country and in Delhi market is growing 40% annually.
- Major markets for cut flowers in India: Delhi, Mumbai, Kolkatta, Bangalore, Chennai, Hyderabad, Ahmedabad, Kharagpur and Pune.

11. History of gardening

- The art and science of growing ornamental dates back to 3000 BC.
- Arboriculture developed in Vedic time during 3000-2000 BC.
- Girls use flowers of champaka and jasmine for decorating their hairs and wear flowers of Siris in ears.

- Botanically, champaka is *Michelia champaca* and Siris is *Albizzia lebbek*.
- Poet Kalidas has made reference of Sandal paste in his writings.
- According to Vatsyayana, house/ Palaces of Kings had a pleasure garden generally known as Vriksavatika and Purpavatika.
- Ashoka tree, known as (*Saraca indica*) relates to Sita whereas Kadamba tree (*Anthocephalus cadamba*) was associated with life of Krishna.
- Description of flowers and gardens in Sanskrit classics like Rigveda (3000-2000 BC); Ramayana (1200-1000 BC) and Mahabharata (500 BC).
- Ashoka tree (*Saraca indica*), Padma tree/ Lotus (*Nelumbo nucifera*), Tulsi (*Ocimum sanctum*) and Peepal (*Ficus religiosa*) found high place in worship.
- Lord Gautam Buddha attains Enlightenment under tree Peepal in Bodh Gaya.
- Sal, Ashoka and Plaksha are associated with Ram.
- Plaskha is scientifically *Butea monosperma*.
- Planting of Avenue tree was taken by Ashoka in 233 BC.
- Concept of developing a Garden in the enclosed space was introduced by Mughals (Babur) in India during 16th and 17th century.
- Babur in Baburnama mentioned some indigenous ornamental trees like *Hibiscus rosa-senensis*, oleander and white jasmine.
- Babur introduced scented Persian rose in India.
- Mother of NurJahan is credited with Otto of rose.

12. Colour schemes

- Natural colour: green, which dominates throughout the year.
- Red colour dominates during winter.
- Yellow colour dominates in spring.

Types of colour schemes: The colour schemes are basically of three types:

i) Monochromatic schemes: Only one colour is used.

ii) Analogous/hormonous colour scheme: According to wavelength of colour.

iii) Contrast colour scheme: Opposite colour of wheel.

VIBGYOR means:

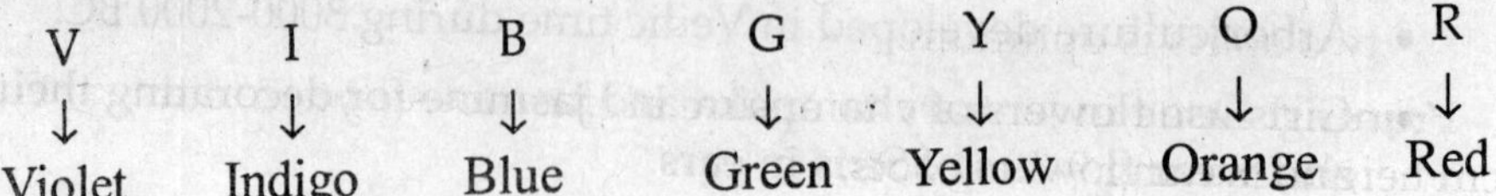

Primary colours: Blue, yellow, red

Secondary colours: Violet, Indigo, Green, Orange

Black + White colour = grey colour

Complimentary/contrast colours: Blue & orange, Red & green, Violet & yellow

13. Cultivation of Jasminum

- Plants are grown as both shrubs and climbers
- Flowers and buds are used for making garlands, bouquets and veni.
- Flowers are also used for production of perfumed hair oils and attars.
- Oil is extracted from *Spanish jasmine* (*J. grandiflorum*).
- *J. sambac* (Arabian jasmine) is reported to be used in China for flavouring tea.
- Out of total world production of Jasmine concrete, 50% is supplied by France alone.
- Origin place of Jasmine is tropical and sub tropical region.
- Three important species used for commercial cultivation are:
  - *J. sambac* (Arabian jasmine): Native to West Indies
  - *J. officinale* (Common white jasmine): Native to Persian origin
  - *J. grandiflorum* : Native to Afghanistan
  - Distribution: *J. auriculatum* (India), *J. flexile* (India), *J. humile* (tropical Asia) and *J. wallichianum* (Nepal).

Cultivation: Warm climate combined with copious rainfall and sunny weather contributes long duration of flowering season.

Soil and climate: Preferred well drained sandy loam to clay loam soil. Cool house species should be kept at 7-13°C and store species at (13-18°C) during September to March. Soil pH: 6.5-7.5.

Fertilizers/ manures

- N 60g + P_2O_5 120 g singly or together enhanced flower and essential oil yield.
- Highest flower yield when treated with N and P_2O_5 350 and 300 kg/ hectare respectively.
- Application of 60:120:120g/plant along with 10 kg of FYM applied in two splits is optimum.

Pruning: Done in January to ensure higher flower yield, cut branches at 90 cm height, leaving 9-11 shoots.

Yield: 1 ton flowers give 2.5 kg concrete.

14. Post harvest management of orchids

Harvesting: Harvesting should be done in the evening. All equipments should be sterilized. When individual *cattelya & cymbidium* flowers are cut, the peduncle should immediately be inserted in a tube of water. In Hawaii and Singapore some *Dendrobium* and *Aranda* growers immerse the entire sprays of flowers in water for 15 minutes before packing and shipping. Orchids are harvested when fully opened.

Grading: No standard grades for orchids. In case of *Cattelya* flower both "Colour and size" are considered while pricing. While grading; spike length, number of open flowers, unopened buds, arrangement of flowers on a spike and number of side shoots/spike are taken into consideration. In solitary flowers like cattelaya, both flower colour and flower size are considered.

Storage: Stored at 5-7°C for 10-14 days. Use of modified atmosphere can often usefully substitute for the low temperature. Most of the orchids are stored at 7-10°C. *Cymbidium* and *Paphio redilum* are stored at -0.5 to 4°C.

Packaging: An ideal package should be airtight, water proof, strong enough to withstand handling. *Cymbidium* spikes are packed "100 flowers' in a box. Standards boxes are used for packaging of *cattelya* flowers. *Dendrobium* is packed in (4 dozon sprays) per box. Orchids have `Non-thermic' properties, hence packed in corrugated boxes of different sizes.

1. Scorpion orchids are packed in bunches of 5-10 while small packages used for dendrobiums.
2. Arenda flowers are individually wrapped in tissue papers and packed.
3. Fan shaped varieties like 'Golden Shower' are packed in such a way that they lie with the flat side on top of each other.
4. Care should be taken when blooms packed individually, few pieces of shredded wax paper is to be put between sepals and petals and around the tip.

Vase-life: Lower 0.75 cm of the peduncle is cut and flower is inserted into tube of water. In spray type orchids, the basal 2.5 cm of the stem is cut upon arrival. Placed in warm water at 38°C with a preservative and hardened off at 5°C. Orchid flowers are sensitive to ethylene. Modified atmosphere storage under 10% CO_2 for 4 days could extend the bench life by 4 days. Foliar application of 500 ppm aluminium chloride lengthens the vase-life of Oncidium.

Transportation: Orchids are sensitive to wilting, hence the cut ends of spike are wrapped with water saturated cotton during long distance transport.

15. Specific use of chemical retardants

Growth retardants: They reduce plant height and are mostly synthetic compounds that either slow down cell division or inhibit cell elongation. They are very specific to plant species in their action. Very old, but little used retardant is Phosphon-D. Foliar sprays of SADH are used commonly in chrysanthemum, azaleas whereas Chlormequat (CCC spray) drenches are used in begonia, geranium and poinsettia. Ancymidol is active in lilies, hyacinths, tulips.

- **Chrysanthemum:** Plant treated with MH (1000 to 2000 ppm) at three time intervals after planting reduces the plant height.
- **Rose:** CCC application at 5000-10,000 ppm to cultivar Celebration decreases plant height.
- **Marigold:** Growth regulation was observed with 500 ppm cycocel and 700 ppm TIBA in seedling of marigold Cv Fantasy.
- **Tuberose**: Etheral sprayed after 40 days of planting noticed reduction in plant height. Rhizome treated with GA_3 (100 ppm) for 24 hours have smaller plant height.
- **Carnation:** Reduction in height of main shoot and length of laterals with 2000 ppm MH is recorded.
- **Daffodils:** A dip of daffodils in BA (100 ppm) + 2, 4-D (22 ppm) retards senescence.

16. Important species as cut flowers

- In *Lilium, Pollyana,* Elite, Grand Paradise are Asiatic type whereas; Star Gazer is oriental type.
- Tulip: Apeldoorn, Golden Apeldoorn are promising.
- Daffodil: Gigantic Star, Carlton & Dutch Master
- Hyacinth: Anna Marie, Jan Bose and Amsterdom, Gypsy Queen.
- Carnation: Red Corso, Espana, Candy.
- Gladiolus: Priscilla, Trader Horn, Wind Song, Marvellous, Yellow Dreams.
- Chrysanthemum: Snowdon, Mountaineer in standard and Ajay, Birbal Sahni in spray.

17. Important species used as pot plant

1) *Crocus species*
2) *Hyacinthus orientalis* (Gypsy Queen, Jan Bose Amsterdom)
3) *Iris hollandica*
4) *Iris reticulata*
5) *Muscari armeniacum*
6) *Narcissus species*

7) *Tulips species* (Apeldoorn, Golden Apeldoorn)

8) Lilies: Pollyana, Elite, Paradise, Star Gazer

18. Foliage plants

These plants are valued for their beautiful foliage and grow well in shade or partial shade. In the garden such conditions are available under the "trees or artificially constructed greenhouse or the buildings". These are also used for interior decoration in pots, wooden crates etc. Important foliage plants are Aspidistra, Chlorophytum, Caladium, Dieffenbachia, Moranta and Monstera.

1) Asparagus: Native to South Africa is tuberose rooted belongs to family liliaceae.

2) *Aspidistra elator* belongs to liliaceae family.

3) *Caladium hortulanum* (Araceae) also called syngonium.

4) *Coleus blumae* (Labiateae) is propagated by seed and terminal cuttings.

5) *Dieffenbachia spp*. (Araceae).

6) Crotons (*Coliaeum variegatum*) belong to Euphorbiaceae family and propagated by air layering.

7) Dracaena (Liliaceae).

8) *Chlorophytum sp* (Ribbon plant) belongs to family liliaceae.

19. Important Parks and Gardens

Name of park/garden	Special features
Sayaji Park, Baroda (Gujarat)-1879	Siyaji park in Baroda named after Maharaja Sayaji Rao to cover 40 hectare area. About 8000 various ornamental trees are there in garden. The garden has a toy train, a grant wheel, children park and traffic training centre for children. The Baroda museum is situated in the park (opened in 1894). The park has a Zoo. The most important attractive part of the garden is the bandstand i.e., on one hectare area. The formal portion of garden has arbour-like band stand, paved walks, and green lawns, music besides changing multi-colour light.
Mandor garden, Jodhpur, (Rajashtan)- 1724-1749 AD.	The garden is 5 km away from Jodhpur. This garden was laid out by Raja Abhai Singh in the desert region of Rajasthan. Lawn, the flower beds, trees, shrubs add beauty to this garden.
Rose Garden, Chandigarh, 1966	The garden is among the biggest rose gardens of the world. Top position goes to Jackson and Perkins of New York. The garden covers 10 hectare area and has more than 36,000 rose types.

contd.

	Other famous Rose gardens - The Rose garden, Parque Bagatelle (Paris) - Parque del oeste Madrid (Spain) have 30,000 roses. - Pare Qe La group (Geneva) - Queen Marryrose garden and Regent park (London) - Golden walk, Cartwell (England)
The Mughal Garden, Pinjore (Haryana)- 17th Century	The garden is situated near Kalka. Lay out by Fidai Khan. The original name of place is Panchapnea or Panjpur has association with five Pandavas. Area under garden is 25 hectare and garden is divided into six terraces. The Main gate is at the highest terrace, while the remaining five appear in a decending order.
Shalimar Garden, Srinagar-1619-1630 AD	Jahangir initiated the garden work and extended by Zafar Khan. The garden is connected with Dal Lake (16 m Canal). On both sides of canal, trees are planted. The garden has three terraces. In two terraces only their stone bases are left while third terrace is meant for ladies, have a magnificent black stone pavilleon and surrounded by a reservoir.
Achabal, 1620	Built by Nur Jahan. The spring air in achabal is the largest in Kashmir. Six vertical waterfalls situated in the garden.
Lal bagh Bangalore (Karnataka), 1760	Lal bagh was built by Hyder Ali in a total area of 50 lakh heactare area.
Governmental botanical garden, Ootacamund- 1848	Situated in Nilgiris hills. The garden has six major sections.
Sim's park, Coonor, Tamil Nadu-1874	The park was established by JD Sim. The total area of garden is 15 hectare.
Botanic garden, Coimbatore, Tamil Nadu- 1908	The garden was established by Department of Agriculture.
The Byrant Park KodaiKanal, Tamil Nadu- 1909	Total area of garden in 10 lakh hectares
The Indian Botanic Garden, Sibpur Kolkatta, (West Bengal)- 1787	The garden is situated in twin city on the opposite side of the river hoogly. 200 year old banyan tree is important feature of this garden. The garden has 26 lakes, the total area of garden is 150 hectare.
Llyod botanic garden Darjeeling, West Bengal-1878	Situated in Middest of the Himalayas. The garden has 24 hectare area. Garden is laid out by Sir George King, the then Superintendent of Royal Botanic Garden.
National Botanical Research Institute (NBRI), Lucknow-1789-1814	The NBRI was laid out by Nawab Sardar Ali Khan and improved by Nawab Wajid Ali Khan and named after his wife Sikander Mahal Begum. The main

contd.

	objective of the garden is to disseminate knowledge for establishing scientifically planned garden.
Horticultural Research Institute, Saharanpur-1750/ 1817	Laid by East India Company in 1817. Falconii, Jameson and Duthies, have worked in this garden
Rashtrapati Bhawan Garden, New Delhi-1929	The architecture of the Palace is a mixture of Indian and Western style. The area under garden is 134 sq meters.
Other gardens	Mediterranean garden- Yalta Osaka garden, Japan Lal bagh, Bangalore-1760 Brindavan garden, Mysore Llyod botanic garden, Darjeeling, 1878 Baradari garden- Patiala Shalimar garden- Lahore Chasma-e-shahi garden- Srinagar Rock garden, Chandigarh Agri-Horticultural Society garden-Kolkatta-1872 Government Botanic garden, Ootacamond-1848

20. Pot (flowering) plants

1) *Calceolaria herberolhybrids* (Pocket book plant) belong to Scrophulariaceae family. Requires cool temperature below 15°C for flower initiation.
2) *Campanula isophylla* (Pocket book plant) belongs to family Campanulaceae. It is a long day plant need 16, 15 & 14 hours at night temperature of 12-15 °C, 18°C, 21°C respectively.
3) *Capsicum sp* and *Solanum pseudocapsicum* (Chrismas cherry) belongs to family solanaceae.
4) *Clerodendron thomsoniae* (bleeding heart) belongs to family Verbenaceae. The development of flowers is delayed under long days.
5) *Exacum affine* (German Violet) belongs to family Gentinaceae, propagated by seed.
6) Shade loving plants are mainly grown in pots is highly prized for their ornamental foliage and called foliage plants or pot plants.
7) Pot mixture: 2 parts garden soil + 1 parts sand + 2 parts leaf mould + 1 part farm yard manure.
8) Re-potting should be done in rainy season or February-March. At the time of repotting, extra shoot cut off. Feed pots with liquid manure containing bone meal and spray systemic fungicide.

21. Famous gardens in india

1. Lalbagh: Bangalore (KN)
2. Brindavan Garden: Mysore (KN) – Biggest formal Garden
3. Sim's Park: Conoor (Tamil Nadu)
4. Byrant Park: Kodaikanal (Tamil Nadu)
5. The Indian Botanical Garden: Sibpur, Calcutta (WB) –
6. Lyod Botanical Garden: Darjeeling (WB)
7. National Botanical Garden: Lucknow (UP)
8. Rastrapathi Bhawan Garden: New Delhi
9. Buddha Jyanti Park: New Delhi
10. Pinjore Garden: Haryana
11. Rose Garden : Chandigarh (Punjab)
12. Mandoor Garden : Jodhpur (Rajasthan)
13. Syaji Park : Baroda (Gujarat) Branching palm
14. Roshana park : New Delhi

22. National flower of the different country

1. Lotus : India, Egypt
2. Rose : England, Iran, New Zealand
3. Narcisuss : China
4. Chrysanthamum : Japan
5. Tulip : Netherlands
6. Lily : Italy, Canada
7. Corn flower : Germany
8. Daffodil : Wales
9. Carnation : Spain
10. Golden rose : USA
11. Cresent : Pakistan
12. Water tily : Bangladesh

23. Flower for different purposes

Name	Purpose	Name	Purpose
Rose	Love	Daffodil	Regard
Carnation (white)	Women's love	Amarylillies	Pride
French Marigold	Jealously/ Sorrow	Iris	Message
African Marigold	Vulgar mind	Lily	Purity
Pansy	Thoughts	Stock	Luxary
Narcisuss	Self esteem	Sweet Pea	Departure

24. Annuals

- Summer Annuals: Seeds are sown during February-March.

  Zinnia, Kochia, Portulaca, Tithonia, Gaillardia, Sunflower, Cosmos, Gomphrena, Coreopsis etc.

- Rainy annuals: Seeds are sown during June-July.

  Balsam, Cock's Comb, Amaranthus, Gaillardia, Gomphrena etc.

- Winter annuals: Seeds are sown during September-October. They are able to tolerate low temperature during winter

  1. For fragrant flower: Mignonette, Carnation, Sweet pea, Sweet Sultan, Sweet William, Sweet Alyssum and Stock.
  2. For hanging Basket: Daisy, Nasturtium, Verbena, Phlox, Portulaca.
  3. For shady situation: Salvia, Cineraria.
  4. For rock garden: Ice plant, Nasturtium, Verbana, Phlox.
  5. For screening purpose: Hollyhock, Sweet pea
  6. For pots: Carnation, Antirrhinum, Aster, Petunia
  7. For dry flower: Statice, Helichrysum, Acroclinum, Lady's lace.

- Blue colour (flower) annuals: Corn flower, blue larkspur, ageratum and Linaria.
- White flower annuals: Allysum, China Aster, Mathiola, Nigelia, Phlox, Papaver, Zinnia and Stock.
- Yellow and orange flower annuals: Pot marigold, *Dimorphetheca*, *Eschacholtiza*, *Tegetes*, Zinnia, Wall flower, Coreopsis and Helichrysum.
- Self pollinated annuals: Lupin, Sweet pea, Salvia.
- Often cross pollinated: Antirrhinum, Larkspur, Linaria, Phlox, Pansy.
- Short long day: Campanula, White Clover
- Tender annual: Oxalis

- Hardy annuals: Digitalis, Rudbeckia, Viola.
- Long day flowers: China aster, Calendula, Delphinium, Gardenia, Stock, Antirrhinum, Petunia, Rudbeckia, Sweet Willium
- Short day flowers: Chrysanthemum, Cosmos, Kalanchoe, Poinsettia Amaranthus, Salvia, Aster.
- Day neutral flowers: Carnation, Balsam, African Violet, Tuberose, Dianthus, Gompherena.

25. Colour Scheme in gardens

1. Green colour dominant throughout year in garden.
2. Warm colour: Red in winter.
3. Yellow colour: in spring.
4. Red, yellow, blue: Primary colour
5. Orange, green, violet: Secondary colour
6. White, black, grey: Neutral colours
7. Cream, pink and shades: Tertiary colours
8. Red, orange and yellow: Warm colours
9. Green and blue: Cool colours

26. Hedge

When shrub is planned on boundary for fencing, it is called as hedge.

- Planting time: July – August.
- Spacing: Tall 60-90 cm, dwarf; 20-30 cm
- When hedge attain height of 15 cm, they whould be topped back to 10 cm height

Classes of hedge

1. **Tall protective** (1-3 mt ht): *Inga dulcus*, Karoda, Bouganvillea, *Accasia ferrestina.*
2. **Dwarf protective** (1 m ht): *Euphorbia bojori, Opuntia spp, Agave spp, Pedilanthus spp.*
3. **Tall ornamental:** Mehandi, *Duranta, Casurina, Hibiscus, Hamelia patens, Thevatia peruviana, Murryaa peniculata.*
4. **Dwarf ornamental:** *Acalypha, Clerodendron, Thumbergia, Lantana spp.*

27. Edge

When low growing plants are grown on the border of plot they are called as edge plant. They hardly grow upto 20-30 cm. Examples are Alterranthera, Justicia, Eupatorium, *Iresine lindenii.*

28. Topiary

It is an art of training the plants into different shapes. Examples are *Duranta plumeri, Sesberia egyptica, Inga dulcus, Acasia modesta, Murraya panniculata.*

29. Lawn (Heart of Garden)

Important grasses

1 Bermuda grass: *Cynadon dactylon* (Doob or Haryali)

2 Korean grass: *Zoysia japonica*

3 Manilla grass: *Zoysia matrella*

4 Korean velvet grass: *Zoysia tenuifolia*

5 Carpet grass: *Axonopus affinis*

Planting of grasses

1 Dibbling of roots: Most common and cheapest method of planting

2 Seedling

3 Turfing: Quickest method

4 Bricking: to replace the few unhealthy patches in well maintained lawns

Disease of lawn

1. Fairy Ring: Caused by fungus *Marasmius ordeades*
2. Pale or yellow lawn: Due to N_2 deficiency
   - 60-75% area of garden should be devoted to lawn
   - Seed rate: 12 kg/ Acre or 25-30 kg/ hac or 25 g/m^2
   - Weeds occur in lawn: *Cypruss rotandus, Euphorbia.*
   - Glyphosate: Most widely used pre-emergance herbicide for lawn
   - In shady region: Kentucy grass is grown

30. Style of Gardening

1. Formal style: Plan is symmetrical. Persian and Mughal Garden are formal.
2. Informal style: Plan is asymmetrical. It reflects naturalistic effect of total view and represents natural beauty. Example : Japanese garden

3. Free style: Combination of both formal and informal style. English Garden and Lal Bagh are free style.

31. Gardens

- Features of Mughal Garden are:

  1. Terraces 2. Running water 3. High protecting wall

  4. Entrance gate 5. Baradari 6. Terminal building
- Symbol of some plants and flower trees

  1. Cypress - immortality

  2. Flowering trees - Renewal of life.

  3. Kachnar - Youth and life.

  4. Running water - Life
- Main features of Japanese Gardens

  1 Trees 2 Ornamental water 3 Garden lanterns

  4 Garden Pagoda 5 Garden Bridges 6 Dry landscape

  7 Gate + fences 8 Wells
- Main features of English Garden

  1. Herbaceous border -discovered by William Robinson

  2. Cottage Garden: - discovered by G Jekyell

  3. Lawn

  4. Rockery
- Persian gardens : Charbagh
- Surken garden : Rastrapati garden

32. Flower arrangement

- Japanese style of gardening: **Ikebana**
- Natural Ikebana where piled flowers are used: **Moribana**
- Free flower arrangement: **Jiyubana**
- English flower arrangements: **Morimona**
- In western style, flowers are 1½ times taller than flower vase.
- Straight material with uneven height are used: **Zeneika**
- Beautiful sculpture is created by using wood, stone, rocks: **Zeneibana**
- Emphasis is given on spritial and religious background, only few flowers are used: **Japanese flower arrangement.**

- Emphasis given on mass flower arrangement: **English flower arrangement.**

33. Bonsai

Japanese art of growing miniature trees and shrubs by extreme dwarfing. Origin of bonsai is China. In Maime bonsal: Plant height is 15-20 cm.

34. Oil extraction

Rose:	i)	*Rosa damascena*: 0.05%
	ii)	*Rosa bourboniana*: 0.04%
	iii)	*Rosa centifolia*: 0.01%
	iv)	*Rosa moschata*: 0.04%
Jasmine:	i)	*Jasminum auriculatum*: 0.29% (Maximum oil recovery)
	ii)	*J. grandiflorum*: 0.25-0.30%

35. Status of aromatic and medicinal plants

- Highest number of medicinal spp are under family – Asteraceae
- Maximum demand in the world market is of Senna leaves, Isabgol seed, and Cassia tora seeds.
- India is largest producer of Kewada oil, Senna, Isabgol.
- India is the largest exporter of – *Psyllium* and Senna leaves
- China is the major producer of Geranium oil and Citronella oil.
- World production of essential oil is dominated by Brazil (40%) followed by USA (20%) and India (15%).
- Essential oil is the odoriferous steam volatile constituents of aromatic plants.
- National Aromatic and Medicinal Plant Board is situated at New Delhi
- Central Institute for Medicinal and Aromatic Plants is located at Lucknow
- National Research Centre for Medicinal and Aromatic Plants is located at Anand –Gujrat.

EXPLANATARY NOTES

LOTUS

(*Nelumbo nucifera*)

Family: Nymphaeaceae/Nelumbonaceae
Origin: Southern Asia
Flower colour: White to deep pink
Plant part used: Flower (almost all parts)
Basic chromosome number: X=8
Somatic chromosome number: 2n =16

- Flower of *antiquity*.
- National flower of *India*.
- Considered as Sacred flower and symbol of Goddess *Lakshmi*.
- The family Nymphaeaceae has two genera *Nymphaea* and *Nelumbo*.
- Water Lilly belongs to Nymphaea whereas Lotus to Nelumbo.
- It is a tropical deep water aquatic plant need, warm climate (20-30ºC).
- Lotus may go into dormancy during coolar climate.
- Nelumbo has two species viz; *N. nucifera* and *N. lutea*
- *N. lutea* (American lotus) with yellow flowers is native to North America.
- *Nelumbo nucifera* is commonly known as Sacred Lotus, the Hindu Lotus, Indian Lotus, the East Indian Lotus or the Chinese Lotus.
- All parts of lotus are usd as food; rhizomes are used as vegetable; eaten as pickle, chips; carpels are also edible and are very nutritious; petals used as soup garnishing etc.
- It is propagated by rhizome divisions.

ROSE

(*Rosa spp.*)

Family: Rosaceae
Origin: North Hemisphere (Himalayas)
Flower colour: Red (commonly)
Plant part used: Flower
Basic chromosome number: X=7
Somatic chromosome number: 2n =14

Queen of flowers.

- National flower of England, Iran, UK.
- Symbol of beauty, convey message of love.
- Commercial method of propagation: T budding
- Best time for budding: November to February
- Rootstock: *R. multiflora* (Edward rose) most commonly used rootstock of western India.
    - *Rosa indica* var *odorata* – most commonly used rootstock in North India.
    - Dog rose: *Rosa canina.*
    - Cabbage rose: *R. centifolia*
    - Thornless rose: *R. pendulina, R. bourboniana*
    - French Rose: *R. gallica*
    - Musk Rose: *R. moschata*
- Good quality blooms are produced in winter.
- Rose requires light throughout the year.
- BK Roy Choudhary: 1st Indian Rose breeder who raised var Dr S D Mukharjee in 1935.
- BS Bhattacharajee (Father of Rose breeding) was 2nd rose breeder, evaluated var Ramkrishnadev.
- Dr BP Pal evolved 1st rose var *Rose Sherbet.*
- Bud union is most susceptible to low temperature than any other part of Rose.
- Winter chilling is necessary in flower bud formation in *Rosa damascena.*
- Preservative solution: 1-3% sugar + 100-300 ppm HQC.
- var 'La France' produced by Guillot (1867).
- About 80% of rose flowers are utilized for rose water, 10% attars and 1-2% pankhuri and 8% for gulrogan and gulkand preparation.
- Hybrid Tea Roses (Hybrid Perpetual × Tea Roses)

  La France is considered as First hybrid tea rose (1867).
- Bedding varieties.
    - Yellow: Vasant, King Ransom, Golden Giant
    - Orange : Scarlet Superstar
    - Pink : Confidence, First Prize, Sonia
    - Red: Crimson Glory, Happiness

- Bronze: Sunset Song
- Lavender: Blue Moon, Anurag
- White: June Bride, Tushar
- Colour blend: CarelessLove, Kiss of Fire

- Hybrid Perpetual: First hybrid perpetual was developed by Princess Helene.
- Floribundas: Hybrid Tea × Polyanthas (1924). Also called Hybrid polyanthas.
    - 1st var-Rodhatte, produced by Poulesen (1912)
    - Red: Week Jock, Jantar-Mantar
    - Orange: Independence, Shola
    - Yellow: Ali Gold, Gold Bunny
    - Pink: Queen Elizabath, Junior Miss
    - White: Iceberg, Himangini
    - Bicolour: Red Gold
    - Colourblend: Banjaran
    - Bicentennial: Charisma Madhura
- Grandiflora: Hybrid Tea × Floribundas
    - 1st var: Buccaneer (1952)
    - Swati Rashmi, Montezuma (1955), Queen Elizabeth (1954).
- Polyantha: *R. multiflora* × *R. wichuriana* × *R. chinensis*
    - 1st var La Paquerette (1875)
- Climbers: Sympathe, Delhi White Pearl, Breath of Life, Golden Shower America, Swan Lake, Delhi Pink Pearl.
- Ramblers: American Pillar (1902), Excelsa (1909), Albertine
- Miniature roses (Baby or fairy roses): Ideal for growing in pots. Desert Charm, Red Flush, Delhi Scarlet, Summer Butter, Party Girl, Puppy Love, Snow Carpet, Yellow Doll, Cindrella.
    - Siriped and hand painted: Sidhartha, Madhosh
    - Exhibition varieties: Christian Dior, Eiffel Tower, Garden Party, Mischief, Pusa Sonia, Show Girl, First Prize, Raktagandha.
    - Scented varieties: Lafrance, Seventh Heaven, Pusa Sugandha, Blue Moon.
    - Cut flower: Gladiator, Happiness, Super Star, Sonia Mercedes, Arjun, Raktagandha, Sindhoor.

- Most of varieties take about 60-75 days for blooming after pruning.
- Wintering of roses is very common in western part of India.
- Pulsing treatment is done to increase shelf-life.
- Most costly oil: Rose oil.
- Miniature roses are resistant to pest and diseases.
- Limp neck – Rose disorder.
- Most common rootstock in European countries: *R. cannina*
- Flowering in hybrid tea roses: 42 days after pruning.
- Flowering in Floribundas: 45 days after pruning.
- The waxy residue left after extraction of essential oil through distillation is known as concrete.
- Die back is the main fungal disease in roses.
- Bent neck is the physiological disorder characterized by bending of cut rose stems after harvesting.

GLADIOLUS

(*Gladiolus tritis*)

Family:	Iridaceae
Origin:	South Africa
Plant part used:	Flower spike
Basic chromosome number:	X= 15
Somatic chromosome number:	2n = 30, 60, 120

- Most popular bulbous flowering plant.
- Gladious a Latin word means sword. It is also known as Sword Lily.
- Gladiolus was coined by Pliny the Elder (AD 23-79).
- Optimum temperature for growth: 16-30ºC
- Optimum temperature for corm storage is 4-5ºC.
- It require open sunny situation.
- Longer day length improves spike quality.
- The point where scale is attached to the corm is called Node.
- Planting time: July-December, spacing 20 x 30 cm^2.
- Corm should be treated with 0-2% Bavistin before plantation.
- Ethylene chlorohydrine is used to break dormancy of corms.
- Gladiolus is a 7 months crop.

- Hilling is important operation of Gladiolus.
- Preservative solution: 20% sucrose + 200 ppm HQC.
- Dormancy of corm broken by storage at 4-5°C for 3-4 month.
- Corm and cormels are the important planting material.
- Seeds require: 15-20 days to germinate.
- For cut spikes storage temperature: 1-2°C for 2 weeks.
- Fluoride toxicity seen on tip of leaves, absorbed from air.
- Toxicity is due to heavy application of super phosphate, rock phosphate which contains hydrogen fluoride.

CARNATION

(*Dianthus caryophyllus*)

Family:	Caryophyllaceae
Origin:	Mediterrarean region
Plant part used:	Flower spike
Basic chromosome number:	X= 15
Somatic chromosome number:	2n = 30

- Quantitatively long day plant. Cyclic lighting is effective.
- It is a cool season crop.
- Ideal temperature range: 10-20°C.
- Night temperature should not be less than 10°C and more than 18°C.
- Carnation occupies a prime position in International cut flower market.
- Pinching is regular practice in carnation.
- Disbudding is regular practice in carnation and is most important in standard varieties.
- Staking is also done in carnation.
- Pre-conditioning of cut flower in solution of $AgNO_3$ is important to avoid ethylene injury and prolong shelf life.
- Sim carnation has great commercial importance.
- Sim group need regular pinching.
- Perpetual flwering carnations are commercially used as cut flowers.
- Calyx splitting is a serious problem affecting quality of flowers.
- Types of carnation:
    - Perpetual: *D. caryophyllus* × *D. chinensis*. These may be standard or spray type, having longer stock length.

- Marguerite: *D. chinensis* × *D. caryophyllus*. Flowers are single or double.
- Malmaison: Flowers are large, double with well filled centre. It has pink flowers. Princess of Wales, Mr Martin Smith
- Royal: Malmaison × Perpetual (Royal Fancy, White Perfection)
- Modern : Pico

- Pinching: 1st : 4th week after planting (July) – (6th pair of leaf)
  2nd: 7th week after planting
  - Single pinching: Below 6th node: to get early crop.
  - Pinch and a half regular pinching + half pinching: Steady production.
  - Double pinch: To delay flowering period

CHRYSANTHEMUM

(*Dendranthema grandiflora*)

Family:	Asteraceae
Origin:	China
Plant part used:	Flower and spike
Flower colour:	Almost all except blue
Basic chromosome number:	X= 9
Somatic chromosome number:	2n = 36, 45, 54.

- It is a short day plant.
- Common name: Guldaudi, Autumn Queen, Glory of East, Queen of East
- Symbol of Royality in Japan.
- National Flower of Japan.
- Disc florets: Centre.
- Ray Florets: Outer.
- Blooming period: September-October.
- Propagation: By root suckers or terminal cuttings.
- Suckers: For small flowered, cuttings for disease free, long time, fails.
- Pinching: To encourage side branches for cut flower.
- Disbudding: To encourage single crown branch for standard flower.
- Yellow, white colours are preferred for cut flowers.
- Urea is not applied as it causes phytotoxicity.

- Use of Alar/Phosphon is very effective in producing better size blooms, on dwarf plants.
- Disc florets are perfect while ray florets are pistillate.
- Axillary shoots produce buds called crown buds
- Harvesting: July-August-September
- Pinching: Most important for cascade (Japanese) formation
- Pinching is also known as stopping.
- Regular incurve, irregular, regular reflex, irregular reflex, intermediate, quilled, spoon, anemone, single and semi double are ray florets arrangement of large chrysanthemum flowers.
- Anemone, button, single Korean, decorative, pompon, semi quilled, quilled, stellate and cineraria are ray florets arrangement of small chrysanthemum flowers.
- It has shallow fibrous root system which is sensitive to water logging.
- Lighting in greenhouse is done for normal growth during inadequate natural light.
- International variety: i) Kokovarouri – Standard type – yellow

  ii) Nanako – Spray type – yellow

MARIGOLD

African (*Tagetes erecta*)

French (*Tagetes petula*)

Family:	Asteraceae/Compositae
Origin:	Mexico (Central America)
Plant part used:	Loose Flowers
Basic chromosome number:	X= 12
Somatic chromosome number:	2n = 24, 48

- Marigold is a quantitative short day plant.
- Flowers are sold in market as loose or as a garland.
- Requires mild climate for luxuriant growth.
- Optimum temperature: 18-30°C
- Nugget is a triploid variety of marigold.
- Seed rate: 1-15 kg/hectare. Seeds count about 300-350 seeds per gram.
- Best flowering noticed during winter months (October to April).
- Weeds are major problem and 3-4 weedings are required.

- Plucking of flowers should be done in cool hours of the day (preferably evening).
- It is a cross pollinated crop.
- Damping off is the major disease of marigold.
- Ketones are the base material for synthesizing aroma chemicals.
- French marigold thrives best in light soil.
- Application of CCC growth retardant @3000ppm prolongs flowering period in African marigold.

JASMINE

(*Jasminum spp*)

Family: Oleaceae
Origin: Mexico
Basic chromosome number: X= 13
Somatic chromosome number: 2n = 26, 39, 52

- It is grown in tropical climate and is known as native of tropical and sub-tropical region.
- It is a perennial crop.
- Jasmine is a climbing, erect shrubby plant may be deciduous or evergreen.
- Poet's jasmine: *J. officinale;* Chameli: *J. grandiflorum*
- Different spp of *Jasminum*
  - *J. sambac*: Arabian Jasmine, Tuscan jasmine, Bela, Mogra.
  - *J. grandiflorum*: Royal or Spanish jasmine, chameli, Mallai, Pitchi (Flowering time: March-September)
  - *J. auriculatum*: Thum, Jai, Mullai (Maximum recovery of oil)
  - *J. multiflorum*: Kakada, Fussy jasmine. (Non-scented jasmine)
  - *J. arborescence*: Tree jasmine, Bela (Flowering: November – May).
  - *J. carophyllum*
  - *J. flexile*: Climbing jasmine.
  - *J. humile*: Yellow jasmine.
- Propagation: By semi hard wood cutting.

  Pruning:
  - *J sambac* (Arabian or Tuscan jasmine): October end.
  - *J grandiflorum* (Spanish/common jasmine): Mid December
  - *J auriculatum*: White flowers in December-January.

- For extraction of Jasmine concentrate – fully open flowers are plucked.
- Flowering in Jasmine starts from second year.

ORCHIDS

(*Cymbidium sp* and *Dendrobium sp*)

Family: Orchidaceae
Origin: Tropical countries

- Bulbophyllum is largest genera of orchids.
- Orchids are the most beautiful flowers in God's creation.
- Group of orchids:
  - Epiphytes : Dendrobium, Vanda, Bulbophyllum
  - Lithophytes (Terrestial): Cymbidium
- Plant morphology
  - Monopodial : Venda, Vanilla, Renanthera
  - Sympodial: Cattleya, Cymbidium, Dendrobium, Bulbophyllum
- Propagation: A) Division: Cattleya, Cymbidium, Dendrobium
  B) Cutting: Venda
- Netherland: Largest producer of temperate orchids (*Cymbidium*).
- Thailand: Largest producer of tropical orchids (*Dendrobium*).
- Orchids include about 800 genera and 35000 species.
- Orchidaceae is the largest family among flowering plants.
- Flower have 3-sepals and 3 petals, hence called as – Tepals.
- Seed – Endosperm absent (Exalbuminous).
- Commercial propagatioin method: Tissue culture.
- In orchids light requirement is 2000-6000 Foot candles.
- Day temperature vary from 15.5-21°C and night temperature 10-15.5°C.
- Epiphytic orchids are commonly grown in media containing tree fern fibre, osmuda fibre, coconut husk, bricks, charcoal etc.
- Most common method for multiplication of sympodial orchids is division.
- Harvesting influence keeping quality
  - Cattleya harvested: 3-5 days after bud split or dehisce.
  - Dendrobium harvested when 2-3 buds are still unopened.
  - During warm weather, blooms are harvested at early development stage.

TUBEROSE

(*Polyanthes tuberosa*)

Order -	Asparagales
Family -	Agavaceae
Origin: -	Mexico

- Latin word tuberose meaning Swollen or tuberous; *Polianthes* means grey flower.
- In Hindi tuberose is called Rajnigandha means *night fragrance* (Rajni = Night, gandha = Fragrance)
- In Bengali – tuberose is called Rajoni-gondha meaning *scent of the night.*
- In Singapore, it is called ye Lai Xiang means *fragrance that comes in night.*

LAVENDULA

(*Lavendula angustifolia*)

Order -	Lamiales
Family -	Lamiaceae
Binomial name -	*Lavendula officinalis* Mill
Origin -	Western Mediterranean region
Plant part used:	Flowers

- *Lavendula angustifolia* is known as common lavender, true lavender or English lavender.

LAVENDER

(*Lavendula species*)

Family:	Lamiaceae
Origin:	Europe
Plant part used:	Flower and flowering tops
Basic chromosome number:	X=6
Somatic chromosome number:	2n = 48, 54

- *Lavendula angustifolia* (True lavender), *L. latifolia* (Spike lavender), *L. intermedia* (Lavendin) are three important species of lavender.
- USSR is a major producer followed by France and Bulgaria.
- *L. angustifolia* is polyploid. Lavender is mostly cross pollinated.
- It is a temperate plant, flowers in long day conditions.
- Light loam to calcareous soils, pH 7.0-8.4.
- Propagation: True lavender by seeds and Lavandin always by cutting (10 cm).

- Oil is obtained from 'Flowering tops' and recovery is 1-2 percent.
- Harvesting: Flower cut with 12 cm stem.
- Main chemical constituent: Linalool (27.6-48.0%).
- Fertilizers: N and P (40:40 kg/ha each) at time of planting. N = 60 kg/ha in 2-3 splits.

ALSTROEMERIA

(*Alstroemeria caryophyllae*)

Family: Alstroemeriaceae
Origin: Tropical America
Plant parts used: Flowers
Basic chromosome number: X=8
Somatic chromosome number: 2n = 16

ANTHURIUM

(*Anthurium acutifolium*)

Family: Araceae
Origin: Columbia and Peru
Plant parts used: Flowers
Basic chromosome number: X=15, 16
Somatic chromosome number: 2n = 30, 32

BIRD OF PARADISE

(*Sterlizia alba*)

Family: Musaceae
Origin: South Africa
Plant parts used: Flowers

CHINA ASTER

(*Callistephus chinensis L.*)

Family: Asteraceae
Origin: China
Plant parts used: Flowers
Basic chromosome number: X=9
Somatic chromosome number: 2n = 18

CROSSANDRA

(*Crossandra undulaefolia*)

Family:	Acanthaceae
Origin:	East Indies
Plant parts used:	Flowers
Basic chromosome number:	X=15, 20
Somatic chromosome number:	2n = 30, 40

DAHLIA

(*Dahlia coccinea*)

Family:	Asteraceae
Origin:	Mexico, Central America
Plant parts used:	Flowers
Basic chromosome number:	X=16
Somatic chromosome number:	2n = 32, 48

NARCISSUS

(*Narcissus astureinsis*)

Family:	Amaryllidaceae
Origin:	Northern France
Plant parts used:	Flowers
Basic chromosome number:	X=7, 10
Somatic chromosome number:	2n = 14, 20

TULIP

(*Tulipa biflora*)

Family:	Liliaceae
Origin:	Asia minor
Plant parts used:	Flowers
Basic chromosome number:	X=12
Somatic chromosome number:	2n = 24

ZINNIA

(*Zinnia elegans*)

Family:	Compositae
Origin:	Mexico
Plant parts used:	Flowers
Basic chromosome number:	X=11, 12
Somatic chromosome number:	2n = 22,24

PALMAROSA

Family:	Gramineae
Origin:	India
Plant part used:	Flower and leaves
Basic chromosome number:	X=10, 20
Somatic chromosome number:	2n = 20 (var. Motia); 2n = 40 (var. Sofia)

- Palmarosa is indigenous to India.
- India is the major producer followed by Brazil, Indonesia.
- Highly cross pollinated.
- *Cymbopogon martini* var motia, *C. martini* var Sofia are two important species belongs to family Gramineae.
- Recovery of oil: 0.4-0.6%
- Geraniol percentage in Motia = (65 to 80%); Sofia = (36 to 60%).
- Propagation: By seeds during May-June.
- Loam to light sandy loam; pH= 9.
- Harvesting: Full bloom stage, 7-10 days after flowering.
- Trishna developed at CIMAP, Lucknow Jamrosa developed at RRL, Jammu.

CITRONELLA

Family:	Gramineae.
Origin:	Sri Lanka
Plant part used:	Leaves
Basic chromosome number:	X=10
Somatic chromosome number:	2n = 20

- Citronella is a tropical plant, thrive in Humid tropical.
- It is a perennial crop and remains for 5 to 6 years.
- *Cymbopogon winterianus* Jowett is java citronella.
- *Java citronella* and *Ceylon citronella* are native to Sri Lanka.
- Source of oil: Leaves oil recovery of citronella is 1%.
- Varieties (*Java citronella*): Manjusha, Mandakii are clonal selection and have 30-40% higher yield.
- New variety: Bio-13.
- Soil: Light loam; pH 5.8 to 8.0.

- Propagation: Propagated by splitting the clumps and each clump must have 1-3 tillers.
- Spacing: 50 cm row to row and 50-60 cm plant to plant.
- Harvest after 3 to 4 months of planting to induce tillering, leaves are harvested 15 cm above ground.
- Only leaf blade is harvested leaving the leaf sheeth.
- Crop yield: 100 kg/hectare (1st year); 150 kg/ hactare (2nd year).
- 20:40:40 kg NPK/hectare is basal dose during planting.
- Main chemical constituent: Citronellol (13.4-15.7%).
- Indonesia, China, Thailand and India are main producers.
- *Java citronella* has 75-85% total alcohol, whereas *Ceylon citronella* has 55-65% total alcohol.

PATCHOULI

(*Pogostemon cablin*)

Family:	Labiatae
Origin:	Phillipines
Plant part used:	Branches and leaves
Basic chromosome number:	X=17
Somatic chromosome number:	2n = 34

- Harvesting starts after 5-6 years of planting at stage when foliage starts turning pale green to light brown and gives typical patchouli odour.
- Only leaves and branches are harvested.
- Well drained, medium loam, fertile soil, rich in organic matter is preferred.
- Moderate temperature (30-35°C) with very high humidity favours the growth.
- Fertilizers: Phosphorus is beneficial in South India.
- Oil yield: 1.8 to 3% oil.
- Major chemical constituent: Patchouli alcohol (33.7%).
- Indonesia is the largest producers of oil account for 95% of world production.
- Leaves have glands which secrets Red oil.
- Real patchouli (*Pogostemon cablin*) never flowers.
- Roots, stems, branches, stalk and leaves all parts contain oil.
- Most of oil is present in top three leaves.

BASIL

(*Ocimum basilicum* Var *glabrata*)

Family:	Lamiaceae
Origin:	India
Plant part used:	Leaves and tender shoot part
Basic chromosome number:	X=12
Somatic chromosome number:	2n = 24

- Basil is derived from Greek word Basilica means Royal plant.
- It is variously called Sweet basil, French basil and Common basil belongs to family Lamiaceae; Sub-family Ocimoideae.
- Parts used for extraction of oil: Leaves and tender part of shoot.
- Long days and high temperature is good for growth and oil products.
- Propagated by seed/tender shoot tip.
- Harvesting stage: Full bloom stage.
- Soil temperature and moisture directly correlated to essential oil content.
- *Ocimum species* are cross pollinated.
- Oil is present in leaves.

FOX GLOVE

(*Digitalis purpurea*)

Family:	Scrophulariaceae
Origin:	Europe
Plant part used:	Leaves

- It is a biennial herb, cross pollinated.
- Honey bees are main pollinators.
- Part used: Leaves.
- Source: Glycoside (0.93-0.99%).
- Harvesting stage is Rosette stage.
- Leaves of Fox glove contains glycosides namely digitoxin and gitoxin.
- Silt loam to clay loam soil is best.
- Temperature required: 20-30°C is good.
- Seed rate is 8kg/hectare.

OPIUM

(*Papaver somniferum* L.)

Family:	Papaveraceae
Origin:	Western Mediterranean Region of Europe
Plant part used:	Green but fully ripe capsule
Basic chromosome number:	X= 11
Somatic chromosome number:	2n = 22

- Opium is known as Joy plant in South France belongs to Family Papaveraceae; Sub family Papaveroideae.
- Type of fruit is Capsule.
- Opium is extracted from green but fully ripe capsule.
- Morphene obtained: 7-17%; Codeine obtained: 21-44%.
- Opium is self pollinated.
- Kirtiman, Chetak, Trishna are important varieties.
- India is the major producer of *Opium* alkaloid in world.
- Capsule contains 70% of total morphine.
- Opium is used in manufacturing of heroines.
- Trishna is resistant to mildew.
- Seed rate: 5-6kg/hectare
- Planting time: Nov. to April
- Spacing: 30 × 10cm

SOLANUM

(*Solanum viarum*)

Family:	Solanaceae
Origin:	India
Plant part used:	Yellow berries
Basic chromosome number:	X= 12
Somatic chromosome number:	2n = 24

- *Solanum viarum* syn *khashianum* belongs to family Solanaceae; sub-family: Leptostemonum.
- Solasodine contents vary from 1.00-1.75% on DWB in berries.
- Fertilizers: N: P: K= 80:40:40 kg/hectare.
- Planting time: February-March.

- Harvesting: Berries are harvested when they turn yellow.
- *S. viarum* is susceptible to *Fusarium oxysporum*.
- Wilt is the major disease.
- Spacing: 50 × 50cm

BELLADONA

(*A. belladonna*)

Family: Solanaceae
Origin: Central and Eastern Europe
Plant part used: Leaves and roots.

- Belladona (*A. belladonna*) is a cross pollinated crop.
- Seed rate: 4 kg/hectare.
- Spacing: 30 × 45cm

SENNA

(*Cassia angustifolia*)

Family: Leguminoseae
Origin: South Africa
Plant part used: Leaves and pods.
Basic chromosome number: X= 13
Somatic chromosome number: 2n = 26

- It is a self pollinated crop.
- Source: Sennosides-A, B, C

ISABGOL

(*Plantago ovata*)

Family: Plantaginaceae
Origin: India
Plant part used: Seed/ husk

- Harvesting: When crop turn yellow and spike turn brownish.

SCENTED GERANIUM

Family: Geraniaceae
Origin: South Africa
Plant parts used: Flowers
Basic chromosome number: X=9
Somatic chromosome number: 2n = 90

LEMONGRASS

Family:	Gramineae
Origin:	Malabar Coast of India.
Plant parts used:	Leaves and seeds
Basic chromosome number:	X=10
Somatic chromosome number:	2n = 20

ROSEMARY

Family:	Labiateae
Origin:	Spain, South Africa.
Plant parts used:	Leaves and seeds
Basic chromosome number:	X=12
Somatic chromosome number:	2n = 24

MULTIPLE CHOICE QUESTIONS

1. Carnation is a

a) Short day plant
b) Day neutral plant
c) Long day plant
d) None of these

2. Lotus in Sanskrit is known as

a) Pankaja
b) Padma
c) Kamala
d) All of these

3. The National flower of India is

a) Rose
b) Jasmine
c) Lotus
d) Kachnar.

4. Rose is the national flower of

a) UK
b) USA
c) Iran
d) All of these

5. National flower of China is

a) Chrysanthemum
b) Narcissus
c) Tulip
d) Lily

6. National flower of Japan is

a) Rose
b) Chrysanthemum
c) Tulip
d) Lily

7. National flower of Netherland is

a) Tiger lily
b) Tulip
c) Daffodil
d) All of these

8. Lily is the national flower of

a) Italy
b) Iraq
c) Turkey
d) All of these

9. Who is the present (year 2011) DDG (Horticulture) in ICAR, New Delhi?

a) Dr KL Chadha
b) Dr BP Pal
c) Dr HP Singh
d) Dr MS Swaminathan

10. Who is the present (year 2011) Director General of ICAR, New Delhi?

a) Dr BP Pal
b) Dr S Ayyappan
c) Dr MS Swaminathan
d) Dr KL Chadha

11. The largest cut flower producing country in the world is

a) Netherland
b) Colombia
c) Armenia
d) USA

12. India contributes nearly_____ percent to the global flower market

a) 15
b) 2
c) 10
d) 0.49

13. The biggest international flower market is located at

a) Alsmeer
b) Colombia
d) New Delhi
d) London

14. The highest per capita consumption of cut flowers is found in

a) India
b) USA
c) Germany
d) Switzerland

15. World trade in foliage plants is about (billion US$)

a) 5
b) 2.5
c) 10
d) 15

16. Name the country which has maximum share of foliage plants in the world market

a) India
b) China
c) Denmark
d) Netherland

17. Which of the following is considered as number one flower in International cut flower market?

a) Rose
b) Chrysanthemum
c) Carnation
d) Orchid

18. Maximum consumption of cut roses is during

a) Valentine's day
b) Mother's day
c) New Year eve
d) Christmas day

19. How many private units are engaged in export of flowers in India?

a) 500 b) 200
c) 100 d) 300

20. In India, the maximum area is in which flower crop?

a) Marigold b) Tuberose
c) Jasmine d) Rose

21. Which one is growing in largest area as long stem cut flower in our country?

a) Chrysanthemum b) Rose
c) Gladiolus d) Orchid

22. Free style garden are nothing but

a) Symmetrical gardens b) Formal gardens
c) Informal gardens d) Mughal gardens

23. Ground layering is most common in

a) Carnation b) Rose
c) Begonia d) Chrysanthemum

24. Herbaceous stem cutting is a propagation method used for

a) Carnation b) Begonia
c) Hollyhock d) All of these

25. Golden shower takes _____ years to flower.

a) 15 b) 10
c) 20 d) 2

26. *Lagerstroemia indica* is a

a) Flowering climber b) Flowering shrub
c) Foliage tree d) Flowering annual

27. Removal of undesirable leaves from the tree is known as

a) Disbudding b) Deblossoming
c) Defoliation d) Defruiting

28. Removal of undesirable flowers from plant is

a) Defruiting b) Deblossoming
c) Defoliation d) Disbudding

29. Removal of undesired branches by picking auxiliary buds is known as.

a) Clipping b) Nipping
c) Topping d) Budding

30. Vista vision is a theme for

a) Landscape b) Japanese garden
c) Persian garden d) Mixed garden

31. Which of the following is/ are cheapest or easiest method for lawn making

a) Turfing b) Turf plastering
c) Dibbling d) None of these

32. First DG of Indian Council of Agricultural Research was.

a) Dr M S Swaminathan b) Dr B P Pal
c) Dr G S Randhawa d) Dr M S Randhawa

33. Which of following is winter season foliage annual?

a) Coleus b) Poinsettia
c) Croton d) Kochia

34. Male sterility is common in

a) Petunia b) Marigold
c) Antirrhinum d) All of these

35. Thimma is an important cultivar of

a) Rose b) Bougainvillea
c) Tulip d) Carnation

36. Corm dormancy in gladiolus is due to

a) Linoleic acid b) Linolenic acid
c) Stearic acid d) All of these

37. Pyrethrum is extracted from.

a) Leaves of *Nicotiana tobaccum* b) Flower of tobacco
c) Flower petals of chrysanthemum d) Stems of carnation

38. Banjaran a cultivar of rose belongs to which category?

a) Floribunda b) Polyantha
c) Hybrid tea d) None of these

39. Dahlia is propagated by

a) Tubers b) Rhizomes
c) Tuberous roots d) Seeds

40. Bending of plants towards light is called

a) Hydrotropism b) Phototropism
c) Chemotropism d) Geotropism

41. Maximum rose oil is produced in

a) Bulgaria b) Alsmeer
c) Italy d) China

42. Gladiolus is asexually propagated by

a) Corms b) Rhizome
c) Bulb d) Tuber

43. Bulbil is a common feature in

a) Tulip b) Gladiolus
c) Dahlia d) Tiger lily

44. Cormel is a swollen end of

a) Fibrous root b) Primary root
c) Stolon d) Auxiliary bud

45. Which of the following is an "English flower arrangement"?

a) Jiyubana b) Ikebana
c) Morimona d) Zeneika

46. Dahlia was introduced by Agri-horticultural society of India for the first time at Kolkata in the year

a) 1935
b) 1857
c) 1882
d) 1905

47. Chrysanthemum in India is known as

a) Daud
b) Harsingar
c) Guldaudi
d) Mum

48. In China and Japan, chrysanthemum is known as

a) Hill queen
b) Autumn queen
c) Japanese queen
d) Guldaudi

49. Dr MA Kher was associated with

a) Chrysanthemum
b) Carnation
c) Rose
d) China aster

50. Bharat Sundari is a famous cultivar of

a) Bougainvillea
b) Hibiscus
c) Rose
d) Carnation

51. Thornless rose rootstock was developed at

a) IARI
b) NBRI
c) IIHR
d) Rose Garden, Chandigarh

52. First cultivar of rose released by Dr BP Pal in the year1962 was

a) Rose Sherbet
b) Aruna
c) Rose Scented
d) Mehak

53. International bougainvillea registration centre is at

a) IIHR
b) IARI
c) NBRI
d) TNAU

54. Which of following is growing as a long stem cut rose in India?

a) Mother Teressa
b) Anurag
c) Mehak
d) Raktagandha

55. Name the floribunda type cultivar of rose which is also used as cut flower

a) Banjaran b) Rose Sherbet
c) Sindhoor d) Mohini

56. Banjaran cultivar of rose belongs to the category

a) Hybrid Tea b) Polyantha
c) Miniature d) Floribunda

57. Pusa Basanti an open pollinated cultivar belongs to

a) Zinnia b) Chrysanthemum
c) Bougainvillea d) Marigold

58. Bottom heating in case of ______ cuttings enhances rooting percentage

a) Hibiscus b) Rose
c) Bougainvillea d) Dahlia

59. Queen Elizabeth is a common cultivar of

a) Rose b) Carnation
c) Chrysanthemum d) Marigold

60. In North Indian plains which of the following is a superior rootstock of rose?

a) *Rosa bourboniana* b) *Rosa multiflora*
c) *Rosa gallica* d) *Rosa indica*

61. Crocus is propagated successfully by

a) Tuber b) Corm
c) Bulb d) Rhizome

62. Birbal Sahani a cultivar developed at NBRI, Lucknow belongs to

a) Tuberose b) Bougainvillea
c) Marigold d) Chrysanthemum

63. Amar Shola is a cultivar of

a) Marigold b) Rose
c) Amaranthus d) Verbena

64. French marigold is a/an__________ in nature

a) Diploid b) Tetraploid
c) Aneuploid d) None of these

65. Diploid chromosome number of gladiolus is

a) 60 b) 30
c) 80 d) 40

66. Samrat is a tetraploid cultivar of

a) Amaryllis b) Tuberose
c) Rose d) Verbena

67. "The Rose in India" is a book written by

a) RS Randhawa b) Vishnu Swarup
c) MS Randhawa d) BP Pal

68. Most of the cultivars of chrysanthemum are

a) Short day b) Long day
c) Day neutral d) None of above

69. Major problem in breeding roses is/are

a) Difficult pollination b) Poor seed setting
c) Absence of rose trials d) All of these

70. Powdery mildew in roses is caused by

a) *Diplodia* b) *Botrytis*
c) *Diplocarpon* d) *Sphaerotheca*

71. Which cultivar of rose is/are resistant to powdery mildew?

a) Spotless Yellow b) Spotless Pink
c) Spotless Gold d) All of these

72. Which of following species is resistant to powdery mildew?

a) *Moschata* b) *Bourboniana*
c) *Rugosa* d) *Indica*

73. Mohini cultivar of rose is famous for its

a) Red colour
b) White colour
c) Chocolate colour
d) Yellow colour

74. Total area under protected cultivation in the world is nearly about ________ thousand hectares

a) 40
b) 50
c) 60
d) 90

75. The growth rate of global floriculture industry is ________ per cent per annum

a) 30
b) 15-20
c) 10-15
d) 20-25

76. Which one of following is number one foliage plant at global level?

a) *Ficus elastica*
b) Cordyline
c) Aglaonema
d) Dieffenbachia

77. The leading cut foliage exporter is

a) USA
b) Netherlands
c) France
d) Italy

78. The largest flowers exporter in Asia is

a) India
b) Korea
c) China
d) Japan

79. The largest flowering plant species family is

a) Asteraceae
b) Rosaceae
c) Brassicaceae
d) Orchidaceae

80. How many species of orchid are native to India?

a) 1600
b) 5000
c) 1000
d) 1800

81. Orchid species which grow on trees are known as

a) Epiphyte
b) Lithophytes
c) Saprophyte
d) Terrestrial

82. Orchid species which grow on moss covered rocks are known as

a) Epiphyte b) Terrestrial
c) Both a and b d) Lithophyte

83. Phaius orchids belongs to the group

a) Saprophyte b) Terrestrial
c) Epiphyte d) Lithophyte

84. Jewel orchids are valued for their beautiful

a) Leaves b) Stamens
c) Flowers d) All of these

85. Gynoecium in orchid flower is known as

a) Stamens b) Tube
c) Endosperm d) Column

86. Orchid seeds are devoid of

a) Seed coat b) Cotyledon
c) Endosperm d) All of these

87. Tissue culture industry in the world has revolutionized by

a) Orchid b) Rose
c) Tulip d) Carnation

88. Which of following flower has longest vase-life?

a) Tulip b) Rose
c) Chrysanthemum d) Paphiopedilum

89. Which of the following alkaloid is not present in orchids?

a) Denrobine b) Pierardine
c) Chysine d) Atrazine

90. A flat like projection between male and female parts in orchid flowers is known as

a) Rostellum b) Column
c) Screen d) None of these

91. Indian shot is the name given to seeds of

a) Dog flower b) Rose
c) Orchid d) Canna

92. Fruit of rose is known as

a) Hip b) Indian shot
c) Nut d) Berry

93. For getting large size flowers which of following operation is important?

a) Pinching b) Disbudding
c) Puncturing d) Disshooting

94. Which one of following is growth retardant?

a) IBA b) IAA
c) B-Nine d) NAA

95. Pigment responsible for blue colour in flowers is

a) Pelargolin b) Delphilidin
c) Lycopene d) None of these

96. Aspermy in chrysanthemum is caused by

a) Fungus b) Bacteria
c) Virus d) All of above

97. Gladiolus belongs to the family

a) Liliaceae b) Rosaceae
c) Begoniaceae d) Iridaceae

98. Which of the following is not a blue colour flowering annual?

a) Larkspur b) Cosmos
c) Ageratum d) Delphinium

99. Corm dormancy in gladiolus is broken by

a) IAA b) GA_3
c) SADH d) 2, 4-D

100. 'Liliput' is a variety of

a) Rose b) Marigold
c) Dahlia d) Chrysanthemum

101. The most serious fungus in gladiolus is

a) Fusarium b) Alternaria
c) Botrytis d) Curvularia

102. Canna is propagated commercially by

a) Corms b) Rhizome
c) Bulb d) Tuber

103. Soil sterilization is done by

a) Formaldehyde b) Chloropicrin
c) Methyl Bromide d) All of these

104. Shoot tip culture is practiced in which of following:

a) Carnation b) Orchid
c) Chrysanthemum d) All of these

105. Lt Governor of Himachal Pradesh Shri Bajrang Bahadur Singh Bahaduri has developed 160 cultivars of

a) Rose b) Gladiolus
c) Dahlia d) Chrysanthemum

106. Dioecy is very common in

a) Asparagus b) Aster
c) Tulip d) Petunia

107. Male sterility is common in

a) Petunia b) Marigold
c) Ageratum d) Aster

108. Self incompatibility is not common in

a) Ageratum b) English daisy
c) Petunia d) Rose

109. 'Yellow Rose' is a scented variety of

a) Rose
b) Gladiolus
c) Tuberose
d) Aster

110. Rose oil is primarily extracted from which of following species ?

a) *Odorata*
b) *Damascena*
c) *Indica*
d) *Gallica*

111. Bonsai culture has originated in which country

a) China
b) Korea
c) India
d) Japan

112. Which of following is most common rooting hormone?

a) IBA
b) NAA
c) 2, 4-D
d) GA

113. Air layering is commonly used to propagate

a) Rose
b) Jasmine
c) Rubber plant
d) Azalea

114. Mame bonsai are normally up to________ feet

a) Two
b) One
c) Half
d) Three

115. Those cultivars of chrysanthemum which produce flower between 10-27°C temperature are grouped in

a) Thermo-zero
b) Thermo-positive
c) Thermo-negative
d) None of these

116. Which of following is not a primary colour?

a) Red
b) Yellow
c) Blue
d) Green

117. Which of following is softer or cooler colour?

a) Green
b) Orange
c) Blue
d) Violet

118. The basic colour is

a) Orange b) Red
c) Grey d) Violet

119. Which of following is not a neutral colour?

a) White b) Grey
c) Black d) Pink

120. Closely related colours are also known as

a) Contrasting colour b) Analogous colour
c) Complimentary colour d) All of these

121. Yellow colour is contrasting to

a) Orange b) Black
c) Blue d) Violet

122. Which country in Asia is the leading exporter of orchids?

a) Malaysia b) India
c) China d) Japan

123. Colours which are placed at opposite ends of triangles of colour wheel are known as

a) Complimentary colour b) Monochromatic
c) Analogous d) None of these

124. Which of following is most suitable for hanging baskets?

a) Rudbeckia b) Cosmos
c) Portulaca d) Rubber plant

125. Which annual can be grown more successfully in shade?

a) Pansy b) Stock
c) Cineraria d) Daisy

126. Which of the following is not a good loose flower?

a) Marigold b) Gailardia
c) Zinnia d) Sweat pea

127. Which of the following is not grown as foliage annual?

a) Kochia
b) Ageratum
c) Coleus
d) Celosia

128. In cryo-preservation, the seeds are immersed in liquid nitrogen at ________°C temperature.

a) 100
b) -196
c) -100
d) 196

129. The seeds of ________ loose viability after drying

a) Mapple
b) Jasmine
c) Rose
d) Quercus

130. Which of the following is seed germination inhibitor?

a) ABA
b) GA
c) BA
d) PBA

131. Seed viability is determined by

a) Direct germination
b) Excised embryo
c) Tetrazolium test
d) All of these

132. Seeds of which of following can not germinate at any temperature?

a) *Cupressus*
b) *Ailanthus*
c) *Casuarina*
d) *All of these*

133. Scarification of seeds is done by

a) Hot water
b) Acid
c) High temperature
d) All of these

134. Seed priming is done by

a) Alcohol
b) Hot water
c) Infusion
d) Acid

135. Non-tunicated bulbs are common in

a) Lilium
b) Narcissus
c) Nerine
d) All of these

136. Scooping is very common practice in

a) Hyacinth b) Rose
c) Lilium d) Crocus

137. Pseudo-bulbs are commonly used to multiply

a) Tulip b) Orchids
c) Gladiolus d) Tuberose

138. Single or multiple node cuttings are taken in

a) Dieffenbachia b) Dracaena
c) Song of India d) All of these

139. Wintering of roses is very common in

a) Delhi b) Mumbai
c) Shimla c) Kolkatta

140. Which of the following is not a common loose flower in India?

a) Jasmine b) Tuberose
c) Marigold d) Carnation

141. Indian cut flowers can be sold throughout the year in

a) Singapore b) South Korea
c) Japan d) China

142. Which of following is propagated by tuberous roots?

a) Eranthes b) Begonia
c) Iris d) Anemone

143. Among bulbous plants maximum area is under which flower

a) Gladiolus b) Tulip
c) Lilium d) All of these

144. Which country is largest exporter of bulbous plants?

a) China b) USA
c) Netherlands d) Israel

145. Aerial bulblets formed in the leaf axils are known as

a) Aerial bulb b) Corms
c) Cormlets d) Bulbils

146. Scoring is very common in

a) Gladiolus b) Begonia
c) Lilium d) Tulip

147. Which of the following is not propagated by rhizome?

a) Canna b) Hydechium
c) Iris d) Lilium

148. Spring flowering bulbous plants are planted during

a) August b) January
c) November d) March

149. Which of following is planted at maximum depth ?

a) Gladiolus b) Tulip
c) Lilium d) Tuberose

150. Which is most sensitive to temperature?

a) Clivia b) Gladiolus
c) Crocus d) Tulip

151. Which of the following cultivar of gladiolus is resistant to Fusarium wilt?

a) Sagar b) Sapna
c) Dhiraj d) Apsara

152. Which of the following is a hybrid of African marigold?

a) Pusa Shankar-I b) Pusa Narangi
c) Pusa Sweta d) Pusa Basanti

153. Which of the following is not a cultivar of China aster?

a) PG Purple b) Poornima
c) PG Violet d) None of these

154. Which of following is not a cultivar of Tuberose?

a) Shringar b) Suvashini
c) Rajat Rekha d) Swarna

155. Which is not a cultivar of *Jasminum auriculatum*?

a) Motia b) Large round
c) Long point d) Pari Mullai

156. Plants which complete their life cycle within one year are known as

a) Annual b) Biennial
c) Perennial d) None of above

157. Rainy season annuals are sown in nursery during

a) February b) June
c) August d) April

158. Which of the following is a foliage annual?

a) Aster b) Salvia
c) Kochia d) Cosmos

159. Which is not grown during summer season?

a) Kochia b) Portulaca
c) Gaillardia d) Pansy

160. Which of following is intermediate day flowering annual?

a) Coleus b) Petunia
c) Gaillardia d) Pansy

161. Which of following is are long day annual?

a) Antirrhinum b) Rudbeckia
c) Petunia d) All of these

162. Which is most tender annual and can not be grown in open in high hills?

a) Stock b) Pansy
c) Statice d) Rudbeckia

163. Seeds of which of following can germinate in dark

a) *Echium* b) *Lobelia*
c) *Nicotiana* d) None of above

164. Seeds of which flower require stratification and scarification

a) Sweat pea b) Nigella
c) Clianthus d) Marigold

165. Direct seed sowing is not economical in

a) Sweat pea b) Petunia
c) Hollyhock d) Balsam

166. Kochia is having a plant form of

a) Informal b) Globular
c) Columnar d) Conical

167. Person made significant contribution in floriculture even being a non-professional

a) MS Randhawa b) GS Randhawa
c) KL Chadha d) BP Pal

168. Bhabha Atomic Research Institute, Bombay has mandate on floriculture especially

a) Rose oil extraction
b) Micro-propagation of ornamentals
c) Landscaping for pollution control
d) Breeding of bulbous ornamentals

169. Research on Nymphaea has been conducted at

a) IIHR, Bangalore b) NBRI, Lucknow
c) IARI, New Delhi d) BSI, Kolkatta

170. Dr Foja Singh made significant contribution in breeding of

a) Chrysanthemum b) Gladiolus
c) Orchids d) Rose

171. In Himachal Pradesh, model floriculture centre is at

a) Chail b) Shimla
c) Rajgarh d) Kandaghat

172. In India, research work on Jasmine is being conducted at

a) IARI b) TNAU
c) IIHR d) None of these

173. *Dendranthema grandiflora* is botanical name of

a) Paper flower b) Chrysanthemum
c) Carnation d) China aster

174. Who is associated with Jasmine breeding?

a) S Muthuswami b) RS Malik
c) BP Pal d) TK Bose

175. Who is associated with Marigold breeding in India?

a) B Singh b) ML Chaudhary
c) RL Mishra d) SPS Raghawa

176. Who is associated with greenhouse cultivation of ornamentals?

a) NK Dahlani b) KR Bhandari
c) P Chandra d) All of above

177. The Temperate Horticulture Research Institute (THRI) is situated at

a) Srinagar b) Almora
c) Kullu d) Shimla

178. Monogenic recessive male sterility is common in

a) Marigold b) Zinnia
c) Calceolaria d) All of above

179. Heterostyly is a common feature in

a) Petunia b) Ageratum
c) Primula d) Gerbera

180. Cytoplasmic male sterility is found in

a) Antirrhinum b) Petunia
c) Ageratum d) Salvia

181. Which of following is not a self pollinated flowering annual?

a) Larkspur b) Sweat pea
c) Lupine d) None of these

182. Cypress in Persian gardens was used as a symbol of

a) Idea of heaven b) Death and Eternity
c) Persian Paradise d) Life and youth

183. Which of following is not often cross pollinated annual?

a) Ageratum b) Lineria
c) Pansy d) Antirrhinum

184. Self-pollination depends on the mechanism of

a) Chasmogamy b) Heterostyly
c) Dichogamy d) Decliny

185. Nugget is a hybrid cultivar of

a) Petunia b) Marigold
c) Zinnia d) Antirrhinum

186. First F-1 hybrid in petunia was developed in Japan during year

a) 1965 b) 1945
c) 1935 d) 1970

187. Marigold has originated in

a) South Africa b) Mexico
c) USA d) UK

188. Gladiolus has originated in

a) South Africa b) Mexico
c) Asia d) UK

189. Which of following tree is not of Indian origin?

a) *Cassia fistula* b) *Michelia champaca*
c) *Grevillea robusta* d) All of these

190. Which of following shrub is not originated in India?

a) *Barleria cristata* b) *Holmskoidia sanguine*
c) *Tecoma stans* d) *Jasminum sombac*

191. Which of following flowering pot plant has originated in India?

a) Azalea b) Crossandra
c) Gardenia d) All of these

192. Genetic male sterility is common in

a) China Aster b) Marigold
c) Gaillardia d) Dahlia

193. Which of following is most common type of sterility in ornamental plants?

a) Genetic
b) Cytoplasmic genetic
c) Cytoplasmic
d) All of above

194. Basic chromosome number (x=) of lotus is

a) 8
b) 10
c) 9
d) 7

195. Basic chromosome number (x=) of rose is

a) 8
b) 7
c) 11
d) 13

196. Basic chromosome number (x=) of orchids is

a) 18
b) 17
c) 20
d) 16

197. Basic chromosome number (x=) of gladiolus is

a) 15
b) 9
c) 8
d) 7

198. Basic chromosome number (x=) of carnation is

a) 9
b) 7
c) 8
d) 15

199. Basic chromosome number (x=) of chrysanthemum is

a) 9
b) 8
c) 7
d) Plenty

200. Basic chromosome number (x=) of jasmine is

a) 15
b) 25
c) 13
d) 9

201. Basic chromosome number (x=) tuberose is

a) 17
b) 15
c) 13
d) Plenty

202. Basic chromosome number (x=) of dahlia is

a) 13 b) 12
c) 15 d) 8

203. Basic chromosome number (x=) of amaryllis is

a) 7 b) 8
c) 11 d) 15

204. Basic chromosome number (x=) of gerbera is

a) 15 b) 13
c) 11 d) 25

205. Basic chromosome number (x=) of anthurium is

a) 15 b) 13
c) 11 d) 25

206. Basic chromosome number (x=) of china aster is

a) 12 b) 9
c) 15 d) 25

207. Basic chromosome number (x=) of marigold is

a) 9 b) 15
c) 12 d) 25

208. Basic chromosome number (x=) of Mentha is

a) 11 b) 12
c) 10 d) 6

209. Basic chromosome number (x=) of Scented geranium is

a) 9 b) 8
c) 12 d) 6

210. Basic chromosome number (x=) of Lavender is

a) 10 b) 8
c) 12 d) 6

211. Basic chromosome number (x=) of Citronella is

a) 6 b) 12
c) 10 d) 16

212. Basic chromosome number (x=) of Palmarosa is

a) 8 b) 6
c) 7 d) 10

213. Basic chromosome number (x=) of Lemongrass is

a) 7 b) 8
c) 10 d) 6

214. Basic chromosome number (x=) of Rosemerry is

a) 10 b) 9
c) 12 d) 8

215. Basic chromosome number (x=) of Patchouli is

a) 17 b) 9
c) 12 d) 8

216. Self-incompatibility is overcome by

a) Bud pollinatioin b) Surgical techniques
c) Irradiation d) All of above

217. Virus free plants can be produced from

a) Anther b) Meristem culture
c) Nodes d) All of these

218. Who designed landscaping of Chandigarh city?

a) MS Randhawa b) Corbusier
c) Maxwell d) Meyer

219. Which of following is most suitable for planting in Rajasthan?

a) *Albizia lebbek* b) *Pongamia glabra*
c) *Butea monosperma* d) *Prosopis juliflora*

220. Mohini, a well known cultivar of rose is __________ in nature

a) Diploid b) Triploid
c) Aneuploid d) Tetraploid

221. One gram seed of petunia contains how many seeds ?

a) 10000 b) 10
c) 1000 d) 100

222. Which garden is regarded as genesis of gardening?

a) Eden b) Brindavan
c) Hampshire d) Osaka

223. Osaka garden is located in

a) UK b) South Korea
c) China d) Japan

224. Vatsyayana did not describe which of following garden

a) Pramadodyan b) Nandanvana
c) Passage garden d) Vrikshavatika

225. Gardens at Nalanda and Takshshila were developed in the time of

a) Mughals b) Aryans
c) Budhists d) None of above

226. 'Char Bagh' the paradise garden is situated in

a) India b) Iran
c) Pakistan d) Turkey

227. Taj Mahal was built by

a) Nur Jahan b) Shah Jahan
c) Jahangir d) Akbar

228. Dilkhush garden of Lahore was built by

a) Fadai Khan b) Jahangir
c) Akbar d) Shah Jahan

229. Moorish garden style was developed in

a) France b) Germany
c) Spain d) Iran

230. Baradari garden of Patiala was developed by

a) Fadai Khan b) Ranjeet Singh
d) Sansaar Chand d) Bhupinder Singh

231. Royal Botanic garden of Kew is located in

a) Germany
b) England
c) USA
d) Australia

232. First Botanical garden in the world was started at Venice during

a) 1621
b) 1543
c) 1840
d) 1759

233. Heart of garden is

a) Hedges
b) Fountains
c) Rose
d) Lawn

234. Baradari is a main feature of

a) Japanese garden
b) Mughal garden
c) Italian garden
d) English garden

235. Mughal style gardening was developed by

a) Shah Jahan
b) Akbar
c) Babar
d) None of these

236. Pagoda is a name of

a) Japanese monument
b) Flowering tree
c) Rock statue
d) Shrub shaping

237. Dry landscape is important feature of

a) Mughal garden
b) Japanese garden
c) English garden
d) Italian garden

238. Oldest botanical garden in Europe is at Leyden in

a) Germany
b) Spain
c) Netherlands
d) None of these

239. Budha Jayanti Park is situated at

a) New Delhi
b) Chandigarh
c) Varanasi
d) Mysore

240. Which of following is not a Japanese type garden?

a) Vertical garden
b) Hill garden
c) Tea garden
d) Flat garden

241. Who gives an idea about informal gardening through his paintings?

a) W Robinson b) Le Notre
c) C Lorain d) H Hoare

242. Which of the following symbolizes death and eternity?

a) Bougainvillea b) Kachnar
c) Chenar d) Cypress

243. ____________ introduced Indian style gardening in Japan.

a) Prof H Mori b) Chinese
c) English trackers d) Budhist Monks

244. Which of following is associated with life of Lord Budha?

a) *Saraca indica* b) *Butea monosperma*
c) *Shorea robusta* d) All of these

245. Mandor garden of Jodhpur was built by

a) Ranjeet Singh b) Abhai Singh
c) Fadai khan d) None of above

246. Mughal garden at Pinjore was laid out by

a) Fadai Khan b) Bajendra Singh
c) Aurangzeb d) Ranjeet Singh

247. Roshanara Park, in New Delhi was built by

a) Prof K Mori b) Heian
c) Nara d) Muromachi

248. Which park belongs to Japanese style?

a) Roshnara park b) Budha Jayanti park
c) PM House at Saldarjung d) All of these

249. Shalimar garden in Kashmir was built by

a) Jahangir b) Akbar
c) Nur Jahan d) Jafar Khan

250. Chasma-e-Shahi garden was built by

a) Fadai Khan b) Ali Mardan Khan
c) Ranbir Singh d) None of above

251. Sand garden is also known as

a) Soto-roji
b) Roji-niwa
c) Ryoanji
d) Rithai-seki

252. Which chemical is used for dehydration of flowers?

a) CaO
b) CaC_2
c) Borax
d) All of these

253. 'White Star' is a variety of

a) Dahlia
b) Chrysanthemum
c) Rose
d) Aster

254. Byrant Park is situated at

a) Coimbatore
b) Trichy
c) Rameshwaram
d) Kodaikanal

255. Lloyd botanic garden, Darjeeling was laid down by

a) Sir George King
b) Dr N Wallich
c) William Llyod
d) Dr CC Calder

256. Stone lanterns are important feature in

a) Japanese garden
b) Persian garden
c) Mughal garden
d) English garden

257. Which of following is/are not formal gardens?

a) English
b) Italian
c) French
d) All of these

258. Which of the following statement is incorrect?

a) Portulaca – Rose moss
b) Kochia – Burning bush
c) Gompherena – Globe amaranth
d) Gaillardia – Summer cypress

259. Which of the following is a winter annual?

a) Calendula
b) Kochia
c) Balsam
d) Portulaca

260. After whom the generic name Kochia has been given

a) SD Koch
b) WDJ Koch
c) AD Koch
d) BDC Koch

261. *Amaranthus caudatus* is commonly called as

a) Rose moss
b) Sun plant
c) Love-lies-Bleeding
d) Blanket flower

262. Wall flower belongs to the family

a) Crucifereae
b) Solanaceae
c) Caryophyllaceae
d) None of these

263. Wall flower is native to

a) Chile and Peru
b) Europe
c) Mediterranean region
d) Mexico

264. Phlox belongs to the family

a) Polemoniaceae
b) Solanaceae
c) Violaceae
d) Rosaceae

265. State which of the following pair is incorrect?

a) *Iberis amara*-Candytuft
b) *Mathiola incana*-Ice plant
c) *Lythyrus odoratus*-Sweet Pea
d) *Limonium sinuatum*- Statice

266. Amaranthus and Cock's Comb belongs to the family

a) Amaranthaceae
b) Balsaminaceae
c) Asteraceae
d) Chenopodiaceae

267. Balsam belongs to the family

a) Amaranthaceae
b) Portulaceae
c) Balsaminaceae
d) Asteraceae

268. Zinnia, Tithonia, Sunflower and Gaillardia belong to the family

a) Portulaceae
b) Asteraceae
c) Chenopodiaceae
d) Amaranthaceae

269. Kochia belongs to the family

a) Asteraceae
b) Balsaminaceae
c) Portulaceae
d) Chenopodiaceae

270. Gaillardia is commonly called as

a) Blanket flower
b) Sun plant
c) Globe amaranth
d) Rose moss

271. Which of following is a floating plant?

a) Azolla
b) Water Hyacinth
c) Duckwood
d) All of above

272. Which is/are the biggest formal garden in India?

a) Vrindhavan garden (Mysore)
b) Rock garden (Chandigarh)
c) Both a and b
d) None of these

273. Which flower is grown in all seasons?

a) Chrysanthemum
b) Candytuft
c) Corn flower
d) Marigold

274. Cutting from broad leaved evergreen trees are usually taken in

a) Early summer
b) Early winter
c) Late summer
d) None of the above

275. Herbaceous stem cuttings for propagation are used in

a) Carnation
b) Begonia
c) Rose
d) Hollyhook

276. Leaf and leaf bud cuttings for propagation are used in

a) Jumpier
b) Begonia
c) Carnation
d) Grape

277. Soft wood cuttings for propagation are used in

a) Dogwood
b) Wisteria
c) Begonia
d) None of these

278. Hard wood cuttings for propagation are used in

a) Dogwood
b) Wisteria
c) Fig
d) Begonia

279. Tip, simple, trench and mound are the kinds of

a) Layering
b) Rootage
c) Budding
d) Grafting

280. Lawn in mughal garden is

a) Sloppy
b) Star shape
c) Terraced
d) Circular

281. Stone lantern was first designed by

a) San-chu-keu
b) Josef
c) Oribe
d) Ashoka

282. Mughal style of gardening was developed by

a) Shahjahan
b) Akbar
c) Babar
d) None of these

283. Shade loving annual flowering plant is

a) Salvia
b) Forget-Me-Not
c) *Dianthus*
d) Anchuja

284. Mucilage in cut flowers is responsible for

a) Improving flower life
b) Decreasing transpiration
c) Bickering of vessels
d) All of these

285. Hogarth course is also known as

a) Line of beauty
b) Circular curve
c) Tangent arrangement
d) None of these

286. Any one type of flowers has

a) Plane disc
b) Curled petals
c) Doom shaped disc
d) Ring around disc

287. Name of annual climber is

a) *Quisqalis indica*
b) *Imqurea pentaphyla*
c) *Lathyrus odoratus*
d) *Tecoma grandis*

288. Pagoda is a name of

a) Japanese flowering tree
b) Japanese monument
c) Statue
d) None of these

289. Botanical name of carnation is

a) *Celosia cristata*
b) *Tagetes errecta*
c) *Dianthus caryophyllus*
d) *Centuria cyathus*

290. Dahlia is best propagated by

a) Layering b) Rhizomes
c) Sucker d) None of these

291. Crescent is a well known

a) Flower arrangement b) Pigment
c) Type of jasmine scent d) English garden feature

292. Peony is a name for the class of

a) Marigold b) Sunflower
c) Chrysanthemum d) Dahlia

293. Which place among the following is known as 'Heaven for orchids'?

a) Shillong b) Cherapunji
c) Kalimpong d) None of these

294. β-Hydroxy quinoline sulphate (HQS) is used in

a) Hormone preparation b) Cut flower solution
c) Micro-nutrient spray d) Weed control

295. Shalimar garden is situated at

a) Bangalore b) Kashmir
c) Hyderabad d) Delhi

296. Which of the following is a well known retardant ?

a) Alar b) Kinetin
c) GA_3 d) IBA

297. Persian style of gardening was introduced in India by

a) Shahjahan b) Babur
c) Akbar d) Noorjahan

298. Which of the following are the kinds of branch pruning ?

a) Heading back b) Thinning
c) Branch tipping d) All of these

299. Which of the following plants are used for boundary tall hedge ?

a) Allysum b) Fresine
c) *Tecoma stans* d) Allocasia

300. Fairy ring is a disease noticed commonly in

a) Calendula b) Chrusanthemum
c) Lawn grasses d) Rose

301. Acacia is planted as

a) Hedge b) Fruits
c) Ornamentals d) None of these

302. *Carissa carandus* is used as

a) Ornamental b) Hedge
c) Fruit d) Fence

303. The term scion and root-stock are used in

a) Layering b) Budding
c) Grafting d) Cutting

304. Bougainvillea is propagated by

a) Budding b) Layering
c) Cutting d) All of these

305. Roses are grown for

a) Perfume or rose oil b) Cut flower
c) Rose water, gulkand d) All of these

306. Chrysanthemum is propagated by means of

a) Suckers b) Cuttings
c) Budding d) Inarching

307. Floral bangles and crowns are made from flowers of

a) Jasmine b) Tuberose
c) Chandni d) All of above

308. Which of following is not commonly seen in painting of Ram and Sita?

a) Garlands b) Bangles
c) Buttonhole d) Bajubandhs

309. Flowers of *Albizia lebbek* are used for decorating

a) Ears
b) Neck
c) Hairs
d) Wrist

310. Which of following is not used for making gajra?

a) Marigold
b) Barieria
c) Michelia
d) Crossandra

311. Veni popular in South India is made from

a) Jasmine
b) Tuberose
c) Crossandra
c) All of above

312. Bouquets are not presented for

a) Birthday
b) Welcoming a guest
c) Departed soul
d) Marriage function

313. Which of following is a free type flower arrangement?

a) Jiyubana
b) Moribana
c) Zenei-ka
d) None of above

314. In Japanese language fillers are known as

a) Shin
b) Soe
c) Jushi
d) Hikae

315. Japanese flower arrangement is based on

a) Religious theme
b) Artistic theme
c) Spiritual theme
d) Social theme

316. English flower arrangement is based on

a) Artistic theme
b) Imaginary theme
c) Spiritual theme
d) All of above

317. Floral clock is important feature at which garden?

a) Pinjore Bagh
b) Lal bagh
c) Nishat Garden
d) None of above

318. Which of the *Jasminum species* contains maximum oil?

a) *Grandiflorum*
b) *Auriculatum*
c) *Narcissus*
d) *Humile*

319. Maximum refineries of oil extraction of Jasmine are located in

a) Kerala b) Tamil Nadu
c) Karnataka d) West Bengal

320. Oldest botanical garden in Europe is at Leyden in

a) Germany b) Spain
c) Netherland d) None of these

321. Which of the following literature mentions the lotus symbol?

a) Jainism b) Buddhist
c) Hinduism d) All of these

322. Which of following is a symbol of self-esteem?

a) Narcissus b) Stock
c) Irish d) Carnation

323. Which of the following is a symbol of purity?

a) Tulip b) Tuberose
c) Lily d) Daffodil

324. Die back, a serious disease of rose indicates

a) Dark brown spot on leaves
b) Raddish orange pustules on petiole
c) Death of plant from top to down
d) Powdery growth on leaves lower sides

325. Die back in rose is due to

a) Virus b) MLO
c) *Diplodia rosarum* d) *Diplocarpon rosae*

326. Rose cultivars resistant to die back is/are

a) White Christmas b) Royal Ascot
c) Blue Moon d) All of these

327. The powdery mildew of rose appears when

a) Days are warm and nights are cool
b) Days are rainy and nights are cool
c) Days are rainy and nights are warm
d) Both days & nights are cool

328. 'Pankhuri' prepared from

a) Rose
b) Gladiolus
c) Carnation
d) None of these

329. Which of the following is a temperate aromatic crop?

a) Palmarosa
b) Lemon grass
c) Lavender
d) Citronella

330. The terms Padma, Kamala and Pankaja relate to

a) Rose
b) Lotus
c) Marigold
d) Jasmine

331. Aquatic flower resembling with lotus is

a) Day lilly
b) Tiger lilly
c) Water lilly
d) Blue African lilly

332. Brahma (the creator), Vishnu (the protector) and Shiva (the destroyer) are associated with

a) Lotus
b) Tuberose
c) Carnation
d) Jasmine

333. Lotus is the symbol of the God/Goddess.

a) Lakshmi
b) Ganesh
c) Shiva
d) Vishnu

334. For which of the following the 'Golden Lotus Prize" is given?

a) Best feature film
b) Best sportsman
c) Best social worker
d) Best Horticulturist

335. Stalks of which of flower are used to make necklace and bracelets in West Bengal.

a) Gladiolus
b) Lotus
c) Carnation
d) Chrysanthemum

336. Optimum temperature for storing gladiolus corms is ______

a) 5-7°C
b) 10-12°C
c) 15-20°C
d) 1-5°C

337. Which of the following is not a fragrant variety of gladiolus?

a) Lucky star b) Sagar
c) Jimmy Boy d) None of these

338. Punjab Gold is a variety of

a) Chrysanthemum b) Tuberose
c) Rose d) Marigold

339. Fluorine injury is very common in

a) Tulip b) Rose
c) Iris d) Gladiolus

340. Negative geotropism a disorder occur during transportation of

a) Tulip b) Rose
c) Carnation d) Gladiolus

341. Storage corm rot in gladiolus is caused by

a) *Fusarium* b) *Rhizoctonia*
c) *Penicillium* d) All of the above

342. Sleepiness a disorder occurs in

a) Gladiolus b) Carnation
c) Chrysanthemum d) Tulip

343. Basic chromosome number of carnation is

a) 20 b) 26
c) 60 d) 15

344. Arthur Sim carnation is highly resistant to

a) Fusarium wilt b) Rust
c) Stem Rot d) Blight

345. The best time of rose pruning in North Indian plains is

a) September-October b) October-November
c) November-December d) June-July

346. Pruning in roses is done twice during November and June at

a) Shimla b) Bangalore
c) Delhi d) Both b and c

347. Which of following is not a Sympodial orchid?

a) Cymbidium
b) Vanda
c) Dendrobium
d) None of these

348. Who started tissue culture in orchids for first time?

a) Morel
b) Kundson
c) Chang
d) None of above

349. Which of following is commonly known as sword lily?

a) Crocus
b) Gladiolus
c) Daffodil
d) Irish

350. In carnation, calyx splitting is a problem due to

a) Genetic factors
b) Nutritional factors
c) Environmental factors
d) All of above

351. In carnation, sleepiness is a problem because of

a) Ethylene
b) CO_2
c) High temperature
d) All of above

352. In carnation, curly tip a disorder is due to

a) Low light
b) Low temperature
c) Nitrogen deficiency
d) All of above

353. __________ is the most serious pest in carnation.

a) Red spider mite
b) Aphid
c) Thrips
d) Moth

354. *Nelumbo lutea* is commonly known as

a) American lotus
b) Kamala
c) Indian lotus
d) None of these

355. Silver thio-sulphate enhances flower longevity in

a) Rose
b) Tulip
c) Lily
d) Carnation

356. __________ tons of roses produces one kg oil.

a) 10
b) 3-4
c) 10-15
d) 1-15

357. Gulkand is a processed product prepared by mixing rose petals and sugar in ratio of

a) 1 : 1 b) 2 : 1
c) 1 : 2 d) 1 : 3

358. Chemical defoliation in roses is done by

a) GA b) Urea
c) Auxin d) Copper sulphate

359. _______ coloured roses are most popular

a) Red b) White
c) Pink d) Yellow

360. Which flower is universally acclaimed as the queen of flowers?

a) Lotus b) Rose
c) Orchid d) Tulip

361. Which type of chrysanthemum looks globular?

a) Incurve b) Pompon
c) Anemone d) Decorative

362. Grey mould in chrysanthemum is caused by

a) *Alternaria* b) *Fusarium*
c) *Botrytis* d) None of these

363. Dahlia is native to

a) Canada b) USA
c) Mexico d) Asia

364. Removal of undesirable auxillary buds at initial flowering stage is known as

a) Notching b) Clipping
c) Deblossoming d) Topiary

365. Bougainvillea belongs to the plant family

a) Nyctaginaceae b) Rosaceae
c) Apocynaceae d) Asteraceae

366. Which of following is bi-coloured cultivar?

a) Splendens b) Lasbenos
c) Snow Queen d) Sonnet

367. CO_2 concentration (ppm) in greenhouse for rose growing should be

a) Upto 500 b) 4000-6000
c) 1000-3000 d) 10000-30000

368. Coals and bark are important constituents of potting media for growing

a) Rose b) Orchid
c) Tulip d) Rubber plant

369. Suitable green house covering material used in hills is

a) Glass b) Polythene
c) Fibber glass d) All of these

370. Most favourable green house structure for hilly areas is

a) Tunnel b) Quonset
c) Ground to ground d) Gable

371. Normal humidity in greenhouses should be

a) 40-50% b) 60-65%
c) 70-80% d) 80-100%

372. The optimum night temperature of chrysanthemum at bud initiation stage should be

a) 10-12ºC b) 15.5-16.5ºC
c) 13.5-15.5 ºC d) 18-20 ºC

373. Which of following is not common name of Gerbera?

a) Transvaal daisy b) Barberton daisy
c) African daisy d) French daisy

374. Gerbera belongs to the family

a) Asteraceae b) Euphorbiaceae
c) Liliaceae d) Rosaceae

375. Air drying of flowers is common in

a) Helichrysum b) Aster
c) Dahlia d) Daisy

376. Which of the following is not a double bract cultivar of bougainvillea?

a) Archana b) Mrs HC Buck
c) Cherry blossom d) None of these

377. Which of the following is variegated bract cultivar of bougainvillea?

a) Archana b) Dr BP Pal
c) Partha d) Shubhra

378. Bougainvillea is propagated by

a) Softwood cutting b) Partially mature cuttings
c) Hardwood cutting d) None of above

379. Which of the following is not a growth retardant

a) SADH b) B-Nine
c) Cycocel d) 2, 4-D

380. The first hybrid tea rose was developed by

a) BP Pal b) Guillot
c) McMillan d) Dhall

381. The source of blue pigmentation in roses are found in the cultivar

a) Blue moon b) Sonia
c) Samba d) Bhim

382. Pigment responsible for blue colour is

a) Pelargolin b) Delphilidin
c) Lycopene d) Roseline

383. Nicki is a hybrid of ______

a) Petunia b) Rose
c) Nicotiana d) Primula

384. Who gave the name Dahlia in 1791?

a) Abbe Cavanilles b) Andreas Dehl
c) Willis d) Pizetti

385. What is the scientific name of Gerbera?

a) *Gerbera viridifolia* b) *G jamesonii*
c) *G aurantiaea* d) *Dendrenthema grandiflora*

386. Common name of *Hemerocallis fulva* is

a) Torch lily b) Water lily
c) Day lily d) Tiger lily

387. Botanical name of bird of paradise is

a) *Sterlitzia reginae* b) *Sterlitzia aungusta*
c) *Sterlitzia kwensis* d) *Sterlitzia nicolai*

388. Bird of paradise is native to

a) India b) Peru
c) China d) South Africa

389. Bird of paradise belongs to family

a) Cannaceae b) Musaceae
c) Iridaceae d) None of above

390. Botanical name of China aster is

a) *Aster chinensis* b) *Callistephus chinensis*
c) *Callistephus hortensis* d) None of above

391. Basic chromosome number of China aster is

a) 10 b) 9
c) 13 d) 18

392. Stock belongs to the family

a) Scrophularaceae b) Brassicaceae
c) Leguminaceae d) None of above

393. Which of the following is known as blanket flower?

a) Limonium b) Gomphrena
c) Gaillardia d) None of these

394. Native place of Gomphrena is

a) Mexico b) India
c) China d) USA

395. Gomphrena belongs to family

a) Gaillardiaceae
b) Amaranthaceae
c) Solanaceae
d) Compositae

396. Solidago is also known as

a) Amaranths
b) Blanket Flower
c) Golden Rod
d) Stock

397. Native place of solidago is

a) India
b) China
c) America
d) Japan

398. Pin and thrum type of flowers are found in

a) Petunia
b) Primula
c) Cyclamen
d) Gompherina

399. Which of the following is not a true species of bougainvillea?

a) *Peruviana*
b) *Buttiana*
c) *Speciabilis*
d) None of these

400. Designing and beautification of a place with definite use of plant to serve certain aesthetic or utility purpose is known as

a) Landscape
b) Landscaping
c) Garden
d) All of above

401. Representation of the structure of any surface is known as

a) Texture
b) Canopy
c) Design
d) Floriculture

402. Which of the following is not an element of landscaping?

a) Line
b) Texture
c) Canopy
d) Rhythm

403. Rhythm in a garden is created through

a) Repetition of shapes
b) Progression of sizes
c) Continuous line movement
d) All of above

404. Which of following have drooping growth habit?

a) *Salix babylonica* b) Bottle brush
c) *Pinus peptula* d) All of these

405. Area of the home which is viewable from the street is known as _____ area.

a) Public b) Front
c) Approach d) All of these

406. Part of home landscape which provide room for necessities is known as ___ area.

a) Service b) Family
c) Approach d) All of above

407. Mobility in garden is created by use of ______

a) Different size b) Evergreen trees
c) Deciduous trees d) Evergreen shrubs

408. Shrubbery borders in home garden are kept around ______%

a) 10-15 b) 20-30
c) 15-20 d) 30-40

409. Accent draws attention of human being through ______

a) Colour b) Shape
c) Texture d) All of these

410. Which of the following is not a part of texture?

a) Fine b) Large
c) Medium d) Coarse

411. Selection of garden style depends upon its

a) Topography b) Location
c) Space d) All of these

412. Largest importer of houseplants is

a) India b) Italy
c) USA d) Germany

413. Optimum water holding capacity of potting medium should be

a) 50-60% b) 40-50%
c) 60-70% d) 20-30%

414. Poor aeration in potting medium is due to

a) Compactation b) Inadequate pore space
c) Over watering d) All of above

415. Which of the following type of containers are cheapest?

a) Earthern b) Concrete
c) Plastic d) Copper

416. For growing cacti, which type of pots is preferred?

a) Earthern b) Copper
c) Concrete d) Plastic

417. Corts are commonly used to multiply

a) Ivy b) Araucaria
c) Chlorophytum d) Maranta

418. Came baskets are suitable for growing ________

a) Ferns b) Orchids
c) Succulents d) Begonias

419. Which of the following is most suitable to dark corner of the house?

a) Aspidistra b) Acalypha
c) Hoya d) Marinate

420. Plants suitable for growing in sunny areas require ______ hours light in winter.

a) 1-2 b) More than 5
c) 2-3 d) Upto 5

421. Optimum temperature during day for house plants should be ______ ºC.

a) 15-20 b) 20-30
c) 10-15 d) 0-2

422. Optimum soil temperature of potting medium should be ______ °C

a) 10-15 b) 20-25
c) 18-21 d) 15-25

423. Optimum relative humidity in room growing house plants should be

a) 30-40% b) 50-60%
c) 70-80% d) 100%

424. Application of fertilizer along with watering is known as ______

a) Fertilizer application b) Liquid fertilization
c) Fertigation d) None of above

425. Which is not commonly propagated by seed?

a) Araucaria b) *Aralia*
c) Dracaena d) Palm

426. Tip cutting having 1-2 nodes is very common in ______

a) Coleus b) Aglaonema
c) Dracaina d) All of above

427. Leaf lamina cutting is very common in ______

a) Rex begonia b) Peperonia
c) Ivy d) Coleus

428. Cane cutting is very common in ______

a) Dieffenbachia b) Araucaria
c) Both a and b d) Philodendron

429. Air layering is not common in ______

a) Dracaena b) Crotion
c) Begonia d) Aglaonema

430. Saddle grafting is very common in

a) Hydrangea b) Rhododendron
c) Rosewood d) Bougainvillea

431. Mound layering is common in

a) Hydrangea b) Cestrum
c) Agave d) Cactus

432. Which of the following is a common rooting hormone

a) IBA
b) NAA
c) IAA
d) GA

433. Offsets are commonly used to propagate

a) Agave
b) Aloe
c) Pandanus
d) All of these

434. Treatment of cut flowers with high concentration of sugar is known as

a) Pulsing
b) Hardening
c) Loading
d) a & b

435. Optimum pH of holding solution should be

a) 7-10
b) 4-5
c) 6-7
d) 2-3

436. Name the flower which is less ethylene sensitive

a) Gerbera
b) Snapdragon
c) Orchids
d) Carnation

437. Which of following is most important ethylene inhibitor?

a) Silver thiosulphate
b) Sugar
c) Citric acid
d) Nickel chloride

438. The most commonly used germicide is

a) Salt of Hydroxy quinoline
b) Silver nitrate
c) Aluminium sulphate
d) Silver thiosulphate

439. Which of the following is not ethylene inhibitor?

a) AVG
b) MVC
c) NAA
d) AOA

440. The strongest senescence stimulators is

a) ABA
b) BA
c) PBA
d) AOA

441. Which of following is used as a wetting agent?

a) Tween 20 b) Soap
c) Washing powder d) None of these

442. Impregnation of cut flower is very common in ______

a) Aster b) Gerbera
c) Carnation d) All of these

443. Which of following is highly ethylene sensitive pot plant?

a) Euphorbia b) Scindapsus
c) Nephrolepis d) None of these

444. Which of following is not highly sensitive to ethylene?

a) Archimedes b) Fuchsia
c) Hibiscus d) Primula

445. Which of following is less sensitive to ethylene?

a) Chrysanthemum b) Kalanchoe
c) Begonia d) All of these

446. Flower highly sensitive to chilling injury is

a) Tulip b) Anthurium
c) Freesia d) Lily

447. Name the flower less sensitive to chilling injury

a) Rose b) Cattleya
c) Poinsettia d) Bird of paradise

448. Optimum light in cold storage is ______ Lux.

a) 2000-5000 b) 100-200
c) 500-1000 d) 1000-15000

449. In home, which of following is used to increase vase-life?

a) Sugar b) Salt
c) Glucose d) All of these

450. Bird of paradise flowers are stored at ______ °C

a) 10-15 b) 8-10
c) 1-2 d) 4-5

451. Water disinfection is done by ______

a) Sodium chloride
b) Sodium hypochloride
c) Potassium chloride
d) Tween 20

452. Which of following is not commonly used as water disinfection?

a) UV rays
b) Aluminium sulphate
c) Sodium hypochloride
d) Copper sulphate

453. Optimum dose of gamma radiation for prolonging vase life is ____ K rad.

a) 10-15
b) 1-2
c) 50-100
d) 30-40

454. In low pressure storage (LPS), the pressure in storage room is reduced to ___ atm.

a) 1
b) 10
c) 5
d) 0.1

455. Which is not suitable for dry transportation?

a) Carnation
b) Chrysanthemum
c) Lily
d) Iris

456. Geotropic bending during transportation is common in______

a) Gladiolus
b) Snapdragon
c) Lupin
d) All of these

457. Flower stems of the following should be normally kept in boiling water for seconds.

a) Rose
b) Poinsettia
c) Lily
d) Tulip

458. 8-Hydroxy Quinoline Citrate works as preservative, it normally

a) Acidify water
b) Improve water balance
c) acts as germicide
d) All of above

459. 'Bull head' roses are produced due to ______

a) Thrips infestation
b) Hard pruning
c) Insufficient carbohydrates
d) All of these

460. Yellow rose cultivars are harvested at

a) Half open stage
b) Slightly loose stage
c) Tight bud stage
d) None of these

461. Which of following is not serious fungus in cut roses?

a) *Pythium*
b) *Botrytis*
c) *Penicillium*
d) *Alternaria*

462. Which of following accelerate senescence in cut carnation?

a) Abscissic acid
b) Ethylene
c) High temperature
d) All of above

463. Quilling of florets is common disorder in

a) Chrysanthemum
b) Carnation
c) Dahlia
d) Tulip

464. Petal burn in chrysanthemum is due to deficiency of _____

a) Copper
b) Boron
c) Calcium
d) Potassium

465. Optimum temperature for long term holding of chrysanthemum is _____ ^{o}C

a) 0-1
b) 2.5
c) 5-9
d) 10-12

466. A lip opposite to odd sepal in orchid flower is known as

a) Column
b) Labellum
c) Keel
d) None of these

467. Orchids under normal conditions can be stored up to 2 weeks at _____ ^{o}C.

a) 5-7
b) 2-5
c) 0-2
d) 10-12

468. Short days at 1-2 leaf stages in gladiolus leads to _______

a) Bud blasting
b) Blind shoot
c) Poor spike
d) Multiple spike

469. Topple disorder in gladiolus is due to deficiency of

a) Potassium
b) Calcium
c) Nitrogen
d) Boron

470. Bud blasting in Iris is caused by

a) Poor light
b) High temperature
c) Water stress
d) All of above

471. Which of the following preservative show phyto-toxicity in daffodil?

a) 8-HQC
b) STS
c) Both a and b
d) Citric acid

472. Epinasty in poinsettia can be controlled by

a) Sugar
b) Silver Nitrate
c) Salt
d) Ancymidol

473. Ground cover of perennial grass which persist under continuous mowing is called as

a) Turf
b) Paving
c) Lawn
d) All of above

474. Lawn can be established perfectly by

a) Plastering
b) Seed
c) Dibbling
d) All of these

475. Rolling, an important operation in lawn is done to

a) Level the ground
b) Touch nodes with ground
c) Break grass
d) All of above

476. Which of following is effective weedicide in *Zoysia* grass?

a) 2, 4-D
b) Sylvex
c) Glyphosate
d) All of above

477. Fairy ring spot is a problem in lawns might be due to

a) Fungus
b) Bacteria
c) Nutrient deficiency
d) Both a and c

478. Which of the following is highly cold tolerant?

a) Rough blue
b) Zoysia
c) Creeping bent
d) All of these

479. Which of the following is least heat tolerant?

a) Rough blue
b) Carpet
c) Zoysia
d) Creeping bent

480. Which of the following is highly tolerant to salinity?

a) Creeping bent
b) Rough blue
c) Carpet
d) Red top

481. Which type of grass has the fastest establishing rate?

a) Kentucky blue
b) Manilla grass
c) Both a and b
d) Bermuda

482. Which of following grasses has medium establishment rate?

a) Creeping bent
b) Red fescue
c) Bahia
d) All of these

483. *Amhersita nobilis* a flowering tree has ________ flowers.

a) Yellow
b) Red
c) White
d) Violet

484. *Ailanthus excelsa* is native to.

a) China
b) India
c) Africa
d) Iran

485. *Peltophorum ferrugenium* a flowering tree has _____ flowers.

a) Pink
b) Red
c) Yellow
d) White

486. *Delonix regia* is commonly known as

a) Gulmohar
b) Yellow Gulmohar
c) Lal Gulmohar
d) None of these

487. Which of the following has beautiful fruits?

a) *Kigellia*
b) *Delonix*
c) Gulmohar
d) *Bauhinia*

488. *Azadirachata indica* belongs to the family

a) Meliaceae
b) Caselpiniaceae
c) Sapindaceae
d) None of above

489. Which of following yield nectar?

a) Bottle brush
b) Neem
c) Horse chestnut
d) All of above

490. Which of following have drooping branches?

a) *Salix bodylonica*
b) Bottle brush
c) *Australian acacia*
d) All of above

491. Which of following is suitable for planting alongside of canals?

a) Bottle brush
b) Jacaranda
c) Silver oak
d) All of above

492. Which of following has beautiful trunk?

a) *Chorisia*
b) *Araucaria*
c) *Bauhinia*
d) *Acacia*

493. Which of following has fragrant flowers?

a) Devil's tree
b) Michelia
c) Magnolia
d) All of above

494. Which of following tree have blotched bark?

a) Pride of India
b) Platanus
c) Eucalyptus
d) All of above

495. Which of following tree has bark with prickles?

a) *Erythrina*
b) *Bombax*
c) *Chorisia*
d) All of above

496. Botanical name of coral tree is

a) *Erythrina indica*
b) *Erythrina suberosa*
c) *Erythrina cristagalli*
d) None of these

497. Which of the following tree is associated with Sita in Ramayana?

a) *Polyalthia longifolia*
b) *Salix spp*
c) *Cedrus deodara*
d) *Saraca indica*

498. Which of the following flower during November?

a) *Bauhinia variegata*
b) *Bauhinia purpurea*
c) *Bauhinia vahli*
d) None of above

499. Which of the following has white flower?

a) *Dillenia indica*
b) *Bauhinia purpurea*
c) *Tecomella undulata*
d) *Ceiba pentandra*

500. Which of the following is most suitable flowering tree for high hills?

a) *Cedrus deodara*
b) *Rhododendron arborerum*
c) *Tecomella undulata*
d) *Ceiba pentandra*

501. Which of following tree is/are grown for cut foliages?

a) Podocarpus
b) Cupressus
c) Thuja
d) All of these

502. To check air pollution the planted foliage should be

a) Fine
b) Thick and shining
c) Glabrous
d) Pubescent

503. Which of following is suitable for alkaline and saline soils?

a) *Casuarina equisetifolia*
b) *Pinus roxburghii*
c) *Salix babylonica*
d) *Grevillea robusta*

504. *Ficus* species grown for religious purpose is

a) *Infectoria*
b) *Retusa*
c) *Religiosa*
d) *Benghalensis*

505. Which of following is a quick growing tree?

a) Eucalyptus hybrid
b) *Ficus benjamina*
c) *Erythrina suberosa*d)
Parkinsonia aculeata

506. Which of following is used as climber, shrub as well as pot plant?

a) Silver oak
b) Bougainvillea
c) Begonia
d) All of these

507. Which of the following climb by means of tendrils?

a) *Jasminum grandiflorum*
b) *Ficus repens*
c) *Ipomoea sp*
d) *Antigonon leptopus*

508. Which of following is a rambler?

a) *Jasminum grandiflora*
b) *Antigonon leptopus*
c) *Quisqualis indica*
d) *Pyrostegia venusta*

509. Which of the following *Tecoma* species is not a climber?

a) *Grandiflora*
b) *Stans*
c) *Capensis*
d) *Jasminoides*

510. Which of following species of *Jasminum* is not a climber?

a) *Grandiflorum*
b) *Dispermum*
c) *Humile*
d) *Officinale*

511. Which of following has coarse texture foliage?

a) *Tecoma grandiflora*
b) *Pyrostegia venusta*
c) *Quisqualis indica*
d) *Thumbergia grandiflora*

512. Name any climber which is commonly used as hedge.

a) *Clitoria ternatea*
b) *Clerodendron splendens*
c) *Clemata paniculata*
d) *Ipomoea sp*

513. Which of following is a foliage climber?

a) *Monstera deliciosa*
b) *Hedera helix*
c) *Scindapsus aureus*
d) All of these

514. Which of following has fragrant flowers?

a) *Lonicera japonica*
b) *Tecoma grandiflora*
c) *Jasminum dispermum*
d) All of above

515. Which of following has Watch shaped flower?

a) *Passiflora caerulea*
b) *Aristolochia elegans*
c) *Ipomoea purpurea*
d) *Tecoma grandiflora*

516. Which of following is not a member of family Bignoniaceae?

a) *Pyrostegia venusta*
b) *Tecoma grandiflora*
c) *Bignona unguiscati*
d) *Begonia sempervirens*

517. *Hiptage benghalensis* belongs to the family

a) Hiptageaceae
b) Malphigiaceae
c) Saxifragaceae
d) Moraceae

518. Which of following has beautiful fruits?

a) *Pyrostegia venusta* b) *Tecoma jasminoides*
c) *Smilax aspera* d) *Lonicera japonica*

519. Which of the following has duck shaped flowers?

a) *Aristolochia elegans* b) *Bignonia unguiscate*
c) *Bauhinia spp* d) *Beaumontia grandiflora*

520. Which of following has orange coloured flowers?

a) *Jasminum grandiflorum* b) *Beaumon sterlitzia*
c) *Bignonia unguiscun* d) *Pyrostegia venusta*

521. Which of following produces white coloured flowers?

a) *Clematis paniculata* b) *Jasminum grandiflorum*
c) *Beaumontia grandiflora* d) All of above

522. Which of following is used for screening walls?

a) *Pyrostegia venusta* b) *Lonicera japonica*
c) *Ficus repens* d) All of above

523. Which of following Ipomoea species is known as Railway creeper?

a) *Alba* b) *Purpurea*
c) *Tuberosa* d) Nore of these

524. Which of following has shining foliage?

a) *Tecoma jasminoides* b) *Thunbergia grandiflora*
c) *Lonicera japonica* d) *Pyrostegia venusta*

525. Climber suitable for pots.

a) Golden shower b) Passion flower
c) Cat's claw d) Bougainvillea

526. Which of following *Solanum* species is known as potato creeper?

a) *Wendlandii* b) *Seaforthianum*
c) *Jasminoides* d) *Tuberosum*

527. Which of the following does not belong to family Leguminosae?

a) *Derris scandens* b) *Wisteria sinensis*
c) *Clematis paniculata* d) None of these

528. Which of the following is classified as light climber?

a) *Solanum wendlandii* b) *Cobaea scandens*
c) *Petrea volubilis* d) *Thumbergia grandiflora*

529. Which of following is cool season climber?

a) *Derris scandens* b) *Quisqualis indica*
c) *Pyrostegia venusta* d) *Tecoma grandiflora*

530. Which of following has blue flower?

a) *Clitoria ternatea* b) *Ipomoea violacea*
c) *Wisteria sinensis* d) All of above

531. Which of following *Bignonia* species is known as cut's claw?

a) *Purpurea* b) *Graclis*
c) *Unguiscan* d) *Speciosa*

532. Duck flower a climber is native to

a) South America b) Brazil
c) India d) Japan

533. Which of following climb by secreting sticky substance?

a) *Clitoria temata* b) *Ficus repens*
c) *Clematis paniculata* d) None of above

534. Which of following is suitable for porches?

a) *Pyrostegia venusta* b) *Ipomoea horsfalliae*
c) *Clerodendron splendens* d) All of above

535. Which of following *Solanum* species is known as potato creeper?

a) *Wendiandii* b) *Seaforthianum*
c) *Jasminoides* d) *Tuberosum*

536. A perennial plant having distinct trunk and crown at top is known as

a) Shrub b) Tree
c) Climber d) Herb

537. A low growing woody or semi-woody perennial plant with little or no trunk having height almost 4 m is known as

a) Climber b) Shrub
c) Tree d) Herb

538. Which of the following has mild odour in flowers and foliage?

a) *Hamiltonia suaveolens* b) *Duranta repens*
c) *Acalypha hispida* d) All of above.

539. Which of the following is night blooming?

a) *Nerium oleander* b) *Hamelia patens*
c) *Nyctanthes arbortritis* d) *Acer palmatum*

540. Which coloured shrubs are grown in night garden?

a) Red b) Blue
c) White d) Yellow

541. Area of garden devoted exclusively to shrubs is known as

a) Border b) Shrubbery
c) Hedge d) None of above

542. Which of the following has bicoloured foliage?

a) Excoecuria b) Nandina
c) Gynura d) All of above

543. Which of the following has beautiful bracts?

a) Bougainvillea b) Mussandra
c) Poinsettia d) All of above

544. In double faced shrubbery tall shrubs are planted in

a) Corner b) Under tree
c) Near wall d) Centre

545. Shrubs when planted at regular interval to form a thick screen is known as

a) Edge b) Shrubbery
c) Hedge d) All of these

546. Low growing shrubs with same qualities as hedge for controlling traffic is known os

a) Edge b) Topiary
c) Shrubbery d) None of these

547. For rockeries shrubs should be________

a) Moisture loving b) Drought loving
c) Deciduous d) Any of above

548. Which of the following is good tall protective hedge?

a) Popular ciliata b) *Cuphea milvillea*
c) *Acacia farnensiana* d) All of above

549. Which of the following is not good dwarf protective hedge?

a) *Agave americana* b) *Jasminum humile*
c) *Euphorbia tetragoria* d) All of above

550. Which is planted as tall ornamental hedge?

a) *Polyalthia longifolia* b) *Putranjiva roxburghii*
c) *Thuja orientalis* d) All of above

551. Formal edging is made off with which one of the following.

a) Tiles b) Bricks
c) Stones d) All of above

552. Informal edging is made from

a) Stones b) Plants
c) Concrete d) All of above

553. Art of training plants into shapes of different statues, birds or animals is known as

a) Edge b) Hedge
c) Topiary d) None of above

554. For making topiary plants should be

a) Quick growing b) Dense branching
c) Small foliage d) All of above

555. Which of the following is used for making topiary?

a) *Thuja orientalis* b) *Cuperssus torulosa*
c) *Clerodendron inerme* d) All of above

556. Which of following is a popular pot plant in international market?

a) Ixora b) Poinsettia
c) Crossandra d) Hibiscus

557. Cycads belong to the family

a) Cycadaceae b) Cupressaseae
c) Conifereae d) Palmaceae

558. Which is grown for cut greens?

a) *Breynia nivosa* b) Bongainvillea
c) *Lantana depressa* d) *Vinca rosea*

559. Which of following has red flowers?

a) *Punica granatum* b) *Lagerstroemia indica*
c) *Acucuba japonica* d) All of above

560. Which of following has dark green branches and red flowers?

a) *Hibiscus rosasinensis* b) *Malvabiscus arboreus*
c) Russelia juncea d) All of these

561. Which of following is not a member of Malvaceae?

a) *Hibiscus syriacus* b) *Malvabiscus arboreus*
c) *Dombeya spectabilis* d) All of above.

562. Which of following is native to India?

a) *Russelia juncea* b) *Hibiscus mutabilis*
c) *Cassia glanca* d) *Hamelia patens*

563. Which of following has black fruits?

a) *Pentas lanceolata* b) *Ochna jabotapita*
c) *Nerium oleander* d) *Punica granatum*

564. Botanical name of Din-ka-raja is

a) *Cestrum diurnum* b) *Cestrum pargui*
c) *Cestrum nocturnum* d) None of these

565. Palms belong to family

a) Palmeae b) Palmaceae
c) Palmideae d) None of these

566. *Hydrangea macrophylla* produces blue flowers in which soil

a) Neutral b) Acidic
c) Alkaline d) All of above

567. *Hydrangea macrophylla* produces pink/red flowers in which soils

a) Acidic b) Neutral
c) Alkaline d) All of these

568. Which is not a cool flowering shrub?

a) *Barleria cristata* b) *Plumbago rosea*
c) *Cassia alata* d) All of above

569. Which of following has not yellow flowers?

a) *Bauhinia tomentosa* b) *Pentas lanceolata*
c) *Ochna squarrosa* d) All of these

570. Botanical name of China shoe flower is

a) *Hibiscus mutabilis* b) *Hibiscus syriacus*
c) *Hibiscus rosa sinensis* d) *Malvabiscus arborcus*

571. Din ka raja is a local name of

a) *Cestrum diurnum* b) *Cestrum parqui*
c) *Cestrum nocturnum* d) None of above

572. How many genera are included a palm group?

a) 100 b) 500
c) 150 d) 50

573. Botanical name of China shoe flower is

a) *Hibiscus syriacus* b) *Malva biscus arborcus*
c) *Hibiscus rosa sinensis* d) *Hibiscus mutabilis*

574. Which of following is not a feather leaved palm.

a) Areca b) Caryota
c) Phoenix d) Livistonia

575. Which is a fan-leaved palm?

a) *Rhapis excelsa*
b) *Livistonia chinensis*
c) *Thrinas argentea*
d) All of above

576. Which of the following plant has beautiful trunk?

a) Rhapis
b) Roystonea
c) Zamia
d) Cyeas

577. Most of palms are propagated by

a) Seed
b) Suckers
c) Cutting
d) Layering

578. The conventional method of propagation in tuberose is

a) Radial cutting of bulbs
b) Seeds
c) Callus of scale stem
d) Bulbs

579. Which of the following statement is incorrect?

a) Banjaran – 1969
b) Raktagandha – 1975
c) Rose sherbet – 1962
d) Swati – 1960

580. Dr Homi Bhabha, a rose cultivar belongs to class

a) Hybrid teas
b) Floribunda
c) Miniatures
d) Climbers

581. Chrysanthemum cultivars Apsara, Birbal Sahni, Jayanti and Kundan were developed at

a) IARI
b) NBRI
c) IIHR
d) TNAU

582. 'No Pinch No Stake' relates to

a) Chrysanthemum
b) Rose
c) Carnation
d) Lotus

583. Rakhee is an open pollinated seedling of

a) Flirt
b) Lord Doonex
c) Indira
d) Red Gold

584. Red Gold, a hybrid of gladiolus is cross between

a) Flirt × Valentine
b) Indira × Rakhee
c) Flirt × Rakhee
d) Indira × Valentine

585. Apsara, Meera, Nazrana, Poonam, Sapna and Shoba are cultivars of

a) Lotus
b) Gladiolus
c) Carnation
d) Tuberose

586. Apsara is a cross between

a) Green wood pecker × Friendship
b) GPI × Friendship
c) Shoba × Sapna
d) Black Jack × Friendship

587. Shoba is a mutant of

a) Sapna
b) Wild Rose
c) Poonam
d) Meera

588. Meera is a cross between

a) GPI × Friendship
b) Poonam × Sapna
c) Shoba × Wild Rose
d) Sapna × Shoba

589. Mirage, a small flower variety of gladiolus was introduced from

a) USA
b) Mexico
c) Japan
d) Germany

590. Sapna is a cross between

a) Poonam × Sapna
b) Black jack × Meera
c) Black jack × Friendship
d) Green wood packer × Frienship

591. Zakariana, Jawahar Lal Nehru, Purple wonder, Sholay, Usha and Dr HB Singh are varieties of

a) Rose
b) Tuberose
c) **Bougainvillea**
d) China aster

592. Dr HB Singh is hybrid between

a) Trinidad × Formosa
b) Formosa × Trinidad
c) Lalbagh × Red Glory
d) Sholay × Purple Wonder

593. Usha is seedling selection of

a) Red Glory
b) Lady Hope
c) Chitravati
d) Formosa

594. Jawahar Lal Nehru is a spontaneous mutant of

a) Lal Bagh
b) Trinidad
c) Red Glory
d) Lady Hope

595. Flower yield in Rose cv Queen Elizabeth can be increased by application of

a) GA (10-100 ppm)
b) GA (500 ppm)
c) GA (400 ppm)
d) Cycocel (200 ppm)

596. Chemical used for enhancing shelf-life of chrysanthemum is

a) Cycocel 50 ppm
b) 8-HQC 200 ppm
c) Both (a) & (b)
d) None of these

597. Growth regulator used to reduce plant height in carnation is

a) Etheral 1500 ppm
b) Etherel (500-1000 ppm)
c) ABA
d) NAA

598. Palm seeds are treated for quick germination with treatment called

a) Scarification
b) Water soaking
c) Mechanical treatment
d) Stratification

599. Sago palm is a species of genus *Cycas*.

a) *revoluta*
b) *rumphii*
c) *cercinalis*
d) None of these

600. Selaginella belongs to the family

a) Selaginelleae
b) Lycopodiaceae
c) Selaginellaceae
d) None of above

601. Selaginellas are commonly known as

a) Club moss
b) Lycopodium
c) Moss
d) None of above

602. Which of following is known as Royal fern?

a) *Osmunda regalis*
b) *Asplemium nidus*
c) *Pteris multifida*
d) *Polystichum aristatum*

603. Drooping cactus is

a) *Echinocereus pentalophus*
b) *Chamaecereus silvestris*
c) *Aporocactus*
d) All of above

604. *Cephalocereus albispinus* is a root stock for which of following.

a) Cleistocactus
b) Notocactus
c) Aporocactus
d) All of above

605. *Echinocactus grusonii* is commonly known as

a) Golden Barrel
b) Rainbow cactus
c) China cactus
d) Tom thumb

606. Which species of *Opuntia* is known as Bunny Ears'?

a) *Tetracantha*
b) *Tunicata*
c) *Microdosys*
d) *Mulgaris*

607. Which of following cactus grown luxuriantly in moist locations?

a) *Rhipsalis*
b) *Opuntia*
c) *Notocactus*
d) *Parodia*

608. Which of following is commonly known as 'century plant'?

a) Aloe
b) Agave
c) Echeveria
d) Lobivia

609. Which of following is known as climbing onion?

a) *Stapelia variegata*
b) *Adenium obesum*
c) *Bowiea volubilis*
d) *Gasteria hybrida*

610. Which of following is known as Slipper plant?

a) *Paphiopedilum*
b) *Pedilanthus*
c) *Pachyveria*
d) *Greenovia*

611. Which is commonly known as Song of India?

a) *Dracaena sanderiana*
b) *Dracaena fragrans*
c) *Pleomele reflexa*
d) *Pleomele reflexa vuriegata*

612. Cacti and succulents are also grouped as

a) Mesophytes
b) Xerophytes
c) Lithophytes
d) Saprophytes

613. Silver dollar is the name of *Crassula*

a) *Arborescens*
b) *Tricolor*
c) Both a and b
d) None of these

614. Botanical genus of rat tail cactus is

a) *Ariocarpus*
b) *Aporocactus*
c) *Zygocactus*
d) *Ferocactus*

615. Which of following is propagated by leaf cuttings?

a) Agave
b) Aloe
c) Kalanchoe
d) Cereus

616. Which of following is propagated by offsets.

a) Agave
b) Notocactus
c) Howonhia
d) All of above

617. Which species of *Opuntia* is known as India fig?

a) *Falcate*
b) *Ficus-indica*
c) *Rufida*
d) *Vitis*

618. Which species of Crassula is known as Silver dollar.

a) *Arborescens*
b) *Falcata*
c) *Tricolor*
d) None of above

619. Inflorescence of which grass is used as cut flower.

a) *Cynodon dactylon*
b) *Agrostis nebulosa*
c) *Ophiopogon intermedius*
d) All of above

620. Which of following medicinal plants are used as ornamental plant?

a) Anise
b) Indian dill
c) Bladderdock
d) All of above

621. Heliconia belongs to the family

a) Bromeliadaceae b) Musaceae
c) Cannaceae d) None of above

622. Palms prefers luxuriantly climate as

a) Cool-humid b) Warm-dry
c) Both a and b d) Warm-humid

623. Which of following methods are used to identify viral diseases?

a) ELISA b) DIBA
c) DAS d) All of these

624. Cultivar (s) of *Rosa damascena* developed at IHBT Palampur is/are

a) Rose Sherbet b) Damascena selection
c) Himroz d) All of these

625. Name the flower(s) suitable for air drying.

a) Helichrysum b) Statice
c) Acroclinum d) All of these

626. Which of the following is most suitable flower for press drying?

a) Gladiolus b) Rose
c) Pansy d) Helichrysum

627. Which of the following desssicant is used for flowers drying?

a) Silica gel b) Borax
c) River sand d) All of these

628. Biggest market for dry flowers is in

a) Germany b) UK
c) Japan d) USA

629. Bleaching of petals during drying is due to

a) Sand b) Silica gel
c) Borax d) Saw dust

630. Which of the following insects damage flowers seriously in greenhouse?

a) Aphids b) Thrips
c) Nematodes d) White fly

631. Nematodes can be controlled by

a) Malathion b) Phorate

c) Chlorpyriphos d) All of these

632. Which of following cultivar of chrysanthemum flowers during July August?

a) Meghdoot b) Birbal Sahni

c) Punjab Gold d) All of these

633. Name the chrysanthemum cultivar flowers during February-March.

a) Sharad Mala b) Maghi

c) Jwala d) None of these

634. Pollen sterility in roses is checked by using

a) Potassium Iodideb) Acetocarmine

c) Ethyl alcohol d) All of these

635. Which of following is not used for making garlands?

a) Orchids b) Crossandra

c) Chrysanthemum d) Marigold

636. The beauty of trees planted along water canals get enhanced due to

a) Reflection b) Refraction

c) Dispersion d) Colourful stem and leaves

637. The native place of rose is

a) England b) USA

c) India d) China

638. Hybrid 77 is a variety of

a) Japanese mint b) Lavender

c) Cetronella d) Jasmine

639. Siwalik is a variety of

a) Lemongrass b) Citronella

c) Lavender d) Japanese mint

640. Mandakani is a variety of

a) Palmarosa
b) Citronella
c) Lavender
d) Patchauli

641. Noor-Jahan is a variety of

a) *Rosa demascena*
b) *Rosa moschata*
c) *Pogostemon cablin*
d) *Pelargonium graveolens*

642. Jasmine belongs to the sub-family

a) Jasminoideae
b) Pomoideae
c) Prunoideae
d) None of these

643. Botanically, the Jasmine fruit is

a) Pome
b) Berry
c) Nut
d) Drupe

644. How many species of Jasmine are known in India?

a) 30
b) 25
c) 50
d) 42

645. CO1 Pitchi, a variety of Jasmine is released by

a) IIHR
b) TNAU
c) IARI
d) CIMAP

646. *Jasminum grandiflorum* is commonly known as

a) French Jasmine
b) Spanish Jasmine
c) Chameli
d) All of these

647. Surabhi is a highly fragrant species released at IIHR belongs to

a) Jasmine
b) Tuberose
c) Rose
d) Carnation

648. Jasmine plant starts flowering after

a) 3 years
b) 4 years
c) 2 years
d) 5 years

649. In North India, flowering period in jasmine crop is

a) October-January
b) June-September
c) November-March
d) December-March

650. Which of the following types of medium is best to plant jasmine cutting?

a) Vermiculite b) Sand
c) Clay d) Moss

651. In Egypt, jasmine is mostly propagated by

a) Layering b) Grafting
c) Cutting d) Seeds

652. Jasmine can be propagated by

a) Layering b) Stem cutting
c) Grafting d) All of these

653. Which of the following flower is universally acclaimed as "Queen of flowers"?

a) Lotus b) Rose
c) Gladiolus d) Carnation

654. Which of the following is National flower of England?

a) Rose b) Lotus
c) Chrysanthemum d) Carnation

655. Rosa species only having four petals and sepals

a) *Serica* b) *Persica*
c) *Damascena* d) *Gallica*

656. The term 'hip' in rose refers to

a) Petals b) Sepals
c) Thalamus d) Ripe fruits

657. Scented geranium needs

a) Moderate rainfall
b) Heavy rainfall
c) Hot summers
d) High humidity and moderate rainfall

658. Black spot is a serious problem in temperate areas having

a) Dull climate
b) High temperature & low rainfall
c) Low temperature & heady rainfall
d) Low temperature & low rainfall

659. Warm and humid climate is considered serious for

a) Stem blight b) Black spot
c) Rose rust d) Die back

660. Which of following is not correctly matched?

a) Die back (*Diplodia rosarum*)
b) Powdery mildew (*Sphaerotheca pannosa var Roseae*)
c) Black spot (*Diplocarpon roseae*)
d) Rose Rust (*Alternaria alternata*)

661. Which of the following is the favourable reason for occurrence of Rose rust?

a) Warm days and cool night
b) Dull cold climate of temperate region
c) Warm and humid areas
d) Improper pruning

662. Among the following diseases, which is caused by *Alternaria alternata*?

a) Die back b) Powdery mildew
c) Black spot d) Leaf spot

663. Rose fruits are rich in

a) Ascorbic acid b) Vitamin-C
c) Vitamin-A d) Both (a) and (b)

664. Miniature roses are propagated by

a) Cutting b) Seed
c) Grafting d) Layering

665. *Nelumbo lutea* is a native of

a) Mexico b) Africa
c) America d) India

666. *Nelumbo nucifera* is synonymous to

a) *Nelumbiun nelumbo*
b) *Nymphea spp*
c) *Nelumbo lutea*
d) None of these

667. In lotus, carpel's maturing into nut like achene's are called

a) Spores
b) Spongy receptacle
c) Filaments
d) Seeds

668. Lotus is propagated by

a) Rhizome
b) Division
c) Seed
d) All of these

669. Quantity of seeds (kg per hectare) required to produce lotus seedlings

a) 5-6
b) 7-8
c) 10-12
d) 8-10

670. Lal bagh is at

a) Bangalore
b) Delhi
c) Mysore
d) Ootacamund

671. Java citronella is native to

a) Pakistan
b) Japan
c) India
d) Sri Lanka

672. Manjusha and Mandakini are clonal selection of

a) Citronella
b) Lavender
c) Jasmine
d) Palmarosa

673. Citronella is vegetatively propagated by

a) Cutting
b) Grafting
c) Clumps
d) Mound layering

674. Citronella is a

a) Diploid
b) Tetraploid
c) Hexaploid
d) Aneuploid

675. In citronella, leaves are harvested __________ cm above ground.

a) 30
b) 25
c) 5
d) 15

676. The major lavender oil producing country in the world is

a) USSR
b) Bulgaria
c) India
d) Sri Lanka

677. Lavender is native to

a) USSR
b) Europe
c) Bulgaria
d) India

678. Lotus belongs to the family

a) Nymphaceae
b) Irridaceae
c) Asteraceae
d) Oleaceae

679. Orchids belong to the family

a) Oleaceae
b) Irridaceae
c) Orchidaceae
d) Nymphaceae

680. Gladiolus belongs to the family

a) Irridaceae
b) Oleaceae
c) Asteraceae
d) Araceae

681. Carnation belongs to the family

a) Oleaceae
b) Irridaceae
c) Carryophyllaceae
d) Asteraceae

682. Chrysanthemum belongs to the family

a) Irridaceae
b) Asteraceae
c) Oleaceae
d) Rosaceae

683. Jasmine belongs to the family

a) Oleaceae
b) Asteraceae
c) Irridaceae
d) Rosaceae

684. Tuberose belongs to the family

a) Irridaceae
b) Amaryllidaceae
c) Rosaceae
d) Nymphaceae

685. Amaryllis belongs to the family

a) Rosaceae
b) Asteraceae
c) Amaryllidaceae
d) Oleaceae

686. Gerbera belongs to the family

a) Oleaceae b) Asteraceae
c) Irridaceae d) Rosaceae

687. Anthurium belongs to the family

a) Araceae b) Asteraceae
c) Irridaceae d) Carryophyllaceae

688. China aster belongs to the family

a) Irridaceae b) Oleaceae
c) Araceae d) Asteraceae

689. Origin place of gladiolus is

a) South Africa b) Mexico
c) Southern France d) Columbia

690. Origin place of carnation is

a) South Africa b) Southern France
c) Asia d) China

691. Origin place of dahlia is

a) Southern France b) India
c) Mexico d) Columbia

692. Origin place of anthurium is

a) Colombia b) Mexico
c) India d) Japan

693. Origin of marigold is

a) India b) Mexico
c) China d) Japan

694. Botanically, tuberose fruit is a

a) Capsule b) Pome
c) Berry d) Aggregate

695. The name 'Tuberose' is derived from

a) Tuberosus b) Tube-rose
c) Tuberosa d) Tuber-ose

696. The 'gardener's dictionary' was written by

a) Phillip miller b) Clusius
c) Linnaeus d) None of these

697. Who among the following kept tuberose under genus *Polyanthus* and species *tuberose*

a) Miller b) Carlos Clusius
c) Palmer d) Linnaeus

698. Which of the following statement about tuberose is incorrect?

a) Gulchari-Hindi b) Rajanigandha-Bengali
c) Sugandhraja-Kannada d) Nilasampangi-Telugu

699. In Hindi, tuberose is known as

a) Rajanigandha b) Gulshabbo
c) Sukandaraji d) Nilasampangi

700. Rajat Rekha and Swarna Rekha are the cultivars of tuberose released at

a) NBRI b) IARI
c) TNAU c) IIHR

701. For a very rapid multiplication, the tuberose is propagated through

a) Bulbs b) Tissue culture
c) Division of bulb d) Seeds

702. Tuberose is mainly propagated by

a) Bulbs b) Seeds
c) Division of bulbs d) Tissue culture

703. Banjaran- a Floribunda rose was released in

a) 1965 b) 1967
c) 1969 d) 1970

704. Madhosh is a mutant of

a) Gulzar b) Kiss of fire
c) Abhisarica d) Banjaran

705. Which of the following rose cultivar has won many prizes in USA?

a) Jantar-Mantar b) Mohini
c) Banjaran d) Rose Sherbet

706. Research on floriculture started at IARI in

a) Late Sixties b) Late Seventies
c) Late Fifties d) Early Fifties

707. The author of book 'Rose in India' is

a) Dr MS Randhawa b) Dr SD Mookherji
c) Dr Homibhaba d) Dr B P Pal

708. 'Rose growing in Tropics' was written by

a) BS Bhattacharji b) Dr B P Pal
c) Dr M S Randhawa d) Dr S D Mookherji

709. 'Rose Sherbet' a variety of floribunda Rose was released in

a) 1965 b) 1962
c) 1960 d) 1975

710. Mohini, floribunda rose is a cross between

a) Akash Sundari x Granda b) Shola x Sea Pearl
c) Super Star x Granda d) Sea Pearl x Shola

711. Shubra is a bud sprout of

a) Sweta b) Mary Palmer
c) Archana d) Shubra

712. Which of the following is sensitive to geotropic bending?

a) Freesia b) Lotus
c) Carnation d) Chrysanthemum

713. Basil is name given to aromatic plants belonging to genus

a) *Ocimum* b) *Cymbopogon*
c) *Basilicum* d) *Rosemarinus*

714. Basil is pollinated by

a) Wind b) Insects
c) Housefly d) Air

715. Trishna and Jamrosa are cultivars of

a) Palmarosa b) Citronella
c) Japanese nut d) Patchouli

716. Basil thrives well under

a) Fair to high rainfall and humid condition
b) Humid conditions
c) High temperature and heavy rainfall
d) Low temp. & heavy rainfall

717. Victoria, Comet, Giant California asters and Branching asters refers to

a) Varieties of asters b) Classification of asters
c) Dwarf varieties of asters d) Tall varieties of asters

718. The word 'Dianthus' is derived from Greek word meaning

a) Devil flower b) God flower
c) Divine flower d) All of these

719. Which of the following species of Jasmine is the chief source of essential oil?

a) *J. grandiflorum* b) *J. sambac*
c) *J. humile* d) *J. auriculatum*

720. Most suitable spacing for *J auriculatum*

a) 2.5 x 2.5 meters b) 1.8 x 1.8 meter
c) 1.2 x 1.2 meters d) 3.0 x 3.0 meters

721. The term 'Phylloidy' is related with

a) Carnation b) Rose
c) Tuberose d) Jasmine

722. The best rooting hormone in jasmine is

a) IBA 4000 ppm b) GA_3
c) CA d) IBA 100 ppm

723. Fossils of roses in USA have been reported _______ million year ago.

a) 10 b) 1
c) 30 d) 100

724. Diploid chromosome number of roses is

a) 10
b) 28
c) 14
d) 20

725. Which of the Rosa species is resistant to cold?

a) *Centiflora*
b) *Rugosa*
c) *Foetida*
d) *Chinensis*

726. *Pelargonidin enthocyanidin* is present in _______ colour.

a) Blue
b) Orange – Red
c) Yellow
d) White

727. Cyandin anthocyanidin is present in ______ colour

a) Black
b) Pink
c) Bluish-Red
d) Yellowish-white

728. Inheritance of pigments is controlled by ______ gene action

a) Additive
b) Dominance
c) Epistasis
d) None of above

729. Fragrance is controlled by _________ gene.

a) Mono
b) Oligo
c) Poly
d) None of these

730. Chemical defoliatioin in roses is done by.

a) Urea
b) Copper sulphate
c) Auxin
d) GA

731. Which fragrant cultivar of roses is grown in greenhouses?

a) Kontetti
b) Cocktail
c) Jacaranda
d) All of above

732. Which is most popular variety of roses in protected cultivation in India?

a) Grand gala
b) First Red
c) Konfetti
d) All of above

733. The layout of Lalbagh was designed by

a) Sim
b) Hyder Ali
c) Sir George King
d) Akbar

734. Which of the following is botanical garden of Karnataka state?

a) Sim's park
b) Brindavan garden
c) Lal bagh
d) Rock garden

735. Lal bagh is the seat of the Directorate of Horticulture of which state of India?

a) Maharashtra
b) Karnataka
c) Kerala
d) Tamil Nadu

736. Government Botanic garden is situated in the

a) Shivalik hills
b) Nilgiri hills
c) Aravalli hills
d) Satpura hills

737. Which of the following is popularly known as 'Sikander Bagh?'

a) NBRI, Lucknow
b) Government botanic garden
c) Botanic garden, Coimbatore
d) The Indian Botanic garden, Sibpur

738. The most interesting plant popularly known as "Living Fossil tree" in Llyod botanic garden is

a) Dawn Red Wood
b) Araucaria
c) Chinar
d) Cupressus

739. Which of the following gardens is connected with dal lake?

a) Rose garden, Chandigarh
b) Shalimar garden, Kashmir
c) Mandor garden, Jodhpur
d) Botanic garden, Coimbatore

740. Diwan-e-Aam and Diwan-e-Khas are concerned with

a) Shalimar bagh
b) Roshanara park
c) Nishant bagh
d) Mandoor garden

741. The Sim's park located at Coonoor was established by

a) D.K. Sim
b) A.S. sim
c) A.K. Sim
d) J.D. Sim

742. The Sim's park was established in the year

a) 1774
b) 1874
c) 1674
d) 1974

743. The Royal botanic garden has been renamed as

a) Indian Botanic garden
b) Government botanic garden
c) Botanic garden
d) None of these

744. The Byrant Park, Kodaikanal is a centre to supply

a) Fruit plants
b) Ornamental plants
c) Nursery plant
d) Rootstocks

745. The Roshanara Park designed by Dr MS Randhawa and Prof K Mori in 1958 is at

a) Chandigarh
b) Mysore
c) Delhi
d) Dehradun

746. State which of the following pairs is incorrect

a) 1st Japanese style garden - Roshanara Park, Delhi
b) Prof K Mori - Famous Japanese landscape architect
c) The Byrant Park - Darjeeling (West Bengal)
d) The Indian Botanic garden - Sibpur (Calcutta)

747. Which of the following is correctly matched?

a) The Byrant park - Kodaikanal (Tamil Nadu)
b) Lal Bagh - Ootacamond
c) Botanic garden - Bangalore
d) Sim's Park - Coimbatore

748. In which State the Satyaji park is situated?

a) Haryana
b) Gujarat
c) Kashmir
d) Uttar Pradesh

749. Which of the following garden were not laid out by Fidai Khan?

a) Mandoor garden
b) Rose garden
c) Llyod botanic garden
d) All of these

750. The credit for developing Mughal gardens in Kashmir goes to

a) Akbar
b) Jahangir
c) Shah Jahan
d) All of these

751. Which of the following is not a Japanese style garden?

a) Nishat Bagh
b) Chasma-e-Shahi
c) Roshanara park
d) None of these

752. The Sayaji Park is named in honour of

a) Maharaja Sayaji Rao III
b) Sayaji Rao II
c) Soayaji Satya Rao
d) None of these

753. The Baroda museum situated in the 'Sayaji Park' was opened in the year

a) 1979
b) 1880
c) 1894
d) 1881

754. Raja Abhai Singh is associated with

a) Mandor garden
b) Rose garden
c) Rock garden
d) Mughal garden, Pinjore

755. Where is Queen Marry rose garden situated?

a) Paris
b) London
c) Spain
d) Chandigarh

756. Which of the following Mughal garden of Kashmir is/are correctly matched

1) Shalimar garden- Jahangir and Zafar Khan
2) Nishat bagh- Asaf Jah
3) Chasma-e-Shahi - Ali-mardan Khan
4) Achabal - Nur Jahan

a) 1 only
b) 2 & 3
c) 2, 3 & 4
d) All of these

757. The Shish Mehal, Rang Mahal and Jal Mahal are magnificent building of

a) Mandoor Garden, Jodhpur
b) Mughal garden, Pinjore
c) Rose garden, Chandigarh
d) . Sayaji Park, Baroda

758. Ornamental plants collection in the Mughal garden, Pinjore goes in the credit of

a) Fidai Khan
b) Dara Shikoh
c) Yadvindra Singh
d) Abhai Singh

759. The Indian Botanic garden sibpur was established on advice of Robert kyad, he was

a) A farmer
b) A confectioner
c) An army men
d) A scientist

760. The 1st Indian to occupy the post of superintendent of Indian Botanic garden, Sibpur.

a) Dr K Biswas
b) Dr M K Randhawa
c) Dr K L Chadha
d) Dr J N Kaul

761. Flower vase should not be kept near _____ in room.

a) Oven
b) Fan
c) Heater
d) All of these

762. Which of following is commonly used to increase vase-life?

a) Salt
b) Oil
c) Sugar
d) Glucose

763. The period for which flowers remains in presentable form is known as _____ of particular flowers.

a) Vase life
b) Shelf life
c) Display life
d) All of these

764. In vase solution, which of following acts as bactericide

a) DICA
b) DDMH
c) 8-Hydroxy quinoline
d) All of these

765. Hypobaric storage is also known as

a) Modified atmospheric storage
b) Low pressure storage
c) Controlled atmospheric storage
d) All of these

766. Preservative that shows toxicity in Daffodil.

a) 8-HQC
b) STS
c) Citric acid
d) Silver nitrate

767. Which of following flowers is/ are suitable for air drying

a) Helichrysum
b) Acraclinum
c) Statice
d) All of these

768. Which of following flowers is/ are suitable for press drying

a) Gladiolus b) Rose
c) Pansy d) All of these

769. Medium used in drying of flowers is/ are

a) Silica gel b) Borax
c) River sand d) All of these

770. In oven drying most of flowers are dried for _____ hours.

a) 10-20 b) 20-30
c) 48-72 d) 72-90

771. Terrarium is

a) Plant grown on terraces
b) Transparent race for keeping flowers
c) Solution for using in flowers
d) Pot for raising plants

772. Plant part of saffron used as spice

a) Bark b) Rhizome
c) Seed d) Flower

773. Chemical content of Safed Musali is

a) Saponins b) Morphine
c) Nicotine d) Reserpine

774. Which medicinal plant is used to cure heart disease?

a) Foxglove b) Henbane
c) Belladona d) Isabgol

775. Medicine to check high blood pressure is obtained from

a) *Cinchona spp.* b) *Rauwolfia serpentina*
c) *Digitalis purpurea* d) *All of these*

776. Medicinal plant used to reduce cholesterol content in blood

a) Guggal b) Isabgol
c) Neem d) None of these

777. Major flowers dried by freeze drying

a) Rose b) Carnation
c) Both (a) & (b) d) None of these

778. Most suitable flowers subjected to glycerin drying

a) Magnolia b) Oak
c) Eucalyptus d) All of these

779. Process of converting ice directly into water vapour

a) Sublimation b) Evaporation
c) Drying d) Dehydration

780. The best drying agent for Anemone, Aster, larkspur flowers

a) White sand b) Silica gel
c) Sand d) Borax

781. Basic steps involved in dry flower production

a) Drying b) Bleaching
c) Dying d) All the above

782. In an ideal preserving mixture to treat the foliage the glycerine and water ratio should be

a) 1 : 2 b) 2 : 2
c) 1 : 1 d) 1 : 4

783. Glycernizing is most suitable special preservation technique for

a) Eucalyptus b) Hydrangia
c) Magnolia d) All of these

784. Floral preservative used as pretreatment to improve the quality of dry flowers

a) Citric acid b) Hydrogen peroxide
c) Sodium hydroxide d) None of these

785. The optimum conditions for hypochlorite bleaching

a) Low temperature b) Low concentration
c) pH d) All of these

786. The best bleaching agent for plant foliage

a) Hydrogen Peroxide b) Sodium chlorite

c) Hypochlorite d) None of these

787. The European Economic Community standard and grades for Carnation flower are based on

a) Stem length b) Stem strength

c) Flower diameter d) Flower colour

788. Bull head in roses is caused due to

a) Insufficient carbohydrate supply to buds

b) High light intensity

c) Excessive fertilizer application

d) High humidity

789. Senescence in rose flowers is associated with

a) Blueing of red petals

b) Decreases in protein content

c) Increase in Ribonuclease activity

d) All of these

790. Exposure of carnation flowers to ethylene causes

a) Sleepiness b) Calyx splitting

c) Uneven opening of flower d) Shedding of flowers

791. Calyx splitting in carnation is a common disorder of

a) Warmer areas b) Temperate areas

c) Dry temperate areas d) None of these

792. A plant hormone having significant role in regulation of senescence in flowers

a) Gibberellic acid b) Abscissic acid

c) Cytokinin d) None of these

793. Calyx splitting & uneven opening of carnation flowers are due to

a) High temperature
b) Nutritional deficiencies
c) Sudden fluctuation in day and night temperature
d) All the above

794. The best harvest stage in tulip

a) Tight bud stage b) Paint brush stage
c) Pink bud stage d) Green bud stage

795. The optimum temperature for long term storage of cut gladiolus

a) 1.7 to 4.4°C b) below 1.0°C
c) 0°C d) 5.8°C

796. TBZ stands for

a) Thiobenzene b) Thiobendize
c) Thiobengene d) Thiobendazole

797. STS stands for

a) Sulphuric-tri-sulphide b) Sulforated-tri-sulphide
c) Silver-Tri-Sulphate d) Silver Thio-sulphate

798. QAS stands for

a) Quarterly Ammonium salt b) Quarternary Amino Salt
c) Quarternary Amino Salt d) None of these

799. HQS stands for

a) Butylated Hydroxy Quinine Sulphide
b) Hydroxy Quinoline Sulphate
c) Hydroxy Quinine Sulphate
d) Hydroxy Quinoline Sulphide

800. BHQC stands for

a) Butylated Hydroxy Quinaline Chlorine
b) Hydroxy Quinoline Chlorate
c) Hydroxy Quinoline Citrate
d) Hydroxy Quick Cis Citride

801. One kg oil is obtained from ______ rose petals

a) 10 ton
b) 10-15 tones
c) 3-4 tones
d) 0.1-10 tones

802. Pelargonidin anthocyanidin pigment is responsible for which of following colour

a) Orange-Red
b) Blue
c) Yellow
d) White

803. Which of the following methods are used to extract rose oil

a) Steam stills
b) Old fashioned field stills
c) Modern direct fire stills
d) All of these

804. Oil percentage in *Rosa damascena*

a) 0.3
b) 0.2
c) 0.03
d) 0.02

805. A treatment given to flowers after harvesting by using water to restore turgidity is

a) Loading
b) Hardening
c) Pulsing
d) Both (b) & (c)

806. Treatment of cut flowers after harvesting by using high concentration of sugar is known as

a) Hardening
b) Loading
c) Pulsing
d) Both (a) & (c)

807. Optimum pH of holding solution should be

a) 2-3
b) 6-7
c) 5-6
d) 4-5

808. Ethylene in cold storage is removed by

a) Ventilation
b) Low pressure
c) UV light
d) All of these

809. Optimum cold storage temperature for carnation storage is ______°C

a) 0-1
b) 1-2
c) 3-5
d) 10-12

810. Flower vase should not be kept near _____ in room.

a) Oven b) Fan
c) Heater d) All of these

811. Which of following is commonly used to increase vase life?

a) Salt b) Oil
c) Sugar d) Glucose

812. The period for which flowers remains in presentable form is known as _____ of particular flowers.

a) Vase life b) Shelf life
c) Display life d) All of these

813. The country having highest Rose oil production

a) Bulgaria b) Italy
c) China d) India

814. Rose oil is primarily extracted from which *Rosa species*

a) *Odorata* b) *Damascena*
c) *Indica* d) *Gallica*

815. In cryo-preservation seeds are preserved in liquid nitrogen at ______°C

a) 100 b) -96
c) -196 d) 0

816. Air drying of flowers is common in

a) Aster b) Dahlia
c) Daisy d) Helichrysum

817. In roses, blue pigmentation source is found in cultivar

a) Blue moon b) Bhim
c) Samba d) Sonia

818. Blue colour pigment is

a) Lycopene b) Delphilidin
c) Pelargolin d) Reseline

819. Lilium bulbs are stored in moist sand at a temperature of

a) 5°C b) 10°C
c) -2°C d) -5°C

820. Sweet pea is a __________ winter annual.

a) Tall b) Medium
c) Dwarf d) Climber

821. Hollyhock is a __________ winter annual.

a) Tall b) Medium
c) Dwarf d) Climber

822. Portulaca is a __________ summer annual.

a) Tall b) Medium
c) Dwarf d) All of these

823. Summer annuals are planted in month of

a) Oct.-November b) Dec.-January
c) February- March d) July-August

824. Winter annuals are planted in month of

a) November-December b) October-November
c) April-May d) July-August

825. Rainy season annuals are planted in month of

a) September-October b) December-January
c) March- April d) June- July

826. Chrysanthemum is planted in the month of

a) July-August b) November-December
c) February- March d) May-June

827. Rose is planted in the month of

a) June-July
b) End of Sept. to Oct. 1st fortnight
c) April- May
d) May-June

828. Brachycome is a ________ winter annual.

a) Tall
b) Medium
c) Dwarf
d) All of these

829. Pot plants need relative humidity (%) of

a) 60-80
b) 40-70
c) 20-40
d) 80-100

830. Most common disease of pot plant is

a) Black rust
b) Botrytis
c) Black spot
d) Die back

831. Yellowing in lawns might be due to

a) Water logging
b) Insect attack
c) Fungus attack
d) Snow-fall

832. Dahlia is a

a) Bulbous plant
b) Tuberous plant
c) Corm
d) Rhizome

833. Daffodil is a

a) Bulbous plant
b) Tuberous plant
c) Corm
d) Rhizome

834. Narcissus is a modified

a) Root
b) Stem
c) Leaf
d) Flower

835. Formal style gardens were originated in

a) Persia
b) India
c) Japan
d) England

836. Informal style gardens were originated in

a) Persia
b) India
c) Japan
d) England

837. Herbaceous border concept was originated in

a) Italy
b) India
c) Japan
d) England

838. Cottage gardens were originated in

a) Italy b) England
c) Japan d) India

839. Which of following is most suitable for hedge making?

a) *Duranta plumieri* b) *Poinsettia pulcherima*
c) *Cassia glauca* d) *Clerodendron inerme*

840. Which of following is most suitable for topiary making?

a) *Duranta plumieri* b) *Nyctanthus arbortristis*
c) *Cestrum nocturnum* d) *Clerodendron inerme*

841. Dibbling method of lawn plantation should be practiced during

a) July-August b) December-January
c) February-March d) May-June

842. Top dressing of lawn is usually done in month of

a) July b) December
c) February d) April

843. Raking in lawn is practiced for

a) Killing weeds b) Aeration
c) Mixing fertilizer d) Hoeing

844. Fairy ring disease of lawn is caused by

a) Nematodes b) Parasites
c) Fungus d) All of these

845. Roses are wintered in month of

a) April-May
b) December-January
c) End of Sept. to Oct. 1st fortnight
d) June-July

846. *Butea monosperma* produces flower in the month of

a) September-October b) February-March
c) December-January d) June-July

847. *Casssia fistula* produces __________ colour flowers.

a) Yellow b) White
c) Blue d) Red

848. *Jasminum grandiflorum* produces __________ colour flowers.

a) Yellow b) White
c) Blue d) Red

849. *Canna indica* is planted in the month of__________.

a) April-May b) February-March
c) November-December d) July-August

850. Money plant is also known as

a) *Hedera halix* b) *Irish ivy*
c) *Scindapsis aureus* d) *Ficus repens*

IMPORTANT CULTIVARS

Plant name	Cultivars
Amaranthus tricolor	**NBRI, Lucknow**: Amar Kiran, Amar Mosaic, Amar Parvarti, Amar Prithu, Amar Raktabhy, Amar Suikiran, Amar Summer King, Amar Summer Queen, Amar Tarang
Amaranthus caudatus	**NBRI, Lucknow**: Amar Shola
Bougainvillea	**Dr BP Pal, New Delhi**: Dr RR Pal, Sonnet, Spring Festival, Summer Time, Stanza. **Agri-Horticultural Society, Calcutta**:- Dr BP Pal **IARI, New Delhi**: Vishakha, Dr RR Pal, Spring Festival, Stanza. **Lalbagh-Bangalore**: Bhabha, Lalbagh, Trinidad, Thimma. **NBRI, Lucknow**: Archana, Begam Sikander, Chitra, Dr BP Pal, Los Benos Beauty Variegata, Mahtma Variegata, Many Palmer Special, Nirmal, Pallavi Parthasarthy, Shubhra, Tetra Mrs McCleans, Wazid Ali Shah. **Soundaraya Nursery, Madras**: Vericolour, Sensation, Flame. **IIHR, Bangalore**: Purple Wonder, Gopal Jaylakshmi and Mahatma Gandhi. Chitravati (1979): Lalbagh × Red glory (Hybrid) Jawahar Lal Nehru (1975): Spontaneous mutant of Lalbagh Purple Wonder: Formosa × Trinidad Sholey(1977): Seedling selection of Red Glory Usha (1977): Seedling selection of Lady Hope DR HB Singh (1977): Trinidad × Formosa (Hybrid).
Chrysanthemum	**Atma Sahay, Allahabad**: Mahatma Gandhi, Modinagar, Mr KB Srivastava, KN Modi. **Barin Gupta, Jamshedpur**: Jamshedji, Jamshedpur Glory, Pride of Jamshedpur, Red Carpet, Steel City Beauty, Sri Ganga. **Chandra Nursery, Sikkim**: Anokha, Chandra's Choice, Rang Mahal. **IIHR, Bangalore**: Chanderkant, Chandrika, Kirti, Nilima, Pankaj, Ravikiran, Yellow Gold and Yellow Star. **Indira** (1980): Hybrid between open pollinated seedlings of Lord Doonex and a hybrid seedling of Flirt × Valentine **Rakhee** (1980): open pollinated seeding of cv Lord Doonex **Red Gold**: Flirt × Valentine **NBRI, LUCKNOW** **Large Flowered Mutant**: Aruna, Asha, Basant, Kanak, Kum Kum, Nirbhaya, Pingal, Pitaka, Pitamber, Rohit, Shefali, Shukla, Shweta, Swarnim, Tamra and Taruni. **Small Flowered Induced Mutant**: Agnishikha, Alankar, Anamika, Basanti, Hemanti, Lohit, Manbhavan, Sharad Har, Sheela, Sonali, Subarna, Surekha Yellow. **Mutant with change in form**: Ashankit, Cosmonaut, Jhalar, Kunchit, Shabnam, Tulika. **Pompon type**: Apsara, Birbal Sahni, Jayanti, Jubilee, Kundan. **No pinch No stake type**: Appu, Apurva, Arun Kumar, Arun Singar, Guldasta, Haldi Ghati, Hemant Singar, Shard Singar, and Suhag Singar. **Off-season blooming cultivars**: Ajaya, Himanshu, Haldi Ghati, Jaya, Jwala, Jyoti, Maghi, Meghdoot, Phuhar, Sarada, SardMala, Sarad Singar, Tushar, Usha, Vasantika. **PAU, Ludhiana**: Basanti, Gul-e-Shair, Punjab Gold, Shanti. **TNAU, Coimbatore**: MDU-1 Chrysanthemum, CO-1, CO-2.

contd.

	Large flowered varieties: Sonar Bangla, Redwest field, Cresta, City beauty, Day Dream, Peach Blossom, Sweet Heart, Green Sensation, Rupsi Bangla, Kirti, Chandarkant, Kasturba Gandhi. **Small flowered varieties:** Gul-a-Sahir, Birbal Shani, King Fisher, Red Star, Stella, Sharad Kumar: No staking or pinching **Off season blooming varieties:** Haldi Ghati, Himanshi, Jwala, Maghi, Meghdoot. **Export varieties:** A) Standard: Dignity, Wild Fire, Detroit News B) Spray: Parliament, Dazzler Florida, Marble C) Pot mums: Fantasy, Albert, Alpine.
Cooperanthus	**Percy Lancaster, Agri-Horticultural Society, Calcutta:** Alipore Beauty, King Emperor, Lancastrian Percy, Sunset, Sydney, The Governor, The President, The Viceroy.
China Aster	**IIHR, Bangalore:** Kamini, Poornima, AST-1, AST-2 and Sashank. **MPKV, Rahuri:** Phule Ganesh Pink, Phule Ganesh Purple, Phule Ganesh Violet, Phule Ganesh White.
Coreopsis	**IARI, New Delhi:** Pusa Tara
Croton	**IIHR, Bangalore:** Akali Phoola Singh, Arkavati, Gnat, Mohan Kumara Mangalam, Lt General Yadavindra Singh of Patiala, Pink Elegans, Pokhran, Sanjay, Shaheed Bhagat Singh, Sonar Bangla, Valmiki, Vijavantha, Vikrant.
Dahlia	**IARI, New Delhi:** Kenya Blue, Kenya White, Kenya Yellow, Manali, Manjushri. **Swami Vinayananda:** Bhikhus Mother, Bhikhus Vivek, Jyotsana, Lord Budha, Sarada Devi, Swami Gauri Swarananda, Swami Madhavananda. **LN Singh Thakur:** Chitchor, Zail Singh **R Mitra:** Manjushri **SC Dey:** Disco, Swami Vinayananda.
Carnation	**Perpetual:** Winter Cheer, Britania, Jokar, Mr. Thomas Lawson, Day Break, Willium Sim, Lipstick, Pink Dona. **Standard or Sim:** Corleone, Empire, Dark Tempo, Regina, Gold Rush, Peterson Red, Scania Red, White Sim, red Diamond. **Malmaison:** Princess of Wales, Mr Martin Smith **Royal:** Royal Fancy, White Perfection **Modern:** Pico
Gladiolus	**IARI, New Delhi:** Agnirekha, Anjali, Archana, Bindiya, Chandani, Chirag, Dhanvantari, Mayur, Neelam, Neelkanth, Noopur, Pusa Suhagin, Sanjeevni, Sarang, Shweta, Suchitra, Sunayana, Vandana. **NBRI, Lucknow:** Archana, Arun, Basant Bahar, Hans, Indrani, Jwala, Kajal, Kalima, Kohra, Manhar, Manisha, Manmohan, Manohar, Monaka, Mohini, Mridula, Mukta, Priyadarshini, Tabassum, Rim Jhim, Sada Bahar, Sanyukta, Sumita, Triloki, Usha. **Lt Gov Shri Bajrang Bahadur Singh Bhadari, Himachal Pradesh:** Bhadri Blue Beauty, Bhadri Bright Red, Bhadri Fortune, Bhadri Lemon Queen, Bhadri Little White, Bhadri Pearl, Bhadri Purple Queen, Bhadri Rose Glory, Bhadri's Simla Sunset, Bhadri Tricolour, Bhadri Yellow Beauty, May Blossom, Raj Niwas Pride, Rose of Heaven, Sakir Hussain. **IHBT (CSIR), Palampur, Himachal Pradesh:** Anurag, Brick Beauty, Palampur Queen, Palampur Princess, Tushar Mauli. **IIHR, Bangalore:** Aarti (1981): Shiley × Melody, Apsara (1981): Black jack × Friendship

contd.

	Poonam (1979) – Gelliber Herald × RN 121 Sapna (1979) - Green Woodpecker × Friendship Shoba (1981) - Mutant of wild rose ***Gladiolus* (IARI-New Delhi):** Agni Rekha, Mayur, Suchitra, Apple Blossom, Melody and Sylvia. Aarti, Darshan, Dhiraj (Resistant to Fusarium), KumKum, Meera, Nazrana, Poonam, Sagar, Shakti, Sindhoor, Jwala, Gazal, Priyadarshani, Melody, Suchitra, Friendship (2n=60), Prabha, Oscar, Hunting Song, Her Majesty, Blue sky, Agni Rekha. **Mutant varieties:** Shobha, Pusa Swasini- mutant of wildrose variety **Export varieties:** Cartago, Priscilla, American Beauty, Mayur.
Hibiscus	**IIHR, Bangalore:** Aikta, Anuradha, Arunodaya, Ashirwad, Basant, Benazeer, Bharat Sundari, Chitralekha, Geetanjali, Jogan, Nartaki, Nazneen, Neelofer, Parkeejah, Phulkari, Priya, Queen of Hesarghatta, Ratna, Red Gold, Red Saturn, Shanti, Smt Indira Gandhi, Smt Kamla Nehru, Tribal Queen. **Lalbagh, Bangalore:** Bangalore-22. **NBRI, Lucknow:** Anjali. **TNAU, Combatore:** Punnagai, Thilagum
Hippeastrum	**IARI, New Delhi:** Suryakiran**BCKV, Nadia, West Bengal:** Anjali **NBRI, Lucknow:** Apollo, Apurb, Charm, Charon, Chitwan, Coquette, Deepali, Diana, Emperor, Garima, Goergeous, Hannibal, Jyoti, Kiran, Lady Lancaster, Man Bhavan, Man Mayur, Minerva, Nizam, Percy Lancaster, Phoenix, Poonam, Raktamanjari (Mutant), Samrat, Saturn, Snow White, Sydney
Hollyhock	**IARI, New Delhi:** Deepika, Dulhan, Gouri, Pusa Gulabi, Pusa Krishna, Pusa Lalima, Pusa Pastel Pink, Pusa Pink Beauty, Pusa Yellow Beauty, Pusa Sweta
Jasmines	*Jasminum auriculatum*: CO 1, CO-2, Parimullai, Large Round, Large Point, Short Point, Medium Point, Long Round. *Jasminum grandiflorum*: CO 1 Pichi, CO 2 Pitchi, Arka Surabhi *Jasminum sambac*: Adukkaumalli, Irubachi, Gungumali, Ramabanam, Virupakshi, Motia, Single Mogra, Double Mogra, Mohra, Sujimalli, Madanbari, Arka Aradhana.
Marigold	**IARI, New Delhi:** Pusa Basanti Gainda, Pusa Narangi Gainda, Pusa Sankar-I. **TNAU Coimbatore:** MDU-1 Marigold **African marigold:** Alaska, Giant Sunset, Golden Age, Honey Comb, Cracker jack, Climax, Golden Age, Crown of Gold, Chrysanthemum Charm, Star Gold, Pusa Narangi Gainda, Pusa Basanti Gainda, Snowbird, Texas, Yellow Climax and Yellow Fluffy. **F_1 hybrids:** Apollo, Climax, First Lady, Moon Light, Orange Lady. **French marigold:** Melody, Orange Flame, Primrose Climax, Rusty Red, Spun Gold, Tangerine Yellow, Butter Scotch, Valencia.
Portulaca	**NBRI, Lucknow:** Jhumka, Lalita, Mukta, atnam, Vibhuti.
Roses	**IARI, New Delhi:** Abhisarika (1975), Anurag (1980), Arjun, Bhim, Chitwan, Dr BP Pal, Gang, Jawahar, Mother Teressa, Mridula, Mrinalini, Nurjahan, Priyadarshini, Pusa Sonia, Raj Kumari, Raktagandha, Rangasala, Surabhi **(Hybrid Tea); Floribunda type:** Arunima, Chandrama, Deepshikha, Himangini, Mohini (1970), Nav

contd.

	Sadabahar, Neelambri, Prema, Sadabahar, Shabanum, Sindhoor, suchitra, Suryodaya. **Miniature**: Delhi Scarlet (1963). **Polyantha:** Swati (1974). **NBRI, Lucknow:** Light Pink Prize, Mrinalini Stripe, Pink Montezuma, Summer Holiday Mutant, Winter Holiday Mutant **(Hybrid Tea)**. **Floribunda type**: Angara, Curio, Pink Contempo, Pink Imperator, Sharada, Sukumari, Twinkle, Yellow Contempo, Zorina Pink **(Miniature)**. **Dr B P Pal:** Akash Sundari, Apsara, Aravali Princess, Ashirwad, Dilruba, Dr Homi Bhabha, Dr MS Randhawa, Dr RR Pal, Hasina, Indian Princess, Kanakangi, Lalima, Lal Makhmal, Mehak, Maharani, Nayika, Nishada, Pahadi Dhun, Poornima, Raat ki Rani, Raja Surendra Singh of Nalagarh, Rajhans, Ranjana, Sandeepani, Surkhab and Uma Rao **(Hybrid Tea)**; Akash Nartaki, Banjaran, Chitchor, Delhi Brightness, Delhi Princess, Deepak, Jantar Mantar, Madhura, Paharan, Parwana, Rangini, Rupali, Suryakiran, **(Floribunda type)**. **MN Hardikar:** Cynosure, First Rose Convention, Flying Tata. **YK Hande**: Ajanta Caves, Gauri, Good Morning, Indian Pearl, Perfumer, Pink Wave. **MS Viraraghavan**: Kanchi, Nefertiti, Priyatama, Rajni, Tamrabarani, Vamsadhara **(Hybrid Tea)**, Amarpali, Bhagmati, First Offering, Mahadev, Vanamali **(Floribunda)**; Kanyakumari **(Climber type)**. **Raja Surendra Singh of Nalagarh:** Ghajal, Nazar-e-Nazar, Yamini Krishnamurthy **(Hybrid Tea)**; Gopika **(Floribunda)**. **Braham Dutt:** Don Nielson, Gond Beauty, Indian Festival, KK Thakur, Price of Nagpur, Soft Touch **(Hybrid Tea)**. **Rose cultivars developed by nurserymen in India:** **BK Roychowdhary:** Bagha Jatin, Dr P Banerjee, Dr S D Mukherjee and Muzibar. **BS Bhattacharji**: Kalima, President Radhakrishnan, Raja Ram Mohan Roy, Ramkrishna Dev, Sugandha **(Hybrid Tea)**; Jai Hind, Menaka, Mukttadhara, Pandit Nehru, Peetmanjari, Sir Jagdish Bose, Urbashi **(Floribunda)**; Rishi Bankim, Tarapunja **(Poliantha)**. **JP Agarwal:** Kasturi Rangan **(Hybrid Tea)**; City of Lucknow **(Floribunda)**. **PL Arun**: Divine Light, Golden Days, Mahak **(Floribunda)**; Dark Beauty **(Miniature)**; Tata Centenary **(TELCO Nursery)**; Pioneering Pilot, Suvarnarekha **(TISCO Nursery)**.
Tuberose	**IIHR, Bangalore:** Shringar (Single), Suvasini (Double); **NBRI, Lucknow:** Rajat Rekha (Single), Swarna Rekha (Double)
Lotus	Alba Striata, Alba White, Angel Wings, Perry Superstar, Alba Grandiflora, Shiroman, Baby Doll, Ben Gibson. *Nelumbo lutea:* Yellow Bird, Carolina Queen, Patricia Garrett, Flavescens.Hybrid cultivars: Embolene, Alexander the Great, Big Ben, Bonnie Clyde.
Orchids	**IIHR, Bangalore:** IIHR-164 (Vanda group), IIHR-38 (Dendrobium group). **Scorpion orchids**: Maggie Oei Yellow, Catherine, Ishbel. **Renanthera**: Brokkie Chandler, Kilauea, Poipu, Tom Thumb. **Sympodial Cattelya**: Bow Bells, Diane Salo, Empress Bells, Estelle.Dendrobium: Sonia-17, Sonia-28, Earsakul, Kasem Gold, Snow White, Jurie Red, Tongchai Blue.

Rose cultivars developed at IARI New Delhi

Hybrid Teas	Abhisarika (1975) - Mutant of Kiss of fire
	Anurag (1980) - Hybrid seedling of Sweet Afton × Gulzar
	Arjun (1980) - Blithe Spirit × Montezuma
	Bhim (1970) - Charles Mallerin × Delhi Princess
	Chitwan (1971) - Western Sun × Golden Splendour
	Ganga (1970) - A seedling of Sabina
	Jawahar (1980) - Sweet Afton × Delhi Princess
	Mridula (1975) - Queen Elizabeth × Sir Henry Segrave
	Mrinalini (1972) - Pink Perfact × Christian DiorNur
	Jahan (1980) - Sweet Afton × Crimson gloryPusa
	Sonia (1968) - A seedling of MC grey yellow
	Raj Kumari (1969)- Charles Mallerin × Delhi Princess
	Raktagandha (1975)- Christian Dior × Seedling of Carrousel
	Surabhi (1975) - Oklahoma × Delhi Princess
	Vasant (1980) - Sweet Afton × Delhi Princess
Floribunda	Arunira (1976) - A seedling of Frolic
	Chandrama (1980) - A hybrid seedling white bouquet × Virgo
	Himangini (1968) - A seedling of Saratoga
	Mohini (1970) - A hybrid seedling of Sea Pearl × Shola
	Nav Sadabahar - Mutant of Sadabahar
	Neelambari - Blue Moon × African Star
	Preema - A hybrid seedling of Sea Pearl × Shola
	Sada bahar (1975)- A seedling of Baby Sylvia
	Sindoor (1980) - Sea Pearl × Suryodaya
	Suchitra (1972) - A hybrid seedling of Lady Frost × Swati
Polyantha	Swati (1968) - A seedling of Winifred Coulter

HINTS FOR SELF-CONFIDENCE

- Harmony is the principle of landscaping.
- Texture is an important element of landscaping.
- Blue is a primary colour.
- Green in a secondary colour.
- Garden furniture is a tangible item.
- Sound of waterfall is a intangible item.
- Pinjore garden was developed by Fadai Khan.
- Roshnara park is of Japanese style.
- Pilkhan is suitable for bonsai.
- *Delonix regia* is a flowering tree.
- Ikebana is a Japanese style flower arrangement.
- Sweet pea is a climbing annual.
- Acalypha is a foliage shrub.
- Gardenia is a flowering shrub
- *Lonicera japonica* is a climber.
- *Agrostis palustris* is a lawn grass.
- Marigold is used for making garlands.
- Veni is made from Jasmine flowers.
- Gladiolus flowers are used for making bouquets.
- Ikebana is an oriental flower arrangement.
- The book 'Ornamental Horticulture' is written by Vishnu Swarup.
- The book 'Planting Design' is written by Brian Hackett.
- The book 'Flower Trees' is written by MS Randhawa.
- Form is an element of landscaping.
- Balance is a principle of landscaping.
- *Lawsonia innermis* is used for edge.
- Cupressus is suitable for topiary.
- Blue colour is due to Delphidin.
- *Haemanthus multiflorus* is called football lily.
- J W Robinson is associated with wild garden.
- Le-Notre is associated with French garden.

- International flower market is situated at Alsmeer in the Netherlands
- HQ of International cut flowers grower association: USA
- HQ of International Society for Horticulture Science: Belgium
- International Registration authority for Rose : USA
- International Registration Authority for Bouganvillia : New Delhi
- Number one foliage plant at global level : Diffenbachia
- Number one cut flower at global level: Rose
- Total area under floriculture in the world: 25 lakh hectare
- Total area under GH floriculture in the world: 60,000 hac
- Total floriculture trade in the world is 20 billion USS/ annum
- India's share in global floriculture trade : 06%
- Total area under floriculture in India : 1 lakh lac (Approximately)
- State having maximum area under floriculture in India : Karnataka
- State having max production under floriculture in India : Tamil Nadu
- In India,total area under GH : 500 hectare
- Largest importer of floriculture product from India : USA (27%)
- Share of dry flower product in India's total export : 60%
- Maximum cut flower production in India : West Bengal
- Division of ornamental crops started at IIHR in: 1989
- Division of floriculture and landscaping started at IARI in : 1983
- In AICRP on floriculture started in 1971.
- Flower crop covering maximum area in India: Jasmine
- Leading Bulbous plant producing country: Netherlands
- Leading Bulbous plant importing country: USA
- India is largest producer of loose flower in the world
- 'Hedra' – No one pot plant in global flower market
- Helichrysum – 1st rank in dried ornamental in global flower market
- Flower capital of world: California, USA
- Foliage capital of the world : Apokka, Florida, USA
- Aspargus rank 1st in cut green in global flower market
- Leading flower seed producing states (i) Punjab (50%) (ii) Haryana (iii) HP

- Area under seed production in India: 800 hectare
- Annual having maximum number of seed/ gram: Petunia and Portulaca (over 10,000)
- Annual having minimum number of seed/ gram: Sweet pea and Sunflower (15-20)
- Bold seed: Holyhock, morning glory, lupin, Nasturtium
- Stevia - 'Wonder Plant' (Sweteners of future)
- 'Beautiful garden' book is written by M S Randhawa
- 'Garden flowers' book is written by V Swarup
- 'Garden through age' book is written by MS Randhawa
- Complete gardening in India is published by Hoseli Press
- Introductory ornamental horticulture is published by Kalyani Publishers
- Hogarth course is also known as line of beauty
- Biggest formal garden : Vrindavan Garden, Mysore
- Heaven of Man – Italian Garden
- Kadam tree is associated with Lord Krishna
- Semal tree is associated with Shiva
- Bauhinia tree is associated with Sarswati
- Amaranthus tree is associated with Kali
- Yellow Amaltas tree is associated with prosperity in trade
- Ashoka, Sal and Palash tree is associated with Buddha
- Babar was 1st Mougul emperor who started gardening in India He made Aram Bagh at Agra
- Akbar : Garden in Fatehpur Sikri (Agra), Tomb Garden is Sikandara (Agra)
- Jhangir – Shalimar Garden (Kashmir), Dilkhush Garden (Lahore)
- Shah-Jhan: Chasma-a-shahi (Sri Nagar). Shalimar Garden (Lahore)
- Taj Mahal Garden (Agra): Redfort (Agra & Delhi)
- Fadai Khan : Pinjore Garden
- King Hyder Ali : Lalbagh Garden (Bangalore)
- Maharaja Ranjit Singh: Garden at Amritsar
- King Bhupinder Singh: Baradari Garden at Patiala

- Peet Kalidas mentioned plant in the play Shkuntla: Madhvi
- Noorjahan discovered otto of rose while taking bath
- Garden which is considered as genesis of gardening: Garden of Eden
- Moorish Garden were developed in Spain
- Famous French garden designer: Le Notre
- Bulgeria is largest producer of rose perfume
- Egypt is largest producer of Jasmine perfume
- France is largest produce of tuberose perfume
- France is largest producer of carnatioin perfume
- Concrete: Non purified form of essential oil obtained by solvent extraction method It contain 45-55% absolute.

❑❑❑

Section – IV

Important Terms Used in Horticulture

Abscission: The shedding of leaves, flowers or fruits as a result of formation of layer of loosely adhering cells at base that breaks apart readily.

Accent: It is created in the garden to avoid the monotonous view. Mostly unusual object like tall fountain, tree, statue etc are used to create the effect

Acre: A unit of measurement of land area equivalent to 4840 square yards or 0.4047 hactare.

Acropetal: Developing sequentially from basal to the apical position.

Acrylic: It is a glassy thermoplastic that is incorporated in rigid plastic to enhance wither ability.

Aestivation: The use of high temperature to promote flowering.

After-ripening: Physiological changes that take place within a dormant seed or bud during dormancy or It is a type of embryo maturation which enables germination of seeds.

Aging: Refers to the Processes acquiring maturity with the passage of time or Normally an increment of time, which may or may not be accompanied by physiological changes including senescence. Aging thus includes a much 'wider span' of physiological processes, which may either "weaken the organism or to be neutral".

Agmark: It is Agriculture Produce Grading & Marketing Act, 1937 & voluntary in nature.

Alcoholic fermentation: Decomposition of sugar by yeast in absence of oxygen called as an anaerobic respiration and represented by following equation:

$$C_6H_{12}O_6 + \text{Yeast} \xrightarrow{\text{Absence of } O_2} 2C_2H_5OH + CO_2$$

Amateur: A person who himself or with assistance maintains gardens and grows plants, flowers for pleasure and enjoyment and not for his livelihood.

Anabolism: Process of building of body tissues from simple raw materials supplied by the products of digestion of food.

Anaerobic respiration: An incomplete oxidation of food to release partial energy takes place in the absence of atmospheric oxygen and occurs in cytoplasm.

Analytical chemistry: Deals with detection and estimation of elements and compounds.

Androecium: It is male sex organ of plant and composed of a number of stamens. Each stamen consists of filament, anther and connective.

Andromonoecious: A sex form where staminate and hermaphrodite flowers are separately produced in the same plant.

Anemone: The ray florets are flat or twisted, may be quiled but the disc florets are prominent.

Annuals: The group of plants which live for one year or less (from seed sowing date till plants die). These plants make its vegetative growth, flowers and produces seed within one year.

Anther: The pollen producing organ of the flower.

Anthesis: The period of life of a flower from opening of bud to the setting of fruit.

Anthocyanin: A class of water-soluble pigments, including most of those imparting red or blue colour to fruit or flowers.

Anti-oxidants: The chemical substances which are used to prevent the oxidative reactions inside the foods. BHT, BHA, Propyl gallate (PG) used as antioxidants.

Apical meristem: The growing point of a stem or shoot or root etc.

Apomixis/asexual: Development of embryo in the ovary without fertilization.

Apple scald: Accumulation of toxic levels of volatile in the skin tissues leading to superficial death and browning of affected tissues.

Aromatic compounds: Compounds contain atleast one benzene ring or a ring of six carbon atom with three double bonds in the alternate position. Examples are benzene, phenol, benzoic acid etc.

Aromatic plants: Plants which possess essential oil in them. These plants have a typical aroma due to presence of organic compounds.

Artificial long days: The extension of natural day length artificially to prevent flower bud initiation of short day plants like chrysanthemum and poinsettia.

Ascorbic acid: Water soluble vitamins found in fruits and vegetables. A good quantity of vitamin C is present in Barbados cherry, aonla and citrus fruits.

Asepsis: It is a technique to keep micro-organisms out and is a natural phenomenon to keep the products like eggs, apples, pumpkins, etc. in bacteriologically inactive state.

Asexual propagation: Reproduction by vegetative means such as cuttings or division.

Asexual propagation: It does not involves the gamete from parent in which vegetative part such as leaf, stem or root are used instead of seed.

Autoclaving: The most practical process for sterilization of a medium, where heat in form of steam under pressure is main killing agent, carried out in autoclave at 121°C for 20 minutes.

Auxin: A substance synthesized by the plant influencing growth at some point other than the point of its synthesis e.g. IAA, NAA, IBA, etc.

Avenue trees: Trees planted on roadsides for shade or for beautiful vision.

Axil: The angle formed by upper side of a leaf with the stem on which it grows.

Axis: In formal style, axis is central whereas in informal style, it is oblique. Axis is an unifying element.

Balance diet: The food taken by human beings is called dict. The diet which contains adequate amount of all essential nutrients like CHO's, fats, proteins, minerals and vitamins sufficient for normal growth of body.

Balance: Means a symmetrical equilibrium of plantation in gardens.

Barley water: Prepared from citrus fruits like lime, lemon and orange, contains atleast 25% juice, 30% TSS and 0.25% barley starch.

Basal dose: Amount of manure or fertilizer applied to the soil just before the crop is sown or planted or transplanted.

Basal plate: It is a perennial modified stem that has a growing point and to which bulb scales and roots are inter-joined.

Basipetal: Developing sequentially from an apical position towards base.

Berry: This term applies to any fleshy fruit in which there is no hard part except the seeds. Seeds are embedded in pulp formed from the various layers of the fruit wall. Berry fruit is multi-seeded derived from a single ovary.

Biennial: These are the group of plants which complete their life span in 2 growing seasons. They remain vegetative in first year and produce flower and seed during second year.

Bio-degradation: Oxidative breakdown of synthetic or natural organic substances by microbial activity.

Biosynthesis: The building up or synthesis of complex compound from simple substances in a living body by living organism.

Bitter pit: A disorder of apple caused by calcium deficiency which is characterized by small, brown, necrotic zone in the flesh, 3-5 mm in cross section, more frequent toward the calyx portion of the fruit and sometimes, visible through the skin as dark brown or brown in flesh.

Black tip: A disorder of mango caused due to brick Kiln fumes and is characterized by blackening and hardening of the distil end of fruits which ripe prematurely.

Blanching: Heat treatment given to fruit and vegetables before processing. Steam cooking followed by a cold dip of 10-12 second also known as scalding, par boiling or pre-cooling.

Blasting (flower): The failure of a bulb to produce a marketable flower even after the floral initiation has took place.

Blend: To mix two or more ingredients so completely that they loose their separate identities, so that individual ingredients can not be seen.

Blindness (flower): The failure of a bulb to produce any floral parts.

Blossom end rot of Grape: A disorder due to calcium deficiency characterized by a black sunken spot develops at the blossom end of the berry which later on spreads with water soaked region around it.

Bolting: Premature emergence of flower stalk in vegetables.

Bonsai: It comprises of a tree or shrub planted in a small container for developing as a miniature plant showing the general appearance of that plant species found in nature.

Bract: A special leaf or leaf like structure usually at base of flower or inflorescence.

Breathing: It is a physical process of intake of air and removal of air.

Brine: 1-2% solution of common salt which is generally used as covering liquid in canning vegetables.

°Brix: A measure of TSS in fruits and vegetables juice in terms of sucrose. 1°Brix = 1% sucrose, measured with refractrometer.

Bromelin: A protein digestive enzyme present in the mature pineapple fruit.

Brown Core: A low temperature disorder in apple where browning and necrosis of flesh occur around the seed cavity and in the flesh underlying the stem cavity.

Brown Staining: A type of chilling injury in grape fruit and mandarin where diffuse irregular superficial discoloration of the Peel occur.

Browning of litchi: A physiological disorder in which discoloration of the pericarp associated with desiccation of fruit and development of off flavour after harvest.

Bud scales: Leaf like structures that surround some flower buds.

Bud: A bud is undeveloped and elongated stems composed of a very short axis of meristem cells from which embryonic leaves, lateral buds, flower parts or other tree parts arises.

Budding: Type of grafting in which a scion (vegetative bud) is placed in the stock plant.

Bulb production phase (1-3 years): All aspects of bulb production, which lead to the sale of forcing sized bulbs.

Bulb: A specialized underground plant organ consists of a greatly reduced stem (basal plate) surrounded by fleshy or modified leaves called scales which contains reserve food.

Bullhead: Spherically shaped flower bud, usually resulting in a malformed flower.

Bullnose: A physiological disorder of Narcissus flower bud (non-opening of buds).

CA storage: Technique for maintaining the quality of produce in an atmosphere that differs from air in respect to the proportion of O_2, CO_2 or N_2. The desired composition of the atmosphere for storing commodities may be obtained by adding or scrubbing O_2 or CO_2 in a tight storage room or container.

Cacti: A group of plants with peculiar shape and size and mostly adapted for desert life.

Cactus: These are the group of plants which have special characteristics to store water in thick fleshy leaves. Cactus is characterized by presence of aeroles, carrying spines or hairs.

Callus: Wounded tissues which develop from cambium of other exposed meristem.

Cambium: Between xylem and phloem there is a thin wall, undilletentiated tissues is known as cambium.

Candy: A fruit product prepared by gradually concentrating fruits in syrup by repeated boiling until the fruit is heavily sugary and fruits are dried to overcome stickiness.

Canning (Appertizing): The preservation of foods in hermetically sealed container by heat. Mostly canning is done in tin cans, steel coated container. Fruit pieces are kept in 33-50% sugar syrup and vegetables in 2-3% brine (salt solution) together with required citric/ ascorbic acid in the can.

Caramelization: Sugar in dry form when heated beyond melting point, decompose and form brown mass known as caramel having bitter taste.

Carbonation: Method of fruit juice preservation with CO_2. It helps to make an mist atmosphere inside bottled juice by displacing oxygen.

Case-cooled bulbs: Bulbs kept under below temperature treatments in the shipping container.

Catabolic process: It is a process in which big molecules are broken into smaller molecules example respiration.

Catabolism: It is the degradation of complex organ molecules into simple molecules and done by oxidative reaction.

Catalyst: Catalysts are substances which accelerates a certain chemical reaction, without being consumed themselves.

Certified seeds: Seeds produced by the breeder, who developed the variety.

Chilling injury of Banana: Low temperature injury which starts at 12-13°C and is characterized by the appearance of sub epidermal brown streaking, loss of flavour, building up of tannins, watery dark green patches on skin, bitterness of fingers and delayed ripening.

Chilling injury of citrus: It is characterized by the appearance of sunken, brown coloured pits on the peel surface when fruits are stored at temperature below 10°C, occurs most frequently on grape fruit, lemon and limes.

Chilling injury: An injury caused by relatively low temperature above freezing point.

Chimera: Plant part consisting of tissue of diverse genetic constitution, often observed in flowers.

Chimera: A grant hybrid is a stem, branch or plant originating from an adventitious bud at the grant union.

Chlorophyll: Green colouring matter in leaves which trap the energy of sun light for photosynthesis. Chlorophyll a ($C_{55}H_{72}O_5N_4Mg$), chlorophyll b ($C_{55}H_{70}O_6N_4Mg$).

Chlorosis: A diseased condition showing yellowing of the plant between the veins on upper side of leaves due to loss of chlorophyll causing its deficiency.

Chutney: A preserved product where fully mature green fruit and green vegetables are peeled, boiled, crushed and mixed with sugar, salt and powdered spices and cooked to a reasonably thick consistency.

Cider: An alcoholic beverage made from fermented juice of apple.

Cleistogamy: A condition in flower plants where the flowers do not open at all.

Climacteric fruit: Climacteric is defined as period in the ontogeny of fruit during which a series of biochemical changes are initiated by the autocatalytic production, making the change from growth to senescence and involving an increase in respiration leading to ripening of fruit.

Climacteric fruits: Fruits in which the respiration rate is minimum at maturity and remains constant even after harvest which gradually increase at the beginning of ripening followed by sharp rise to the peak and then slowly decline e.g. tomato, muskmelon.

Climacteric peak: The maximum point of respiration rate of mature fruit.

Climber: Group of plant which possesses special structures to climb over a support. These special structures may be thorns, tendrils or rootlets.

Clinching: Partially seaming by a single first roller action of a double seamer where lid is remaining sufficiently loose to permit the escape of dissolved as well as free air from content.

Cloudy jelly: Cloudy appearance as a defective form of jelly instead of clear jelly which happens due to the use of improper clarified juice, over cooking, over cooling or faulty pouring into containers.

Coagulation: Process of change colloidal state into insoluble precipitate.

Coconut water: It is used for manufacture of vinegar and also for beverage manufacture.

Co-enzyme: It is a non-proteinaceous portion of enzyme loosely bond with enzyme and without their presence it could not work.

Cold treatments: A cold moist treatment given to bulbs prior to planting, which induces rapid shoot elongation and flowering.

Concentration: Exact quantity of solute present in exact amount of solvent or exact amount of solution.

Concrete: Waxy essence obtained by extracting odorous material (like jasmine, rose, tuberoses) dissolved in volatile solvents (petroleum ether, hexane etc) followed by separation of solvent by evaporation.

Condensation: Union of two or more molecules of same or different substances with or without the elimination of water.

Conditioning: Means a cooling treatment of cut flower before shipment to restore turgidity of flowers.

Conduction: It is the process of transmission of heat through a substance without any detectable motion of heated particles of the substance. In thick puree, sauces, soups, fruit juice concentrate heating is by conduction.

Contrast: It is most useful in emphasizing the best features of an object.

Controlled atmospheric storage: It is a technique for holding fresh commodities in a atmosphere that differs from normal air in respect of the proportion of nitrogen, oxygen and carbon dioxide.

Convection: It is the process of transmission of heat from one place to another by actual mass movement of heated particle of liquid or gas. In most of juices, thin soup, canned fruits and vegetables heating by convection.

Convenience foods: Products which reduce preparation time at home would naturally be purchased by busy high income consumer.

Conveyors: These are used for conveying fruits, vegetables and can cases etc. They may be slat conveyers, chain conveyers or of any other design as per requirement.

Cool chain: Practice in which the produce is maintained in low temperature environment from field to consumer in a fresh form. It implies to the construction of cold storage in the production zone, refrigerated truck or rail, refrigerated ships and development of cold storage at retail shops.

Cordial: This is a sparkling, clear, sweetened juice from which all pulp and other suspended materials have been completely eliminated. It contains 25% juice, 30% TSS and 350 ppm SO_2.

Cormels: Small corms arising on stolons which develop between mother and daughter corms.

Corms: A specialized underground stem having short, fleshy, vertical axis (internodes) covered with dry scale like leaves e.g., gladiolus.

Corolla: These are the inner perianth (petals) of a flower.

Corrosion: It is the process of gradual deterioration of a metal from its surface due to unwanted chemical or electrochemical interaction of metal with its environment.

Critical day length: The day length above which a plant will flower, depending on condition that the plant is a short or long day plant

Crown: The base of a plant where the stem and roots meet.

Cuttings: A detached portion of a plant placed in suitable medium like sand, soil or saw dust in order that it may produces roots and shoots to form a new plant.

Cyathium: Inflorescence of plants like Poinsettia. Relatively inconspicuous but bears pistils stamens and nectar glands.

Cyme: A relatively flat-topped determinate flower cluster (spray) where the central flowers or inflorescence first to open.

Deaeration: The process of removal of oxygen along with other gases dissolved in juices during processing, to prevent oxidative deterioration.

Deciduous plants: Deciduous plants shed their leaves once in year during dormant season. Examples; Apple, pear, peach etc.

Deep Fat Frying: Food is totally immersed in hot oil and cooked vigorously by convection currents and cooking is uniform on all the sides of food

Dehiscent fruits: Such type fruits brust, open automatically on ripening and discharge their seeds. These may be classified further depending on mode of dehiscence like legume or pod, siliqua, capsule etc.

Dehydration: It is the drying by artificially produced heat under carefully controlled condition of temperature, humidity and air flow.

Dehydration: It is a drying process where moisture of foods is removed by artificially produced heat under controlled conditions of temperature humidity and air flow.

Dehydro-freezing: It is an efficient storage procedure of the perishables where half the weight of the produce is reduced by warm air drying prior to their freezing.

Deshooting: Removal of newly formed shoots to prevent them from becoming branches. It is also known as summer pruning.

Determinate type: A growth habit where the main axis of the plant terminates with a flower cluster the cessation of elongation in this point.

Dieback: Death of shoots, originating at the shoot tips.

Diploid: An organism or cell with two genomes or two sets of chromosome (2x).

Disbudding: The removal of lateral flower buds of plants like carnation and chrysanthemum.

Disc florets: Florets present in centre of chrysanthemum inflorescence, conspicuous in daisy or anemone-flowered types.

Disorders: Abnormal growth and development patterns brought about by sub-optimal environment conditions.

Division: Separation of root system of parent plant into several units (asexual propagation).

Domestication: The process of bringing a wild species under human management.

Dominance: Ability of an allele to express itself in heterozygous state.

Dormancy: The period of inactivity in bud, bulbs or seeds when growth stops and the growth will be resumed after desirable changes in environment.

Drupe/stone fruits: Normally it is one seeded fruit with its pericarp well differentiated into an outer skin like epicarp, a middle fleshy or fibrous mesocarp and an inner stony hard endocarp. It is derived entirely from an ovary.

Dry pack storage: The storage of cut flowers usually at 0°C in vapour-proof containers with the stems not kept in water.

ELISA: Enzyme Linked Immuno-Sorbent Assay used for testing the viral diseases in plants.

Emasculation: A cultural operation consisting of removal of immature anthers from hermaphrodite flowers.

Enzyme: It is a specialized protein produced within an organism which is capable of catalyzing a specific chemical reaction. Since it acts as a catalyst sometimes and referred to as a bio-catalyst.

Epiphyte: An organism growing upon a plant for support without establishment of a parasite host relationship.

Essential oil: Essential oils are the odoriferous steam volatile constituent of the aromatic plants. They are mainly a complex mixture of acyclic and cyclic mono terpenoids. The terpenes are basically secondary metabolites and they have no apparent function in the plant primary metabolism.

Ethephon: (2-chloro-ethyl-phodphonic acid): The active ingredient in the commercial products. Etheral and Floral, which is metabolized to ethylene in the plant.

Ethylene scrubbers: Chemicals used to remove ethylene from the atmosphere.

Evapo-transpiration: Total amount of water loss due to transpiration by a crop and evaporation from the surface of soil during a specified time from a particular area.

Evergreen plants: Do not have definite resting season and retain functional leaves throughout the year. Example; Mango, lime, sapota, orange etc.

False berry (*Epigynous*): A multi-seeded fruit derived from the fusion of ovary and receptacle. Example is blue berry.

False fruit: Develops from other floral members of the flower.

Family: A group of plants having many common floral and vegetative characters.

Fascination: The fusion of two floral stalks to form a single floral stalk.

Fermentation: The process which is carried out aerobically and anaerobically for breaking down of complex matter into simpler ones with the aid of enzymes and bacteria

Fermented Fruit Beverage: A fruit juice which has undergone alcoholic fermentation by yeast containing varying amounts of alcohols, e.g. grape wine, apple cider, berry wine etc.

Fertility: Ability to produce viable progeny.

Fertilization: The act of fusion of pollen nucleus and the ovule following pollination to form seed.

Field Heat: It is the heat of the produce after harvesting from fields which can be determined by the thermal energy removed from the produce in cooling.

Filler trees: Tree placed in between permanent trees at the time of planting for getting some returns from them up to the stage when permanent trees start production.

Fleshy or edible fruits: These usually remain succulent and juicy even when fully mature.

Floater-sinker: A method used for separating healthy bulbs from those with basal rot.

Floral bud: Immature flower that consists of petals, stamens and pistil.

Floriculture: It is an aesthetic branch of horticulture which deals not only with commercial growing of ornamentals, annuals or perennials but also arrangement of flowers and marketing etc.

Floriculture: The cultivation of flowers and ornamental plants for commercial purposes or merely for getting pleasure and as a hobby.

Flower bud adoption: Cessation of floral bud development at any stages of development.

Flower bud development: Progressive change in flower bud from transition to flowering.

Flower differentiation: Complete morphological development of the floral organs following initiation.

Flower induction: An unobservable preparatory step occurs prior to flower bud initiation.

Flower initiation: Visible organization of flower buds at the stem apex.

Foliage plants: Any plant grown primarily for its foliage and utilized for interior decoration or landscape purposes.

Food Additives: Substance or mixture of substances other than food stuff incorporated in food either directly or indirectly during production, processing, storage, packaging to improve nutritional value, consumer acceptability and keeping quality e.g. acid, alkali, emulsifying agent, sterilizing agent, colour nutrient, clarifying ages.

Food Adulteration: It is the term used to describe a food product having the ingredients of inferior quality or the one with prohibited material in it.

Food chain: Transfer of food energy from plants through a series of organism with repeated eating and being eaten

Food infection: An illness caused by the infection produced by invasion, growth and damage to the tissues of the host by the pathogenic organism carried by food.

Food Poisoning: Illness or disease caused due to intake of foods contaminated by micro-organisms and their poisonous metabolites, and those resulting from infection of host through the intestinal tract.

Food safety: Means assurance that food is acceptable for human consumption according to its intended use.

Food Science: Deals chiefly with the acquiring of new knowledge to elucidate the course of reactions or changes occurs in food whether natural or induced by handling procedures.

Food security: All people at all time must have an access to safe and nutritious food which necessitates that individuals must have physical and economic access to food.

Food technology: The science and technology which permits the conservation of the desirable qualities of a food in more or less stabilized form to permit their widespread distribution to meet the needs of people wherever they may be on earth, on the moon or even on other planets and as needed.

Foods and Nutrition: It is the science of foods, the nutrients and other substances therein, their action interactions, and balance in relationship to health and diseases

Forcing: Acceleration of flowering by manipulating environmental conditions.

Formal gardening: It is the application of garden method and material geometrically balanced based on the bilateral symmetry.

Freezing: It means reduction of temperature of the product to such an extent that the activities of micro-organism stops.

Fruit and vegetable processing: Change of fresh fruits and vegetable into new or more usable forms and makes them more convenient to prepare

Fruit drink (RTS): A type of fruit beverage which contains juice content not less than 10%, commercially juice is 15%, TSS <15°Brix. For good quality juice quantity may be increased up to 80-90% or nearly 100% e.g. sugarcane juice, cashew apple juice etc.

Fruit juice concentrate: This is a fruit juice which is concentrated by removal of water either by heat or freezing. TSS not less than 32°B, juice content 100%.

Fruit juice cordial: (Lime juice cordial) juice content not less than 25%, TSS not less than 30°B, acidity 1.3-1.5%. This is similar to squash but differs only to that it is prepared from clarified juice.

Fruit juice squash: This consists essentially of strained juice containing moderate quantities of fruit pulp to which sugar is added. The squash must contain: fruit juice not less than 25%, TSS not less than 45%, acidity 1.3 to 1.5% and is served after dilution 1:3.

Fruit Juice: A natural juice pressed out of a fruit, strained and kept practically unaltered in its composition during preparation and preservation. It is 100% natural juice.

Fruit Nectar: Ready to serve beverage containing strained fruit juice or pulp to which sugar is added and as per FPO specification, it should contain not less than 20% pulp/ juice and TSS not less than 15%.

Fruit syrup: The sweetened water extract of a fruit or about 25% sweetened juice of a fruit with high concentration of sugar (minimum 65%) with low acid contents.

Fruit: Fruit is a characteristic feature of flowering plant usually, it develops after fertilization. But, it may develop without fertilization such a fruit is termed as *Parthenocarpic fruit*.

Functional foods: Food which contain adequate amount of one or combination of components, which affects the function in body so as to have positive cellular and physiological effects. The term functional food seems to have coined in Japan in late 1980. It is used to denote a food imparting health benefits beyond that of basic nutrition.

Garden: A plot or land devoted to the growing of flower, shrubs, flowering and shade the creepers herbs, other ornamental plants, fruit trees and vegetables in certain manners.

Geotropic bending: Upward curvature of tips of spike flowers like gladiolus when held horizontally on the ground surface.

Germplasm: The sum total of hereditary material or genes present in a species.

Glabrous: Smooth and hairless plants.

Gooseneck: The proper stage of flower development to cut daffodils.

Grading: Classification of plants and flowers on basis of size and quality done before marketing.

Graftage: It is the process of joining a part of plant with another in such a way that both will unite to work as a unit and until will continue to growth.

Graphical tracking: The proper utilization of greenhouse temperature and exogenous plant growth regulators to grow a crop to a desired marketable height.

Grassy growth: Excessive and noticeable production of axillary branches on stem. Example; Snapdragon.

Green pruning: Pruning of actively grown rose plants without benefit of a dormant period.

Green Revolution: The self sufficiency in food grain was revolutionalized by the use of high yielding varieties, seeds, chemical fertilizers, plant protection measures and irrigation along with use of agriculture machinery

Green-house effect: Heating of air caused by allowing solar radiations but inhibition of outgoing radiations. The warm air inside the greenhouse causes heating.

Growth regulators: Applied to organic compounds other than nutrients, which when used in minute quantities can inhibit, stimulate or alter growth.

Gynandrium: The structure in the orchid flower, which results from the fusion of the male and female portions of the flower.

Gyno-monoecious: A sex form where pistillate and hermaphrodite flowers are separately produced in the same plant.

Hanging baskets: Containers usually suspended with supports in greenhouse and used to suspend the plants in garden.

Harmony: It is overall effect of various features, styles and colour schemes of the total scene.

Harvest: Single deliberate action to separate the food stuff/ commodity from its growth medium e.g. picking of fruits from tree, lifting of fish from water and all succeeding actions are defined as the post-harvest action.

Hazard: Means a biological, chemical and physiological agent in condition of food with the potential to cause an adverse health effect. The biological hazards include pathogenic microbes (bacteria, viruses) and chemical hazards include pesticides, cleaning compounds, heavy metals and additives.

Head Space: Space between surface of cap/ cork/ lid and the upper surface of liquid, which helps to accumulates CO_2 & SO_2.

Health foods: Foods often sold in Special Retail outlets called Health food stores. Contain more fiber, less refined or contain constituent ingredients (e.g. salt or alcohol, animal food) that are less likely to be associated with disease.

Health: It refers to condition of body includes physical, mental and emotional fitness.

Heat: Something which produces hotness in bodies and gives us the sensation of warmth commonly measured in kilo joules or Btu.

Herbarium: A collection and arrangements of plant specimens, according to taxonomy.

Hesperidium: This is also like a berry but it develops from a multi-carpellery and syncarpous pistil axial placentation. Epicarp and Mesocarp form a leathery skin while endocarp projects inwards farming distinct chambers with juicy hairy i.e. citrus fruits.

Heterosis: Superiority of heterozygote in respect to one or more traits in comparison with their parents.

Hibernation: The induction of a state of dormancy by low temperature.

High tech nurseries: A modern system of raising the seedling in the plastic trays in soil less media under controlled environmental conditions.

High-tech Horticultural technologies: The technologies which are modern, less environment dependent, capital intensive and have the capacity to improve the productivity and quality of the produce.

Horizontal resistance: Partial resistance equally effective against all races of a pathogen.

Hormone: Any organic substance which is produced in one part of plant and translocated to another part where they are necessary for specific physiological or bio-chemical processes.

Horticultural Maturity: The stage of development of a plant or plant part which possesses the necessary pre-requisites for utilization by consumer for a particular purpose and it depends upon particular crop

Horticulture: Horticulture can be defined as culture of fruits, vegetables, flowers and ornamental plants and its preservation for long time. Horticulture is a word derived from two Latin words *Hortus* and *culture.*

Host: A plant that is invaded by a parasite and from which the parasite obtains its food material.

Hydroponics: The growth of plant in water without soil and supplied nutrient is known as hydroponics.

Hypobaric Storage: Preservation of foods under low pressure. The commodities are kept in vacuum tight and refrigerated containers. Low pressure inside container reduces oxygen tension and removal of ethylene by decreasing respiration.

Hypotonic solution: If water potential of the surrounding solution is less (negative) than that of cell sap.

Indehiscent fruits: Such type of fruit never dehisces. The pericarp is dry. These types of fruits include caryopsis, cypsela, nut or schizocarpic.

Indeterminate type: A growth habit where the main axis of the plant continues to grow indefinitely i.e. emergence of inflorescence and elongation of the stem go on side by side.

Index plants: Plants tested by pathological methods and found to be free of known pathogens.

Indoor gardening: Defined as growing, arrangement and display of house plants for interior decoration of a room or house.

Infestation: The attack of insect-pest on the host plant.

Informal gardening: It is defined as the application of garden method and materials for the improvement of any area on which it is possible and desirable to developed new face.

Inter-cropping: The programme should be fixed in such a manner that the main fruit crop does not suffer in any way on account of inter-cropping.

Interveinal chlorosis: Yellowing of leaf tissues between leaf veins.

Interveinal: Area between the veins of a leaf.

Isogenic lines: Lines identical in genotypes except one gene.

Isolation distance: A distance which is to be maintained between the seed crop and the contaminants.

Jam: It is a product prepared by boiling the fruit pulp with sufficient quantity of sugar to a considerable thick consistency, firm enough to hold the fruit tissue in position.

Jam: Product prepared by boiling pectin containing fruit pulp with required amount of sugar, water and acid to reasonably thick consistency, firm enough to hold fruit tissue in position.

Jelly: It is a product prepared by boiling the fruit with or without water, straining, mixing the strained and clear juice extract with sugar and boiling the mixture to a stage at which it will be set to a clear gel.

Jelly: Product prepared by boiling clear fruit extract with sugar. It is transparent, well set and when cut it retains shape and shows clear cut surface.

Ketchup: A concentrated juice/ pulp without seed and skin wherein spices, salt, sugar, vinegar etc. are added to an extent that it contains not less than 12% fruit and vegetable solids and 28% total solids.

Knuckling: A disorder of tulips in which the shoot grows back into the bulb scales instead of upward in a normal growth pattern.

Label: Any tag, mark, brand, pictorial or other descriptive matter, written, printed, marked, embossed, graphic, perforated, stenciled, stamped or immersed on or attached to container, cover, lid or crown of any food package.

Labeling: It helps to identify a product, grade a produce, describe and promote a product through its attractive graphics

Lacquer: It is colloidal dispersion of a solution of cellulose derivative, resin and plasticizer in solvent and diluents, wherein all these constituents principally dry in air by evaporation of solvents, yielding a transparent, hard and water proof film

Lacquering: Providing a living of resinous material inside can to prevent discolouration of food due to formation of black stains of iron sulphide. Generally, it is of two types Acid resistant, R-enamel cans (used for acid foods) and sulphur resistant, C-enamel cans (used for non-acid foods).

Landscape architecture: An art of arranging land and landscape for human use, convenience and enjoyment.

Landscape gardening: Planning and planting of outdoor space, by the application of garden forms and material for improving landscape design. It secures the most desirable relationship between architect and plants at best to meet the human needs for beauty and function.

Landscape plants: The plants planted with the objective of beautifying surroundings. They must serve certain functional, architectural or engineering aspects/purposes.

Landscape: It is the general appearance of a portion of land/garden which attracts the eye at once.

Landscaping: Design and alteration of a portion of land by use of planting material and land reconstruction.

Latex: Milky juice fluid found in stems, foliage and bracts of poinsettia.

Lath house: A propagating structure made up of wood lath or plastic screen for protecting plants from excessive sunlight or frost.

Lawn: Lawn is an open area with green grass of the garden e.g. *Cynodon dactylon*.

Layering: A vegetative method of propagation in which a part of the plant is allowed to bear root for detaching it from the mother plants.

Leaf scorch: Crescent shaped necrotic areas that develop along the margin and tips of leaves as a result of physiological imbalances.

Light (Lux): It is a measure of light spectrum or the duration of light.

Light compensation point: Light intensity at which the respiration and photosynthesis of the entire plant are balanced.

Long day plant: Plant that flower when the day length is longer than the critical.

Mat watering: Substrates in which plants are grown. It includes soil, sand, peat, moss, vermiculite, pine bark humus *etc*.

Matrix: A place on the root stock that are prepared for joining the scion or bud.

Maturation: The stage of development leading to the attainment of physiological and horticultural maturity.

Mature: The stage of development of fruit, which still remain attached to plant, that will ensure completion of ripening and acceptable palatability after harvest.

Maturity index: Means stage of maturity at which the fruit if harvested, will give optimum quality and yield. It is determined by different means i.e. Visual means (colour, size, shape), physical (firmness, softness), chemical (sugar, acid content), computation (Heat units) and physiological means (respiration).

Meristem: Growing point where cell divisions occur. The undifferentiated plant tissue from which new cells arise by division.

Mesophyll: Large parenchyma cells located within the epidermis layers of N a leaf.

Micronutrients: Elements required in small amount for plant growth and flowering.

Molality (m): Number of moles of solute dissolved in 1000 gm of the solvent is known as molality and is represented by m.

Molarity (M): Number of gram molecular weight (moles) of the solute dissolved per litre of the solution.

Mole fraction: Ratio of number of moles of one component (solute or solvent) to the total number of moles present is the solution.

Monoecious: A plant having both male and female flowers on the same plant but at different locations.

Monopodial: A plant with a primary upright stem that continues growth year after year i.e., Vanda-orchid.

Mono-saccharides: Carbohydrates which can not be hydrolyzed into simple units. They only contain one aldehyde or ketone group in the molecules and are called sugars, e.g. glucose, fructose, galactose, mannose etc..

Mother bulb: That portion of the bulb, which is currently flowering and producing a daughter bulb in the axial of a scale subtending the mother axis.

Multi-branched plant: One plant with several shoots and flowers, which is achieved by pinching.

Mutation: Sudden heritable change in the genetic potential of a cell.

NAA: Naphthalene acetic acid, an auxin used as a rooting hormone.

Natural cooling: Technique in which non pre-cooled commercial bulbs are planted immediately and grown under cool natural conditions, but with frost protection, prior to being placed in the greenhouse.

Necrosis: Symptom of plant injury caused by spray damage, insect or disease injury or other causes, which is characterized by dead, discoloured cells and tissues.

Nematodes: Worm like organisms that can affect roots, stem and foliage.

Node: The point on the stem where the leaf is attached.

Non-climacteric fruit: These fruits show neither a rise in respiration nor an associated production of ethylene during ripening process and called non-climacteric fruit. The ripening is normally completed on the parent plant and fruit contain no or a very low starch i.e. pineapple, rose apple, java plum, litchi, lemon, lime, olive.

Non-cooled bulb: Bulb that is delivered direct to the forcer and has not received a cold treatment.

Non-reducing sugars: When two or more mono-saccharides are linked together through their aldehyde or ketone group so that these reducing groups not free and are non-reducing sugars example maltose.

Non-traditional flowers: The flowers included in the non-traditional flowers are used strictly for decorative purposes. These flowers are referred as cut flowers and are generally harvested with a long stem. The flowers in non-traditional use are arranged in vases, pots, bouquets and are mostly consumed during social functions. These flowers are also known as modern flowers.

Nutrient film technique: It is a new water system based on simple principle of circulating a shallow plant of film of nutrient solution over the roots of growing plants to provide an adequate supply of water, nutrients and oxygen.

Offsets: Bulblets that are formed in the interior of a bulb and enlarge to commercial sized bulbs.

Orchard: A group of fruit trees grown in a specified area.

Ornamental garden: An area established with valuable and pleasurable plants adjacent to a house or other building.

Osmocote: Slow-release encapsulated fertilizer.

Parthenocarpy: The development of fruit without fertilization or the phenomenon of seedless fruit production.

Parthenogenesis: The development of new individuals from an egg cell without fertilization.

Parts per million (ppm): It is equivalent to milligram per litre.

Pasteurization: It is a heat treatment given to eliminate harmful pathogens where the temperature usually does not exceed 82°C.

Pasteurization: It is heat treatment of a food at a sufficient high temperature to kill the majority, though not all, of micro-organisms i.e. Bacteria, mould, yeast present in food and air, water prevent their access to food inside can by sealing the containers hermetically, thereby prolonging normal keeping quality.

Peat moss: Partially decayed plant material often used as an ingredient in a growing medium, which is acidic in nature.

Pectin: A complex carbohydrate derived from pectose in the process of ripening.

Pedicel: The support of a single flower in an inflorescence (stalk).

Peduncle: The stalk supporting either an inflorescence or a solitary flower.

Pepo: This is like berry but develop from an interior, multi-carpellary and syncarpous ovary with parental placentation as in cucurbits.

Percent strength: Number of parts by weight of solute present per 100 parts by weight of solution.

Perennial flowers: The flowers those have life span extending beyond one calendar year and do not need replacement year after year are categorized as perennial crops. The life span could range from 2 years to over 10 years.

Perennial: Plant that lives for more than two years. Vegetative growth for first year and productive for second year.

Perianth: The collective coloured petals of the flower.

Perlite: These are expanded porous aggregates used in growing media to facilitate proper drainage and also improve aeration.

Pesticide: A chemical used for controlling undesirable organisms.

PFA: It is Prevention of Food Adulteration Act, 1954 & Rules 1955. Enact to protect the consumer against the supply of inferior quality or adulterated foods. It is mandatory in nature.

PGR: Plant growth regulators modify plant physiological process.

pH: pH is a measure of acidity or alkalinity expressed as negative log of hydrogen ion concentration. pH of 7.0 is neutral, less than 7.0 is acidic and more than 7.0 is alkaline.

Photoperiod: The length of the day used in reference to its effect on growth and flowering.

Photoperiodic response: Behaviour of an organism to the length of day.

Photoperiodism: Response of plants to the daily duration of light.

Photosynthesis: It is a bio-chemical process by which plants manufacture their food using carbon dioxide and water as raw material in presence of sunlight and chlorophyll, green leaves have chloroplast which contains chlorophyll and it is used to convert solar energy into chemical energy.

Phyllotaxy: The arrangement of leaves on the stem. It is of three types viz; alternate, opposite and whorled.

Physiological disorders: Undesirable affects caused by a non-pathogenic agent.

Physiological loss in weight (PLW): Weight loss of fresh fruits and vegetables attributed to many physiological activities like transpiration and respiration etc. which depends on temperature, RH and other storage environment.

Physiological maturity: Refers to the stage of development of fruit or vegetable when maximum growth and maturation has occurred.

Phytochrome: It is applied to those hormones which are exclusively produced inside a living plant.

Phyto-pathogenic: Term applicable to a micro-organism that can incite in plants.

Pickle: Processed fruits and vegetables in common salt, vinegar or edible oil with the addition of spices and condiments may be unfermented (Indian) and fermented (western pickle) e.g. sauerkraut and dill pickle fermented.

Pickling: Preservation of fruits and vegetables in common salt or vinegar is called pickling.

Pinching: Removal of the shoots apex to overcome apical dominance and promote lateral shoot development.

Plant hormone: Organic compound synthesized in one part of plant and translocated to another part wherein very low concentration, it causes a physiological response.

Plastochron: The time interval between two successive similar occurrences as rhythmic initiation of leaves by the meristem.

Polyembryony: Some seeds contain more than one embryo is known as poly-embryony.

Pome fruits: This is a false fruit as it is surrounded by a fleshy and edible thalamus. It is derived from the fusion of ovary and receptacle (Thalamus). It develops from inferior, multi-carpellary and syncarpous ovary.

Pomology: The science of growing fruits crops is called Pomology. It is an important branch of horticulture deals with various aspects of fruit starting from raising sapling to harvesting, ripening and marketing.

Post harvest handling: The process carried out with harvested vegetables in course of making them available to the consumers, grading, packaging, marketing, etc.

Precooling: Dry storage of bulb at temperature between 2° and 9° C after floral initiation.

Preservatives: A chemical additive which preserve some desired characteristic of food making certain chemical structures more stable by retarding microbial growth.

Probiotic foods: To select probiotic as a compound it should be absorbed or hydrolyzed in upper gastro intestinal tract besides inducting the growth of beneficial bacteria.

Processing: Series of operations performed in order to make a good, tasty or relishable products from raw materials done by washing, cooking, mixing of additives, preparation of different products, carbonation etc.

Processing: The fundamental principle of preserving the foods by heat is known as processing. It consists basically application of heat in varying degrees to the food in closed container for sufficient time to sterilize the content before they are hermitically sealed.

Proportion: It is the relation of one thing to another in magnitude.

Protective Foods: Green leafy vegetables, yellow and orange fruits and vegetables, aonla, harar and bahera are a group of foods that contain chemical substances necessary for normal growth and health.

Pruning: It is the art and science of cutting away a portion of a plant to improve its shape to influence growth, flowering and fruitfulncss to improve the quality of the product.

Rejuvenilization: Stimulation of new growth of old plants usually accomplished with pruning.

Reverse osmosis: Reverse osmosis is a process where water from aqueous solution is removed without change of phase by permeation, through a suitable membrane by applying pressure higher than osmotic pressure of liquid to be concentrated.

Reversible reaction: A reaction in which the products react to give back the reactants is called reversible reaction

Rhythm: Repetition of same object at equidistance in a garden is known as rhythm.

Ripe: Condition of maximum edible quality attained by the fruit following harvest.

Ripeness: State of complete maturation prior to breakdown

Ripening: Involves a series of changes occurring during the early stage of senescence of fruit in which composition of unripe fruit is altered, so that it becomes acceptable to eat.

Ripening: Sequential changes in sensory factors like colour, flavour, texture and taste which render the fruits acceptable to eat.

Risk: Risk in relation to any article of food means the probability of an adverse effect on the health of consumer of such food and the severity of that effect, consequential to a food hazard.

Saprophyte: An organism that uses dead organic material for food.

Scaling: Scaling is a technique used to propagate foundation stock, where the scale of a bulb are removed and planted. This produces numerous scale bulb lets from a single mother scale.

Scape: Peduncle originating at the base of the plant and bearing one or more flowers at the apex.

Scion: The upper part of plant union is called scion.

Scooping: A method of propagating hyacinths and other bulbs by scooping out the basal plate, the main goal is to eradicate apical dominance.

Seasonal flowers: The flowers those complete their life cycle with in one calendar year and need to replant every year. These flowers are short span crops and include Marigold, chrysanthemum, gladiolus and aster.

Self-branching: The growth of axillary buds taking place without pinching.

Senescence: Aging of the plant parts, such as the flower. It is usually the stage from full maturity to death.

Senescence: Senescence is the final phase in the ontogeny of the organ, in which a series of normally irreversible events are, initiated that leads to the cellular breakdown and death of organ. Senescence is also defined as the deteriorative processes that are natural cause of death.

Senescence: Senescence of plant organ can be defined as the final phase in its ontogeny in which a series of normally (essentially) irreversible events is initiated that leads to cellular break down and death.

Sensible heat: Amount of heat which causes increase or decrease in temperature of body without change in its state.

Sensory evaluation: A synonym for subjective evaluation of a product measurements determined by using senses of sight, smell, taste and touch.

Sepal: A unit of calyx, the first formed series of the floral parts of green colour.

Sherbat: A clear sugar syrup which has been artificially flavoured having TSS < 65%, Juice <10%.

Sherry: Spanish wine matured by placing the barrels for 3-4 months in sun light, where temperature is as high as 40-60°C

Shoot: Upright stem, often arising from axillary position following a pinch.

Short day plants: Plants that flower when the day length is shorter than the critical.

Shrub: Shrub may be defined as a perennial plant having many woody branches arising from the base of the plant.

Simple fruits: Developed from singled pistil of a single flower with or without accessory organ.

Slipping stage: The time when the inflorescence emerges from the leaf sheaths.

Slow releasing fertilizer: Fertilizer not immediately soluble or readily available to the plant roots because of coating of the granule.

Sod culture: Cultivation of grass in orchards to maintain moisture is called sod culture.

Sodium hypochlorite: Common household bleach used for commercial sterilization of greenhouse benches and tools.

Soft scald of apple: A low temperature disorder where symptoms appear as smooth, brown, irregular shaped well defined areas of skin irrespective of the skin colour but usually not at the calyx end

Soft smell: A can with buldged ends but gas pressure inside cans is low enough to permit ends to be dented by pressure of fingures and with the release of pressure they will get back.

Soft water: Water that produces lather with soap solution readily is called soft water, e.g. distilled water, rain water, demineralized water.

Soil less culture: Growing of plants without soil by providing nutrients essential for the proper growth and different media such as coarse sand, crushed bricks, vermiculite, etc. for holding plants roots.

Solute: The substance which is dissolved in liquid.

Solution: Homogenous mixture of two or more pure substances whose composition can be varied within certain limits.

Solvent: Liquid in which the solute is dissolved to form true solution.

Sorbitol: A white crystalline alcohol found in certain fruits and berries and manufactured by catalytic hydrogenation of sucrose used as sweetener.

Spadix: A succulent stalks bearing an inflorescence as in aroid family.

Species: A group of individuals having similar characteristics and able to sexually reproduce among themselves.

Specific Gravity: Ratio of weight of certain volume of substance at 1°C to the weight of same volume of water at 4°C.

Specific heat: The heat required to raise the temperature of a given weight of any other material to that required to cause an equivalent use in the same weight of water.

Spike: A flower head in which flowers are virtually stalkless e.g., gladiolus, stock, lily, *etc.*

Spitting: In hyacinths, the abscission or release of the entire floral stalk and inflorescence from the basal plate during forcing.

Spoilage of food: These are physical and chemical changes brought about in food through the activities of enzymes, moulds, yeasts and bacteria.

Spoilage: Physical and chemical changes brought about in food through the activities of enzymes, moulds, yeast and bacteria.

Sport: A mutant that is inherited and transmitted to progeny.

Spray treatment: Removal of apical flower bud to stimulate development of lateral flowers.

Sprouting or germination: This process increases digestibility, as complex substances are converted into simple substances

Squash: Unfermented fruit juice beverage which consists essentially of strained juice containing fruit pulp to which sugar is added for sweetening. It should contain 25% juice and 40-45% TSS, & 1.0% acidity.

Stage 'G': The term used to indicate that the gynoecium (pistil) has formed in the flower of tulip in the bulb itself.

Standard forcing: A technique used for cold treatment given after planting of the bulbs. Rooting takes place during the programming phases of forcing.

Standard solution: A solution of known concentration or known normality.

Staple food: The main food that we eat to provide us energy. Example; rice, roti, etc.

Stem topples: In tulips, the physiological disorder that is characterized by the collapse of a small portion of the inter-node of the flower stalk located just underneath the flower.

Stock plant: Plants from which cuttings are taken for propagation.

Stock: It is the part of a plant which has the roots and which support the growth made by the other component scion.

Stolon: A creeping underground stem.

Stripping: Chlorotic stripes that can be caused by pesticidal phytotoxicity or nutrient deficiencies.

Succulents: These are the juicy plants are among the most specialized form and they are the expression of peculiar condition of soil and climate.

Sun scald: Injury caused by excessively high light intensity and radiant heat.

Sweetening: A term used to denote the odour of lilies after storage under anaerobic conditions.

Sympodial: Plants with a main stem or axis that ceases growth each year and new growth arises from the base ie *Cattleya orchid* .

Synthetic variety: In cross pollinated species a varietv obtained by mating in all possible combinations.

Syringing: Spraying of water on the foliage done to reduce transpiration, to reduce leaf temperature.

Systemic: A term used to describe pesticides as disease that enters and is distributed and act within the plants.

Tapka: A maturity index for mango harvesting indicated by fall of ripe fruits naturally from the tree.

Taste: Sensation caused in the tongue by things placed in at with the help of taste buds. Four basic tastes like sweet, salt, sour and bitter.

Taxonomy: The science of classification of plants and animals.

Tensiometer: Instrument used to measure tension with which water is held in the growing medium.

Terrarium: A closed type of glass container used to provide usual environment for the growth of plants.

TIBA: 2, 3, 6-tri, iodobenzoic acid, a synthetic plant growth regulator.

Traditional flowers: The flowers which are offered in religious and social ceremonies, used as an adornment by womens, offered for worship at home or temples.

Traditional foods: Food involves somé degree of acquired skill, elaborate, more time consuming process, besides being highly perishables.

Training: Means developing a desired shape of the tree with particular objectives by controlling the habit of growth.

Transpiration: The loss of water through the leaf stomata.

Tropical fruits: Require hot and humid climate in summer and mild in winter.

True fruit: Fruits develops only from the ovary of the flower.

Truss: Main supporting structure of GH roof.

Tuber: A thickened, often short, subterranean stem, enabling the plant to be asexually propagated.

Tuberous roots: Enlarged roots generally having primordial at proximal end and root primordial at the distal ends.

Tunic: The dry papery scales that surround the fleshy organs of a bulb or corm.

Twig: Stem one year old or less without leaves.

Tyndel effect: Scattering of light by the particles of colloidal solution in the path of light.

Ultra-filtration (UF): It is a fractionation process separating molecules species on basis of size, using membranes which allow water and other molecules to pass and retaining the large molecules.

Under-stock: The lower portion of a budded or grafted plant, which develops into the root system.

Vacuole: In cells, the cell sap surrounded by protoplasm

Vacuum Cooling: A technique of cooling vegetables having a high surface to volume ratio rapidly and uniformly by boiling off some of their water at 1°C and at low pressure (5 mm mercury) into sealed container. The produce is cooled by evaporation of water from tissue surface and is more rapid than hydro-cooling.

Vacuum drier: A drier used to dry heat sensitive products where low pressure lowers the temperature helps to retain natural flavour and minimize browning.

Vacuum: It is the pressure condition inside a hermetic food container and is a measure of extent to which air has been eliminated from the container prior to processing.

Vapour pressure: It is the pressure exerted by the vapours above the liquid surface in equilibrium with the liquid at a given temperature.

Variety: A group of strains or single strain of closely related parts of common origin which have similar characteristics and can be differentiated on the basis of structural and functional characters from another group of plants.

Vase life: Potential useful longevity of flowers at final consumption stage of in the vase.

Vector: Any organism able to transmit a pathogen.

Vegetable forcing: This is a type of gardening which is concerned with the production of vegetables out of their normal season.

Vegetable forcing: A specialized type of vegetable farming where vegetables are grown out of their normal season. It requires some special structures like GH, hot beds, etc.

Vegetable: Herbaceous plant or part of plant which are use for culinary purposes.

Vermi compost: Compost produced from digestion and discharge of refuse and other organic wastes by earthworms.

Vermiculite: Mica platelets formed by heating to about 738°C and used as an ingredient in growing media.

Vernalization: Cold moist treatment of a seed, plant or bulb to induce or hasten the development of the capacity for flowering.

Vernalization: It is technique of inducing early flowering in plants by pre-treatment of propagating material with very low temperature.

Vertical resistance: Complete resistance to some races of a pathogen but not to others.

Viability: Capacity of seed to germinate is called viability.

Vinegar: Vinegar is an acidulous liquid prepared from sugary or starchy materials by first alcoholic and subsequently acetic acid fermentation. It should contain 4% acetic acid.

Viroids: Small, low-molecular weight ribonucleic acids (RNA) that can infest plant cells, replicate themselves and cause disease.

Virus: A sub-microscopic obligate parasite consisting of nucleic acid and proteins.

Viscosity: Property of liquids by virtue of which it offers resistance to its own flow measured by viscometer. Viscosity units are: Centipoise, Millipoise and Micropoise.

Vista: It is a three dimensional confined view of terminal building or dominant element of feature. Best example of man-made vista is a view of main building of Taj Mahal from the entrance gate and Hanging Garden of Babylon.

Vitality: The strength or vigour of growth is called vitality.

Water activity (aw): It is ratio of the water vapour presence of food to the vapour pressure of pure water measured at the same temperature. It may be expressed in terms of available water for growth of micro-organisms.

Water core: A pre-harvest disorder of apple characterized by the presence of translucent liquid infused tissues around the vascular bundles only or affecting additional tissues within or outside the core area. In severe case, most of the tissues may be damaged even to the extent that the lenticles secrets droplets of sap.

Water Solubility Index (WSI): Amount of dried solid recovered by evaporating the supernatant from the WAI test.

Water sprouts: These are shoots growing from latent adventitious buds on stems or branches.

Watt: Power of an agent working at the rate of 1 joule or 10-7 ergs per second.

Wave length: Distance between two peaks of waves (cm).

Waxes: Waxes are the lipids which contain in them large amount of esters of long chain monohydric alcohols (C16-C36) with higher fatty acids.

Waxing: A short term storage technique of fresh produce under ambied condition by applying wax imulsion containing paraffin wax, triethanol and aleic acid. It reduces respiration and transpiration resulting increase shelf-life.

Web bulb thermometer: This gives a temperature reading at a given space with cent per cent saturated vapour content at that temperature.

Wilting point: It is a point at which soil contains so little water that it is unable to supply water at a rate sufficient to prevent permanent wilting of the plants.

Wine: Undistilled liquor produced by alcoholic fermentation of juice of ripe grape by *Saccharomyces cerevisae* yeast culture.

Wrenching: Cutting of roots of a plant prior to lifting from the growing area.

Xanthin: A basic nitrogenous compound related to uric acid, one of the purines. Insoluble part of yellow colouring matter of flowers and soluble part of the yellow colouring matter of flowers is xantheine.

Xanthophyll: A carotenoid pigment responsible for the pigmentation of skin. Associated with chlorophyll and carotene in plants imparting a golden yellow to ivory colour according to concentration.

Yearlings: Lily planting stock at the end of the first growing season from a bulblet.

Year-round flowering: Control of day length and temperature to produce flowering plants throughout the year.

Yeast: Unicellular plant body, very minute in size containing cell wall, cytoplasm with one vacuoles and a single nucleus cause alcoholic fermentation.

Zero energy cool chambers: It is based on the principle of direct evaporation cooling and hence does not require any electricity or power to operate. A cool chamber used to enhance the shelf-life of fresh fruits and vegetables by maintaining temperature and RH, naturally used to make the cool chamber (brick, sand, bamboo and khuskhus etc) are easily available and cheap.

Zero-vacuum: The pressure in the headspace is equal to atmospheric pressure whereas a vacuum of 30 inch of mercury would indicate that all gas had been removed from the container. Vacuum gauge is used (inches in mercury) for measuring.

Z-value: Mathematically this value is equal to reciprocal of the slope of TDT curve, hence Z-value provides information on the relative resistant of micro-organisms to different destructive temperature.

Section – V

Miscellaneous

- Edaphology is the study of soil properties in relation to plant higher production.
- Pedology refers to study of origin of soils in their natural environment, classification and description.
- pH is the negative logarithm of the concentration of H^+ ions in soil solution.
- Soil profile is a vertical exposure of horizon sequence.
- Soil texture is not changed by cultural management.
- Cation exchange capacity (CEC) is defined as sum total of exchangeable cations that a soil can absorb.
- Sandy soils have lower CEC than clay soils.
- Anion exchange together with cation exchange largely determines ability of soils to provide nutrients to plants promptly.
- Nematodes, commonly thread worms are found almost in all soils.
- Clubfoot in cabbage may be controlled by increasing pH to 7.0 and above.
- The conditions encourage adsorption will discourage leaching.
- Acid rain (precipitation) water contains nitric and sulphuric acid.
- The soil is primary source of *Radon gas*, which can cause *lung cancer*.
- Radon Gas = Radioactive decay of Radium (breakdown of uranium).

- When a plant is under soil moisture stress, the roots shrink in size (shrinkage).
- In no-tillage systems, the surface soil layers have higher bulk density.
- The diameter of moist erodible soil particles is 0.1 mm.
- Herbicides are more mobile than fungicides and insecticides.
- Barley, Rape, Cotton are high salt tolerant crops.
- Among fruits lemon, apple, plum are placed in low salt tolerance group.
- Excess N_2 supply in apple delay maturity (help growth).
- Pure Line Selection widely used to select new varieties from old 'land' varieties.
- Male sterility is a device to produce large quantities of seeds of hybrid varieties.
- Homozygosity within families increases with continuous self fertilization.
- Density of ice is lower than density of water.
- Adhesion is the attraction between unlike molecules.
- Surface tension = a falling water drop becomes spherical.
- Whip tail of cabbage and broccoli due to Molybdenum deficiency.
- Growth is defined as progressive development of an organism.
- Environment is defined as aggregate of all the external conditions and influences affecting tip of an organism.
- Excess nitrogen fertilizer reduces sugar contents of sugarbeets.
- Susceptibility of tomato to Boron-deficiency is controlled by a single recessive gene.
- Agronomy = Agros (field) + nomas (manage).
- Cereal = Ceres (Roman goddess) + giver (grain).
- Multi-storeyed cropping means cultivation of different crops of different canopy heights simultaneously in the same field.
- Breeder's seed refers to seed/ propagation material directly controlled by originating or sponsoring plant breeder.
- Purity of certified seed should be 99% against 99.5% for foundation seeds.
- A herbicide moves faster in young plant than in old plants.
- Zero Tillage system was 1st used successfully in 1950 in Pasteur renovation in USA.

- CAZRI, Zodhpur (Rajasthan) established in 1959.
- ICARDA was established in 1977.
- Zinc deficiency in Rice cause Khaira disease.
- Weed competition in rice is more in direct seeded crops.
- Centre of origin of wheat is South Western Asia.
- Fruit of mustard and rapeseed is silique (cruciferae family).
- Fruit of Linseed is seed ball, belongs to family Linaceae.
- Most destructive disease of sugarcane is Red Rot.
- Marigold has been used in biological control of nematodes (*Meloidogyneae and Paratylanchus*).
- *Cucurbitacin* compound in cucurbits acts as repellent for Namatodes.
- The Food Corporation of India was set up in 1965.
- NABARD Act passed in March and came into existence on July 12, 1982.
- 1st KVV at Pondicherry was established in 1974.
- 1st Agricultural University came into existence at Pantnagar (UP) in 1960.
- Lemon does not belong to temperate region.
- Walnut is a temperate fruit.
- Sapota is a tropical fruit crop.
- Ground layering is most common in rose.
- Air layering is most common in litchi.
- Root cutting is a material used for propagation in pomegranate.
- Soft wood cutting is a propagating material used in coleus.
- Veneer grafting is the kind of detached grafting.
- Ring budding is a kind of budding.
- In grafting, the lower part of plant is known as stock.
- In grafting, the upper part of plant is known as scion.
- IBA growth promoter can develop the roots in mango.
- BA is a growth inhibitor.
- Removal of undesirable leaves from the tree is known as defoliation.
- Removal of undesirable flowers from the plants is called deblossoming.
- The nitrogen requirement of one year old plant is 50 grams.

- Apple is a self-incompatibility fruit crop.
- Litchi is a hetero-styled fruit tree.
- In hexagonal method of plantation about 15% more trees can be planted than triangular method.
- Rectangular system of planting is most common in grape.
- Age of the plants at planting time should be 2-3 years.
- Mango malformation disease is caused by boron deficiency.
- Amrapali variety of mango is developed by crossing Neelam and Dashehari.
- Pseudostem is upper stem of banana.
- Maximum production of banana is in Tamilnadu.
- Fruits of banana mature after 3-4 months of fruit setting.
- The origin place of Papaya is South America.
- Chi-square is an index of dispersion.
- The use of 5% and 1% level of significance is simply a convention working.
- A null hypothesis is specific hypothesis about a population that is being tested by means of the same results.
- Standard error and standard deviations are synonymous.
- The coefficient of variation is often between 5 and 15%.
- The coefficient of variation denotes ratio of average having same units of measurement and hence is independent of unit.
- In normal distribution mean = medium = mode.
- Range of distribution = difference between largest and smallest observations.
- Correlation coefficient lies between -1 and +1.
- Coefficient of variation is useful for comparison between different populations.
- In a normal distribution, the Mean, medium and mode are equal.
- Latin square is the experimental design suitable for situation where fertility variation in the field is in two directions at right angles.
- Range of distribution is the difference between largest and smallest observations.
- Correlation coefficient always lies between -1 and +1.

- Coefficient of variation is useful for comparison between different population
- Biometry deals with the collection of observations.
- Standard deviation is expressed in the same unit of measurements.
- The test of significance of differences between two means in small sample is known as t-test.
- F-test is used for testing the significance of several differences.
- When two variables change together in such a way that an increase in one variable is accompanied by an increase in the other. The variables are said to be positively correlated.
- $\div^2$ test is applied for qualitative observations.
- Indian Agricultural Research Institute (IARI) was founded in 1905 at Pusa, District Darbhanga (now Samastipur), Bihar.
- IARI before independence (1947) was known as Imperial Agricultural Research Institute (IARI).
- The annual rate of soil erosion is one centimeter of surface soil.
- In India, economically non-viable holdings comprise 76 per cent of the total holdings.
- Grow More Food Committee was constituted in 1952.
- The National Seeds Corporation (NSC) of India was established in 1963 having headquartered at New Delhi.
- High yielding varieties programme (HYVP) was launched in India in 1966.
- Indian Society of 'Agronomy' was established in 1955.
- Indian Society of 'Seed Science' was established in 1971.
- India receives 73.7 percent of the total annual rainfall through South West monsoon.
- When the annual average rainfall is more than 20 percent, it taken as excess rainfall.
- If the annual rainfall is either 19 percent or less, it is regarded as normal rainfall.
- The departments of Agriculture were established in 1874 at provisional level in India.
- Dr BP Pal was appointed as the first Director General of ICAR on May 14, 1965.

- Dr MS Swaminathan was the first Agriculture Scientist to become Secretary to the Government of India.
- IARI, New Delhi was accorded the status of a "Deemed University" by the University Grants Commission (UGC) in 1955.
- Diwan Bahadur Sir, T. Vijay Raghavacharya was the first Vice Chairman of ICAR.

❑❑❑

Keys for MCQ
Fruit Science

1. (a) 2. (d) 3. (b) 4. (c) 5. (d) 6. (a)

7. (c) 8. (b) 9. (b) 10. (a) 11. (c) 12. (b)

13. (a) 14. (b) 15. (c) 16. (a) 17. (b) 18. (c)

19. (b) 20. (d) 21. (a) 22. (a) 23. (c) 24. (a)

25. (c) 26. (b) 27. (b) 28. (c) 29. (a) 30. (b)

31. (d) 32. (b) 33. (d) 34. (b) 35. (a) 36. (b)

37. (a) 38. (c) 39. (b) 40. (a) 41. (b) 42. (a)

43. (c) 44. (a) 45. (b) 46. (a) 47. (b) 48. (c)

49. (d) 50. (a) 51. (b) 52. (d) 53. (a) 54. (b)

55. (a) 56. (b) 57. (c) 58. (a) 59. (b) 60. (c)

61. (c) 62. (a) 63. (c) 64. (b) 65. (a) 66. (b)

67. (b) 68. (a) 69. (a) 70. (b) 71. (a) 72. (b)

73. (b) 74. (a) 75. (a) 76. (c) 77. (a) 78. (b)

79. (b) 80. (d) 81. (a) 82. (a) 83. (b) 84. (c)

85. (a) 86. (a) 87. (a) 88. (c) 89. (a) 90. (b)

91. (a) 92. (d) 93. (a) 94. (b) 95. (b) 96. (c)

97. (a) 98. (d) 99. (b) 100. (b) 101. (b) 102. (d)

103. (b) 104. (d) 105. (b) 106. (a) 107. (c) 108. (a)

109. (d) 110. (b) 111. (b) 112. (d) 113. (b) 114. (a)

115. (b) 116. (c) 117. (c) 118. (c) 119. (c) 120. (d)

121. (d) 122. (a) 123. (b) 124. (c) 125. (a) 126. (b)

127. (a) 128. (b) 129. (c) 130. (a) 131. (c) 132. (a)

133. (b) 134. (a) 135. (c) 136. (b) 137. (a) 138. (b)

139. (a) 140. (d) 141. (d) 142. (a) 143. (a) 144. (c)

145. (b) 146. (d) 147. (b) 148. (b) 149. (a) 150. (a)

151. (c) 152. (d) 153. (b) 154. (c) 155. (a) 156. (a)

157. (d) 158. (b) 159. (a) 160. (b) 161. (d) 162. (a)

163. (d) 164. (a) 165. (c) 166. (a) 167. (c) 168. (a)

169. (b) 170. (a) 171. (b) 172. (a) 173. (a) 174. (c)

175. (b) 176. (a) 177. (b) 178. (a) 179. (b) 180. (a)

181. (d) 182. (a) 183. (a) 184. (d) 185. (a) 186. (a)

187. (a) 188. (c) 189. (c) 190. (d) 191. (d) 192. (d)

193. (a) 194. (b) 195. (b) 196. (b) 197. (d) 198. (d)

199.	(d)	200.	(c)	201.	(c)	202.	(c)	203.	(a)	204.	(c)
205.	(a)	206.	(d)	207.	(c)	208.	(d)	209.	(b)	210.	(a)
211.	(c)	212.	(b)	213.	(d)	214.	(b)	215.	(c)	216.	(a)
217.	(b)	218.	(c)	219.	(d)	220.	(a)	221.	(c)	222.	(b)
223.	(a)	224.	(a)	225.	(d)	226.	(a)	227.	(d)	228.	(d)
229.	(a)	230.	(d)	231.	(c)	232.	(a)	233.	(b)	234.	(c)
235.	(a)	236.	(d)	237.	(c)	238.	(c)	239.	(a)	240.	(b)
241.	(d)	242.	(a)	243.	(b)	244.	(c)	245.	(a)	246.	(d)
247.	(a)	248.	(b)	249.	(c)	250.	(a)	251.	(d)	252.	(b)
253.	(a)	254.	(a)	255.	(d)	256.	(a)	257.	(a)	258.	(b)
259.	(a)	260.	(d)	261.	(a)	262.	(b)	263.	(a)	264.	(b)
265.	(a)	266.	(b)	267.	(c)	268.	(b)	269.	(a)	270.	(d)
271.	(c)	272.	(d)	273.	(a)	274.	(d)	275.	(b)	276.	(a)
277.	(c)	278.	(b)	279.	(a)	280.	(c)	281.	(c)	282.	(b)
283.	(c)	284.	(a)	285.	(c)	286.	(d)	287.	(b)	288.	(a)
289.	(d)	290.	(a)	291.	(d)	292.	(a)	293.	(b)	294.	(a)
295.	(a)	296.	(c)	297.	(a)	298.	(c)	299.	(a)	300.	(d)
301.	(a)	302.	(b)	303.	(a)	304.	(a)	305.	(d)	306.	(a)
307.	(b)	308.	(a)	309.	(a)	310.	(a)	311.	(c)	312.	(d)
313.	(a)	314.	(c)	315.	(b)	316.	(c)	317.	(d)	318.	(c)
319.	(b)	320.	(d)	321.	(a)	322.	(b)	323.	(d)	324.	(d)
325.	(a)	326.	(d)	327.	(d)	328.	(a)	329.	(b)	330.	(c)
331.	(b)	332.	(d)	333.	(b)	334.	(d)	335.	(a)	336.	(c)
337.	(c)	338.	(b)	339.	(c)	340.	(c)	341.	(c)	342.	(a)
343.	(b)	344.	(b)	345.	(c)	346.	(a)	347.	(c)	348.	(a)
349.	(b)	350.	(a)	351.	(d)	352.	(b)	353.	(a)	354.	(b)
355.	(c)	356.	(a)	357.	(c)	358.	(b)	359.	(a)	360.	(d)
361.	(c)	362.	(b)	363.	(a)	364.	(c)	365.	(a)	366.	(b)
367.	(c)	368.	(a)	369.	(b)	370.	(b)	371.	(a)	372.	(d)
373.	(a)	374.	(d)	375.	(a)	376.	(a)	377.	(c)	378.	(a)
379.	(d)	380.	(b)	381.	(a)	382.	(a)	383.	(b)	384.	(a)
385.	(d)	386.	(d)	387.	(b)	388.	(a)	389.	(b)	390.	(d)
391.	(d)	392.	(b)	393.	(a)	394.	(c)	395.	(a)	396.	(d)
397.	(b)	398.	(b)	399.	(b)	400.	(b)	401.	(d)	402.	(a)
403.	(d)	404.	(d)	405.	(a)	406.	(a)	407.	(a)	408.	(d)
409.	(a)	410.	(d)	411.	(b)	412.	(c)	413.	(a)	414.	(c)
415.	(a)	416.	(a)	417.	(d)	418.	(a)	419.	(b)	420.	(d)
421.	(a)	422.	(b)	423.	(b)	424.	(c)	425.	(b)	426.	(c)

427.	(b)	428.	(d)	429.	(c)	430.	(a)	431.	(c)	432.	(b)
433.	(b)	434.	(d)	435.	(b)	436.	(b)	437.	(b)	438.	(d)
439.	(a)	440.	(a)	441.	(c)	442.	(b)	443.	(d)	444.	(a)
445.	(b)	446.	(d)	447.	(b)	448.	(a)	449.	(b)	450.	(c)
451.	(b)	452.	(a)	453.	(c)	454.	(d)	455.	(a)	456.	(c)
457.	(a)	458.	(b)	459.	(d)	460.	(b)	461.	(a)	462.	(a)
463.	(d)	464.	(a)	465.	(b)	466.	(c)	467.	(b)	468.	(d)
469.	(a)	470.	(b)	471.	(c)	472.	(b)	473.	(a)	474.	(d)
475.	(a)	476.	(a)	477.	(b)	478.	(c)	479.	(a)	480.	(b)
481.	(a)	482.	(b)	483.	(a)	484.	(a)	485.	(c)	486.	(b)
487.	(c)	488.	(c)	489.	(c)	490.	(a)	491.	(b)	492.	(a)
493.	(b)	494.	(d)	495.	(a)	496.	(b)	497.	(c)	498.	(b)
499.	(a)	500.	(a)	501.	(a)	502.	(a)	503.	(d)	504.	(b)
505.	(c)	506.	(a)	507.	(b)	508.	(b)	509.	(c)	510.	(c)
511.	(d)	512.	(d)	513.	(a)	514.	(d)	515.	(a)	516.	(b)
517.	(a)	518.	(b)	519.	(a)	520.	(d)	521.	(a)	522.	(b)
523.	(a)	524.	(d)	525.	(c)	526.	(c)	527.	(b)	528.	(a)
529.	(a)	530.	(c)	531.	(b)	532.	(c)	533.	(a)	534.	(b)
535.	(a)	536.	(d)	537.	(c)	538.	(a)	539.	(b)	540.	(b)
541.	(a)	542.	(c)	543.	(a)	544.	(a)	545.	(b)	546.	(c)
547.	(d)	548.	(b)	549.	(a)	550.	(c)	551.	(b)	552.	(a)
553.	(d)	554.	(b)	555.	(a)	556.	(b)	557.	(a)	558.	(b)
559.	(a)	560.	(c)	561.	(c)	562.	(d)	563.	(c)	564.	(d)
565.	(c)	566.	(c)	567.	(a)	568.	(c)	569.	(d)	570.	(d)
571.	(d)	572.	(a)	573.	(a)	574.	(a)	575.	(a)	576.	(a)
577.	(a)	578.	(d)	579.	(a)	580.	(d)	581.	(d)	582.	(c)
583.	(a)	584.	(d)	585.	(d)	586.	(b)	587.	(a)	588.	(c)
589.	(c)	590.	(a)	591.	(c)	592.	(a)	593.	(d)	594.	(c)
595.	(a)	596.	(b)	597.	(b)	598.	(b)	599.	(c)	600.	(b)
601.	(d)	602.	(c)	603.	(a)	604.	(b)	605.	(a)	606.	(b)
607.	(a)	608.	(a)	609.	(b)	610.	(d)	611.	(c)	612.	(a)
613.	(a)	614.	(b)	615.	(d)	616.	(a)	617.	(b)	618.	(a)
619.	(c)	620.	(a)	621.	(d)	622.	(d)	623.	(a)	624.	(b)
625.	(b)	626.	(d)	627.	(a)	628.	(a)	629.	(d)	630.	(b)
631.	(d)	632.	(a)	633.	(c)	634.	(a)	635.	(a)	636.	(c)
637.	(b)	638.	(d)	639.	(d)	640.	(b)	641.	(a)	642.	(a)
643.	(d)	644.	(b)	645.	(a)	646.	(b)	647.	(c)	648.	(c)
649.	(b)	650.	(b)								

Vegetable Science

1.	(b)	2.	(c)	3.	(b)	4.	(a)	5.	(d)	6.	(a)
7.	(d)	8.	(b)	9.	(c)	10.	(c)	11.	(a)	12.	(b)
13.	(b)	14.	(a)	15.	(c)	16.	(b)	17.	(d)	18.	(c)
19.	(a)	20.	(d)	21.	(a)	22.	(b)	23.	(c)	24.	(c)
25.	(a)	26.	(b)	27.	(d)	28.	(a)	29.	(c)	30.	(d)
31.	(b)	32.	(c)	33.	(a)	34.	(d)	35.	(c)	36.	(d)
37.	(b)	38.	(c)	39.	(a)	40.	(b)	41.	(a)	42.	(d)
43.	(a)	44.	(a)	45.	(b)	46.	(c)	47.	(d)	48.	(a)
49.	(b)	50.	(b)	51.	(d)	52.	(b)	53.	(b)	54.	(d)
55.	(a)	56.	(d)	57.	(a)	58.	(b)	59.	(d)	60.	(a)
61.	(c)	62.	(d)	63.	(a)	64.	(d)	65.	(a)	66.	(c)
67.	(b)	68.	(a)	69.	(d)	70.	(b)	71.	(c)	72.	(b)
73.	(c)	74.	(c)	75.	(a)	76.	(b)	77.	(a)	78.	(c)
79.	(b)	80.	(c)	81.	(b)	82.	(d)	83.	(a)	84.	(c)
85.	(c)	86.	(b)	87.	(d)	88.	(b)	89.	(d)	90.	(c)
91.	(b)	92.	(b)	93.	(b)	94.	(c)	95.	(a)	96.	(b)
97.	(c)	98.	(a)	99.	(a)	100.	(a)	101.	(d)	102.	(b)
103.	(d)	104.	(d)	105.	(b)	106.	(b)	107.	(c)	108.	(c)
109.	(b)	110.	(b)	111.	(c)	112.	(b)	113.	(b)	114.	(c)
115.	(b)	116.	(c)	117.	(c)	118.	(c)	119.	(a)	120.	(d)
121.	(c)	122.	(c)	123.	(b)	124.	(b)	125.	(b)	126.	(c)
127.	(b)	128.	(b)	129.	(b)	130.	(d)	131.	(b)	132.	(b)
133.	(a)	134.	(b)	135.	(b)	136.	(c)	137.	(b)	138.	(c)
139.	(b)	140.	(b)	141.	(b)	142.	(d)	143.	(c)	144.	(b)
145.	(b)	146.	(b)	147.	(a)	148.	(a)	149.	(c)	150.	(d)
151.	(c)	152.	(b)	153.	(b)	154.	(b)	155.	(c)	156.	(b)
157.	(a)	158.	(b)	159.	(b)	160.	(b)	161.	(b)	162.	(c)
163.	(d)	164.	(b)	165.	(c)	166.	(b)	167.	(c)	168.	(c)
169.	(b)	170.	(a)	171.	(b)	172.	(b)	173.	(b)	174.	(b)
175.	(b)	176.	(b)	177.	(b)	178.	(a)	179.	(b)	180.	(a)
181.	(a)	182.	(a)	183.	(b)	184.	(c)	185.	(a)	186.	(d)
187.	(a)	188.	(d)	189.	(c)	190.	(b)	191.	(a)	192.	(d)

193.	(d)	194.	(b)	195.	(d)	196.	(b)	197.	(d)	198.	(b)
199.	(b)	200.	(b)	201.	(b)	202.	(d)	203.	(a)	204.	(c)
205.	(d)	206.	(a)	207.	(a)	208.	(d)	209.	(c)	210.	(a)
211.	(a)	212.	(d)	213.	(b)	214.	(a)	215.	(b)	216.	(a)
217.	(d)	218.	(b)	219.	(d)	220.	(a)	221.	(c)	222.	(c)
223.	(c)	224.	(a)	225.	(d)	226.	(a)	227.	(d)	228.	(b)
229.	(b)	230.	(c)	231.	(b)	232.	(b)	233.	(a)	234.	(d)
235.	(b)	236.	(b)	237.	(b)	238.	(b)	239.	(c)	240.	(b)
241.	(c)	242.	(a)	243.	(c)	244.	(a)	245.	(b)	246.	(c)
247.	(d)	248.	(d)	249.	(c)	250.	(a)	251.	(c)	252.	(d)
253.	(c)	254.	(c)	255.	(d)	256.	(a)	257.	(b)	258.	(c)
259.	(a)	260.	(d)	261.	(c)	262.	(a)	263.	(c)	264.	(c)
265.	(a)	266.	(a)	267.	(b)	268.	(c)	269.	(c)	270.	(b)
271.	(a)	272.	(d)	273.	(a)	274.	(b)	275.	(b)	276.	(d)
277.	(d)	278.	(d)	279.	(d)	280.	(a)	281.	(c)	282.	(a)
283.	(d)	284.	(b)	285.	(d)	286.	(b)	287.	(a)	288.	(c)
289.	(b)	290.	(a)	291.	(c)	292.	(c)	293.	(a)	294.	(b)
295.	(b)	296.	(d)	297.	(c)	298.	(c)	299.	(b)	300.	(a)
301.	(b)	302.	(c)	303.	(b)	304.	(d)	305.	(b)	306.	(a)
307.	(a)	308.	(d)	309.	(a)	310.	(a)	311.	(b)	312.	(a)
313.	(d)	314.	(a)	315.	(d)	316.	(b)	317.	(d)	318.	(a)
319.	(b)	320.	(c)	321.	(d)	322.	(c)	323.	(c)	324.	(c)
325.	(d)	326.	(b)	327.	(b)	328.	(a)	329.	(b)	330.	(d)
331.	(d)	332.	(b)	333.	(b)	334.	(a)	335.	(d)	336.	(c)
337.	(b)	338.	(d)	339.	(c)	340.	(a)	341.	(a)	342.	(a)
343.	(c)	344.	(c)	345.	(d)	346.	(a)	347.	(a)	348.	(c)
349.	(c)	350.	(c)	351.	(d)	352.	(b)	353.	(b)	354.	(c)
355.	(c)	356.	(a)	357.	(b)	358.	(b)	359.	(c)	360.	(b)
361.	(d)	362.	(b)	363.	(d)	364.	(a)	365.	(a)	366.	(c)
367.	(c)	368.	(a)	369.	(a)	370.	(b)	371.	(b)	372.	(a)
373.	(d)	374.	(a)	375.	(a)	376.	(c)	377.	(a)	378.	(c)
379.	(a)	380.	(c)	381.	(b)	382.	(b)	383.	(b)	384.	(d)
385.	(d)	386.	(b)	387.	(b)	388.	(b)	389.	(c)	390.	(a)
391.	(b)	392.	(b)	393.	(a)	394.	(d)	395.	(c)	396.	(a)
397.	(a)	398.	(a)	399.	(b)	400.	(a)	401.	(a)	402.	(a)

403. (c) 404. (a) 405. (c) 406. (a) 407. (d) 408. (a)
409. (c) 410. (a) 411. (a) 412. (d) 413. (c) 414. (a)
415. (d) 416. (a) 417. (a) 418. (a) 419. (a) 420. (a)
421. (a) 422. (a) 423. (a) 424. (a) 425. (d) 426. (d)
427. (b) 428. (d) 429. (a) 430. (b) 431. (b) 432. (a)
433. (a) 434. (d) 435. (c) 436. (a) 437. (a) 438. (d)
439. (a) 440. (c) 441. (b) 442. (d) 443. (a) 444. (a)
445. (b) 446. (a) 447. (a) 448. (b) 449. (c) 450. (d)
451. (c) 452. (d) 453. (c) 454. (c) 455. (a) 456. (a)
457. (a) 458. (d) 459. (d) 460. (c) 461. (b) 462. (a)
463. (a) 464. (c) 465. (c) 466. (d) 467. (a) 468. (b)
469. (b) 470. (b) 471. (a) 472. (d) 473. (a) 474. (a)
475. (a) 476. (d) 477. (a) 478. (a) 479. (a) 480. (a)
481. (a) 482. (a) 483. (a) 484. (c) 485. (c) 486. (a)
487. (a) 488. (a) 489. (b) 490. (b) 491. (a) 492. (b)
493. (a) 494. (b) 495. (a) 496. (a) 497. (d) 498. (c)
499. (d) 500. (a) 501. (a) 502. (c) 503. (a) 504. (a)
505. (a) 506. (a) 507. (b) 508. (b) 509. (c) 510. (a)
511. (d) 512. (d) 513. (a) 514. (a) 515. (a) 516. (a)
517. (d) 518. (a) 519. (a) 520. (a) 521. (d) 522. (a)
523. (a) 524. (a) 525. (a) 526. (a) 527. (d) 528. (a)
529. (a) 530. (a) 531. (a) 532. (a) 533. (a) 534. (a)
535. (a) 536. (d) 537. (a) 538. (a) 539. (c) 540. (a)
541. (a) 542. (a) 543. (a) 544. (a) 545. (b) 546. (a)
547. (d) 548. (a) 549. (a) 550. (c) 551. (a) 552. (a)
553. (a) 554. (a) 555. (a) 556. (a) 557. (a) 558. (a)
559. (b) 560. (a) 561. (a) 562. (a) 563. (a) 564. (c)
565. (a) 566. (a) 567. (a) 568. (a) 569. (a) 570. (a)
571. (d) 572. (a) 573. (a) 574. (a) 575. (c) 576. (d)
577. (a) 578. (d) 579. (a) 580. (a) 581. (a) 582. (d)
583. (a) 584. (a) 585. (d) 586. (c) 587. (a) 588. (d)
589. (a) 590. (a) 591. (c) 592. (b) 593. (a) 594. (b)
595. (a) 596. (a) 597. (d) 598. (d) 599. (c) 600. (c)
601. (b) 602. (c) 603. (c) 604. (c) 605. (c) 606. (c)
607. (a) 608. (a) 609. (b) 610. (a) 611. (b) 612. (c)
613. (b) 614. (a) 615. (b) 616. (c) 617. (c) 618. (c)

619.	(a)	620.	(b)	621.	(a)	622.	(c)	623.	(a)	624.	(c)
625.	(c)	626.	(b)	627.	(a)	628.	(d)	629.	(b)	630.	(c)
631.	(c)	632.	(a)	633.	(d)	634.	(b)	635.	(c)	636.	(d)
637.	(b)	638.	(c)	639.	(b)	640.	(a)	641.	(a)	642.	(d)
643.	(c)	644.	(b)	645.	(a)	646.	(a)	647.	(c)	648.	(b)
649.	(b)	650.	(c)	651.	(a)	652.	(d)	653.	(b)	654.	(a)
655.	(a)	656.	(c)	657.	(a)	658.	(d)	659.	(b)	660.	(c)
661.	(a)	662.	(a)	663.	(c)	664.	(b)	665.	(a)	666.	(c)
667.	(a)	668.	(c)	669.	(c)	670.	(b)	671.	(d)	678.	(a)
679.	(b)	680.	(a)	681.	(b)	682.	(d)	683.	(c)	684.	(c)
685.	(b)	686.	(a)	687.	(a)	688.	(b)	689.	(b)	690.	(b)
691.	(b)	692.	(b)	693.	(d)	694.	(c)	695.	(a)	696.	(c)
697.	(c)	698.	(b)	699.	(b)	700.	(a)	701.	(a)	702.	(d)
703.	(b)	704.	(d)	705.	(c)	706.	(b)	707.	(a)	708.	(d)
709.	(b)	710.	(c)	711.	(c)	712.	(d)	713.	(b)	714.	(a)
715.	(c)	716.	(d)	717.	(b)	718.	(b)	719.	(c)	720.	(a)
721.	(b)	722.	(c)	723.	(a)	724.	(d)	725.	(a)	726.	(c)
727.	(b)	728.	(c)	729.	(b)	730.	(a)	731.	(d)	732.	(b)
733.	(a)	734.	(b)	735.	(c)	736.	(b)	737.	(a)	738.	(a)
739.	(c)	740.	(a)	741.	(b)	742.	(b)	743.	(c)	744.	(a)
745.	(c)	746.	(a)	747.	(b)	748.	(b)	749.	(a)	750.	(d)
751.	(b)	752.	(c)	753.	(b)	754.	(b)	755.	(a)	756.	(c)
757.	(b)	758.	(d)	759.	(b)	760.	(b)	761.	(d)	762.	(a)
763.	(c)	764.	(b)	765.	(d)	766.	(a)	767.	(b)	768.	(d)
769.	(b)	770.	(b)	771.	(a)	772.	(b)	773.	(b)	774.	(b)
775.	(c)	776.	(b)	777.	(a)	778.	(c)	779.	(b)	780.	(a)
781.	(c)	782.	(d)	783.	(a)	784.	(c)	785.	(c)	786.	(b)
787.	(c)	788.	(b)	789.	(a)	790.	(c)	791.	(b)	792.	(c)
793.	(b)	794.	(c)	795.	(a)	796.	(c)	797.	(a)	798.	(a)
799.	(a)	800.	(d)	801.	(a)	802.	(c)	803.	(a)	804.	(d)
805.	(b)	806.	(c)	807.	(a)	808.	(d)	809.	(b)	810.	(d)
811.	(a)	812.	(a)	813.	(c)	814.	(a)	815.	(c)	816.	(a)
817.	(a)	818.	(b)	819.	(d)	820.	(d)	821.	(d)	822.	(d)
823.	(a)	824.	(a)	825.	(a)	826.	(a)	827.	(b)	828.	(c)
829.	(a)	830.	(d)	831.	(b)	832.	(b)	833.	(c)	834.	(c)
835.	(d)	836.	(d)	837.	(a)	838.	(d)	839.	(d)	840.	(b)

841.	(a)	842.	(d)	843.	(c)	844.	(a)	845.	(a)	846.	(c)
847.	(a)	848.	(d)	849.	(a)	850.	(d)	851.	(b)	852.	(c)
853.	(c)	854.	(a)	855.	(a)	856.	(a)	857.	(a)	858.	(c)
859.	(c)	860.	(c)	861.	(c)	862.	(a)	863.	(c)	864.	(d)
865.	(a)	866.	(a)	867.	(c)	868.	(d)	869.	(a)	870.	(a)
871.	(c)	872.	(d)	873.	(a)	874.	(b)	875.	(a)	876.	(a)
877.	(a)	878.	(c)	879.	(a)	880.	(a)	881.	(d)	882.	(a)
883.	(a)	884.	(a)	885.	(a)	886.	(a)	887.	(a)	888.	(a)
889.	(a)	890.	(a)	891.	(a)	892.	(a)	893.	(a)	894.	(a)
895.	(a)	896.	(a)	897.	(a)	898.	(a)	899.	(b)	900.	(b)
901.	(b)	902.	(c)	903.	(a)	904.	(b)	905.	(a)	906.	(a)
907.	(a)	908.	(d)	909.	(a)	910.	(b)	911.	(a)	912.	(b)
913.	(a)	914.	(a)	915.	(a)	916.	(d)	917.	(d)	918.	(c)
919.	(d)	920.	(c)	921.	(c)	922.	(d)	923.	(a)	924.	(c)
925.	(a)	926.	(a)	927.	(a)	928.	(a)	929.	(a)	930.	(a)
931.	(a)	932.	(a)	933.	(a)	934.	(a)	935.	(b)	936.	(b)
937.	(d)	938.	(d)	939.	(d)	940.	(a)	941.	(a)	942.	(b)
943.	(a)	944.	(c)	945.	(a)	946.	(b)	947.	(a)	948.	(a)
949.	(a)	950.	(a)	951.	(a)	952.	(d)	953.	(a)	954.	(a)
955.	(a)	956.	(a)	957.	(a)	958.	(c)	959.	(b)	960.	(a)
961.	(a)	962.	(c)	963.	(a)	964.	(a)	965.	(a)	966.	(b)
967.	(d)	968.	(a)	969.	(a)	970.	(b)	971.	(c)	972.	(b)
973.	(d)	974.	(a)	975.	(b)	976.	(b)	977.	(c)	978.	(a)
979.	(b)	980.	(b)	981.	(a)	982.	(b)	983.	(a)	984.	(d)
985.	(a)	986.	(c)	987.	(d)	988.	(d)	989.	(a)	990.	(a)
991.	(a)	992.	(a)	993.	(a)	994.	(a)	995.	(a)	996.	(a)
997.	(c)	998.	(b)	999.	(d)	1000.	(a)	1001.	(b)	1002.	(d)
1003.	(c)	1004.	(a)	1005.	(b)	1006.	(d)	1007.	(d)	1008.	(d)
1009.	(d)	1010.	(d)	1011.	(a)	1012.	(c)	1013.	(a)	1014.	(d)
1015.	(b)	1016.	(a)	1017.	(d)	1018.	(b)	1019.	(c)	1020.	(b)
1021.	(d)	1022.	(b)	1023.	(c)	1024.	(a)	1025.	(d)	1026.	(c)
1027.	(a)	1028.	(c)	1029.	(d)	1030.	(c)	1031.	(b)	1032.	(d)
1033.	(d)	1034.	(b)	1035.	(d)	1036.	(d)	1037.	(d)	1038.	(a)
1039.	(d)	1040.	(a)	1041.	(a)	1042.	(b)	1043.	(c)	1044.	(a)
1045.	(b)	1046.	(c)	1047.	(b)	1048.	(c)	1049.	(d)	1050	(d)
1051.	(d)	1052.	(a)	1053.	(d)	1054.	(a)	1055.	(b)	1056.	(c)

1057.	(d)	1058.	(a)	1059.	(a)	1060.	(c)	1061.	(d)	1062.	(b)
1063.	(d)	1064.	(b)	1065.	(c)	1066.	(b)	1067.	(d)	1068.	(b)
1069.	(a)	1070.	(a)	1071.	(a)	1072.	(a)	1073.	(a)	1074.	(d)
1075.	(b)	1076.	(a)	1077.	(b)	1078.	(d)	1079.	(a)	1080.	(d)
1081.	(a)	1082.	(d)	1083.	(b)	1084.	(c)	1085.	(b)	1086.	(a)
1087.	(b)	1088.	(b)	1089.	(c)	1090.	(a)	1091.	(b)	1092.	(d)
1093.	(b)	1094.	(a)	1095.	(d)	1096.	(a)	1097.	(d)	1098.	(c)
1099.	(b)	1100.	(d)	1101.	(d)	1102.	(a)	1103.	(c)	1104.	(c)
1105.	(c)	1106.	(b)	1107.	(c)	1108.	(d)	1109.	(b)	1110.	(c)
1111.	(d)	1112.	(c)	1113.	(d)	1114.	(d)	1115.	(c)	1116.	(c)
1117.	(b)	1118.	(a)	1119.	(d)	1120.	(b)	1121.	(b)	1122.	(a)
1123.	(d)	1124.	(a)	1125.	(c)	1126.	(a)	1127.	(b)	1128.	(a)
1129.	(a)	1130.	(b)	1131.	(d)	1132.	(c)	1133.	(d)	1134.	(d)
1135.	(d)	1136.	(d)	1137.	(b)	1138.	(b)	1139.	(b)	1140.	(b)
1141.	(d)	1142.	(a)	1143.	(b)	1144.	(b)	1145.	(d)	1146.	(b)
1147.	(c)	1148.	(b)	1149.	(d)	1150.	(a)	1151.	(b)	1152.	(a)
1153.	(b)	1154.	(b)	1155.	(b)	1156.	(a)	1157.	(c)	1158.	(c)
1159.	(a)	1160.	(c)	1161.	(d)	1162.	(d)	1163.	(d)	1164.	(b)
1165.	(b)	1166.	(a)	1167.	(d)	1168.	(b)	1169.	(b)	1170.	(b)
1171.	(c)	1172.	(d)	1173.	(a)	1174.	(d)	1175.	(c)	1176.	(b)
1177.	(c)	1178.	(a)	1179.	(b)	1180.	(c)	1181.	(d)	1182.	(c)
1183.	(a)	1184.	(b)	1185.	(d)	1186.	(d)	1187.	(b)	1188.	(c)
1189.	(b)	1190.	(b)	1191.	(c)	1192.	(a)	1193.	(a)	1194.	(b)
1195.	(b)	1196.	(d)	1197.	(c)	1198.	(c)	1199.	(a)	1200.	(c)
1201.	(b)	1202.	(c)	1203.	(c)	1204.	(d)	1205.	(a)	1206.	(c)
1207.	(a)	1208.	(b)	1209.	(d)	1210.	(d)	1211.	(a)	1212.	(d)
1213.	(b)	1214.	(b)	1215.	(b)	1216.	(d)	1217.	(a)	1218.	(a)
1219.	(d)	1220.	(c)	1221.	(b)	1222.	(b)	1223.	(b)	1224.	(a)
1225.	(b)	1226.	(d)	1227.	(d)	1228.	(c)	1229.	(d)	1230.	(a)
1231.	(a)	1232.	(b)	1233.	(b)	1234.	(c)	1235.	(a)	1236.	(d)
1237.	(a)	1238.	(b)	1239.	(b)	1240.	(c)	1241.	(b)	1242.	(d)
1243.	(a)	1244.	(a)	1245.	(c)	1246.	(d)	1247.	(d)	1248.	(d)
1249.	(d)	1250.	(b)	1251.	(b)	1252.	(d)	1253.	(b)	1254.	(a)
1255.	(d)	1256.	(d)	1257.	(a)	1258.	(a)	1259.	(d)	1260.	(a)
1261.	(b)	1262.	(a)	1263.	(c)	1264.	(d)	1265.	(d)	1266.	(a)
1267.	(b)	1268.	(a)	1269.	(c)	1270.	(b)	1271.	(b)	1272.	(d)

1273.	(a)	1274.	(a)	1275.	(c)	1276.	(c)	1277.	(b)	1278.	(c)
1279.	(d)	1280.	(b)	1281.	(a)	1282.	(a)	1283.	(b)	1284.	(a)
1285.	(b)	1286.	(a)	1287.	(a)	1288.	(a)	1289.	(c)	1290.	(a)
1291.	(b)	1292.	(a)	1293.	(b)	1294.	(b)	1295.	(d)	1296.	(d)
1297.	(b)	1298.	(b)	1299.	(a)	1300.	(c)	1301.	(d)	1302.	(c)
1303.	(b)	1304.	(d)	1305.	(a)	1306.	(c)	1307.	(d)	1308.	(c)
1309.	(b)	1310.	(a)	1311.	(b)	1312.	(c)	1313.	(c)	1314.	(a)
1315.	(b)	1316.	(c)	1317.	(d)	1318.	(b)	1319.	(d)	1320.	(b)
1321.	(c)	1322.	(b)	1323.	(d)	1324.	(a)	1325.	(c)	1326.	(b)
1327.	(c)	1328.	(c)	1329.	(a)	1330.	(d)	1331.	(d)	1332.	(b)
1333.	(b)	1334.	(d)	1335.	(d)	1336.	(c)	1337.	(d)	1338.	(d)
1339.	(d)	1340.	(a)	1341.	(a)	1342.	(b)	1343.	(a)	1344.	(d)
1345.	(a)	1346.	(a)	1347.	(d)	1348.	(a)	1349.	(a)	1350.	(a)
1351.	(c)	1352.	(c)	1353.	(b)	1354.	(d)	1355.	(c)	1356.	(d)
1357.	(a)	1358.	(b)	1359.	(c)	1360.	(c)	1361.	(d)	1362.	(d)
1363.	(d)	1364.	(a)	1365.	(b)	1366.	(c)	1367.	(a)	1368.	(b)
1369.	(d)	1370.	(c)	1371.	(a)	1372.	(c)	1373.	(c)	1374.	(b)
1375.	(a)	1376.	(a)	1377.	(a)	1378.	(a)	1379.	(d)	1380.	(b)
1381.	(a)	1382.	(b)	1383.	(d)	1384.	(c)	1385.	(d)	1386.	(b)
1387.	(d)	1388.	(c)	1389.	(c)	1390.	(a)	1391.	(d)	1392.	(d)
1393.	(d)	1394.	(d)	1395.	(a)	1396.	(a)	1397.	(d)	1398.	(b)
1399.	(a)	1400.	(d)	1401.	(b)	1402.	(c)	1403.	(a)	1404.	(d)
1405.	(c)	1406.	(a)	1407.	(b)	1408.	(a)	1409.	(d)	1410.	(a)
1411.	(c)	1412.	(d)	1413.	(c)	1414.	(b)	1415.	(d)	1416.	(b)
1417.	(b)	1418.	(d)	1419.	(b)	1420.	(d)	1421.	(a)	1422.	(c)
1423.	(b)	1424.	(d)	1425.	(b)	1426.	(c)	1427.	(a)	1428.	(d)
1429.	(c)	1430.	(d)	1431.	(d)	1432.	(c)	1433.	(a)	1434.	(a)
1435.	(d)	1436.	(b)	1437.	(d)	1438.	(a)	1439.	(b)	1440.	(a)
1441.	(c)	1442.	(b)	1443.	(c)	1444.	(a)	1445.	(d)	1446.	(b)
1447.	(a)	1448.	(c)	1449.	(a)	1450.	(a)	1451.	(c)	1452.	(b)
1453.	(d)	1454.	(d)	1455.	(b)	1456.	(b)	1457.	(b)	1458.	(a)
1459.	(d)	1460.	(d)	1461.	(b)	1462.	(c)	1463.	(c)	1464.	(d)
1465.	(d)	1466.	(a)	1467.	(c)	1468.	(d)	1469.	(a)	1470.	(a)
1471.	(d)	1472.	(a)	1473.	(c)	1474.	(a)	1475.	(b)	1476.	(c)
1477.	(b)	1478.	(b)	1479.	(c)	1480.	(c)	1481.	(b)	1482.	(c)
1483.	(c)	1484.	(b)	1485.	(b)	1486.	(a)	1487.	(c)	1488.	(a)

1489. (a)	1490. (d)	1491. (b)	1492. (b)	1493. (a)	1494. (d)
1495. (d)	1496. (c)	1497. (d)	1498. (d)	1499. (b)	1500. (b)
1501. (c)	1502. (b)	1503. (b)	1504. (c)	1505. (b)	1506. (b)
1507. (c)	1508. (d)	1509. (d)	1510. (d)	1511. (d)	1512. (c)
1513. (d)	1514. (c)	1515. (c)	1516. (c)	1517. (c)	1518. (c)
1519. (d)	1520. (d)	1521. (d)	1522. (b)	1523. (b)	1524. (d)
1525. (b)	1526. (c)	1527. (b)	1528. (b)	1529. (c)	1530. (b)
1531. (b)	1532. (c)	1533. (a)	1534. (b)	1535. (d)	1536. (c)
1537. (c)	1538. (d)	1539. (b)	1540. (a)	1541. (b)	1542. (c)
1543. (c)	1544. (d)	1545. (c)	1546. (c)	1547. (c)	1548. (d)
1549. (b)	1550. (a)	1551. (d)	1552. (d)	1553. (c)	1554. (a)
1555. (a)	1556. (b)	1557. (b)	1558. (c)	1559. (b)	1560. (b)
1561. (a)	1562. (a)	1563. (b)	1564. (c)	1565. (b)	1566. (c)
1567. (d)	1568. (a)	1569. (a)	1570. (d)	1571. (b)	1572. (a)
1573. (c)	1574. (b)	1575. (b)	1576. (c)	1577. (b)	1578. (d)
1579. (b)	1580. (a)	1581. (b)	1582. (b)	1583. (b)	1584. (a)
1585. (b)	1586. (a)	1587. (c)	1588. (c)	1589. (a)	1590. (b)
1591. (a)	1592. (d)	1593. (b)	1594. (b)	1595. (a)	1596. (d)
1597. (c)	1598. (b)	1599. (a)	1600. (a)	1601. (d)	1602. (b)
1603. (c)	1604. (a)	1605. (a)	1606. (b)	1607. (b)	1608. (a)
1609. (b)	1610. (d)	1611. (b)	1612. (c)	1613. (a)	1614. (c)
1615. (c)	1616. (c)	1617. (c)	1618. (a)	1619. (b)	1620. (a)
1621. (b)	1622. (c)	1623. (b)	1624. (c)	1625. (a)	1626. (a)
1627. (a)	1628. (a)	1629. (a)	1630. (a)	1631. (b)	1632. (a)
1633. (a)	1634. (a)	1635. (c)	1636. (c)	1637. (a)	1638. (b)
1639. (d)	1640. (a)	1641. (a)	1642. (d)	1643. (a)	1644. (c)
1645. (a)	1646. (c)	1647. (b)	1648. (d)	1649. (a)	1650. (b)
1651. (c)	1652. (c)	1653. (b)	1654. (d)	1655. (b)	1656. (b)
1657. (a)	1658. (b)	1659. (c)	1660. (d)	1661. (b)	1662. (b)
1663. (a)	1664. (b)	1665. (a)	1666. (b)	1667. (b)	1668. (b)
1669. (a)	1670. (c)	1671. (b)	1672. (c)	1673. (b)	1674. (c)
1675. (c)	1676. (c)	1677. (a)	1678. (a)	1679. (c)	1680. (c)
1681. (a)	1682. (a)	1683. (d)	1684. (b)	1685. (a)	1686. (d)
1687. (a)	1688. (b)	1689. (a)	1690. (a)	1691. (c)	1692. (d)
1693. (b)	1694. (b)	1695. (a)	1696. (d)	1697. (a)	1698. (a)
1699. (d)	1700. (a)				

Floriculture

1. (c)	2. (d)	3. (c)	4. (d)	5. (b)	6. (b)
7. (b)	8. (a)	9. (c)	10. (b)	11. (a)	12. (d)
13. (a)	14. (d)	15. (b)	16. (d)	17. (a)	18. (a)
19. (b)	20. (c)	21. (b)	22. (c)	23. (b)	24. (a)
25. (b)	26. (b)	27. (c)	28. (b)	29. (b)	30. (a)
31. (a)	32. (b)	33. (a)	34. (d)	35. (b)	36. (d)
37. (c)	38. (a)	39. (c)	40. (b)	41. (a)	42. (a)
43. (d)	44. (c)	45. (c)	46. (b)	47. (c)	48. (b)
49. (a)	50. (b)	51. (c)	52. (a)	53. (b)	54. (d)
55. (c)	56. (d)	57. (d)	58. (c)	59. (a)	60. (d)
61. (b)	62. (d)	63. (c)	64. (b)	65. (a)	66. (a)
67. (d)	68. (a)	69. (b)	70. (d)	71. (d)	72. (c)
73. (c)	74. (c)	75. (c)	76. (d)	77. (a)	78. (d)
79. (d)	80. (a)	81. (a)	82. (d)	83. (b)	84. (a)
85. (d)	86. (c)	87. (a)	88. (d)	89. (d)	90. (a)
91. (d)	92. (a)	93. (b)	94. (c)	95. (b)	96. (c)
97. (d)	98. (b)	99. (b)	100. (d)	101. (a)	102. (b)
103. (d)	104. (d)	105. (b)	106. (a)	107. (d)	108. (d)
109. (a)	110. (b)	111. (a)	112. (a)	113. (c)	114. (c)
115. (a)	116. (d)	117. (c)	118. (b)	119. (d)	120. (b)
121. (d)	122. (a)	123. (a)	124. (c)	125. (c)	126. (d)
127. (b)	128. (b)	129. (d)	130. (a)	131. (d)	132. (b)
133. (d)	134. (c)	135. (a)	136. (a)	137. (b)	138. (d)
139. (b)	140. (d)	141. (c)	142. (a)	143. (b)	144. (c)
145. (d)	146. (a)	147. (d)	148. (c)	149. (b)	150. (d)
151. (c)	152. (a)	153. (b)	154. (d)	155. (a)	156. (a)
157. (b)	158. (d)	159. (d)	160. (a)	161. (d)	162. (a)
163. (d)	164. (c)	165. (b)	166. (c)	167. (a)	168. (b)
169. (d)	170. (c)	171. (a)	172. (b)	173. (b)	174. (a)
175. (d)	176. (d)	177. (a)	178. (d)	179. (c)	180. (b)
181. (a)	182. (b)	183. (a)	184. (a)	185. (b)	186. (b)
187. (b)	188. (a)	189. (c)	190. (c)	191. (b)	192. (b)

193.	(c)	194.	(a)	195.	(c)	196.	(c)	197.	(a)	198.	(d)
199.	(a)	200.	(c)	201.	(b)	202.	(d)	203.	(c)	204.	(d)
205.	(a)	206.	(b)	207.	(c)	208.	(b)	209.	(a)	210.	(d)
211.	(c)	212.	(d)	213.	(c)	214.	(c)	215.	(a)	216.	(d)
217.	(b)	218.	(b)	219.	(d)	220.	(c)	221.	(a)	222.	(a)
223.	(d)	224.	(b)	225.	(c)	226.	(a)	227.	(b)	228.	(b)
229.	(a)	230.	(d)	231.	(b)	232.	(b)	233.	(d)	234.	(b)
235.	(c)	236.	(a)	237.	(b)	238.	(c)	239.	(a)	240.	(a)
241.	(c)	242.	(d)	243.	(d)	244.	(a)	245.	(b)	246.	(a)
247.	(a)	248.	(d)	249.	(a)	250.	(b)	251.	(c)	252.	(c)
253.	(a)	254.	(d)	255.	(a)	256.	(a)	257.	(a)	258.	(d)
259.	(a)	260.	(b)	261.	(c)	262.	(a)	263.	(b)	264.	(a)
265.	(b)	266.	(a)	267.	(c)	268.	(b)	269.	(d)	270.	(a)
271.	(d)	272.	(a)	273.	(d)	274.	(c)	275.	(a)	276.	(b)
277.	(a)	278.	(b)	279.	(a)	280.	(c)	281.	(c)	282.	(c)
283.	(c)	284.	(c)	285.	(a)	286.	(c)	287.	(c)	288.	(b)
289.	(c)	290.	(d)	291.	(a)	292.	(d)	293.	(c)	294.	(b)
295.	(b)	296.	(a)	297.	(b)	298.	(d)	299.	(d)	300.	(c)
301.	(a)	302.	(b)	303.	(c)	304.	(d)	305.	(d)	306.	(a)
307.	(d)	308.	(c)	309.	(a)	310.	(a)	311.	(c)	312.	(c)
313.	(a)	314.	(c)	315.	(c)	316.	(d)	317.	(c)	318.	(a)
319.	(b)	320.	(c)	321.	(d)	322.	(a)	323.	(c)	324.	(c)
325.	(c)	326.	(d)	327.	(a)	328.	(a)	329.	(c)	330.	(b)
331.	(c)	332.	(a)	333.	(a)	334.	(a)	335.	(b)	336.	(a)
337.	(b)	338.	(a)	339.	(d)	340.	(d)	341.	(c)	342.	(b)
343.	(d)	344.	(b)	345.	(b)	346.	(b)	347.	(b)	348.	(a)
349.	(b)	350.	(d)	351.	(a)	352.	(d)	353.	(a)	354.	(a)
355.	(d)	356.	(b)	357.	(a)	358.	(c)	359.	(a)	360.	(b)
361.	(b)	362.	(c)	363.	(c)	364.	(b)	365.	(a)	366.	(c)
367.	(c)	368.	(b)	369.	(a)	370.	(d)	371.	(b)	372.	(b)
373.	(d)	374.	(a)	375.	(a)	376.	(b)	377.	(c)	378.	(c)
379.	(d)	380.	(b)	381.	(c)	382.	(b)	383.	(c)	384.	(a)
385.	(b)	386.	(c)	387.	(a)	388.	(d)	389.	(b)	390.	(b)
391.	(b)	392.	(b)	393.	(c)	394.	(b)	395.	(b)	396.	(c)
397.	(c)	398.	(b)	399.	(b)	400.	(b)	401.	(a)	402.	(d)
403.	(d)	404.	(d)	405.	(d)	406.	(a)	407.	(c)	408.	(c)

409.	(d)	410.	(b)	411.	(d)	412.	(d)	413.	(a)	414.	(d)
415.	(a)	416.	(b)	417.	(c)	418.	(b)	419.	(a)	420.	(b)
421.	(b)	422.	(c)	423.	(b)	424.	(c)	425.	(c)	426.	(d)
427.	(a)	428.	(a)	429.	(c)	430.	(b)	431.	(b)	432.	(a)
433.	(d)	434.	(a)	435.	(b)	436.	(a)	437.	(a)	438.	(a)
439.	(c)	440.	(a)	441.	(a)	442.	(d)	443.	(a)	444.	(d)
445.	(a)	446.	(b)	447.	(a)	448.	(c)	449.	(a)	450.	(b)
451.	(b)	452.	(d)	453.	(a)	454.	(d)	455.	(d)	456.	(d)
457.	(b)	458.	(d)	459.	(d)	460.	(c)	461.	(a)	462.	(d)
463.	(a)	464.	(b)	465.	(b)	466.	(b)	467.	(a)	468.	(b)
469.	(b)	470.	(b)	471.	(a)	472.	(b)	473.	(a)	474.	(c)
475.	(b)	476.	(b)	477.	(a)	478.	(d)	479.	(a)	480.	(a)
481.	(d)	482.	(d)	483.	(b)	484.	(b)	485.	(c)	486.	(c)
487.	(a)	488.	(a)	489.	(d)	490.	(d)	491.	(a)	492.	(a)
493.	(d)	494.	(d)	495.	(d)	496.	(a)	497.	(d)	498.	(b)
499.	(a)	500.	(b)	501.	(d)	502.	(b)	503.	(a)	504.	(c)
505.	(a)	506.	(b)	507.	(b)	508.	(c)	509.	(b)	510.	(c)
511.	(d)	512.	(b)	513.	(d)	514.	(d)	515.	(a)	516.	(d)
517.	(b)	518.	(b)	519.	(a)	520.	(d)	521.	(d)	522.	(c)
523.	(a)	524.	(a)	525.	(d)	526.	(b)	527.	(c)	528.	(b)
529.	(c)	530.	(d)	531.	(c)	532.	(a)	533.	(b)	534.	(d)
535.	(b)	536.	(b)	537.	(b)	538.	(a)	539.	(c)	540.	(c)
541.	(b)	542.	(a)	543.	(d)	544.	(d)	545.	(c)	546.	(a)
547.	(b)	548.	(c)	549.	(b)	550.	(d)	551.	(d)	552.	(b)
553.	(c)	554.	(d)	555.	(d)	556.	(d)	557.	(a)	558.	(a)
559.	(a)	560.	(b)	561.	(c)	562.	(a)	563.	(b)	564.	(a)
565.	(b)	566.	(b)	567.	(c)	568.	(d)	569.	(b)	570.	(c)
571.	(a)	572.	(c)	573.	(c)	574.	(d)	575.	(a)	576.	(b)
577.	(a)	578.	(b)	579.	(d)	580.	(d)	581.	(b)	582.	(a)
583.	(b)	584.	(a)	585.	(b)	586.	(d)	587.	(b)	588.	(a)
589.	(a)	590.	(d)	591.	(c)	592.	(a)	593.	(b)	594.	(d)
595.	(a)	596.	(c)	597.	(b)	598.	(d)	599.	(a)	600.	(c)
601.	(b)	602.	(a)	603.	(d)	604.	(d)	605.	(a)	606.	(c)
607.	(a)	608.	(b)	609.	(c)	610.	(b)	611.	(d)	612.	(b)
613.	(a)	614.	(b)	615.	(c)	616.	(d)	617.	(b)	618.	(a)
619.	(b)	620.	(d)	621.	(b)	622.	(d)	623.	(d)	624.	(c)

625.	(d)	626.	(c)	627.	(d)	628.	(b)	629.	(c)	630.	(d)
631.	(b)	632.	(a)	633.	(b)	634.	(b)	635.	(c)	636.	(a)
637.	(a)	638.	(a)	639.	(d)	640.	(b)	641.	(a)	642.	(a)
643.	(b)	644.	(d)	645.	(b)	646.	(d)	647.	(a)	648.	(c)
649.	(b)	650.	(a)	651.	(a)	652.	(d)	653.	(b)	654.	(a)
655.	(a)	656.	(d)	657.	(a)	658.	(a)	659.	(c)	660.	(d)
661.	(c)	662.	(d)	663.	(d)	664.	(a)	665.	(c)	666.	(a)
667.	(d)	668.	(d)	669.	(c)	670.	(a)	671.	(d)	678.	(a)
679.	(c)	680.	(a)	681.	(c)	682.	(b)	683.	(a)	684.	(b)
685.	(c)	686.	(b)	687.	(a)	688.	(d)	689.	(a)	690.	(b)
691.	(c)	692.	(a)	693.	(b)	694.	(a)	695.	(c)	696.	(a)
697.	(b)	698.	(d)	699.	(b)	700.	(a)	701.	(b)	702.	(a)
703.	(c)	704.	(a)	705.	(b)	706.	(c)	707.	(d)	708.	(a)
709.	(b)	710.	(d)	711.	(b)	712.	(a)	713.	(a)	714.	(b)
715.	(a)	716.	(a)	717.	(b)	718.	(c)	719.	(a)	720.	(b)
721.	(d)	722.	(a)	723.	(c)	724.	(c)	725.	(b)	726.	(b)
727.	(c)	728.	(a)	729.	(c)	730.	(c)	731.	(d)	732.	(b)
733.	(b)	734.	(c)	735.	(b)	736.	(b)	737.	(a)	738.	(a)
739.	(b)	740.	(a)	741.	(d)	742.	(b)	743.	(a)	744.	(b)
745.	(c)	746.	(c)	747.	(a)	748.	(b)	749.	(d)	750.	(d)
751.	(d)	752.	(a)	753.	(c)	754.	(a)	755.	(b)	756.	(d)
757.	(b)	758.	(c)	759.	(c)	760.	(a)	761.	(d)	762.	(c)
763.	(a)	764.	(d)	765.	(b)	766.	(a)	767.	(d)	768.	(c)
769.	(d)	770.	(c)	771.	(b)	772.	(d)	773.	(a)	774.	(a)
775.	(b)	776.	(a)	777.	(c)	778.	(d)	779.	(a)	780.	(b)
781.	(d)	782.	(a)	783.	(d)	784.	(a)	785.	(d)	786.	(b)
787.	(a)	788.	(a)	789.	(d)	790.	(a)	791.	(a)	792.	(b)
793.	(d)	794.	(d)	795.	(a)	796.	(d)	797.	(d)	798.	(a)
799.	(b)	800.	(c)	801.	(c)	802.	(a)	803.	(d)	804.	(c)
805.	(b)	806.	(c)	807.	(d)	808.	(d)	809.	(a)	810.	(d)
811.	(c)	812.	(a)	813.	(a)	814.	(b)	815.	(c)	816.	(d)
817.	(c)	818.	(b)	819.	(c)	820.	(d)	821.	(a)	822.	(c)
823.	(c)	824.	(b)	825.	(d)	826.	(a)	827.	(b)	828.	(c)
829.	(a)	830.	(b)	831.	(a)	832.	(b)	833.	(a)	834.	(c)
835.	(a)	836.	(c)	837.	(d)	838.	(b)	839.	(a)	840.	(d)
841.	(a)	842.	(c)	843.	(b)	844.	(c)	845.	(c)	846.	(b)
847.	(a)	848.	(b)	849.	(d)	850.	(c)